Managerial Economics

Fourth edition

Managerial Economics

A European text

W. DUNCAN REEKIE AND JONATHAN N. CROOK

FINANCIAL TIMES
Prentice Hall

An imprint of **Pearson Education**

Harlow, England · London · New York · Reading, Massachusetts · San Francisco · Toronto · Don Mills, Ontario · Sydney
Tokyo · Singapore · Hong Kong · Seoul · Taipei · Cape Town · Madrid · Mexico City · Amsterdam · Munich · Paris · Milan

First published 1995 by
Prentice Hall Europe

Pearson Education Limited
Edinburgh Gate,
Harlow
Essex, CM20 2JE
England
and Associated Companies throughout the world

Visit us on the World Wide Web at:
http://www.pearsoneduc.com

Typeset in 9./12pt Palatino
by Mathematical Composition Setters Ltd, Salisbury

Printed and bound by Antony Rowe Ltd, Eastbourne

Library of Congress Cataloging-in-Publication Data

Reekie, W. Duncan.
    Managerial economics / W. Duncan Reekie, Jonathan N. Crook. – 4th ed.
      p.   cm.
    Includes bibliographical references and index.
    ISBN 0-13-100520-0
    1. Managerial economics.   Crook, Jonathan N. II. Title.
    HD30.22.R39 1994
    338.5′024′658–dc20
                                            94-894
                                               CIP

British Library Cataloguing in Publication Data

A catalogue record for this book is available from the British Library

ISBN 0-13-100520-0

---

10 9 8 7 6 5 4 3 2
04 03 02 01 00

For Ruth and Kate

Contents

Preface

This book has passed the market test of colleagues (students and teachers) who have read and prescribed earlier editions for nearly two decades in all five continents. For their support we are grateful. We must also express our thanks to our own students over the years and to fellow instructors who have pointed out inadequacies, errors and omissions in earlier editions. We have taken on board many of their suggestions.

This edition has been thoroughly revised. Indeed a comparison with the first edition or with Joel Dean's 1949 classic of the same name would show how far the subject of managerial economics has progressed in recent years. This, of course, is to be expected of any discipline taught in a university where teaching and research go hand in hand.

The book has evolved with the journal literature and indeed managerial economics has been well served in this way, not only is research in the area published in finance, law and economics, industrial organisation and some marketing journals, but one of us established the now leading journal in the area *Managerial and Decision Economics* in the late 1970s. Fifteen years of specific research activity has found its way into the following chapters.

New features of this edition include an emphasis on the work which started with Ronald Coase and was continued by Oliver Williamson on why entrepreneurs create firms. Why do firms exist? When is management within the firm more efficient (less costly in transactions costs terms) than exchange across markets? As James Buchanan put it economics is not only a science of choice but also a science of contracts. Even within the firm the latter approach can be used to view firms as a nexus of contracts with the manager playing the central role between customers, capital providers and risk bearers, suppliers of labour and of tangible inputs: in short managers must optimise the interests of all stakeholders, including regulators and the public at large.

Another strand of literature which has been expanded upon is that of principal and agent. If economics is a science of contracts how are contracts drawn up within and between firms which minimise agency and attenuate transaction costs? The obverse of these problems are strategic decisions in situations of rivalry. Corporate strategists not only attempt to optimise the firm's financial position as such, they must do so in a situation of rivalry where one ancillary objective is to minimise the range of choices open to competitors. Strategic theory consequently occupies an important place in the text.

Where such activities operate against the public interest regulation impinges – for example by way of monopolies and mergers policies or through regulatory agencies with industry specific remits (particularly in the privatised sector).

The book continues unconventionally to have chapters where economic methods (the application of marginal equivalency principles) are applied to decisions where only non-transaction data are available in real life. This is particularly true of advertising where economists have always been loath to tread. (For no understandable reason except their conventional emphasis on the transactions data of prices paid and sales achieved which, of course, are absent *ex ante*, but for which a wealth of market research proxies are available).

A further new feature is the expansion of the discussion on why firms go multinational. Although present in the third edition, some instructors believe we placed too little emphasis on the origins of that literature in trade theory. We had jumped too rapidly to the purely intuitive approach – which might be satisfactory for executive programmes but was less so for MBA and the advanced Bachelor's students who form our major readership.

A major new expository innovation in this edition is the addition to the expanded highly practical chapter end questions (for which worked solutions are available to instructors) of mini-cases scattered throughout each chapter. These mini-cases are taken from relevant real life business situations pertinent to the surrounding discussion, or are, in some instances, synopses of major theoretical papers which illustrate why the surrounding pages are of disciplinary relevance and what their genesis has been. Also new to this edition is a supporting teacher's manual compiled by Sinclair Davidson, lecturer in the School of Economic and Business Studies at Wits University. The teacher's manual is available on request and contains additional questions, problems, discussion aids, expository guidance for teachers as well as master overhead projector acetates for lecturers.

We hope readers will agree that these changes represent a move towards a still higher optimum in this, our fourth edition. We hope also they continue to feed back their reactions to us so that we can continue to adapt and improve the product to meet tomorrow's market requirements.

W.D.R.
J.N.C.
August 1994

Abbreviations

AC	average cost curve		*LTrC*	least transport cost
AFC	average fixed cost		*M*	multidivisional
AR	average revenue curve		MA	moving average
BARB	Broadcasters' Audience Research		MC	marginal cost
	Board		MM	Modigliani and Miller
BFS	basic feasible solution		MMC	Monopolies and Mergers
BOT	Board of Trade			Commission
CAPM	capital asset pricing model		*MMD*	*mutatis mutandis* demand
CML	capital market line		MNE	multinational enterprise
CRS	computer reservation system *or*		*MR*	marginal revenue
	constant returns to scale		MRPC	Monopolies and Restrictive
CTC	clinical trail certificate			Practices Commission
DCF	discounted cash flow		MRPT	marginal rate of product
DGFT	Director General of Fair Trading			transformation
DRS	decreasing returns to scale		MRS	marginal rate of substitution
DW	Durbin–Watson		*MU*	marginal utility
EC	European Commission		*NMR*	net marginal revenue
EMV	expected monetary value		*NPV*	net present value
FDI	foreign direct investment		NRS	National Readership Survey
FIFO	first in first out		NRV	net realisable value
GDP	gross domestic product		OLS	ordinary least squares
GNP	gross national product		OTH	opportunity to hear
GRP	Gross Rating Point		OTS	opportunity to see
IO	input–output		OTV	opportunity to view
IRR	internal rate of return		p.d.f.	probability density function
IRS	increasing returns to scale		PDI	personal disposable income
LAAC	locus of average advertising costs		PERT	programme evaluation and review
LAC	long-run average cost			technique
LCM	least common multiplier		*PIL*	physical investment line
LIFO	last in first out		*PV*	present value
LMC	long-run marginal cost		*PYI*	Paasche Year Index
LP	linear programming		RC	replacement cost
LTC	long-run total cost		ROCE	return on capital employed

ROR	rate of return	*STC*	short-run total costs
RPI	retail price index	*STVC*	short-run total variable costs
RTPC	Restrictive Trade Practices Court	*TC*	total cost
SATC	sort-run average total costs	*TFC*	short-run total fixed costs
SAVC	short-run average variable costs	*TR*	total revenue
SMC	short-run marginal costs	*U*	unitary
SML	security market line	VNM	Von Neumann and Morgenstern
SMP	system marginal price	*WACC*	weighted average cost of capital
SSD	semi-standard deviation		

Part I

Basic concepts

Chapter 1

What is managerial economics?

Managerial economics is the application of economic concepts and methods of thought to the decision making process within the firm or organisation. The relevance of the subject stretches beyond the business firm. Managerial economics can often be applied in public sector or government organisations just as it can in commercial ones. It cannot, however, be extended in scope to the planning or management of the total, aggregate economy (Box 1.1). Rather it is restricted to management decisions in individual firms.

Historically economics has viewed the firm as a 'black box' and hence decision taking within firms has apparently been beyond the purview of the discipline. But Eugene Fama (1980) sees a firm as a 'nexus of contracts' where different participants meet to fulfil or carry out contracts drawn up with each other. Managers take decisions to achieve corporate objectives given the firm's relationships with customers and suppliers in an environment where competing firms exist; where the future is uncertain or unknowable; and where governmental regulation acts as a constraint. Figure 1.1 illustrates this.

The firm is far more than just one group of participants. The different participants, however, only join together as a firm incompletely – they have other interests in life, they trade with other firms, spend time at leisure and engage in other activities apart from any express or implied contractual relationship within the one firm of the diagram. Moreover, the roles identified in the diagram can overlap. Thus managers can be employees. Capital providers can be managers. Risk bearers can provide capital. Suppliers can be risk bearers, and customers can be capital providers, to name but a few overlaps in practice. However, to enable us to adopt the nexus of contracts approach it is helpful to distinguish these different activities.

If the nexus of contracts approach is valid the firm need not be regarded as a 'black box' into which we cannot peer and to which we cannot apply economic analysis. It is not simply an entity to which we can apply stimuli and possibly predict responses. Rather, modern economics as it has developed since, say post-1970, can help explain why certain responses occur, what the responses should be, and indeed can even suggest what stimuli should be sought for by businessmen, and which stimuli they might try to apply to their competitors. All of this is far

---

Box 1.1

What managerial economics is not about

Managerial economics is an aid to decentralised decision taking at the level of the firm. It is *not* about central planning of a total economy. Decentralised planning (managerial economics) is distinct from central planning.

In 1938 Lange and Taylor (1938, pp. 59–61) argued that central planning 'is a problem of choice between alternatives. To solve ... three data are needed: (a) a preference scale which guides the acts of choice; (b) knowledge of the terms on which alternatives are offered; (c) knowledge of the amount of resources available.'

In fact, Lange and Taylor go on, if only (a) and (c) – preferences and resources are known – or as they put it 'established by the judgement of the authorities' – then the system will work. This, of course, is true. Hayek (1945, pp. 519–30) pointed out that once preferences and means are given the remaining problem is 'purely one of logic' (or in technical jargon it is one of computing the point where the marginal rates of substitution between any two commodities or inputs are the same in all their different uses).

But knowledge of resources and preferences are never given to a single mind, and even if conceptually they could be, preferences and technologies are continuously changing as individuals adjust their tastes and knowledge of how better to achieve their individually preferred ends. Individuals and groups of individuals such as firms) *plan* to achieve their own objectives. There is competition between decentralised planners. It is these planners that the discipline of managerial economics is designed to assist.

It begins rather than ends with attempting to determine or ascertain prices (what Lange and Taylor called 'knowledge of the terms on which alternatives are offered') since it is these which reveal information on today's unknown and tomorrow's unknowable demands and supplies. These prices – and the incentives of profits and the penalties of losses which they reveal – not the 'judgement of the authorities' drive decentralised managerial decisions.

---

removed from the static textbook picture of the 'perfectly competitive equilibrium' of Economic Principles courses where the firm is an artefact with little autonomous life of its own. A few writers such as Joel Dean – who wrote the seminal textbook *Managerial Economics* in 1951 tried to fight against this, but the paradigm of the firm as 'black box' has dominated most of twentieth-century economics. Only recently has the subject returned to the richer, more empirically based foundations of examining what goes on within real firms in real life industries – a tradition and an approach which was never ignored by earlier – and diverse – writers less bewitched by academic abstraction such as Adam Smith, Karl Marx and Alfred Marshall (Box 1.2).

All of the participants in the firm are unique in different ways. There is, however, one peculiarly distinguishing feature of managers. They have the unique task of

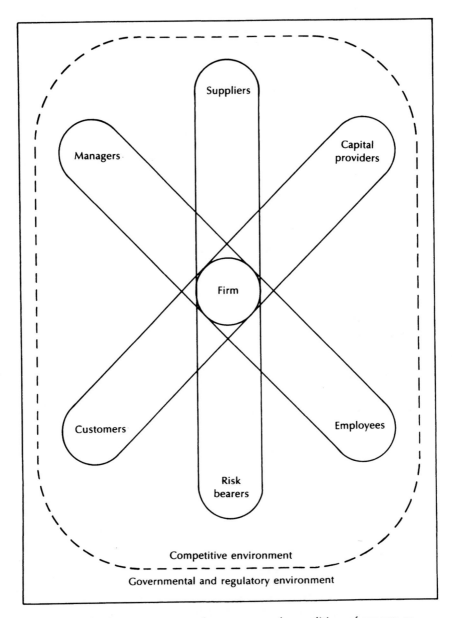

Figure 1.1 The firm as a nexus of contracts and a coalition of groups as participants

Box 1.2

Why firms exist and why managers are different

It is easy to view the firm as a necessary accompaniment to large-scale production. Surely production-line activity (for example) cannot be conducted 'democratically' by independent workers buying and selling from each other and renting floor space from a factory owner? Such a division of labour would be chaotic. Nobel prize-winner Ronald Coase (1937) argued that this was not so. The price system alone would avoid confusion. Suppliers always have their customers' requirements in mind and rising or falling prices let them know what customers think of their product offerings and vice versa. The relevant question is why on some occasions the integrating force is a firm, and on others it is a transaction carried out in the market? Coase concluded that the costs of using the price mechanism vary. Transactions are not homogeneous. When transaction costs rise too far, when the costs of negotiating and contracting become excessive, firms come into being. A firm then, is that area of activity where the economies of internal organisation exceed the economies of market relationships.

Firms are teams of people (and other resources) and groups must be co-ordinated. Moreover, although co-operative team production may result in an output which exceeds the total output which could be achieved by each team member operating in isolation, and although this excess may be greater than the costs of co-ordination, there remains the problem of monitoring.

Alchian and Demsetz (1972) view the monitoring of effort and the rewarding of productivity as the two major problems in firm production. The interdependence of team production means that it is difficult to ascertain what part of total output is attributable to any one team member's efforts.

Conversely, shirking may go unobserved. In individual work the individual reaps all the benefits of his efforts; if he shirks he bears all the costs. But in team work, the costs of shirking are borne by the full team. Everyone admits he is better off if no one shirks, but everyone also realises that if he alone shirks, the cost to him will be small: he can get a 'free ride' on the efforts of other team members.

More shirking will therefore occur in firms than in individual market transactions. The team members can get over the problem by hiring another member to monitor the productive activity of the whole team. To be effective, the monitor must have disciplinary powers over shirkers which can be used without disbanding the team. In short, he must be able to fire a shirker. The monitor watches and directs other team members by their common consent. Any contract, express or implied, is two-way. Whether the monitor initially hired the team or the team initially hired him is irrelevant. Team members enter into such contracts since they know a monitor is essential to maximise output. They want to maximise output since only in that way can they bargain for larger rewards when contracts come up for renegotiation.

Alchian and Demsetz then pose the question: who monitors the monitor? How can team members ensure that he is diligent, that he does not shirk? One way is to make him a residual claimant. All team members agree to work for a specific amount; any income remaining at the end of some arbitrary period is his. He is consequently motivated to make this residual as large as possible. A residual claim

$\rightarrow$

is a property right. Alchian and Demsetz condense their discussion by asserting that the bundle of property rights listed below must be vested in the monitor:

1. To be a residual claimant (i.e. of revenues after payment of legal obligatory costs).
2. To observe input behaviour.
3. To be the central party common to all contracts with inputs.
4. To alter the membership of the team.
5. To sell these rights.

These rights and their incentive effects explain the hierarchy of the traditional, entrepreneur-founded and controlled firm.

There the owner/manager has the property rights of a *residual claimant* (1), and those of a *residual controller* (5). Residual rights arise because as Milgrom and Roberts point out (1992, p. 288) it is impossible in complex transacting to write complete contracts specifying what should be done under every possible contingency. As firms have grown so this complexity has increased and the owner/manager role itself has become diffused across different individuals.

drawing-up, executing and enforcing the contracts between the firm and all other participants. Managers concern themselves with:

1. whether the firm should have a contract with particular participants;
2. what the terms of that contract should be;
3. whether that contract should be
   (a) spot (a one-off buy–sell relationship);
   (b) long-term (for example a leasing or employment, contract) or;
   (c) unified and permanent for example vertical integration into one firm with a customer or supplier);
4. arranging the optimal execution of the contract; and
5. choosing the appropriate method and level of monitoring and evaluation necessary to ensure contract execution.

Even among writers sympathetic to the managerial economics approach the tendency has been to emphasise only point (4) – (what Matthews (1986) termed production costs). Matthews defines the activities covered by the remaining points (1–3) as *ex ante* transaction costs and by (5) as *ex post* transaction costs.

Study of transaction costs is critical if we view the firm as an organisation of different people who have come together contractually. Voluntary groupings such as firms arise because people believe they will be (as individuals) better off in the organisation than they would have been acting in isolation. Ronald Coase put it another way. Firms exist because it is less costly (in transaction cost terms) to carry out activities within firms, rather than by purchase and sale across markets. When this is not so market transactions replace unitary organisations. Cyert and March (1967) term the firm an 'organisational coalition' of managers, workers, share-holders, customers and so on. Each coalition member will have an individual goal which may well conflict with the goal of another member. For the firm as an organisation to remain in existence, the coalition members must then be satisfied with less than their maximum objectives since the resources are not available to satisfy them all. People will only be prepared to 'sub-optimise' in this way if by doing so they get closer to their objectives than they would have acting as individuals outside the organisation. So, since this conflict of objectives exists, the final set of goals of the firm will, at least partly, be the outcome of a political or bargaining process.

In short the nexus of contracts which makes up the firm is arrived at through bargaining between individuals and because individuals differ and have different goals the resulting organisation will have one single goal or single clearly defined objective function only to the extent that the contracts themselves have some underlying and probably fairly restricted common denominator.

Furthermore, since the contracts managers write with the other participants are written today for execution some time in the future there are several elements of uncertainty involved with predicting the outcome from any given decisions. The future is unknown; the objectives of members of the coalition will rarely be coincident; the writing of contracts to maximise coincidence does not guarantee compliance of action; not every future contingency can be foreseen and so a fully detailed contract cannot be drawn up which would specify what actions to take to ensure objective coincidence and action compliance if circumstances alter; and, to complete the circle, given differing individual objectives, enthusiastic contract compliance is not necessarily to be expected. There are *ex ante* and *ex post* transaction costs.

Managerial economics puts an orderly framework around this complex reality of business decisions. Figure 1.2 summarises the subject diagrammatically. It commences with the type of problems managers are faced with in normal business life. These stretch from short- to medium-term decisions, such as deciding what prices to set and what quantities to produce, what production techniques to employ and what type or level of sales promotion should be engaged in; to medium- to long-term decisions such as the level and mix of financing instruments which should be employed, and the degree to which the firm should strategically diversify into other product lines or alternative national markets.

To address these problems of which contracts to enter into, on what terms to draw them up, on what modes of execution should be selected, and on what means of monitoring and evaluation should be chosen most efficiently to align the incentives and so the activities of the various members of the firm managerial economics draws on four main disciplines.

Neo-classical positive economics examines how firms and consumers behave. Traditionally it is descriptive and not prescriptive, and assumes consumers and producers operate in conditions of perfect information with given objective functions (profits in the case of firms, utility or satisfaction in the case of consumers). The descriptions of 'what is' are modified when different types of industry structures (for example monopoly) are introduced into the theory.

Statistics and mathematics can be used to complement positive economics. They can be employed to show how firms gather and process information in order to take

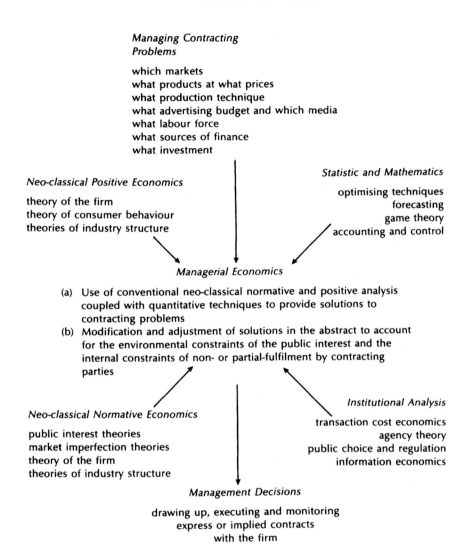

Managing Contracting Problems

which markets
what products at what prices
what production technique
what advertising budget and which media
what labour force
what sources of finance
what investment

Neo-classical Positive Economics

theory of the firm
theory of consumer behaviour
theories of industry structure

Statistic and Mathematics

optimising techniques
forecasting
game theory
accounting and control

Managerial Economics

(a) Use of conventional neo-classical normative and positive analysis coupled with quantitative techniques to provide solutions to contracting problems
(b) Modification and adjustment of solutions in the abstract to account for the environmental constraints of the public interest and the internal constraints of non- or partial-fulfilment by contracting parties

Neo-classical Normative Economics

public interest theories
market imperfection theories
theory of the firm
theories of industry structure

Institutional Analysis

transaction cost economics
agency theory
public choice and regulation
information economics

Management Decisions

drawing up, executing and monitoring
express or implied contracts
with the firm

Figure 1.2 Managerial economics uses neoclassical economics, statistics and mathematics, and institutional analysis to arrive at managerial decisions

the optimal decisions predicted by positive theory. More recent developments such as game theory permit the introduction into the analysis of more complex types of industry structure such as oligopoly and the dynamics of industry entry. Accounting and managerial data gathering and processing activities such as market research are some of the more common tools used, and in turn this facilitates the drawing-up and monitoring of the firm's contracts. In traditional neo-classical positive economics such transaction costs are assumed away.

Institutional analysis, however, explicitly recognises such costs. According to North and Wallis (1986) transaction costs have grown in importance from a (non-negligible) 25 per cent of total gross national product (GNP) 'resource use' in 1870 to over 50 per cent in 1970. Their explicit recognition in managerial economics is long overdue. A good illustration of transaction costs are the costs of agency. For example, the relationship between the juridical owners of a modern firm (i.e. the shareholders) and its senior executives is typical of many between principals and agents which are found throughout society. When managers are not the sole owners of a firm they are often regarded as agents making decisions on behalf of the owners or principals. The principals reward the agents for making these decisions out of the profits which result from the agents' decisions. But there are a number of difficulties associated with this relationship as far as the principals are concerned. The agent has far more information about the firm's costs, rivals, market potential, etc. than the principals. The latter cannot then know whether the agents are doing the best possible job of managing the firm which is facing say, declining demand, or are instead pursuing their own objectives at the expense of the principals. There is information asymmetry, i.e. the agents have specialised knowledge not available to the principals.

Because of information asymmetry there is a monitoring problem. This simply means it will be impractical or too costly to police all aspects of an agency relationship. Some 'inefficiency' must therefore be tolerated because the monitoring costs would exceed the benefits. Economists then argue that the most efficient form of organisation – and therefore that most likely to survive in the long run – is the one which, *ceteris paribus*, minimises the sum of agency costs.

Information asymmetry lies at the heart of agency relationships (within firms), and is crucial to competitive relationships (between firms). It also impacts on governmental regulation of firms. Neo-classical normative economics has traditionally viewed government as a benevolent platonic guardian which would intervene in inter- and intra-firm relationships when markets fail. The public interest view of government as regulator justifies intervention from this standpoint in areas as diverse as monopoly policy, privatisation and regulation of corporate behaviour in order to protect consumers, the environment, employees, shareholders or other firm members from the effects of imperfectly drawn-up contracts (or what is traditionally called 'market failure').

But public choice analysis (in contrast to the public interest view) suggests that there are good reasons why governments also fail. Politicians and bureaucrats, no less than anyone else, pursue their own self-interest. They do so in an institutional environment which makes it not impossible that it will be at the expense of the public. Again, the role of information is important. The price mechanism provides private financiers with the information about shortages and surpluses they need for their decisions. It also provides the incentive to seek out the information, which government officials do not have. The latter have no property rights in the gains created from exploiting a profitable trade. Nor do they suffer directly the losses from error in misdirecting the flows of capital or labour. They may not be so alert to the best opportunities and will be less likely to exercise caution in the face of unpromising alternatives.

Then there is the phenomenon economists have come to call 'rent seeking', that is, the use of government power by interest groups and individuals to obtain special privileges for themselves. Successful rent seekers gain above-market returns by deliberate contrivance, by successfully lobbying government for favours. Lobbies representing small particular interest groups are likely to have a disproportionately large influence on government while the interest of large groups, especially consumers and society at large, are likely to be underrepresented.

Finally neo-classical economics is drawn on in normative fashion to show how firms should behave – in different structural environments in order to maximise profits. The principles of marginal equivalency, commonly used by welfare economists are adapted to providing initial answers to the basic management contracting problems of what prices to set, where goods should be sold, how they should be manufactured and how the manufacturing process should be financed.

1.1 Outline of the book

Chapter 2 outlines the basic neo-classical concepts of marginal equivalency, profit and the importance of time on which managerial economics rests. Chapter 3 deals with the problem of maximisation (which marginal equivalency apparently 'solves') given that decisions are taken and contracts are drawn up today relating to a future which is unknown, uncertain or risky. Chapter 4 expands on contract construction, execution and monitoring when decisions about contracts are taken. What are the transaction costs and how are they minimised when the nexus of contracts is constructed? Chapter 5 expands on the question: what is it that different groups within a firm wish to maximise? How are the differing objectives of the differing members of firms – the agency problem – dealt with?

Given that sales affect the degree to which certain of the objectives of owners, managers and workers alike are achieved and that the future level of sales is uncertain, Chapter 6 asks: how can managers predict future sales? Chapter 7 examines one aspect of markets – customers – and questions how the firm can ascertain what makes up the utility function of these stakeholders in the firm. Chapter 8 operationalises the concepts of Chapter 7 by explaining techniques which specialists within a firm can use to estimate the effects of causal factors on the amount of a product or service demanded.

Chapter 9 considers the mechanics of production. How is output related to different amounts of input? What is the optimum combination of inputs to use? How do costs – foregone benefits when money is spent on producing a product – vary with the amount of that product which is produced? How can we discover these relationships in practice? In Chapter 10 we again provide tools to operationalise the concepts of a previous chapter. In this case we show how linear programming can be, and is being used to answer the second question above and the question as to the optimum amount of product to produce.

Chapter 11 examines pricing decisions using both traditional neo-classical analysis and newer theories of market behaviour. Chapter 12 relates mainly to regulated utilities and adopts a similar approach, namely it commences with the traditional welfare economic approach of marginal cost pricing, popular in the 1960s and 1970s, but moves on to discuss the recent developments in price-cap, or RPI-X regulation.

Chapter 13 examines advertising decisions. In particular this chapter emphasises how economists – if they are to contribute to managerial decision making – must not rely exclusively on data from actual outcomes, often called market data or transactions data. Businesses must usually act before transaction data are available, 'and often would benefit from data that will *never* be revealed in transactions' (Calfee and Rubin 1993, p. 164). Advertising is a good example of a business situation where decisions must be made before the transactions occur. Chapter 13 illustrates how economists can obtain and use 'non-transactional data' for taking decisions which will impact on transactions (i.e. purchases and sales) in the future. Chapter 14 explains how a manager can decide whether to engage in a transaction today which has lasting effects into the future. £1 received next year is worth less than £1 received today because one could invest today's pound for one year to earn interest. So the stream of benefits and costs from transactions over time must be made comparable. We explain the optimum mix of finance which a firm should use for the benefit of its shareholders. We also consider formally how the riskiness of a transaction affects the correspondence of today's pounds with those received tomorrow.

Chapter 15 examines traditional and transactions cost reasons for vertical integration and the control and managerial problems which it gives rise to or which it attenuates. Setting transfer prices is one issue related to integration, while setting prices of products within a range is a related issue when companies diversify. Diversification itself brings together not only pricing issues, but also the concepts of risk and portfolio management as well as the product life cycle and learning curve where costs of production (and often also of consumption) fall as output accumulates through time. In short the subject of diversification brings together these (and other) topics from earlier chapters and hence the shorthand phrase of 'corporate strategy' is not inappropriately included in the chapter heading. Finally, the chapter concludes by examining the causes, direction and nature of international business activity. Chapter 16 examines where firms should locate plants, factories and retail outlets.

Chapters 17 and 18 study government regulation of industry. Chapter 17 discusses competition policy legislation as it relates to transactions within the domestic economy and to those between European economies. What are the social benefits and disbenefits of monopoly power which transactors may seek? What legislation impinges on entrepreneurs when they engage in actions which may restrict competition? Is the legislation effective in achieving its intended aims? Chapter 18 examines the topical issues of the environment and pollution. These problems are not transient and managers must understand them in order to respond constructively. The Coase Theorem, introduced in Chapter 4, is essential for this purpose. Our final chapter, Chapter 19 expands on our earlier distinction between the accountant's definition of cost and that of the economist. We then explain how cost, revenue and various accounting ratios may be used for the purposes of control by a manager.

Bibliography

Alchian, A. and Demsetz, H. (1972) 'Production, information costs and economic organis- ation', *American Economic Review*, vol. 62.

Calfee, J. E. and Rubin, P. (1993) 'Non-Transactional Data in Managerial Economics and Marketing', *Managerial and Decision Economics*, vol. 14.

Coase, R. H. (1937) 'The nature of the firm', *Economica*, vol. 4.

Cyert, R. M. and March J. G. (1963) *A Behavioural Theory of the Firm*, Prentice Hall.

Dean, J. (1951) *Managerial Economics*, Prentice Hall.

Fama, E. (1980) 'Agency Problems and the Theory of the Firm', *Journal of Political Economy*, vol. 88.

Hayek, F. A. (1945) 'The use of knowledge in society', *American Economic Review*, **35**.

Lange, O. and Taylor, F. M. (1938) 'On the economic theory of socialism', in D. E. Lippencott (ed.), *On the Economic Theory of Socialism*, University of Minnesota Press.

Matthews, R. C. O. (1986) 'The Economics of Institutions and the Sources of Growth', *Economic Journal*, **96**.

Milgrom, P. and Roberts, J. (1992) *Economic Organisation and Management*, Prentice Hall.

North, D. C. and Wallis, J. J. (1986) 'Measuring the Transactions Sector in the American Economy, 1870–1970', in S. L. Engerman and R. E. Gallmand (eds), *Long-Term Factors in American Economic Growth*, Chicago University Press.

Chapter 2

Introduction to maximisation and optimisation

Business firms provide an investment home for the savings of individuals (directly or via the institutions); they provide employment for managers and workers; but first and foremost they exist to produce goods or services which meet the requirements and needs of their actual or potential customers. Profits are the ultimate yardstick of management's ability to co-ordinate, plan and act in the interest of the consumer. The word 'profit' however, means different things to economists, to accountants, to businessmen, to politicians and to tax collectors. What is profit?

2.1 The meaning of profit

In income distribution theory all income is classified according to source. Wages are income from direct labour; interest is income from allowing others to use one's money; rent is the excess of the value produced by a productive factor over the payment required to induce it to work; and profit is the excess of income over the cost of production. In a perfectly competitive economy in a state of equilibrium, profits do not exist. But in reality, competition is dynamic, not static. Given this, three main groups of theories have arisen to explain the presence of profits.

First, there is the view that profits are a reward for bearing risks and uncertainties. Most people prefer to avoid these, yet in general, businessmen are unable to do so. Firms must take actions today with a view to satisfying consumer wants in a risky or uncertain tomorrow. Consequently, a higher reward is required as the risk and/or uncertainty in the situation increases. Without this reward firms would avoid such situations and so market wants tomorrow would remain unsatisfied. A second theory is that profits are the result of market frictions and imperfections. They exist because of disequilibrium and imperfect competition. They tend to persist because the economy can rarely adjust instantaneously to changes in cost and demand conditions. This is the monopoly theory of profit. Third, there is the view that profits are the reward for innovation. Innovations are those new products or processes (Schumpeter (1987) went so far as to include all 'different things') which increase national income more than they increase national costs. The difference is profit. All factors of production involved in producing the innovation are paid their opportunity costs and the entrepreneur who crystallised and organised the new idea into a marketable good or service receives this surplus of income over costs as reward. After a time imitators will appear (what Schumpeter colourfully called the 'Perennial Gale of Creative Destruction' p. 87), price levels will tend to be forced down to a perfectly competitive level and the innovative profits will be 'washed away'. More realistically, of course, a further innovation will appear on the scene before equilibrium is attained and the cycle will commence again.

2.1.1 Rent, quasi-rent and profits

These latter two views of profit – monopoly and innovation – overlap partly with the concept of rent. Recall rent is that part of a resource's reward in excess of that required to induce it to move to its next best alternative employment. Pure economic rent is derived from rare and valuable qualities of nature. Thus a firm's profits may include economic rent earned consequential on its possessing a monopoly of a given natural resource (say a particularly rich and productive vineyard), or because it was the first to introduce a new singer or entertainer to the market place (thus the profits earned by Time-Warner on Madonna's books, films and records include an element of rent, as do her own fees and royalties – she has a naturally endowed and unusual talent whose next best alternative employment would provide both her employer and herself with a very much smaller gross income). The distribution of these rents between the various coalition members into profits for capital provided, excess salaries for managers, excess wages for the vineyard farmers and fees for modelling erotic photographs depend on comparable bargaining strengths.

Most rents are not pure economic rents, however, but are quasi-rents. These too can be included in profit under the monopoly or innovation explanations. Unlike pure rents, *quasi-rents* are not the result of naturally occurring scarcity but are the result of *specialised investments*. Investments can be specific to firms, individuals, occupations or industries. Once committed, specialised resources cannot be transferred to alternative uses without loss of value. Alchian (1984, p. 35) argues that 'part of the value of a successful team (firm) is the value of having assembled a successful team (firm) – that is the avoidance of future costs of *searching for* a successful team'. Thus for example, Xerox earned monopoly and innovative profits embodying significant quasi-rents which persisted until other photocopying firms were assembled to compete them away. How much of these rents were appropriated by Edwin Land (the inventor), Xerox shareholders for profits, Xerox managers for salaries or workers (earning higher wages than they would have from competing employers requiring similar skills in different industries in the same towns as the Xerox plants) is, of course, an empirical and historical question.

2.1.2 Economic costs and accounting costs

Profits to an economist are the excess of income over opportunity costs. But the cost concepts used by accountants differ from those which would be used by economists. The accountant ignores opportunity costs.

One obvious example of this discrepancy is in the treatment of interest on the shareholder's capital. The accountant does not deduct this as a cost. The economist would impute it as a cost to be deducted from revenues in order to arrive at the profit figure. The rate of interest the economist chooses might be the market rate on 'risk-free' investments such as gilt-edged securities, or it might be a rate which reflects the risk and uncertainty of the operations of the firm in question. In the latter case, any remaining profit would presumably arise only from the rewards of innovation or the presence of market imperfections. Another common example is the case of smaller, owner-managed firms. There the accountant ignores the opportunity cost of the income that owners could earn if working elsewhere. Thus accounting profits, represent an exaggeration of 'true' profits.

In addition to any failure to impute opportunity costs rents and quasi-rents, there are even more serious errors arising out of deficiencies in accounting techniques themselves. These all have a common root concerning the length of time over which income and costs are calculated. The 'true' profitability of any investment or business cannot be determined until the ownership of that investment or business has been fully terminated. That is, until all income and costs over the relevant period of ownership have been calculated. Yet accountants must produce interim profit figures for shareholders (who need information on the progress of their investment), for managers (who need information upon which to judge past or base future decisions), and for the Inland Revenue (who need information to calculate a firm's tax liability). As a consequence, accounting figures are produced which are based upon an arbitrary allocation of both revenues and costs to a given accounting period. There is a major conceptual conflict here. Economists look to the future when placing a value on today's assets. To them, and for that matter to the business man or woman, the past is irrelevant. Profit, in an economic sense, is the *difference between the cash value of the enterprise today and its cash value at the end of its existence.*

In the case of economic profit sunk costs are regarded irrelevant and forecasts of net income into the indefinite future must be made. On the other hand, accountants define profits as the difference between revenues and costs over a given period, say a year. Both revenues and costs are calculated on an accrued basis, they are allocated to the time period in which they are earned or incurred, not necessarily the period in which they are earned or paid. Historical, not anticipated, cost and revenue data are used for the calculation. In balance sheet terms, profits calculated in this way represent *the difference between a firm's net worth* (i.e. total assets minus reserves and liabilities) *at the beginning and end of a year.*

These two definitions of costs highlight some of the differences and similarities between accounting and economic profits. The economist is concerned with income expectations: the accountant aims at producing historical records within the constraints of company law and professional practice.

2.2 Maximising the value of the firm

Throughout this book we assume that the objective of the firm is to maximise profits. Other objectives have been attributed to managers and we shall discuss these in Chapter 5. Optimisation is the most desirable allocation of resources from the manager's point of view, given whatever goals he or she has. However, total optimisation, even by a profit-maximising firm, is so complex that we generally discuss only partial optimisation of one or a small number of the firm's activities. In the remaining chapters we often concentrate on maximising the value of the firm by taking price decisions, investment decisions, manufacturing decisions or whatever, on the assumption that conditions ruling elsewhere within the firm are held constant. Accountants view profits as the excess of revenues over costs in the short run. Economists view profit as the value of the firm (i.e. profit taking into account the time dimension). It is with this latter concept of profit that we are now primarily concerned. The issues of incomplete information, risk and uncertainty are deferred until Chapters 3 and 4. Algebraically, the value of the firm can be expressed as follows:

Value of the firm = present value of expected future profits

or

$$PV_\pi = \frac{\pi_1}{1+r} + \frac{\pi_2}{(1+r)^2} + \frac{\pi_3}{(1+r)^3} + \ldots + \frac{\pi_n}{(1+r)^n}$$

$$= \sum_{t=1}^{n} \frac{\pi_t}{(1+r)^t} = \sum_{t=1}^{n} \frac{(TR - TC)_t}{(1+r)^t}$$

where $\pi_1, \pi_2 \ldots \pi_n$ are the expected profits for each year from 1 to n; r is the appropriate interest rate; and TR and TC are total revenues and total costs respectively.

Clearly, to maximise long-term profits in this way requires an understanding not only of what is meant by TR, TC and r, but also of the variables which can influence their magnitudes. The ability to control such variables, comprehend those which are beyond the firm's control, understand their interrelationships, and foresee or initiate changes in their values is the task of the manager and subject matter of this book.

2.2.1 Present value

Money has a time value. £1 received today is worth more than £1 to be received in the future. The sooner we receive money, the better off we are because the sooner we can invest it to earn interest. But how much more today's £1 is worth compared with £1 due in the future depends on the time interval and what can be done with the £1 in the interval. (At this point we are not discussing the impact of inflation on the real value of money. This is a separate issue.)

Suppose we have currently available a sum of £1,000 which we will term its present value or PV. We can invest this sum in the bank at, say, an interest rate,

r, of 10 per cent. After one year we could withdraw from the bank both the original deposit and the accumulated interest; this would be our future receipt in year one, or R_1. That is:

$$R_1 = £1000 + (0.1)\ 1000 = £1100$$

Box 2.1

The importance of development time in the profitability of innovation of over-the-counter medicines

Proprietary, non-prescription over-the-counter medicines include products such as Enos Fruit Salts, Panadol, Aspro and Beecham's Powders. Over the years new products are continuously introduced. For example in the cough and cold segment flavoured and soothing remedies such as Lemsip improved upon the straightforward pills or powders which only subdued symptoms. In turn soothing remedies were overtaken themselves by others such as Vick's Medinite or Night Nurse which relieved symptoms, and soothed but also aided sleep. Profits were gained as a consequence of innovation.

In the 1970s, however, the industry was subject to increased regulation arising from the implementation of the 1968 Medicines Act. The time required to carry out formulation studies and clinical testing was increased as more and more information was required to obtain the government awarded clinical trial certificate (CTC) and product license necessary before trials and, if successful, subsequently marketing of any product to the public was to be permitted. (On average development lead times rose from $2\frac{1}{4}$ to $4\frac{1}{2}$ years.)

The consequence was that the present value of profits which could have been computed thus:

$$PV_\pi = \frac{C_1}{1+r} + \frac{C_2}{(1+r)^2} + \frac{\pi_3}{(1+r)^3} \cdots + \frac{\pi_n}{(1+r)^n}$$

altered to:

$$PV_\pi = \frac{C_1}{1+r} + \frac{C_2}{(1+r)^2} + \frac{C_3}{(1+r)^3} + \frac{C_4}{(1+r)^4} + \frac{\pi_5}{(1+r)^5} \cdots + \frac{\pi_n}{(1+r)^n}$$

Where C is research and development and other set-up costs. Positive profits only begin to emerge in year 5 instead of year 3 (assuming revenues exceeded other costs in launch year). It is clear that, other things equal, PV_π, would be much less in 1978 than it would have been in 1970. One study of the industry converted this to percentages and showed that the expected rate of return in the industry to innovative investment in new products fell from 18.1 per cent in 1970 to 10 per cent in 1978. The drop was due not simply to an increase in costs, but to the fact that positive values for π were deferred still further into the future – and hence made even less valuable being divided by the term $(1 + r)$ at higher powers in 1978 than in 1970.

Source Reekie 1980.

Generally

$$R_1 = PV + r(PV) = PV(1 + r)$$

Alternatively, if we did not withdraw the money but left it on deposit for a further year, then at the end of year two we could withdraw the following:

$$R_2 = £1100 + (0.1)\ 1100 = £1210$$

Generally

$$R_2 = R_1 + (r)R_1 = R_1(1 + r) = PV(1 + r)^2$$

In like manner, R at the end of year three would be:

$$R_3 = PV(1 + r)^3$$

and at the of year n;

$$R_n = PV(1 + r)^n$$

This process is called compounding. The above general formula is the compound interest formula, and it tells us the magnitude of a future receipt if we already know its present value and the interest rate.

The reverse procedure, where the future receipt and the interest rate are known, and the present value remains to be found, is known as discounting. The discounting formula can be stated as:

$$PV = R_n/(1 + r)^n$$

This tells us the PV of a sum of money to be received in n years hence, given a discount rate of r. When a stream of future receipts is expected, occurring at annual intervals, then the PV of the stream is the sum of the PVs of each receipt. That is:

$$\frac{R_1}{(1 + r)} + \frac{R_2}{(1 + r)^2} + \frac{R_3}{(1 + r)^3} + \dots + \frac{R_n}{(1 + r)^n} = \sum_{i=1}^{n} \frac{R_i}{(1 + r)^i}$$

Box 2.1 provides an example of how lengthening the time required before an investment provides positive cash flows reduces the PV of profits.

2.3 Two rules of marginal equivalency

To indicate conditions of profit maximisation within a firm two general questions must be faced. Firstly, to what extent should a course of action be pursued; and secondly, if insufficient funds prevent all actions from being carried out at the optimum level, to what degree should each be pursued? The two theorems of marginal equivalency answer these questions:

Theorem 1   A course of action should be pursued until its marginal benefits equal its marginal costs, that is, where its marginal net benefits equal zero.

Theorem 2 If no action can be pursued to the optimum extent, each different action should be pursued until they all yield the same marginal benefits per unit of cost.

2.3.1 Total, average and marginal relationships

Theorem 1 is explained by reference to Table 2.1 (for simplicity we ignore the issue of time and of discounting). There we have hypothetical total, average and marginal profit functions of a firm. Note that, if we know the total profit function, the average and marginal values can be readily derived. The marginal value is merely the total value at that level less the total value at the immediately preceding output level. In other words, any total value is equal to the sum of all preceding marginal values.

Given this it is clear that if the marginal value is positive, then the total value will be rising. If the marginal value is negative, the total value will be falling. Therefore Theorem 1 is substantiated.

2.3.2 Diminishing marginal returns

Theorem 2 cannot be fully explained without reference to the law of diminishing marginal returns. Briefly, the law states that if the quantities of all inputs are held constant, but that of one input is increased, then the marginal output of that input will eventually decrease.

Suppose a business man or woman is pursuing two courses of action, A and B, and the marginal profit for the expenditure of £1 on A is £3.00 and on B is £3.50. It would be worth while to transfer £1 of expenditure from A to B. So doing he or she would forfeit £3.00 of profits but gain 50 pence for no extra cost. It would pay to continue reallocating expenditure until both A and B provided the same marginal profit per pound. If he or she could not pursue each action to the extent that its marginal profit equalled zero, the final marginal profits would be positive.

Table 2.1

Units of output	Total profits	Average profits	Marginal profits
1	5	5.0	5
2	16	8.0	11
3	31	10.33	15
4	49	12.25	18
5	63	12.6	14
6	72	12.0	9
7	74	10.57	2
8	67	8.37	−7

Box 2.2

Why newspapers advertise to advertisers

Most newspapers, magazines, radio and television stations depend on advertising revenues for income. Typically they in turn advertise in trade and business magazines to alert business men and women to the types of readers or audiences they attract. For example, if a manufacturer wishes to sell his or her product to upper middle-income earners living in central Scotland he will be better advised to place ads in the *Scotsman* and not the *Yorkshire Post*. Advertisements for these newspapers make this point to potential advertisers.

More recently in South Africa the Newspaper Press Union (a body representing the press) has been placing advertisements designed to attract business men or women not to spend all their advertising budget on television. The copy ran as follows:

> We're not questioning the efficiency of TV. But the latest Media Synergy research now proves that there is a high wastage factor in investing one's adspend exclusively in the box. It was found that advertisers who invested a minimum of 50% in print, combined with 50% in the electronic media, enjoyed a market share of 21% above the average.

The 'synergy' is due to application of marginal equivalency Theorem 2. More specifically it implies that production isoquants (or as we term them in Chapter 13 – sales response isoquants) display a diminishing marginal rate of technical substitution.

Due to the law of diminishing returns, *B*'s marginal yield relative to that of *A* would fall as more resources were allocated to it. Simultaneously as fewer resources were allocated to *A*, *A*'s marginal yield would rise relative to that of *B*. Hence ultimately the optimal position of marginal equivalency would be reached. Box 2.2 illustrates the theorem's application.

2.4 Mathematical methods

Relationships between economic variables can be expressed verbally, in a table, graphically or algebraically.

2.4.1 Marginal analysis and geometry

The relationships of Table 2.1 are expressed geometrically in Figure 2.1. The relationships between average profits and output (Q) and between marginal π and Q can be derived from the relationship between total π and Q.

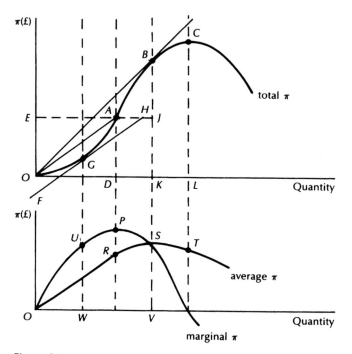

Figure 2.1

2.4.2 Marginal and average values

Average π are total π divided by Q. So in Figure 2.1 average π at output OD equals (distance AD/distance OD). Now the general formula for the slope of a straight line between two points, say A with coordinates (x_1, y_1) and B with coordinates (x_2, y_2) is $(y_2 - y_1)/(x_2 - x_1)$. Therefore since total π corresponds to the ys and Q to the xs, average π at OD equals the slope of OA. At any point on a total curve the corresponding average is the slope of the straight line from the origin to that point. Given this, we can see that the slopes (and hence average values) of straight lines from the origin to the total curve increase until output equals OK. Thereafter they decrease.

Marginal π is the increase in total π which results from a 1-unit increase in Q. Hence if AJ represented one unit, marginal π at output OD would equal BJ/AJ. If AJ was very much less than 1 unit, BJ would also be smaller and BJ/AJ would approximate the slope of a tangent to the total π curve at A. In general

$$\text{Marginal } y = \frac{y_2 - y_1}{x_2 - x_1} = \frac{\Delta y}{\Delta x}$$
(2.1)

where 'Δ' means 'change in'.

Now the slope of a curve at any point equals the slope of the tangent to the curve at that point. Thus at any point on the total curve the corresponding marginal figure is given by the slope of the line drawn tangent to the curve at that point. Marginal π at G is equal to the slope of FH, which equals WU in the lower half of the figure. Marginal π at B is equal to the slope of OB which equals VS in the lower figure. Marginal π at C would equal zero, since there the total π curve is neither rising nor falling and so its slope would be zero. This is the point of maximum total π. After point C the slope of the total π curve is negative with corresponding implications for the marginal π curve.

Notice that at outputs up to OD, the gradient of the total π curve increases as Q increases, but thereafter the gradient decreases. Hence marginal π is maximised at OD.

Average π and marginal π are equal at S, where the tangent to total π and the line from the origin to the output level on total π curve at any point is greater than the slope of the line drawn from the origin to that point. After B, the reverse holds true. Consequently, up to point B, or S on the lower figure, the fact that marginal values are higher than average will result in continuously increasing average values. After S, since marginal values are lower than average the average curve will fall away.

Figure 2.2 shows the familiar marginal cost (MC) and average cost (AC) curves of elementary texts. In Figure 2.1 we showed how it was possible to obtain marginal and average values from a total curve. Here we will illustrate how total values can be derived from the average or marginal curves. (The arguments we will use would be equally applicable to Figure 2.1.) Since total cost equals average (unit) cost multiplied by the number of units produced, then at Q_1 total cost equals $OA \times OQ_1$ which is the rectangle OQ_1CA. At any point on an average curve the total value is equal to the rectangle inscribed under that curve which has the axes for one set of sides and the origin and the point on the curve as diagonally opposite points.

We have already defined a total value as the sum of all preceding marginal values. Thus the total cost of producing Q_1 (8 units) is the sum of the eight thin

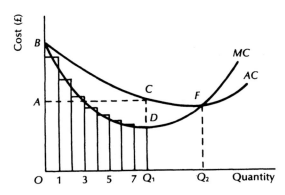

Figure 2.2

rectangles by which the MC curve is plotted, area $OBDQ_1$. At any point on a marginal curve the total value is equal to the area under the curve to the left of a vertical line dropped from the point on the curve to the x, or horizontal axis.

The above two propositions enable us to find a marginal curve when only an average curve is known. Consider Figure 2.3 where we have a linear demand, or average revenue curve (AR). At Q_1 we know that total revenue is equal to the area contained by the rectangle $OACQ_1$. To draw in the (unknown) marginal revenue (MR) curve, we must do so in such a way that at Q_1 the total revenue represented by $OBDQ_1$ is equal to $OACQ_1$. This will only be so if the two triangles ABE and CDE are equal in area. Both triangles already have two angles of equal magnitude, irrespective of where BD cuts AC. (Each has a right angle, and the angles at E are the opposite angles of a vertex.) Consequently, for the two triangles to be of equal size and shape they now merely need to have an equal side. This is obtained by ensuring that BD cuts AC at its midpoint so that $AE = EC$. Given a linear average curve, the corresponding marginal curve is found by drawing in the straight line which begins where the average curve cuts the vertical, or y, axis and passes through the midpoint of any horizontal line from the average curve to the y axis.

The problem of constructing a marginal curve from a non-linear average curve is more complex. For example, in Figure 2.4, we are given the average cost curve AC. Rather than finding the marginal cost curve, MC, as such, we must approximate it by discovering a number of individual points on it. At output level Q_1, the corresponding marginal value for X is Y. This is found by drawing AB, the tangent to X. This can be regarded as a proxy linear average curve passing through X and relevant to Q_1. The corresponding linear marginal curve to AB is AD. At Q_1, AD has a value of Y. Similarly, at output level Q_2, the average value of W has a corresponding marginal value of Z. This value was found by constructing the lines EF and EG in the same way as AB and AD. This process can be repeated at different output levels until the position of MC is known with confidence.

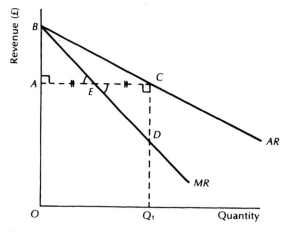

Figure 2.3

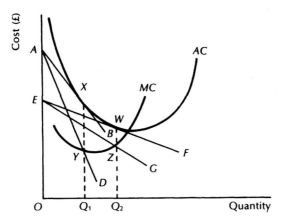

Figure 2.4

2.4.2 Marginal analysis and calculus

Often by representing a relationship by an equation we can find specific answers to certain problems. In these cases, calculus may be useful to locate maximum and minimum values. In this section we list some rules which are used in differential calculus.

2.4.3 Functions of one variable

Earlier we argued that in our formula for marginal y, equation (2.1), as we reduced the size of the change in x, distance AJ in Figure 2.1 would become smaller and BJ/AJ would become a closer and closer approximation to the gradient of the total π curve at A. Now a derivative is a precise specification of the general marginal relationship $\Delta y/\Delta x$ when Δx is infinitesimally small. In this case we write:

$$\frac{dy}{dx} = \lim_{\Delta x \to 0} \left(\frac{\Delta y}{\Delta x}\right)$$

Hence if we know a total cost equation we can find the marginal cost at any output.

To find the derivative of a function we follow the rules which are given in Table 2.2. The proofs of these rules can be found in any calculus text.

To see how calculus allows us to find the maximum or minimum values of a function, consider Figure 2.5. At outputs less than OQ_1 the gradient of the total curve is negative, at OQ_1 its gradient is zero, at outputs Q_1 to Q_3 it is positive and at outputs greater than OQ_3, it is negative again. Therefore we can draw the curve representing the gradient, or first derivative or marginal values. At OQ_1 total π has a local minimum (*local* because there may be lower minima at outputs for which we have not drawn the curve): as Q increases from just below Q_1 to just beyond it π

Table 2.2 Some simple rules of differentiation

Rule	Examples	Derivatives
1. *Constant Rule* The derivative of a constant is zero.	$y = a$ $y = 9$	$dy/dx = 0$ $dy/dx = 0$
2. *Power Rule* The derivative of a power function is the power times any original constant times the independent variable to its original power less one.	$y = ax^n$ $y = 9x$ $y = 9x^2$ $y = 9x^3$	$dy/dx = nax^{n-1}$ $dy/dx = 9$ $dy/dx = 18x$ $dy/dx = 27x^2$
3. *Sums and Differences Rule* The derivative of a sum (difference between) of several terms is the sum (difference between) of the derivatives of these terms.	$y = g(x) + h(x)$ $y = 10 + 4x^2 - 3x^3$	$\dfrac{dy}{dx} = \dfrac{dg}{dx} + \dfrac{dh}{dx}$ $\dfrac{dy}{dx} = 8x - 9x^2$
4. *Product Rule* The derivative of the product of two terms is the first term multiplied by the derivative of the second, plus the second term multiplied by the derivative of the first.	$y = g(x)h(x)$ $y = 9x^2(2 - x)$	$\dfrac{dy}{dx} = g(x)\dfrac{dh}{dx} + h(x)\dfrac{dy}{dx}$ $\dfrac{dy}{dx} = 9x^2(-1) + (2 - x)18x$ $= -9x^2 + 36x - 18x^2$ $= 36x - 27x^2$
5. *Quotient Rule* The derivative of a ratio function, equals the denominator multiplied by the derivative of the numerator, minus the numerator multiplied by the derivative of the denominator, all divided by the denominator squared.	$y = u/v$ where $u = g(x)$ $v = h(x)$ $y = (2 - x)/9x^2$	$\dfrac{dy}{dx} = \dfrac{1}{v^2}\left(v\dfrac{du}{dx} - u\dfrac{dv}{dx}\right)$ $\dfrac{dy}{dx} = \dfrac{9x^2(-1) - (2 - x)18x}{81x^4}$ $= \dfrac{-9x^2 - 36x + 18x^2}{81x^4}$ $= \dfrac{9x^2 - 36x}{81x^4} = \dfrac{x - 4}{9x^3}$
6. *Chain Rule* The derivative of a function of a function, such as $y = f(u)$ when $u = g(x)$, with respect to x, is equal to the derivative of y with respect to u, multiplied by the derivative of u with respect to x.	$y = f(u)$ where $u = g(x)$ $y = 2t^2$ where $t = x^3$	$\dfrac{dy}{dx} = \dfrac{dy}{du} \times \dfrac{du}{dx}$ $\dfrac{dy}{dx} = 4t \times 3x^2$ $= 4x^3 \times 3x^2 = 12x^5$

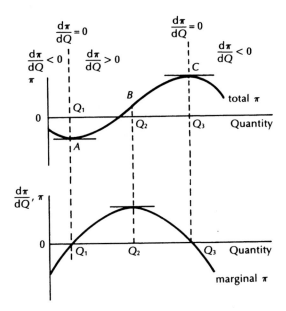

Figure 2.5

decreases but then rises. At C total π has a local maximum: as output increases from just below OQ_3 to just above OQ_3, total π rises at first but then decreases. Since at A and C the gradient is zero (because if we change Q by ΔQ, $\Delta \pi$ is zero, hence $\Delta \pi / \Delta Q$ is zero) if we set $d\pi/dQ = 0$ we have a necessary condition for a maximum or a minimum.

To distinguish between which of a maximum or a minimum we have, we use our observations about the gradients of the total curve at the outputs just below and just above OQ_1 and OQ_3. Since in the former case as Q increased, the gradient changed from being negative to positive, so it must be *increasing*. But in the case of OQ_3 as Q increased, the gradient changed from being positive to negative, so it must be *decreasing*. If the gradient is increasing as Q increases, the *gradient of the gradient* must be positive whereas if the gradient decreases as Q increases, the *gradient of the gradient* must be negative.

To find the gradient of the gradient of a function we find the first derivative of the first derivative, called the second order derivative and written $d^2\pi/dQ^2$ in this particular case. So we simply apply the rules of Table 2.2 to the first derivative.

For example

$$\pi = aQ + bQ^2 - cQ^3$$

$$\frac{d\pi}{dQ} = a + 2bQ - 3cQ^2$$

$$\frac{d^2\pi}{dQ^2} = 2b - 6cQ$$

Our argument is summarised thus: if $y = f(x)$ a maximum is found if the first derivative is zero and the second derivative is negative; a minimum is found if the first derivative is zero and the second derivative is positive.

2.4.4 Functions of several variables

Unconstrained optimisation

In many cases a dependent variable depends on the values of *several* independent variables. For example a demand function:

$$Q = f(A, P)$$

where Q represents quantity demanded per period, A advertising per period and P, price.

To find the marginal effects of each independent variable on the dependent variable whilst holding the effects of the other variables constant we use partial derivatives. A first order partial derivative of $Q = f(K, L)$ with respect to K is

$$\frac{\partial Q}{\partial K} = \lim_{\Delta K \to 0} \left(\frac{\Delta Q}{\Delta K} \right) \text{ where } L \text{ is held constant.}$$

This is analogous to the first derivative of a function of one variable which we explained above.

To interpret a partial derivative geometrically consider Figure 2.6 where $Q = f(K, L)$ represents a surface. If we hold L constant at L_0, then Q can change only if K is changed. These changes are shown by the 'slice' BPL_0. The partial derivative $\partial Q / \partial K$ at a point equals the gradient of this slice at that point because from the above definition of $\partial Q / \partial K$ we can see it is the change in Q divided by the change in K when this tends to zero and L is held constant. Similarly $\partial Q / \partial K$ at a point represents the gradient of the slice $K_0 PC$ at that point if K is fixed at K_0.

To find a first order partial derivative we treat all of the independent variables as constants except for that with respect to which we are differentiating. We then simply apply the rules of Table 2.2. For example:

$$z = 25 + 3x^2 + 5xy - 2y$$

$$\frac{\partial z}{\partial x} = 6x + 5y$$

$$\frac{\partial z}{\partial y} = 5x - 2$$

To find the maximum of say, Q as in Figure 2.6 we are geometrically trying to locate point P. We set $\partial Q / \partial L$ and $\partial Q / \partial K$ equal to zero. These conditions are necessary because if either was positive (negative) we could increase Q by increasing (decreasing) the relevant independent variable. In terms of Figure 2.6 we can see that the gradient of both of the slices $K_0 PC$ and BPL_0 equals zero at P, whereas at D, for example, $\partial Q / \partial K$ is positive so by increasing K we could increase Q. Hence D

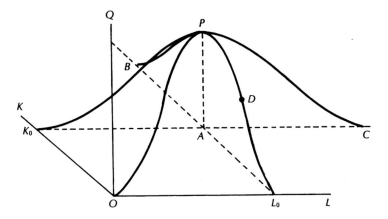

Figure 2.6

does not represent a maximum value of Q. However, note that we have explained only the necessary conditions for a maximum here. For the necessary *and* sufficient conditions the reader is referred to the Bibliography on page 31.

Constrained optimisation

Managers often wish to maximise or minimise a function of certain variables given certain constraints on those variables. For example, minimising total cost (depends on the quantities of inputs and their prices) subject to output being equal to a fixed level.

Two techniques can be used: the reduction method and the Lagrangian multiplier method. Before describing each, however, let us again use a geometric interpretation of the problem. If we are given an equation $Q = f(K, L)$ which we wish to maximise given that $4K + 2L = 100$, the first equation may represent a dome and the

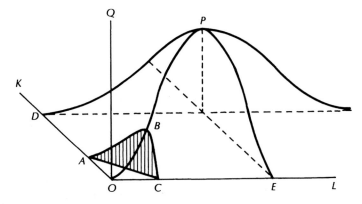

Figure 2.7

constraint, a line, because it contains only two variables, K and L, and not three. This dome is represented in Figure 2.7 and the constraint by AC. Geometrically the problem is to locate a point on the dome which is furthest up from the base but verti- cally above AC. That is if we slice the dome by moving a knife vertically through it so that it cuts along AC, where will it touch the dome first?

The reduction method

To consider both methods consider the problem:

$$\text{Maximise } z = 20x + 15y + 8xy - y^2 - x^2 \text{ subject to } 4x + 2y = 100.$$

Using the reduction method we would make, say, y the subject of the constraint equation, substitute it into the z function and treat the result as an unconstrained maximisation problem of one variable. Hence $y = 50 - 2x$

$$\therefore z = 20x + 15(50 - 2x) + 8x(50 - 2x) - (50 - 2x)^2 - x^2$$

$$= -1750 + 590x - 21x^2$$

$$\frac{\partial z}{\partial x} = 590 - 42x = 0 \quad \therefore x = 14.05$$

$$\frac{\partial^2 z}{\partial x^2} = -42 < 0 \quad \therefore \text{ a maximum.}$$

Substituting $x = 14.05$ into the constraint gives the optimum value of y to be 21.9. By substituting both of these values into the z function the maximum value of z is found to be 2394.05.

Notice that z could have been output; x and y quantities of capital and labour, and their coefficients 4 and 2 could have been their prices, with total cost equal to the 100. But often the constraints encountered are too numerous or too complex for the reduction technique to be practical, for example if in the last case we had had four independent variables and constraints a simpler method would have been the Lagrangian multiplier method.

Lagrange multiplier method

In this technique the constrained optimisation problem is converted into an unconstrained problem. The technique is to rearrange the constraint so that on one side we have the value zero, to multiply the resulting equation by an undetermined variable – the Lagrangian multiplier – and to add this to the objective function. Hence for our last problem:

$$Z_\lambda = 20x + 15y + 8xy - y^2 - x^2 + \lambda(100 - 4x - 2y)$$

where Z_λ is the Lagrangian function and λ the Lagrangian multiplier. We then differentiate Z_λ with respect to $x, y,$ and λ and equate each derivative to zero to obtain three equations in these three unknowns. These equations are then solved simultaneously. Recall that we wish to find values of x and y which give the largest possible value of z while still satisfying the constraint $100 - 4x - 2y = 0$. If only values of x and y which fulfil the constraint are considered, the expression in brackets in the Z_λ is zero, and those values from this restricted set which maximise Z_λ will also maximise z (and do so subject to the constraint). Therefore, the constraint is fulfilled, and we can treat the problem of finding x and y which give the constrained maximum of z as the same as finding x and y to give the unconstrained maximum of Z_λ. Hence we partially differentiate Z_λ with respect to each of x, y, and λ and equate the partial derivatives to zero. The multiplication of the rearranged constraint by λ guarantees that the constraint is fulfilled because, when Z_λ is differentiated with respect to λ and equated to zero, the constraint is obtained as one of the necessary conditions. Differentiation with respect to x and y completes the requirements for maximisation. Hence:

$$\partial Z_\lambda / \partial x = 20 + 8y - 2x - 4\lambda = 0$$

$$\partial Z_\lambda / \partial y = 15 + 8x - 2y - 2\lambda = 0$$

$$\partial Z_\lambda / \partial \lambda = 100 - 4x - 2y \quad = 0$$

Solving simultaneously gives $x = 14.05$, $y = 21.9$ and $z = 2394.05$, the same solutions as from the reduction method. If further constraints existed we would rearrange each, apply a different Lagrange multiplier to each and proceed as before. (Note that λ represents the marginal change in z when the constraint – in the example, 100 – changes by one unit. Thus if z represents output and x and y are capital and labour with prices of £4 and £2 respectively, and the constraint represents the available budget to be spent on both inputs, then λ has a value of 41.8. If we increased the budget by £1 and allocated this optimally between additional x and y, output would rise to 2436.01 units or approximately 42 units above its previous level. We would hire an additional 0.14 units of x and 0.30 units of y.)

Bibliography

Alchian, A. (1984) 'Specificity, specialisation, and coalitions', *Journal of Institutional and Theoretical Economics*, vol. 1.

Archibald, G. C. and Lipsey, R. (1967) *An Introduction to a Mathematical Treatment of Economics*, Weidenfeld & Nicholson.

Birchenhall, C. and Grout, P. (1984) *Mathematics for Modern Economics*, Philip Allan.

Casson, M. (1973) *Introduction to Mathematical Economics*, Thomas Nelson.

Chiang, A. C. (1984) *Fundamental Methods of Mathematical Economics*, McGraw-Hill.

Dowling, E. T. (1980) *Mathematics for Economists*, McGraw-Hill.

Glass, J. Colin (1980) *An Introduction to Mathematical Methods in Economics*, McGraw-Hill.

Huang, D. S. (1964) *Introduction to the Use of Mathematics in Economic Analysis*, John Wiley.

Reekie, W. D. (1980) 'Legislative change and industrial performance', *Scottish Journal of Political Economy*, vol. 27.

Schumpeter, J. (1987) *Capitalism, Socialism and Democracy*, Unwin Paperbacks.

Yamane, T. (1968) *Mathematics for Economists: An elementary survey*, Prentice Hall.

Chapter 3

Decision analysis under risk and uncertainty

The previous chapter emphasised that profits must not only be carefully defined but that they must be discounted for time. Profit maximisers are misnamed. They should really be termed wealth maximisers. Time is not the only factor for which profit calculations should be adjusted. Most managerial decisions involve risk or uncertainty. In this chapter we set out a framework for explaining decision theory, discuss the nature of certainty, risk and uncertainty, and finally show how the present value wealth maximising formula can be adjusted to account for the phenomena.

3.1 A framework for decision making

Suppose a decision maker wishes to choose between two alternative actions. The outcome of each will depend on both which is chosen and which 'state of nature' occurs. A state of nature is a set of environmental factors which affect the value of an outcome. For example, the manager may wish to decide on which of two projects to pursue where the profits resulting from each depend on which of the following occurs: recession, normal conditions, and boom.

We can represent this decision maker's situation diagrammatically as in Table 3.1 where S_1 to S_3 represent the states of the economy, A_1 and A_2 represent the projects and $O_{11} \ldots O_{23}$ represent outcomes.

This matrix can be generalised for any number of actions $A_1 \ldots A_n$ and any number of states of nature $S_1 \ldots S_q$. We assume the states of nature are mutually exclusive and independent of the choice of action. The outcomes can be measured in money units or utility units as we discuss in Section 3.3.

3.2 The nature of certainty, risk and uncertainty

Decision making situations may be classified in two ways: the degree of strategic interdependence between different decision makers and the degree of knowledge

Table 3.1

Actions	States of nature		
	S_1	S_2	S_3
A_1	O_{11}	O_{12}	O_{13}
A_2	O_{21}	O_{22}	O_{23}

which a decision maker has about the occurrence of each state of nature. Strategic interdependence exists if the actions of other firms are explicitly taken into account by the first firm. It is absent if the actions chosen by other firms are simply regarded as a state of the environment. For example in oligopoly strategic interdependence would exist because each firm would try to predict its competitor's action. In this chapter we ignore strategic interdependence.

There are three degrees of knowledge which a decision maker can have about the occurrence of each state of nature: certainty, risk and uncertainty. *Certainty* exists if the decision maker has complete knowledge of every relevant aspect of the decision and knows which outcome will result from each action. *Risk* exists if each action leads to one of several possible outcomes where the manager knows the probability of occurrence of each state of nature. He or she does not know which state of nature he *will* face but only the proportion of the total number of occasions on which each state of nature will exist if it frequently recurs.

The probability of occurrence of a state of nature may be calculated either a priori: before the states have occurred, or a posteriori: after the states have occurred on a certain number of occasions. In the former the probability may be deduced. For example, the probability of the occurrence of a head when an unbiased coin is tossed may be deduced in advance to be one half. In the a posteriori case, a historic sample of occasions on which states of nature occurred is taken and the relative frequency of each is calculated. This assumes that the relative frequency of each state in the past is identical to that in the future. Alternatively a subjective probability may be attributed to each state of nature based on, for example, one's experiences of similar past events. *Uncertainty* exists if the probability of each outcome occurring when any one action is chosen is either completely unknown or is not even meaningful.

Thus the cases of certainty and uncertainty are two extremes of the degree of knowledge which a decision maker has as to the probability of occurrence of each state of nature. As confidence in estimates of these probabilities changes, the situation moves from one extreme to the other. Most decisions are taken in situations between the two.

3.3 Measurement of risk

One common way to explain risk is to use a probability distribution of outcomes resulting from a decision. This relates the value of each possible outcome to the probability of its occurrence.

Consider an example where a manager has to choose between two projects where the profits from each depend on the forthcoming state of the economy. Suppose the manager knows the probability of occurrence of each state of the economy as in Table 3.2.

Given that only five states of nature can occur, Figure 3.1 represents the probability distribution of the outcomes of each project. If there were a very large number of states of the economy then the number of columns in Table 3.2 would be much greater. With a very large number of points in the figure each representing a different pay-off and each with a specific probability of occurrence, the probability of any particular value is much lower than in Figure 3.1. The resulting large number of points may then be approximated by a continuous line as in Figure 3.2.

Measures of the risk associated with an action relate to certain characteristics of the probability distribution of outcomes for that action. Crudely, the riskiness of any decision is measured in terms of the variability of its outcomes. The less dispersed the possible outcomes are from the expected value (i.e. the mean), the greater the probability that the actual outcome will be within a given range of that expected value and hence the less risky the project.

Table 3.2

	States of nature					
Actions	Deep recession	Stagnation	Normal	Mild boom	Extreme boom	Expected value (Mean)
Probability	0.10	0.20	0.40	0.20	0.10	
Project A	1.00	3.00	5.00	7.00	9.00	5.00
Project B	4.50	4.75	5.00	5.25	5.50	5.00

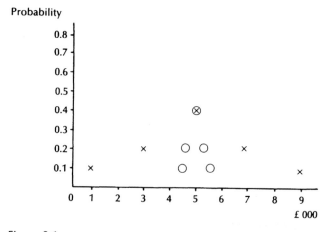

Figure 3.1

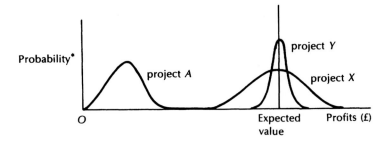

*More accurately 'probability density' (since the probability of any specific
π value occurring is near zero, yet the area under the curve between two
π values gives the probability of a π value in that range).

Figure 3.2

3.3.1 Standard deviation

The most common measures of risk are the standard deviation and coefficient of
variation. The former is calculated thus:

$$\sigma = \sqrt{\sum_{i=1}^{n} P_i(X_i - \overline{X})^2}$$

where P_i = probability of outcome i
      X_i = value of outcome i
      n = number of outcomes
      $\overline{X}$ = mean value of all outcomes
      σ = standard deviation

The lower the standard deviation, the tighter the probability distribution of
outcomes and the lower the risk, whereas the higher the standard deviation the
greater the risk. From Table 3.2 we can see that in terms of standard deviations,
project A is riskier than project B and in Figure 3.2 project X is riskier than project Y.

One criticism of this measure is that a conservative manager may be more
concerned with avoiding outcomes below the expected value than with achieving
outcomes above. Therefore a measure of risk which more accurately corresponds to
that experienced by a manager would be a measure which included only pay-offs
below the expected value. An example of such a measure is the 'semi-standard deviation' which is calculated as:

$$SSD = \sqrt{\sum_{i=1}^{k} P_i(X_i - \overline{X})^2}$$

where P_i = probability of outcome i
      X_i = value of outcome i

$i = 1 \ldots k =$ the set of outcomes whose values are less than $\overline{X}$
$\overline{X} =$ mean of all outcomes

However, it is usual for the standard deviation and semi-standard deviation to be correlated, so the latter may add little information.

A second criticism of the standard deviation is that two alternative actions may have probability distributions which intuitively seem to differ in riskiness but which have the same standard deviation. For example, suppose projects A and X in Figure 3.2 have the same standard deviation of £1,000 but A has an expected profit of £10,000, whereas X has an expected profit of £100,000. Using the standard deviation as a measure of risk, both A and X are equally risky, but this measure has not taken into account the greater expected return of X in comparison with A.

3.3.2 Coefficient of variation

To standardise for different magnitudes of expected outcomes one can calculate the coefficient of variation for each project:

$$V = \frac{\sigma}{E(\pi)}$$

where $E(\pi)$ denotes expected profits. Using this criterion project A is more risky than project X.

A limitation of these measures is that neither σ nor V gives indications of other aspects of the probability distribution such as shape, yet shape may affect risk. For example, both distributions in Figure 3.3 share the same values for σ and V but the adoption of project A may result in profits between π_0 and π_2 whereas project B would not result in profits below π_1 but could result in profits as high as π_3. Therefore a more accurate assessment of the riskiness of a project may depend not only on σ and V, but also on the degree of skewness of the distribution, its range, modal outcome and so on.

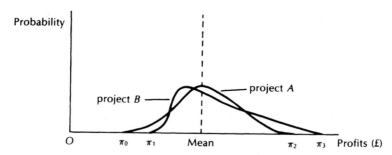

Figure 3.3

3.4 Decision criteria under certainty

Here the decision maker knows which state of nature will occur. Therefore the lower pay-offs can be ignored which are possible for each action. He can then simply choose the action with the largest pay-off.

3.5 Decision criteria under risk

In this case the manager uses the probability distribution.

3.5.1 Expected monetary value (*EMV*)

The decision maker chooses the action with the largest *EMV*. *EMV* is calculated as:

$$EMV(A_i) = P_1\pi_{i1} + P_2\pi_{i2} + \ldots + P_n\pi_{in}$$

$$= \sum_{j=1}^{n} P_j\pi_{ij}$$

where P_j is the probability of state of nature j

   π_{ij} is the pay-off which results from action i and state of nature j.

A criticism of the ranking of projects based on *EMV* is that it ignores the riskiness of each project. This was illustrated in Table 3.1 where two projects had the same *EMV*, but different distributions of possible pay-offs.

3.5.2 Managers as risk averters and risk preferrers

In the above case the manager is presumed to be risk-neutral. That is, he or she has a constant marginal utility of money. In Figure 3.4a increasing the monetary value of an outcome from Y to $2Y$ would simply double the manager's utility. However, managers may be risk preferrers (people who gamble on horses or roulette are risk preferrers) with an increasing marginal utility of money; or risk averters with a diminishing marginal utility of money (people who insure against their home catching fire are risk averse). Clearly the same individual can be both a risk averter and risk preferrer at different times or at different levels of possible wealth gain. Similarly different individuals will display different degrees of preference or aversion (thus different degrees of motor accident coverage are common ranging from third-party cover to fully comprehensive). Figures 3.4b and 3.4c show individual utility functions displaying increasing and decreasing marginal utility of money respectively. In Figure 3.4b doubling Y more than doubles the utility received by the individual. In Figure 3.4c doubling income increases total utility less than proportionately.

(a) Risk neutrality – constant marginal utility of money

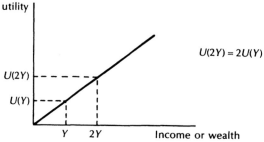

(b) Risk preference – increasing marginal utility of money

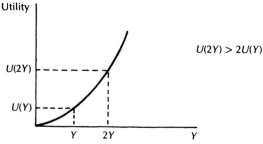

(c) Risk aversion – decreasing marginal utility of money

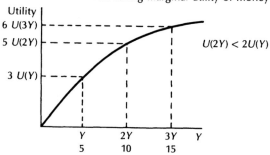

Figure 3.4

Generally decision makers are presumed to be risk averse. Why is risk aversion linked to a diminishing marginal utility of money? Consider Figure 3.4c. Values have been attached to the axes, in money values for Y and in 'utils' for utility. A manager (risk averse) can choose between a project (X) which produces £10 with certainty or an alternative project (Z) which has two alternative pay-offs of £5 or £15 with a 50:50 probability of either outcome. Which will be chosen?

$$EMV_X = £10$$

$$EMV_Z = £5 - Z(0.5) + £15(0.5)$$

$$= £10$$

The *EMVs* are identical. If the manager is risk-averse he or she will choose project X because the expected utilities differ consequent on his or her having a diminishing marginal utility of money. Thus:

$$EUV_X = 5 \text{ utils}$$

$$EUV_Z = 3(0.5)\text{utils} + 6(0.5)\text{utils}$$

$$= 4.5 \text{ utils}.$$

X is preferred, not simply intuitively as observation of the probability distribution would suggest, but numerically and unambiguously.

The practical problem is how to obtain such utility values. Or, put differently, how can utility values be injected into a pay-off matrix like Table 3.1? Readers can experiment for themselves with Figure 3.4 and show risk preferrers display an increasing marginal utility of money.

3.5.3 Converting monetary values into utility values

Von Neumann and Morganstern (VNM) developed a means of devising a cardinal utility index.

Neo-classical cardinal utility (see Chapter 7) measures the intensity of satisfaction which an individual derives from an action. But VNM cardinal utility is different (despite the identical use of words). It is a number associated with a pay-off which enables one to rank pay-offs in terms of those more and those less preferred by a decision maker. In what sense is the measure cardinal? To explain this we must distinguish between different types of measure.

Measures may be ordinal or cardinal. The first allows one to rank phenomena in terms of a measure. But it does not allow one to combine two or more rankings to produce an index which would be valid for the phenomena jointly. For example, suppose we have two ladders. Using a measure which ranks only height we would award a higher number to the taller ladder and a lower number to the shorter. Provided we always give a higher number to the taller ladder the actual numbers used do not matter. The measure will still rank the ladders correctly. But one cannot necessarily *combine* the actual numbers to compare this pair of ladders with another pairing of ladders. The second (cardinal) measure does allow one to combine the indices of a characteristic of two phenomena to predict whether or not the characteristics of the two together do or do not exceed the characteristics of another two. Such an index, for example metres, would enable us to predict whether the height of the two ladders, one extended from the other, would or would not exceed the height of a ceiling. The VNM index is a cardinal index in this sense. It permits the combination of utility indices of more than one pay-off so that one can assess whether or not one set of joint pay-offs is to be preferred to other combinations.

3.5.4 The VNM standard gamble technique

Here we construct the VNM utility index for a risky pay-off and, secondly, for a certain pay-off. Suppose an entrepreneur is trying to decide between manufacturing denim jeans or cord trousers. Suppose the possible pay-offs depend only on whether consumers' tastes are predominantly in favour of denim or of cords. Let the money pay-offs (in £ 000) in each case be those shown in Table 3.3.

If, for jeans, the utility index of the £100,000 pay-off is 1000 utils and 500 utils for the £40,000, and the respective probabilities are 0.7 and 0.3, then the expected utility of the introduction of this product is $0.7 \times 1000 + 0.3 \times 500 = 850$ utils. Similarly, in the case of the introduction of cords, if the utility index for each pay-off is 690 utils for the £60,000 and 880 utils for the £80,000 then the expected utility for this product is $0.7 \times 690 + 0.3 \times 880 = 747$ utils. In general, the expected utility of a risky action, A, $EUV(A)$, with two pay-offs, π_1 and π_2 is:

$$EUV(A) = pU(\pi_1) + (1-p)U(\pi_2) \tag{3.1}$$

where p and $(1-p)$ denote the probabilities of π_1 and π_2 occurring respectively, and $U(\pi_1)$ and $U(\pi_2)$ denote the utility indices for π_1 and π_2. But how does one evaluate $U(\pi_1)$ and $U(\pi_2)$?

To ascribe a utility number to a specific money pay-off, say π_1, the decision maker is presented with a 'standard gamble' comparison. A risky action, say A_1, is considered as the yardstick for comparison. Its possible outcomes, X_1 and X_2, have probabilities of occurrence q and $(1-q)$ respectively. Arbitrarily chosen utility indices are then awarded to X_1 and X_2 so that the higher index is attributed to the outcome the decision maker prefers. Next, the decision maker is presented with a series of choices between the risky action, A_1, and the action A_2, which has the certain outcome of π_1 to which we wish to ascribe a measure of utility. That is, the decision maker is asked to compare

$$EUV(A_1) = qU(X_1) + (1-q)U(X_2) \text{ and } EUV(A_2) = 1 \times U(\pi_1)$$

This choice situation is represented in Table 3.4. The value of q is altered in the series of choice situations until the decision maker is indifferent between the two actions.

Table 3.3

	Tastes in favour of denim	Tastes in favour of cords
Probability	0.7	0.3
Denim jeans	100	40
Cords	60	80

Table 3.4

Actions	State of nature		Expected utility
	S_1	S_2	
Probability	q	$(1-q)$	
A_1	$U(X_1)$	$U(X_2)$	$qU(X_1) + (1-q)U(X_2)$
A_2	$U(\pi_1)$	$U(\pi_1)$	$1 \times U(\pi_1)$

If $U(X_1)$ is less than $U(X_2)$ then, as q increases from 0 to 1, the probability of gaining X_1 rather than X_2 is increased and $EUV(A_1)$ decreases from $U(X_2)$ to $U(X_1)$. At the value of q which renders the decision maker indifferent between the actions, both have the same utility index. So $EUV(A_1) = EUV(A_2)$ and therefore

$$U(\pi_1) = q \times U(X_1) + (1-q)U(X_2)$$

But, since $U(X_1)$ and $U(X_2)$ are known, albeit with arbitrarily chosen values, and q has been found by experiment, $U(\pi_1)$ can be calculated. The process can be repeated for $U(\pi_2)$. Both indices can then be substituted into equation (3.1) to find the utility index for action A.

Returning to the jeans and cords example, suppose we wish to find the utility which the entrepreneur associates with £100,000. We could formulate the standard gamble as a risky action with pay-offs of £10m and £10. Suppose the entrepreneur expresses a preference for £10m to £10: we would arbitrarily assign utilities of, say, 19,620 and 20 utils to each respectively. The entrepreneur is then given a series of choices between, on the one hand, the standard gamble and on the other hand a certain £100,000 where q, the probability of gaining the £10m in the standard gamble, is progressively reduced until he or she is indifferent between the two. Suppose this value of q is 0.05. Then:

$$EUV(£100,000) = EUV \text{ (standard gamble)}$$

$$= qU(£10 \text{ million}) + (1-q)U(£10)$$

$$= (0.05 \times 19620) + (0.95 \times 20)$$

$$= 1000 \text{ utils}$$

The same procedure could be performed for the other possible outcome of the denim product and both 'utility' values substituted into an expression analogous to equation (3.1) to gain the EUV for denim jeans. In similar fashion Figure 3.4a–Figure 3.4c can be constructed for different decision makers with different attitudes to risk (and hence differing marginal utilities of money).

3.5.5 The certainty-equivalent or expected return–risk analysis approach

An alternative to using VNM cardinal utility values is the use of expected return–risk analysis. The *EMV* and the risk of each action may be plotted on a diagram. Risk may be measured using any of the indices already explained. Figure 3.5 shows the results for the actions represented in Table 3.5. The manager's preferences may be represented by indifference curves, for examples lines I_1, I_2, I_3. Each indifference curve joins different combinations of *EMV* and risk between which the manager is indifferent. If the manager prefers a greater *EMV* with a given level of risk and also a lower level of risk given an *EMV*, then the indifference curves will have a positive slope. Combinations on curves closer to the top left-hand corner represent *EMV*–risk combinations which are preferred to those on curves closer to the lower right-hand corner because with any given level of risk the former curves indicate greater *EMV* than the latter. To accept greater risk and remain indifferent to their initial position a manager is assumed to require a proportionately greater *EMV*; that is, the manager is risk-averse. Given the indifference curves in Figure 3.5 we predict that the manager would prefer action A_2. (Note that we have ignored the possibility that the earnings resulting from one action may be correlated with those of others. This possibility is considered in Chapter 14.)

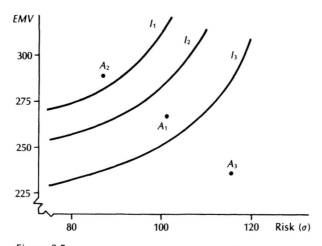

Figure 3.5

Table 3.5

| | States of nature | | | |
Actions	S_1	S_2	S_3	EMV
Probability	0.25	0.35	0.40	
A_1	100	300	350	270
A_2	300	400	200	295
A_3	400	100	250	235

The position of the indifference curves can be found by quizzing managers in a manner analogous to the VNM standard gamble approach. Thus for any curve such as I_1, and any risk–return combination on that curve the manager would initially be asked what certain equivalent *EMV* (i.e. what point on the *EMV* axis with zero risk) would provide him with identical utility. This process could be repeated for points on I_2 and I_3.

3.6 Decision criteria under uncertainty

Several techniques can be used when the probability of each state of nature is unknown: for example, the maximin (or Wald) criterion, the minimax regret (Savage) criterion, the maximax criterion, the Hurwicz and Laplace criteria. For each we shall use as an example the choice situation of Table 3.6.

3.6.1 Maximin criterion

For each strategy the decision maker identifies the lowest pay-off. The strategy with the largest of these 'lowest pay-offs' is selected. In the example the lowest pay-offs for strategies A_1, A_2 and A_3 are 1.0, −2.0 and 3.0 respectively. The decision maker would select A_3.

This criterion is 'conservative' or 'pessimistic' because it is a rule whereby the decision maker avoids the worst outcome. Some argue that since the criterion does not take account of the value of every pay-off it can lead to unreasonable conclusions. For example, in Table 3.7 action A_3 would be chosen despite the very large possible pay-offs of the alternatives.

3.6.2 Minimax regret criterion

Here the decision maker asked what would be the sacrifice if a particular state of nature occurred, but instead of having chosen the strategy with the greatest pay-off given that state, he or she had chosen another. Hence, for each state of nature the difference between the maximum pay-off and that for each action is calculated and placed in a new 'regret' matrix. For each action the largest regret is calculated and

Table 3.6

Actions	States of nature		
	S_1	S_2	S_3
A_1	1.0	2.0	9.0
A_2	−2.0	5.0	11.0
A_3	3.0	3.5	4.5

Table 3.7

Actions	States of nature		
	S_1	S_2	S_3
A_1	2.9	10^4	10^7
A_2	2.9	10^4	10^{10}
A_3	3.0	3.1	3.1

the action with the smallest of these is selected. Adoption of the criterion, therefore, avoids the greatest sacrifice of pay-off if the chosen strategy turns out not to be the one with the highest pay-off, given the state of nature which occurs. Thus this criterion can also be regarded as 'pessimistic'.

In the example, the regret matrix is shown in Table 3.8 and strategy A_1 would be chosen. Several criticisms have been made of this criterion. Firstly, it ignores information; specifically, it ignores all regrets except the largest for each strategy. But the action with the smallest of these may have regrets all of a similar size whereas the rejected actions may, apart from the largest regret, have much smaller ones than those of the chosen strategy. In this situation the criterion may be unreasonable.

Secondly, the criterion may select a strategy from a group of alternatives but would select a different strategy if the original group were depleted by one which was initially rejected. For example consider the case in Table 3.9. If all three strategies were available A_3 would be selected, as shown by the 'Regrets 1' matrix. But if only strategies A_2 and A_3 were available A_2 would be chosen, not A_3, the original and still available choice.

Table 3.8

Actions	States of nature			
	S_1	S_2	S_3	Row maxima
A_1	2.0	3.0	2.0	3.0
A_2	5.0	0.0	0.0	5.0
A_3	0.0	1.5	6.5	6.5

Table 3.9

Actions	Pay-offs			Regrets 1				Regrets 2			
	S_1	S_2	S_3	S_1	S_2	S_3	Row maxima	S_1	S_2	S_3	Row maxima
A_1	21	11	1	0	11	18	18				
A_2	1	22	8	20	0	11	20	10	0	11	11
A_3	11	5	19	10	17	0	17	0	17	0	17

3.6.3 Maximax criterion

Here the decision maker selects the largest pay-off for each action and the action with the largest of these maxima. In Table 3.6 the largest pay-offs are 9.0, 11.0 and 4.5 respectively. Hence the decision maker would select A_2. This criterion also ignores information: it would select a strategy even if the maximum pay-off for that strategy only marginally exceeded that of others, even if the other possible outcomes from the selected action were very much or even dangerously lower.

3.6.4 Hurwicz α-criterion

The maximin criterion selected only the worst outcome for each action whereas the maximax selected only the best. The Hurwicz α-criterion is an attempt to use both. For each action an α-index, αI_i, is calculated where:

$$\alpha I_i = \alpha M_i + (1 - \alpha) L_i$$
$M_i, L_i =$ the least and largest pay-offs for action i respectively
$\alpha = $ a pessimism–optimism index.

The action with the largest α-index is selected. For example if $\alpha = \frac{1}{4}$ the α-indices for each action in the original example are 7, $7\frac{3}{4}$ and $4\frac{1}{8}$ for A_1, A_2 and A_3 respectively, hence A_2 would be chosen. The value of α may be derived by presenting the decision maker with hypothetical choices between A_1 and A_2 as in Table 3.10. The value of z is increased from 0 until the decision maker is indifferent between the two actions.

Again this is analogous to the standard gamble approach. The pay-offs of 0 and 100 for A_1 are hypothetical. The α-index for A_1 is

$$\alpha I = \alpha (0) + (1 - \alpha) \, 100$$

$$= 100 - 100\alpha$$

When indifference is reached, the actions are assumed to have the same α-index. Hence $100 (1 - \alpha) = z$ so, given z, α can be calculated.

A criticism of this technique is that it also ignores information: only the largest and smallest pay-offs are considered. Hence one action may be chosen in preference to the others despite the fact that all of its intermediate pay-offs may be less than those of any other strategy.

Table 3.10

	States of nature		
Actions	S_1	S_2	αI
A_1	0	100	$100 - 100\alpha$
A_2	z	z	z

3.6.5 Principle of Insufficient Reason (Laplace criterion or Bayes's criterion)

This states that if one has no idea which state of nature is most likely to occur, then one should ascribe the same probability of occurrence to each. Hence if there are n states of nature, the probability of $1/n$ is ascribed to each, and the expected value for each strategy calculated. The strategy with the greatest expected value is chosen.

A criticism of this technique is that in practice there may be many different ways of listing states of nature where each way is complete and each state mutually exclusive. For example, the states of nature which affected the outcomes to the denim jeans/cords choice were given as 'tastes in favour of denim' and 'tastes in favour of cords'; hence using the Laplace criterion, each state would have a probability of $\frac{1}{2}$, but possibly one should consider three relevant states: 'tastes strongly in favour of denim'; 'tastes mildly in favour of denim'; 'tastes in favour of cords', each being ascribed a probability of $\frac{1}{3}$ and so on.

3.6.6 Mixed strategies

Instead of choosing a pure strategy the decision maker could choose each strategy on a fixed proportion of occasions, the choice on each occasion being determined randomly. The pay-offs for each state of nature in the mixed strategies would be those expected from the combination of actions. The pure strategies and the mixed strategies could all be compared on a maximin or minimax regret criterion for selection. For example, if the mixed strategy in Table 3.11 (taking a different example to that of Table 3.6) consists of A_1 and A_2 with probabilities $\frac{1}{3}$ and $\frac{2}{3}$ respectively, the pay-offs for each state of nature are the sum of $\frac{1}{3}$ and $\frac{2}{3}$ times those of the pure strategies. When the maximin criterion is applied to this augmented matrix the chosen action is A_2.

3.6.7 Cautionary note

Note that in all of our pay-off matrices the VNM utility index value could be substituted for each monetary value for use with any of our criteria. But of these

Table 3.11

Actions	States of nature	
	S_1	S_2
A_1	30	15
A_2	60	30
$\frac{1}{3}A_1 + \frac{2}{3}A_2$	50	25

criteria, the Principle of Insufficient Reason is the only one which is consistent with all of VNM's underlying theoretical assumptions (see Baumol 1977).

3.7 Sequential decisions: decision trees

A manager often has to decide between strategies where the outcomes depend on chance events and/or future choices whose outcomes themselves depend on chance and/or future choices and so on. Provided there is sufficient information concerning the probabilities of the outcomes of each chance event and of the values of every final outcome, decision trees are a method of calculating the EMV of each strategy.

Suppose a manager has to decide whether or not to develop a new product which has emerged from the firm's research laboratory. The manager believes that the probability of successfully doing so in two years is 0.7 and hence the probability of either technological failure or inability to keep to the budgeted time span is 0.3. If successful, the pattern of net cash inflow will depend on whether the project is launched with high or low advertising, or whether it is abandoned. In the former two cases, demand may be high, medium or low with probabilities 0.5, 0.3 and 0.2 respectively if advertising is high, but 0.2, 0.3 and 0.5 respectively if advertising is low. High, medium and low levels of demand give net cash inflows of £8,000, £5,000 and £3,000 if advertising is high, but £8,500, £5,500 and £2,500 if it is low. Abandonment at this stage results in a loss of £1,000.

If, however, the development fails after two years, the manager must decide whether or not to engage in further efforts. If development is authorised this may also succeed or fail. Suppose the probabilities of these outcomes occurring, given earlier failure, are 0.3 and 0.7 respectively. If the development is successful on this occasion, again the manager must decide whether to launch and advertise heavily, advertise lightly or abandon. In the first two cases the probabilities of high, medium and low demand are 0.5, 0.3, 0.2 and 0.2, 0.3 and 0.5 respectively with corresponding cash inflows of £7,000, £4,000, £2000 and £4,500, £2,500 and £1,500. Abandonment at this stage results in a loss of £2,000. Abandonment in the very first instance results in neither profit nor loss, whereas abandonment after an initial development failure results in a loss of £1,000.

The problem facing the manager is represented by the decision tree of Figure 3.6. Each square box represents a 'decision node', the branches from it indicating *decisions* made. The circles represent 'chance nodes', the branches represent *outcomes* which result from earlier decisions and which occur with certain probabilities. The numbers above the lines represent the probability of the next outcome occurring given that the previous chance node has been reached.

To make the decision on the basis of EMVs, the EMV for each action is calculated and the action with the greatest EMV is chosen. Each EMV is calculated on the basis that whenever a decision has to be made, the manager will choose that with the highest EMV. The method of analysing this type of problem is called 'rollback' or 'foldback' and consists of working from right to left, calculating the EMV of the outcomes for each decision and choosing the action with the highest EMV when the

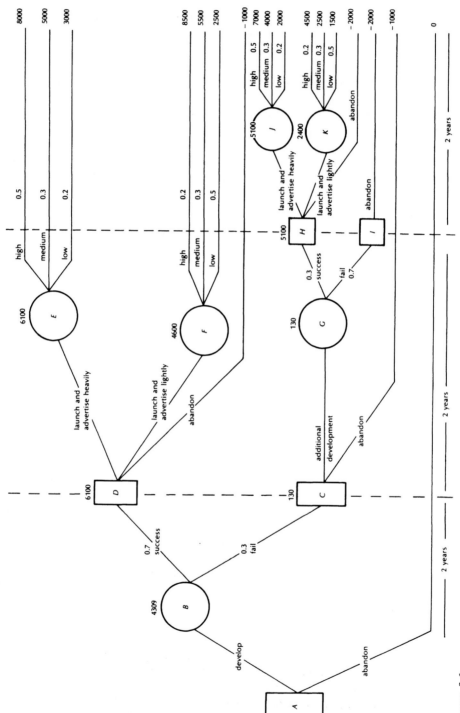

Figure 3.6

decision node is reached. This *EMV* is then applied to the probability of the outcome which led to the decision for which this *EMV* has been calculated, and so on until each of the original actions has an *EMV* attached to it.

Returning to the example and beginning in the top half of the figure, given that the development research was successful, the *EMV* of a heavily advertised launch is £6,100 (i.e. $0.5 \times 8000 + 0.3 \times 5000 + 0.2 \times 3000$). For similar reasons the *EMV* of a lightly advertised launch is £4,600. Since the *EMV* of abandonment at this stage is − £1,000, the largest *EMV* of a successful development stage is £6,100. In the central section, given an initial development failure, further research and eventual success, the *EMVs* of heavily and lightly advertised launches are £5,100 and £2,400 respectively, whereas abandonment results in a £2,000 loss. The largest of these *EMVs* i.e. at node *H* is £5,100. Since success in the second research attempt has an *EMV* of £5,100 and probability 0.3, whereas failure has an *EMV* of − £2,000 and probability of 0.7, the *EMV* of additional development is £130, i.e. $(0.3 \times £5,100 + 0.7 \times − £2,000)$. The largest of the *EMVs* of additional development (£130) versus abandonment (− £1,000) is the former. Hence this is the *EMV* at node *C*. By weighting the *EMVs* at node *C* and *D*, that of pursuing development initially is calculated. By comparing this (£4,309) with that of initial abandonment (£0) the manager can decide on his strategy.

3.8 Adjusting the present value formula for risk

In Chapter 2 we defined the value of the firm as:

$$PV\pi = \sum_{t=1}^{n} \pi_t/(1+r)^t \qquad (3.2)$$

However, π_t relates to expected, not certain, value: in the event, another value may occur. Hence, suppose a manager wished to choose between two projects. Let both projects have the same lifespan and the same expected profits in each year. But assume the risk associated with the annual earnings of one project is much greater than that of the other. The values of $PV\pi$ calculated using (3.2) would be equal, but if the manager is risk-averse, he would prefer the lower-risk project. Hence, ranking $PV\pi$ values would not indicate the manager's preferred project. Here we explain three out of many methods which have been proposed to adjust equation (3.2) to rank projects accurately when each project involves different levels of risk.[1]

3.8.1 Certainty equivalent method

Using this method the manager attempts to derive a hypothetical value for $PV\pi$ where the π_ts are received with certainty such that he or she is indifferent between this $PV\pi$ and that of the risky stream. The expected profit for each year is estimated together with its degree of risk. These expected values are converted to their hypothetical certainty equivalent values (that is, the value of π_t to be received with certainty and between which and the risky profit the manager would be indifferent). The *PV* of the stream of certainty equivalent values is then calculated.

The derivation of the certainty equivalent values can be explained by referring to an expected return–risk diagram. For example, in Figure 3.7 an expected return–risk indifference curve is presented. It shows combinations of expected return and risk between which the manager is indifferent and has the same properties as that shown in Figure 3.5.

If the manager is risk-averse, the curve will slope upwards; if the manager is indifferent to risk, the curve would be horizontal and if he or she enjoys risk, the curve would slope downwards. In the first case, curves further towards the top left-hand corner would represent combinations which the manager would prefer to those on the line we have drawn.

Returning to the certainty equivalent technique, if the risk level associated with a given level or expected profits is V_1 and the expected profits of a project in a particular year are £10,500 then if these points are both located on the curve, the manager is indifferent between the risky value and profits of £5,000 with no risk, i.e. certainty. Hence a risky £10,500 would be replaced by a certain £5,000 in the $PV\pi$ stream.

In general, if π_t represents the risky return and π_t^* the certainty equivalent value of this, the *PV* formula would be modified to:

$$PV\pi = \pi_0^* + \frac{\pi_1^*}{(1+i)} + \frac{\pi_2^*}{(1+i)^2} + \dots + \frac{\pi_n^*}{(1+i)^n}$$

(3.3)

where i equals the risk-free discount rate. The risk-free discount rate is used because the replacement of the risky return by its certainty equivalent fully compensates for any risk and so there is no need to make any further adjustment.

The certainty equivalent of £A with risk can be derived by repeatedly presenting the manager with choices between receiving this value with risk and successively smaller amounts to be received with certainty until indifference is reached.

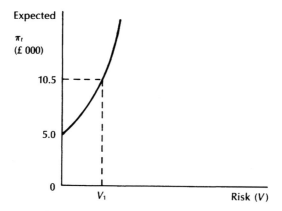

Figure 3.7

Consider further the relationship between π_t and π_t^*. The certainty equivalent coefficient is defined as:

$$\alpha = \frac{\pi_t^*}{\pi_t} = \frac{\text{certain profits}}{\text{risky profits}} \Rightarrow \pi_t^* = \alpha_t \pi_t$$

Hence, if we knew the value of α_t and π_t, we could calculate π_t^*. Now, α is dependent on, amongst other things, the level of risk. In the above example with risk of V_1, $\alpha_t = 0.48$. If risk were higher than V_1, the risky profits, which have the same preference ranking as the certain £5,000, would be higher. Therefore the corresponding α would be lower (£5,000 divided by a number larger than £10,500). If the level of risk were less than V_1, the risky profits on the same indifference curve as the £5,000 would be less than £10,500; the value of α would be higher. Hence α lies between 1 (zero risk) and 0 (very high level of risk). Plotting this relationship as in Figure 3.8 gives the 'α curve'.

If we knew that for a given level of risk the ratio of risky profit to its certainty equivalent, (α), was always the same regardless of the value of the certain profits or their time of receipt, i.e. the risk-return indifference curves were parallel in the vertical direction, then we could read off the α value for an anticipated level of risk. For example, with risk of V_1, the α value is 0.48. Hence the $PV\pi$ formula, equation (3.3) would be written and calculated as:

$$PV\pi = \alpha_0 \pi_0 + \frac{\alpha_1 \pi_1}{(1+i)} + \frac{\alpha_2 \pi_2}{(1+i)^2} + \ldots + \frac{\alpha_n \pi_n}{(1+i)^n}$$

However, it is possible that as a firm's circumstances change over time, the certainty equivalent of a specific risky return may change: that is, the α curve shifts and the α value changes. We would then need a new α curve for each time period.

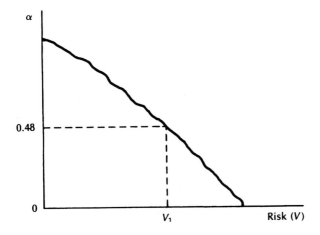

Figure 3.8

3.8.2 Risk adjusted discount rates

In this approach the discount rate is increased above the riskless rate, that is, the rate of return which could be gained for certain, by an amount depending on the degree of risk. Assuming that less rather than more risk is preferred, a risk premium is added to the riskless rate such that, given the level of risk, the manager is indifferent between the riskless rate and the adjusted rate with the premium added. We represent the relationship between the two in Figure 3.9. Here the manager is indifferent between a riskless rate, i, of 10% and the risk-adjusted rate $i + k$, of 14% received with risk level V_1. The PV formula is modified to be:

$$PV = \pi_0 + \frac{\pi_1}{(1 + i_1 + k_1)} + \frac{\pi_2}{(1 + i_2 + k_2)^2} + \ldots + \frac{\pi_n}{(1 + i_n + k_n)^n}$$

where the values of i and k may differ between time periods.

This technique has a number of limitations when used in practice. Firstly, firms often group projects together according to their riskiness, potential investments in each group being ascribed the same value of k_t. The probability distributions of returns in each year are often not considered when the risk of each project is assessed. Secondly, the relevant risk–return indifference curve is not derived to calculate the appropriate value of k for each level of risk: the choice of k is often somewhat arbitrary. Thirdly, firms often apply the same values of i for every time period and likewise for k. This implies that the manager believes that the riskiness of expected future values of profits increases with time and at a constant rate. In fact, it might not. To understand this implication, remember that both the certainty equivalent and risk-adjusted discount rate give the same present value of a risky profit which is expected to be received in a given year. (They must do because they both adjust the PV of a risky receipt to equal that of a certain receipt which gives the same utility as the risky one.) Hence:

$$\frac{\alpha_t \pi_t}{(1 + i)^t} = \frac{\pi_t}{(1 + i + k)^t}$$

where

α_t = certainty equivalent coefficient
i, k = risk-free discount rate and risk premium respectively: both assumed constant for all periods

Cross-multiplication and cancelling π_t gives:

$$\alpha_t = \left(\frac{1 + i}{1 + i + k} \right)^t \tag{3.4}$$

Hence

$$\alpha_1 = \frac{1 + i}{1 + i + k}$$

and by substituting this into (3.4): $\alpha_t = (\alpha_1)^t$. Verbally, the further into the future we

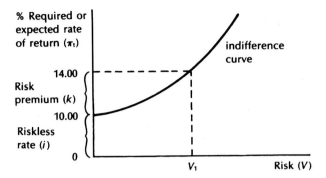

Figure 3.9

consider, the greater the adjustment to the risky profits that is implied to gain their certainty equivalent value. Further, since the adjustment for one further period is α_t multiplied by α_1,

$$\alpha_{t+1} = (\alpha_1)^{t+1}$$

$$= (\alpha_1)^t \times \alpha_1$$

$$= \alpha_t \, \alpha_1 \qquad\qquad\qquad \text{(from equation (3.4))}$$

the adjustment is at a constant rate (α_1) for each additional period into the future we consider.

3.8.3 Probability distribution approach

Using this technique, an expected *NPV*-standard deviation indifference map is drawn and points representing each project placed in it.[2] The possible values of cash flow in each year are each ascribed a probability of occurrence. These probabilities are conditional on the occurrence of a given cash flow in the preceding year. The overall probability of *NPV* for all the years is calculated and the expected *NPV* estimated using the formula:

$$E(NPV) = \sum_{i=1}^{n} NPV_i P(NPV_i)$$

where $P(NPV_i)$ = probability of NPV_i occurring and NPV_i = net present value, estimate i. The standard deviation of the possible *NPV*s is calculated as:

$$\sigma(NPV) = \sqrt{\left[\sum_i (NPV_i - E(NPV))^2 \, P(NPV_i) \right]} \qquad\qquad (3.5)$$

To illustrate, consider a firm deciding whether it should market a large or a small car. For simplicity, assume the former operation will last only two years and that only three possible cash inflows can exist, given the value in the previous year. In year 0 the three cash inflows for the large car are £50, £75 and £100 with probabilities assessed by the management at 0.3, 0.4 and 0.3. In year 1, given that the previous year's figure was £50 and the possibilities of £75, £100, £125, the management estimates the probabilities of each as 0.2, 0.6, and 0.2.[3] This procedure is repeated for the other two possible values for year 0. The probability of each cash inflow in year 1 is the product of the probabilities that it and the previous year's value occurred. The situation is shown in the tree Figure 3.10.

The NPV of each pair of pay-offs (in years 0 and 1) is calculated by discounting. Hence the first figure in column 3, 118.18, is the NPV of receipts of £50 in year 0 and £75 in year 1, i.e. $118.18 = 50 + 75/(1.1)$. Notice that the pay-offs received in the current period (period 0) have not been discounted because there is no delay in their receipt, so no foregone interest has been lost. The remainder of the column is calculated similarly. The expected NPV is found by summing the products of each NPV

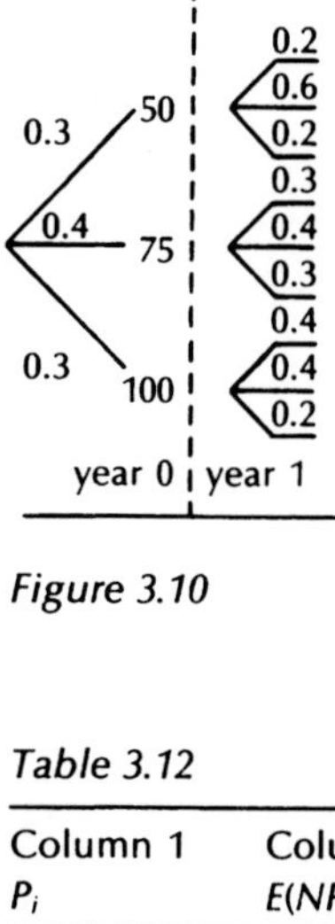

	Outcome	Probability of outcome	$NPV_i = r = 10\%$	$P(NPV_i) \times NPV_i$
0.2	75	$0.2 \times 0.3 = 0.06$	118.18	7.09
0.6	100	$0.6 \times 0.3 = 0.18$	140.91	25.36
0.2	125	$0.2 \times 0.3 = 0.06$	163.64	8.82
0.3	100	$0.3 \times 0.4 = 0.12$	165.91	19.91
0.4	150	$0.4 \times 0.4 = 0.16$	211.36	33.82
0.3	180	$0.3 \times 0.4 = 0.12$	238.64	28.64
0.4	200	$0.4 \times 0.3 = 0.12$	281.82	33.82
0.4	210	$0.4 \times 0.3 = 0.12$	290.91	34.91
0.2	229	$0.2 \times 0.3 = 0.06$	300.00	18.00
				211.37

year 0 | year 1

Figure 3.10

Table 3.12

Column 1 P_i	Column 2 E(NPV)	Column 3 NPV_i	Column 4 $(NPV_i - E(NPV))^2$	Column 5 Column 4 × $P(NPV_i)$
0.06	211.37	118.18	8684.38	521.06
0.18	211.37	140.91	4964.61	893.63
0.06	211.37	163.64	2278.15	136.69
0.12	211.37	165.91	2066.61	413.32
0.16	211.37	211.36	0	0
0.12	211.37	238.64	743.65	89.24
0.12	211.37	281.82	4963.20	595.58
0.12	211.37	290.91	6326.61	759.19
0.06	211.37	300.00	7855.28	471.32
				3880.03

$\sigma(NPV) = \sqrt{3880.03} = 62.29$

and its probability of occurrence, the first figure in column 4 equalling 0.06×118.18 and so on. The expected value is 211.37. The stages in calculating the standard deviation of the possible *NPV* values are shown in Table 3.12. Hence the expected value and standard deviation for the large car may be plotted in a figure, each axis measuring each of these variables. Corresponding values may be calculated and plotted for the small car or any other investment. Indifference curves may be placed on the figure to establish a ranking of preferences between projects.

Notes

1. We have ignored the possibility that the earnings of one project may be correlated with those of others. This possibility is considered in Chapter 14.

2. $NPV = -C_0 + \dfrac{\pi_1}{1+r} + \dfrac{\pi_2}{(1+r)^2} + \ldots + \dfrac{\pi_n}{(1+r)^n}$

   where C_0 = initial capital outlay of a project
   r = discount rate
   π_n = net cash inflow in year n, i.e. profits net of operating costs (see Chapter 14).

3. Notice that these probabilities are conditional on the cash inflow in the previous period. If the cash flows between periods are independent or perfectly correlated, equation (3.5) can be simplified.

Additional reading

Allen, D. E. (1983) *Finance: A Theoretical Introduction*, Martin Robinson.

Baker, A. J. (1981) *Business Decision Making*, Croom Helm.

Baumol, W. J. (1977) *Economic Theory and Operations Analysis*, Prentice Hall.

Berry, R. H. and Dyason, R. G. (1980) 'On the negative risk premium for risk adjusted discount rates', *Journal of Business Finance and Investment*, vol. 53.

Bussey, L. E. (1978) *The Economic Analysis of Industrial Projects*, Prentice Hall.

Clark, J. J., Hundelang, T. J. and Pritchard, R. E. (1979) *Capital Budgeting: Planning and control of capital expenditures*, Prentice Hall.

Friedman, M. and Savage, L. J. (1948) 'The utility analysis of choices involving risk', *Journal of Political Economy*, vol. 56.

Luce, R. D. and Raiffa, H. (1957) *Games and Decisions*, John Wiley.

McGuigan, J. and Moyer, R. C. (1979) *Managerial Economics*, Castle House.

Magee, J. F. (1964) 'Decision trees for decision making', *Harvard Business Review*, vol. 42.

Magee, J. F. (1966) 'How to use decision tress in capital budgeting', *Harvard Business Review*, vol. 44.

Moore, P. G. (1972) *Risk in Business Decision*, Longman.

Moore, P. G. (1976) *Anatomy of Decisions*, Penguin Books.

Pratt, J. W., Raiffa, H. and Schlaifer, R. (1964) 'The foundations of decision making under uncertainty, an elementary exposition', *Journal of the American Statistical Association*, vol. 59.
Robichek, A. A. and Myers, S. C. (1965) *Optimal Financing Decisions*, Prentice Hall.
Ryan, T. (1978) *Theory of Portfolio Selection*, Macmillan.
Van Horne, J. (1977) *Financial Management and Policy*, Prentice Hall.

Chapter 4

Strategic decision taking and transactions costs

In the previous chapter we analysed decision taking under conditions of risk and uncertainty, and generally incomplete information. We excluded the possibility of strategic interdependence between the decision taker and his or her rivals and or between the decision taker and his or her suppliers and/or customers. In essence we took the state of nature as given and unaffected by the decision itself. Here, we continue to defer discussion of oligopolistic or other direct inter-firm rivalry where the firms are competing for the same custom or supply. In this chapter what we do examine is decision taking which may impact on the environment as represented by the market itself (either customers or suppliers). To do this we revert to our earlier discussion of Ronald Coase and draw on later contributions to the literature of transactions costs and agency theory.

4.1 The Coase Theorem and value maximisation

Coase argued that firms (hierarchies) would exist and replace market transactions when the costs of transacting exceeded the cost of internal organisation. On this foundation the theory of the firm as a juridical entity was left in its traditional form. However, the nexus of contracts approach sees the firm as embracing both external market relationships as well as internal contracts. Coase's original 1937 paper was concerned with explaining only the traditional view of the firm.

A later paper by Coase (1960) provided the starting point for transactions cost analysis from which both internal and external contracting, and on a different dimension, implicit and explicit contracts could be enlarged. In his 1960 paper Coase assumed that the parties to any contract will have value maximisation as an objective (i.e. the present value of the stream of discounted future net revenues). He then went on to demonstrate, in what is now called the Coase Theorem, that any set of contracting parties will, if they bargain efficiently, namely if they bargain until there is no further possibility of mutual benefit, draw up a contract which maximises the aggregate value achievable by all the parties to the contract.[1] The distribution of that aggregate value, how the net benefits are divided, would be affected by the

---

Box 4.1

Proving the Coase Theorem

When transaction costs are absent, joint or aggregate value maximising decisions and courses of action will result from efficient contracting – either outside or inside the juridical firm. This is true whatever the original split of resources between two parties to a trade – only the division of the incremental value will be affected by the initial endowments.

Consider an example used by Coase himself. There is a strip of unowned and unfenced land between the properties of a grain and of a cattle farmer. The grain farmer would like to plant crops on it but the cattle would damage the crops so he does not cultivate the land. This may or may not be a joint value maximising decision, that would depend on the profits he had forfeited and on the profits accruing to the cattle farmer.

Assume we do not know which stream of profits is the larger but that the grain farmer takes a chance that he can plant grain and obtain profits from at least some undamaged portion of it, and that he also decides to sue the cattle farmer for damages to the remainder of his crop. Neither farmer has rights to the unowned strip of land so a court must make a value judgement as to which farmer to assign the user rights. In Table B4.1 we look at both alternative assignations of 'original' rights to the use of the land, and we look at two alternative profit streams (one where the cattle farmer's profits from using the strip of land exceed the grain farmer's, and vice versa).

Table B4.1

| | Land use rights awarded to | |
	Cattle farmer	Grain farmer
Profits on cattle £1,000 Profits on grain £600	Cattle will be farmed earning cattle farmer £1,000	Cattle will be farmed. Cattle farmer will pay grain farmer a rental of > £600 and < £1,000
Profits on cattle £600 Profits on grain £1,000	Grain will be farmed. Grain farmer will pay cattle farmer a rental of > £600 and < £1,000	Grain will be farmed earning grain farmer £1,000

Once property rights are assigned, contracts can be entered into by the two farmers. If transaction costs are absent and knowledge of the outcomes of any contracts is given then *the decision taken will always maximise joint profits*, irrespective of who owns the land. Land ownership will only impact on how the joint profits are shared. So the Coase Theorem is proved.

→

Transaction costs will not be absent, however. Most obviously in the example, fencing costs will be required to keep the cattle off the grain if the scenario in the second row of the matrix occurred. Which farmer pays for the fencing is not relevant to the joint profits, only the amount. The cattle farmer would be motivated to fence in order to avoid paying for lost grain, the grain farmer would be motivated to fence to avoid losing grain. What fencing by the grain farmer would affect is the upper limit he would be willing to pay as rental.

initial assets or bargaining power each party brings to the negotiations, but not the total. Or to put it another way, when transaction costs are absent, value maximising behaviour is achieved by efficient contracting. Efficient contracting may take place within the juridical firm or outside of it in the market place (within the firm as a nexus of contracts). Which route is chosen depends on the unavoidable presence of transaction costs in real life and on which form of contracting results in them being minimised (see Box 4.1). Coase, however, did not explore the nature of such costs in detail and it was left to later writers, in particular Oliver Williamson in his book *Markets and Hierarchies* (1976), to develop the theory of which organisational mode, the juridical firm or outside market purchase and sale best economises on these costs.

4.2 Transaction costs

Transaction costs fall into two main categories: co-ordination costs and motivation costs. Both apply within and outside of the traditional concept of the firm. Co-ordination costs outside the firm are the costs of using the price system including the gathering of information about what markets best to supply and where it is optimal to purchase inputs from. Within the firm, co-ordination costs include the transmission downwards of directions to dispersed sections of the firm and the gathering and transmission of information upwards to enable central decision makers to monitor the carrying out of centrally determined plans. These costs include time delays as well as the possibilities of information distortion, incompleteness and bounded rationality.

Motivation costs can be further subdivided into those arising from two sources; information asymmetries and imperfect commitments. In a perfect market with complete information, the motivation to trade is provided by the incentive of profits arising from price differentials. When the parties to a potential trade do not have access to the same information, value maximising contracts may not occur because one or other party fears being adversely exploited, or the costs of avoiding such exploitation resulting from opportunistic behaviour are deemed to be too high.

Imperfect commitments arise when the parties to a trade, having agreed on rewards for contract fulfilment and penalties for breach, fear the agreement can be readily breached and hence shy away from value maximising decision making. Again the fear is of opportunistic behaviour but this time in the future. For example, a sausage manufacturer may be offered a six-month contract to supply Snooks's retail butcheries provided he or she invests in a particular high cost, highly hygienic production process. This may be a joint value maximising decision but if the manufacturer feels – all contractual detail notwithstanding – that once the expenditure on the new process is sunk Snooks may go out of business in the interim, or take a lower throughput, or attempt to lower the price of supply, then he or she may not undertake the investment at all. To the contrary if the retailer was not Snooks but Marks & Spencer and was able to call on reputation effects of many successful similar contract completions in the past with other suppliers then the manufacturer might well be more willing to sink funds into a highly specific asset for manufacturing St Michael brand sausages.

4.3 Transaction dimensions

At least five dimensions for transactions are necessary fully to understand transaction cost analysis. First, transactions that require costly investments in idiosyncratic or *specific assets* that would lose most of their value outside the specific transaction require that costs be incurred contractually or organisationally to protect the investor against opportunistic behaviour in the future. Such transaction costs can be much lower when assets are non-specific and the investor can either sell and recoup his or her expenditures if the contract is not fulfilled (the costs are not sunk) or the asset can readily be transferred to some other function.

Second, contract *frequency and duration* impact on transaction costs. Thus when a trade is of a one-off nature the least cost method of contracting may well be to use existing legal frameworks for drawing up and enforcing contracts. When the trade is carried out frequently over a long period of time the traders are more likely to develop routines and procedures specific to themselves (which could range from a formal firm understanding to an informal – but well-informed – understanding) where each knows what is required and expected of the other without detailed or written routines. Such close but unique relationships would have lower transaction costs than drawing up separate spot-market contract documents on each occasion a value maximising decision is taken.

Similarly, the *more standardised, certain and uncomplex* is the product traded the more economical it is to write a performance contract on each occasion a trade is made. Thus gold is traded with contracts specifying date of delivery and price and very little else.

When a complex product is traded it is much more difficult and costly to specify every possible contingency and parameter. Contracts then tend to emphasise performance attributes less. Rather, rights, obligations and procedures which should be followed if certain parameters are not met are emphasised more. For example in ordering an oil rig from a construction firm an oil company will insert penalty clauses for late delivery, the construction company may insert open-ended clauses relating to the (unknown) cost of restoring the environment of the coastline or countryside after the construction is complete, while since neither purchaser nor builder can forecast what additional construction costs may ultimately be required if maritime regulators change spillage or safety regulations the contract will have to have sufficient flexibility to cater for such unknowns.

Fourth, when *performance measurement is difficult* contracts will tend to be written differently than when it is easy. The issues here relate to incentives and the problems of principal and agent to be discussed later (see Section 4.7). When performance can be readily gauged, rewards will often be linked to results which intuitively would appear to provide appropriate incentives for contract fulfilment. When results do not only depend upon effort, however, contracts are either more complex and/or parties to a trade spend resources searching for suitable alternatives which either make measurement easier or reduce its importance. Thus, for example, success as a restaurant manager is partly dependent on the manager's efforts, but it is also dependent on the vagaries of the weather, of consumer tastes, location and advertising as well as on the difficult-to-measure managerial attributes of ensuring the staff are well trained as cooks, or waiters and are pleasant to the public. Restaurant owners such as Kentucky Fried Chicken and Macdonalds thus own some of their outlets, paying managers by results (turnover or profit), but in most cases franchise the outlets to owner/managers. Unobservable but poor managerial performance is then a cost borne by the franchisee owner/manager of the outlet. Owner/managers are thus motivated not to perform poorly as managers even if their poor performance is not directly measurable, since now the costs of their poor performance is borne directly by themselves.

Finally transactions may be *design connected*. A classic example of design connection is motor vehicle assembly. The two standard ways to handle the problem are to have the firm fully integrated and centralised, so that all components are designed to be assembled into the given model. The same firm manufactures speedometers, seats, body shells and fuel gauges. Strong central co-ordination is required to minimise transaction costs. The alternative, if market transactions replace the single firm, is to have close frequent liaison meetings, between supplying and purchasing firms. The former approach was typical of the British industry in the 1950s, the latter was more common in Japan in the 1960s and 1970s. Which approach minimises transaction costs in any given industry at any given time requires case-by-case analysis.

This discussion of the dimensions of transactions hints at the nature of transaction cost analyses. They are not precise computations at the margins like calculus-based economics. Rather it is sufficient 'to demonstrate an inequality between two (total) quantities' (Simon 1978, pp. 1–16).

4.4 Bounded rationality and strategic behaviour

Rarely are the parties to a trade fully informed. Rather they are boundedly rational. They attempt to satisfice rather than maximise. That is they attempt, within the limits of the information available to them, to achieve a satisfactory level of performance which may be, but is accepted not to be, the best possible outcome. It is rational to settle for such satisficing behaviour since the costs of searching out the information to maximise are acknowledged to be – and probably are – unacceptably high.

Furthermore, each party to a trade in real life will admit that not only is he or she not fully informed but there is information asymmetry between a party and his or her fellow trader. The information each possess differs. However, since each is attempting to satisfice, or optimise within constraints of information, then strategic or opportunistic behaviour will also be expected. That is each presumes the other will indulge in what Oliver Williamson called 'self-seeking with guile' (1985, p. 30).

Absent bounded rationality and opportunism traders can write explicit complex and detailed classical contracts where all possible contingencies in contract execution are foreseen and plans of action for each are agreed upon in advance and it is known that it will be easy to ascertain whether the contract's terms are being met and, if not, each trader is willing and able to enforce agreed performance. The alternative to a complete classical contract is a spot-market contract where goods are exchanged on the spot and it is known that there will be little likelihood of a change in circumstances before the rapid conclusion of the contract that would alter the appropriateness of the trade.

Neo-classical contracting (where formal legal contracts are involved and a third party, the civil law, is used to aid in both contract construction and execution) is another means of economising on transaction costs. Contracts are less than complete and an agreed arbiter is introduced in advance in order to minimise or discourage opportunistic behaviour during execution and to save on information search costs during contract write-up.

Table 4.1 Economising on opportunism and bounded rationality by selecting governance structure according to transaction

| | Characteristics of traded good | | |
	Non-specific	Mixed	Specific and idiosyncratic
Occasional purchase	e.g. standard equipment	e.g. customised equipment	e.g. construction of building or plant
	Spot-market trade or *classical contract*	*Neo-classical contract*	*Neo-classical contract*
Recurrent purchase	e.g. standard equipment	e.g. customised component parts	e.g. site-specific transfer of partly finished product intended for further processing
	Spot market trade or *classical contract*	*Bilateral relational contract*	*Unified relational contract*

Source: adapted from Williamson 1979.

Relational contracts are those where the parties settle for a framework which merely defines the relationship. It is suitable where bounded rationality is a problem but opportunism is less likely. Williamson (1979) subdivides relational contracts into two – bilateral and unified. As opportunism becomes more of a danger, unified governance rather than independence of operation may be the least costly alternative. Table 4.1 summarises much of the discussion to this point.

Contracts are designed to minimise the transaction costs of strategic behaviour and bounded rationality by aligning the incentives of the contracting parties. Incomplete contracts, however, have limitations in achieving this coincidence of motivations. One or other party may renege and the fear of this may result in value maximising decisions not being taken at all. This is known as *post-contractual opportunism* consequent on hidden or unforeseeable action. *Pre-contractual opportunism* due to hidden information may also result in value maximising trades not occurring. These two types of strategy behaviour will be examined in turn.

4.5 Pre-contractual opportunism and adverse selection

Adverse selection is an *ex ante* information asymmetry problem. It arises because one set of parties to a trade conceals or misrepresents information about itself. The phrase 'adverse selection' originated in the insurance industry to describe a situation where the insurer ends up with a set of clients, non-randomly selected (by themselves) in the high risk proportion of the population. To remain in business and meet claims the insurer would then have to raise his or her rates, but in so doing would lose his or her clientele. The classic example in the economics literature was Akerlof's 'lemons' (see Box 4.2).

An example of adverse selection arises with life insurance. Those seeking cover will have better knowledge about risk factors such as hereditary health risks, smoking, drinking and dangerous sport habits than the insurance company. They have no incentive to reveal this knowledge, as it would be harmful to them. They would have to pay a higher premium or even be refused cover. On the contrary such people who have such private knowledge have the incentives both to apply for cover and to keep silent about their information. Of course, insurance companies will try to elicit such information if they can by interview, by medical examination, and by contractual refusals to pay claims *ex post* should such opportunism be discovered. These activities, however, are costly in themselves and if excessively so, might result in value maximising trading not occurring.

Another example is in the new car market. All manufacturers provide guarantees on their product for a given length of time or a given mileage. Some, however, will, at a price, provide extended warranties for longer periods or distances. There is an incentive here for only those purchasers who drive their vehicles hard to purchase the warranty. Those who do not drive on rough roads, engage in motor sports, tow caravans or heavy trailers, or engage in consistent long distance driving are less likely to buy the extended guarantee.

Box 4.2

Adverse selection and 'lemons'

George Akerlof (1970) provided a classic example of adverse selection from the second hand car market. He began by asking why there is such a large price difference between a brand new car and a second-hand car which has only recently left the showroom? The answer starts from the premise that there are good and bad new cars – for example those assembled at week beginning are allegedly inferior to those assembled mid-week (known as 'Monday morning' cars in the United Kingdom or 'lemons' in the United States. Every buyer of a new car runs the risk of buying a 'lemon'. Neither the buyer nor the seller (the car dealer) is aware which cars are lemons. There is no information asymmetry. After owning a car, however, an owner who becomes aware that he has bought a lemon (because of actual or threatened problems) has more information than a potential purchaser from him. Second-hand buyers are aware of this information asymmetry but cannot distinguish lemons from other cars. Both lemons and non-lemons must therefore sell at the same price in the second-hand market. But at this price owners of non-lemons have little incentive to sell, while owners of lemons may still find the price acceptable. As a consequence the probability of a car being a lemon is higher on the second-hand market than on the new market. This risk is reflected in the price. The basic problem is unobservable information about the true quality of a used car from a buyer's perspective. Sellers have no incentive to transmit information on faults. Bad risks self select into the second-hand car market.

Source abstracted from Akerlof (1970).

4.5.1 Bargaining

The Coase Theorem asserts that without transaction costs, joint value maximising decisions will be taken and trades will occur. Information asymmetries and pre-contractual opportunism, however, are just the sorts of transaction costs which can discourage or prevent agreements which would be judged as efficient given complete information. We start by explaining the case with information asymmetry only and then we explain the case where pre-contractual opportunism is exercised.

4.5.2 Information asymmetry

Consider the following simplified situation with one seller and one buyer of a product. All the possible values which the two parties place on the product are shown in Table 4.2. Assume no bounded rationality so the two parties *know* the valuation which each places on the product. Assume also no strategic behaviour. Then, for any given pair of product valuations, either trading will occur or it will not. The price at which trading will occur will lie between the lowest of the buyer's and the highest of the seller's valuations such that both parties are better off.

Table 4.2

Buyer's valuations	Seller's valuations	
	£1 (0.4)	£3 (0.6)
£2 (0.5)	Trade occurs	No trade
£4 (0.5)	Trade occurs	Trade occurs

The Coase Theorem does not indicate the agreed price but it does imply that joint value maximisation decisions will take place. This is because whatever the values placed on the product, if the buyer places a higher value on the product than the seller then trade will occur so that the person with the highest valuation eventually owns the good. The actual transaction price will depend on the comparative bargaining strengths of the two parties but irrespective of agreed price joint value maximising behaviour will take place.

Let us now introduce bounded rationality into Table 4.2 so that each party knows his or her own valuation of the product but is *uncertain* of the *other* party's valuation. For example, each partner assigns the probabilities of valuation to the values of the other as indicated in Table 4.2. If the actual valuations are £2 for the buyer and £1 for the seller then as before 'trade' would occur between these prices and joint value would be maximised. However, thanks to bounded rationality, this joint value maximising outcome *will not* consistently occur but will occur only on those 20 per cent (0.5×0.4) of occasions when the negotiated prices are within the limits of the actual valuations.

4.5.3 Pre-contractual opportunism

There is worse to come. Given information asymmetries there are problems with the bargainers trying to misrepresent their actual valuation in order to get a better price. In the previous example, the seller may claim that £3 is his or her actual valuation, not £1. This carries the danger that in the bargaining situation, if the seller carries conviction, the two parties may always end up in the no-trade cell. To overcome these transaction costs each party must be convinced that full revelation of actual valuation is as worthwhile as concealment or misrepresentation.

The aim is, given the claimed values by the buyer and seller, to impose rules on the bargaining process and to calculate trading prices which discourage the buyer from falsely claiming a low valuation and the seller a high valuation. To accomplish this a rule is imposed that a seller who claims a value of £3 must be offered that figure, but no more, as an incentive to participate in trade while a buyer who only values a product at £2 must be asked for no more but only be allowed to claim a value of £2 when trade occurs. This figure also can be regarded as a participation incentive constraint. Table 4.3 shows the possibilities for the buyer and seller of Table 4.2. The problem is now to find a value for the price x, which will encourage both parties to be truthful when the claimed values are £4 and £1.

Table 4.3 Prices to encourage information disclosure and value maximisation

Buyer's values	Seller's values	
	£1 (0.4)	£3 (0.6)
£2 (0.5)	2	No trade
£4 (0.5)	x	3

Consider first the buyer. If the buyer is honest and says he or she values the good at £4 he or she would pay £3 when the seller values the product at £3 and x when the seller claims his or her value is £1. This gains the buyer a benefit of 0.6 $(4-3) + 0.4 \ (4-x) = 2.2 - 0.4x$. If the buyer engages in opportunism and claims he or she values the product at only £2 not £4 the buyer trades only on these occasions when £2 exceeds the seller's value. This will occur when the seller values the good at £1 which happens only on 40 per cent of trading occasions. The buyer will gain only £2, given the rule chosen so his or her expected pay-off from opportunism is $0.4 (4-2) = £0.8$. To make it worthwhile not to engage in opportunism $£0.8 \leqslant £2.2 - 0.4x$, or $£1.4 \leqslant £0.4x$ or $x \leqslant £3.5$.

A similar computation can be done for the seller. Given an honestly declared £1 valuation the seller accepts £2 when the buyer offers £2 and x when the buyer values the product at £4. Honesty results in an expected pay-off of $0.5(2-1) + 0.5(x-1) = 0.5x$. Dissembling results in a pay-off $0.5 (3-1) = £1$. $£1 \leqslant £0.5x$ to discourage opportunism, or $x \leqslant £2$.

Thus it is possible to devise incentive compatibility constraints, £3, £2 and $(£2 \leqslant x \leqslant £3.50)$ which would make it more costly to dissemble than to trade openly and honestly.[2] This is a situation which is known as incentive efficient.

So it is possible – even if not consistently so – for participation incentive constraints to be introduced to overcome pre-contractual strategic behaviour and so permit joint value maximising trade. According to the Coase Theorem, traders should seek out such mechanisms if there are net gains. The issue then is: how do the gross gains compare with the costs of finding and improving such constraints? Theoreticians have still to solve the issue and little can be inferred other than that misrepresentation is always likely because of information asymmetry. On the other hand, if the potential gains from trade are large then incentive constraints and other transactions costs such as bargaining or haggling costs together with performance measurement costs would have to be very important to inhibit value maximising behaviour. Box 4.3 shows how one large selling organisation has successfully minimised such transaction costs.

Market breakdown or collapse due to adverse selection is a real possibility. Several ways have been devised to overcome this. The De Beers example (Box 4.3) is one case. Another example comes from the banking industry. We noted in insurance that due to non-random self-selection by clients the firm could become unprofitable as claims of above average frequency and amount arise – leading to higher premiums and still higher claims as the 'better risks' of the already adversely

---

Box 4.3

The central selling organisation and De Beers

The De Beers diamond company through the Central Selling Organisation (CSO) in London operates the world's longest-standing and most successful trading cartel. Why the cartel has survived given the presence of independent producers in Russia, Australia, Zaire and Libya is a story still to be told. Nevertheless even the independents tend to sell through the CSO and not on the market.

The CSO economises on pre-contractual opportunism, information search costs, measurement costs and bargaining costs as follows. It restricts buyers to selected and approved dealers who have indicated interests in purchasing stones of particular sizes and qualities. They are offered a packet, or 'sight' of such stones roughly corresponding to their wants on a strict take-it-or-leave-it basis at a price based on gross characteristics. Neither the contents nor the price of the package is negotiable and refusal to purchase results in exclusion from participation in future 'sights' and hence effective exclusion from the trade.

This does not explain why the cartel operates successfully as a cartel. It does explain *how* the cartel minimises transaction costs. Bargaining and value assessment stone by stone would be time consuming and costly (the gems have not yet been cut hence value to either buyer or seller would be difficult to determine). Buyers need not inspect too carefully since the packages have not been rejected by other buyers as deficient in quality, while the seller, by refusing to bargain on penalty of withdrawal of future sight rights saves on bargaining costs today being used as an opportunistic basis for possibly dishonest claims that higher prices would be offered in future. (Thus forcing buyers to forego and hence save on their bargaining costs.)

---

selected clients drop out of the market. In banking likewise a bank may prefer not to raise its interest rates if the general cost of money in the economy rises since it might then only attract borrowers with the highest risk of default. Instead it may hold its lending rate and *screen* out or ration to low default risk borrowers only. Another example is where the buyer invests in an attribute which *signals* that he or she is a low-risk trading partner. The original example of this comes from the labour market where potential employees invest in education not necessarily to attain pertinent knowledge for a specific job but to signal that they are hard working, committed and productive individuals to whom employers can safely (on average) pay higher productivity wages than to less well educated competitors for the job. Provided the signal is credible, that is provided less well educated competitors for jobs are in fact less productive and less able, then educational attainments can act as (proxy) signals for productivity reducing adverse selection and information asymmetry costs. To persist, this type of signal must also be cheaper – or easier to obtain for the high productivity worker than the low, or they too would make the same signal.

Signalling in non-labour markets includes dividend distribution (in the capital market) to signal financial soundness; guarantees and brand-name advertising (in

---

Box 4.4

Signalling commitment that reneging post-contractually is unlikely: branding as a device to minimise moral hazard

Economist Sir Dennis Robertson in his book *Lectures on Economic Principles* said 'There is a real spiritual comfort in buying a known and trusted brand of cocoa rather than a shovelful of brown powder of uncertain origin.' (1966, p. 169) If a product is unsatisfactory a brand makes it readily identifiable and so avoidable. Branding and the advertising expenditure which goes with it implies that the advertiser has 'posted a bond', past expenditure on promotion resulting in goodwill which will be forfeited if post-contractually the products are found not to live up to expectations. An unsatisfactory product will have to be withdrawn from the market place much more quickly than a non-branded equivalent if post-contractual opportunism takes place. The consumer will know which product to avoid. Branding identifies. A brand can be avoided or chosen. An unidentified brand does not provide the information that the consumer will receive the same quality or satisfaction on next purchase irrespective of time or place of sale. Branding provides an implicit guarantee and hence commitment that a contract will be fulfilled. The manufacturer has an incentive not to forfeit the bond.

The value of brands was well illustrated by the very high premium price Nestlé were willing to pay for Rowntree-Mackintosh's stable of Smarties, KitKat and Black Magic. The price was well above the book value of Rowntree's manufacturing assets.

---

the product market) to signal product quality (see Box 4.4); low prices set a signal to potential competitors to deter entry; and high levels of investment in fixed assets not easily transferable to other uses, signals to competitors that a particular market will not be given up without a costly fight.

4.6 Post-contractual opportunism and moral hazard

Moral hazard is also a problem of information asymmetry. It is an *ex post* concept and refers to opportunistic hidden action occurring after contracts are entered into rather than the concealment of information before the event. Again, like adverse selection the term originated in the insurance industry but is now part of the vocabulary of transaction cost economics.

Once an insurance contract is entered into and cover is provided there is an incentive for the client to behave with less caution than if uninsured. Information asymmetry means that the insurance company cannot tell whether loss or damage has been caused by some uncontrollable event such as a fire or robbery or whether the insured began to exercise less care in providing fire prevention or securing his or her property against theft after cover had been obtained. The insurer is unable to observe the behaviour of the insured, and the insured's incentives have changed after cover is obtained.

Contracts, insurance or otherwise, are rarely complete. They consequently fail fully to align the incentive of both parties. Their levels of commitment to achieving the same goals are not identical and reneging on the contract, or attempting to renegotiate *ex post* becomes probable. This type of behaviour is known as post-contractual opportunism, *ex post* strategic behaviour or moral hazard. Finally, even if moral hazard has been detected, incomplete contracts generally imply that enforceability is difficult, certainly costly and perhaps impossible.

One serious type of moral hazard is the *hold-up* problem. This is particularly probable when assets are specific to a particular use and are exceptionally valuable only in that use. For example, an aluminium smelter may be constructed in an isolated location close to a deep-water harbour. The smelting firm may negotiate with British Rail to construct a line connecting the smelter with the main rail network and agree to particular freight rates per ton. Both the spur line and the smelter are highly specific and this gives rise to the possibility of hold-up. Post-contract, either party could attempt to renegotiate rates in its own favour. For example the smelter could threaten that if rates were not reduced it would transfer its transportation contract to road haulage. A pre-contractual fear of post-contractual hold-up may lead to non-joint value maximising behaviour. The railroad may simply refuse to build the track in the first instance and the resulting total value (which might be less) would then be shared by the smelter and (less efficient) truck firms. Conversely if the smelter fears that rail rates would rise (particularly if road haulage was not a viable alternative) it might locate its investment elsewhere at a higher cost, or not construct the smelter at all.

Table 4.1 suggests that one way to economise on bounded rationality and opportunism in such a situation is to adopt the governance structure of a 'unified relational contract', in other words common or joint ownership of both assets, namely vertical integration. In this way incentives are aligned and the incentives for hold-up are removed.

Table 4.4 expresses the hold-up problem in matrix form (it is a type of Prisoner's Dilemma game, see Chapter 11) – with pay-offs to the smelting company in the

Table 4.4

		Railway		Minimum outcomes for smelter
		Hold-up	No hold-up	
Smelter	Hold-up	−1 / −1	−2 / 4	−1
	No hold-up	4 / −2	3 / 3	−2
Minimum outcomes for railway		−1	−2	

lower left-hand corner and the pay-offs to the railway in the upper right-hand corner of every cell. In this illustration the two firms' decisions and outcomes are provided on the same matrix, and instead of states of nature being plotted against decision choices (as in Chapter 3) the other party's actions are the alternative states. Assume that agreement between the smelter and the railway would provide joint value maximisation of £10, for an investment by each of £2, yielding an evenly split profit of £3 each. Assume no hold-up by either party, then the situation in the bottom-right cell will exist. Now assume hold-up by either party costs £4, which if successful yields all of the profits $(10-2-4) = £4$ to the party carrying out the hold-up. In this case the party held-up invests £2 for no return (-2). If both the smelter and the railroad engage in hold-up behaviour simultaneously each earns 50 per cent of $(10-4-8) = -1$.

Clearly applying the maximin rule, the conservative assumption of the presence of moral hazard would result in both parties ending up in the top-left cell and the investment would not take place. The threat of opportunism destroys the incentives to do so. A unified relational contract is more likely to inculcate feelings of mutual trust than is a bilateral one.

4.7 The theory of principal and agent

Moral hazard, adverse selection and information asymmetry also underlie the relatively new theories of principal and agent. These theories have also been developed to overcome the problems identified in the previous section. Namely how contracts can be written under such circumstances to ensure goal congruence when interests diverge; what incentives can be injected into the contracts to assist in achieving this aim if performance is unobservable wholly or in part; and how this can be done given that the parties to a contract may differ in their attitudes to risk and uncertainty and therefore have to be rewarded at different monetary levels to induce them to inject similar amounts of effort for similar outcomes.

Principal and agent theory, therefore tackles a sub-case of the strategic behaviour:bounded rationality problem – namely that where risk preferences differ. Examples of agency relationships are pervasive. Obvious ones include those between employer and employee, shareholder and manager, insurer and insured, client and professional adviser. In short the agent is someone who carries out a task on behalf of another, the principal.

It is conventional to assume that the principal is the risk-neutral party while the agent is the risk-averse one. This is not unrealistic where the principal can (as in most of the examples given) keep his wealth in well-diversified portfolios. Employers have many customers, employees only one job. Shareholders may invest in many firms, managers' salaries are tied to one. Insurers spread risks by defini-tion, the insured is seeking to shed his or her risk. Thus principal and agent theory is dealing with a somewhat different contractual problem from that where both parties had either no or similar risk preferences (as was the case with the bilateral hold-up example where each trader was concerned about the default possibility of the other).

Consider a situation where there is a risk-neutral sales manager who is the principal, P, concerned with maximising expected firm sales. The manager has several salespersons reporting to him or her each responsible for a different sales territory. Any one salesperson can be regarded as an agent, A, who is risk averse and also unwilling to provide effort without suitable reward. Such an agent's objective function is not to maximise his or her territory's expected sales but rather to maximise his or her own utility. We can write the agent's utility function as follows:

$$U = f(w, e)$$

That is, the agent's satisfaction depends on w, the agent's wage, and e, his or her effort. Or, specifying the equation,

$$U = w^{1/2} - e^2 \qquad (4.1)$$

The term $w^{1/2}$ in equation (4.1) indicates that the agent has a diminishing marginal utility of income or money.

$$\partial U / \partial w = 0.5 \, w^{-0.5}$$

is the slope of the utility function and injecting successively large values of w into the equation for slope would provide ever diminishing values of $\partial U / \partial w$, or marginal utility. Figure 3.4c indicated that this is characteristic of a risk averter. The term e^2 is the cost of effort and the negative sign implies that A is also effort averse. Suppose the agent has a choice of two effort levels, the higher effort it is assumed will result in greater expected sales but actual sales will also depend on unknown risky or uncertain environmental factors which neither P nor A can control.

For example in Table 4.5 when $e = 1$, expected sales are £233, when e is twice as great expected sales are £366. But neither P nor A can influence the state of the economy to be in boom, slump or normal conditions. Furthermore the agent must receive a guaranteed opportunity wage providing a minimum level of expected utility otherwise he or she would work elsewhere. For simplicity assume this minimum level of utility is $EU_A = 2$ (or a reservation wage of £9 given $e = 1$, see (4.1) above, $EU_A = 9^{1/2} - 1 = 2$).

If information asymmetries did not exist, if P could observe A's efforts the solution would be to specify an effort input of $e = 2$. This would maximise P's utility of expected sales at £366. The only remaining question would be whether this is

Table 4.5

Sales	Boom $p = 0.333$	Normal $p = 0.333$	Slump $p = 333$	Expected sales
$e = 1$	500	100	100	233
$e = 2$	500	500	100	366

sufficiently far above £233 to make it worth P's while to pay A to provide $e = 2$. Such a contract would have a fixed wage w and A, if he provided $e = 2$ would bear no risk. Risk would be borne entirely by P since the actual sales achieved would remain random. Risk would then be efficiently allocated, borne entirely by risk neutral P. The wage needed to get A to work is determined by deriving A's minimum reservation wage given the knowledge that A's overall utility function must at least equal 2. Thus:

$$w^{1/2} - e^2 = w^{1/2} - 4 \geqslant 2$$

or $w \geqslant 36$

The answer is therefore in the affirmative.

P's expected sales are £366 providing P with a profit of £330 (net of A's pay), and providing A with an incentive bonus of £27. This is a joint value maximising contract since the alternative (to pay A only £9) results in an expected net profit of £224.

The Coase Theorem's prediction that joint value maximising contracts will be entered into absent transactions costs does not hold, however, if effort is non-observable and P is unable to insist that A exerts effort equal to $e = 2$. With P able only to observe the outcome of A's actions, a self-interested A with a fixed remuneration would select $e = 1$ and blame the external economic environment if £100 not £500 was the observed outcome. A bad outcome could be the result of luck or shirking. A good outcome could be independent of e. P must therefore design a contract which exposes A to some risk so that it is in A's self-interest to implement P's desired effort level.

If P wants $e = 2$ then EU_A must exceed that which P would earn if he or she shirked. The incentive contract can only be drawn up on the basis of observed outcomes. Let y be the remuneration if £100 is the outcome and z be the remuneration when sales receipts are £500. Then (from equation (4.1)):

$$EU_A(e = 1) = 0.666\,(y^{1/2} - 1) + 0.333\,(z^{1/2} - 1)$$

$$EU_A(e = 2) = 0.666\,(z^{1/2} - 4) + 0.333\,(y^{1/2} - 4)$$

For the agent to be willing to pick $e = 2$ the second expression must equal or exceed the first

$$0.666\,y^{1/2} - 0.666 + 0.333\,z^{1/2} - 0.333 \leqslant 0.666\,z^{1/2} - 2.666 + 0.333\,y^{1/2} - 1.333$$

which simplifies to

$$0.333\,y^{1/2} \leqslant 0.333\,z^{1/2} - 3$$

$$y^{1/2} \leqslant z^{1/2} - 9.$$

This is the incentive compatability constraint. Simultaneously P must also draw up the contract to meet the participation constraint (recall that minimum $EU_A = 3$):

$$0.666(y^{1/2} - 1) + 0.333(z^{1/2} - 1) \geqslant 3 \text{ or}$$

$$0.666y^{1/2} \geqslant 4 - 0.333z^{1/2}$$

$$2y^{1/2} \geqslant 12 - z^{1/2}$$

The principal's problem is to find values for y and z which will meet both these constraints, and since A is not to be penalised for environmental conditions, y and z must > 0. Expressing the two inequalities as equations and solving simultaneously we have $y = £1$ and $z = £100$ (i.e. a basic wage of £1 can be offered and a bonus of £99 provided on the occasions when £500 of sales are achieved).

Now drawing the threads together the principal–agent problem in this illustration is a situation of information asymmetry where the principal cannot observe behaviour but only outcomes. The problem facing the principal was to devise a contract which would induce the agent to operate in the principal's interest. To do this, incentives had to be provided so that the agent's income was at least partly dependent on the agent's own efforts and not only on the environment. This required an efficient sharing of risk (in a full-information setting the risk-averse agent efficiently bore no risk and the risk-neutral principal bore all the risk). In a situation of bounded rationality some risk had to be shifted to provide an appropriate incentive alignment situation.

Did the evolution of such a contract justify the Coase Theorem assertion that joint value maximisation would be achieved provided the costs of contracting were not too great?

Absent appropriate contracting and given agency problems the principal would have settled for expected sales of £233 (net profit of £224 and a £9 agency wage). With contracting at $e = 2$ expected sales rise to £366 and the agent's expected wage rises from £9 to $0.666 \times £99 + 0.333 \times £1 = £66.33$, giving the principal net profits of £299.66.

Joint value maximisation has occurred given construction of the appropriate incentive contract. Of course, it might not have been possible to do this. Just as in Box 4.1 where we discussed the Coase Theorem, optimal transacting would not have occurred if fencing costs had exceeded £400. Here also, if we had adjusted our parameters, we would not have been able to design an appropriate incentive contract. Joint value maximisation would not then occur. A further point is that had we relaxed the assumption of risk neutrality of the principal then again the optimal risk sharing proportions would have been altered.

Finally consider one additional example – a multidivisional corporation with divisions reporting to a central head office. This is a situation with one principal and several agents operating through time. Most head offices will evaluate divisional management performance on the basis of yardsticks such as return on capital or market share in the last accounting period, on how performance measured by those yardsticks has improved over earlier periods, and on how the division compares using these yardsticks in comparison with other divisions. All divisions will be affected more or less equally by general economic conditions and the objective of head office is to align the incentives of the divisional managers with those of the central group. The theory of principal and agent highlights the difficulties involved in maximising in this type of situation and why. Later chapters show how these difficulties (and those of some of the other principal–agent problems mentioned earlier, such as shareholder–manager relations, credit–borrower linkages, transfer pricing and other contracts in the nexus of contracts called the firm) are better understood and resolved with an appropriate understanding of both transaction costs and the theory of principal and agent.

Notes

1. The Coase Theorem assumes that there are no wealth effects present in the contracting process. This assumption is valid for most business situations. 'No wealth effects' implies three conditions. First, that there is always some monetary amount which would compensate a party to a transaction for a change in circumstances. Second, any unexpected increases in the firm's existing asset values will not affect the firm's pricing or investment decisions. (This seems plausible, but could not be applied, for example, to the behaviour pattern of an individual who had unexpectedly won £$\frac{1}{2}$ million on the football pools. On the other hand recall our discussion of the diminishing marginal utility of money, risk aversion, and consequent modification of the value maximising formula.) Third, the decision maker must always have sufficient capital available willingly to pay for any switch from a less preferred to a more preferred transacting outcome.
2. The reader can check that if the probabilities had been reversed this outcome would not have been possible. (x would either be $\geqslant £2$ or $\leqslant £1.666$.) In that type of circumstance it is impossible for the parties' interests to coincide, not to dissemble and to trade even when trade is value maximising.

Bibliography

Akerlof, G. (1970) 'The market for "lemons": qualitative uncertainty and the market mechanism', Quarterly Journal of Economics, vol. 95.

Coase, R. H. (1937) 'The nature of the firm', Economica, vol. 4.

Coase, R. H. (1960) 'The problem of social cost', Journal of Law and Economics, vol. 2.

Robertson, D. H. (1966) Lectures on Economic Principles, Fontana Library.

Simon, H. A. (1978) 'Rationality as process and as product of thought', American Economic Review, vol. 58.

Williamson, O. E. (1976) Markets and Hierarchies, Free Press.

Williamson, O. E. (1979) 'Transaction cost economics: the governance of contractual relations', Journal of Law and Economics, vol. 22.

Williamson, O. E. (1985) The Economic Institutions of Capitalism, Free Press.

Chapter 5

Business objectives

In this chapter we explain several models of the firm, each based on a different assumption concerning the managerial objective. We do this for two reasons. Firstly, these explanations help to clarify the reader's understanding of the necessary conditions which management must fulfil given sufficient information and varying objectives. Secondly, models help deduce comparative static predictions for a 'typical firm'. That is, a prediction of the qualitative changes in the equilibrium values of endogenous variables (those which the model explains) when exogenous variables (those outside the model) change. Examples of exogenous variables are taxes, costs, and demand conditions. Such predictions, for example, that when a lump sum tax rises, the 'typical firm' will reduce output, would be useful to the government economist and to the trade association economist. If a firm believed that others in its markets fulfilled the assumptions of a particular model, then that model would allow it to make predictions as to their average response to such changes. Correspondingly, if a firm believes that it conforms to a particular model, then the predictions show in which direction managers should adjust their policy variables to continue to achieve their chosen goal.

Thirdly, since the firm is a nexus of contracts consisting of people with different interests, then apparently conflicting objectives may exist within the firm, whether it is viewed as it is by some as an organisational coalition, or by others, as a series of examples of the principal and agent problem. When the firm is regarded as an organisational coalition examining satisficing behaviour would be the appropriate mode of analysis. When the firm is viewed as a series of principal and agent problems, the devising of appropriate incentive compatible contracts in the presence of transaction costs such as opportunism and bounded rationality would be the relevant framework.

In this chapter we rely heavily but not exclusively on models. A model is merely a description of reality in a simplified and highly abstract form. The number of factors which can affect firms' responses to an exogenous change is so large that it would be impossible to include them all. Therefore only the most essential factors can be included.

The factors which one includes are those which enable the model to fulfil the purpose for which it was designed. Therefore, firstly, when the *prediction* of other firms' responses is the aim, the model adopted should be that which has achieved this aim more frequently than any other model. Secondly, when normative *prescriptions* are to be deduced, the model which assumes the goal most desired by management should be chosen.

One may divide models into those with single-period and those with multi-period goals. In the former we consider models based on each of three maximising goals: profits, sales revenue and Oliver Williamson's utility model. The concept of satisficing is also discussed. In the second case we consider long-run maximisation of profit, sales and Marris's utility model. The latter model explicitly looks at attenuating the problem implicit in most of the others: namely that while share-holders generally wish firms to maximise wealth, managers may have other objectives. One way to align incentives is to resort to the market in corporate control. This issue leads into the positive theory of agency associated with the work of Jensen and Meckling.

5.1 The single-period profit-maximising model

We assume here that the firm is a monopolist. The total revenue (TR) and total cost (TC) functions are as in Figure 5.1. To maximise profits, the firm must determine the output level at which the vertical distance between TR and TC is greatest. Geometrically this occurs where the gradients of the two curves are equal, as at Q_2. At outputs less than Q_2, a one unit increase in Q increases TR by more than TC, so such an increase would increase profits, π. At outputs above Q_2, an increase in Q would increase TR by less than TC: π would fall. Since the gradients of TR and TC are the values of marginal revenue and marginal cost, profit maximisation requires equality of these marginal values. The firm's total profit curve is obtained by subtracting TC from TR at each output level as shown in the lower part of Figure 5.1.

Maximum profits occur where the profits curve peaks. The level of profit-maximising output can be derived using the calculus of Chapter 2. Suppose the TR and TC functions are:

$$TR = 41Q - 2Q^2$$

$$TC = 4 + 5Q - 118Q^2 + 0.033Q^3$$

Now

$$\pi = TR - TC$$

$$= 41Q - 2Q^2 - (4 + 5Q - 118Q^2 + 0.033Q^3)$$

$$= 36Q + 116Q^2 - 0.033Q^3 - 4$$

$$\frac{d\pi}{dQ} = 36 + 232Q - 0.1Q^2 = 0 \text{ for max.}$$

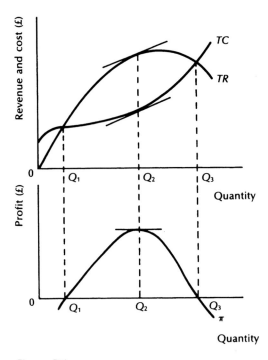

Figure 5.1

Solving for Q, one obtains -0.16 or 2320.16. Since output can never be negative, the profit-maximising rate of output is 2320.16 units.

$$d^2\pi/dQ^2 = 232 - 0.2Q$$

This is negative when $Q = 2320$. Therefore a maximum rather than a minimum value of profit has been found. Notice that since the first derivatives of TR and TC are MR and MC and that equality of MR and MC is necessary for profit maximisation, the equilibrium output can be found by equating these values.

The model may be used to predict what the response of management should be if an exogenous factor changes and if managers wish to continue maximising profits. If fixed costs, for example, rent or rates, rise or if a lump sum tax is imposed, TC rises by the same amount at every output level. Therefore the change in TC, when one additional unit of output is produced (i.e. MC) is unaltered at each output level. Since MR is unchanged, MC equals MR at the original output. So output should remain the same.

If variable costs such as the wage rate rise, or if a tax on every unit of output is levied, the cost of producing one additional unit will be greater at every output level than it was originally. That is, the MC curve will rise. Since the MR curve remains the same, MC will equal MR at a lower output.

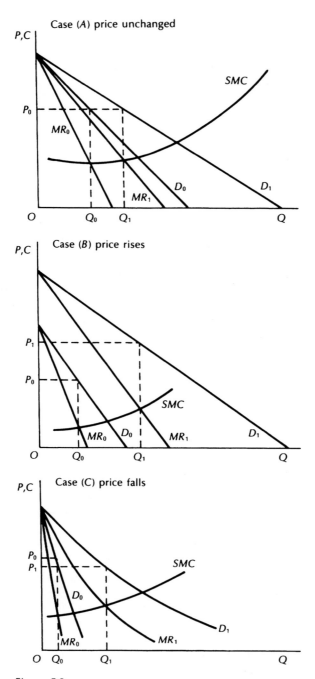

Figure 5.2

If the tax on profits is increased, the post-tax profits curve would shift closer to the Q axis by an amount proportional to the original profits level. But since the tax increase is by the same percentage at every level of profits, the curve will still peak at the same output as before the tax rise. The profit-maximising output should remain the same. If the demand curve shifts, the profit-maximising output may fall, rise, or remain unchanged depending on the exact shift in the curve as is shown in Figure 5.2. In each case the demand curve shifts from D_0 to D_1, *ceteris paribus*, while the marginal revenue curve intersects with the short run marginal cost curve (SMC) above Q_0 and Q_1 as indicated.

5.2 Single-period managerial models

Frequent criticisms were made of the profit-maximising model and managerial models were proposed as substitutes. One criticism was that profit maximising did not describe the goal to which managers aspired. Four main reasons were put forward. First, firms may not be constrained by external forces to maximise profits. Studies have shown that in the large modern corporation there may be a divorce of ownership from control. Shareholders are diffuse and/or lacking in knowledge of the industries in which they invest. In addition an absence of competitive policies by existing firms can permit departures from profit-maximising behaviour by others. Second, it has been argued that firms do not and/or cannot actually maximise profits because managers do not know and cannot determine the concepts of expected marginal revenue and marginal costs. They cannot predict the relevant future values. They are risk averse and that, together with intrafirm communication difficulties, may prevent profit maximisation. Third, it has been argued both on the basis of evidence and *ad hoc* reasoning, that managers have goals other than single-period profits which they try to attain. A further criticism of the assumption has been that some of the comparative static predictions which may be deduced from it have been observed less frequently than those derived from alternative hypotheses. For example, the profit-maximising prediction that price and output would remain unchanged if fixed costs rose appears to be less frequently observed than the prediction that such a rise would lead to a price rise, a prediction to be derived from Baumol's single-period model, to which we now turn.

5.2.1 Baumol's single-period sales-maximising model

Baumol (1959) has argued that business men, particularly in oligopolistic industries, aim to maximise their sales revenue. His assertion is based on public statements by business men and on a number of a priori arguments as to the disadvantages of declining sales: for example, fear of customers shunning a less popular product, less favourable treatment from banks, loss of distributors and a poorer ability to adopt a counter-strategy against a competitor. In Figure 5.3, the position is equal to an

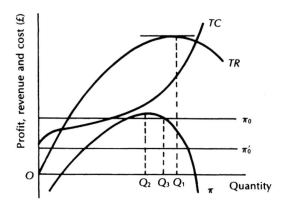

Figure 5.3

output level of Q_1 where the slope of the TR curve (marginal revenue) equals zero. In comparison, the profit-maximising output occurs when $MR = MC$, that is Q_2.

However, as it stands, this argument is incomplete. Baumol argued that there is some minimum level of profits, a profits constraint, which must be earned. This level is determined by a firm's desire to keep its dividends and share prices suffi-ciently high to keep existing shareholders quiescent and to enable it to raise new capital at a future date. Only after this profits constraint has been earned do profits become subordinate to sales in the firm's hierarchy of goals. This constraint is the line π_0 in Figure 5.3. If π_0 is above the level of profits which occur when $MR = 0$, as in the figure, the revenue maximiser is 'constrained'. The constrained maximiser in Figure 5.3 will produce at output level Q_3 where the constraint, π_0, is met. If π_0 was less than the profit where $MR = 0$, for example, π_0' in Figure 5.3, then the revenue maximiser would be unconstrained and produce Q_1. Provided that π_0 is less than maximum profits, the sales maximiser will produce a greater output than the profit maximiser.

The first main difference between the profit maximiser and a constrained sales maximiser is that the latter will charge a lower price to sell the extra $(Q_3 - Q_2)$ output. If both have the same demand curve this must be true.

A second implication is that the sales maximiser will spend more on advertising than the profit-maximising firm. In Baumol's simplified explanation it is assumed that advertising does not affect a product's price. It does, however, lead to increased output sold (with diminishing returns) and it is assumed that advertising will always lead to a rise in TR; MR will never become negative. By assuming that advertising does not affect total non-advertising costs, and by measuring advertising expendi-ture also along the vertical axis, the TC line of Figure 5.4 is derived. Since advertising will always increase TR, the business man will increase advertising until prevented by the profits constraint. In Figure 5.4, A_1 is the profit-maximising level of advertising expenditure. While if π_0 is less than maximum profits, A_1 will always be less than the constrained revenue maximiser's expenditure, A_2. Of course, if

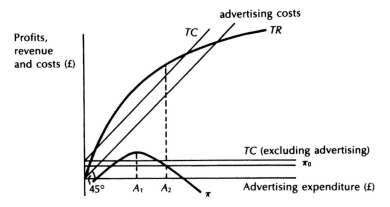

advertising costs
TC
TR
Profits,
revenue
and costs (£)
TC (excluding advertising)
π_0
45° A_1 A_2
π
Advertising expenditure (£)

Figure 5.4

advertising leads to greater output sold, non-advertising costs would be expected to rise. For simplicity, we have omitted this treatment but consider it in Chapter 13.

The comparative static predictions (ignoring advertising) are derived as follows. Assume an initial equilibrium in Figure 5.5 of output Q_1 for the constrained sales maximiser, and Q_3 for the profit maximiser, with the profits curve π_1. If fixed costs (or a lump sum tax) rise, the TC curve would rise by the same amount at each output, and the profits curve would fall parallel to its original position. Therefore the gradient of the profits curve is still zero at Q_3, the final profit-maximising output, but the profits constraint can be met only at a lower output, Q_2, the final constrained revenue maximiser's output. Since demand is unchanged, the constrained revenue maximiser would raise the price to sell the reduced output, the profit maximiser would not.

If, *ceteris paribus*, variable costs or an output tax rose, both the profit maximiser and constrained revenue maximiser would reduce output. If variable costs rose, the cost of each additional unit of output would be greater than previously. Therefore the TC curve would pivot upwards about its intersection with the vertical axis. Hence the profits curve would fall and by a greater amount the larger the output

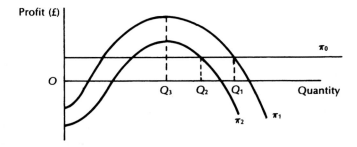

Profit (£)
π_0
O
Q_3 Q_2 Q_1 Quantity
π_2 π_1

Figure 5.5

(because *TC* will have risen by an ever greater amount). This shift is shown in Figure 5.6. The outputs of both the profit maximiser and the constrained revenue maximiser will both fall from Q_2 to Q_1 and Q_4 to Q_3 respectively.

Figure 5.7 shows that a similar situation arises when the rate of corporation tax increases. Compared with Figures 5.5 and 5.6, a corporation tax increase only shifts the profits curve downwards at each level of *profitable output*, and does it by the percentage tax increase (a varying absolute amount) not by a lump sum. Again, the constrained sales maximiser will raise his price and reduce his output, from Q_1 to Q_2, in order to meet the externally imposed profit constraint. The profit maximiser, however, must continue to produce at Q_3. Although his after-tax profits curve has now fallen from π_1 to π_2, Q_3 is still the output level at which the slope of π_2 equals zero.

Finally, the constrained revenue-maximising model predicts that a rise in demand will lead to a rise in output since the profits curve will shift upwards and cut the profits constraint at a greater output. The effect on price is unclear because the relative prices indicated by the 'before' and 'after' outputs depend on the position and shape of the initial and final demand curves. These positions and shapes we have not specified. The same predictions hold in the case of the profit maximiser.

5.2.2 Oliver Williamson's model of managerial discretion

Williamson's (1967) model depends on many of the assumptions of Baumol's:

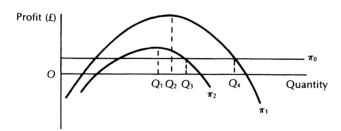

Figure 5.6

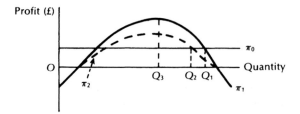

Figure 5.7

a weakly competitive environment, a divorce of ownership from control, and a capital market imposed minimum profit constraint. Williamson argues that the most important motives of business men are desires for salary, security, dominance and professional excellence. These can be gained by additional expenditures on staff, S, managerial emoluments, M, and discretionary investment, I_D. It is argued that these provide additional utility and it is utility, U, which managers aim to maximise. Hence the manager's goal is to maximise U where:

$$U = f(S, M, I_D)$$

The quality and number of staff (S) reporting to a manager enables the manager to gain promotion, salary and dominance and also security through greater confidence as to his department's survival, and greater professional excellence due to the better services which a larger staff can provide. Managerial emoluments (M), represent the type and amount of perquisites the manager receives (the lavish offices, personal secretary, expense account, and so on) beyond the level necessary for efficient operation. The greater is M, it is argued, the greater the manager's status, prestige and satisfaction. Discretionary investment expenditure (I_D) is investment which exceeds that necessary to achieve the minimum post-tax profits demanded by shareholders (denoted π_0). Such spending allows managers to pursue their pet projects, personal investment preferences and to exercise their power – hence it provides utility.

Unlike the models presented earlier, Williamson's firm announces only 'reported' profits, whereas Baumol's and the profit-maximising firm report actual profits. Reported profits, the profits admitted by the firm, equal actual profits less M. M is deducted because it is an expenditure made and is also tax deductible. Notice that in Williamson's model, *actual* profits may not equal *maximum* profits if, as the model predicts, S exceeds the profit-maximisation level.

Before explaining a simplification of the model, it is useful to outline these relationships using the above notation and where:

R = Revenue
C = Production cost
T = Tax
Actual profit: $\pi = R - C - S$
Reported profit: $\pi_R = \pi - M = R - C - S - M$
Minimum (post-tax profit constraint): π_0
Discretionary investment: $I_D = \pi_R - \pi_0 - T$

Since the objective function of a Williamson firm consists of four variables, a completely satisfactory geometric treatment is not possible. Instead we present a simplified diagrammatic analysis of the equilibrium and comparative static predictions. Williamson's model was originally presented mathematically.

We begin our illustration of the equilibrium of the model by considering perks and ignoring expenditure on staff and π_0. Since $\pi_R = \pi - M$, if the maximum level of actual profit a firm could earn is given and π takes on this value, one could represent this relationship as in Figure 5.8. Because each £1 spent on perks reduces π_R by £1,

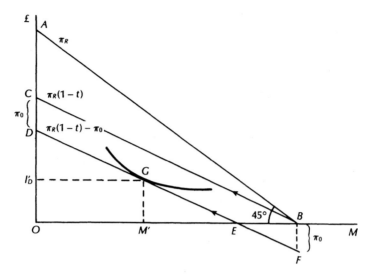

Figure 5.8

this curve will have a gradient of −1 and is shown by the upper line. If a profits tax, rate t, is levied on π_R the curve AB will pivot anticlockwise about point B. This is because, for every £1 diverted from perks to π_R, reported profit will increase by £1, but after tax, post-tax π_R will increase by only £$(1-t)$ because of the tax paid out by the firm. Therefore the slope of the new constraint is $-(1-t)$ which has a value which is closer to zero than AB. Finally, subtract a given profits constraint, π_0, from post-tax reported profit. Since at each level of perks post-tax reported profit decreases by the same amount, we arrive at a final constraint which is line DE, parallel to CB, but lower by the value of π_0. Along the vertical axis this line represents post-tax reported profit in excess of the minimum profits constraint which, by definition, is discretionary investment. Therefore line DE shows how management may exchange I_D for M and vice versa (given the maximum level of profits achieved) and still be sure of attaining the minimum profits constraint.

Now suppose that managerial utility depends only on perks and I_D and that the marginal utility of each is positive. If a manager is to retain the same level of utility when sacrificing I_D, he must take additional M. We can represent this trade-off by an 'indifference curve' as shown by the curved line in Figure 5.8. Such a curve shows combinations of M and I_D between which the manager is indifferent. If we assume that for each additional £1 taken as perks, management is prepared to give up only smaller and smaller amounts of I_D to remain equally satisfied, the indifference curves will be curved inwards as shown. Williamson assumed that management wishes to maximise its utility, and because both I_D and M yield utility, wishes to attain a combination of these which is on the highest indifference curve possible. However, management can only gain combinations of I_D and M on the lowest line of Figure 5.8. Therefore the combination where this constraint line is tangential to the highest indifference curve possible denotes the utility maxi-mising point: point G with I_D of I_b and perks of M'.

We now turn to the staff expenditure and I_D trade-off and temporarily assume that there is no expenditure on perks. If sales staff expenditure, S, increases, output sold will increase. As S increases, reported profit will at first rise since each extra salesman increases output sold more than his or her predecessor. But eventually further sales effort will be less productive, leading to greater wage costs than revenue brought in. Therefore the relationship between reported profits and S is an inverted U-shape, as shown by P in Figure 5.9.

To derive the relationship between S and I_D instead of π_R, suppose that a profits tax is subtracted from the levels of profits shown by line P in Figure 5.9. The curve would become 'flatter' and at each level of S, the maximum post-tax value of π_R would be less, as shown by the dotted curve P' in Figure 5.9. But the level of S which corresponds to π_R of zero is unchanged, since the tax could not reduce a zero-reported profit. Hence curve P' in Figure 5.9 would have the same intercepts as originally. Finally, suppose that the minimum profits constraint is subtracted from P'. Then the level of adjusted profits corresponding to each value of S would be uniformly lower. Curve P' would shift downwards to give curve P''. Since the vertical axis of Figure 5.9 now represents post-tax reported profits in excess of the profits constraint, we have a curve showing the manager's trade-off between I_D and S given π, π_0 and t. By applying an indifference curve to Figure 5.9, one can predict the utility-maximising combination of I_D and S: point E.

Now graphically put together the concepts of Figures 5.8 and 5.9 as shown in Figure 5.10. Since I_D is represented by the vertical axis in both cases, when the manager is maximising his utility, the value of I_D must be the same in both cases. The analysis of Figure 5.9 assumed no perks. This is shown by PH_1 in Figure 5.10b, the same as P' in Figure 5.9. But if management decides to take perks, as it would if its utility-maximising position is shown as point X in Figure 5.10a, the level of I_D corresponding to each level of S in Figure 5.10b, would be reduced by that level of perks, in this case M'', from PH_1 to PH_2. Recall that I_D is calculated after perks have been subtracted. So corresponding to each level of perks, there is a different level of the profit hill. Secondly, the original (Figure 5.8) analysis of Figure 5.10a assumed

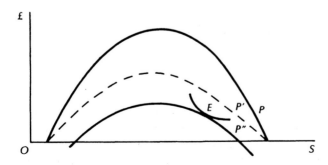

Figure 5.9

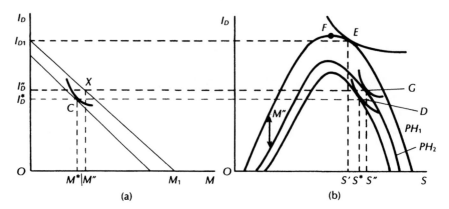

Figure 5.10

a gives π (and so a fixed and known S). If S changes from the profit-maximising level of S_0 (as it would if G in Figure 5.10b were the new combination), π decreases. If S rises, say to S'', the $I_D M$ curve would shift downwards parallel to itself, that is, to a line below $I_{D1}M_1$. This may affect the profit hill yet again, and so on. When the constraint lines in each figure are tangential to the highest indifference curve which can be reached, at the same level of I_D, then the indicated values of I_D, M and S are the utility-maximising levels, given π_0 and t. Such combinations are shown by points C and D in Figure 5.10.

Notice that by definition a profit maximiser takes $M = 0$ (because M is defined as emoluments *in excess* of the profit-maximising value). If the management also has no preference for staff over and above the profit-maximising level, the values of I_D and S taken would be shown by point F in Figure 5.10b. If management has a preference for staff but not for emoluments, point E in Figures 5.9 and 5.10b would locate the optimum combination. If as in the Williamson firm, management has a preference for I_D, S and M, then points C and D are chosen for reasons given earlier. If we assume that the indifference curves in both diagrams have the convex downwards shape attributed to them, then in the Williamson firm the level of perks taken must be positive, and point D in Figure 5.10b must lie to the right and below point F. Therefore, the Williamson manager chooses a positive value of M, whereas the profit maximiser chooses a zero value, and the former also takes a higher value of S and a lower value of I_D than the latter. Finally a higher value of S corresponds to a higher value of output produced. Hence, since a Williamson firm would choose a higher S value than a profit-maximising firm, it would choose to produce a higher output.

Due to their complexity we merely explain the comparative static predictions of this model intuitively and summarise them in Table 5.1. This table compares the qualitative predictions which have been deduced from all the single period models which have been explained.

Table 5.1 Comparative static predictions concerning output

Model	Increase in	Lump sum tax ($T\uparrow$)	Fixed costs ($FC\uparrow$)	Output tax ($Q_t\uparrow$)	Variable costs ($V\uparrow$)	Corporation tax ($t\uparrow$)	Demand ($D\uparrow$)
Profit Maximiser	Changes in Q:	0	0	$\downarrow$	$\downarrow$	0	$\uparrow$
Baumol's sales revenue maximiser		$\downarrow$	$\downarrow$	$\downarrow$	$\downarrow$	$\downarrow$	$\uparrow$
Williamson's utility maximiser		$\downarrow$	$\downarrow$	$\downarrow$	$\downarrow$	$\uparrow$	$\uparrow$

Note: $\uparrow$ = increase $\downarrow$ = decrease 0 = no change.

One of the more interesting predictions is that all 3 models differ in outcome when a rise (or fall) in corporation tax is imposed. We can intuitively understand the outcome of a rise in t in the Williamson case if we recall that

$$U = f(S, M, I_D)$$

which implies that at the margin for each pound of profits allocated by management

$$MU_S = MU_m = MU_{ID} (1 - t).$$

where MU is marginal utility and I_D is expenditure incurred or available for incurring after the imposition of t, profits tax. If this condition did not hold, utility could be increased by reallocating profit between S, M and I_D. Now if t is raised:

$$MU_s = MU_m > MU_{ID} (1 - t).$$

Thus to restore marginal equivalency, discretionary investment must be reduced by switching pounds from I_D (raising $MU_{ID} (1 - t)$) towards S and M, reducing MU_s and MU_m, but, since Williamson, by assumption, argued that expenditure on M or S had a similar effect on sales as would promotional or advertising expenditure, then sales would increase.

5.3 Satisficing and the organisational coalition

Dissatisfaction with the profit-maximising model of economics prompted other writers to develop non-neoclassical models of the firm. One of the first of these was Simon in 1959. Simon (1959) argues that managers must always have imperfect knowledge on which to base decisions; that, if full knowledge was available, the calculations involved in decision making would be too complex to be practicable; and that, given this and the other inevitable uncertainties surrounding decision making in reality, business men can never know whether they are maximising profits or not. Instead, he says, business men 'satisfice', they do not maximise, they aim merely at satisfactory profits. They act with 'bounded rationality'.

What the satisfactory aspiration levels of profit will be depends on past experience and will take account of future uncertainties. If it is easily attained, the aspiration level will be raised, if it proves difficult to attain, it will be revised downwards. In either event managers will instigate 'search' behaviour to find out why actual performance differs from that aspired to so that remedial action can be taken. However, because of the cost of gleaning information, not all alternatives will be explored. A satisfactory alternative course of action will be selected – this probably will *not* be the profit-maximising alternative. (The cynic would argue that this is merely marginalist behaviour. One searches for the *best* course of action (*not* the satisfactory course), but only until the marginal cost of search equals the marginal benefits to be attained from the search.)

If neither search behaviour, nor the lowering of aspiration levels results promptly enough in the achievement of a 'satisfactory' situation then, Simon alleges, the manager's behaviour pattern will become one of apathy or of aggression. This model may seem a long way removed from managerial usefulness. This may be true, but it represents a major departure from traditional ways of thinking about how firms operate and may yet spawn results of utility. For example, it does knit in with the facts where business men price on a full cost basis, adding a satisfactory margin of profit, not knowing where the $MR = MC$ price and output combination is. It does help explain why some firms, faced with a falling market share, act more vigorously than competitors, in an attempt to halt the decline while others, conversely, in the same situation, act as though they were commercially moribund.

In their book, *Behavioural Theory of the Firm* (1963), Cyert and March examined the particular individuals who take decisions in firms, rather than looking at the firm's behaviour as such. They were more interested in the decision making process than in the motivation, profit maximising or satisficing, of the firm.

Firms, in the Cyert and March model, are composed of individuals who make up the 'organisational coalition'. These include managers, workers, shareholders and customers. Each coalition member will have an individual goal which may well conflict with the goal of another member. For the firm, as an organisation, to remain in existence, the coalition members must be satisfied with less than their maximum objectives since the resources are not available to satisfy them all. People will be prepared to 'sub-optimise' in this way if by so doing they get closer to their objectives than they would if acting as individuals outside the organisation. So, since this conflict of objectives exists, the final set of goals of the firm will, at least partly, be the outcome of a political decision.

Cyert and March suggest that firms are always being run at a level below maximum efficiency and so more expensively than need be. 'Organisational slack' exists. This consists of 'payments to members of the coalition in excess of what is required to maintain the organisation'. Slack exists because first, it is difficult to ascertain the minimum acceptable reward to coalition members. Second, assets tend to be underexploited since it is difficult to know the maximum productivity of a human or a machine. Third, since the market's characteristics can never be fully known, less than optimal price, product and promotion policies will probably be pursued. Moreover, adaptations to changes in circumstances at any of these levels will probably be slow and imperfect.

Although the number of sub-goals a firm can have is infinite under this model, Cyert and March concentrate on five. These are production, inventory, sales, market-share and profit. The production goal is of consequence to those members of the coalition concerned with production (such as workers and factory managers). It will reflect the desire for such things as stable employment, ease of scheduling, and so on. The inventory goal will be of importance to customers and salespersons who are interested in the firm having both an adequate breadth (for choice) and depth (for fluctuating demand) of stock. The sales goal will be of consequence to salespersons where the market share will be of importance to top sales managers interested in comparative measures of performance. While the profit goal will be highly relevant to shareholders, top managers, creditors who require assurance of payment, and sub-units of the firm, whose budgets for expansion may well depend on the overall firm's profitability.

These various sub-goals will often conflict, and their relative order of achievement will depend on the explicit or implicit bargaining power of the various interest groups in the coalition. Simon, Cyert and March wrote before the appearance of principal and agent theory in the literature. Their work stressing bounded rationality, satisficing behaviour and the tolerance of members of the organisational coalition of organisational slack all foreshadowed the view of the firm as a nexus of contracts where there are transactions costs of bounded rationality and opportunism and where efficient contract writing involves optimising the alignment of incentives.

The difficulties involved in value-maximising behaviour given transaction costs are highlighted in Box 5.1.

In times of high demand, greater slack will be created and the resources will go to those who are the first to spot the opportunity. This will usually be those most intimately involved on a full-time basis with the organisation, such as the management group and the workers. Conversely, if some goal is not being satisfied, then either aspiration levels can be lowered, *pace* Simon, or slack can be reduced. For example, if profits were low then a special effort might be made to reduce costs. Or if demand was weak, the firm might be willing to reduce its profit margin and lower prices.

Some of the conclusions of this model are not particularly different from those of the traditional profit maximising model. There are three major variations, however. The Cyert and March model illustrates the process of decision making; the marginalist, profit-maximising model merely indicates the decision which *must* be taken to achieve a desired outcome. It does not show how the decision is arrived at. Second, organisational slack does not exist in the profit-maximising model. It is assumed that least cost input combinations are already being used. Finally, the Cyert and March model may not merit the status of a theory, if by a theory we mean a model which is capable of verification and of universal applicability.

Should we then discard the behavioural non-marginalist models of the firm as being of little value to the manager? They have made several valuable contributions.

Box 5.1

Decision making by committee and Arrow's Impossibility Theorem

Consider a three-person committee. First, the sales manager who wants maximum product range depth and breadth in order to aid him or her maximise sales. This requires the carrying of large inventories and the production of a heterogeneous product range. Second, a production manager who wishes to minimise production costs by specialising on volume production of a narrow range of products during any given production period. The production manager is unconcerned that this implies large inventories to meet fluctuating demands in those periods a particular good is not manufactured, and he or she is similarly unconcerned, indeed would prefer to persistently produce only a narrow range of goods. Finally, the firm's finance manager wishes to hold inventories (and hence working capital to a minimum). The finance manager is less concerned about running out of stock and failing to meet customer requirements, and also relatively unconcerned about the production manager's desire to avoid short production runs.

The committee of three can only combine these conflicting objectives into one value-maximisation function if they are combined as follows:

$$V = \alpha M + \beta P + \gamma F$$

where M is the marketing manager's sub-goal (sales maximisation), P, the production manager's sub-goal (cost minimisation), and F, the finance manager's sub-goal (capital outlay minimisation). The three must accept each other's sub-goals and must agree on the weights (the relative importance) α, β and γ of each.

Kenneth Arrow (1950) demonstrated this type of problem in what is termed the Impossibility Theorem. If Table B5.1 shows the individual's sub-goals in order of preference then, if the three managers vote in committee, none will achieve his or her objective. One vote will be cast for each policy choice. If only two choices are available (say M and F) the result is totally unstable. Production and Finance prefer F to M and F will be chosen in a 2 to 1 vote. But Arrow showed that this is an impossible outcome since if only M and P had been available Marketing and Finance would have voted for M by 2 to 1 (winning over F). Similarly P would have won over F if M had not been available.

Two possible alternatives are a dictatorial general manager selecting the value maximising choice or information on α, β and γ to permit a voluntary joint value-maximising choice to be made.

The values of α, β and γ would, of course, still be open to the problems of information asymmetry and a satisficing agreement (one which meets all three unknown aspiration levels) is a likely solution permitting a unanimous, non-value-maximising agreement with consequential organisational slack.

Table B5.1

	1st choice	2nd choice	3rd choice
Marketing manager	M	P	F
Production manager	P	F	M
Finance manager	F	M	P

First, they have highlighted the problem of organisational slack. From the national economic viewpoint, resources are not being fully utilised if slack exists. The citizen as consumer and shareholder (directly or indirectly through the institutions) loses in terms of overall living standards if managers, as administrators of the nation's real resources, fail to minimise slack. From the individual manager's viewpoint, the concepts of slack and the organisational coalition have emphasised that the management task is more difficult and complex, but probably more interesting, than solely technocratic models of the firm might at first indicate.

Second, by their *lack* of general applicability they have shown again how it is possible to reconcile profit maximisation models with rule of thumb techniques such as the full cost pricing model. Rules of thumb in pricing (or in other) decisions help minimise the costs of search and so are perfectly consistent with a maximisation approach. The behavioural models explain how the rule of thumb chosen must obtain support from within the organisation. They fail, however, to explain how the rule of thumb is itself selected, and how such a rule will change as conditions in the market place or elsewhere vary.

Third, although they pre-date the writings on transaction costs, they emphasise again how and why the development of principal and agent theory, and viewing the firm as a nexus of contracts and not a black box is vital further to undertake understanding of the problems managerial economics must address. Before returning to that discussion, however, recall that profit maximising itself as an objective has been modified not only to take account of information asymmetries, but also time. Hence in Section 5.4 we reintroduce time into the profit objective. In Section 5.5 as in earlier sections, we look at alternatives to the objective of maximising profits over time (value maximising) and in Section 5.6 we return to principal and agent theory to see how more modern writings have adopted the principles of marginal equivalency to account for the transaction costs hinted at in the behavioural theories of Simon, Cyert and March.

5.4 The multi-period profit-maximising model

Observation of management behaviour and the business press has led several writers to argue that management goals are growth-centred. These writers have built a range of dynamic models which differ from the so-called 'static' models of the firm which we have examined so far, and which help to deduce the optimum values of policy instruments for expansion-minded firms. Thus, if we introduce the time factor into the profit-maximising model, the firm will be assumed to act in a manner which will maximise the present value of expected future profits, $[PV(\pi)]$.

Consider Figure 5.11 derived by Baumol (1962). $PV(\pi)$ equals the difference between the present values of total revenue and total costs, $PV(TR)$ and $PV(TC)$ respectively. $PV(TR)$ and $PV(TC)$ are assumed to depend on the firm's growth rate of output, g. The firm chooses the value of g which maximises $PV(\pi)$. The $PV(TC)$ function is composed of two types of cost; output costs and expansion costs. They are composed of fixed and variable costs; and if we assume constant returns to scale

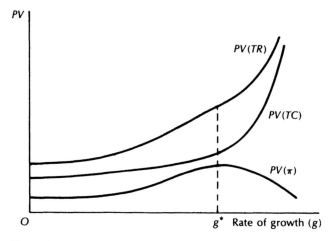

Figure 5.11

they will rise in a linear fashion as the firm's annual rate of growth rises. (If the firm has identified the optimum scale of plant, it can replicate that plant as often as required to meet any output growth needs.) On the other hand, expansion costs can be expected to rise more than proportionately as the rate of growth increases.

It is for this reason that the $PV(TC)$ function is displaying non-linear properties. One major reason for the disproportionate rise in expansion costs is the limited ability of management to administer efficiently a growing entity. Growth entails recruitment of new personnel at all levels of the firm. These must be trained and assimilated into the organisation. While new staff are being trained and gaining experience, inefficiencies arise. The greater the training task and the more new employees there are, then – given the fixed size of the original management team – the higher these inefficiencies become, and the firm's expansion costs rise accordingly. Expansion costs also rise disproportionately if the firm tries to shortcut the time required to build new plant capacity.

'Crash programmes' invariably raise unit costs. Also, ever more rapid growth requires ever more capital to finance the expansion. Beyond some level, the cost of capital will rise. For example, frequent issues of shares to raise funds will force the price of equity down and so its cost of servicing up.

The $PV(TR)$ function also rises at an increasing rate as g increases. That is, a firm which continuously grows at a relatively high rate will expect a more than proportionately greater discounted sum of future revenue than a firm which grows at a relatively low rate. This can be seen by formulating the $PV(TR)$ equation:

Let R_t = revenue in period t
t = 0: current period
g = continuous growth rate of revenue and output

Then[1] $PV(TR) = R_0 + \dfrac{R_1}{(1+r)} + \dfrac{R_2}{(1+r)^2} + \ldots$

But $R_1 = R_0 + R_0 \times g = R_0(1 + g)$

$R_2 = R_1 + R_1 \times g = R_1(1 + g) = R_0(1 + g)^2$

and so on.

So $PV(TR) = R_0 + \dfrac{R_0(1 + g)}{(1 + r)} + \dfrac{R_0(1 + g)^2}{(1 + r)^2} + \ldots$

$$= R_0 \left\{ \dfrac{1}{1 - (1 + g)/(1 + r)} \right\} = R_0 \left\{ \dfrac{(1 + r)}{(r - g)} \right\} \qquad (5.1)$$

$$= R_0(1 + r)(r - g)^{-1}$$

(The sum of the geometric series $a + ak + ak^2 + \ldots + ak^n$ as $n \to \infty$ where 'a' is a constant and k, a multiplicative factor, is $[a/(1 - k)]$.)

If we partially differentiate this with respect to g, using rule 6 of Table 2.2 we derive:

$$\frac{\partial PV(TR)}{\partial g} = R_0(1 + r)(r - g)^{-2}$$

which is positive because R_0 and $r > 0$ (assuming $r > g$). So the $PV(TR)$ curve has a positive gradient. Now

$$\frac{\partial^2 PV(TR)}{\partial g^2} = 2R_0(1 + r)(r - g)^{-3}$$

is positive for the same reason. So the gradient of the $PV(TR)$ curve increases as g increases, that is the $PV(TR)$ curve bends upwards as shown in the figure.

The growth rate which achieves the management's goal is that where $PV(TR)$ exceeds $PV(TC)$ by the greatest amount: g^* in Figure 5.11. If g is increased beyond g^*, the increase in $PV(TR)$ is less than that of $PV(TC)$, so $PV(\pi)$ would fall. Marginal $PV(TR)$ is less than marginal $PV(TC)$. If g is below g^* but increased, $PV(TR)$ would increase by more than $PV(TC)$, so $PV(\pi)$ would rise. Marginal $PV(TR)$ exceeds marginal $PV(TC)$. So $PV(\pi)$ is maximised where these marginal present values are equal.

5.5 Marris's multi-period managerial model

Marris has argued that managers aim to maximise their utility, which in this model depends only on the firm's growth rate, subject to a security constraint. Stock-holders are assumed to be wealth maximisers. That is, they wish to maximise the present value of future expected dividends plus share price when they realise their shares:

$$S_0 = \sum_{t=0}^{n} d_t/(1+r)^t + S_n/(1+r)^n$$

$$= \sum_{t=0}^{\infty} d_t/(1+r)^k \tag{5.2}$$

where S_0 = current share price
d_t = dividend per share received in year t
S_n = share price in year n
r = discount rate

Our discussion follows Radice's simplification (Radice 1971). Marris assumes that the firm's growth rate, g, once chosen, remains fixed indefinitely and that it relates to all characteristics of the firm: assets, profits, revenue, dividends and so on. Hence all ratios of these 'state' variables remain constant. (Only the number of shares (N) is assumed constant.) Therefore we can rewrite equation (5.2) as:

$$S_0 = \sum_{t=0}^{\infty} \frac{d_0(1+g)^t}{(1+r)^t}$$

using similar reasoning as that preceding equation (5.1). Hence, since $d_0 = D_0/N$ where D_0 = total dividend payment, we can write:

$$S_0 = \sum_{t=0}^{\infty} \frac{D_0(1+g)^t}{N(1+r)^t} \tag{5.3}$$

Marris argues that there is a two-way relationship between g and profitability, P. In equation form:

$$g = f(P) \ldots \text{(supply–growth relationship)} \tag{5.4}$$

$$P = \phi(g) \ldots \text{(demand–growth relationship)} \tag{5.5}$$

Consider the supply–growth relationship, Greater profitability allows faster growth because it allows more to be retained per period if the retention ratio is given, and hence more to be reinvested. Similarly Marris argued that the greater the profitability the greater the amounts of debt and equity which would be taken by the capital market per period. The supply growth function is presented as a straight line as in Figure 5.12.

Consider now the demand growth equation. Marris argued that the main form of firm growth is diversification rather than increasing revenue from existing products. A new product may be a success, a failure, or in between. In the first case, revenue rises over time and eventually reaches a high level which increases only at the rate at which the market for the product increases. In the second case, revenue would rise only to a low level and then decrease. We assume that all products are successful.

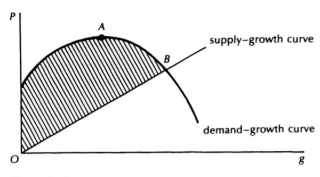

Figure 5.12

If a firm adopts the maximum diversification rate consistent with a given level of profitability, at relatively low rates of growth the relationship between P and g is direct. Several reasons are put forward for this. Firstly, growth and diversification at a slow rate rather than not at all will allow the relatively high profits of those products which are continually being introduced to be gained, rather than just the relatively low profits of old products. There would then always be some new products earning (temporarily high) monopoly profits. Secondly, up to a certain growth rate, managerial efficiency may increase with the firm's growth rate, because growth allows managers to face new interesting situations, and enables them to gain additional prestige and to exercise their ability, unlike the management of a firm with no growth.

However, eventually, greater rates of diversification result in successively lower profitability. Firstly, the methods of increasing the diversification rate reduce profitability by reducing total revenue or increasing total costs, relative to firm size. Such methods are: increasing advertising expenditure; greater R&D expenditure or lower prices. Secondly, as mentioned in Section 5.4 faster growth would require a faster growth rate of skilled management. This would mean that less time was spent by experienced staff in performing their original tasks and inefficiencies would arise. These factors would outweigh those causing a direct relationship at lower growth rates. Hence as the growth rate increases, profitability would decrease.

For these reasons, equation (5.5) forms an inverted U-shape as shown in Figure 5.12. Since both equations (5.4) and (5.5) must be satisfied (there can only be one value for each of g and P) the chosen growth rate and profitability must be where both the demand–growth and supply–growth lines intersect, that is point B in Figure 5.12.

However, the exact position of the supply–growth curve merits more explanation. Its location depends on the subjective preferences of the management for security and tenure. At any level of profitability, the maximum growth rate depends on the level of retentions, increase in new debt and the rate of increase of new equity. Suppose the retention ratio is initially low and growth rate minimal. As the retention ratio rises, current dividends would fall if profitability remained unchanged, but their growth rate would increase. As the retention ratio (R)

increases, the supply–growth curve will pivot clockwise since with no external finance: $g = R \times P$, that is $P = (1/R)g$. Now at first at successively higher retention ratios, the profitability increase, as predicted by Figure 5.12 would outweigh the reduction in dividends which would otherwise occur. Dividends and their growth rate rise and so, given the discount rate which shareholders apply to future receipts, the value of each share rises.

When the retention ratio has reached a level such that the supply–growth line passes through A, the firm will be maximising profitability. If retentions are further increased, current dividends will be lower due to lower profits and pay-out ratio, but their growth rate will outweigh this and the firm's market value will still increase. Eventually, still higher retention ratios would cause the decrease in dividends to outweigh the increase in growth rate in the share value formula (equation (5.3)), and hence cause share value to fall. When the rate of increase of debt or new equity per period is increased, the analysis is more complex but the same results apply.

Marris explains the significance of a lower share price in terms of the 'valuation ratio'. A valuation ratio equals the total market value of the firm's shares (number of shares times their market price) divided by the book value of the firm's assets (valued at replacement cost).

Remembering that if by adopting a higher retention ratio etc., the higher growth rate eventually causes a lower share price, then given the number of shares and the book value of assets, the valuation ratio would be lower. If the actual valuation ratio falls below the subjective valuation ratio put on the firm by a potential bidder, the latter will take over the firm. In short, a firm will be taken over if a buyer believes he or she can make more profitable use of the existing assets than the current managerial team and so increase its share price and valuation ratio. Since a takeover will jeopardise the jobs of those managers who opted for growth in the first place, managers will wish to keep their valuation ratio above a level where a takeover is thought 'likely'.

Referring back to Figure 5.12 since management wishes to maximise the firm's growth rate subject to a minimum valuation ratio constraint, the relevant supply–growth line is that which is pivoted as far clockwise as managers believe leaves their firm safe from takeover. Policies which involve higher valuation ratios are also safe and therefore retention policies leading to supply–growth curves anywhere within the shaded areas of the figure are 'safe'.

Figure 5.13 presents the same arguments in a more explicit form. Point X indicates the point of maximum shareholder utility given that they wish to maximise their wealth and so make some trade-offs between current dividends and capital gains. At point X equation (5.3) is maximised, share price is at its highest possible level and thus by definition so also is the firm's valuation ratio (as indicated by Figure 5.13). Managers too, however, are in a trade-off situation. They are not, like shareholders, comparing current dividends with future dividends, but rather job security against corporate growth. Their indifference curves are indicated by the lines labelled M_1, M_2 and M_3. Given the indifference curves of the figure, the managers of the firm will choose point B' and the appropriate growth

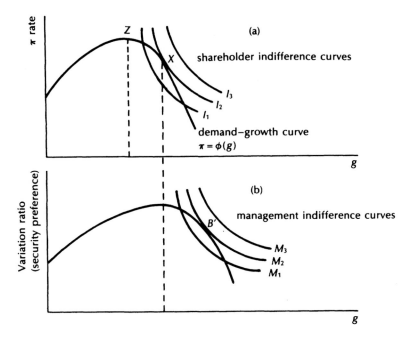

Figure 5.13

rate/valuation rate combination. (B' in Figure 5.14 implies the same growth rate as B in Figure 5.12.)

However, managerial utility (M) is a function of security (the valuation ratio), and if the threat of takeover is high enough, the indifference curves labelled M will be close to horizontal and B' and X will coincide vertically (in Figure 5.13) and in Figure 5.12 the supply–growth line will pivot to the left maintaining the implication that B and B' still result in equal growth rates.

5.6 The positive theory of agency

The theory of principal and agent discussed in Chapter 4 is aimed at designing optimal contracts to raise the incentives of the agent so that his actions coincide with the objectives of the principal. Given that the firm is a nexus of contracts how should such contracts be written?

The positive theory of agency discussed here, arises from a less mathematical literature base and attempts to ask why certain contractual types of governance structure exist? It is directed at explaining the contracts and organisational forms of the real world rather than at prescribing them. It tends to rely on the Coase Theorem and presumes that joint value-maximising behaviour patterns already do exist (net of transaction costs) since, if they did not, alternative behavioural or organisational patterns would have superseded them.

None the less, the theory of the firm and the positive theory of agency have much in common. In particular, the theory of the firm developed to embrace the notions that managers and owners may have differing objectives, that while managers may make strategic decisions, owners receive the bulk of any residual profits, and – crucially – most shareholders are unable to exercise meaningful control over managers. Thus the managerial and behavioural theories of the firm discussed earlier in this chapter can more appropriately be replaced or complemented by one or other of the two branches of agency theory. The relationship between 'owners' and 'managers' is simply a special example of an 'agency relationship'. That is, it is a contract where principals (owners) engage agents (managers) to perform services on their behalf and in so doing delegate considerable decision making authority to them. Assuming both principals and agents are utility maximisers, it is likely that an agent will act in such a way that, while maximising his or her own utility, the agent will not maximise that of the principal. For example, in Williamson's model, managers took more than the profit-maximising level of perks, and in Marris's model, managers set a growth rate in excess of that which maximised the valuation ratio. The monetary value of the benefits foregone by the principal because the agent does not maximise his or her utility is called the agency cost or 'residual loss' due to the relationship.

Jensen and Meckling (1976) represented the magnitude of the residual loss diagrammatically as follows. Assume that the manager gains utility from both money wages and the present value of perks. With a given technology and demand, any chosen combination of policy variables, e.g. price, output, etc., will result in particular cash inflows in future periods which in turn will determine the market value of the firm. Given the manager's money wage, if the manager took only the value-maximising level of perks and chose the value-maximising level of price etc., the firm's value would be maximised at, say, point $\bar{V}$ in Figure 5.14 where the

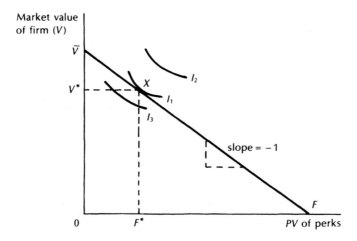

Figure 5.14

downward-sloping line meets the vertical axis. But the manager may take more perks than the level which maximises the firm's market value. If he or she does, and given the maximum market value of the firm, its *actual* market value will decrease because, by definition

$$V = \bar{V} - P \qquad (5.6)$$

where V = market value of firm
P = PV of perks
$\bar{V}$ = maximum market value of firm

Therefore, for each additional £1 by which the manager increases the PV of his or her perks, the market value of the firm decreases by £1. Similarly, from equation (5.6) we can deduce that if the manager takes all of the PV of profits as perks, the value of the firm would be reduced to zero: point F in Figure 5.14. (Of course, for each scale of firm there would be a different $\bar{V}F$ line parallel to the one shown. The $\bar{V}F$ line is analogous to the budget constraint of demand and cost theory discussed in Chapters 7 and 9.)

To illustrate the magnitude of the agency 'residual loss' we shall compare the value of a firm where the owner is also the manager (and hence, by definition, there is no agency relationship) with a case where there is such an agency relationship. Suppose, first, that the manager owns 100 per cent of the equity of the firm. Then the maximum market value of the manager's (100 per cent) share in the firm, given any level of perks, is shown by $\bar{V}F$ in Figure 5.14. This is because, if the manager increases the PV of his perks by £1, the latter is *his or her* loss of wealth: he or she owns the entire firm. Suppose also that the manager's indifference curves between utility and perks are as shown. To maximise his or her utility the manager will choose to take the PV of perks equal to F^* and correspondingly the value of the firm will be V^*: point X.

Now suppose the owner (already at point X) sells some of his or her shares in the firm to an outsider but retains a proportion, α, of the firm's equity. In this case, if the owner – still being the manager – increases the PV of perks taken by £1, the market value of the firm decreases by £1. But, since the owner only owns α of the firm, the cost to *him or her* of taking extra perks is now lower than it was when he or she was the owner. The market value of *his or her* share decreases only by α£1, and α is less than 1.0. Hence the constraint which the manager (and now only part owner) faces in his or her choice of PV perks and MV firm has a slope of $-\alpha$, not -1. This constraint $V_1 P_1$ must also pass through point X. This is because, if the individual wishes, he or she can still have that combination of perks and MV which the individual had before selling his or her shares.

The share sale provides the manager with cash receipts $(1 - \alpha)V^*$, the MV of the manager's remaining shares αV^* and perks corresponding to F^*. The new constraint is shown as $V_1 P_1$ in Figure 5.15. If the manager's indifference curves are unchanged, he or she will choose a greater PV of perks, F^0, (point Y) than when he or she owned the whole firm. Given equation (5.6), since the PV of perks has increased, the actual market value of the firm will decrease by this amount, i.e. from V^* to V^0.

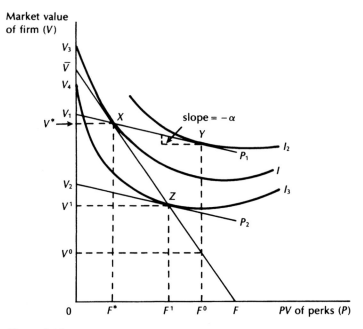

Figure 5.15

However, share purchasers are not naive. If they believe that after purchase the manager will take perks in excess of F^*, and consequently that the value of the firm will then fall below V^*, they will only, at most, be prepared to pay $(1-\alpha)$ times the new expected value of the firm. That is less than $(1-\alpha)V^*$ for the shares.

Similarly, the owner/manager is aware that, with chosen perks of F^0, the firm would only have a value of V^0 and, while the owner/manager is willing to sell for $(1-\alpha)V^*$, he or she is not prepared to sell for $(1-\alpha)V^0$. He will only be prepared to sell for $(1-\alpha)$ times the new expected value of the firm, or above.

Given that the owner/manager wishes to sell $(1-\alpha)$ of the firm, what price will be satisfactory to both parties to the trade? Jensen and Meckling show that it must be V^1, on a constraint line V_2P_2 which passes through Z, a particular point on $\overline{V}F$ where the owner/manager has an indifference curve I_3, tangential to it.

Point Z is unique in that it is firstly possible (it lies on $\overline{V}F$) for the resources of the firm to provide the perks: MV combination shown; while secondly, it lies on a constraint line with a slope of $-\alpha$ and thirdly, and simultaneously lies on an indifference curve with that same slope. Or to put it differently it is only at Z that the owner/manager's marginal utility from spending an extra £1 on on-the-job consumption (perks) equals the marginal utility of forfeiting £1 of personal wealth in the form of firm market value (whilst still remaining on the overall constraint line VF).

Algebraically at Z:

$$\text{slope of } I_3 = \frac{MU_{\text{perks}}}{MU_{MV}}$$

$$= \frac{\text{price of perks}}{\text{price of } MV} = \frac{-\alpha}{1}$$

$$= \text{slope of } V_2 P_2 \text{ or}$$

$$MU_{\text{perks}} = \alpha MU_{MV}$$

In summary, we see that when a manager owns all the shares of a firm, the firm's value is V^*. But when a manager owns only α of the shares, because he or she takes more perks than when the sole owner, the value of the firm and of the manager's wealth is less than V^*: it is V^1. This reduction in the value of the firm is the 'residual loss' of the agency relationship which was created when the owner/manager sold some of his or her shares. (Although, as Jensen and Meckling point out, this 'loss' is perfectly consistent with economic efficiency since the owner/manager would only incur it if he or she believed that using the cash receipts $(1-\alpha)V^1$ elsewhere would make him- or herself better off. The owner/manager has, after all, moved from a higher to a lower indifference curve, namely I to I_3. Similarly, shareholders will only pay for the shares purchased if, in their judgement, this is the best alternative use of their cash resources.)

5.7 Managerial discipline

Agency relationships, then, can result in agents – in this context managers – behaving in a way which does not maximise the welfare of principals – owners (at least as measured by V). The question arises as to whether there are any mechanisms which constrain the agent's behaviour to be as close to that of joint wealth-maximisation as possible. Four main constraints have been proposed. We have already discussed one: the takeover mechanism embodied in the Marris model. Manne (1965) called this the *market in corporate control*. Box 5.2 provides an illustration of the market in corporate control in operation.

We have also discussed a second – appropriate contract design in order to minimise transaction costs (in Chapter 4). This as we saw involves monitoring of agents to avoid shirking in the presence of asymmetric information. Positive agency theory has added a further gloss to this. Owners can monitor managers and by spending resources on observation (for example by appointing a board of directors,

---

Box 5.2

The market in corporate control: takeovers and takeover threats as means of disciplining management

The ICI–Hanson case

It represents more than half a century of British industrial history. It boasts a handful of the world's most important inventions in chemicals, plastics and drugs. It is one of Britain's biggest manufacturers, one of its most international firms and, over the long run, one of the more successful. That is why the mere idea that Hanson might make a hostile bid for Imperial Chemical Industries has caused a mighty stir in boardrooms, plenums and pubs. Yet the response from ICI's board has been haughty: denigrating the bidder, while arguing that it should be left to get on with its own plans for reshaping the company ... alongside its modest half-yearly results. This will not – and should not – be enough to make shareholders immune to the temptations of the takeover.

There is more at issue in the battle for ICI than the pride of its chairman ... and his board. Although on May 14th Hanson merely revealed that it had bought 2.8% of ICI, the implicit threat of a takeover also offered a classic case of why such hostile bids are at once both regrettable and unavoidable. Regrettable because they are disruptive ... while battle is fought ... only the firm's competitors can gain. But unavoidable because, in the absence of any other source of pressure, boards take their time over making necessary changes, leaning on their oars while another study is done and another year goes by.

... ICI is not a failure. For a start, its half-yearly results, announced at the trough of a British recession, are better than its performance in 1980–82 during Britain's previous recession. But that modest success reveals a firm that has much to be modest about. Its troubles in the early 1980s arose from being in many of the wrong businesses, in the wrong countries, and run by a cumbersome bureaucracy. It had arrived there after decades of passable drift. It responded in the right way – by shaking itself up – but for too short a time. Big, old, bureaucracies hate change. They resist it, and once the shaking has stopped they 'consolidate' – i.e. they sit back. That is what happened at ICI ...

It was a missed opportunity, for when change is so hard to get going, the last thing a firm should do is to stop it prematurely. The pause left ICI still a bureaucratic place, and still with many of the classic weaknesses of the conglomerate. Each of its businesses, ranging from paints to pharmaceuticals, has its strengths, and there are undoubted synergies between them. But they also detract from one another, both because of the bureaucracy and because winners subsidise losers. The drugs business, which provides almost half ICI's profits, is typical: a good, successful firm that needs more attention than it gets inside ICI. This conglomerate, stripped down though it is compared with the 1970s, has resisted further stripping, to its own detriment.

The arrival of Hanson, however, offers a fresh opportunity to get change started again. Even the staunchest of opponents of hostile bids admits that Hanson's attentions are likely to improve ICI, whatever the outcome, by concentrating directors' minds ...

→

The ICI board has made three serious mistakes. It let it be known that the firm has a break-up value of at least £15 billion ($26 billion), well above its current market value. Intended to show Hanson how costly a bid would be, this was a tacit admission that the board was failing to do its job. Second, it attacked Hanson with a series of small smears, winning publicity but losing ammunition and perhaps even some respect. The third mistake is the worst, however ... it is missing the chance to strike a new deal with its shareholders.

The problem faced by any incumbent board during a takeover bid is that to propose big changes is to admit past failures. Given that the cards are stacked in ICI's favour, however, its board could afford to be both humble and brave – especially before a bid has actually been made. It could go to its shareholders and say, in effect, that Hanson has a point: ICI is not doing as well, and is not worth as much, as it could be.

This takeover threat did not materialise but the reader should study the history of ICI's managerial decisions since this 1991 report. (© *The Economist*, London 27 July 1991)

and by having the firm's books checked by an external auditor) they can reduce on-the-job consumption of perks. Alternatively the agent, management, can 'post a bond'. The difference between monitoring and bonding is simply a question of where the initiative lies. Owners take the initiative in monitoring activities. Agents (in this case, managers) take the initiative in bonding. The posting of a bond is simply a gesture of intent stating that if an agreement is defaulted upon the bond will be forfeited. In this case, managers bond themselves to be monitored by a board and by auditors. In either event both bonding and monitoring costs are borne by the principal.

To explain this assertion reconsider Figure 5.15. The original owner absorbed the full cost of any on-the-job consumption of perks ($\bar{V} - V^*$). If the owner can convince potential buyers that he or she will consume (after sale of $(1 - \alpha)$ per cent of shares) less than F^1 in perks then he or she will be able to sell the shares for an amount greater than $(1 - \alpha)$ per cent of V^1. If the owner consumes less, the value of the firm rises, that is V^1 rises, and it is the agent as seller (the original owner, soon to be owner/manager) who captures this increase in his or her selling price not the outside buyers (soon to be principals) who pay it. So it could be in the manager's interest credibly to promise (to post a bond) that he or she will restrict consumption of perks below F^1. By consuming less than F^1 the manager can increase his or her utility (receiving a price for his or her shares above $(1 - \alpha)V^1$).

But bonding and/or monitoring costs such as auditing of books and employment of a board of directors cost money – reducing the value of the firm. Thus the original owner's budget constraint is no longer V_2P_2 but a curve above it like SZ (see Figure 5.16). At Z monitoring and bonding costs are zero. Left of Z they increase, but they also raise the price at which the firm's shares can be sold, doing so ultimately at a diminishing rate. Although these costs must be borne to overcome an information asymmetry which did not previously exist (when the firm was 100% owner-managed

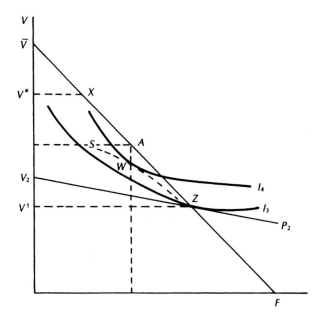

Figure 5.16

there was no information asymmetry), SZ cannot lie above $\overline{V}F$, which is an absolute resource constraint.

At some point, such as W, there is an optimal amount of monitoring and bonding where by reducing perks below F^1 a utility level such as I_4 can be achieved, above I_3 and below I. At W the owner/manager spends WA on monitoring and bonding costs. Agency costs, which in Figure 5.15 equalled V^*V^1 have been reduced to the vertical V^*A (in Figure 5.16), or, including bonding and monitoring, a total residual loss of V^*W.

A third form of managerial discipline was described by Fama (1980). He argued that managerial performance is encouraged by the existence of managerial labour markets within and between firms. Fama also viewed the firm as a nexus of contracts between factors of production which specify what each input will do, how it relates to other inputs to produce outputs and how receipts from the outputs are divided between the inputs. A manager has a contract with the firm to supply his or her skills for an agreed rent – his or her wage.

High managerial performance is stimulated and opportunistic behaviour attenuated by *internal and external labour markets*. Management is not a monolith, but rather a group of self-interested persons seeking to displace others. Managers are in competition with fellow incumbents and outside challengers. As Fama (1980, pp. 291–4) points out, managers rent their wealth, or human capital, to the firm and the 'rental rates ... signalled by the management labour market ... depend on the success or failure of the firm'. Managers are 'sorted and compensated' (*ibid.*, p. 292) according to performance. Since the firm is always in the market for new managers it must be able to explain to recruits how they will be rewarded. If the reward system is not responsive to performance, the firm will not be able either to recruit or to retain the best managers. Conversely, but by the same argument, managers, especially top managers, have a stake in the firm's performance since the external market uses that as a means of determining their opportunity wage. In the internal management market, monitoring lower levels of management, gauging their performance and rewarding them is a normal management task. And this monitoring process operates upwards as well:

> Lower managers perceive that they can gain by stepping over shirking or less competent [seniors] . . . [while] in the nexus of contracts . . . each manager is concerned with the performance of managers above and below him since his marginal product is likely to be a positive function of theirs. (*ibid.*, p. 293)

Finally, managers can be disciplined or controlled by various organisational devices which permit owners to retain strong proprietorial interests and control even when juridical ownership share is proportionally small (see Box 5.3). For example pyramidal holding companies can permit an owner to have a 50 per cent plus 1 interest and so control in a small holding company which in turn controls a second twice the size of the first. This process can continue down the pyramid until an owner of a relatively small amount of capital can control large volumes of capital far in excess of twice his original 50 per cent. Such arrangements are difficult to organise legally in the United States or the United Kingdom but are common in many other countries where founding families wish to retain control of the managers of enterprises now far in excess of their original size. (For example, in Switzerland's Roche, Sweden's Electrolux, South Africa's Anglo-American, Holland's Philips, and many others, proprietorial control is retained in this manner – thus minimising agency

---

Box 5.3

Swedish proprietorial power: an alternative to the market in corporate control?

When Peter Wallenberg became head of one of the world's biggest industrial empires in 1982 following the death of his father, sceptics doubted whether he would be able to hold it together. So far, the 67-year-old Swede has proved them wrong, seeing off raiders and progressively tightening his grip on many of the family's firms.

The Wallenberg empire accounts for some 40% of the Swedish stockmarket – a concentration of economic power unequalled in Europe. Alongside the shares owned by Investor, the family's key holding company, the Wallenbergs have also built up a maze of alliances with other Swedish investors. Their fief includes ASEA, which owns half of ASEA Brown Boveri, a Swedish-Swiss electrical-engineering giant; SKF, the world's biggest ball-bearing producer; and Stora, Europe's biggest papermaker.

The growth of these firms is testimony to the Wallenbergs' patience. By giving managers considerable independence, the family has attracted and kept talented

→

bosses such as Percy Barnevik, the chief executive of ASEA Brown Boveri. And the family has always been international in its outlook. In stark contrast to the recent decision by Volvo, a Swedish car maker, to turn its back on a partnership with France's Renault, many Wallenerg companies already think and act as Europeans. Today roughly 80% of their SKr450 billion ($54 billion) in sales are outside Sweden, primarily in other European countries.

The Saab-Scania saga has exposed cracks in the family's industrial edifice. The Wallenbergs rarely own a majority shareholding in their companies [see Table B5.2]. Instead, they rely on share structures that give some classes of shares up to 1,000 times as many votes as others, and on Swedish allies – 'the Wallenberg sphere' – to stand by them. Despite the sphere, in 1990 Sven Olof Johansson, a property developer, built up a 22% stake in Saab-Scania before the shaken Wallenbergs bought him out at a hefty premium. To avoid more such greenmail attempts, the family took the company private in 1991.

The past year has been an uncomfortable one for the Wallenbergs. Might not 1994 be a better vintage? Mikael Sjowall of Barclays de Zoete Wedd, a London broker, reckons that Wallenberg firms, alongside other big Swedish exporters, will soon benefit from the sharp depreciation of the krona. However, as the Saab-Scania debacle has illustrated, the family also has to cope with bigger challenges. These include shaking up Investor, refocusing their empire into larger stakes in a smaller number of firms and managing a smooth transition to the next generation of the family.

Take Investor first. Though it is the family's main vehicle, the Wallenbergs still find it hard to convince investors that they will get a better deal from a stake in the holding company than from shares in its subsidiaries. Investor's complex structure, designed to perpetuate the family's control rather than to maximise its value, explains why it trades at a discount to net asset value of around 20%. Wary foreigners own just 6% of Investor's voting stock, compared with, say, 39% of Astra, a fast-growing drug firm. (© The Economist, London, 25 December 1993)

Table B5.2 Principal Wallenberg companies

	Sector	Sept. 1993	
		% of votes	% of equity
ASEA*	Electrical engineering	33	25
Astra	Pharmaceuticals	12	10
Atlas Copco	Industrial equipment	22	15
Ericsson	Telecommunications	22	2
Electrolux*	Household appliances	93	6
Incentive	Diversified holding	34	26
Saab-Scania	Aerospace and vehicles	100	100
SKF	Ball bearings	38	14
Stora	Forest products	20	16

Source: Investor
*Including shares owned by Incentive

costs.) Another similar device, also difficult to use for legal reasons in the United Kingdom and United States is issuing non-voting shares. (Marks & Spencer was one UK company which adopted this practice.)

In conclusion we can assert only that it is debatable whether profit maximisation, value maximisation, joint value maximisation or other objective functions are accurate descriptions of managerial behaviour. However, value maximisation subject to transaction costs is an operational objective and will be the one assumed to hold in most of our remaining chapters.

Note

1. In this formula we begin at $t = 0$, not $t = 1$ as in Chapter 1. This is because we assume here that revenue is currently being earned, whereas in Chapter 2 we assumed that initial earnings were received at the end of period 1.

Bibliography

Arrow, K. J. (1950) 'A difficulty in the concept of social welfare', *Journal of Political Economy*, vol. 58.

Baumol, W. J. (1959) *Business Behaviour, Value and Growth*, Macmillan.

Baumol, W. J. (1962) 'On the theory of the expansion of the firm', *American Economic Review*, vol. 52.

Cyert, R. M. and March, J. G. (1963) *A Behavioural Theory of the Firm*, Prentice Hall.

Fama, E. (1980) 'Agency problems and the theory of the firm', *Journal of Political Economy*, vol. 88.

Jensen, M. C. and Meckling, W. H. (1976) 'Theory of the firm: managerial behaviour, agency costs and ownership structure', *Journal of Financial Economics*, vol. 3.

Manne, H. M. (1965) 'Mergers and the market for corporate control', *Journal of Political Economy*, vol. 71.

Radice, M. (1971) 'Control type, profitability and growth in large firms', *Economic Journal*, vol. 81.

Simon, H. A. (1959) 'Theories of decision making in economics', *American Economic Review*, vol. 49.

Williamson, O. E. (1967) *The Economics of Discretionary Behaviour*, Markham.

Part II

Knowing the market

Chapter 6

Forecasting

By definition the future is unknown. Yet managers must take decisions today which either depend on or affect conditions ruling tomorrow. Such decisions can be in the fields of investment, research and development, price, advertising, recruitment, and so on, and involve the future values of variables like output demanded, wage rates, interest rates, consumers' income and the likely state of technology.

Business forecasting aims to reduce uncertainty about tomorrow, so that more effective decisions can be made today by providing predictions of future values of variables from past and present information. Usually future sales are predicted first, followed by other areas of corporate forecasting and planning.

In this chapter, several techniques for forecasting future values of many different variables are reviewed. Forecasting methods vary widely in their accuracy and sophistication (not necessarily synonymous terms) when applied to most variables. The manager's problem is, given the choice of variable to be predicted, to choose the most accurate technique subject to the nature of the forecast required, the availability of finance, data and expertise.

6.1 Surveys

Survey techniques can be used to provide short- to medium-term forecasts (up to 2 years hence) based on what people say they intend to do or what they expect will occur under specific circumstances. It is assumed that people's intentions and expectations can be accurately established and that attitudes can be collected in a way which enables predictions to be made. We present firstly the methodology of sales forecasting, and secondly a brief list of surveys of variables relating to UK macroeconomic activity.

6.1.1 Sales forecasting

Despite the title of this section, it is to be emphasised that analogous procedures may be applied to forecasting future levels of wages, interest rates, fuel prices and so on. When forecasting sales, surveys (unlike the techniques described in Section 6.3 onward) have the advantage of being applicable to new, as well as established, products. A new product could be described to the respondent and the respondent's views towards it recorded.

1. *Surveys of Buyer Intentions*:   Customers are asked what they will purchase under various conditions, for example, price and income levels. However, this technique has many disadvantages. Firstly, response error may be significant. Buyers may be *unwilling*, to give correct answers, either for reasons of privacy or commercial secrecy. They may be *unable* to give correct information because they have uncertain intentions or may change their minds after the survey. Because of the way in which the questions are phrased, or the way in which they are asked, or answers recorded, 'interviewer bias' my occur.

Secondly, these surveys are costly. Costs can be reduced by combining with other firms which are not competitors, sharing a questionnaire and hence asking fewer questions relating to one particular firm. But the amount of information obtained is then much less than using a firm-specific questionnaire. However, these 'omnibus' surveys can be useful to evaluate consumers' awareness of price, quality and other differences between products.

2. *Surveys of Sales Forces*:   Superficially, this technique has many advantages. Those who are closest to the market are questioned and their responses aggregated. It is cheap and easy to do, with the possible spin-off benefit of a self-selected target which may increase the motivation of the salesperson.

However, disadvantages exist. Sales representatives suffer from either optimism or pessimism. One would expect this: the former because of a desire to appear dynamic, the latter because payments may depend on the amount by which actual sales exceed quotas based on forecasts. Hence estimates may be biased upwards or downwards. To correct these biases a record could be kept of each person's forecasts and achievements over a period. Possibly a consistent over- or under-prediction pattern will emerge. This 'normal' discrepancy for each could then be applied as a correction factor to each person's forecasts before aggregation, though care would have to be taken that the raw estimate did not contain any unusual factors specific to one person's territory, to which the correction should not apply. Other accuracy-improving techniques are often used. For example: informing each salesperson of the accuracy of his or her past forecasts, providing each salesperson with an independent forecast of GNP, basing part of the salesperson's remuneration on the accuracy of his or her forecast and arranging for the salesperson to discuss the reasons for his or her forecast with the immediate superior. In each case over-optimism or over-pessimism would be expected to be reduced.

3. *Surveys of Experts*:   Obtaining views from a group of specialists either outside the firm – for example, investment analysts, academics, consultants, or inside – for example, executives, has the possible advantages of speed and cheapness. (At its simplest, a succession of telephone calls may produce the required information.)

And in intractable areas, such as forecasting future technological states where basic data are non-existent, it can provide, at worst, a range of different views to which the manager can adapt his or her thinking.

4. *Surveys Relating to Aggregated Items*: A number of surveys of aggregated variables are published regularly in the United Kingdom. Whilst these may not relate to a manager's particular brand or inputs, they may relate to the product group of which his or her brand is a member, or to the type of inputs the manager uses. Examples of these surveys are shown in Table 6.1.

6.1.2 Techniques

Individuals may be simply asked for estimates of future values of a variable under certain conditions or a range of values may be elicited from them and reduced to one value by the surveyor. Several techniques of the latter variety are used.

Table 6.1

Name of survey	Publisher/ location	Regularity	Examples of variables included Expectations/intentions relating to:
Industrial Trends	CBI	Monthly	Company's exports capital expenditure, new orders, numbers employed, output, stocks, average costs, average prices
Distributive Trades Survey	*Financial Times*	Monthly	Sales
Business Survey	CBI/EC	Monthly	Company's employment, stocks of raw materials, stocks of finished products, production, selling price, direction of change of new orders, direction of change of exports
Consumer's Confidence Survey	Gallup	Monthly	Consumer's expectations as to direction of change of income, the macroeconomy, prices, unemployment

PERT method (Programme Evaluation and Review Technique)

The respondent is asked for an optimistic, X_1, a most likely, X_2, and a pessimistic, X_3, estimate. A single estimate is derived by finding the weighted average of these three values. The weights 1, 4, 1 respectively for X_1, X_2 and X_3 are commonly used and based on past experience. Hence:

$$EV = (X_1 + 4X_2 + X_3)/6$$
$$\sigma \ = (X_3 - X_1)/6$$
$\sigma \ $ = standard deviation
EV = expected value of X

This technique has the limitations that it is assumed that the respondent can produce three realistic estimates of the required types, which the respondent may not be able to do. Secondly, it assumes that the optimistic, most probable and pessimistic values are normally distributed. If the respondent is biased this may not be so.

Decision theory

In this case the respondent is asked both for several estimates of sales and the probability of each under different uncontrollable situations (states of nature). The expected value is calculated (see Section 2.6). Defects of this technique are that the assumptions that the executive can identify the relevant states of nature, and can estimate the probabilities of each, may not be valid. But the technique is based on value judgements with a more consistent basis than pure guesses.

Utility theory

By presenting the respondent with a number of choice situations, the probability which he or she associates with each of several forecasts is formed. The most likely forecast is taken. For example the subject is told that his or her job depends on his accurate forecasting. The respondent is presented with a choice between accepting two forecasts: (a) a 100% chance (certainty) of sales being £10,000 and (b) 1% probability of achieving sales of £50,000 (the estimate for which a probability is required) and 99% chance of nothing. If the subject chooses (b) the probability of the £50,000 forecast is raised until indifference between (a) and (b) is reached. This probability is assumed to be that associated with £50,000. A major problem with using this technique is the large amount of time required. It is useful when, say, executives are required to provide accurate forecasts from experience.

Delphi technique

One way of increasing the accuracy of answers may be to provide feedback as in the Delphi technique. At its simplest, members of, for example, an executive panel are asked by letter to give their predictions of the likelihood of occurrence of specified events. Postal anonymity from other panel members minimises the impact of personal inhibitions on the making of speculations about the future. Panel members are then informed by letter of the outcome and in particular of the consensus. Dissenters are invited to explain their reasons for diverging and/or to modify their forecasts. This process may be repeated again, and the final range of outcomes regarded as a probabilistic forecast. At worst, however, the firm may have nothing better as a result of this exercise than a mere consensus of ignorance.

6.2 Experiments

Experiments can be used for deriving forecasts, especially when no information concerning consumers' past purchases of a product is available as, for example, when a new product is to be launched. Two main types are in use: test marketing and laboratory experiments.

6.2.1 Test marketing

The firm finds a test area which is thought accurately to represent the market into which the product is to be introduced. The product is launched in the test market in a manner identical to that which the firm intends to use when and if the product is launched nationally. If more than one test area is used, alternative marketing tactics can be compared. For example, price, advertising, packaging and other controllable variables in the demand function can differ area by area. Sales can be compared at different levels of price, advertising and so on, or with different pack designs.

A major limitation of this technique is its high expense in both time and money. When examining a new product, a full-scale marketing exercise is required and a significant amount of output has to be manufactured. The test must last long enough to cover the repurchase cycle, otherwise false conclusions as to the demand beyond initial purchases may be drawn. For example, when a new product is launched sales might be higher than after the initial round of purchases (see Figure 6.1) because of the effect of unusually high initial advertising and novelty interest. When it is time to repurchase, both of these factors may be lower, but the consequent lower sales may not be predicted if the test exercise is prematurely terminated. The length of the cycle will of course vary with the nature of the product and may be so long, as in the case of consumer durables, as to preclude use of this technique.

Secondly, use of the technique increases the chances of prompt imitation on a national scale by a competitor. Thirdly, it is often difficult to find an area which accurately represents the intended total market. Similarities should be present in socio-economic breakdown, age, occupational grouping, advertising media availability and so on. If no area which is sufficiently representative is found, adjustments, which enable further inaccuracies to creep in, must be made. In the United Kingdom, television regions are frequently chosen because the expenditure on

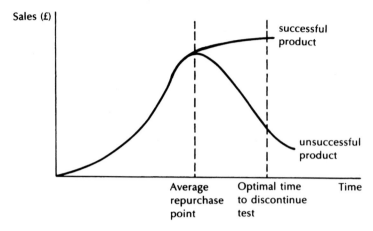

Figure 6.1

advertising offered to the known population can be easily measured. Fourthly, if one considers only one market over time and unusual conditions occur during the test – for example, strikes by raw material suppliers, lay-offs by a major local employer – the results may not be representative of 'normal' conditions. Further, it is common for competitors to respond to a test marketing exercise with atypical behaviour. Competitors may lower prices or increase advertising so that again the test market results obtained are not representative of 'normality'. Finally if, for example, price is raised during the experiment, customers may be lost never to return when the product is nationally launched. However, the technique does enable one to draw conclusions from what customers do, as opposed to what they *say they will do*, as in the survey approach. Box 6.1 illustrates the use of test marketing in the case of Olivio, a new brand of spread.

6.2.2 Experiments in laboratories

One method of preventing unusual factors from making the results of a test marketing exercise unrepresentative of 'normal' demand conditions is to ask subjects to undergo shopping trips in a laboratory store and to record which and how much of each brand they would buy at different prices. Typically a sample of subjects is selected as being representative of the intended target market. Secondly each subject is asked to assess his or her relative preferences towards different existing brands of the product and is then exposed to advertising materials for both the new and established brands. Next, the subjects are given a fixed amount of money and asked to buy some of the product from a simulated store designed to be as close to a real shopping experience as possible. The quantity of the new brand purchased is recorded. Those respondents who choose the new brand are allowed to take it home and a later questionnaire records their repurchase intentions. The product's prices or other characteristics may be altered and the experiment

---

Box 6.1

Case study

In February 1991 Van den Berghs Food, a subsidiary of Unilever, the producer of Flora, test marketed a new brand of spread: Olivio. Unlike other spreads, including Flora, Olivio had a relatively high content of olive oil: 24%. The test market chosen was the London area because, according to *Marketing* (December 1990), '21% of households now buy olive oil and the market is growing at 33% year on year, 40% of all olive oils are bought in the London area.' The product was targeted at socio-economic groups ABC1 (skilled and professional workers, see page 149). The price set was very close to that of butter: 55p and 59p for 250 g., respectively. The former was 13p higher than Flora. Within a week of launch three 20-second TV commercials not mentioning the brand were shown. In the following week a 40-second film which did emphasise the brand was screened. The advertising spend for these two weeks was reported as being equivalent to a national spend of £2.3 million.

---

repeated. Alternatively, a subject may be asked to undertake a number of hypothetical shopping trips whilst at a desk. Each is told they can imagine they have a given amount of money to spend. They are then asked how much of each item they would buy on each of a number of shopping trips from printed lists of available products.

One of the earliest proponents of these techniques was Pessemier who used it to obtain price–quantity combinations and so demand curves for various goods. However, the results may be biased by testing and selection effects. The former occurs when subjects alter their behaviour because they realise they are part of an experiment and their behaviour is being recorded. The latter occurs if the subjects who agree to take part are atypical of those in a potential market because they consist of those who are prepared to take part in tests.

6.3 Time series analysis

Each of this group of techniques uses only past values of a variable or the time period number to predict future values. There is no attempt to represent factors which causally affect the values of the variable. In the first two cases which we describe it is assumed that the historic relationship between past and future values will continue to hold.

6.3.1 Naive methods

Many naive methods exist, their main advantage being their simplicity and cheapness. Examples are:

1. $\hat{X}_{t+1} = X_t + \Delta X_t$

2. $\Delta \hat{X}_{t+1} = k \, \Delta X_t$ the 'proportional change' model
3. $\hat{X}_{t+1} = \alpha + \beta(t+1)$ the 'linear trend' model

where $\hat{X}_{t+1}$ = the value of X which is forecast for period $t+1$

$\Delta X_t = X_t - X_{t-1}$.
k, α and β are constants to be estimated.

A value of k may be estimated by plotting ΔX_{t+1} against ΔX_t; values of α and β may be gained by plotting X_{t+1} against $(t+1)$. In all cases a line may be fitted to the data by eye or by using regression techniques (see Chapter 8). k and β are the slopes of these lines respectively, α is the intercept of model (3). Notice that model (3) assumes that as time passes by one unit the value of X always increases by the same amount.

Box 6.2

A motor car manufacturer wishes to forecast the sales of motor cars in Great Britain for Quarter 3 in 1992. Initially the marketing department make estimates using naive methods. Data on new registrations is obtained from the Department of Transport as in Table B6.1.

Table B6.1 New registrations of private cars

Year	Quarter	Numbers (000)	Year	Quarter	Numbers (000)
1984	1	167.0	1988	1	192.8
	2	146.7		2	170.9
	3	167.8		3	243.4
	4	104.9		4	129.7
1985	1	167.3	1989	1	209.4
	2	144.7		2	187.2
	3	187.5		3	241.3
	4	114.4		4	130.4
1986	1	167.0	1990	1	193.2
	2	151.3		2	158.5
	3	192.8		3	210.6
	4	116.5		4	106.1
1987	1	174.7	1991	1	152.8
	2	156.5		2	113.1
	3	212.9		3	177.9
	4	128.1		4	89.7
			1992	1	134.7
				2	120.2

Source: CSO, *Economic Trends Annual Supplement 1993*, HMSO, Table 8, Series FHCH.

The forecasters plot this data as in Figure 6.2.

→

Implementing each of the naive methods their forecasts for 1992 quarter 3 are as follows:

Method 1

$$X_{t+1} = X_t + \Delta X_t = X_{92Q3} \quad = 120.2 + (120.2 - 134.7)$$
$$= 105.7$$

Method 2

$$\Delta X_{t+1} = k \; \Delta X_t = X_{92Q3} \quad = 120.2 - 0.8309 \,(120.2 - 134.7)$$
$$= 132.2$$

where *k* has been established by regression using all of the above observations.

Method 3

$$X_{t+1} = \alpha + \beta(t+1) = X_{92Q3} = 165.5 - (0.2787 \times 31)$$
$$= 156.9$$

where α and β have again been estimated by regression.
These estimates are also plotted in Figure 6.2.

Limitations of these methods are firstly that the assumed relationship may not accurately fit past values and so may not produce accurate forecasts. For example, it can be seen in Box 6.2 that all models omit to consider the past occurrence that new registrations in Quarter 3 are the largest of the year and that new registrations in Quarter 4 are the lowest. This pattern is probably due to the change in registration letter in UK number plates which occurs in Quarter 3 and purchasers waiting until the beginning of a new year in which to register their car.

Secondly, because no causal factors are separately included, forecasts based on these techniques would not reflect unusual changes in such factors. For example, if competitors increased their advertising suddenly and greatly, a firm's sales might then no longer be forecasted accurately by this technique.

6.3.2 Time series decomposition

Figure 6.2 shows that the number of new car registrations varied in a regular manner within each year, that is, its values show seasonal variation. The data also showed a long-term trend and variation about the trend over several years. This is not an uncommon pattern, yet the naive methods omit to account for all three types of variation. Use of time series decomposition unlike the naive methods, assumes that the value of a variable at a point in time can be decomposed into one or more of trend *T*, seasonal, *S* and cyclical, *C*, elements and a random element *E*. Variation due to each component may be represented graphically as in Figure 6.3 for the case of sales. Trend variation relates to long-term changes in, say, sales, due for example,

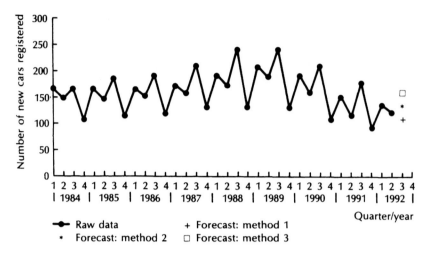

Figure 6.2

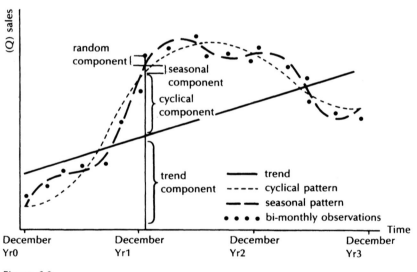

Figure 6.3

to changes in population or technology, etc. Cyclical variation occurs over a few years and is often due to changes in income. Seasonal fluctuations occur within fixed intervals, such as a year and are often attributed to the weather (in the case of fuel) or government regulations (such as car registrations). Random variations are those which may not be classified into other categories and may be due to unique events, such as fires, war, strikes, and so on. The forecaster assumes a relationship between the components, for example:

$$X_t = T_t + C_t + S_t \text{ or } X_t = T_t \times C_t \times S_t$$

Values of T, C and S are predicted for the next period and substituted into these equations to give a predicted value for X, $\hat{X}$. But how are these predictions derived? We shall explain this for the second (and most commonly used) equation.

Stage 1: The T and C components are removed to estimate the values of S and E for each season. To do this a moving average (see Section 6.3.3) is calculated where the number of terms equals the number of seasons in a year.

Because high values in a year have been averaged with low values, the variation in the data between seasons and due to random fluctuations is removed. So M_t, the moving average values, consist only of trend and cyclical components: $M_t = T_t \times C_t$. Dividing the actual values of X by the corresponding moving average gives S and E because:

$$X_t/M_t = (T_t \times C_t \times S_t \times E_t)/(T_t \times C_t) = S_t \times E_t$$

Stage 2: The randomness of the $E \times S$ series is now removed and the average index for each period is calculated. To do this the quarterly values of X_t/M_t are examined (for example) for spring, summer, autumn and winter of each of the last, say, seven years. The largest and lowest values for each quarter are deleted and the average for each quarter calculated (medial average). Both procedures remove randomness since this is more likely to be observed in the outliers than in more regular seasonal observations and the averaging procedure distributes randomness evenly over the elements in each average. These medial averages are scaled so that their sum equals 4 (i.e. their sum, on average, for each quarter). The M series represents the cyclical and trend pattern in the data (see Figure 6.3). The M series *multiplied by the seasonal indices* gives the seasonal pattern because each seasonal index equals the average (over several years) ratio of the corresponding seasonal value (i.e. $T_t \times C_t \times S_t$) to the cyclical and trend value ($T_t \times C_t$). If the seasonal indices did not total 4, the average for the seasonal values within one year would not then equal the average cyclical and trend values over that year. That is, the average multiplicative factor applied to the M (cyclical and trend) values over one year would not equal 1. To ensure that they do, the quarterly medial averages are scaled.

Stage 3: Remember that the moving average values consist of $T_t \times C_t$. We now wish to remove the cyclical factor for each quarter. To do this the trend value is calculated first. A common method of calculating a trend value is to estimate a and b in:

$$T_t = a + bt \tag{6.1}$$

where t = time period, using regression or some other method. The value of M_t is then divided by T_t to give C_t:

$$\frac{M_t}{T_t} = \frac{T_t \times C_t}{T_t} = C_t$$

Stage 4:   To forecast we calculate

$$X_{t+1} = T_{t+1} \times C_{t+1} \times S_{t+1}$$

where S_{t+1} is the average index which was calculated earlier for the relevant, say, quarter. T_{t+1} is calculated using the above equation. C_{t+1} is calculated frequently from judgement based on a consideration of past cyclical components.

Time series decomposition requires only past values of the variables which are usually readily available. The calculations can be performed quickly using a computer, the forecaster needing only moderate analytical skills, and the performance of these techniques for 12-month forecasts has in the past been good. But a limitation of these techniques is that any causal factor which in the past has changed regularly (or remained constant) may change irregularly in the future (or vary), but the effects of these changes would not be allowed for by these models. For example, suppose that the government imposed a very large reduction in car tax (as in the United Kingdom in 1993) we would expect the sales of cars to increase considerably, yet no such reductions had occurred in a regular way in the past. Secondly, since past information must be available, the demand for new products cannot be calculated. Furthermore, the prediction of the cyclical component requires an additional technique such as an indicator (see Section 6.4) or a survey of expert opinion. Box 6.3 illustrates the use of times series decomposition to forecast the sales of cars.

Box 6.3

The marketing director of the car manufacturer has decided that the naive methods do not represent the patterns in the data sufficiently accurately and instead the forecaster is instructed to use time series decomposition. The observed new car registration data is shown in the left-hand section of Table 6.2. The simple four quarter moving averages are shown in the middle section. The right-hand section shows the calculation of the medial index. Each observed value of new registrations is divided by the corresponding moving average. The largest and smallest number in each column is deleted and the mean value of each column (the medial average) calculated. Because these four medial averages do not sum to 4.000, each is divided by 4.005. The result is the seasonal index for each quarter. Moving to stage 3, use of regression analysis gives estimates of a and b in the trend equation (6.1) so that it may be written as:

$$T_t = 165.5 - 0.2787t$$

Finally, suppose the car manufacturer believes that the value of C in quarter 3 1993 will be 1.000. The manufacturer can now make the forecast as

$$X_{Q393} = 156.9 \times 1.000 \times 1.257 = 197.2.$$

Table 6.2

Year	Quarter	Observed values				4 Quarter moving averages (MAs)				(Actual/4 Quarter MAs[1]) = SE²				Total
		1	2	3	4	1	2	3	4	1	2	3	4	
1984		167.0	146.7	167.8	104.9			146.600	146.675			1.145	0.715	
1985		167.3	144.7	187.5	114.4	146.175	151.100	153.475	153.400	1.145	0.958	1.222	0.746	
1986		167.0	151.3	192.8	116.5	155.05	156.375	156.900	158.825	1.077	0.968	1.229	0.734	
1987		174.7	156.5	212.9	128.1	160.125	165.150	168.050	172.575	1.091	0.948	1.267	0.742	
1988		192.8	170.9	243.4	129.7	176.175	183.800	184.200	188.350	1.094	0.930	1.321	0.689	
1989		209.4	187.2	241.3	130.4	192.425	191.900	192.075	188.025	1.088	0.976	1.256	0.694	
1990		193.2	158.5	210.6	106.1	180.850	173.175	167.100	157.000	1.068	0.915	1.260	0.676	
1991		152.8	113.1	177.9	89.7	145.650	137.475	133.375	128.850	1.049	0.823	1.334	0.696	
1992		134.7	120.2			130.625				1.031				
	Medial average									1.078	0.956	1.259	0.712	4.005
	Seasonal index									1.077	0.955	1.257	0.711	4.000

Notes:
1. Since these are quarterly MAs they should be centred at quarter 2½ in every 4-quarter period. But because the observed values are divided by these MAs, the latter have been positioned at quarter 3.
2. SE means seasonal index multiplied by random element.

6.3.3 Smoothing techniques

Moving averages

Use of these techniques also assumes that each observed value consists of a regular element and a random element. By averaging several successive values the random element is assumed to be removed. Various methods may be followed, but at their simplest the most recent smoothed value is used as the forecast. If a four-period moving average is used, each value is calculated according to the formula:

$$M_t = \tfrac{1}{4}q_t + \tfrac{1}{4}q_{t-1} + \tfrac{1}{4}q_{t-2} + \tfrac{1}{4}q_{t-3} \tag{6.2}$$

For example, consider the data in Table 6.3. The last moving average can be used as the forecast for January 1995. This is a short-term forecasting method. If the most recent moving average is taken as the forecast for the succeeding March or June, the errors would be likely to be larger than for forecasts for earlier months since no observations nearer the forecast date than December would enter the calculation.

One limitation of the simple moving average is that, if the observed values begin to follow a steeper trend between periods t and $t+1$, the moving average which includes the tth observation will be below this observed value for period $t+1$. This is because the forecast for period $t+1$ is the moving average of the six previous (and, on average, lower) values. If the trend continues to remain upwards, the moving averages used as a forecast will always be below the line joining the observations. This is because, when used as a forecast one month into the future, the moving average for six values will be placed one month after the most recent value. But, given the upward trend, the observed value in period $t+1$ will be above the average of the previous six observations. This is shown in Figure 6.4 (which uses different observations compared with Table 6.3). Forecast A is the average of observations

Table 6.3

	Month		Forecast 6-month moving average
1994	January	20	
	February	15	
	March	40	
	April	20	
	May	40	
	June	60	
	July	40	32.5
	August	45	35.8
	September	70	40.8
	October	50	45.8
	November	90	50.8
	December	70	59.2
1995	January		60.8

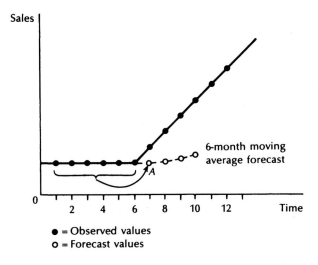

Figure 6.4

1 to 6 and so is below observation 7. For this reason simple moving averages are most suited to short-term (up to three months hence) forecasts when the trend is less likely to be significant than over longer periods. Corrections for a rising or falling trend may be used, and the reader is referred to the Bibliography for these.

Exponential smoothing

In the example shown in Table 6.3 the forecast for January equalled the average of the observed sales for July to December where *each had the same weight*. This is generally the case with simple moving averages (see equation (6.2)). But any change in trend will be observed in the most recent figures before earlier ones. Therefore a more accurate forecast would be obtained if the most recent observations were given greater weights than more distant observations. A formula which achieves this would be:

$$M_t = a_1 q_t + a_2 q_{t-1} + \ldots + a_{12} q_{t-11} \tag{6.3}$$

where $a_1 > a_2 > a_3 > \ldots > a_{12}$

and in order that M_t may be a true average,

$$a_1 + a_2 + a_3 + \ldots + a_{12} = 1.0$$

To forecast sales, the same procedure as in the simple moving average case is followed except that the weights in the moving average formula are exponentially declining. To do this, the value given to each *a* is typically chosen to form a geometric progression – each is chosen to be a constant fraction of the one preceding it. Thus, if the fraction were 0.8, then:

$$a_1 = 0.2, \quad a_2 = 0.2(1 - 0.2) = 0.16, \quad a_3 = 0.2(1 - 0.2)^2 = 0.128, \text{ and so on.}$$

The equation for the moving average would then be written:

$$M_t = 0.2 [q_t + 0.8q_{t-1} + (0.8)^2 q_{t-2} + \dots + (0.8)^n q_{t-n}]$$

and M_t would be taken as the forecast for period $t + 1$.

Adaptive filtering

The last two types of moving averages both use equation (6.3) to smooth past observations. In both cases the weights are subjectively chosen by the forecaster and then remain fixed for every moving average which is calculated for a given set of data. Alternatively, when adaptive filtering is used, the magnitude of the forecast error when one moving average is calculated is used to adjust the weights to calculate the next moving average. To explain further, consider a forecast for period $t + 1$ which equals the moving average calculated for the preceding three periods:

$$F_{t+1} = a_1 q_t + a_2 q_{t-1} + a_3 q_{t-3}$$

Using any set of weights, the first moving average is calculated using observations for periods 1, 2 and 3, giving a forecast for period 4. This forecast is compared with the observed value in period 4. The magnitude of the error is inserted into a formula which will select values for a_1, a_2 and a_3 which will minimise this error. The new weights are used to calculate the forecast for period 5 using observations for periods 2, 3 and 4 and the process is repeated.

Whilst this method is likely to be more accurate than the other moving average techniques described, it is also less tractable. As with all moving average techniques, it does not allow the manager to predict the seasonal or cyclical component of the sales levels.

6.4 Barometric techniques

Mechanical extrapolation implies that the future is some sort of extension of the past. Barometric techniques, however, are based on the idea that the future can be predicted from certain events occurring in the present. Formally, they involve statistical indicators, usually time series, which, when combined in certain ways, provide indications of the direction in which the economy, or certain industries in it, is going.

6.4.1 Leading indicators

These tend to reflect future changes. For example, a bookshop may use the number of first year Business students registered for a course in July to predict the number of copies of a textbook to stock in October. In Figure 6.5 data on both the number of registered students in July and sales of the textbook are plotted and a lagged correlation coefficient could be calculated.

Leading indicators are often used to forecast cyclical changes in macroeconomic variables. Common leaders of overall business cycle movements include stock market prices, the average working week in manufacturing and new orders for machine tools. Many indices are published in *Economic Trends*, the *National Institute of Economic and Social Research Review*, *The Economist* and the *Financial Times*. Examples of longer and shorter indices published by *Economic Trends* are given in Table 6.4.

A major problem in using this technique is to find the relevant indicator for the purpose. Since past values are required if one wishes to forecast using this technique, it cannot be used for new product forecasts. Moreover, an unusual change in a factor which is causally related to the forecasted variable, but not the indicator, may render predictions by the latter very inaccurate. For example, if another bookshop opens closer to the university, or the lecturer for the course decides to recommend a different book, the forecast indicated by the number of accepted students will be incorrect. A company which cans vegetables may plan capacity on the acreage devoted to vegetables but may find that poor weather or a crop disease reduces the actual yield well below its forecast. Alternatively, for the same reason, the lag between indicator and event usually varies. For example, between 1973 and 1989 total dwellings started led gross domestic product (GDP)

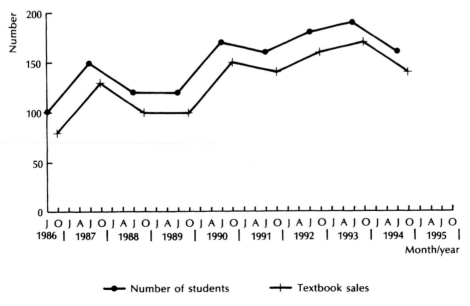

Figure 6.5

Table 6.4 Shorter and longer leading indicators

Longer leading

Financial surplus/deficit, industrial and commercial companies, divided by GDP deflator
Confederation of British Industry (CBI) quarterly survey: change in optimism
Financial Times – Actuaries 500 share index
Rate of interest, 3 months prime bank bills
Total dwellings started

Shorter leading

Credit extended by finance houses, retailers and other credit grantors
Gross trading profits of companies excluding stock appreciation and mineral and natural
   gas extraction, divided by GDP deflator
New car registrations
CBI quarterly survey: change in new orders
CBI survey: expected change in stocks of materials

---

usually by 11 months but sometimes by as little as 1 month and as far as 40 months. Thirdly, an indicator may move, a manager may react but find too late that the movement was merely a quirk of no real significance. Fourthly, in practice, indicators have not always accurately shown the magnitude of changes in forecast variables, even when and if they have indicated turning points.

6.4.2 Coincident indicators and lagging indicators

These coincide with or fall behind general economic activity or market trends. Their value is not in forecasting but rather in confirming, or refuting a few months afterwards the validity of the leading indicator used as an indicator of business cycles. Common examples of coinciding indicators are GDP itself, change in raw material stocks, industrial production and retail sales. Common examples of laggards are manufacturers' stock levels and consumer credit outstanding.

6.4.3 Diffusion indices

Diffusion indices were developed to try to overcome the problem that a movement in one indicator is of unknown significance at first. To calculate a diffusion index, the percentage of a group of chosen leading indicators which have risen (or fallen) over the last period is plotted against time. When the index exceeds (or falls below) 50%, most of the indicators have risen (fallen or remained unchanged) and hence predict a rise (fall or no change) in the forecast variable. So by combining several indicators, a small movement of no consequence in one would be outweighed by others. If the indicators used are sub-units of one larger one, for example house-building starts in each county, where all counties are equally significant, the diffusion index resembles the rate of change of the aggregated variable. Hence the percentage of, say, regional or county house-start indicators showing growth would decrease when the rate of increase of national house-starts decreases, (albeit total house-starts may still be increasing). Since the *rate of increase* would decrease before *total house-starts fall*, the diffusion index which shows this rate would decrease before the aggregate house-starts indicator falls.

A limitation of these indices, when used in the United States to forecast business cycles, has been that the lead time between changes in those indicators which have usually been chosen, and turning points in the business cycle, has been very short: many peak early in the cycle, remain stable and then fall dramatically during the downturn. The inclusion of more indicators to increase the lead time has rendered their interpretation difficult. Secondly, a decrease in the index may be erroneously taken as an indication of a downturn in the forecast variable, if for example, it decreases but still remains above 50%. But a manager would not, at the time of the decrease, be aware of the value to which it eventually is to descend. For these reasons diffusion indices should complement not replace other forecasting techniques.

6.4.4 Composite indicators

These consist of a weighted average of several indicators. The inclusion of several indicators reduces the likelihood that a movement in it is insignificant or random.

The use of composite indices to forecast business cycles in the United Kingdom has been studied by O'Dea (1975) and the Central Statistical Office (CSO), the latter producing indicator series quarterly. O'Dea removed the trend and then smoothed each indicator series using a moving average method. Secondly, he subjectively ascribed weights to each of five desirable indicator characteristics and attributed scores to each indicator according to the degree to which it fulfilled each characteristic. These characteristics were economic significance, cyclical conformity, timing stability, smoothness and currency. By multiplying an indicator's score on a characteristic by the appropriate weight and summing, the overall weight for the indicator in the composite was obtained.

The CSO removed the trend from a large number of possible indicators and selected a small number which were leading, coincident with and lagged the reference cycle according to nine characteristics. Each was inverted where appropriate and adjusted to form an index with a common amplitude about 100. Each composite indicator was then formed using equal weights for each constituent series. *Economic Trends* currently publishes monthly values of longer and shorter leading indicators as well as coincident and lagging indicators.

6.5 Econometric models

When using these techniques one is trying to predict a future value of a variable by examining future values of other variables which are causally related to it. For example, to predict the future demand for a model of a car ($\hat{Q}^D_{t+1}$) one would substitute the future values of factors which are causally related to it, say, its price ($\hat{P}_{t+1}$), advertising by the manufacturer ($\hat{A}_{t+1}$), competitors' advertising (A_{Ct+1}), and aggregate personal disposable income ($\hat{Y}_{t+1}$), into a formula which relates demand to these variables.

The first stage in the method is to hypothesise which variables causally affect the forecast variable and the form of the mathematical relationship between them. Such hypotheses may be deduced from economic theory or proposed on the basis of past empirical evidence. For example one might hypothesise a linear form for the above demand problem:

$$Q^D_t = \alpha + \beta_1 P_t + \beta_2 A_t + \beta_3 AC_t + \beta_4 Y_t + \varepsilon_t$$

Secondly the values of α, β_1, and so on are estimated. (See Chapter 8 for an explanation of regression techniques.) The equation which best represents behaviour in the past is assumed to represent it in the future. Future values of P_t and so on are then predicted and substituted into the equation.

Notice that the equation does not include *every* possible independent variable which might determine the value of Q^D_t, it is an abstraction. So even if the linear form accurately represents the relationship (which it may not), substitution of values of P_t, A_t, AC_t and Y_t into the model may not give values for Q^D_t which equal those realised. The differences are represented by the ε_t (error) variable. This is a general property of regression models. Box 6.4 illustrates the use of an econometric model to forecast the number of tourist visits from the UK to Spain.

Econometric models may consist of only one equation (a single equation model) if such a form represents the causal relationship sufficiently adequately for the purpose in hand. But often theory may predict that an independent variable in one equation will causally affect the dependent variable *and vice versa*. In these cases a complete system of equations representing the causal relationships between these variables must be specified: a simultaneous model.

Simultaneous models consist of two types of variables: endogenous and exogenous and two types of equations: behavioural equations and identities. Endogenous variables are those which are explained or predicted by the model and exogenous variables are those which are determined by factors which are not predicted by the system. Behavioural equations represent how people or physical processes are expected to behave – allowing for the possibility that they might not do so in the hypothesised way – whereas identities are relationships which are necessarily always correct.

To illustrate such a model consider the following simplified model of the economy where GNP is defined as the sum of consumption, investment and government expenditure:

$$Y_t = C_t + I_t + G_t \tag{6.4}$$

Consumption is hypothesised to be positively related to GNP:

$$C_t = \alpha + \beta Y_t + \varepsilon_t \tag{6.5}$$

Box 6.4

Forecasting the demand for tourism

Forecasts of the demand for tourist visits from one country to another are of special interest to airlines, railways, coach operators, hotel chains, manufacturers of goods purchased by tourists and governments. If the demand for such visits can be predicted then the appropriate capacity planning can be engaged in by all such sectors: thus airlines and railways can plan an appropriate number of journeys on particular routes, hotel chains can decide whether in the long term to increase the number of rooms and to hire more or less staff. In the early 1990s Witt and Witt (1992) developed various forecasting models, including econometric models to forecast the demand for tourist visits between different countries. In each case the relevant explanatory variables were proposed and regression equations were estimated. Each equation differed according to the identity of the various explanatory variables included. In the case of visits from the United Kingdom to Spain, a simplified version of the best model in terms of the size of the R^2, and the consistency and significance of the coefficient on each variable with economic theory was as follows:

$$\log \frac{V_t}{P_t} = -23.6 \qquad + 1.8 \log Y_t \qquad + 0.64 \log EX_t$$

$$(-4.21) \qquad\qquad (1.97) \qquad\qquad (1.18)$$

$$-0.16 \log TS_t + 0.92 \log TSS_t - 0.02 \, DVI_t$$

$$(-0.26) \qquad\qquad (1.10) \qquad\qquad (0.26)$$

$$\bar{R}^2 = 0.840 \qquad DW = 1.73$$

where V_t = number of tourist visits from the UK to Spain in year t
Y_t = personal disposable income (PDI) per head in UK in year t
P_t = population in UK in year t
EX_t = rate of exchange between pounds sterling and pesetas in year t
TS_t = cost of travel by surface from UK to Spain (constant prices) in year t
TSS_t = weighted average of the cost of travel by surface to substitute destinations from UK in year t (constant prices)
DVI_t = dummy variable to account for oil price rise in 1973
t values in brackets.
DW is the Durbin Watson statistic, see page 204.

This equation was estimated using data for the period 1965–80. The equation was re-estimated for 1965–84 and forecast values for each explanatory variable for 1985 were substituted in to derive a prediction of tourist visits per head in 1985. This was compared with the observed number to assess the accuracy of the model.

Investment is hypothesised to be negatively related to the interest rate but positively related to past periods' profits:

$$I_t = \gamma - \delta r_t + \theta \pi_{t-1} + \varepsilon_t \qquad (6.6)$$

where
Y_t = GNP in period t
C_t = Actual consumption in period t
I_t = Actual net capital investment in period t
G_t = Actual government expenditure in period t
π_{t-1} = Actual profits in period $t-1$
ε_t = Disturbance term in period t
$\alpha, \beta, \gamma, \delta, \theta$ = constants, which in practice will be estimated.

Equation (6.4) represents the definition of GNP, hence it is an identity. Equations (6.5) and (6.6) represent causal relationships which are simplifications and abstractions: for example values of Y_t substituted into equation (6.5) will not very often give completely accurate predictions for C_t because of random disturbances (ε_ts). Hence these equations are behavioural. Notice that in equation (6.5) values of Y_t determine values of C_t but from equation (6.4) an increase in the value of C_t will increase Y_t, *ceteris paribus*.

The advantages of these models are firstly, that they attempt to explain why a variable attains different values and hence can include unusual changes in independent variables unlike the other techniques discussed so far. Secondly, unlike the time series approach, the econometric approach may enable managers to forecast the effects of changes in policy variables if they are included as independent variables. Thirdly, unlike barometric models, estimates of the *values* of variables are predicted. Fourthly, the accuracy of the model can be improved as predicted values are compared with realised values.

Finally, it is important to note that the use of econometric models and that of surveys and experiments are not necessarily alternatives. Surveys and experiments *may* be used to derive the data which can be used to estimate the coefficients of an econometric model. In addition, if the model requires values of exogenous variables for the period of the forecast, some method of deriving these values must be used, for example, surveys, indicators, time series and so on.

6.6 Input–output (IO) analysis

By examining the industrial source of inputs into the production process of every industry in an economy, and by making certain assumptions about the production function in each, the use of IO analysis enables managers to gain an indication of the likely effects on the demand for the output of their industry (and of others) of a change in final demand by consumers, the government and foreign countries. To understand how this is achieved, the nature of certain IO matrices and their use in forecasting is explained.

Suppose, for simplicity, that an economy consists of two industries: manufacturing and services, and also governmental, exports, and household sectors. (For simplicity, we have assumed that imports are zero.) Suppose that the revenue and expense accounts of each of the two industrial sectors are as shown in Table 6.5. This table shows, in the case of manufacturing, for example, the values of inputs purchased from all other industries including itself, the expenditure it made on wages and taxes, and the resulting profits. Also shown are sales to each industry and to households, the government and foreign countries.

But rearranging the information in Table 6.5, an IO *transactions matrix* may be constructed (Table 6.6). This shows the values of transactions which have occurred between any two sectors over a given period. The value of transactions may be shown in terms of quantities or money. Each sector listed vertically represents the origin of an input and each column its destination. The table can be divided into four quadrants. The top left-hand corner represents transactions between industries. The equivalent quadrant for the United Kingdom has 99 industries included and so a 101 row by 101 column quadrant is required. The top right-hand corner shows the

Table 6.5

───────── Manufacturing ─────────			
Purchases from manufacturing	30	Sales to manufacturing	30
Purchases from services	15	Sales to services	10
Government (taxes)	60	Exports	30
Wages	145	Sales to government	90
Profits and depreciation	40	Sales to households	130
Total	290	Total	290

───────── Services ─────────			
Purchases from manufacturing	10	Sales to manufacturing	15
Purchases from services	5	Sales to services	5
Government (taxes)	30	Exports	10
Wages	91	Sales to government	40
Profits and depreciation	20	Sales of households	86
Total	156	Total	156

───────── GNP accounts ─────────			
Income		Expenditure	
From government (taxes)	90	Exports	40
From wages	236	By government	130
From profits and depreciation	60	By households	216
Total	386	Total	386

Note: Expressed in £ million.

Table 6.6 IO transactions matrix (£ million)

	Producers		Final demand			Gross output
	Inputs to manufacturing	Inputs to services	Exports	Government	Households	
Manufacturing	30	10	30	90	130	290
Services	15	5	10	40	86	156
Government	60	30				90 ⎫
Wages	145	91				236 ⎬ GNP = 386
Profits and depreciation	40	20				60 ⎭
Gross input	290	156				

GNP = 386

values of outputs of each industry which were finally demanded. The lower left-hand corner shows the payments which were made for primary inputs to the two industries (i.e. value added), that is, inputs not produced by industries shown in the top left-hand corner. GNP may be calculated by either summing the final demand – export expenditure plus government expenditure plus household expenditure – or by summing the total value added (equals total factor payments). The lower right-hand corner would show values of primary inputs taken by the final demand sectors. (We have assumed that these figures equal zero for simplicity.)

To understand how IO aids the forecaster, it is useful to explain the *direct inputs technology matrix*. This is a matrix in which each value shows the amount of an input required to produce £1's worth of the corresponding output. To construct this matrix and to use it to forecast, it is assumed that prices and technology remain constant over the forecast period, that factor inputs are used in constant pro-portions, and that constant returns to scale prevail. Table 6.7 shows the *direct inputs technology matrix* for Table 6.6. Each value has been derived by dividing the corresponding value in the transactions matrix by the gross input (= gross output) of the relevant industry, i.e. by the row or column total. For example, to produce £1 of manufacturing output, £(15/290) = £0.052 of service output is needed. Since prices are always constant by assumption, this ratio always represents the same quantity, and since a constant state of technology and constant returns are assumed, this quantity will not vary due to technological change or with the magnitude of total manufacturing output.

Suppose now that the demand for manufacturing goods by the *final demand* sectors is forecast to increase by £1 million and that for services is expected to remain the same. By multiplying this value by each coefficient in the technology matrix, the initial increase in the input from each industry, which is necessary to produce this additional manufacturing output, is calculated. Hence £(1m. × 0.103) = £103,000 of additional manufacturing output (as well as the £1 million) will have to be produced; as will £(1m. × 0.052) = £52,000 of additional service industry output. However, this is just the first round of increases. Each of these increases will require additional inputs from the other sector. The additional £103,000 of manufacturing output will require £(103,000 × 0.013) = £10,609 of manufacturing inputs and further service inputs. The additional £52,000 of service inputs would need further service and manufacturing inputs. Each of these further inputs would need ever more inputs from each sector, though the requirements diminish as we consider successive rounds. An analogous argument would apply if, instead of the final demand for one industry changing, those of several industries changed.

When the first and all successive increments in each industry's outputs is included we obtain the direct and indirect inputs technology matrix per £1 of final

Table 6.7 Direct inputs technology matrix

	Inputs to manufacturing	Inputs to services
Manufacturing	0.103	0.064
Services	0.052	0.032

Table 6.8 Direct and indirect inputs technology matrix

	Inputs to manufacturing	Inputs to services
Manufacturing	1.119	0.074
Services	0.060	1.037

demand.[1] This is analogous to the direct inputs technology matrix except that the values show the total (i.e. first round plus all future round effects) inputs per unit of final demand produced. The direct plus indirect matrix for Table 6.6 is shown in Table 6.8. By multiplying the value of final demand for any industry's output by each value separately down the corresponding column, and summing these products, the gross output from that industry which is necessary to supply the final demand is estimated. Hence, to supply a final demand of £1m. for manufacturing and zero for services requires £1.119m. and £0.60m. of manufacturing and service industry outputs respectively.

The costs of data collection for the construction of an IO transactions matrix are too great in relation to the benefits for collection by individual firms. Consequently, firms use the tables published by government statistical agencies, which only produce information at the industry, not the firm, level. Hence the technique will not give predictions of the quantity demanded from an individual firm. However, the technique will produce predictions of the demand for industry outputs which in turn may help a firm predict its own demand. A firm can also compare the identities of its customers with those of its industry as a whole and similarly those of its suppliers. Such comparisons may suggest where potential customers may be gained or generate ideas for combining inputs in different and more efficient proportions.

IO has other limitations as a forecasting tool. Firstly, the assumption of constant returns to scale may not hold in all industries, so the expansion of one industry's output may not have the predicted effect on that of another. Secondly, relative prices of different industry outputs may change between the date on which the transaction matrix was assembled and the date of the forecast. In response, the actual physical flows of outputs in the transactions matrix and so the direct and indirect inputs technology matrix may have changed. In addition, since technology matrices are calculated in money values, such a change in relative prices would mean that the forecast of future money values of each industry's output was based on the wrong ratio in the transactions matrix. Thirdly, if technology changed over time, the inputs from one industry per unit output of another might change; again, the forecast would be based on an inappropriate transactions matrix. Whilst techniques have been developed to reduce at least the last two sources of error, they cannot remove it entirely.

6.7 Markov chains

When highly simplified, the Markov chain method of prediction is to multiply current values by the proportion by which they are expected to change, in order to derive their expected value for the next period. To explain the procedure we consider the example of the sellers of each of three brands (the only brands of the product which are sold) where each wishes to predict his market share at the end of the next – say – month, which is March.

6.7.1 Transition probabilities

Suppose that the seller of each brand notices that between 31 January and 28 February, sales of his or her brand have changed. Suppose also that each seller has been able to discover the original and final brand which each switching customer previously bought and now buys. A table (similar in construction to an input–output transactions matrix) may be used to represent the known flow of customers: Table 6.9. The number of customers on 31 January and 28 February for each brand are shown in the left-hand and right-hand columns and the difference between these two consists of the difference between customers gained (shown in the second column) and those lost (shown in the third column). Hence the value '100' of 'A' row, 'B' column in the losses section shows that 100 customers switched from brand A to brand B. Some customers will be retained. They will number the difference between the original number and those lost, as shown in Table 6.10.

Since each figure in the losses section of Table 6.9 shows the number of customers which switched from each particular brand to another, the probability that any one customer will switch from one particular brand to another may be calculated by dividing the relevant figure in the loss section of Table 6.9 by the row total for January. Hence the probability that any one customer would switch from brand A

Table 6.9   Flow of customers

Brand	Number of customers on 31 Jan.	Gains from			Losses to			Number of customers on 28 Feb.
		A	B	C	A	B	C	
A	800	0	150	200	0	100	150	900
B	1000	100	0	100	150	0	300	750
C	1400	150	300	0	200	100	0	1550

Table 6.10   Derivation of retentions

Brand	Number of customers on 31 Jan.	Gains	Losses	Number of customers on 28 Feb.	Retentions
A	800	350	250	900	550
B	1000	200	450	750	550
C	1400	450	300	1550	1100

to brand B between January and February was 0.125 ($= 100/800$) and that for a switch from brand A to brand C was 0.188 ($= 150/800$).

The probability that any customer will be retained by a brand equals the number retained by that brand divided by the number who originally bought the brand. Hence the probability of retention between January and February for brands A, B and C was, respectively 550/800, 550/1000, and 1100/1400.

If we place each of the probabilities which we have derived in the last two paragraphs in the same position as the numerator in their calculation was placed in the *losses to* section of Table 6.9, we obtain the *transition probability matrix*: Table 6.11.

6.7.2 Prediction

One period

To predict market shares it may be assumed that their future values depend only on customers' switching behaviour over the last period (a first order Markov chain), on behaviour over the last two periods (a second order Markov chain) *or* on behaviour over even more past periods. In this chapter we discuss only a first order process; the reader is referred to the Bibliography for higher-order chains. Hence it is assumed that the probability that a customer switched from one specific brand to another brand in the last period *equals* the probability that the customer will make that switch in the next period.

Therefore to predict the market share of, say, brand A on 31 March we calculate:

$$\left\{ \begin{array}{l} A\text{'s expected market} \\ \text{share constituted by} \\ \text{customers retained} \\ \text{by } A \end{array} \right\} + \left\{ \begin{array}{l} A\text{'s expected market} \\ \text{share constituted by} \\ \text{customers expected} \\ \text{to switch from } B \text{ to} \\ A \end{array} \right\} + \left\{ \begin{array}{l} A\text{'s expected market} \\ \text{share constituted by} \\ \text{customers expected} \\ \text{to switch from } C \text{ to} \\ A \end{array} \right\}$$

Table 6.11 Transition probability matrix

Brand	A	B	C
A	$0.688 \left(= \dfrac{550}{800} \right)$	$0.125 \left(= \dfrac{100}{800} \right)$	$0.188 \left(= \dfrac{150}{800} \right)$
B	$0.150 \left(= \dfrac{150}{1000} \right)$	$0.550 \left(= \dfrac{550}{1000} \right)$	$0.300 \left(= \dfrac{300}{1000} \right)$
C	$0.143 \left(= \dfrac{200}{1400} \right)$	$0.071 \left(= \dfrac{100}{1400} \right)$	$0.786 \left(= \dfrac{1100}{1400} \right)$

Now

A's expected market share constituted by customers retained by A	= (A's propensity to retain customers) $\times$ (A's current market share)	= 0.688×0.281 = 0.193
A's expected market share constituted by customers expected to switch from B to A	= (A's propensity to attract customers from B) $\times$ (B's current market share)	= 0.150×0.234 = 0.035
A's expected market share constituted by customers expected to switch from C to A	= (A's propensity to attract customers from C) $\times$ (C's current market share)	= 0.143×0.484 = 0.069 Total = 0.297

Notice that A's propensities to retain customers, to attract them from B and to attract them from C are the probabilities given in the first column of the transition probability matrix.

To predict the market share of brand B on 31 March we would similarly calculate:

$$\left\{\begin{array}{l} B\text{'s expected} \\ \text{market share} \\ \text{constituted by} \\ \text{customers retained} \\ \text{by } B \end{array}\right\} + \left\{\begin{array}{l} B\text{'s expected market} \\ \text{share constituted by} \\ \text{customers expected} \\ \text{to switch from } A \text{ to} \\ B \end{array}\right\} + \left\{\begin{array}{l} B\text{'s expected market} \\ \text{share constituted by} \\ \text{customers expected} \\ \text{to switch from } C \text{ to} \\ B \end{array}\right\}$$

and for C:

$$\left\{\begin{array}{l} C\text{'s expected} \\ \text{market share} \\ \text{constituted by} \\ \text{customers retained} \\ \text{by } C \end{array}\right\} + \left\{\begin{array}{l} C\text{'s expected market} \\ \text{share constituted} \\ \text{by customers} \\ \text{expected to switch} \\ \text{from } A \text{ to } C \end{array}\right\} + \left\{\begin{array}{l} C\text{'s expected market} \\ \text{share constituted} \\ \text{by customers} \\ \text{expected to switch} \\ \text{from } B \text{ to } C \end{array}\right\}$$

Each of these terms would be calculated in the analogous way to that explained for A.

Instead of setting out the problem in this spacious way one could use matrix algebra. The predicted market shares could be calculated as the product of the row vector of current shares (for example of A, B and C) times the transition probabilities matrix. (A row vector is simply a collection of numbers which are arranged side by side in a row.) In the case of the example:

$$(0.281\ 0.234\ 0.484) \begin{pmatrix} 0.688\ 0.125\ 0.188 \\ 0.150\ 0.550\ 0.300 \\ 0.143\ 0.071\ 0.786 \end{pmatrix} = (0.297\ 0.198\ 0.503)$$

(6.7)

By performing this multiplication we would derive:[2]

$$
\left\{
\begin{array}{ccc}
0.281 \times 0.688 & 0.281 \times 0.125 & 0.281 \times 0.188 \\
+0.234 \times 0.150 & +0.234 \times 0.550 & +0.234 \times 0.300 \\
+0.484 \times 0.143 & +0.484 \times 0.071 & +0.484 \times 0.786
\end{array}
\right\}
$$
$$
= \quad (0.297 \qquad\qquad 0.198 \qquad\qquad 0.503)
$$

The left column of this matrix is identical to the arithmetic above for the prediction of A's share. This is because this matrix representation is simply a graphically different, though logically the same, way of presenting the calculation. The second and third columns are identical to the arithmetic which we would, if space was allowed, have written to predict the future shares of B and C.

Further periods

The above method is general for the prediction of, say, market shares, one period into the future. For convenience let us represent the row vector for the current period t by $\underline{Z}_t$ and the matrix of transition probabilities which relate to the changes between t and $t+1$ by $P_{t,t+1}$. Then generalising equation (6.7) we have

$$\underline{Z}_t \times P_{t,t+1} = \underline{Z}_{t+1} \tag{6.8}$$

Therefore, if a prediction two periods into the future, say to April in the above example, is required, one would apply the method for a one-period prediction to the forecasted value for March. If the transition probabilities are assumed to remain the same between April and March as between February and March, then the shares for April could be predicted as:

$$
(0.297\ 0.198\ 0.503)
\left\{
\begin{array}{ccc}
0.688 & 0.125 & 0.188 \\
0.150 & 0.550 & 0.300 \\
0.143 & 0.071 & 0.786
\end{array}
\right\}
= (0.304\ 0.182\ 0.511) \tag{6.9}
$$

The left-hand row vector shows the predicted shares for March. Therefore it is the product of the row vector of shares for February (the current period) times the transition probability matrix. Hence to derive equation (6.9) the current period shares have been multiplied by the transition probability matrix twice. That is:

$$\underline{Z}_{\text{Apr.}} = \underline{Z}_{\text{Feb.}}\, P_{\text{Feb.,Mar.}}\, P_{\text{Mar.,Apr.}} = \underline{Z}_{\text{Feb.}}\, P^2_{\text{Feb.,Mar.}}\ \text{if } P_{\text{Feb.,Mar.}} = P_{\text{Mar.,Apr.}}$$

In general

$$\underline{Z}_{t+n} = \underline{Z}_t \times P^n_{t,t+1}$$
$$\text{if } P_{t,t+1} = P_{t+1,t+2} = P_{t+2,t+3} \ldots P_{t+n-1,t+n} \tag{6.10}$$

6.7.3 Equilibrium conditions

Suppose the transition probability values are assumed to remain constant and that values of say, market shares, are predicted further and further into the future. After a large number of predictions, forecast shares may not change between one period's values and those predicted for the next period. An equilibrium would exist. For example, if the market shares of our three brands are predicted for later months using the same transition probabilities matrix the forecasts are as shown in Table 6.12. From this table it can be seen that the absolute difference between the predicted share for each month and its predecessor decreases the further into the future the forecast month is.

To find the possible equilibrium values consider equation (6.10) (which it is recalled is a generalisation of all the previous prediction manipulations). If we consider how to predict the values of our market shares, just one period hence say, $t+1$, but now call that future period the period when values reach their equilibrium values, we have:

$$\underline{Z}_{t \, = \, \text{equil period}} = \underline{Z}_{t-1=(\text{equil period})-1} \times \underline{P}_{t-1,t}$$

Expanding this and substituting the market shares transition probability matrix for P we have:

$$(A_t B_t C_t) = (A_{t-1} B_{t-1} C_{t-1}) \begin{pmatrix} 0.688 & 0.125 & 0.188 \\ 0.150 & 0.550 & 0.300 \\ 0.143 & 0.071 & 0.786 \end{pmatrix}$$

where A_t, B_t, C_t are the market shares of A, B and C respectively, in period t. Hence by matrix multiplication:

$$A_t = A_{t-1}0.688 + B_{t-1}0.150 + C_{t-1}0.143$$
$$B_t = A_{t-1}0.125 + B_{t-1}0.550 + C_{t-1}0.071$$
$$C_t = A_{t-1}0.188 + B_{t-1}0.300 + C_{t-1}0.786$$

But in equilibrium, predictions of successive values are the same, that is $A_t = A_{t-1}$, $B_t = B_{t-1}$ and $C_t = C_{t-1}$. Hence:

$$A = 0.688A + 0.150B + 0.143C \Rightarrow -0.312A + 0.150B + 0.143C = 0 \qquad (6.11)$$

$$B = 0.125A + 0.550B + 0.071C \Rightarrow 0.125A - 0.450B + 0.071C = 0 \qquad (6.12)$$

$$C = 0.188A + 0.300B + 0.786C \Rightarrow 0.188A + 0.300B - 0.214C = 0 \qquad (6.13)$$

Table 6.12

		A Share in one month minus share in previous		B Share in one month minus share in previous		C Share in one month minus share in previous	
	Share	month		Share	month		Share	month
February	0.281			0.234			0.484	
March	0.297	+0.016		0.198	−0.036		0.503	+0.019
April	0.304	+0.007		0.182	−0.016		0.511	+0.008
May	0.310	+0.006		0.174	−0.012		0.513	+0.002

and since the sum of all market shares equals 1.000:

$$A + B + C = 1 \Rightarrow A + B + C - 1 = 0 \tag{6.14}$$

Hence there are three unknowns, A, B and C, and four equations. Dropping one equation and solving the remaining three simultaneously gives the equilibrium market shares of brands A, B, and C as 0.316, 0.169 and 0.515 respectively. (A note of caution is in order. Equilibrium values may not exist and/or may not be unique. The reader is referred to the Bibliography for a discussion of the conditions under which this occurs.)

6.7.4 Evaluation

One limitation of the use of Markov chains as a predictive device is that the variable to be forecast must relate to one of a finite number of known states where the sum of all values for each state totals 1. For example, the market share of 1 of 3 brands may be forecast, the sum of shares equalling 1. Thus the prediction of future sales in £s *per se* is not suitable for the technique. In addition it follows that it must be conceptually possible for the system to move from one state to another. Thus customers could move as above from brand A to brands B and/or C. But how the future level of own or rival prices could be predicted using the technique is not possible to ascertain as the technique is described here.

Thirdly, the technique is expensive. Information concerning the initial values of variables as well as the transition probabilities must be acquired. In the case of market share information this may necessitate a costly market research study.

6.8 Usage

A number of studies have examined the popularity of different forecasting techniques and the contexts in which they are used. These studies differ in the techniques considered, size of firms in the sample, the function of the respondents within their company, the variables to be forecast, and the results presented. However, Table 6.13 presents the results of two recent studies. In both surveys the jury of executive opinion, and various mechanistic extrapolation techniques, were popular. But the British firms used econometric models and sophisticated time series models (Box–Jenkins techniques) far less than their American counterparts. The British survey concludes that, whilst American firms had 'by the mid 1970s . . . made substantial progress in the application of forecasting methods . . . the same cannot by said for British firms', and it found 'a lack of knowledge of specific techniques' in the British sample.

Table 6.14 reports the techniques which Sparkes and McHugh (1984) found were being used by a sample of British managers for each of four types of variables. Of the techniques shown in the table the most frequently used to forecast market size

Table 6.13 Wheelwright–Clarke and Sparkes–McHugh surveys

Authors Country Publication date	Wheelwright & Clarke USA 1976		Sparkes & McHugh GB 1984	
	% who use it	% of those familiar with it who use it	% who use it	% of those with an awareness & working knowledge who use it
Salesforce estimates	67	74	n/a	n/a
Juries of executive opinion	77	82	72	76
Customer surveys	48	57	57	n/a
Naive, trend extrapolation,			58	63
Moving averages,	65	75	57	58
Exponential smoothing,			11	13
Adaptive filtering, time series decomposition				
Box–Jenkins[1]	24	40		
Econometric methods				
Single equation	70	76	10	12
Simultaneous models	57	65		

Note: The Box–Jenkins technique is a highly complex method whereby a forecast value of, say, sales is based on sales in various past periods and past values of a variable whose value on any one occasion was randomly determined. An example of the model used is:

$S_t = \phi_1 S_{t-1} + K + e_t + \theta_1 e_{t-1}$ where S_t is sales in period t, e_t is a random variable, K, ϕ_1 and θ_1 being constants to be estimated.

Table 6.14 Techniques: number of responses

	Executive assessment	Trend analysis	Moving averages	Surveys	Exponential smoothing	Regression & correlation
Market size	2	1	0	15	2	2
Market share	32	17	12	6	0	0
Production/ stock control	10	3	8	0	2	0
Financial planning	20	3	3	0	1	0

and share were 'surveys' and 'executive assessment' respectively. The most popular technique used for forecasts for production/stock control and for financial planning was also 'executive assessment'. Unfortunately, the sample relates to large firms (most had sales above £5m. per annum), was sent only to accountants within firms, and was small (around 65 respondents).[3]

Table 6.15

	Test Surveys markets	Naive	Simple moving averages	Exponential moving averages	Time series decomp.	Adaptive filters	Box–Jenkins	Single equation econometrics	Simultaneous equation econometrics	Leading indicators	Input–output
Time horizon											
1 month	n/a	✓	✓	✓	✓	✓	✓				
1–3 months	✓	✓	✓	✓	✓	✓	✓	✓	✓	✓	
less than 2 years	✓				✓		✓	✓	✓		
more than 2 years	✓							✓	✓		✓
Accuracy											
Predicting pattern	5	1	2	3.5	5	7	10	8	10	0	6
Predicting turning points	8	3	0	0	3	6	8	4	6	5	0
(0 = lowest, 10 = highest)											
Costs											
Development	n/a	0	1	0.5	4	4	8	6	8	0	10
Running	n/a	n/a	1	0	4	7	10	6	8	n/a	10
(0 = lowest, 10 = highest)											

Source: Adapted, with changes from Wheelwright and Makridakis 1980, Table 15.1.

6.9 Managerial revisions of forecasts

It is important to realise that, in view of the limitations described in this chapter, the methods described act merely as *aids* to managerial forecasting. Many forecasters such as Armstrong (1981) have argued that managers should accept the forecasts given by quantitative models without adjustment. Early research (Kelly and Fiske 1950; and Carbone *et al.* 1983) found empirically that managerial revisions did not improve and in some cases reduced the accuracy of forecasts yielded by quantitative techniques. However, this is not always the case. Mathews and Diamantopoulos (1989, 1992) studied the sales forecasts by a UK health care company which sells 900 products to institutional buyers. Forecasts were produced two quarters in advance by a variant of Holt's exponential smoothing technique. These were revised by product managers who used only their experience and data on previous demand to make the revision. Mathews and Diamantopoulos found firstly, that the revision increased the accuracy of the forecasts; secondly, that the managers chose for revision forecasts which, if unrevised, would have been particularly inaccurate but, thirdly, revised forecasts were typically just as accurate as forecasts which were considered accurate before revisions and so were not altered.

6.10 Summary

A number of forecasting techniques have been reviewed, mainly in the context of sales forecasting. It has been emphasised that different techniques are applicable in different situations. However, a comparison of the techniques, in general, according to different criteria is given in Table 6.15.[4]

Appendix 6

New product forecasts

Test marketing and consumer surveys are examples of techniques already discussed which can be used to help in forecasting sales of new products before national launch. Another technique is life cycle segmentation analysis.

Life cycle segmentation analysis

Market segmentation is always useful but is especially so for difficult problems such as new product sales forecasts. Business tactics differ at each stage of the product life cycle, so we want to know when the product will be at any one stage of this cycle. But the cycle will be proceeding at different rates in different market segments, so timing of tactics will differ also according to the segment concerned.

All products were once new to the market-place. As time passes their sales rise from zero to a maximum after which they go into a decline situation, when they will ultimately be withdrawn from the market.

New product sales tend to follow an S-shaped curve. Such curves fit the sigmoidal formula $R = k/(1 + e^{-(a+b)t})$, where k, a, b and e are constants determined from the data, R is sales revenue, and t is time. But this formula is almost useless in predicting the course of such a curve until it at least begins to turn over at the top, or unless maximum sales, the compulsory turning point and its timing can be forecast with confidence.

In short, mathematics is apparently of little help in forecasting what a product's sales will be, since almost all of the product life-cycle curve must be known before a formula can be applied to it. This may be of historic interest but is clearly of little value to the manager who wants to know how to react to or to influence the future course of events.

Figure A6.1 shows a typical life-cycle curve divided into five stages. The length of each stage will vary product by product. Some products, such as Rubik cubes, which are heavily dominated by fashion, may pass through all five in a matter of months. Others, like the motor car, may last for several years, with decline arrested (or even reversed) by the regular introduction of new models or the tapping of new market segments.

The phenomenon of market segmentation gives a clue as to how the product life-cycle concept can be practically harnessed for marketing decisions. First, we shall examine what elements of the mix are important at different stages of the cycle, and second, how segmentation can help identify which stage of the cycle we are at and hence which tactic or tactics to concentrate on.

Mickwitz has suggested that the relevant elements in the marketing mix are as follows:

1. Introduction: quality has the greatest marketing impact, then advertising; price and service have the least.
2. Growth: early adopters have now already purchased, buyer resistance is now being met, advertising is the most effective weapon, then quality.
3. Maturity: most price-insensitive buyers have now bought, rivals have entered the market, so price elasticity has become very much higher, then advertising, quality and service.
4. Saturation: price is no longer important, because it is already low; product differentiation, in quality, packaging, or intangibly through advertising becomes important, as does service.
5. Decline: the problem now is to find new product uses and advertise them; quality and service will have some impact; price very little.

Market segmentation is always useful, but is especially so for difficult problems such as product life-cycle analysis. Business tactics differ at each stage of the product life cycle, so we want to know when the product will be at any one stage of this cycle. But the cycle will be proceeding at different rates in different market segments, so timing of tactics will differ also according to the segment concerned.

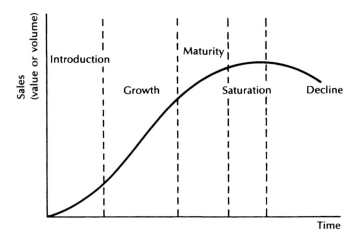

Figure A6.1

The problem of projecting the curve into the future, and so helping to answer the question of what tactics to adopt, can be simplified if we ask an associated question. Who should these tactics be directed at during the course of the cycle? By segmenting the market it may be possible to find well-developed curves in one or two segments, providing some indication of how less-developed curves in other sectors may be expected to progress.

If one knows the total market potential and the total potential in each segment, and if one knows how quickly the first segment is maturing, one can make estimates of similar or modified diffusion rates for the remaining segments and so, in aggregate, for the total market.

A major problem is to pinpoint the early adopters and then define the segment through which the new product will next diffuse. Will it be a trickle effect down the social classes? Or through, up or down, the age groups? Or will it be diffused broadly through middle and skilled working classes, as with TV, rather than through the poor or very rich classes? The example in Figure A6.2 of the life cycle for a new consumer durable shows saturation occurring earliest in the upper socio-economic (AB, followed by C_1) groupings. The social grade definitions are based on those used by the British Institute of Practitioners in Advertising. These are:

AB   higher managerial, administrative or professional;
B   intermediate managerial, administrative or professional;
C_1 supervisory or clerical, junior managerial, administrative or
          professional;
C_2 skilled manual workers;
DE   D semi- and unskilled manual workers;
       E state pensioners or widows (no other earner), casual or lowest
          grade workers.

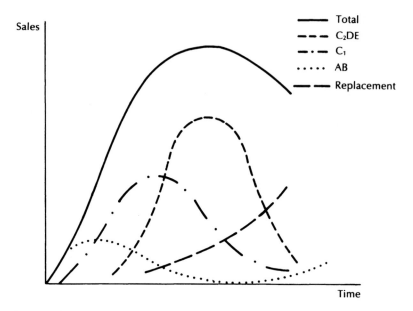

Figure A6.2

Notes

1. The values of the necessary increase in gross output of each industry to fulfil any increase in final demand may be derived by solving certain simultaneous equations. The input of industry i, per unit of output by industry j, a_{ij}, (the values in the direct inputs technology matrix), when multiplied by the output of the purchasing industry, X_j equals the *total* input into j by i, that is, $a_{ij}X_j$. Hence by adding such values for every industry which purchases from one specific industry, and also the final demand for that industry, F_i, the gross output from i is obtained. Hence the transactions matrix of Table 6.6 can be represented as:

$$a_{11}X_1 + a_{12}X_2 + F_1 = X_1 \qquad\qquad\qquad (i)$$
$$a_{21}X_1 + a_{22}X_2 + F_2 = X_2 \qquad\qquad\qquad (ii)$$

and in general $\sum_{j=1}^{n} a_{ij}X_j + F_i = X_i$

where a_{12} = value of input 1 necessary to produce £1 of output 2, and so on; X_1 = gross output of industry 1, and so on; F_1 = total final demand for industry 1, and so on. In general, the transactions matrix can be written as:

$$A\underline{X} + \underline{F} = \underline{X}$$

where A is an $n \times n$ matrix of direct input technical coefficients
$\underline{X}$ is an $1 \times n$ vector of industry outputs

and $\underline{F}$ is an $1 \times n$ vector of final demands.

Rearranging gives:

$$\underline{F} = (I - A)\underline{X} \Rightarrow (I - A)^{-1}\underline{F} = \underline{X}$$

where I is the unitary matrix. The 'direct and indirect inputs technology matrix per £1 of final demand' is $(I - A)^{-1}$. So, given a vector of forecasted future final demands and the a_{ij}s of the direct input technology matrix, the vector of industry outputs can be calculated.

2. The formula for the product of a 1×3 matrix times a 3×3 matrix is:

$$(a_{11}a_{12}a13)\begin{pmatrix} b_{11} & b_{12} & b_{13} \\ b_{21} & b_{22} & b_{23} \\ b_{31} & b_{32} & b_{33} \end{pmatrix}$$

$$= (a_{11}b_{11} + a_{12}b_{21} + a_{13}b_{31} + a_{11}b_{12} + a_{12}b_{22} + a_{13}b_{32} + a_{11}b_{13} + a_{12}b_{23} + a_{13}b_{33})$$

3. This survey is the most up-to-date British survey with which the authors are familiar. For a more specific study relating to sales forecasting techniques, see Mentzer and Cox 1984.

4. For a comparison of characteristics of forecasting techniques for sales forecasting, see Chambers, Mullick and Smith 1971, pp. 45–74. We have not reproduced this here because it is now a little dated.

Bibliography

Aaker, D. A. and Day, G. S. (1983) *Marketing Research*, 2nd edn., John Wiley.

Armstrong, J. S. (1978) *Long Range Forecasting: From crystal ball to computer*, Columbia University Press.

Armstrong, J. S. (1981) 'What to ask about management's forecasts', *Directors and Boards*.

Bails, D. G. and Peppers, L. C. (1993) *Business Fluctuations*, Prentice Hall.

Barker, T. (1985) 'Forecasting the economic recession in the United Kingdom, 1979–1982: a comparison of model-based ex ante forecasts', *Journal of Forecasting*, vol. V, 2.

Bolt, G. (1994) *Market and Sales Forecasting: A total approach*, 3rd edn, Kogan Page.

Butler, W. F. and Kavesh, R. A. (eds) (1966) *How Business Economists Forecast*, Prentice Hall.

Carbone, R., Anderson, A., Corrueau, C. and Corsan, P. P. (1983) 'Comparing for different time series methods and value of technical expertise, individualised analysis and judgemental adjustment', *Management Science*, vol. 29.

Chambers, J., Mullick, S. K. and Smith, D. D. (1971) 'How to choose the right forecasting techniques', *Harvard Business Review*, pp. 45–74.

Chisholm, R. K. and Whitaker, G. R. (1971) *Forecasting Methods*, Richard D. Irwin.

Easingwood, C. J. (1989) 'An analogical approach to the long term forecasting of major new product sales', *International Journal of Forecasting* vol. 5, 1.

Economic Trends (1975) no. 257, March, HMSO.

Georgoff, D. M. and Murdick, R. G. (1986) 'A manager's guide to forecasting', *Harvard Business Review*, vol. 64, January–February.

Gordon, R. A. (1962) 'Alternative approaches to forecasting: the recent work of the National Bureau', *Review of Economics and Statistics*, vol. 44, 3.

Granger, C. W. J. (1989) *Forecasting in Business and Economics*, 2nd edn, Boston Academic Press.

Gross, C. W. and Peterson, R. T. (1976) *Business Forecasting*, Houghton Mifflin.

Hadley, G. and Kemp, M. C. (1972) *Finite Mathematics in Business and Economics*, North Holland.

Haitovsky, Y., Treyz, G. and Su, V. (1974) *Forecasts with Quarterly Macroeconometric Models*, National Bureau of Economic Research.

Hanke, J. E. and Reitch, A. G. (1989) *Business Forecasting*, 3rd edn, Allyn and Bacon.

Jarrett, J. (1991) *Business Forecasting Methods*, Blackwell.

Kotler, P. (1971) *Market Decision Making*, Holt, Rhinehart & Winston.

Levin, R. I. and Kirkpatrick, C. A. (1982) *Quantitative Approaches to Management*, McGraw-Hill.

Lewis, J. P. (1962) 'Short-term general business conditions forecasting: some comments on method', *Journal of Business*, vol. 35, 4.

Makridakis, S. and Wheelwright, S. (1989) *Forecasting Methods for Management*, 5th edn, John Wiley.

Makridakis, S., Wheelright, S. C. and McGee (1983) *Forecasting: Methods and applications*, John Wiley.

Mathews, B. and Diamantopoulos, A. (1989) 'Judgemental revision of forecasts: a longitudinal extension', *Journal of Forecasting*, vol. 8.

Mathews, B. and Diamantopoulos, A. (1992) 'Judgemental revision of sales forecasts: the relative performance of judgementally revised versus non-revised forecasts', *Journal of Forecasting*, vol. 11.

Mentzer, J. T. and Cox, J. E. (1984) 'Familiarity, application and performance of sales forecasting techniques', *Journal of Forecasting*, vol. 3, 1.

Miernyk, W. H. (1965) *The Elements of Input–Output Analysis*, Random House.

Nevin, J. R. (1974) 'Laboratory experiments for estimating consumer demand: a validation study', *Journal of Marketing Research*, vol. 11.

O'Dea, D. J. (1975) *Cyclical Indicators for the Postwar British Economy*, Cambridge University Press.

Pessemier, E. (1960) 'An experimental method of estimating demand', *Journal of Business*, vol. 33.

Saunders, J. A., Sharp, J. A. and Witt, S. F. (1987) *Practical Business Forecasting*, Gower.

Sawyer, A. G., Worthing, P. M. and Sendak, P. E. (1979) 'The role of laboratory experiments to test marketing strategies', *Journal of Marketing*, vol. 43.

Schreiber, M. M. (1983) 'Forecasting Crest Sales', *Business Economics*, January.

Sparkes, J. R. and McHugh, A. K. (1984) 'Awareness and use of forecasting techniques in British industry', *Journal of Forecasting*, vol. 3, 1.

Suits, D. B. (1962) 'Forecasting and analysis with an econometric model', *American Economic Review*, no. 52.

Surrey, M. J. C. (1971) *Analysis and Forecasting of the British Economy*, Cambridge University Press.

Tull, D. S. and Hawkins, D. I. (1992) *Marketing Research: Measurement and method*, 5th edn, Macmillan.

Wallis, K. F., Andrews, M. J., Bell, D. N. F., Fisher, P. G. and Whitley, J. D. (1984) *Models of the UK Economy*, Oxford University Press.

Watson, M. W., Pastuszek, L. M. and Cody, E. (1987) 'Forecasting commerical electricity sales', *Journal of Forecasting*, vol. 6.

Wheelwright, S. C. and Makridakis, S. (1980) *Forecasting Methods for Management*, 3rd edn, John Wiley.

Witt, S. F. and Witt, C. A. (1992) *Modelling and Forecasting Demand in Tourism*, Academic Press.

Chapter 7

Demand theory

Demand in the market-place is the foundation on which all of a manager's decisions must ultimately rest. Failure to meet market demand is the ultimate management failure. In this chapter we examine the theory of demand. We begin in the traditional manner by analysing the individual's (or the individual household's) demand and then move on to an examination of total market demand. In practice, of course, it is not individual demand which managers are interested in, but either total market demand or demand in the market for the firm's products. Market behaviour is merely the behaviour of aggregates of individuals. Acknowledging this enables us to apply demand theory to simple decision taking in the market-place. Chapter 8 examines the complexities of empirical demand analysis in further detail.

7.1 Traditional consumer theory

The satisfaction a consumer gets from a good or service is called utility. A consumer will allocate his or her expenditure among a range of purchase options facing that consumer in such a way that his or her total utility is maximised. The two theories of demand we present to support this statement, however, differ in their approach to utility. The cardinal theory assumes that the satisfaction a consumer gets from a range of products can be measured by cardinal numbers in units designated as 'utils'. Thus a consumer might get 6 utils of satisfaction from one unit of product *A* and only 4 utils from one unit of product *B*. The ordinal theory, more realistically, argues that satisfaction is subjective and incapable of precise measurement. One can only distinguish between greater and lesser levels of utility. It is assumed only that the consumer can rank, not measure, the degree of satisfaction associated with a range of commodities.

7.1.1 The cardinal approach

Although it may not be realistic to measure utility, we can make plausible assumptions about how utility changes as consumption alters. In any given time period an increase in consumption of a product will provide an increase in total utility.

After a certain consumption rate (satiation) total satisfaction will decrease as ever more of the product is consumed. There will also be a point where, as consumption increases, total utility increases, but at a decreasing rate. Diminishing marginal utility will exist. An increase in consumption of one unit of the product results in an increase in total utility less than that provided by the previous unit. A consumer may derive considerable satisfaction from purchasing a television set. The same, or even greater, (marginal) satisfaction may be obtained from a second set, as family squabbles over which channel should be viewed can now be avoided. A third set, however, while it might provide the added convenience of bedroom viewing, would have a lower marginal utility than the first two sets. The basic satisfaction of owning a TV, the opportunity to view where no opportunity had previously existed, would not be provided. A fourth set would have a still lower marginal utility. Extra sets might take the total utility function beyond the satiation rate. The consumer would be in the situation of having more sets than rooms in the house.

Figure 7.1 displays the type of utility surface we have been discussing for two products, A and B. The points of inflection indicate where diminishing marginal utility for both A and B occurs (other things equal). The maximum values similarly indicate satiation.

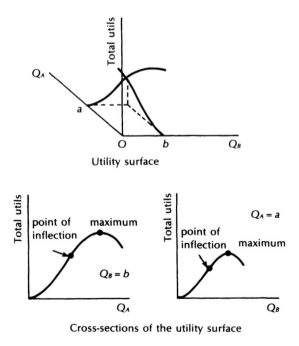

Figure 7.1

How much of each of the products facing a consumer will he or she choose to purchase? Since the consumer will have a given budget to spend, it is unlikely that he or she will be satiated. Assume the consumer is faced with a choice of n products. The total utility the consumer would receive in a given period depends on the quantities he or she consumes of those goods. The consumer's utility function is:

$$TU = f(Q_1, Q_2, \ldots, Q_n$$

where TU is total utility, and Q is the quantity consumed per period of any commodity from 1 to n.

The consumer's budget, however, will impose the following constraint on his or her utility function:

$$M = P_1Q_1 + P_2Q_2 \ldots + P_nQ_n$$

where M is the total amount of money available to the consumer and P the price of any commodity from 1 to n. To maximise utility is a standard optimisation problem. The decision variables are Q_1 to Q_n and M is a constraint on the Q_n choices. Set up the following Lagrangian equation

$$TU_\lambda = f(Q_1, Q_2 \ldots, Q_n) + \lambda(P_1Q_1 + P_2Q_2 + \ldots + P_nQ_n - M)$$

To find the values of Q_1 to Q_n, and of λ, which maximise TU, take the first derivatives of TU with respect to each and set the results equal to zero. Thus:

$$\frac{\partial TU_\lambda}{\partial Q_1} = \frac{\partial f}{\partial Q_1} + \lambda P_1 = 0 \tag{7.1}$$

$$\frac{\partial TU_\lambda}{\partial Q_2} = \frac{\partial f}{\partial Q_2} + \lambda P_2 = 0 \tag{7.2}$$

$$\ldots \ldots \ldots \ldots$$

$$\frac{\partial TU_\lambda}{\partial Q_n} = \frac{\partial f}{\partial Q_n} + \lambda P_n = 0$$

$$\frac{\partial TU_\lambda}{\partial \lambda} = P_1Q_1 + P_2Q_2 \ldots + P_nQ_n - M = 0$$

In principle, a solution can be found (provided second order conditions are also satisfied) and values for Q_1 to Q_n obtained accordingly. In practice, inability to measure utility generally makes this an impossible empirical exercise. However, we obtain useful insights from manipulation of equations (7.1) and (7.2). Transfer the second term to the right-hand side in each, divide the first equation by the second, and we obtain:

$$\frac{\partial f/\partial Q_1}{\partial f/\partial Q_2} = \frac{P_1}{P_2}$$

But $\partial f/\partial Q_1$ is the marginal utility (MU_1) of commodity 1 (by definition), and $\partial f/\partial Q_2$ is the marginal utility (MU_2) of commodity 2. So:

$$\frac{MU_1}{MU_2} = \frac{P_1}{P_2} \text{ and } \frac{MU_1}{P_1} = \frac{MU_2}{P_2}$$

From these results we can say that the consumer will allocate his or her budget between two (or more) products, so that the MUs of the products are proportional to their prices. Or, alternatively, the MUs should have the same ratio to each other as do the prices of the products.

Finally, to illustrate, award the following numbers to this last equation:

$$10/£2 \neq 15/£4$$

In this situation, where equality does not hold, the consumer should reallocate his or her spending away from A towards B. £2 more spent on B provides additional marginal utility of 10. £4 less on A results only in a utility sacrifice of 15. This process of reallocation of spending should continue until marginal equivalency per pound spent is again attained. Diminishing marginal utility ultimately will reduce the MU attainable from B and conversely, raise that attainable from A.

7.1.2 The ordinal approach

The use of consumer indifference curves enables us to adopt the ordinal approach to demand theory. Here the consumer is called on only to rank his or her preferences, not to measure them.

Consider Figure 7.2 which is an indifference map for the only two available goods, A and B. An indifference curve such as JJ is defined as the locus of points, each of which represents a combination of commodities such that the consumer is indifferent between any of these combinations. Thus the consumer will receive the same level of satisfaction or utility at either point R (5 units of A and 2 of B) or point X (2 units of A and 8 of B). In Figure 7.2 we assume, first, that the consumer has not passed the satiation rate of consumption. The consumer will always prefer to have more of A and/or B. Thus any indifference curve which lies above and to the right of another represents some higher level of satisfaction. Also, as a result of this, each indifference curve must have a negative slope (for example, if R and T present identical utilities, but R involves a higher level of consumption of good A, then T must involve a higher consumption of good B to compensate for the lower total utility provided by A).

Second, we assume that our consumer's choice is rational. In other words, if T, X and Z are any three product combinations, and if the consumer is indifferent between T and X, and between X and Z, then the consumer is also indifferent between T and Z. There is consistency in, and transitivity between the consumer's preferences. As a result, indifference curves cannot intersect. (Consider the indifference curves LL and KK intersecting at D. Point F is preferred to point E, since it lies above and to the right of E. But the consumer is indifferent between F and

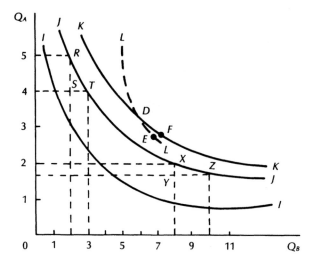

Figure 7.2

D, since they both lie on *KK*, and in turn is indifferent between *D* and *E*, since *they* both lie on *LL*. Thus, by our rationality assumption, the consumer must be indifferent between *E* and *F*. Since he or she cannot both prefer *F* to *E* and be indifferent between them, indifference curve intersection is an impossible contradiction.)

Third, a diminishing marginal rate of substitution (*MRS*) is assumed. The *MRS* of product *B* for product *A* is the number of units of *A* whose satisfaction can be made up for by a unit gain in *B*. For a particular combination of *A* and *B* this equals the absolute value of the slope of the indifference curve at that point. Alternatively, consider the arc *RT*, the *MRS* (*B* for *A*) is *RS/ST*. Now consider two points such as *R* and *X*. At *R*, the consumer has a relatively large supply of *A* and a small supply of *B*. At *X* the converse holds. Therefore, at *R* the marginal utility (*MU*) of *B* will be high, relative to that of *A*, the commodity in plentiful supply. At *X* the *MU* of *A* will be higher relative to that of *B*. So at *R* the consumer is willing to give up one unit of *A* to obtain one unit of *B*. But at *X*, where *A* is scarcer and *B* more plentiful than at *R*, he or she is only willing to forfeit *XY/2* units of *A* to obtain one unit of *B*. As a consequence of this diminishing *MRS*(*RS/ST* > *XY/YZ*) of *B* for *A*, indifference curves are convex to the origin.

Finally, we will show that the *MRS* of *B* for *A* is equal to the ratio of their marginal utilities.

If arc *RT* is sufficiently small, the utility loss in moving from *R* to *T* is $MU_A \times RS$ (the number of units of *A* given up). Similarly, the utility gain in moving from *R* to *T* is $MU_B \times ST$. Since the consumer is indifferent between *R* and *T*, the gain and loss offset each other:

$$MU_A \times RS = MU_B \times ST \text{ thus } RS/ST = MU_B/MU_A$$

and so *MRS* ≡ the slope of $JJ = \Delta A/\Delta B \equiv MU_B/MU_A$. (Remember that since the movement R to S involves a reduction in Q_A, RS is negative. But we defined the MRS to equal the absolute value of the slope of the indifference curve, so we have written $MRS \equiv$ the slope of JJ. Similarly ΔA is negative but marginal utilities positive. So we have written $\Delta A/\Delta B \equiv MU_B/MU_A$.)

The ordinal approach to demand theory requires two more pieces of information, the income of the consumer and the prices of the commodities. This information is provided by the budget line (or price line) $M/P_AM/P_B$ in Figure 7.3. The budget line is the locus of combinations of A and B which can be purchased when the consumer spends his or her entire money income and the prices of A and B are given. Any point within the area $OM/P_AM/P_B$ is a possible choice of combinations for the consumer, but there he or she will not have spent all of the available budget. The point M/P_A indicates the number of units of A the consumer can buy if he or she spends the entire budget, M, on commodity A at the price P_A. Similarly M/P_B indicates the maximum units of B he could purchase.

The (negative) slope of the budget line is numerically equal to the inverse of the ratio of the prices of A and B. Thus:

$$\text{slope} = \frac{\Delta A}{\Delta B_A} = \left(\frac{M}{P_A} \middle/ \frac{M}{P_B}\right) = \frac{P_B}{P_A}$$

Given an income for an individual, plus the related utility function, can we say what purchase combination will be most satisfying for this individual? The optimal position is that which yields highest utility. Within the range of choice available, the highest attainable indifference curve will be the one tangential to the price line. At point C the MRS is such that the individual can give EC units of B in the market and obtain DE units of A in exchange. But the individual is better off at D than at C. He or she is on a higher indifference curve. Consequently the individual will move to point D. Moreover, he or she will not stop at D. The individual will only reach equilibrium, the position which cannot be improved on, when he or she reaches F.

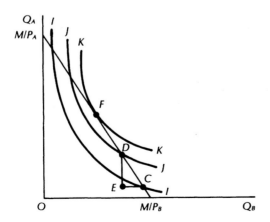

Figure 7.3

At F the slope of the indifference curve KK and the budget line are equal. But the slope of KK at F is equal to the MRS of B for A at that point and:

$$MRS = MU_B/MU_A = \Delta A/\Delta B$$

And the slope of the price line at F equals P_B/P_A. Therefore, in equilibrium:

$$\frac{MU_B}{MU_A} = \frac{P_B}{P_A} \text{ or } \frac{MU_B}{P_B} = \frac{MU_A}{P_A} \tag{7.3}$$

which is the position of marginal equivalency arrived at using the cardinal utility approach.

7.1.3 Income and price changes

Figure 7.4 summarises the impact on the budget line of an income change and of a price change. After an income increase, the original budget line MT moves out along each axis to $M'T'$, and does so parallel to the original line. OM' can now be bought of A, or OT' of B, rather than OM or OT. On the other hand, if the price of commodity B were to decrease then the effect would be the same as an increase in income. The budget line would move to the right, to T', but would do so pivoting around the original point M. More of B could now be bought, OT' rather than OT, but the maximum amount of A which could be purchased would remain OM.

Now examine Figure 7.5. Here we have the family of budget lines MT, $M'T'$ and $M''T''$ tangential to a family of indifference curves. Through the points of tangency we have drawn the income–consumption curve. This shows the way in which consumption varies when income increases and prices remain constant. Such lines generally slope up and to the right. Sometimes, in the case of inferior goods, they will eventually bend back towards the left as the good is replaced by higher quality goods when income increases. (If the inferior good is plotted on the y-axis, of

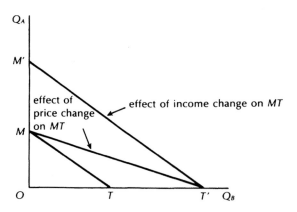

Figure 7.4

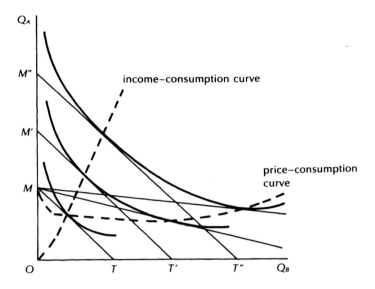

Figure 7.5

course, this line will bend down to the right.) Examples of these could be the replacement of mince by steaks in a family's diet, or the use of air travel rather than long-distance bus journeys.

From the income–consumption curve we can derive an Engel curve: named after the nineteenth-century statistician who investigated the effects of income changes on consumer expenditure patterns. Engel curves for each of commodities A and B can be obtained from Figure 7.5. The points of tangency through which the income–consumption curve passes each provide three pieces of information: income, consumption of A, and consumption of B. Plotting consumption against income for any one commodity, other things held constant, provides an Engel curve.

If we now assume money income to be fixed, Figure. 7.5 shows the effects of a price change. Here, product B is reduced in price on two occasions. Again, the points of tangency between the indifference curves and the three price lines (on this occasion pivoted around M) are joined to trace the price–consumption curve.

As we move from lower to higher indifference curves, the price–consumption curve lies to the right of the income–consumption curve. This highlights the fact that not only does the fall in price of a commodity have a similar effect to an income increase but it also changes relative prices. In other words, the optimal MRS of B for A must also alter if $MU_B/MU_A = P_B/P_A$ is still to hold. There is, therefore, a tendency to substitute the commodity whose price has fallen for others whose price has not fallen as much or at all. The former effect is the *income effect* of a price change; the latter is the *substitution effect*.

In Figure 7.6 we show how these two effects can be separated from each other. The consumer's budget is M, and the price of A is P_{A1} and of B, P_{B1}. Equilibrium

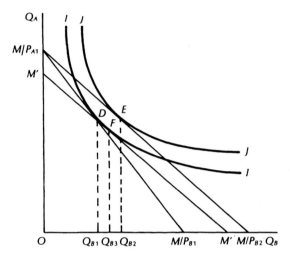

Figure 7.6

is originally at point D on curve II, where Q_{B1} units of B are bought. When P_{B1} falls to P_{B2} the budget line pivots to the right and the new equilibrium point is E, on curve JJ, where Q_{B2} is purchased. This movement, Q_{B1} to Q_{B2} is the *total effect* of the price change.

One way to isolate the substitution effect is to identify what substitution would take place if the final price ratio were to reign with no change in the consumer's real income (or utility). To do this we draw in price line $M'M'$, parallel to $M/P_{A1}M/P_{B2}$. This is tangential to II at F, the same indifference curve as that on which point D lies. The distance from Q_{B1} to Q_{B3} is the substitution effect. It is the change in quantity demanded of B resulting from a change in B's price, holding constant the consumer's real income (or satisfaction).

The distance Q_{B3} to Q_{B2} is the income effect. Formally, it is the change in quantity demanded, exclusively associated with a change in real income, commodity prices and money income being held constant (that is the MRS and the price ratio are the same at both F and E).

7.1.4 Deriving the demand curve

Figure 7.7 depicts the manner in which the demand curve is derived from this analytic system. In the upper half of the figure a price–consumption curve is traced in, by connecting the three points where the family of price lines are tangential to the family of indifference curves. The three price lines MT, MT' and MT'', are drawn given a fixed price for commodity A and prices P_1, P_2 and P_3 respectively for commodity B.

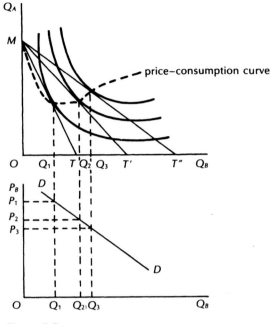

Figure 7.7

In the lower half of the figure the quantity scale for commodity B is reproduced. The vertical axis, however, is now used to plot the relevant prices of B. If we connect the points P_1Q_1, P_2Q_2 and P_3Q_3 we obtain the demand curve for B.

This demand curve illustrates the first law of demand, namely that the quantity demanded will vary inversely with price, other things being equal (and ignoring the exception of those inferior goods where the negative income effect is so strong it outweighs any negative substitution effects; such goods, a peculiar type of inferior good known as Giffen goods are rarely, if ever encountered).

7.1.5 The additive properties of individual demand schedules

The usual assumption is that individual demand curves can be horizontally summed to produce a market demand curve for the good concerned. This approach assumes that each consumer's satisfaction associated with the consumption of the good is completely independent of the number of other consumers purchasing the same good. Liebenstein (1950) terms this approach a functional view of demand, which interprets demand as being based upon qualities inherent in the commodity itself. But what if there are external or non-functional effects? He suggests the following have an impact on utility: (a) the bandwagon effect; (b) the snob effect; and (c) the Veblen effect.

7.1.6 Liebenstein's reservations

The bandwagon effect

The bandwagon effect refers to the extent to which the demand for a commodity is increased because other people are purchasing the same good. It represents the desire to be fashionable. Given this assumption, each individual consumer's demand schedule is likely to be influenced by the level of overall demand in the market. We could analyse this by drawing up such individual demand curves under the assumption that each person thinks that the market demand will be at a given level. The summing of all these demand schedules in the usual fashion gives us a market demand such as curve D_a in Figure 7.8. D_a is drawn on the consumer's assumption that market demand will be OA. On the other hand, if consumers assume market demand to be OB, then D_b is the outcome. And, likewise, D_n is the sum of the individual curves when consumers assume a market demand of ON.

If consumers are right in their expectation that OA will be the level of market demand, then the price in the market would be P_1 at point E_a. Curve D_a then traces out demand at various market prices, given that assumption. But if market demand turns out to be, say, OB, then as soon as consumers realise this they will start operating on demand curve D_b since this is consistent with the view that overall demand is OB. Again, if they are correct in this, there is only one price which is consistent with demand curve D_b and a level of market demand OB and that is price P_2. Given knowledge of market demand, one point only on each of these 'demand curves' is operative and a line joining these unique points, marked D_M traces out the true market demand curve taking into account the bandwagon effect.

The effect in this case leads to a market demand curve which is much more responsive to changes in price (i.e. is more elastic) than the simple adding of individuals' demand schedules would suggest.

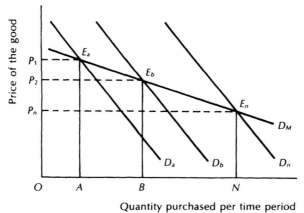

Figure 7.8 The bandwagon effect

The snob effect

The snob effect can be seen as the reverse of the bandwagon effect. Once again we assume that the demand schedule of an individual consumer is influenced both by the price of the good and by the consumer's estimate of the size of the overall market demand. But in this case the relationship between the size of the market and the quantity demanded is reversed. The snob prefers exclusivity and hence the larger the estimated size of the market the less inclined he or she is to buy. The analysis proceeds exactly as before. It is assumed that it is possible to draw up an individual's demand schedule on the basis that market demand is expected to be at a particular level, and that all such individual curves can be summed to produce a market demand curve. Thus D_a in Figure 7.9 represents the market demand for the good given the consumer's expectation that the overall market size is OA, and so on, as previously. Once again only one price is consistent with curves D_a, D_b and D_n respectively. This is so since consumers switch to the relevant alternative demand curve once they realise that market size is different from either OA, OB or ON. The only difference from the bandwagon effect is that, as the level of market size increases, the true market demand schedule falls more rapidly, at all prices as some snobs drop out of the market which they regard as becoming less exclusive.

Once again, Liebenstein concludes that simply adding individual demand schedules, ignoring what he calls external effects, leads to an inaccurate estimation of demand and, in this case demand is less responsive (i.e. less elastic; see later in this chapter) to a price change than otherwise would be predicted.

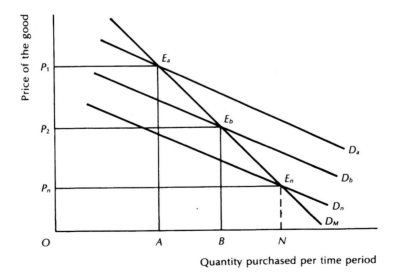

Figure 7.9 The snob effect

The Veblen effect

Finally, Liebenstein describes the Veblen (1899) effect, which is based upon Veblen's theory of conspicuous consumption. Here we distinguish between the good's functional utility and the utility attached to its price; the latter may be considered the conspicuous consumption element. It is this conspicuous component of price which allegedly matters; it is assumed that the higher the conspicuous price the more other people are impressed, and so the greater the satisfaction of the purchaser.

Each consumer has a demand schedule. On the basis of expected conspicuousness of price, prices could be termed P_1, P_2 and P_n, and these curves can be aggregated to produce market demand curves D_1, D_2 and D_n, depending on the conspicuous price. Again, only one point on these aggregated demand curves is relevant, as shown in Figure 7.10. If consumers expect the conspicuous price to be P_1, the demand curve will be D_1, but if it turns out to be P_2, they will move up to operate on demand curve D_2, and so on. If conspicuous consumption is an important determinant of demand for the good, the higher the conspicuous price the higher the demand at all price levels. A line can then be drawn through the expected conspicuous price level of each of these demand curves and this produces the 'true' demand curve D_v. The remarkable feature of this demand curve is that it is upward-sloping. This suggests that an upward-sloping demand curve is conceivable, at least for certain ranges of prices on certain luxury goods. If the price of the good is reduced sufficiently we might expect more normal consumers to enter the market; they will not be concerned with conspicuous effects, the Veblen effect will be reduced to zero, and the customary downward-sloping demand curve will emerge.

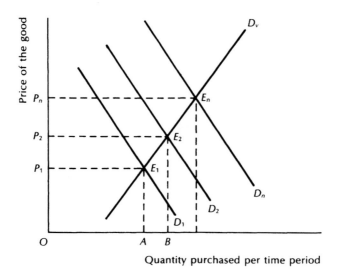

Figure 7.10 The Veblen effect

We have seen that, in certain circumstances, demand curves might indeed slope upwards, that adding individual demand schedules does not necessarily lead to a clear picture of market demand if there are external effects. It is also conceivable that all these external effects might be simultaneously operating and, to a certain extent, counterbalancing. However, these effects explicitly occur only when other things are not equal, so the first law of demand still holds.

It is true also that short-term speculative effects might lead to a temporary increase in quantity demanded, as people lay in stocks in anticipation of a price rise. Even here, however, the first law is not violated, since people are buying more today at a lower price than tomorrow's price is expected to be.

7.2 Becker's development of demand theory

Up to this juncture we have developed the theory of market demand upon the assumption that the individual consumers who go to make up the market in aggregate are rational in their behaviour (that is they display consistency in and transitivity between their preferences). This assumption is not proven but is generally accepted on the grounds that whatever irrationality any one individual may display, the behaviour of large numbers of such individuals in the market closely approximates what it would be if each of them were rational.

Gary Becker (1962) has provided a theoretical basis for the law of demand for the market (that is that quantity demanded is inversely related to price) which does not require the assumption of individual rationality. Rather it rests on probabilistic expectations of aggregate behaviour; his theory can thus be applied using the consumer panel data which is a common tool of market researchers.

Another attraction of the Becker model is that it enables demand curves to be derived which examine the impact on quantity demanded of a price change alone. Only the substitution effect is of interest. Unlike Figure 7.7 where money income was held constant, in Becker's analysis real income is held constant. Since it is the real income constant version of the demand curve which is estimated in most econometric studies of demand relationships, it seems appropriate to place emphasis on theory which is immediately relevant rather than on the combined income substitution effect demand curve of Figure 7.7.

Moreover, Becker, when maintaining real income constant in order to isolate the substitution effect, uses a different device from that employed in Figure 7.6. There real income was equated with constant utility. An 'income-compensated' price line $M'M'$ was drawn in, parallel to $M/P_{A1}M/P_{B2}$, thus reflecting the new relative prices, but tangential to the original indifference curve II, so maintaining real income, or at least utility. An alternative approach (developed originally by Slutsky, as opposed to the constant utility approach just described which was developed by Hicks) is to draw in an income-compensated price line which would enable the consumer to buy the same 'basket of goods'. Real income represents purchasing power, and if the consumer's purchasing power is retained unchanged, after a shift in relative prices, then real income is constant. Again, since it is the ability to buy a measurable 'basket of goods' and not reach a hypothetical indifference curve which is the aim of income compensation, the Becker approach is yet another step nearer to managerial applicability than the conventional ordinal and cardinal approaches already discussed.

Consider Figure 7.11. The original budget line pivots to the left as the result of a price rise from P_{B1} to P_{B2} for product B. The original basket of goods purchased is represented by point X. Now assume that there is no change in the consumer's real income as a result of the price change. To do this we draw in the budget line MM' passing through X and parallel to $M/P_{A1}M/P_{B2}$. In other words, $OM'M''$ encloses the purchase opportunity combination open to the consumer after an income-compensated increase in the price of commodity B. Since $M'M''$ has a higher relative price for B and a lower one for A than does $M/P_{A1}M/P_{B1}$, the set it encloses offers more opportunity to consume A and less opportunity to consume B than does the set enclosed within $OM/P_{A1}M/P_{B1}$. Now, no matter what the consumer's decision rule, $OM'M''$ offers a smaller *opportunity* to consume more than B_0 of B, and a greater *opportunity* to consume more than A_0 of A.

Any rational decision rule which relates choice to 'availability' would necessarily lead the consumer to choose less of B than B_0 and more of A than A_0 out of $OM'M''$. The market demand curve would have a negative slope.

What of the 'irrational' decision rules which are said to be so prevalent amongst consumers? What of the impulse purchaser, the inert consumer, the otherwise inefficient consumer?

Becker regards the impulse purchaser as not being subject to a preference system. Such a consumer 'consults' only a probability mechanism. The individual's decisions cannot be determined in advance, but the average consumption of a large number

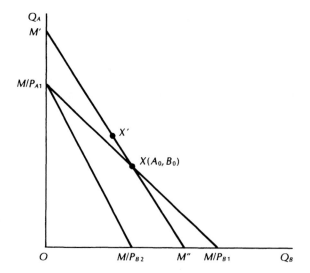

Figure 7.11

of independent consumers would tend to be at the middle of the price line (say X) which is the statistically expected purchase combination pattern of a single consumer. However, after an income-compensated price rise in B, the budget line becomes $M'M''$, the mid-point of which is X', the average location of individual consumers distributed along it. X' is to the left of X and must always be so. Thus the downward sloping to the right of the demand curve is also implied by impulsive behaviour, at least in markets with large numbers of consumers (or for an individual consumer over a sufficiently long series of purchases).

This may perhaps be better understood using numbers. Assume 1,000 consumers with identical incomes of £100 can each purchase goods A or B, both priced at £1. In total 100,000 As or 100,000 Bs could be bought. But given random distribution of preferences 50,000 of each good will be purchased (some consumers buying more of one than the other but the law of large numbers will ensure this averages out over the total). If the price of B is now increased to £2, only 50,000 Bs can be bought or 100,000 As. However, given the original market basket of 50,000 of each good, a new budget of £150 would have to be awarded to each consumer to enable them to maintain their real incomes. Such a budget would enable the consumers as a whole to purchase 150,000 As or 75,000 Bs at either extreme of the budget line. If incomes are again spent randomly the result would be a market basket of 75,000 As and 37,500 Bs.

What of the inert consumer? The brand-loyal purchaser who apparently will purchase nothing but a particular product and always avoid all others? After a price change, consumers originally in the region $M/P_{A1}X$ may wish to remain there. But those along XM/P_{B1} are now denied this possibility since it lies outside $OM'M''$. Those consumers, who have above average consumption of B would have to reduce their purchases, since OM'' is the maximum permitted by $M'M''$. Those relatively less inert consumers driven out of the area $XM''M/P_{B1}$ will be forced into $M'XM/P_{A1}$. So even inert behaviour leads to negatively inclined market demand curves.

7.3 Lancaster's characteristics approach

A further approach to demand theory, also amenable to market research data was developed by Lancaster (1966). He begins with the claim that the satisfactions which consumers desire are provided by the attributes or characteristics of goods, and not by the products themselves. A product, in short, is a bundle of satisfactions or characteristics, and not merely a good or service, *qua* good or service.

The demand for tins of Irish stew, for example, depends on characteristics such as the quantity of meat and the quantity of vegetables in each tin as well as on the product price. Table 7.1 gives a hypothetical characteristic rating for three brands, and two characteristics.

In Figure 7.12 the three brands are depicted in characteristics space as rays emanating from the origin. The slope of each ray is determined by the ratio of characteristic I to characteristic II. A consumer of brand A, for example, would

Table 7.1

	Price of can	(I) Quantity of meat	(II) Quantity of vegetables	Ratio	Cans per £10
Brand A	£1.00	80	40	2.0	10
Brand B	£0.80	40	80	0.5	12.5
Brand C	£0.95	60	60	1.0	10.5

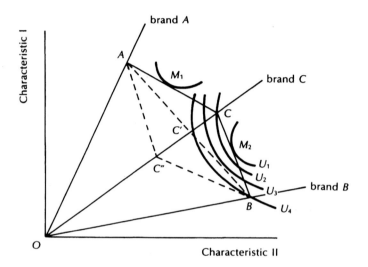

Figure 7.12

always 'consume' these characteristics at a ratio of 2:1 no matter how much of brand A he or she bought. The points A, C and B represent respectively the characteristics the consumer could purchase were he or she to allocate the entire budget to any one brand. Thus points A, C and B depend on his or her (fixed) budget and the (different) brand prices. The line joining points A, C and B is called the *efficiency*, or *characteristics possibility frontier*. Not only do points A, C and B themselves represent an exhaustion of the individual's budget, but so too would any inter-mediate points such as M_1 or M_2. This is so since it is assumed (unrealistically, but as we shall see, usefully) that the characteristics themselves are separable and therefore, hypothetically at least, can be bought in whatever proportions the consumer subjectively desires. Thus if only brands C and B were available, the line CB, if extended to the characteristics axes, is analogous to the price line of normal consumer theory. The consumer's *subjective* tastes for bundles of characteristics can be introduced using conventional indifference curves. To maximise his or her utility, for example, the consumer might select point M_2.

But M_2, while hypothetically attainable using all of the consumer's budget to buy characteristics I and II, is apparently unobtainable in fact. No brand exists which provides this bundle of characteristics in the proportion the consumer wishes. But, in fact, the model is analogous to linear programming and production theory. Characteristics are viewed as the inputs into a production process of which the output is consumer utility, while the goods are the 'processes' by which this output is obtained. The consumer's individual preference determines which combinations of characteristics he or she wishes to provide him- or herself with and in what quantities. But there is also an objective 'consumption technology' which relates inputs with processes. This technology is available to each consumer and he or she will try to attain the characteristics frontier given his or her subjective tastes. If the consumer is willing to combine brands, however, he or she can attain a characteristics bundle equivalent to that at M_2. The brand mix can be found, by drawing a line from M_2, parallel to OB until it hits OC as in Figure 7.13. Similarly another line, parallel to OC is drawn from M_2 until it meets OB. The budget is thus spent on brand C until the consumer reaches point X, when he or she will have acquired y units of characteristic I and x units of characteristic II. The consumer will switch to brand B and spend his or her remaining budget on it to acquire in total the characteristics ratio indicated at point M_2 (namely $y':x'$). This will be accomplished since the line XM_2 along which the consumer is now moving provides the characteristics in the same proportion as brand B (it has the same slope). This move provides him or her with an extra $(y' - y = y'')$ units of I and $(x' - x = x'')$ units of II to add to the y and x units he or she already has at point X. This is so since the move from X to M_2, is, as the opposite side of a parallelogram, equal to OY in characteristics space. By similar reasoning he could consume the brands along the path OYM_2, consuming brand B first. Either pathway exhausts the consumer's budget, given the position and slope of CB.

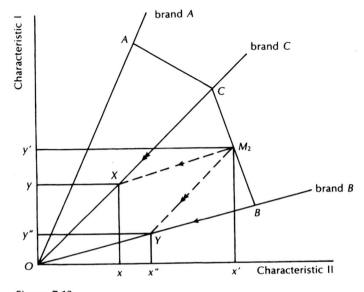

Figure 7.13

Returning to Figure 7.12 we can see the effect of a price change on consumer behaviour. Depending on his or her preferences the consumer will be lying on the line ACB. At M_1 he or she will combine brands A and C, at M_2 C and B. The consumer will reject the possibility of combining brands A and B alone, since this would not enable him or her to purchase the highest possible characteristic combination. If the price of C increases so that only OC' can be bought with the given budget, the frontier becomes $AC'B$ and combinations of A and B also become efficient. If the price rises still further so that only OC'' can be bought, then only combinations of A and B are efficient, combinations A and C, and B and C now lying within the AB frontier. As a corollary any budget increase would shift ACB outwards to the right.

Two factors emerge from this discussion of particular relevance to product policy. First, the concept of brand loyalty can now be better understood. For example it is definitely not the case that consumers will always and for each product type be willing or able to mix brands to attain a desired characteristic bundle. There are at least two reasons for this. In the case of low-price, frequently purchased goods, the consumer may be brand loyal and so may be unwilling to alternate purchases over time to achieve the optimal attribute mix. In the case of high priced items, for example cars or TV sets, the purchase will be discrete and so the consumer may not only be unwilling but also be unable 'optimally' to blend attributes from different brands.

Thus consider again Figure 7.12 with only brands C and B available. The highest indifference curve, U_1 passing through M_2 is hypothetically attainable but brand mixing is unacceptable to the consumer. Instead the consumer will spend his or her budget entirely on brand C, achieving U_2. Now C can be progressively raised in price but the consumer will continue to spend his or her budget on it alone. Given a fixed expenditure he or she is forced on to progressively lower indifference curves, but not until C's price has risen so that OC' exhausts his or her budget, will he consider switching brands to B to achieve the same satisfaction on U_4.

Second, if M_2 cannot be achieved in reality by combining brands, then provided there are sufficient customers, it may well pay a firm to launch a new brand, say brand D, which combines characteristics I and II in the proportions shown at M_2. A ray OD would then be drawn on Figure 7.12 passing through M_2, and provided the brand was priced so that the consumer's budget was exhausted at point M_2, or more accurately, anywhere upwards and to the right of U_2 on ray OD, then brand C would be dropped by the consumer in favour of D.

As with the previous three demand theories we have examined, holding income constant but raising price reduces the quantity demanded. The first law of demand is not violated. A rise in the price of C (for example) shifts the efficiency frontier down along the OC ray closer to the origin (the consumer can then travel less far out along OC). If the frontier is pushed as far down as OC' (as we saw earlier) brand C is even priced out of the market.

The characteristics approach is also applicable to inferior goods (where consumption falls as income rises): as, for example, with long-distance bus travel relative to air or train. Consider Figure 7.14. The attributes are speed and comfort with rail

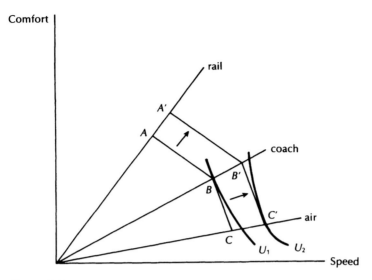

Figure 7.14

possessing the highest comfort:speed ratio and air the reverse, while coach travel is neither a particularly comfortable nor a particularly rapid form of transport.

Assume coach travel is the inferior good so that when income rises less is demanded and consumers shift to air travel (to gain speed) while others shift to rail travel (to gain comfort). Figure 7.14 illustrates the former. The original efficiency frontier is ABC which, with unchanged prices moves out to A' $B'C'$ as a given consumer's income rises. The consumer's original maximum attainable utility curve was U_1 (where he or she purchased coach travel alone) while after the increase in income coach travel ceased to be purchased and air travel at point C' maximised utility on U_2.

One last advantage of Lancaster's theory over cardinal theory can be stressed here. That is, it permits us to distinguish between the impact of advertising on *perceptions* of product attributes and *changes in taste* for different attributes.

The cardinal approach blends these two together and encompasses them both by suggesting that advertising could reposition a consumer's indifference curves by changing the *MRS* so that the highest is tangential to the budget line at a different point. The consumer's corresponding demand curve thus shifts in some way. Sometimes this is claimed to be simply a taste change induced by advertising. Such a move, however could also include a perception change about the product and its characteristics. Figure 7.15 shows how these two effects can be disentangled. We retain the view that advertising may be able to *alter preferences* (whether by information or persuasion) and so impact on the slope of the consumer's indifference curves. This phenomenon is well explained and understood in standard texts and so we do not elaborate on it further here except to emphasise that in Lancastrian theory a change in the *MRS* is due to a change in taste only.

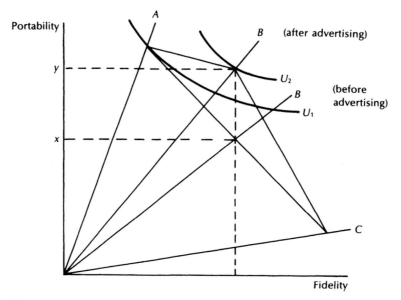

Figure 7.15

If, however, the advertising, *alters perceptions of the attributes* (again by either persuasion or information) then it is not the *MRS* of one attribute for another which changes, rather it is the position of the product ray itself. Figure 7.15 illustrates this. Say an advertising campaign alters the perception that a particular brand of personal CD stereo (brand *B*) is more readily carried in a jogger's shirt pocket than had previously been believed. Assume that the characteristics sought from such products are portability and sound fidelity. The original situation would have seen a consumer purchasing brand *A* rather than *B*, on utility curve U_1. After advertising (with no taste change) the consumer will switch to brand *B*, thanks to the perception change alone. The consumer perceives he or she will gain portability of *xy* units by so switching. Certainly the consumer still perceives *A* to be relatively more portable but given his or her unchanged portability:fidelity preferences, his or her unchanged income, the unchanged product price and the perceived change in the portability of *B* (with unchanged sound fidelity – only the characteristics ratio has changed) he will gain more satisfaction, $U_2 > U_1$, by switching to brand *B* consequential on the advertising.

Like the Becker model, the Lancaster model is amenable to empirical market-research data. Either objective characteristics can be plotted on the axes, or subjective ones gained from behavioural research (for example, in cars contrast objective economy – miles per gallon – with appearance, a psychological measure). Certainly the analysis becomes more complex with more than 2 attributes – *n* alternative brands or products are required to meet consumer wants if *n* attributes are desired. However, once a firm has identified *which* attributes consumers value highly in making their choices it can then adjust its advertising, product and pricing strategies in a more informed way.

7.4 The demand function

We are now in a position to move from demand theory for an individual to that for a market, and from the market demand curve to the demand function. The first of these is conceptually simple. The market demand curve is obtained by horizontally aggregating all of the individual demand curves. Clearly, if any of the individual curves shift or change shape, the market demand curve will respond accordingly. Moreover, the market curve could also shift as a result of a change in the number of consumers in the market.

The demand function specifies the relationship between quantity demanded and all the variables which determine demand. The demand curve is merely that part of the function which relates price and quantity demanded.

7.4.1 The determinants of demand

The following nine variables are likely to be influential in determining the demand for most commodities:

P the market price of the good
T consumer tastes and preferences
Y the level of consumer incomes
P_s the prices of substitutes
P_c the prices of complements
E consumer expectations regarding prices, income and product availability
N number of potential consumers
O all other factors which may influence demand related to the product's specific characteristics.

The effect of these on demand can be expressed in the form of the following non-specified equation:

$$Q = f(P, T, Y, P_s, P_c, E, N, O)$$

where Q is quantity demanded. Demand functions can be specified either for an individual firm or for the entire market in which the firm operates. The list of independent variables would differ in each case. One important difference would be the inclusion of variables representing competitors' activities in the firm's demand function (for example, competitors' advertising levels would probably be negatively related to the firm's demand). Even where a variable is common to the two functions, the parameter would probably differ. For example, suppose we had the following linear specified demand function:

$$Q = \hat{\alpha} + \hat{\beta}_1 P + \hat{\beta}_2 Y + \hat{\beta}_3 P_c + \hat{\beta}_4 N + e$$

The terms $\hat{\alpha}$, $\hat{\beta}_1$, $\hat{\beta}_2$, $\hat{\beta}_3$, $\hat{\beta}_4$ and e are constants, or parameters, calculated from past data. The value of $\hat{\beta}_4$ will be different if the function is for the market or for the firm – in the case of the firm $\hat{\beta}_4$ will be smaller. Only if the firm was a monopoly controlling the entire market would N, number of consumers, have an identical impact on the quantity demanded.

We will now expand on a number of these variables, and also on some additional determinants of demand.

7.4.2 Price, income and price indices

Price is the amount of money given in exchange for a good or service. Money, however, is not a reliable yardstick with which to measure what must be given up to activate a trade. In consequence economists usually think of prices and incomes as measured in terms of some standard real good or *numeraire*. In a two-good world, with goods A and B given pound prices of £6 and £2 respectively, then if one A is bought £6 is given up, which could have been used to buy 3 Bs. Thus the B price of A is 3 Bs, or $P_A/P_B = 3$. Where there are n goods there are $(n-1)$ other non-money goods than the one under study. In reality then it is customary to express the real (or relative) price of a good as the ratio of its absolute money price to some average price of all other goods. The average used is usually one of the various available price indices.

In cross-section studies of a demand function (that is studies at a point in time) the numeraire can frequently be ignored. In time series studies (i.e. over time) the numeraire is critical, since not only may general price inflation be present, but there is no reason why relative prices should move in step with the average. For example, if between 1980 and 1990 the money level of a person's salary doubled, but the retail price index rose from 100 to 150, is that individual better or worse off? Clearly he or she is better off. The individual's real wage, the real price at which he or she is selling his or her labour has risen, not by 100% certainly, but by 33.33%. Where the individual earned £100, he or she now earns £200, but that £200 in 1990 will not buy £200 of 1980 goods, it, will only buy £200 of 1990 goods. The price index increase tells us that in 1990 he or she must give up £150 to buy the equivalent of real goods which £100 could have bought in 1980. But even after maintaining his or her real purchases in 1990 by spending £150, our hypothetical individual still has £50 left, he or she is 33.33% better off than in 1980.

Similarly two products whose money prices had risen from £50 to £65 and from £100 to £155 between 1980 and 1990 can be compared. Both experienced a monetary, absolute price rise. To ascertain whether or not their real prices rose it is necessary to divide by the relevant numeraire. Thus the first product rose in price from £50/1.0 to £65/1.5 = £43.33 in 1980 pounds. The second rose from £100/1.0 to

£155/1.5 = £103.33 in 1980 pounds. In 1990 fewer real goods and services would have to be given up to acquire the first good than were given up in 1980 (the amount fewer being represented by what £6.66 could buy in 1980). Conversely the second product had risen in price in real terms by over 3% in 1980 goods and services.

Two main price indices used by econometricians are the retail price index (RPI) and the gross domestic product (GDP) deflator. The first is essentially a Laspeyres or base-weighted index, the second is a variant of the Paasche or current year index. The RPI is constructed from sample family expenditures in a given base year. At its most simplistic the base year value (of 100) is then compared with some succeeding year's value, the only variables which are assumed to change being the prices of the original sample market basket. Thus:

$$RPI_0 = \frac{\sum\limits_{i}^{n} P_{io}Q_{io}}{\sum\limits_{i}^{n} P_{io}Q_{io}} \times 100 = 100 \quad \text{and} \quad RPI_t = \frac{\sum\limits_{i}^{n} P_{it}Q_{io}}{\sum\limits_{i}^{n} P_{io}Q_{io}} \times 100$$

where P_i is the money price of good i, Q_i is the quantity bought, the subscript o is the base year and t is some future period. Clearly changes in the composition of the market basket due to innovation, obsolescence and product improvement are ignored. More subtly, the very fact that some prices rise or fall relative to others means people buy less or more of the good in question. This first law of demand is ignored by base year indices. It assumes that relatively higher priced items will continue to be bought in the same quantities as before. Substitution is ignored and thus the impact of average price inflation is exaggerated by the RPI. The defects of the current year index are the inverse of those of the base year index. Average price inflation is understated. The commodities bought in the current period are different in kind and quality from those bought in an earlier period. It is calculated thus:

$$\text{Paasche year index}_t = \frac{\sum\limits_{i}^{n} P_{it}Q_{it}}{\sum\limits_{i}^{n} P_{io}Q_{it}} \times 100$$

which, for the base year, 0, is:

$$PYI_0 = \frac{\sum\limits_{i}^{n} P_{io}Q_{io}}{\sum\limits_{i}^{n} P_{io}Q_{io}} \times 100 = 100$$

where t is the current year.

7.4.3 Tastes and preferences

Factors that shape consumers' preferences (that is influence the nature of the indifference map) embrace many determinants of consumption. For example, they include socio-economic factors such as age, sex, education, marital status, position in the domestic life cycle (for example, newly married, growing family, or middle aged with no child dependants), and financial factors such as the disposition of wealth between liquid and illiquid assets. Tastes can change as a result of innovation and of advertising, and more fundamentally, as a consequence of changing values and priorities and rising living standards. Conversely, the existence of stable behaviour patterns, namely habits, means that changes in prices or incomes, or other variables may not have an immediate effect on demand but will be subject to a time lag.

7.4.4 Expectations

A consumer's expectations may influence his or her purchase behaviour. Thus if a consumer anticipates that prices will rise in the near future, he or she may purchase now to avoid paying the higher price. Similarly, he or she may make a large value purchase now with a view to paying for it later out of expected increases in income.

7.4.5 Derived demand

The demand for some goods is derived from the demand for others. The demand for newsprint is derived from the demand for newspapers. The demand for type-writers is derived from the demand for secretaries. In other words, when examining the demand for intermediate goods or capital goods (newsprint and typewriters, say) it will prove worthwhile also to study demand in the markets for the final goods (newspapers and secretaries) to which they are related.

7.4.6 Elasticities: their meaning and value

A typical demand function for a commodity may be written thus:

$$Q = f(P, Y, P_s, P_c) \tag{7.4}$$

What the manager wants to know is how sensitive demand is to changes in the independent variables in the firm's demand function. The measure of responsiveness we use in demand analysis is elasticity. The general definition is that elasticity equals the percentage change in quantity demanded attributable to a given percentage change in an independent variable. So for any variable X, elasticity is given by:

$$\frac{\Delta X/Q}{\Delta X/X} \frac{100}{100} = \frac{\Delta Q}{\Delta X} \frac{X}{Q}$$

This equation measures arc elasticity, namely the elasticity over some finite range of the function. There is consequently more than one value for both X and Q.

Generally, the average value of both X and Q over the range in question will be used, thus:

$$\text{arc elasticity} = \frac{\Delta Q}{\Delta X} \frac{(X_2 + X_1)/2}{(Q_2 + Q_1)/2} = \frac{\Delta Q}{\Delta X} \frac{X_2 + X_1}{Q_2 + Q_1}$$

At the limit, where ΔX is very small, $\Delta Q / \Delta X = \partial Q / \partial X$. This enables us to calculate elasticity at a point, such as X_1, Q_1:

$$\text{point elasticity} = \frac{\partial Q}{\partial X} \frac{X_1}{Q_1}$$

The partial derivative sign is used since we are interested in finding out the impact on quantity demanded of a change in X, holding all other factors constant.

7.4.7 Price elasticity

Point price elasticity of demand, η is:

$$\eta = \frac{\partial Q_1 P_1}{\partial P_1 Q_1}$$

Before examining the importance of this concept it is worth discussing how a value for η, or any other elasticity, can be obtained in practice.

Our non-specified demand equation (7.4) becomes a model when it is expressed in mathematical form. The two most common specified demand equations are those which assume a linear relationship between Q and the independent variables, and those which assume a multiplicative association. For these two, equation (7.4) would be expressed respectively as:

$$Q = \alpha + \beta_1 P + \beta_2 Y + \beta_3 P_s + \beta_4 P_c + \varepsilon \tag{7.5}$$

and

$$Q = \alpha, P^{\beta_1} Y^{\beta_2} P_s^{\beta_3} P_c^{\beta_4} \varepsilon \tag{7.6}$$

which transforms to the linear logarithmic equation:

$$\log Q = \log \alpha + \beta_1 \log P + \beta_2 \log Y + \beta_3 \log P_s + \beta_4 \log P_c + \omega \tag{7.7}$$

where $\log \alpha$, β_1, β_2, β_3 and β_4 are constants to be calculated from past data. Multiple regression equations of this sort are to the managerial economist what the laboratory is to the chemist. They permit the equivalent of controlled experimentation. They have the attribute that other variables can be held constant when the relationship between a pair of variables is being studied.

We can calculate the point price elasticity from equation (7.5) by taking its partial derivative with respect to price, thus:

$$\frac{\partial Q}{\partial P} = \hat{\beta}_1 \text{ therefore } \eta = \frac{\partial Q}{\partial P}\frac{P}{Q} = \hat{\beta}_1 \times \frac{P}{Q} \tag{7.8}$$

where $\hat{\beta}_1$ is the estimated value of β_1.

Thus point elasticity can always be obtained from a linear demand function for variable X by multiplying the regression coefficient or parameter of variable X by the value of X/Q at that point. Given that the value of P/Q on a linear demand curve will vary, being higher at higher prices and lower at lower prices, η in turn will also vary in a similar fashion.

Since equation (7.6) can be transformed into the linear logarithmic equation (7.7), it can still be estimated using linear least squares regression techniques. Another useful factor of multiplicative demand functions is that they have constant elasticities over their full range. These elasticities are given by the coefficients estimated in the regression analysis. For example, writing the estimated form of equation (7.6) as:

$$Q = \hat{\alpha} \times P^{\hat{\beta}_1} \times Y^{\hat{\beta}_2} \times P_s^{\hat{\beta}_3} \times P_c^{\hat{\beta}_4} \times e \tag{7.9}$$

and differentiating this with respect to price, we obtain:

$$\frac{\partial Q}{\partial P} = \hat{\beta}_1 \times P^{\hat{\beta}_1 - 1} \times \alpha \times Y^{\hat{\beta}_2} \times P_s^{\hat{\beta}_3} \times P_c^{\hat{\beta}_4} \times e$$

and so, multiplying both sides by P/Q, we obtain:

$$\frac{P}{Q}\frac{\partial Q}{\partial P} = \eta = \hat{\beta}_1 \times P^{\hat{\beta}_1 - 1} \times \alpha \times Y^{\hat{\beta}_2} \times P_s^{\hat{\beta}_3} \times P_c^{\hat{\beta}_4} \times e \frac{P}{Q} \tag{7.10}$$

If we now substitute equation (7.9) for Q in equation (7.10) we have:

$$\eta = \hat{\beta}_1 \times P^{\hat{\beta}_1 - 1} \times Y^{\hat{\beta}_2} \times P_s^{\hat{\beta}_3} \times P_c^{\hat{\beta}_4} \times e \frac{P}{P^{\hat{\beta}_1} \times Y^{\hat{\beta}_2} \times P_s^{\hat{\beta}_3} \times P_c^{\hat{\beta}_4} \times e}$$

which on cancellation is simply $\eta = \beta_1$. So $\eta = \beta_1$, the exponent of price in equation (7.6). Since this is not a function of the P/Q ratio, it is constant. This constancy applies for all the variables in a multiplicative demand relationship. Clearly, a demand function cannot be forced into a curvilinear relationship, but when it does occur, it removes the problem of variable elasticities from the manager's decision situation.

As shown above, when a multiplicative demand function is estimated, the question of the price at which we wish to calculate elasticity does not arise, η has the same value at all prices. But as equation (7.8) shows, this is not the case with a linear demand curve.

Often price elasticity is calculated at the mean values of P and Q which occur in the sample of observations when the coefficients were estimated. Hence the mean value of Q, $\bar{Q}$ – and of P, $\bar{P}$, – would be substituted in equation (7.8) to give:

$$\eta = \beta_1 \frac{\bar{P}}{\bar{Q}}$$

Price elasticity is of prime importance in indicating the effect on revenue of a price change. Revenue can rise, fall or remain the same after a price change. There are three ranges of price elasticity, and two limiting cases. These are:[1]

1. $\eta = \infty$ This is the case of the perfectly elastic demand curve. Elasticity is infinite. The demand curve is a horizontal line, parallel to the quantity axis.
2. $\eta > 1$ The case of elastic demand. A reduction in price will result in a more than proportionate increase in quantity demanded. Total revenue will rise.
3. $\eta = 1$ The case of unitary elasticity. The demand curve is a rectangular hyperbola. The product of P and Q (total revenue) is constant, irrespective of the level of P.
4. $\eta < 1$ The case of inelastic demand. A reduction in price will result in a less than proportionate increase in quantity demanded. Total revenue will fall.
5. $\eta = 0$ The case of the completely inelastic demand curve. Elasticity is infinitely inelastic. The demand curve is a vertical line, parallel to the price axis.

The key factor, then, is the effect of a price change on revenue. Figure 7.16 depicts a linear demand curve of varying elasticity from $\eta = \infty$ to $\eta = 0$. Marginal revenue (MR) is positive so long as total revenue (TR) is rising, and becomes negative when TR falls. If one knows price and price elasticity of demand at a point, then the value of MR can also be computed. Thus:

$$TR = PQ$$

$$MR = \frac{dTR}{dQ} = P\frac{dQ}{dQ} + Q\frac{dP}{dQ} = P + Q\frac{dP}{dQ}$$

Multiply throughout by P/P

$$MR = P\left(1 + \frac{Q}{P}\frac{dP}{dQ}\right) = P\left(1 + \frac{1}{\eta}\right) \tag{7.11}$$

which is our desired result.

No profit-maximising business man or woman would lower his or her prices in the inelastic range of his or her demand curve. Elasticity measures are vital information in the taking of price decisions. Some products, such as necessities, will have relatively inelastic demand. Within limits they must be bought whatever the price. Others, such as luxury items, will have much more elastic demands, and the market place will be more price sensitive.

Absolutely inexpensive products will have less elastic demand curves than more expensive ones. It will not be worth the consumer's while to waste a large amount of time and energy worrying about price. Derived demand will be less elastic than

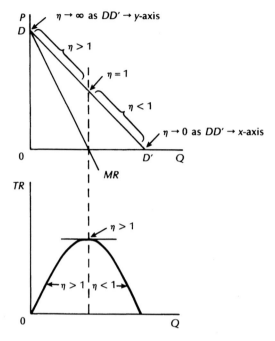

Figure 7.16

primary demand. A rise in the price of machine tools will result in only a relatively small fall in the quantity demanded. Buyers of machine tools will find it difficult, at least in the short run, to find substitutes for machine tools with which to manufacture their final products.

Elasticities of demand are also used in public policy decisions. For example, over the years the tobacco and liquor industries have argued that demand for their products was relatively elastic. So any increase in excise duty by the government would merely result in a decreased quantity demanded and so a lower revenue for both the industries and the government. The government, on the other hand, has argued that demand is relatively inelastic, and that a gross price increase would raise the revenue of the Exchequer.

7.4.8 Income elasticity

The income elasticity of demand, η_y, can be calculated from equation (7.5) by taking its partial derivative with respect to income, thus:

$$\frac{\partial Q}{\partial Y} = b \text{ so } \eta_y = \frac{\partial Q}{\partial Y} \frac{Y}{Q} = b \frac{Y}{Q}$$

Income and quantity purchased typically move in the same direction. So η_y is generally positive. The exceptions to this generalisation are inferior goods. When 'income' is included in a demand equation it can be measured on an aggregate, *per capita* or a per household basis.

'Income' can be national income, or GNP, personal income, disposable (after tax) income, or discretionary income (the surplus remaining after regular commitments on food, housing and other essential recurring expenses). GNP may be the most suitable measure of income in a demand model for machine tools; disposable income may be apposite for a clothing demand model; and discretionary income may well be the most suitable in a model of the demand for beer.

Knowledge of income elasticity is a vital piece of management information. Low income elasticity ($\eta_y < 1$) implies that the company will to some degree be insulated from the vicissitudes of business activity in the economy as a whole. This is the case, for example, with most necessities such as foodstuffs. High income elasticity, however, implies that a rise in income will be accompanied by a more than proportionate rise in the quantity demanded of the product concerned ($\eta_y > 1$). This will be the case with the demand for luxury commodities such as holidays abroad, audio equipment, expensive restaurants, and so on. Firms whose demand functions have high income elasticity of demand will pay particular attention to forecasting and tabulating expected levels of future economic activity.

Figure 7.17 shows a set of three Engel curves for a hypothetical household. For non-durable luxuries no expenditure is recorded at the lowest income levels. When expenditure commences it rises faster than income ($\eta_y > 1$). The income elasticity of necessities, however, is less than unity. In the case of durable luxuries, such as colour TVs, η_y is again greater than unity, but the Engel curve is stepped, indicating threshold levels of demand. Up to a certain level of income there is virtually no demand for the product, but beyond it will almost certainly be acquired. Similarly, demand for a second set barely exists until another threshold income level is attained.

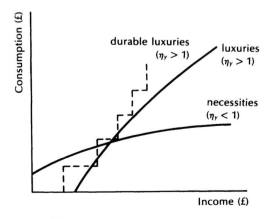

Figure 7.17

7.4.9 Cross-elasticity

The demand for most goods is influenced by the prices of other commodities. Thus the demand for butter is influenced by the price of margarine (a substitute). The demand for cassettes is influenced by the price of tape decks (a complementary good). As the price of cassette decks falls, their quantity demanded will rise and, in turn, the demand for tapes will increase.

Again using equation (7.5) we can calculate the cross-elasticity of demand with respect to a substitute good (η_{xs}) and with respect to a complementary good (η_{xc}) as follows:

$$\eta_{xs} = \frac{\partial Q}{\partial P_s} \frac{P_s}{Q} \text{ and } \eta_{xc} = \frac{\partial Q}{\partial P_c} \frac{P_c}{Q}$$

The cross-elasticity of demand for substitutes is always positive. Q and P_s will always move in the same direction. Conversely, the cross-elasticity of demand for complements is negative. Q and P_c will be inversely related. When two commodities are unrelated, cross-elasticity of demand will be zero or near-zero. Box 7.1 illustrates these concepts in practice.

Box 7.1

A practical example of elasticity analysis

A firm has collected the following data (Table B7.1) from its own records and from market research, where:

> *FIRQ* = its own quarterly sales by volume
> *FIRP* = its own prices
> *RIVP* = the average prices of its competitors
> *AVPR* = the average prices of both itself and its rivals
> *INC* = income per head in the relevant market
> *MKTQ* = total market sales by volume

Table B7.1

OBS.	FIRQ	FIRP	RIVP	AVPR	INC	MKTO
1993Q3	20.0000	5.0000	5.0000	5.0000	2620.0	80.0000
1993Q4	16.0000	5.2000	4.8000	4.8700	2733.0	86.0000
1994Q1	16.0000	5.3200	4.8000	4.8600	2898.0	93.0000
1994Q2	14.0000	5.4800	4.5000	4.7900	3056.0	99.0000
1994Q3	16.0000	5.6000	4.4400	4.7900	3271.0	106.0000
1994Q4	19.0000	5.8000	4.5500	4.8700	3479.0	107.0000
1995Q1	17.0000	6.0300	4.6000	5.0100	3736.0	109.0000
1995Q2	18.0000	6.0100	4.8500	5.3100	3868.0	110.0000
1995Q3	21.0000	5.9200	5.1000	5.5500	4016.0	111.0000
1995Q4	26.0000	5.9000	5.4000	5.7200	4152.0	113.0000
1996Q1	30.0000	5.8500	5.0000	5.7400	4336.0	110.0000
1996Q2	26.0000	5.8000	4.9500	5.5900	4477.0	112.0000
1996Q3	27.0000	5.8500	5.0000	5.5000	4619.0	131.0000
1996Q4	29.0000	5.8000	5.0000	5.4800	4764.0	136.0000

→

Sample period   : 1993Q3 to 1996Q4

Variable(s)	:	FIRQ	FIRP	RIVP	AVPR	INC	MKTQ
Maximum	:	30.0000	6.0300	5.4000	5.7400	4764.0	136.0000
Minimum	:	14.0000	5.0000	4.4400	4.7900	2620.0	80.0000
Mean	:	21.0714	5.6829	4.8564	5.2200	3716.1	107.3571
Std deviation	:	5.4415	.31709	.26494	.36765	718.29160	15.051700
Skewness	:	.39958	−.93419	.10399	.13031	−.11294	.077784
Kurtosis 1	:	−1.3379	−.34210	−.44493	−1.65580	−1.30220	−.090269
Coefficient of variation	:	.25824	.055797	.054555	.070432	.193290	.140200

A glance at the data shows that the firm has a more highly priced product than its competitors and holds a volume market share of approximately one fifth. How can this information be used?

First the firm could compute a linear equation similar to (7.5). A software computer package such as MICROFIT provides output as follows:

Ordinary Least Squares Estimation

****

Dependent variable is FIRQ
14 observations used for estimation from 1993Q3 to 1996Q4

****

Regressor	Coefficient	Standard Error	T-Ratio[Prob]
C	15.9393	20.7687	0.76746[.461]
FIRP	−9.0574	3.1193	−2.9037[.016]
INC	.0085781	.0015457	5.5497[.000]
RIVP	5.0917	2.5816	1.9723[.077]

****

R-Squared	.89759	F-statistic F(3, 10)	29.2161[.000]
R-Bar-Squared	.86687	S.E. of Regression	1.985
Residual Sum of Squares	39.4199	Mean of Dependent Variable	21.071
S.D. of Dependent Variable	5.4415	Maximum of Log-likelihood	−27.111
DW-statistic	1.8137		

****

Chapter 8 describes many of the statistical technicalities. Here we look at the simple results. C, which has a value of 15.9 is the constant α. The estimate of the price coefficient, β_1, has a value of −9.1. The estimate of the income coefficient, β_2, has a value of 0.01, while the estimated coefficient of the price of competing products, β_3, takes on a value of 5.1. All of these estimated β values are statistically significant (the t-statistic takes on a value of approximately 2 or more, ignoring the arithmetic signs). Further, changes in the variables in the equation, FIRP, INC and RIVP, provide a good explanation for any changes in FIRQ. The coefficient of determination, R^2, at nearly 0.9 suggests they 'explain' 90 per cent of any variations in FIRQ. Colloquially the equation provides a 'good fit'.

→

The equation provides two main pieces of information. It can answer 'What if?' questions and it can provide elasticity values.

An example of a 'What if?' question is if the firm wishes to estimate *FIRQ* in 1997, quarter 1, given an assumed income increase to 5000, a *FIRP* rise to £6 and *RIVP* unchanged at £5. Then by substitution:

$$FIRQ = 15.9 - 9.1(6) + 0.01(5000) + 5.1(5)$$

$$= 36.8$$

Examples of firm elasticity calculations at the mean values of the variables are:

$$\eta \quad = -9.1 \times \frac{5.7}{21.1} = -2.5$$

$$\eta_y \quad = 0.01 \times \frac{3716}{21.1} = 1.76$$

$$\eta_{XR} \quad = 5.1 \times \frac{4.9}{21.1} = 1.2$$

As expected price elasticity is negative and cross elasticity is positive.

The firm can also compute a similar set of results for the market as a whole by regressing MKTQ against AVPR and INC. Thus:

Ordinary Least Squares Estimation

****

Dependent variable is MKTQ
14 observations used for estimation from 1993Q3 to 1996Q4

****

Regressor	Coefficient	Standard Error	T-Ratio [Prob]
C	119.5390	20.9141	5.7157 [.000]
AVPR	− 23.1977	5.5567	− 4.1748 [.002]
INC	.029308	.0028442	10.3046 [.000]

****

R-Squared	.94131	F-statistic $F(2, 11)$	88.2126 [.000]
R-Bar-Squared	.93064	S.E. of Regression	3.964
Residual Sum of Squares	172.8549	Mean of Dependent Variable	107.357
S.D. of Dependent Variable	15.0517	Maximum of Log-likelihood	− 37.458
DW-statistic	1.7510		

****

→

Again the coefficients are significant (see the *t*-statistics) and the model is a powerful explanator (see the R^2). The relevant market elasticities at the means are:

$$\eta_M = -23.2 \times \frac{5.2}{107.4} = -1.1$$

$$\eta_{MY} = 0.03 \times \frac{3716}{107.4} = 1.0$$

Firm price elasticity is higher than market-price sensitivity which is to be expected since consumers can always switch to rival's products if firm price rises too much. If the average market price rises a similar amount, consumers would have to either continue buying (albeit in smaller volumes) or switch consumption patterns away to some totally different commodity altogether. Our firm's product is comparatively highly priced so one would expect demand for it to be more income sensitive than demand in the market as a whole. This prediction is also borne out by the results (η_y at 1.76 > η_{MY} at 1.0).

We noted that equation (7.5) could also be expressed as a curvilinear expression, equation (7.7). This involves transforming the data to logarithms. For example in Table B7.2:

LOGFQ = log *FIRQ*

LOGFP = log *FIRP*

LOGRP = log *RIVP* and

LOGY = log *INC*

Table B7.2

OBS.	LOGFQ	LOGFP	LOGRP	LOGY
1993Q3	2.9957	1.6094	1.6094	7.8709
1993Q4	2.7726	1.6487	1.5686	7.9132
1994Q1	2.7726	1.6715	1.5686	7.9718
1994Q2	2.6391	1.7011	1.5041	8.0249
1994Q3	2.7726	1.7228	1.4907	8.0929
1994Q4	2.9444	1.7579	1.5151	8.1545
1995Q1	2.8332	1.7967	1.5261	8.2258
1995Q2	2.8904	1.7934	1.5790	8.2605
1995Q3	3.0445	1.7783	1.6292	8.2980
1995Q4	3.2581	1.7750	1.6864	8.3313
1996Q1	3.4012	1.7664	1.6094	8.3747
1996Q2	3.2581	1.7579	1.5994	8.4067
1996Q3	3.2958	1.7664	1.6094	8.4379
1996Q4	3.3673	1.7579	1.6094	8.4688

$\rightarrow$

If we now carry out a linear regression on these variables the output is as follows:

Ordinary Least Squares Estimation

****

Dependent variable is LOGFQ
14 observations used for estimation from 1993Q3 to 1996Q4

****

Regressor	Coefficient	Standard Error	T-Ratio [Prob]
C	−6.7558	1.0913	−6.1903 [.000]
LOGFP	−2.7549	.92200	−2.9879 [.014]
LOGY	1.5119	.29224	5.1735 [.000]
LOGRP	1.3645	.58910	2.3162 [.043]

****

R-Squared	.89954	F-statistic $F(3, 10)$	29.8472 [.000]
R-Bar-Squared	.86940	S.E. of Regression	.09200
Residual Sum of Squares	.084653	Mean of Dependent Variable	3.017
S.D. of Dependent Variable	.25460	Maximum of Log-likelihood	15.892
DW-statistic	1.6954		

****

This is a statistically more appropriate and probably more accurate estimate of firm demand than our first equation. All of the t-statistics rise above their non-logarithmic equivalents. The same 'what if' exercises can be carried out as before. The elasticities, however, are easier to obtain, and are constant, not varying by the values chosen for *FIRQ*, *FIRP*, *RIVP* or *INC*. They are simply the coefficients (see page 178). Thus:

$$\eta = -2.8$$
$$\eta_Y = 1.5 \text{ and}$$
$$\eta_{XR} = 1.4$$

7.5 Conclusions

In this chapter the theory of demand has been outlined. The first law of demand: that quantity demanded is inversely related to price (other things equal) was stated and explained. (Alleged exceptions such as 'snob' goods or 'prestige' goods assume that the characteristics of the good as perceived by the consumer change as prices change: other things are not equal. Similarly, Giffen goods – if they exist – confuse income and substitution effects. The law of demand relates only to substitution effects. A further 'exception' was mentioned when consumer expectations were discussed. If people buy more today because they expect prices to be higher tomorrow, even if today's price is unchanged, then the first law is actually affirmed not denied.

Recall that 'price' is relative price. Relative to expected prices, today's prices are lower and consistent with the first law of demand – people will buy more.)

The second law of demand, that consumers will be more responsive to a price change in the long than in the short run was also mentioned but not detailed. Long-run price elasticity is greater than short-run price elasticity. First, it takes time for people to adjust their buying patterns. Second, time must pass before people notice a price change. Thus a rise in home heating costs will result first in people cutting consumption of the relevant fuel. In the longer term, however, they will switch their fuel source and change the type of heating equipment they have in their houses: so cutting the consumption of the relatively expensive fuel still further.

In Chapter 8 it will be shown how the principles learned here can be put into effect.

Note

1. Since $\Delta Q / \Delta P$ is negative, η always has a negative value. Conventionally, however, the algebraic sign is ignored.

Bibliography

Baird, C.W. (1975) *Prices and Markets: Microeconomics*, West.

Baumol, W.J. (1977) *Economic Theory and Operations Analysis*, 4th edn, Prentice Hall.

Becker, G.S. (1962) 'Irrational behaviour and economic theory', *Journal of Political Economy*, vol. 70.

Lancaster, K. (1966) 'A new approach to consumer theory', *Journal of Political Economy*, vol. 74.

Liebenstein, H. (1950) 'Bandwagon, snob and Veblen effects in the theory of consumer's demand', *Quarterly Journal of Economics*, vol. 64, 2.

Palda, K.S. (1969) *Economic Analysis for Marketing Decisions*, Prentice Hall.

Pesaran, M.H. and Pesaran, B. (1991) *Microfit 3.0*, Oxford University Press.

Veblen, T. (1899) *The Theory of the Leisure Class*, Allen & Unwin, 1971.

Chapter 8

Techniques for demand estimation

In Chapter 2 it was shown that to maximise profits a manager must produce that output at which $MR = MC$. In the last chapter it was shown that one method of deriving the MR function was to estimate the coefficients in the demand function, make price the subject of the equation, multiply it by Q and differentiate with respect to Q. If the value of MR was required at a particular value of Q, that Q value could be substituted into the MR function, or alternatively, the value of P and the price elasticity of demand, as in equation (7.11). However, knowledge of demand price elasticity requires knowledge of the coefficient of P. The coefficients of the other independent variables must also be known to predict their profit-maximising levels (if they are policy variables) or to predict the likely effects on TR and profits of changes in these variables (if they are exogenous).

The question arises as to how these coefficients may be estimated. This is the subject of this chapter. Chapter 9 will include a section on the measurement of cost functions, so the reader then has an idea as to how he might determine the profit-maximising values of certain policy variables for his firm.

8.1 Survey and experimental methods

These techniques may be used to derive values of the quantity demanded at different values of the independent variables. In the case of surveys, these quantities relate to intended purchases, whereas in the case of experiments they relate to actual purchases under known or partially known conditions. (Often a firm may have to estimate the values of competing firms' policy variables rather than receiving this information from competitors.) In either case sufficient information may be collected from which to estimate arc elasticities of demand by deriving values of quantity demanded at say, different prices, whilst holding constant all other variables which could affect demand. Where the experiment is in the field and not in the laboratory, however, the manager is unlikely to be able to derive even one elasticity of demand from the information gained, since other relevant variables in addition to, say, own price, are likely to have varied when price was changed.

These techniques give arc rather than point elasticities. They do not provide us with coefficients in the demand function. Hence they do not prescribe a method for predicting the quantity demanded for combinations of values of explanatory variables other than those on which the manager already has information. The most commonly used methods of deriving the coefficients of a firm's demand function *given* the information which has been collected by, for example, surveys of consumers, experts suppliers or by experiments, come under the heading of 'regression techniques'.

8.2 Regression techniques

In this section we firstly explain the technique when the quantity demanded in a period, t, is hypothesised to depend on only one independent variable, say price, in the same period. Secondly, the method is generalised to the case of several independent variables. Thirdly, some complications are explained. Fourthly, the identification problem is considered; and fifthly, two examples are explained.

8.2.1 Overview

Suppose it is believed that the demand function for a product is of the form:

$$Q^D = \alpha + \beta P \tag{8.1}$$

where Q^D denotes quantity demanded and P denotes price.

Observations on the price and corresponding quantity demanded in each of, say, 30 weeks have been collected. We may plot these observations as in Figure 8.1. To obtain a value for each of α and β we wish to find a straight line which according

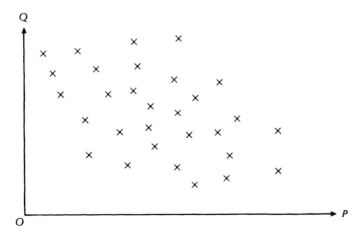

Figure 8.1

to some criterion 'best fits' these points. One of the most commonly used criteria is the method of ordinary least squares (OLS). The use of OLS is based on a statistical model.

In this statistical model it is assumed that, for any given value of price, P_t, the corresponding quantity demanded, Q_t, is given by the equation:

$$Q_t = \alpha + \beta P_t + \varepsilon_t \qquad (8.2)$$

where ε_t is a stochastic term. That is, on any one occasion (i.e. value of t) the value of ε is determined by chance, but the distribution of its possible values is assumed to have certain characteristics (to be explained later). In fact, ε could take on any one of an infinite number of *possible* values. Therefore, for a given price, Q_t could also take on one of an infinite number of *possible* values.

But why *in practice* might we think that a stochastic term should be added to equation (8.1)? Well, for every observation to fit equation (8.1) we would require that Q_t is affected only by P_t, that all persons in the groups to which the equation relates always behave exactly according to the equation (in the sense of always having the same values of α and β), that the true function is linear, and that all observed values of Q_t and P_t are measured completely accurately.

In reality, these conditions are unlikely to hold. Firstly, it is likely that equation (8.1) omits variables which affect Q_t, such as advertising and so on. For completely accurate representation of behaviour the model would have to include every variable which could possibly affect Q_t. So the equation would have to include a very large number of variables. Either in theory or in practice it may not be possible to include them all and to estimate their coefficients, for several reasons. For example, some of these variables may not be known. Secondly, there may be no technique to measure them – for example, tastes, expectations, and so on. Thirdly, the influence of each may be so small that conventional computational techniques would round their coefficient down to zero. Another major reason why the observations may not exactly fit the hypothetical model is that the true relationship may be nonlinear. Finally, the observed values may have been inaccurately measured. So even if equation (8.1) were the true relationship, the erroneous observations would misfit it.

Returning to the statistical model, equation (8.2) may be represented graphically, as in Figure 8.2. In the figure, equation (8.2) is represented by the continuous line which, let us assume, could theoretically be fitted to *every possible* sample of pairs of values of P_t and Q_t generated by consumers' behaviour. Figure 8.2 also shows a pair of P, Q values from this infinite number of possible pairs. For any such pair, for a given value of P_t, the value of Q differs from that on the continuous line by ε_t. For example, for P_1 the statistical model shows a value for Q_1 of $Q_1^* (= \alpha + \beta P_1)$ whereas the value in the sample which corresponds to P_1 is Q_1. Notice that Q_1 differs from Q_1^* by ε_1.

We have said that the continuous line in Figure 8.2 represented the linear equation which fits *every possible* sample of pairs of values of P_t and Q_t. Such a collection of values is called the *population*. The *population* of P_t and Q_t values is hypothetical in the sense that in practice no one could possibly observe every pair:

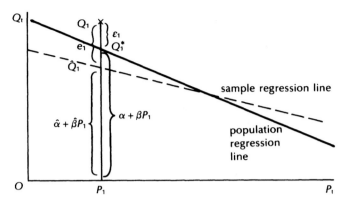

Figure 8.2

there is an infinite number of them. What is observed is a sample of P_t, Q_t values such as, for example, over the last 30 weeks. However, when using OLS, we assume that equation (8.2) represents the process generating each sample. Furthermore, statisticians have proved that, given certain characteristics of the ε term in equation (8.2), we can make inferences about the α and β using merely a *sample of P_t, Q_t values. The manager's aim therefore is to estimate values of α and β which relate to the population of P_t and Q_t values using only a given sample of observations.*

Suppose we 'fit' a straight line to the sample data. It is highly unlikely that each P_t, Q_t pair will lie on the line: there will be an error called a residual, e_t. For example, in Figure 8.2, if P_1, Q_1 is an observed pair of values, Q_1 differs from the value predicted by the sample regression line for P_1 by the amount e_1. The residual values reflect both the factors which were assumed to affect ε_1 and the difference between the line fitted to the sample data and that assumed to apply to the population. These two lines differ because the former is calculated from a *sample* of observations, whereas the latter relates to the population of *all possible values*.

For clarity, a model which generates the *population* is denoted:

$$Q_t = \alpha + \beta P_t + \varepsilon_t \tag{8.3}$$

The equation which has been 'fitted' to a *sample* is denoted:

$$Q_t = \hat{\alpha} + \hat{\beta} P_t + e_t \tag{8.4}$$

Since $\hat{\alpha}$ and $\hat{\beta}$, pronounced 'alpha hat' and 'beta hat' respectively, may not equal α and β respectively, for a given value of P_t, e_t may not be equal ε_t.

8.2.2 Procedural stages

When using regression analysis the procedural stages are as follows:

1. *Choice of variables:* in this stage the manager decides on the variables which he

believes are included in the population model. A manager may derive a list of the variables to be included in a number of ways. For example, economic theory of the consumer, as explained in Chapter 7, predicts that an individual's demand for a good is related to its price, the prices of other goods, his or her income and tastes. Tastes can rarely be measured, but since advertising of own and rival products may affect tastes, advertising expenditure may be included instead. Alternatively, a priori reasoning or evidence either from casual observation or from studies of the demand for other goods or services may suggest further variables. Typically an assumed model would include the above variables. Additional variables, which may differ according to the product of interest, may be added. For example, the demand for volume drinks and ice cream is likely to be related to the weather, whereas that for washing-up liquid is not. The demand for a consumer durable is likely to be related to the interest rate on consumer credit and anticipated future income. The demand for investment goods is likely to be related to company profitability. For consumer products population may be a relevant variable. Finally, it should be noted that, for reasons to be explained, the identity of variables to be included in the model may be restricted by statistical considerations.

2. *Form of the model*: at this stage the manager decides on the functional form of the assumed model. Many alternative forms are available. Two examples, the linear and multiplicative forms, were discussed in Chapter 7 (see equations (7.5) and (7.6) respectively). If the manager is to use the OLS technique, his choice of form is constrained to one which, in the version to be estimated, is linear. Hence OLS can be applied to the multiplicative demand function (equation 7.6) because it can be converted to a linear form by taking logarithms of both sides. However, some functional forms cannot be linearised.

3. *Obtaining the data*: for some variables, e.g. personal disposable income, data can be obtained from government agencies (e.g. the Central Statistical Office) or private data-collecting companies (e.g. advertising data from MEAL).[1] But for some variables the data may not be available at all, or at a sufficiently disaggregate level for the model. In these cases it may have to be collected by survey or experiment.

4. *Estimating the parameters of the model*: suppose that the manager strongly believes that the statistical population model relating every possible quantity demanded to given values of his product's price can be represented by:

$$Q_t = \alpha + \beta P_t + \varepsilon_t$$

(We have deliberately chosen only one right-hand side variable for simplicity.) Estimates of α and β, $\hat{\alpha}$ and $\hat{\beta}$ respectively can be calculated by certain formulae, the *OLS estimators* of α and β. These estimates are based on finding those values of $\hat{\alpha}$ and $\hat{\beta}$ which minimise the sum of *squared* residual values. (Remember that for a given value of P, the residual is the difference between an observed value of Q and that predicted by the sample as shown in Figure 8.2.) Hence:

$$e_t = Q_t - \hat{\alpha} - \hat{\beta} P_t \text{ (from equation 8.4)}$$

$$\Rightarrow \sum_{t=1}^{n} e_t^2 = \Sigma (Q_t - \hat{\alpha} - \hat{\beta} P_t)^2$$

Differentiating with respect to $\hat{\alpha}$ and $\hat{\beta}$ and solving for $\hat{\beta}$ and $\hat{\alpha}$ gives[2]

$$\hat{\beta} = \frac{n\left(\sum_{t=1}^{n} P_t \times Q_t\right) - \left(\sum_{t=1}^{n} P_t\right)\left(\sum_{t=1}^{n} Q_t\right)}{n\left(\sum_{t=1}^{n} P_t^2\right) - \left(\sum_{t=1}^{n} P_t\right)^2} \tag{8.5}$$

and

$$\hat{\alpha} = \frac{\Sigma Q_t}{n} - \hat{\beta}\frac{\Sigma P_t}{n} \tag{8.6}$$

into which equation (8.5) or the estimated value of $\hat{\beta}$ is substituted. An example of the calculation of $\hat{\alpha}$ and $\hat{\beta}$ using these estimators is given in Table 8.1.

In practice, a manager would not perform these calculations by hand but would use one of a large number of statistical packages which are available for use on personal computers, mainframes or both. Examples of such packages are: TSP, MICROFIT, Rats, Shazam, Mystat, SAS and SPSS, all of which have PC versions. Such packages not only produce values of $\hat{\alpha}$ and $\hat{\beta}$ but also a large number of interpretive statistics which may be used to assess the applicability of the population model to the situation in hand.

The fifth stage is to interpret the estimated sample regression line. This is sufficiently important to occupy an entire section of our chapter, but is rather difficult. The reader may skip this section with only a small loss of continuity.

Table 8.1

Q	P	PQ	P²
10	2	20	4
7	3	21	9
8	6	48	36
6	7	42	49
7	10	70	100
4	11	44	121
42	39	245	319

$$\bar{Q} = 7 \quad \bar{P} = 6.5$$

Using formulae (8.5) and (8.6)

$$\hat{\beta} = \frac{6(245) - (39)(42)}{6(319) - (39)^2} = \frac{1470 - 1638}{1914 - 1521} = -0.427$$

$$\hat{\alpha} = 7 + (0.427)(6.5) = 9.776$$

$$Q = 9.776 - 0.427P$$

This example is used to illustrate the calculation of $\hat{\alpha}$ and $\hat{\beta}$ from sample data. When used in practice, many more observations would be needed.

8.2.3 Interpretative statistics

We begin this section by considering in depth the assumptions which form the classical linear regression model, the statistical model behind OLS.

Assumptions of the classical linear regression model

When using a model like:

$$Q_t = \alpha + \beta P_t + \varepsilon_t$$

We make the following assumptions about the way the P_t values are generated:

(A1) For any given set of values of t, the values of P_t are prescribed (or fixed).

Therefore the corresponding values of Q_t consist of the sum of two parts:

(a) a prescribed quantity, $\alpha + \beta P_t$; and
(b) an unpredictable deviation from (a), ε_t, which, a priori, can take on any one of an infinite number of possible values. The probability of each value of ε_t occurring is given by a particular probability distribution.[3]

We also make assumptions about ε_t. If these assumptions together with (A1) are valid, then one can make inferences about the *population values* of α and β from *mere sample observations*. We now outline these assumptions because if real world data suggests they are not valid then very serious difficulties arise in the interpretation of a manager's estimates of α and β. The assumptions made are:

(A2) For any given value of t, the possible values of ε_t are normally distributed.
(A3) For any given value of t, the expected value of ε_t is zero.
(A4) The variances of the distributions of ε_ts for different values of t are all the same.

The implications of these assumptions may be represented graphically as in Figure 8.3 where three specific values of P_t have been chosen. The straight line is simply a demand curve and the curved line at each price shows the distribution of the errors made when predicting quantity. If all the possible hypothetical population values of ε_t associated with each P_t could be recorded and their distribution constructed, it would be normal in each case and have the same variance, and a mean of zero.

(A5) The ε_ts associated with one value of P_t are independent of those associated with any other value of P_t.

This implies that the values of the ε_ts at different ts are uncorrelated. If the population demand curve underpredicts demand in one period, for example because of a sudden fall in a competitor's price, this does not make it any more likely that it will under or over estimate it in the next period.

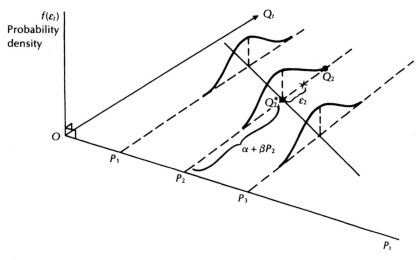

Figure 8.3

These assumptions allow the population model to be written as

$$E(Q_t) = \alpha + \beta P_t \qquad (8.7)$$

where $E(Q_t)$ is the mean of all possible Q_t values given P_t. Therefore the straight line in Figure 8.3 which can be labelled as equation (8.7), the population model, cuts each dotted line corresponding to a specific P_t at the average value of Q_t associated with it. So Q_2^* is the mean of all possible Q_2 values which are associated with P_2.

Significance of the coefficients

If different samples are taken from the population and the value for $\hat{\beta}$ calculated in each case they are almost certain to differ from each other and from that which would fit the population. Similarly, this is likely for $\hat{\alpha}$.

It can be shown that, given certain of the assumptions above:

- if every possible sample of size n is taken and the values of $\hat{\alpha}$ and $\hat{\beta}$ calculated for each, the average of the $\hat{\beta}$ values would equal the value of the desired population coefficient (and similarly for $\hat{\alpha}$); and
- the calculated values of $\hat{\alpha}$ and $\hat{\beta}$ from repeated samples are *normally distributed* if n is large (conventionally 'large' is over 30).

Therefore the distribution of, say, $\hat{\beta}$ values calculated from many different samples may be shown as in Figure 8.4. In addition the standard deviation of this distribution of $\hat{\beta}$ values and that of the distribution of $\hat{\alpha}$ values from the sample data may be estimated. These values are called standard errors and we will denote them as $S_{\hat{\alpha}}$ and $S_{\hat{\beta}}$ for $\hat{\alpha}$ and $\hat{\beta}$ respectively.

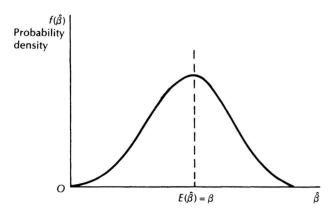

Figure 8.4

In practice, estimates of α and β are gained from a single sample and each sample may give a different estimate. Therefore the manager wishes to know whether, in the light of a single sample, she or he can accept the hypothesis that α and/or β are really specific values which she or he may choose. This is done using a 't' test.

If $\hat{\alpha}$ and $\hat{\beta}$ are calculated from a sample, one can transform these estimates to form t-statistics:

$$t_{\hat{\alpha}} = \frac{\hat{\alpha} - \alpha^*}{S_{\hat{\alpha}}} \sim t_{\phi = n - K} \text{ for } \hat{\alpha} \tag{8.8}$$

$$t_{\hat{\beta}} = \frac{\hat{\beta} - \beta^*}{S_{\hat{\beta}}} \sim t_{\phi = n - K} \text{ for } \hat{\beta} \tag{8.9}$$

each having $n - K$ degrees of freedom where n is the sample size and K is the number of estimated parameters. In the case of our single independent variable model and $K = 2$ ($\hat{\alpha}$ and $\hat{\beta}$).

The t-distribution is a probability distribution.[4] That is, the area between any two values of t is the probability that a value of t derived from a random sample will lie between these values, the total area under the curve equalling one. This point is represented diagrammatically in Figure 8.5 which shows a t-distribution (with $\phi = 20$ degrees of freedom). The probability that a value of t exceeds 2.086, $P(t > 2.086)$, is 0.025. Similarly

$$P(-t < -2.086) = 0.025$$

because the t-distribution is symmetric. These and other values of t can be obtained from Student's t-tables in any statistics text.

To test the hypothesis that the population value, β, is a specific value, β^*, despite the value estimated from the sample being $\hat{\beta}$, one tests the null hypothesis:

$$H_0: \beta = \beta^*$$

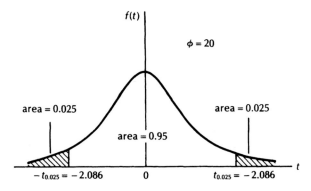

Figure 8.5

against one of the following alternative hypotheses:

H_1: $\beta = \beta^*$ two-tail test
H_1: $\beta > \beta^*$ one-tail test
H_1: $\beta < \beta^*$ one-tail test

depending on which alternative relationship is of interest. In practice H_1 is the hypothesis whose validity we wish to establish whereas H_0 is everything else.

Next, we calculate the t-statistic of equation (8.9) and compare it with the critical t-value from the theoretical t-distribution (given in the tables in any statistics text). The comparison made depends on which alternative hypothesis we put forward.

Suppose the manager wishes to know whether the coefficient for income equals $+0.8$ or whether it differs (either being larger or smaller) from this. That is suppose H_1 is $\beta \neq 0.8$, the 'true' value of β is larger or smaller than 0.8. If the calculated t-statistic in absolute value exceeds the critical t value, where

$$P(t > t_{\text{critical}} \text{ or } -t < -t_{\text{critical}}) = 0.05,$$

for example, if $t > 2.086$ in Figure 8.5, then the probability that the calculated t-value would be observed if $\beta = 0.8$ is less than 0.05. So if we have such a t-value, and we reject the hypothesis that $\beta = 0.8$, there is a probability of less than 0.05 that we have done the wrong thing. If we accept that a probability of rejecting a hypothesis when it is true (a 'type I error') of 0.05 is sufficiently low to accept this risk, we reject H_0: $\beta = \beta^*$ 'at the 5% level' and accept H_1. Notice that we have compared our calculated t with both positive and negative values of t_{critical}. This was done because our alternative hypothesis was β is larger or smaller than β^* ($\beta \neq \beta^*$) and so it did not matter if β fell in either tail of the theoretical distribution.

Suppose, on the other hand, the manager wishes to know whether the coefficient for income equals 0.8 or whether it is larger than this, then he is adopting the second alternative hypothesis: H_1: $\beta > 0.8$. Then he would only be interested in whether or not the population value of β is greater than 0.8, not whether it is greater or smaller. In this case the t-statistic is compared with a t_{critical} which cuts an area of 0.05 from only the right-hand tail of the theoretical t-distribution. If the sample $\hat{\beta}$

were less than β^* and so the calculated t were negative, the test would not be performed: one could not accept H_1 that β is greater than β^* regardless of the value of t.

Finally, if H_1 was: $\beta < \beta^*$ and if the calculated t was negative (because $\beta - \beta^*$ was negative) this would be compared with minus $t_{critical}$ which cuts 0.05 from the *left hand* tail of the t-distribution. The same procedure is used to test corresponding hypotheses about α.

Often the manager may wish to test whether or not β is equal to or differs from zero. That is he may wish to test: H_0: $\beta = 0$ against H_1: $\beta \neq 0$. This would be done by following the above procedure and substituting $\beta^* = 0$ into the t-calculation. The economic relevance of this test is that if one could reject H_0, then the independent variable would be accepted as affecting the dependent variable. If H_0 could not be rejected, then one would accept that the independent variable does not affect quantity demanded. So even if the estimated $\hat{\beta}$ gave a large elasticity of demand (see Section 7.3) we could not reject the idea that, because the scatter of observations was so wide, and hence $S_{\hat{\beta}}$ so large, the elasticity was in fact zero. The importance of this test will become especially apparent when multiple regression is explained and some independent variables, which are less likely than price to be related to Q_t are also included. Examples of the testing of β are shown in Box 8.1.

Goodness of fit

The coefficient of determination, R^2, allows one to examine how closely the estimated equation fits the sample data. Suppose we plot sample observations of Q_t and P_t, one combination of which is shown in Figure 8.6. For each observation the difference between the observed Q_t and the mean of the sample values, $\bar{Q}$, may

---

Box 8.1

Consider a company which is considering the possibility of applying for a franchise to operate trains following the privatisation of British Rail. The Marketing Department wishes to discover how sensitive rail travel is to the price of rail tickets and the prices of competing forms of travel. Initially the analyst strongly believes that the quantity of rail travel demanded is related only to its own real price (price of rail tickets relative to a price index of all goods and services). Over the last five years, the price of rail tickets has risen, but so has that of goods in general, so following our considerations in Chapter 7 the relevant price is that of rail travel divided by the price of all other goods. (Since rail travel is a relatively small proportion of expenditure we have approximated the price of all other goods by the price of all goods).

$\rightarrow$

The marketing analyst has collected data from the *Monthly Digest of Statistics* and has estimated a regression equation using MICROFIT. A portion of the results are shown below.

Ordinary Least Squares Estimation

****

Dependent variable is   PASS
25 observations used for estimation from 1987Q1 to 1993Q1

****

Regressor	Coefficient	Standard Error	T-Ratio [Prob]
C	14880.0	1741.9	8.5422 [.000]
RPRAIL	− 6471.1	1682.0	− 3.8473 [.001]

****

PASS   = British Rail and London Underground Transport passenger kilometres in each quarter
C   = constant
RPRAIL = Retail price index of rail travel/retail price index for all items

The meaning of the variables is given in the table. The figures in the column headed Coefficient are the estimates of α and β. The analyst wishes to know whether he or she can be confident that a change in the relative price of rail travel will have an effect on demand. That is can the analyst reject the idea that β, the population coefficient on price, equals zero and accept the view that β differs from zero. To do this the analyst states the null and alternative hypotheses:

H_0: $\beta = 0$

H_1: $\beta \neq 0$

The alternative hypothesis implies a two-tail test is needed. Setting the probability of a type I error at 5%, the analyst looks up the critical value of the t-distribution which has $25 - 2 = 23$ degrees of freedom such that the tails at each end of the distribution each contain 2.5% of the total area under the distribution. From a statistics text he or she finds this value to be 2.069. The analyst then calculates the t-statistic for β:

$$t_{\phi = 23} = \frac{\hat{\beta} - 0}{S_{\hat{\beta}}} = \frac{-6471.1}{1682.0} = -3.8473$$

Clearly $t = 3.85$ is greater than $t_{critical} = 2.069$. Therefore the null hypothesis is rejected and the alternative hypothesis is accepted. The analyst concludes that relative price is negatively related to the number of passenger kilometres travelled.

Notice that the results from the software package include the t-statistic under the null hypothesis that $\beta = 0$ and also the two-tail probability that a value larger or smaller than the t-statistic would be observed. If this probability is less than 0.05 (i.e. 5%) then the null hypothesis is rejected.

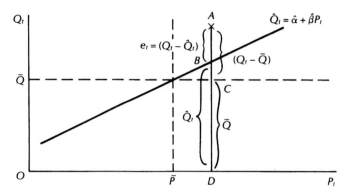

Figure 8.6

be calculated. These differences are due to differences in P_t and to differences in e_ts as is shown in the figure. This may be understood by noting that:

AC	$= BC$	$+ AB$
$(Q_t - \bar{Q})$	$= (\hat{Q}_t - \bar{Q})$	$+ e_t$
Difference between actual and mean	Difference between predicted (that explained by regression line) and mean	Residual

In general terms we wish to measure how much of the total variation in AC values is made up of variation in BC values (that is changes predicted by the sample line) and how much is made up of variation in AB values (that is unexplained residuals).

To do this we use the coefficient of determination which is defined as the proportion of total variation which is explained by the estimated regression line and hence by variations in P_t:

$$R^2 = \frac{\sum_{t=1}^{n} (\hat{Q}_t - \bar{Q})^2}{\sum_{t=1}^{n} (Q_t - \bar{Q})^2} \qquad (8.10)$$

Hence an R^2 of 0.8 means that 80% of the total variation in the sample data about its mean was accounted for by variation in P_t about its mean. If our observations all lie on the regression line, $Q_t = \hat{Q}_t$, so by equation (8.10) $R^2 = 1$. The regression line explains 100% of the variation in Q_t. Since all of the points lie on the regression line, this is the value of R^2 one would expect.

At the other extreme R^2 could equal zero. A necessary condition for this is that changes in the value of P_t would not lead to a change in the predicted value of Q_t, $\hat{Q}_t$. That is, the sample regression line would have a slope of zero: $\hat{\beta} = 0$. Then, the BC values of Figure 8.6 would be zero, so from equation (8.10) R^2 would be zero. Examples of cases where the sample regression line would have a zero slope are shown in Figure 8.7. Notice that in Figure 8.7b, despite $R^2 = 0$, there is a systematic relationship between P_t and Q_t, but it is not a linear one.

F-test

On pages 195–8 we explained how, with reference to equation (8.2), the null hypothesis H_0: $\beta = 0$ could be tested using a t-test. A different test statistic, the F-statistic, could also be used to test exactly the same hypothesis against the two-tail alternative. Briefly, it can be shown that:

$$\frac{\Sigma(\hat{Q}_t - \bar{Q})^2/(K-1)}{\Sigma(Q_t - \hat{Q})^2/(N-K)} \sim F_{\phi 1 = K-1, \ \phi 2 = N-K}$$

where K = number of estimated constants
$\quad\quad N$ = number of observations

The F-statistic has a different probability distribution for every combination of degrees of freedom. Given the degrees of freedom, a calculated value of F is compared with a critical value which cuts off an area under one tail of the F-distribution equal to the chosen probability of a type I error. This means that, if this probability is set at 5% then, given the null hypothesis, the chance of obtaining an F-value in excess of $F_{critical}$ is 5% or less. This is too low a probability to accept, so we reject the null hypothesis with the probability of having done the wrong thing of 5% or less.

For example, consider the demand calculations in Box 8.1. The null hypothesis is H_0: $\beta = 0$ against H_1: $\beta \neq 0$. The probability of a type I error is set at 5%. The $F_{calculated}$ is 14.80 with $(2-1) = 1$ and $(25-2) = 23$ degrees of freedom. The value of $F_{critical, 1, 23} = 4.28$ (see any statistics text). Since $F_{calculated} > F_{critical}$ the null hypothesis is rejected. Again we conclude that price is negatively related to passenger kilometres travelled.

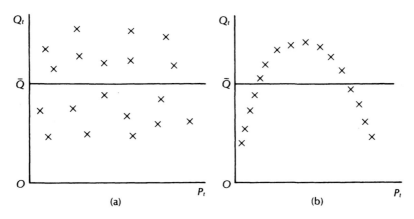

Figure 8.7

This F-test allows an inference to be made concerning R^2. For each sample of P and Q values an R^2 may be calculated. These will almost certainly differ between samples: there will be a population of an infinite number of possible values of R^2. How does the manager know, despite a R^2 above zero, if the R^2 of the population is zero. The answer is as follows. We argued above that if $\beta = 0$ then $R^2 = 0$, so we say that if $\beta = 0$, R^2 *in the population* is zero. That is, none of the variation in Q is explained by variation in P. If the null hypothesis can be rejected, R^2 in the population is not equal to zero and variation in P 'explains' a statistically significant proportion of the variation in Q. So the F-test above is a test of the null hypothesis that R^2 in the population is zero.

8.2.4 Multiple regression

So far we have discussed demand functions with only one explanatory variable. But the theory from Chapter 7 and *ad hoc* theorising suggest that the quantity demanded is likely to be determined by several independent variables in addition to price, such as advertising expenditure, consumers' incomes, etc. The use of OLS estimators in such cases is just an extension of the one explanatory variable case. A population model assumed by a manager might be:

$$Q_t = \alpha + \beta_1 P_t + \beta_2 A_t + \beta_3 Y_t + \varepsilon_t$$

where P_t = price of own good in period t; A_t = advertising expenditure in period t; Y_t = consumers' income; ε_t = error term; and values of α, β_1, β_2 and β_3 are estimated from a sample of observations. The estimated relationship is:

$$Q_t = \hat{\alpha} + \hat{\beta}_1 P_t + \hat{\beta}_2 A_t + \hat{\beta}_3 Y_t + e_t \qquad (8.11)$$

The *OLS* estimators of the coefficients are derived in the same way in these cases as in the one independent variable case. e_t is made the subject of equation (8.11), both sides of the equation are squared, summed and differentiated with respect to α, β_1, β_2, etc. The assumptions of the statistical model are analogous to those for the single-variable case, with two additions. These are, firstly, that there is no exact linear relationship between any two independent variables and, secondly, that the number of observations on each variable exceeds the number of coefficients to be estimated.

In addition, as in the single-variable case, each sample is likely to give a different value for the same coefficient. To test whether the population value differs significantly from a given value, the same procedures are used, although the formulae for the denominator of each t-statistic, $S_{\hat{\alpha}}$, $S_{\hat{\beta}_1}$, $S_{\hat{\beta}_2}$ etc., incorporate terms which relate to the additional variables. The F-statistic may also be used to test the null hypothesis H_0: $\beta_1 = \beta_2 = \beta_3 = \ldots = 0$ against the alternative hypothesis that this is not true. If this null hypothesis is accepted, the manager would conclude that any variation in any or all of the independent variables would have no effect on Q. If the null hypothesis is rejected, then the manager would conclude that the variation in any or all of the independent variables would have an effect on Q.

The R^2 may be used to indicate how well the estimated equation fits the sample data but notice that if the number of explanatory variables increases, R^2 will stay the same or increase. Refer back to Figure 8.6. Intuitively, if an additional explanatory variable is included in the estimated equation, the value of e_t will, on average, decrease because part of this value is now being explained by changes in the additional variable. Thus we could add as many additional variables as our number of observations would allow and so increase the R^2 regardless of whether or not the additional variables are statistically significant. A partial solution to this difficulty is to use the adjusted R^2, denoted $\bar{R}^2$, which is defined as follows:

$$\bar{R}^2 = 1 - \left(\frac{N-1}{N-K}\right)(1-R^2)$$

If more explanatory variables are included, given the number of observations, $N - K$ will decrease so the value of the first bracket becomes larger and R^2 becomes smaller if R^2 stays the same.

8.2.5 Violations of assumptions

In practice, the behaviour patterns of consumers may not correspond to the assumptions of the statistical model. In these situations the statistical tests we have outlined are not valid. In particular there are the problems of autocorrelation, heteroscedasticity and multicollinearity.

Autocorrelation

Autocorrelation is said to occur when the population values do not fulfil assumption (A5) that the ε_ts associated with any one value of P_t are independent of those associated with any other values of P_t. (If P_t takes on only one value per t, then autocorrelation would occur if ε_t was correlated with ε_{t-1}.) If we take the residuals, the e_ts, as proxies for the ε_ts of the population we can illustrate the phenomenon as follows. If the model's over- or underprediction varied cyclically about zero, e.g. due to the competing price changing in a cyclical manner, the inaccuracy this month would be correlated with that for next month, the month after that, etc. Autocorrelation is then said to exist.

If the error in this period is correlated only with that of last period, then *first order* autocorrelation is said to occur. If the error of this period is correlated with that in the last period *and* in the previous period too, *second order* is said to exist.

Further understanding of the nature of autocorrelation can be gained by considering how it can be detected. One can distinguish between positive and negative autocorrelation. Positive autocorrelation occurs when, as claimed above, an error in one period is relatively high and so is that in the next period, or when an error in one period is relatively low, and so is that in the next period. Hence if we plotted e_ts against time (and taking e_ts as proxies for ε_ts) we would expect a 'herd like' pattern. [5] Such a case is shown in Figure 8.8.

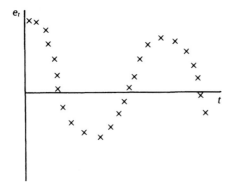

Figure 8.8

Since autocorrelation can vary in degree, examining a figure may not give a very clear indication of its existence. Fortunately, a more accurate test for first order autocorrelation is available: the Durbin–Watson test. The DW statistic is:

$$d = \frac{\sum_{t=2}^{n} (e_t - e_{t-1})^2}{\sum_{t=1}^{n} e_t^2}$$

It can be shown that if the e_ts are free of first order autocorrelation then $d = 2$. However, the test is slightly different from comparing the calculated d with 2. The following rules have been established where $d^* =$ the calculated value of d:

if $d^* < d_L$: accept that first order positive autocorrelation exists
if $d^* > d_u$: accept that no first order autocorrelation exists
if $d_L < d^* < d_u$: the test is inconclusive

where d_u and d_L are given in the DW statistic table in any econometric text for the relevant number of observations, n, and number of independent variables, K'. (We have considered only the commonest type of autocorrelation: positive. Tests for negative autocorrelation are similar – see the Bibliography. Tests in addition to the DW test are also available.)

If autocorrelation exists, then the variance of the $\hat{\beta}$ values which could be derived from every different sample of P_t and Q_t would be likely to be underestimated. Since this is the denominator in the t-statistic relating to the significance of the difference between the estimated β in our sample and that of the population, this t-statistic is likely to be overestimated. So the t-statistic might suggest we should reject the idea that, say, $\beta = 0$, when in fact we should not.

Several methods of reducing autocorrelation have been proposed depending on its cause. In the competitor's price example above the cause was the omission of an important autocorrelated variable. In this case one should add the missing term. If the cause is that one has estimated a linear equation when a multiplicative equation would be more appropriate then the latter should be estimated. If, however, we believe the autocorrelation would not be solved in these ways, various methods of estimating first difference equations can be used.

Heteroscedasticity

Heteroscedasticity occurs when the population values do not fulfil assumption (A4): that is the ε_is associated with each P_t have the same variance. For example, if in the context of the model, $Q_t = \alpha + \beta P_t + \varepsilon_t$, the population variance of the quantity demanded was larger at higher values of price than at lower values, heteroscedasticity would exist. The possible Q_t values would be more dispersed around the regression line at higher levels of P_t than at lower levels of P_t, as shown in Figure 8.9.

If heteroscedasticity exists, it can be shown that the formulae for the variances of the OLS estimators $\hat{\alpha}$ and $\hat{\beta}$ are incorrect. Hence one could not use these variances to perform t-tests of the significance of these coefficients.

For proposed tests for the existence of heteroscedasticity and possible solutions to the problem the reader is referred to the Bibliography. However, notice from its definition that if heteroscedasticity exists then one would also expect the observed residuals to be, say, more widely dispersed at a specific high value of P_t than at a low value.

Multicollinearity

Multicollinearity can occur only in models with more than one independent variable. Multicollinearity exists if any independent variable is correlated with

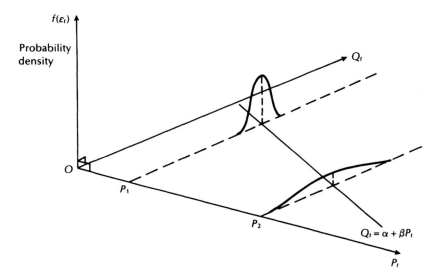

Figure 8.9

Box 8.2

Reconsider the marketing analyst from Box 8.1. Suppose the analyst changes his mind and now believes that the demand for rail travel is related to the following explanatory variables as well as the own relative price: the real level of personal disposable income and the relative prices of competing forms of travel: bus and coach travel and motoring. The analyst formulates a linear model, collects further data from the *Monthly Digest of Statistics* and again uses the MICROFIT package for estimation. The results obtained were:[1]

Ordinary Least Squares Estimation
****
Dependent variable is PASS
21 observations used for estimation from 1988Q1 to 1993Q1
****

Regressor	Coefficient	Standard Error	T-Ratio [Prob]
C	11384.2	4795.6	2.3739 [.030]
RPRAIL	−7392.0	3488.2	−2.1192 [.050]
RPBC	−2942.3	4574.2	−.64323 [.529]
RPMOT	3504.2	4030.7	.86938 [.397]
RPDI87	5.4614	5.0177	1.0884 [.293]

****

R-Squared	.67532	F-statistic F(4, 16)	8.3197 [.001]
R-Bar-Squared	.59415	S.E. of Regression	312.0531
Residual Sum of Squares	1558035	Mean of Dependent Variable	8204.8
S.D. of Dependent Variable	489.8289		
DW-statistic	1.9976		

****

PASS   = British Rail and London Underground Transport passenger kilometres in each quarter

C   = constant

RPRAIL = Retail price index of rail travel/retail price index for all items in each quarter

RPBC   = Retail price index of bus and coach travel/retail price index for all items in each quarter

RPMOT = Retail price index for motoring expenditure/retail price index for all items in each quarter

RPDI87 = Real personal disposable income (1987 prices) in each quarter

The *F*-statistic tests the null hypothesis that none of the population coefficients are significantly different from zero. Since the $F_{critical}$ value for (4,16) degrees of freedom is 3.01 (from any statistics text) whilst the $F_{calculated}$ value is 8.32, the null hypothesis is rejected and the analyst concludes that at least one coefficient is statistically different from zero. Notice that the package automatically gives the probability of a type I error for this test.

→

The R^2 statistic suggests that 67.5% of the variation in passenger kilometres is explained by the explanatory variables together but when adjusted this falls to 59.4%.

The DW-statistic tests the null hypothesis that the population errors are not first order autocorrelated. With 25 observations and 4 explanatory variables the critical values are $d_L = 0.94$, $d_U = 1.65$. The calculated value of the DW statistic is 1.998 which clearly exceeds d_U and so the analyst accepts that no first order auto-correlation exists. The analyst then considered the t-ratios (or t-statistics). The analyst noted that the null hypothesis that the population coefficient equalled zero against an alternative hypothesis that it differed from zero could be rejected only for the constant and the relative price of rail travel. The analyst therefore accepted the idea that changes in the relative price of bus and coach travel and of motoring expenditure and PDI had no effect on the quantity of rail travel demanded.

To discover the relative own price elasticity of demand the analyst found the mean values of the passenger kilometres and relative own price (both calculated by the software package) and so used equation (7.8) (see page 178). Thus

$$\eta = -7392.0 \times \frac{1.0437}{8204.8} = -0.9403$$

This means that if the company raised the relative price of rail travel by 1%, demand would decrease by 0.9403 %.

1. For simplicity we have omitted some of the statistics which MICROFIT would normally produce.

---

another or is linearly related to several others. For example, suppose our hypothesised demand model contained both advertising expenditure by our firm and that by our competitors as two separate variables. Since in reality the advertising expenditures of most firms in the same market usually rise and fall together, these two variables are likely to be correlated. If multicollinearity exists, the variance of the estimates of β_1, β_2, and so on, is greater than if there is no multicollinearity. So if we estimate β_1, β_2, etc., these estimates, and hence the corresponding elasticities of demand, could be *very* different from those in the population.

Notice that since most independent variables which one might wish to include in a demand function are correlated to some extent, the problem is not whether it exists but how serious it is. Multicollinearity is very difficult to remove. One might remove one or more of the correlated variables, relying on those retained to represent the changes in those omitted. Alternatively one might combine variables together. Either way, estimates of separate regression coefficients for each variable and hence the elasticity of each could not then be calculated.

Box 8.2 expands our example of the demand for rail travel in Box 8.1 to illustrate the use of the statistics we have just explained. Box 8.3 also illustrates the estimation of a demand function, in this case the demand for beer.

Box 8.3

Reekie and Blight: the demand for beer

Reekie and Blight (1982) proposed the following model for the demand for beer in the UK:

$$Q_t = \alpha + \beta_1 \frac{P_{Bt}}{P_{At}} + \beta_2 \frac{A_{Bt}}{A_{At}} + \beta_3 \frac{A_{Ct}}{A_{At}} + \beta_4 W_t + \beta_5 \frac{Y_t}{Y_{At}}$$

$$+ \beta_6 T_t + \beta_7 S_t + \beta_8 \frac{P_{Ct}}{P_{At}} + \varepsilon_t$$

where

P_{Bt} = retail price index of beer in period t
P_{At} = retail price index for all goods other than beer, period t
P_{Ct} = retail price index for all other alcoholic drinks, period t
A_{Bt} = advertising expenditure on beer, period t
A_{Ct} = advertising expenditure on all other alcoholic drinks, period t
A_{At} = advertising price index for TV and press, period t
W_t = daily mean temperature, period t
Y_t = personal disposable income per head, period t
Y_{At} = retail price index for all goods, period t
T_t = trend dummy variable
    = 0: January–March and July–September
      1: April–June
      2: October–December

Notice that this model includes variables which would be predicted by consumer theory: product price, price of substitutes and income. Tastes are difficult to measure in practice but one would use advertising messages to affect them. Similarly the trend dummy variables were included to represent any long-term changes in tastes towards or away from beer.

Reekie and Blight's model includes variables which we would expect to be excluded from the supply function, for example, advertising and income. Similarly, it excludes variables which we would expect to be included in a supply function, for example: prices of inputs, wage rates, interest rates and so on. Therefore we would expect the parameters of the model to relate to the *demand* function rather than to the supply function, i.e. it is identified.

Using OLS, the following estimated equation was obtained:

$$Q_t = 3.18 - \underset{(0.64)}{1.355} \left(\frac{P_B}{P_A}\right)_t + \underset{(0.32)}{0.004} \left(\frac{A_B}{A_A}\right)_t + \underset{(2.66)^*}{0.019} \left(\frac{A_C}{A_A}\right)_t$$

$$+ \underset{(5.84)^*}{0.057} W_t + \underset{(1.10)}{0.085} \left(\frac{Y}{YA}\right)_t + \underset{(1.22)}{0.085} T_t$$

$$+ \underset{(0.287)}{0.019} S_t + \underset{(0.173)}{0.371} \left(\frac{P_C}{P_A}\right)_t \qquad \begin{aligned} R^2 &= 0.57 \\ DW &= 2.05 \\ N &= 60 \end{aligned}$$

→

The estimated coefficients all have the signs which one would expect, except for the real advertising of competing products variable. However, by comparing the critical t-statistic (2.00 for a two-tail alternative hypothesis) with those calculated, it can be seen that the null hypothesis that the population coefficient equals zero can be rejected only for two variables: temperature and competitors' advertising. Comparison of the calculated Durbin–Watson statistic with the corresponding theoretical values in DW tables indicates that the errors are not autocorrelated. A priori, one might expect that the advertising variables may be correlated and so might the price variables. It is possible therefore that the insignificance of some of these variables is due to multicollinearity. Further analysis of the data would be needed to confirm this view.

8.2.6 The identification problem

One can never be quite sure in the statistical measurement of demand that what one is measuring is 'demand'. For example, we are not justified in considering the line AB in Figure 8.10 to be a demand curve. The four price:quantity points which AB connects were recorded historically and may, but need not, represent points on the same demand curve. The data available are insufficient to make such an assertion.

AB may represent a stable demand curve intersecting a shifting supply curve at four different points (Figure 8.10), or it may merely be a regression line produced by the movement of both demand and supply (Figure 8.11). This regression line has no meaningful equivalent in static theory. A demand curve shows the relationship between price and quantity demanded, all other things being equal. A supply curve shows the relationship between price and quantity supplied, all other things being equal. In Figure 8.11 non-price variables in both the supply and demand functions have changed between the points in time when the data were observed.

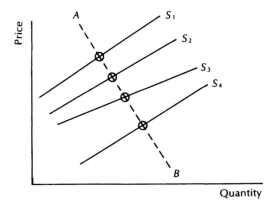

Figure 8.10

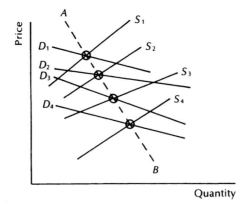

Figure 8.11

If we erroneously interpret *AB* as the demand curve, nonsense forecasts can result. A price rise, if *AB* was the demand curve, might appear an attractive proposition. In Figure 8.12, raising price from P_4 to P_3 would apparently result in a fall in sales of only Q_4 to Q_3. Given the price increase, a quantity reduction of this magnitude may well be justified. In reality, of course, such a price rise, given the demand conditions of D_4, would be unacceptable to the market-place.

Given this simultaneous relationship how can the demand function be unscrambled (or identified) and separated from the other relationships present? Identification is possible only in certain circumstances.

First, identification is not possible if, over a period of time, neither of the two curves change their shape or position. In such a situation all the intersection points would coincide, or at least cluster so close together that no discernible pattern would result.

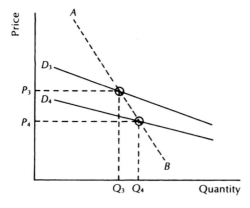

Figure 8.12

Second, identification of demand is not possible if the supply curve remains unchanged over time but the demand curve alters its position. A series of intersection points would be produced, but they will describe only the shape of the supply curve (which is thus identified) but not the demand curve.

Third, identification of demand is possible if the demand curve remains unchanged but the supply curve changes its position over time. This would be the situation in Figure 8.10 if *AB* was the demand curve, drawn from the relevant intersection points. But in Figure 8.10 the supply curve would then be unidentifiable.

Fourth, identification of demand is possible if information exists to explain why and by how much each curve has shifted between data observations. For example, the position of the demand curve may be affected by *per capita* disposable income. The position of the supply curve may be affected by the price level of a basic raw material. (If cost conditions in an industry rise or fall markedly in a period of stable demand, then a situation similar to Figure 8.10 may arise.)

A simultaneous equation estimation procedure can then be employed to establish what relationship exists between the four variables: quantity, price, *per capita* disposable income and raw material cost. The system is identified if it is possible to obtain by so doing an equation representing either of the demand Q_t^D or supply Q_t^s functions:

$$Q_t^D = f(p_t, Y_t) \quad Q_t^s = f(p_t, C_t)$$

where Y_t = personal disposable income in period t and C_t = raw material cost in period t.

If, however, the calculations provide an equation containing all four variables then the system is not identified. A mongrel function has been obtained. *A priori* our verbal model of the preceding paragraphs tells us that neither the demand nor supply functions contain both of the independent variables, raw material cost and *per capita* disposable income.

The corollary of this argument is that one of a pair of simultaneous relationships will be identified if it lacks a variable which is present in the other relationship.

The foregoing can also be illustrated graphically and intuitively. Consider the following historical data:

Year	1	2	3	4	5	6	7	8	9	10
Quantity demanded ('000)	3.0	12.0	4.0	8.0	8.8	10.0	6.6	2.5	1.0	4.5
Price (£)	2.3	4.0	1.5	4.5	3.3	6.0	7.1	6.5	8.0	8.0
Personal disposable income *per capita* (PDI)(£)	3000	6200	3500	5200	5000	6200	5900	4000	4000	5200
Raw material cost (per unit)(£)	2.0	1.0	1.5	1.5	1.0	1.5	2.2	2.7	3.1	2.7

The price and quantity information is plotted in Figure 8.13. We know that the points observed are the result of the interaction of supply and demand but as yet

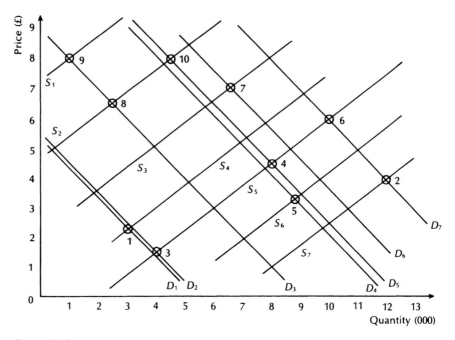

Figure 8.13

the relationship is unidentified. Quantity demanded however, is a function not only of price but also of income. Moreover, it seems reasonable to assume that income is not present in the supply function. Quantity supplied, on the other hand, is a function of price and raw material cost. The latter is unlikely to affect demand. (We are ignoring any correlation between personal disposable income per head and raw material cost.)

If this is so and we are convinced that income is the only variable which makes for substantial shifts in the demand curve, then it follows that points 2 and 6 are on one demand curve; points 4 and 10 are on a second and 8 and 9 are on a third. In each case PDI is the same. The remaining points are all on separate demand curves. Similarly, if we are convinced that raw material cost is the only variable which can lead to shifts in the supply curve then points 3, 4 and 6 are on one supply curve, and 8 and 10 are on another, while the other points are each on different supply curves.

Now consider points 2 and 6. Since they are on the same demand curve they have been located by shifts in the supply curve. But the supply curve shifted whilst the demand curve remained stationary because the level of raw material cost changed and raw material costs affect quantity supplied *not* quantity demanded. A similar explanation applies to points 4 and 10 and 8 and 9. (In fact, in the cases of the remaining points, 1, 2, 5 and 7, we believe they lie on separate demand curves because of differences in income.) Now notice that it is because a variable which shifts the supply curve is excluded from the demand function that we are able to 'identify' the latter. (A similar explanation applies to the supply function. Because the supply function *excluded* income, a variable which the demand function *includes*, the former is also thus identified.)

Notes

1. Media Expenditure Analysis Ltd.
2. See any standard econometrics text for the intervening steps.
3. Strictly speaking, we should refer to a 'probability density function' (p.d.f.). A p.d.f. encloses an area equal to 1. The area under the curve and between two values equals the probability that x will take on a value in that range. The probability of x taking values in a given small range around any given value, x_0, is proportional to $f(x_0)$.
4. Strictly speaking a probability density function.
5. Negative autocorrelation occurs if a relatively high error in one period is typically followed by a relatively low error in the following period, and vice versa. If we then plotted e_ts against time we would expect a 'saw-tooth' pattern.

Bibliography

Acton, J. P and Vogelsang, I. (1992) 'Telephone demand over the Atlantic: evidence from country-pair data', *Journal of Industrial Economics*, vol. XL, 3.

Berndt, E. R. (1991) *The Practice of Econometrics: Classical and contemporary*, Addison-Wesley.

Blundell, R., Pashardes, P. and Weber, G. (1993) 'What do we learn about consumer demand patterns from micro data', *American Economic Review*, vol. 83, 3.

Crook, J. N. (1989) 'The demand for retailer financed instalment credit: an econometric analysis', *Managerial and Decision Economics*, vol. 10.

De Pelsmacker, P. (1990) 'A structural model of the demand for cars in Belgium' *Applied Economics*, vol. 22.

Dougherty, C. (1992) *Introduction to Econometrics*, Oxford University Press.

Eastman, B. D. (1984) *Interpreting Mathematical Economics and Econometrics*, Macmillan.

Gujarati, D. (1988) *Basic Econometrics*, 2nd edn, McGraw-Hill.

Haines, B. (1978) *Introduction to Quantitative Economics*, Allen & Unwin.

Harris, A, McAvinchey, I. D. and Yannopoulos, Y. (1993) 'The demand for labour, capital, fuels and electricity: a sectorial model for the United Kingdom economy', *Journal of Economic Studies*, vol. 20, 3.

Koutsoyiannis, A. (1977) *Theory of Econometrics*, 2nd edn, Macmillan.

Naylor, T. H. (1981) 'Experience with corporate econometric models: a survey', *Business Economics*, January.

Propper, C. (1989) 'Econometric analysis of the demand for private health insurance in England and Wales', *Applied Economics*, vol. 21.

Ramanathan, R. (1992) *Introductory Econometrics*, 2nd edn, Dryden.

Reekie, W. D. and Blight, C. (1982) 'An analysis of the demand for beer in the United Kingdom', *Journal of Industrial Affairs*, vol. 9, 2.

Stewart, J. (1991) *Econometrics*, Philip Allan.

Thomas, R. L. (1985) *Applied Demand Analysis*, Longman.

Working, E. J. (1927) 'What do statistical demand curves show', *Quarterly Journal of Economics*, vol. 41.

Short-/medium-term decisions

Chapter 9

Cost theory and measurement

The traditional theory of costs is derived from, amongst other things, the theory of production. Hence we discuss production theory prior to cost theory. Production theory concerns the relationship between factor inputs and output and allows us to derive the conditions to be fulfilled for an output to be produced at minimum costs. Cost theory concerns the relationship between various measures of costs – marginal, average and total – and their determinants, such as output, and so on. To apply these concepts to a particular firm, its cost function must be estimated. Thus the final section of this chapter is devoted to techniques of cost function measurement.

9.1 Production theory

In economic terms production is an activity which creates or adds value or utility. Therefore production theory can be applied to storage, distribution and service activities as well as to manufacturing. Various non-manufacturing production activities add utility by, for example, changing place, ownership or saving time whereas manufacturing adds utility by changing the form of inputs.

A production function is a mathematical relationship which specifies the maximum quantity of output which can be obtained with a given quantity of each input. When presenting a production function two assumptions are made. Firstly, technology is invariant. (Technological change would alter the relationship between inputs and outputs which is represented by a production function which excludes a 'state of technology' term. If technology changes are also to be related to outputs, a variable representing this factor would have to be included in the function.) Secondly, it is assumed that inputs are used at maximum levels of efficiency.

Notice that since the production function relates inputs to *maximum* outputs, production processes, which for certain combinations of inputs do not produce as much output as another process, would not be represented by the function.

In general a production function may be represented as:

$$Q = f(K, L, Z_1 \ldots Z_n, \lambda)$$

where Q = maximum quantity of output per period; K = quantity of capital used per period; L = quantity of labour used per period; $Z_1 \ldots Z_n$ = quantities of other inputs used per period; and λ = a returns to scale parameter (to be explained below). For simplicity consider only a one output, two input case.

Figure 9.1 shows a production function in graphical form. It forms a surface OK_0XL_0. For example, suppose inputs of L_1 and K_0 of labour and capital respectively produce a maximum output of Q_1. The point representing this L, K, Q combination may be located by drawing a line up vertically by an amount representing Q_1 from the point where perpendiculars to each axis from K_0 and L_1 intersect. Repeating this process for every different L and K combination gives the surface.

Before we explain why the surface has the shape ascribed to it, notice that it can be represented in two rather than three dimensions by the use of isoquants. An *isoquant* is a locus of points, each representing a combination of quantities of two inputs and all such combinations producing the same output. (They are analogous to indifference curves in Chapter 7.) Since all points on any one isoquant represent the same output, they must all be on the surface at the same distance in the vertical direction from the base.

Such points can be located by passing a series of planes through the production surface parallel to the OKL plane. Each such plane would represent a different level of output. For example, planes have been passed through the surface at output heights Q_1 and Q_2. Any point along the curve Q_1Q_1, or along the curve Q_2Q_2, represents an equal output quantity of Q_1 and Q_2 respectively. When these output curves are transposed vertically downwards on to the OKL plane and indicated by the dashed curves $Q_1'Q_1'$ and $Q_2'Q_2'$, we have begun to construct an isoquant map. In geographic terminology, each such isoquant is a contour line on the hill of production.

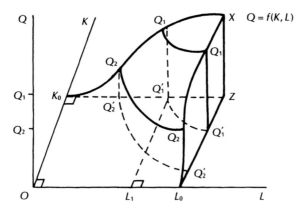

Figure 9.1

The gradient of an isoquant (a negative value since it generally slopes from left to right) at a particular point equals the marginal rate of technical substitution of labour for capital at that point. The MRTS of L for K is the amount of K that must be given up for every one additional unit of L taken on such that output remains unchanged i.e. MRTS (L for K) $= -\Delta K / \Delta L$. The minus sign is added because ΔK is negative but the amount of K *given up* in the MRTS is a positive amount. As ΔL becomes very small this ratio becomes (minus) the gradient of an isoquant, $-\mathrm{d}K/\mathrm{d}L$.

The MRTS of L for K equals the ratio of the marginal product of labour to the marginal product of capital. To understand this, suppose the input of K is reduced. The input of L must be increased if output is to remain unchanged and both the initial and final combinations of K and L are to remain on the same isoquant. The decrease in output due to the reduction in K (if L is not increased) is: $\mathrm{d}Q = MP_K \mathrm{d}K$, where MP_K is the marginal product of K, and $\mathrm{d}Q$ and $\mathrm{d}K$ are very small changes in Q and K respectively. If L is increased (but K remains fixed), the increase in output is $\mathrm{d}Q = MP_L \mathrm{d}L$ where MP_L is the marginal product of labour. $\mathrm{d}K$ and $\mathrm{d}L$ (both greatly magnified) are shown in Figure 9.2. For both initial and final combinations to be on the same isoquant:

$$MP_L \, \mathrm{d}L + MP_K \, \mathrm{d}K = 0 \Rightarrow \frac{MP_L}{MP_K} = -\frac{\mathrm{d}K}{\mathrm{d}L} = MRTS_{L \text{ for } K}$$

The minus sign is initially introduced here since the output reduction due to the reduction in K definitionally equals the output *increase* from the compensating L taken on.

Since (minus) the gradient of an isoquant equals MP_L/MP_K, when MP_L is zero, so is the gradient of the isoquant, i.e. it is horizontal. If MP_K is zero, the isoquant has an infinite gradient, i.e. it is vertical. If we join points on successive isoquants where each marginal product is zero, the enclosed area is called the economic region of production. This is shown in Figure 9.3 where the lines Q_1, Q_2, Q_3 denote isoquants.

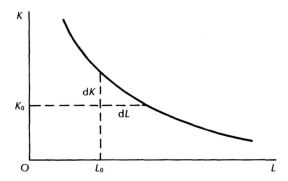

Figure 9.2

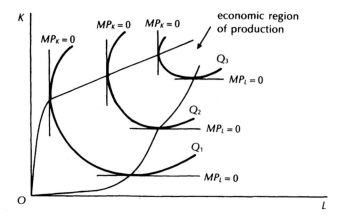

Figure 9.3

Within the economic region of production, isoquants have certain properties:

1. The *MRTS* of *L* for *K* along any isoquant decreases as the quantity of *L* taken increases.

   As *K* is decreased by, say d*K* in Figure 9.2, but *L* is held constant, MP_K increases according to the 'law' of diminishing returns. But, for the same reason if *L* is increased by, say, d*L* in Figure 9.2 MP_L decreases. Hence if *K* is decreased and *L* is increased by these amounts simultaneously MP_L/MP_K must then decrease and so *MRTS* decreases.

2. Isoquants further from the origin indicate greater output. Within the economic region, the marginal products of both factors are positive by assumption. Therefore increasing one factor, holding the other fixed, will increase output. But plotting the new combination on an isoquant map places it further from the origin than the original combination.

3. Isoquants have a negative slope. Since the marginal products of both factors are positive, so is their ratio. But as shown above, the ratio of marginal products equals the negative of the gradient of an isoquant, so minus the ratio of marginal products equals the gradient.

Finally, notice that regardless of whether they are in the economic region of production or not, isoquants cannot intersect, for analogous reasons to those which explain why indifference curves cannot intersect.

9.1.1 Short-run analysis: the law of diminishing returns

The 'law' of diminishing returns states that as additional units of one factor are employed, all other input quantities held constant, a point will eventually be reached where each additional unit of that input will yield diminishing increases in total product, i.e. the marginal product of that factor will decrease.

This 'law' is a generalisation from observed events. On a priori grounds it is highly plausible. If a field or factory is held constant in size, the continued addition of labour cannot be expected to produce constant increments in output. At its most trite, the men will get in each other's way.

The 'law' can be represented graphically. Since a marginal value of a function is the gradient of that function, the gradient of the graph of output against inputs of, say, labour will eventually decrease as labour is increased. This is shown in Figure 9.4a. In Figure 9.4a it is assumed that increasing returns to labour occur at low levels of labour input. In terms of Figure 9.1, if capital input is held constant at K_0, and only the input of labour varied, a curve of the shape of that in Figure 9.4a would be traced as is shown (in Figure 9.1), by the 'slice' K_0XZ. As L is increased, the curve shows initially the assumed increasing returns to labour and eventually diminishing returns. The increase in output when one factor is fixed and the other increased can be shown in an isoquant diagram. In Figure 9.4b, the input of capital is fixed at $\bar{K}$, and the output produced when different levels of L are employed is shown by line $\bar{K}B$. Finally note that the 'law' relates to any factor, not just labour. Hence the same assumed relationships are shown by the 'slices', L_0XZ, $L_1Q_1Q_1'$, etc.

9.1.2 Long-run analysis: returns to scale

In the long run, the quantities of all factors can be varied. Returns to scale relate to changes in output when all inputs change by the same proportion. Three alternative possibilities exist:

1. Increasing returns to scale (*IRS*): the proportionate change in output is greater than the proportionate change in inputs.
2. Constant returns to scale (*CRS*): the proportionate change in output equals the proportionate change in inputs.
3. Decreasing returns to scale (*DRS*): the proportionate change in output is less than the proportionate change in inputs.

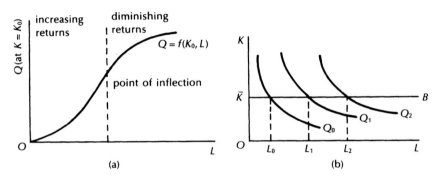

Figure 9.4

Each case may be represented graphically. In Figure 9.5 a ray, OZ, from the origin with constant gradient joins combinations of K and L where K/L is constant. Therefore if both factors changed by the same proportion the ray would indicate both the final and original combinations simultaneously. Suppose the firm initially uses K_0 and L_0 of capital and labour to produce Q_0 output. Now suppose quantities of both inputs are doubled, $2K_0$ and $2L_0$ being represented by OB. If IRS exist, output would now exceed $2Q_0$. Therefore the $2Q_0$ isoquant would lie closer to the origin along OZ than OB since less than $2K_0$ and $2L_0$ would be needed to produce it. If CRS exist, output would equal $2Q_0$ so the $2Q_0$ isoquant would go through point B. If DRS exist, output would be less than $2Q_0$. Therefore the $2Q_0$ isoquant would intersect OZ further from the origin than OB since more than $2K_0$ and $2L_0$ would be needed to produce it.

A production function can exhibit IRS, CRS and DRS over different ranges of input levels. It can also show IRS if inputs were changed by a given common multiple; and DRS if the inputs were changed by the same multiple. This apparent paradox is due to the fact that the former property relates to one ray whereas the latter can only be observed on two different rays.

9.1.3 Homogeneous production functions

Some production functions have the property of *homogeneity*. That is, if all inputs are multiplied by a constant, λ, the new output is λ to the power V times its original value. Hence suppose: $Q = f(L, K)$. If $Q^* = f(\lambda L, \lambda K)$ implies $Q^* = \lambda^V \times f(L, K) = \lambda^V \times Q$, then the production function is defined as homogeneous of degree V.

It can be seen that, if $V = 1$, the function exhibits CRS because multiplying all inputs by λ results in λ times as much output. If V is less than 1, then DRS exist since multiplying all inputs by λ results in less than λ times as much output, whilst V greater than 1 indicates IRS.

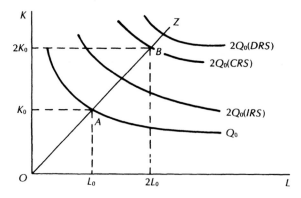

Figure 9.5

Example

One specific form of homogeneous function frequently discussed is the Cobb–Douglas production function:

$$Q = a \times L^b \times K^c \tag{9.1}$$

where a, b and c are constants, and where b plus c sums to unity. To see that this is homogeneous, multiply both inputs by a constant, λ. Hence the new output, Q^1, equals

$$Q^1 = a(\lambda L)^b (\lambda K)^c = a\lambda^b L^b \lambda^c K^c = \lambda^{(b+c)} a L^b L^c$$

$$= \lambda^{(b+c)} Q \qquad = \lambda Q \text{ (when } (b+c) \text{ equals unity)}$$

When $(b+c)$ equals unity, this function is homogeneous of degree one, so it exhibits CRS.[1]

If equation (9.1) is differentiated with respect to L and K (separately), we obtain the marginal products of L and K respectively. Thus:

$$\partial Q / \partial L = baL^{b-1} K^c \text{ and } \partial Q / \partial K = caL^b K^{c-1}$$

It can be seen that the marginal products are functions of L and K; a result which has often been observed in reality. Note also that the Cobb–Douglas function has the desirable property that when logarithms are taken of both sides of the equation a linear equation results to which the regression techniques of Chapter 8 may be applied to estimate a, b and c.

9.1.4 The cost minimising combination of inputs

Managers may wish to determine the combination of inputs to gain the maximum output that can be produced, given total cost, or the combination of inputs which minimises the total cost (TC) of producing a given output. To do this, given the production function, the manager needs the prices of factors. Given these prices, different combinations of two inputs which all have the same TC, can be represented by an isocost line. Since the total cost of each input equals its (given) price times the quantity of it used, we may (in the case of 2 inputs, K and L) write:

$$TC = P_K K + P_L L \tag{9.2}$$

If TC is fixed at TC_0 regardless of the quantities of inputs used, as along any isocost (or budget) line, equation (9.2) is a straight line. If $K = 0$, then $L = TC_0/P_L$. If $L = 0$ then $K = TC_0/P_K$. The slope of the line is $-P_L/P_K$ which is constant for all quantities of each input because their prices are constant. Such a line is shown in Figure 9.6. If TC is increased to TC_1, the intercepts of the line move further from the origin because $(TC_1/P_L) > (TC_0/P_L)$ etc. Hence isocost lines further from the origin denote greater total costs, given factor prices.

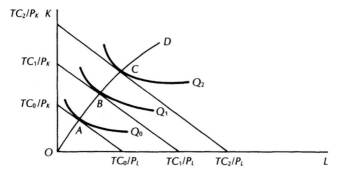

Figure 9.6

Given the production function and factor prices, the input combination which would result in a given output being produced at least total cost occurs where the relevant isoquant is just tangential to the lowest isocost curve possible. If an isocost line lies anywhere above the relevant isoquant, there exists a still lower isocost line which relates to less of both inputs to produce the chosen output. Hence it relates to lower total costs. Such a combination is shown by point A in Figure 9.6 for output Q_0; B for Q_1 and so on. Conversely to produce the maximum output given TC, the input combination corresponding to the isoquant furthest from the origin, which is also tangential to the relevant isocost line, is chosen. If an isoquant lies anywhere below the chosen isocost line, there exists another which just touches the isocost and which is further from the origin and so represents greater output. Such input combinations are also shown by points A to C in Figure 9.6.

Since each of these conditions is fulfilled when an isocost is tangential to an isoquant, and since the gradient of an isocost is $-P_L/P_K$ and that of an isoquant $-MP_L/MP_K$, these conditions are fulfilled when

$$-\frac{P_L}{P_K} = -\frac{MP_L}{MP_K} \Rightarrow \frac{MP_K}{P_K} = \frac{MP_L}{P_L} \tag{9.3}$$

This result can be derived mathematically in the case of any finite number of factors (not just two). We show this in Appendix 9.

If the prices of some, but not all, inputs change, factor substitution is likely. Consider initially the *maximisation of output, given total cost*. Suppose, in a two-input production function such as Figure 9.7, that the price of input L decreased. Then the slope of the isocost line (with quantities of K and L on the vertical and horizontal axes respectively) equals $-P_L/P_K$ and, following a decrease in P_L, will pivot from AB to AC. The initial combination of inputs which maximises output for a given total cost changes from L_0K_0 to L_1K_1 (X to Z).

This change can be decomposed into substitution and output effects analogous to the substitution and income effects of indifference curve theory. The former is the change in the quantities of inputs due purely to a change in their relative prices. The latter is the change in the quantities of inputs required to produce the new output

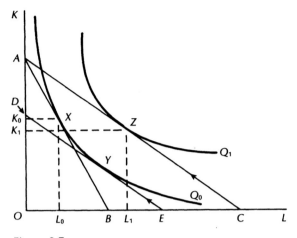

Figure 9.7

which the total cost can now pay for. To isolate each effect diagrammatically, construct a hypothetical isocost line (DE) with the same slope as AC, but tangent to the Q_0 isoquant, e.g. at Y. Since DE is parallel to AC, its slope represents the new input price ratio, and since it is tangent to the original isoquant, its point of tangency with Q_0 indicates inputs needed to produce the original output. The change in inputs from point X to point Y is the substitution effect. The difference between lines DE and AC is purely due to the change in output, since their slope (the input price ratio) is the same. The remaining change in inputs (from Y to Z) represents the output effect.

Alternatively, *minimising total cost given output* would involve only the substitution effect. Here the new isocost line would be tangent to the original isoquant. Hence in Figure 9.7 the movement from X to Y with the new budget line DE represents lower total costs than AB (because it is lower than AC, which in turn represents the same budget as AB, given the new lower price of L).

However, neither of these explanations is complete. A change in a factor price may shift the marginal cost curve which in turn would alter the profit-maximising output. This further output change must be taken into account.

Finally, a change in demand, factor prices given, may also cause the profit-maximising output to change. Depending on the production function and hence the pattern of isoquants, this may cause a change in the ratio of factor inputs. The locus of points where different isocost lines with the same factor prices are tangential to successive isoquants is called the 'long-run expansion path' of the firm. In Figure 9.6 the line ABC is an expansion path.

Optimum input combinations

Whilst the fulfilment of equation (9.3) guarantees that any *chosen* output is produced at minimum total cost, this is not sufficient for profit maximisation. This is because the fulfilment of equation (9.3) is not sufficient to imply that the profit-maximising output is being produced. Equation (9.3) is necessary but not sufficient for profit maximisation. To deduce the *profit-maximising* levels of each input, notice that the inverse of the terms in equation (9.3) also equal marginal cost of output (MC_Q):

$$\frac{P_K}{MP_K} = \frac{P_L}{MP_L} = \ldots = MC_Q \tag{9.4}$$

To prove this, suppose an additional ΔL units of L are hired and its output is, say, ΔQ (the input of K is kept constant). The cost of the additional ΔL units is $P_L \Delta L$ (where P_L is fixed, assuming that each input is bought in a perfectly competitive market). Therefore, the change in total cost per unit change in output, i.e. MC_Q, equals:

$$\frac{P_L \Delta L}{\Delta Q} = \frac{P_L \times 1}{\Delta Q / \Delta L} = \frac{P_L}{MP_L}$$

QED

The profit-maximising output requires that $MR_Q = MC_Q$. Hence, from equation (9.4):

$$\frac{P_K}{MP_K} = \frac{P_L}{MP_L} = \ldots = MC_Q = MR_Q \tag{9.5}$$

$$\Rightarrow P_K = MP_K \times MR_Q = MRP_K \tag{9.6}$$

$$P_L = MP_L \times MR_Q = MRP_L \tag{9.7}$$

where MRP_K and MRP_L denote the marginal revenue products of capital and labour respectively. Since equation (9.5) implies that the firm is producing the profit-maximising level of output and is using the combination of inputs which does this at minimum cost, fulfilment of equation (9.5) is necessary and sufficient for profit maximisation. Note that equation (9.7) is simply the condition that the marginal cost of labour (P_L) equals the marginal revenue of an additional unit of labour, the latter being the change in total output when a unit of labour is hired times the change in total revenue received when that number of additional output units is sold. Equation (9.6) has the same interpretation for capital.

9.2 Cost curves

When considering costs it must be remembered that the economist's concept of cost cannot be obtained from normal accounting data. The economist views cost as opportunity cost whereas the accountant measures cost historically (see Chapter 2).

9.2.1 Traditional Theory

In the Traditional Theory of costs, the same distinction is made between short- and long-run costs as was mentioned briefly in our discussion of production theory. Recapping, the short run is a period of time which is so short that quantities of only certain factors of production can be changed. The long run is a time period which is sufficiently long for the quantities of all factors to be varied. Examples of inputs which are fixed in the short run are: plant, certain administrative and managerial personnel and land. Examples of inputs which can be varied in the short run are raw materials, operating personnel and fuel. The long run may vary in length between industries because the length of time required to gain certain inputs may vary with their nature. For example, 'premises' to an aluminium smelting works may take years to acquire because they may have to be built, whereas 'premises' to a market research agency may either be built more quickly, or because of the relatively more readily available supply of office space, they could also be rented more easily than an aluminium smelter.

Derivation of cost curves

Total costs, *TC*, depend on the quantities of inputs used by a production process, and their prices. They also assume that inputs are combined in the most productive way to obtain the outputs; as implied by the production function. Therefore total costs can be said to depend on the level of output, input prices and technology (which the production function assumes is fixed and so omits). This is the case when all inputs can be varied in quantity. But if some inputs are immediately variable, whilst others have fixed and specific values, output may be *less than it could be* from the quantities of inputs used. The former situation relates to the long run and the later to the short run because of the variability of some inputs and fixity of others. Cost curves represent the relationship between output and cost, other variables such as technology and input prices, being assumed constant.

Short-run cost curves

Short-run total costs (*STC*) at each output equal the sum of short-run total fixed costs, (*TFC*) and short-run total variable costs (*STVC*).

1. Total fixed costs (*TFC*) consist of the *TC* of factors which cannot be varied in the short run. This being so, *TFC* do not differ with output, but are constant. Fixed costs do not exist in the long run, when all inputs can be varied.
2. Short-run total variable costs, (*STVC*) consist of the *TC* of factors which can be varied in the short run and hence differ at different levels of output. The shape of the *STVC* curve can be derived graphically from the expansion path of the firm *provided* both factors on the axes of the isoquant diagram are the only variable

inputs in the short run. Assuming this to be the case, as in Figure 9.8 where all inputs other than fuel and wage labour are assumed constant, the *STVC* can be derived by plotting the *STVC* values, TVC_0, TVC_1, TVC_2, etc, against the corresponding output levels. The results are shown in Figure 9.9a.

The deduction of the shape of the *TVC* curve from a production function is *most simply* illustrated if we assume that only one factor (say wage labour), is variable and all others fixed. Assuming increasing returns to this factor at low levels of utilisation, and that eventually the law of diminishing returns applies, the relation between total output and labour input was shown in Figure 9.4a. If the horizontal axis is multiplied by the (constant) wage rate P_L, it now measures *STVC*. To obtain the *STVC* curve in its conventional position simply rotate Figure 9.4a anticlockwise by $90°$ about the origin and then turn it over about the *STVC* ($= P_L \times L$) axis (now vertical) as if it were the left-hand page of a book and we wished to examine the previous page. A curve of similar shape to that in Figure 9.9a is obtained.

The shape of the *STVC* curve is determined by the productivity of the variable factor(s). Up to Q_1 in Figure 9.9a, *STVC* increases at a decreasing rate, because, with constant input prices, the marginal productivity of the variable input(s) is increasing. Beyond Q_1, the *STVC* increases at an increasing rate as the marginal productivity of the variable input(s) decreases. Below Q_1 the fixed input(s) are being underutilised by the variable input, beyond Q_1 the fixed input(s) are being over-utilised.

3. Average fixed costs (*AFC*), are defined as: $AFC = TFC/Q$.
4. Short-run average variable costs (*SAVC*), are defined as: $SAVC = SATC/Q$.
5. Short-run average total costs (*SATC*), are defined as: $SATC = STC/Q$.
6. Short-run marginal costs (*SMC*), are defined as the change in *TC* resulting from a one unit change in *Q*: $SMC = d(STC)/dQ$.

Since *TFC* does not vary with output, *SMC* equals the derivative of *STVC*: $SMC = d(STVC)/dQ$.

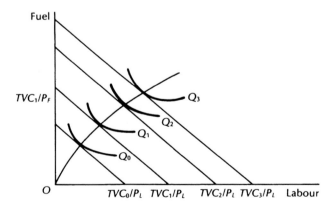

Figure 9.8

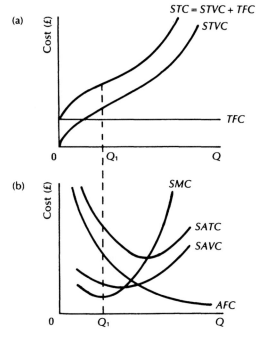

Figure 9.9

Graphically the AFC, SAVC, SATC and SMC curves can be derived from the corresponding TC and TVC curves in the way shown in Chapter 2. The AFC curve takes the shape shown because the fixed TFC level is being spread over an increasing level of output.

The long run

In the long run all costs are variable, there is no fixed cost curve. The long-run total cost curve (TC), can also be derived graphically from an isoquant diagram if there are only two inputs. For example, suppose the only two inputs are capital and labour as shown in Figure 9.6. Assuming that factor prices are constant, the LTC curve may be derived by plotting each output against the corresponding level of TC: TC_0, TC_1, TC_2, etc. The LTC curve shows the minimum level of total cost for which each output can be produced when any combination of inputs may be chosen.

The LTC curve can be related to the STC curve in the case of two inputs by using isoquants. In Figure 9.10 with capital fixed at $\bar{K}$, AB shows quantities of L, which together with $\bar{K}$, are necessary to produce each output. For example, L_1^s of L is necessary to produce Q_1. In the long run with K variable, OC shows the quantities of each input necessary for each output. Hence L_1^l of labour with K_1^l of capital is necessary to produce Q_1. But the total cost of K_1^l and L_1^l is TC_1 whereas that of $\bar{K}$

Box 9.1

Why are US airlines making such a large loss?

Figures from the Air Transport Association show that US scheduled airlines made a collective loss in 1992 of around $4bn. In 1990 the loss was almost as large and in 1991 around $2bn. Losses by some very large airlines such as Pan Am led them to leave the industry. On the other hand the *Financial Times* reported that stock market analysts were predicting that Southwest Airlines, a relatively small airline based in Dallas, would increase its profits by 50% during 1993 to make it the most profitable American airline. What is the cause?

Tomkins (1993) argues that there are several reasons such as an economic recession reducing demand and so leading to overcapacity and the US bankruptcy laws which enable poorly performing firms to continue in business. However he argues that the main reason is increased competition from newly entered companies which offer basic no-frills service at very low prices – sometimes as low as one third of those of large carriers. Why can such companies offer such low prices?

Tomkins says there are several reasons but they ultimately are the result of lower costs. Large US airlines operate a hub and spoke system whereby planes fly from peripheral locations along spokes to specific large central airports – hubs – then back again. Passengers wishing to fly from one peripheral point to another, fly to the hub, change planes and fly along a different spoke to their destination. This is not true of the smaller airlines which operate shuttle flights between pairs of cities without any one city being a hub. The costs of operating a hub and spoke system are much greater than regional shuttle services. In the hub and spoke system, aircraft have to arrive at each hub at the same time so that passengers can make connections. This means that sufficient staff have to be employed to cope with this peak load, but that at all other times they have considerably less to do. In the case of the smaller airlines, planes arrive in series, so fewer staff are needed and they are always occupied.

In addition, Tomkins notes that a further reason why costs are lower in smaller airlines is that labour is used more flexibly than in larger airlines. For example, cabin staff, rather than contract cleaners, clean their plane. Pilots are paid only when flying an aircraft. Tomkins notes that in order to cut costs, some airlines have been willing to sell large amounts of equity to labour unions and cites the cases of Northwest Airlines (37.5% owned by unions) and Trans World Airlines (45% owned by unions) as examples.

As a result of its shuttle fast-turnaround no-frills services operated by highly motivated individuals, Tomkins argues that Southwestern's operating costs per available seat mile are 26% lower than the average for large airlines.

Source summarised from Tomkins 1993.

and L_1^s is TC_2. Because the isoquant marked Q_1 has an increasing gradient as L increases, TC_1 is less than TC_2. Moreover since isoquants generally have increasing gradients at higher levels of L (as drawn), the short-run expansion path involves a higher total cost for a given output than the long-run expansion path, except at one combination of K and L. In the case of plant scale $\bar{K}$, this exception occurs at output

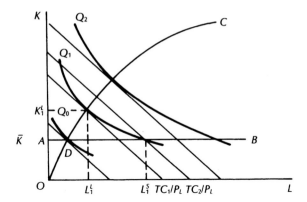

Figure 9.10

Q_0 where long-run and short-run expansion paths intersect. Now since with plant $\bar{K}$, STC exceed LTC at outputs above and (it can be similarly shown) below Q_0, we can state that with K fixed at $\bar{K}$ the STC curve will lie above the LTC curve at all outputs except Q_0. By repeating this argument, it can be shown that for each level of K there is an STC curve which is tangential to the LTC curve at one output level but is otherwise above the LTC. Since there are many different values of K along an expansion path, each usually corresponding to a different value of Q, the tangencies occur at different outputs.

The LAC curve can be derived from the LTC curve using the methodology of Chapter 2. It can also be derived by forming the envelope of different STC curves, each relating to different quantities of fixed factors. Consider Figure 9.11. A firm is faced with the choice of renting one of four factories for a period of a year. The ATC curves for the four factories over a period of a year are ATC_1, ATC_2, ATC_3 and ATC_4 in respective order of increasing size of plant. Suppose the firm expects to produce output level Q_3. Then it will pay to rent the plant with cost curve ATC_3. Both plants ATC_2 and ATC_4 are capable of producing Q_3, but could only do so at a much higher unit cost. Given that it has rented ATC_3 then, this becomes the firm's short-run AC curve for the period of the year. Suppose, however, that it ends up producing output level Q_2, then its unit cost will be represented by the distance Q_2A. If output Q_2 persists, then in the long run (i.e. after the expiry of the one-year rental) it will pay the firm to rent plant size ATC_2 and produce at unit cost level Q_2B.

Thus, in the long run, the firm's long-run average cost curve is represented by the tangential segments of all the short-run curves. When the choice of plant size is infinite, as might be the case when the firm can design and build from scratch a new plant, then the tangential points of these short-run curves become one smooth (envelope) curve of the type indicated by LAC.

The optimum size of plant is ATC_3. The minimum point on ATC_3 is tangential with the minimum of LAC. This is the case for no other plant size. Thus, for example, while no plant would be as efficient at ATC_1 in producing output Q_1 (the

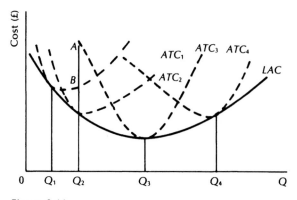

Figure 9.11

point of tangency between *LAC* and *ATC*$_1$) other plants *would* be more efficient than *ATC*$_1$ in producing output level Q_3 where *ATC*$_3$ is at a minimum. Only at the optimum plant size (of *ATC*$_3$) will it ever pay a firm to produce at minimum unit cost!

So far we have not explained why the traditional theory of costs predicts that the *LAC* is U-shaped. This is our next task.

Economies of scale   The traditional theory of costs predicts that the *LAC* will decline as output is initially increased because of the occurrence of economies of scale. These may be real or pecuniary. Real economies of scale occur when, due to the technology of available processes, with given input prices the average input per unit of output measured in terms of average cost declines. It is this phenomenon that the traditional theory of costs derives from production theory. The theory of costs derives the *LAC* under the assumption of constant factor prices. However, in practice, pecuniary economies – lower input prices for bulk purchases – have been observed. The incorporation of such phenomena into the theory of production would complicate matters, but would contribute to an even more steeply sloped *LAC* than that predicted by the traditional theory. Several causes of real economies of scale have been proposed as shown under the next four headings:

1. *Specialisation*   The larger the output, the greater will be the opportunities for, and advantages of, specialisation of labour and machinery. The division of labour into specialised tasks permits the hiring of people with greater skills/knowledge of their one function rather than the hiring of persons with a range of skills and consequently a possibly lower level of expertise for each function. Specialists could not be hired at lower outputs because they would then be underutilised. Secondly, specialisation reduces the time spent moving between types of work. Thirdly,

---

Box 9.2

Economies of scale from a merger

The desire to gain economies of scale is often given as the reason why one firm wishes to acquire another. This was true of the proposed Renault/Volvo merger of 1993.

Renault, the French car and truck manufacturer, was 79% state owned. Volvo was privately owned. It produces cars, trucks, aero and marine engines and also includes food processing businesses. The market shares between January and September 1993 of each company in Western Europe were:

	Cars	Trucks (over 6 tonnes gross vehicle weight)
Renault	10.6%	9.3%
Volvo	1.5%	8.9%

Source: *Financial Times*, 3 September 1993.

In 1992 Renault made a pre-tax profit of $1.13bn on a turnover of $30.7bn. and Volvo a pretax loss of $406m. on a turnover of $10.2bn.

In February 1990, the two companies agreed to share components. On 6 September 1993, they announced a proposed merger between Renault and the automotive divisions of Volvo. In the case of cars Renault produced for all market segments from the Renault 5 and Clio to the Safrane, a large five-seater model. Volvo produced only for the luxury car markets. Volvo had a very small market share in the United States (0.7%). Renault had no share. Hence the merger would have resulted in an increased European market share. In the case of trucks, Renault produced all sizes whilst Volvo produced mainly heavy trucks and no light commercial vehicles. Together with Mercedes Benz, Renault and Volvo supplied 44% of the US truck market.

One of the reasons given for the proposed merger was the reduction of costs. *The Economist* (11 November 1993) stated that the companies hoped the gains would come in three areas. Firstly, gains were expected in marketing since the product portfolios complement each other well. Renault had a particular ability to manufacture small cars (such as the Clio, European Car of the Year 1993); Volvo to produce large cars. Secondly, in production Renault was reported as having stated that by the year 2000 costs could be reduced by $5.3bn. It was intended that this would be achieved by combining their orders for components to gain lower prices, and by combining their planning of future models so having more components common to the models of both manufacturers. *The Economist* suggested that the Volvo 850 saloon and the Renault Safrane may become variations of the same product. This would reduce not only sourcing costs but R&D costs also.

On 2 December the merger was called off.

Source 'Whose driving Renault – Volvo?' *The Economist*, 11 September 1993, pp. 77–8; Done 1993.

specialised workers are more likely to have ideas for more efficient techniques or machines to increase their efficiency than less specialised workers.

2. *Indivisibilities*   A plant is indivisible if, when its output is reduced below a certain level, the required inputs remain constant. At high outputs a large plant may be more efficient than a small plant, but at outputs below its threshold a large plant's productivity will decrease eventually to below that of a smaller plant. To understand this, suppose that to produce a product two alternative processes can be used, one large, one small, with the following production function:

	Input of K	Input of L	Output of Q	TC $P_K = 1, P_L = 1$	AC (= TC/Q)
Process A	1	1	1	2	2
Process B	10	10	20	20	1

Both processes are assumed to have constant returns to scale. Each process can be used to produce any output rate. Given *CRS*, doubling inputs will always double the output for each process. Therefore, given input prices, the average cost of process A will be £2 for all levels of output above zero. Process B has a constant average cost of £1 per unit for outputs above 20. For outputs less than 20, however, the same amount of L and K is required as at 20, i.e. 10 of labour and 10 capital; therefore its total cost remains constant. With lower output[2] AC therefore rises. It can be seen that, when output is as low as 10, the AC of process B equals that of A, whereas at lower outputs still, the AC of B would be even higher than that of A. The LAC curve predicted by these arguments is shown in Figure 9.12.

3. *Geometric relationships*   For many types of equipment, running and construction costs are approximately proportional to equipment surface area, whilst output is approximately proportional to capacity. Examples are tanks, pressure vessels, ships, pipes and other containers. Because of the form of the mathematical relationship between surface area and volume, multiplying the surface area by k will lead to volume increasing by a multiple greater than k. Hence the ratio (surface area/volume) will decrease and correspondingly so will average cost. For example, if the length of each side of a rectangular tank is doubled, the surface area will increase four times, but its volume will increase eight times. In the case of a sphere, the surface area varies with volume to the power 2/3 so costs may be expected to be proportional to output to the power two thirds. Much empirical evidence supports this two-thirds relationship which is used by engineers when designing process equipment.

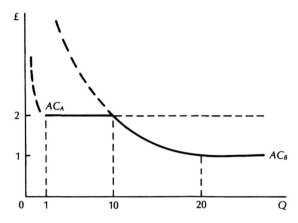

Figure 9.12

4. *Stochastic economies*   Stochastic economies occur when a firm wishes to hedge against an uncertain event. For example, if a firm wishes to maintain a spare machine to be used if a breakdown among a large number of machines occurs, then it can be shown that the proportionate increase in the number of spare machines is less than that of the number of machines actually in service. Likewise, a firm using several identical machines will have to stock proportionately fewer spare parts than firms with only one, and similar economies can exist for stocks of raw materials, finished goods, labour and monetary resources.

Diseconomies of scale   The traditional cost theory predicts that the *LAC* curve will, after a certain output, slope upwards due to diseconomics of scale. *Technical factors* are unlikely to produce diseconomies of scale. If inefficiencies arise as a result of overlarge plant size, they can be avoided by replicating units of plant of a smaller size. (One example of this is turbine blades. If an overlarge turbine is constructed, the ends of the blades will travel at a speed near that of sound. The strains imposed on the blades at this speed increase more than proportionately with turbine capacity.) Technical factors are more likely to limit the sources of scale economies than act as a source of diseconomies. However sources of diseconomies are arguably associated with managerial problems and labour relations.

1. *Management problems*   It is often argued that co-ordination costs increase more than proportionately with output. Firstly, as the number of hierarchical levels of decision taking from supervisor upwards increases, information may be distorted

as it passes up to or down from the relevant decision maker even if all individuals have cost minimisation as their aim. Secondly, the number of decisions which require Board or a co-ordinator's approval will increase with scale while the capacity of the Board or decision maker to make decisions remains fixed, i.e. the peak co-ordinator suffers from 'bounded rationality' (see Williamson 1970) – limits on the rate at which he or she can absorb and process information. Less time per decision is allocated, with poorer decisions likely. These two reasons have been called 'control loss' by Williamson (1967). Thirdly, if those lower in the hierarchy have goals other than profit maximisation, they may follow them to a greater extent in large firms when they are less closely monitored (as they may be if there are many hierarchical levels between them and their managerial monitor).

Counter-arguments have been made to some of the points. Scherer argues that the accuracy of information passing from operative to decision maker has improved greatly over the last few decades due to technological innovation, better techniques of accounting and budgetary control, computer-supported management information systems. But it is unclear, a priori, whether the improvement has led to equal degrees of managerial efficiency at all output rates.

Changes in organisation structure may also affect efficiency. We need not restrict the analysis to single-division or one-product firms. Williamson (1975) has distinguished between several types of structure. The U (Unitary) form structure consists of each function being organised into a separate division, each answering to the Chief Executive as shown in Figure 9.13a.

Alternatively, the M (Multidivisional) form structure consists of separate divisions reporting to the Head Office, each division having within it subsections which perform each function, as shown in Figure 9.13b. An important characteristic is that operating and strategic decision making processes are separated and the appropriate mechanisms for control are used.

Williamson argues that the U-form is the appropriate structure for small to medium-sized firms. But at medium to large firm sizes, the M-form becomes more efficient. If further hierarchical levels are introduced into a U-form firm's structure, then at large sizes 'control loss' increases. Bounded rationality limits the ability of the Head Office to make efficient decisions. Further, the heads of each functional division may liaise with Head Office in order to increase its capacity – this is likely to change the decisions in favour of the more politically persuasive divisions and not necessarily the optimal profit-maximising ones. In addition, due to control loss, individual division heads may have greater scope for following their own non-profit objectives such as sales, staff expenditure, discretionary investment, and perks (see Chapters 4 and 5). Product and capital market competition may restrict this discretion but will do so to a lesser degree in markets where monopoly power exists or where shareholders lack the information necessary to assess their managers' performance accurately.

If the U-form is replaced by the M-form structure, efficiency is (ceteris paribus) likely to be greater. Firstly, operating decisions are made by each separate division, not by the Head Office. The Head Office therefore has more time to devote to the

(a)

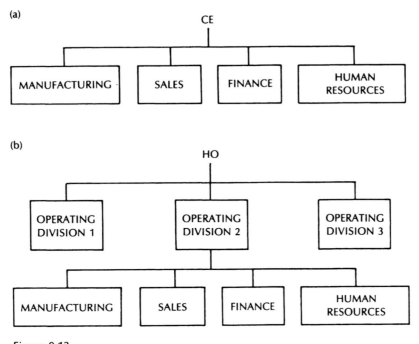

Figure 9.13

(fewer) strategic decisions, and information (up or down the organisation) needs to pass through fewer hierarchical levels.

Secondly, the Head Office advises on and monitors the performance of each division, so increasing the control over divisional behaviour. Thirdly, the divisions compete between themselves for resources, so encouraging greater efficiency in current resource usage and also better allocation of resources for future use. This will be so if proposals for investment in new projects or expansion are evaluated by the Head Office on the basis of the rate of return on past and current projects. Since managers often want to expand (see Chapter 5) they will operate as efficiently as possible today in order to attain resources to grow tomorrow. Fourthly, since the divisional heads do not enter into Head Office decision making, less partisan decisions are made.

2. *Labour relations* Some have argued that, as scale increases and operatives become separated by a greater number of hierarchical levels from decision makers, they become more alienated and morale decreases. In this case strikes may be expected to be more frequent than in small firms and the control loss due to firm size may make it more difficult for decision makers to deal with such dissension. Secondly, if a large firm requires more labour than a smaller firm, it may bid up

local wages compared with a smaller firm and/or it may have higher transport costs because of the need to transport workers over a greater distance to the plant.

9.2.2 Andrews' theory of costs

Some writers have argued that the actual cost curves which firms face have different shapes from those of the Traditional Theory. In particular, Andrews (1949) has argued that for all practical purposes *SACs* are downward-sloping with firms planning excess capacity and that the *LAC* never turns up.

Short run

The short run is the maximum period of time which is too short for the machine with the largest capacity to be replaced. Costs are divided into indirect costs which do not vary continuously with output, and direct costs relating to inputs which do so vary.

Average indirect costs   Indirect costs include: the salaries of administrative staff and of all managers, wear and tear of machinery and plant, and the cost of premises and of the land on which they are located. It is argued that each machine will have a maximum possible output per period. If several processes are involved in manufacture, several small machines at one stage of the process may be required to produce the required output for a larger-capacity machine either earlier or later in the production process.

Andrews argues that the largest machine is installed with capacity in excess of that of the smaller processes which supply it. There are two reasons for this. Firstly, reserve capacity will be required to maintain output when breakdowns occur. Secondly, very large plant is time-consuming and disruptive to install. Capital in excess of planned output is installed so as to meet any demand expansion with less disruption and delay than replacement would involve.

Small machines will have less reserve capacity in proportion to planned output than the largest machine because the former can be replaced much more quickly than the latter. Secondly, stochastic economies will necessitate a smaller proportion of such small machines to be held in reserve for breakdowns than for the largest machine.

If, in the short run, capacity is kept constant, the total cost of such inputs is constant. Hence if output increases, average indirect costs (*AIC*) decrease. When the capacity of smaller machines is reached, say at Q_1 in Figure 9.14, then either multiple labour shifts will be worked, which will increase average direct (not *indirect*) costs, or additional lower capacity machines will have to be installed. If the former decision is taken, the *AIC* will continue to decrease until output Q_0, the capacity of the largest machine, is achieved, say, at point *B*. If the latter decision is

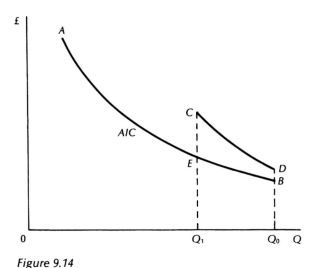

Figure 9.14

taken, the total indirect costs will increase at Q_1 so their average value will increase – as shown by curve *CD*. The *AIC* curve would then be *AECD* and not *AB*. When the total capacity of the smaller machines reaches that of the largest, further output expansion is precluded in the short run.

Average direct costs   Direct costs are those of inputs whose quantities vary with output: employees engaged in manufacturing processes, and raw materials. Andrews argued that the *ADC* curve has a 'flat-bottomed' *U* shape as shown in Figure 9.15. Considering labour costs first, at low and intermediate levels of output (below *Q'*), if additional direct labour is hired by hiring a greater number of individuals, their productivity will remain constant. This is because the capacity of small machines with which they work can be increased and because there is excess capacity in the largest process. Therefore the diminishing returns to labour which were predicted by the traditional theory do not occur. Hence, if the wage rate is constant, the *ADC* of labour is constant. If very high rates of output were considered, e.g. above *Q'* in Figure 9.15, this may necessitate hiring the same individuals *for longer periods per day*, i.e. overtime. This may be necessary because the capacity of the largest machine when using a single shift has been reached, or because of a lack of available labour. In this case we would expect their average productivity to be lower than without overtime and the average wage rate to be higher. Hence average direct labour costs would be higher. Secondly, average direct raw material costs are predicted to be constant at intermediate outputs given their price, but to be greater at very low[3] output rates, e.g. below *Q''*, due to greater wastage. Hence, at outputs below *Q''*, the *ADC* is decreasing, so the *MC* must be below *ADC*; and from a consideration of the total cost curve it can be shown that the *MC* is rising.[4]

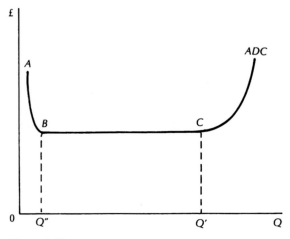

Figure 9.15

Between Q'' and Q' ADC is constant and so equals MC. Above Q' ADC increases so MC is above ADC and it can be shown that MC is increasing as well.

Average total costs ATC are derived by adding the ADC and AIC values at each output. The ATC will decrease with increases in output until just after Q' where the effects of reserve capacity are exhausted, and increase thereafter (see Figure 9.16).

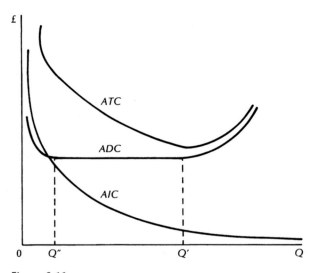

Figure 9.16

(As in the Traditional Theory, normal profits are included in the AIC values.) The minimum level of ATC will occur at a slightly larger output than Q' because, if output is increased slightly beyond Q', the decrease in AIC will at first exceed the increase in ADC. For larger increases in output beyond Q' the reverse is true, hence the ATC will rise.

Long-run costs

In the long run the firm can vary the quantity of all inputs including the largest capacity machine. Andrews distinguishes between technical and managerial costs of production.

Technical costs These are the costs of all inputs other than management. Average technical costs decrease – firstly, due to specialisation and indivisibilities. Secondly, average repair costs may decrease due to stochastic economies (referred to above) and specialisation of labour. Thirdly, at high output rates the firm may make its own raw materials or inputs. Hence it may benefit from any economies of scale in this earlier activity if before expansion the benefits of such scale economies were retained by the supplier due to any monopoly power.

Managerial costs These are defined as all costs except technical costs. Andrews argued that a firm contained several managerial levels. For each level there is an appropriate management technique and each technique is applicable to a range of output rates. Within the output range to which a technique is appropriate, average managerial costs will decrease as output increases since the costs of the same-sized managerial group are divided by greater levels of output. If a larger output range for which a new technique is most appropriate is considered, initially average managerial costs will exceed those relating to the size of the management group using the previous technique. This is because the number of managers has increased greatly, but output by only a relatively small amount. But, again, average managerial costs decrease as output within this range rises. If the scale of output increases greatly, average managerial costs are argued to decrease and eventually to increase but at a decreasing rate as more levels of management are inserted. If the technical and managerial costs are summed, Andrews predicts that, as scale increases, then at first average costs decrease: both types of costs decrease; but eventually average costs become constant as falling technical costs are offset by rising managerial costs. This L-shaped LAC curve is shown in Figure 9.17.

Empirical work by Bain (1956) and others has suggested that firms actually do produce below 100% capacity. (Depending on authors, the estimates range from an average of 66% up to 80%.) At any output, the LAC level (see Koutsoyiannis 1979)

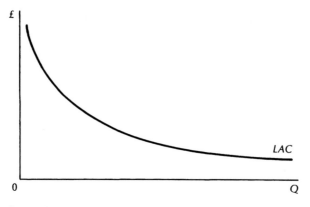

Figure 9.17

is that corresponding to a plant used at such a proportion of its capacity. Hence the actual level of costs, when this proportion of excess capacity exists (by design) and when the firm can choose any combination of inputs (i.e. the long run), will be as shown in Figure 9.18. The *LAC* cuts the *SAC* curves at 66% of the capacity of the latter; points *A*, *B*, and *C* on the three *SAC*s shown. It would be possible to produce a level of output above that indicated by the fitted *LAC*. But firms typically do not do this because it would reduce their excess capacity which is required for the reasons explained on page 238.

9.2.3 Economies of scope

Most firms produce several products. In many such cases at least one input is shared between the products. If a result of this sharing is that the total costs of producing these products or services at any level of output is lower than they would be if the goods were produced separately then an economy of scope exists. This is often expressed as:

$$C(Q_1, Q_2) < C(Q_1, 0) + C(0, Q_2)$$

where $C(Q_1, Q_2)$ denotes the total costs of producing Q_1 of good 1 and Q_2 of good 2 together, and $C(Q_1, 0)$ denotes the total cost of producing Q_1 of good 1 alone.

There are several sources of economies of scope. Firstly, there may be spare capacity in an indivisible resource. For example an indivisible production facility may exist whereby using the plant at capacity would exceed the demand but using a smaller plant would increase average costs. Thus a fridge storing meat may be used to store frozen vegetables, a research engineer may have ideas for additional new products apart from those relating to the product for which he or she was hired. A marketing department may have transferable and unused skills enabling new products to be introduced. Secondly, an input may be 'public' in the sense that production of good 2 does not reduce the output of good 1, as it would in the first

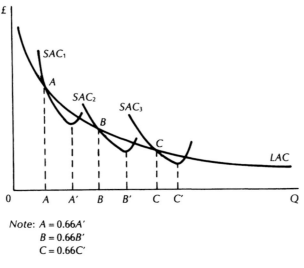

Note: $A = 0.66A'$
$B = 0.66B'$
$C = 0.66C'$

Figure 9.18

case. Examples here consist of inputs with peak load capacities which can be used at other times but without the capital costs of their acquisition. Thus electricity generators whose capacity is large enough to meet the peak hours demand for electricity and which could produce electricity at non-peak hours at a lower cost than if installed for non-peak use only. A similar example is that of buses used for service routes at peak hours and private hire at other times. Thirdly, cases where if the marginal costs of producing one product decrease as the output of the other rises. Examples include producing petrol and paraffin from crude oil rather than just petrol; producing orange juice as well as orange flesh for canning.

The managerial implications of scope economies relate to its product strategy which is considered in depth in Chapter 15. Briefly, managers should remember that since total costs from two products may be less than those of producing the two goods separately they should look out for products where there are spare inputs and calculate the profit for a package of products, not just a single product. They should look for products to produce together, thus fully utilising any spare capacity. If the firm could use such spare capacity and lower costs below those of separate production it may be able to undercut specialised firms in both markets.

9.2.4 The learning curve

In the above theories of costs it has been assumed that the level of labour force skill applicable at each output rate is given. However, empirical evidence suggests that even if the output *per period of time* is constant, as a greater cumulated output is produced, the productivity of labour increases. Hence the level of *LAC* decreases with cumulated output *over time*.

This phenomenon was originally observed by Alchian (1963) for the US aircraft manufacturing industry. He found that the general empirical relationship which best fitted his data was of the form:

$$\log L = a + b \log N \qquad (9.8)$$

where L denotes labour input per unit of output and N denotes the cumulated number of airframes produced. Diagrammatically, this is shown in Figure 9.19. (Other studies have found slightly different equations to be more appropriate.)

Baloff (1966) argues that the learning curve relates to the initial start-up phases of a product's manufacture, and is horizontal by the time the 'steady-state' phase of operation is reached. In the long run the manager would wish to know the equilibrium level of productivity level k in Figure 9.19, and therefore would wish to estimate the value of a in equation (9.8)

There are several reasons why productivity initially increases: for example, the development of greater skill and short cuts by a large range of personnel including machine operators, supervisors, salesmen, quality control and maintenance personnel. Engineers may redesign process machinery: for example, Abell and Hammond (1979) report that the semiconductor industry's average cost falls by 70–80% when cumulated output doubles. Product specifications may be changed slightly, perhaps to conserve raw materials or reduce machine time per item.

Apart from the relatively labour-intensive US airframe construction industry, Baloff quotes many US industries where equation (9.8), albeit with different values of b, is consistent with productivity growth – for example, in the highly mechanised manufacturing industries such as steel, glass, containers, and electrical conductors. The Boston Consulting Group has estimated learning curve equations for a range of products to which we shall return in Chapter 15.

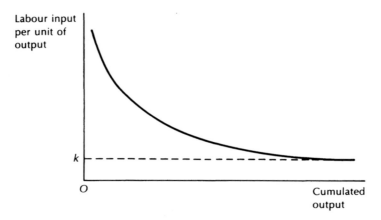

Figure 9.19

Box 9.3

The learning curve of the production of semiconductor memory chips

Memory chips are manufactured in a batch process: 'wafers' with components implanted are produced, each containing tens of chips. The main raw material used is silicon which is expensive. As a company increases its experience of producing wafers the ratio of usable to non-usable chips on each wafer increases. Thus, with experience, the output per unit of silicon and labour inputs increases and the average costs of production decrease.

Gruber (1992) has estimated the learning curves for different types of memory chips. He argues that average costs of a particular type of chip depends not just on the cumulated output of chips but also on (a) the output rate per period – indicating the magnitude of economies of scale and thus the position on a given *LAC* curve at which production occurred; and (b) how long a particular type of chip has been produced. (New generations of a type of chip are introduced every 18 to 36 months depending on the type of chip.) Due to data access difficulties the dependent variable is price but Gruber gives good reasons why this is an accurate proxy for unit cost.

Gruber found a 78% curve for EPROMS (Extended Programmable Read Only Memories). That is if cumulative output is doubled, average cost is reduced by 22%. The equation he estimated was:

$$\log P_t = 2.55 + 0.04 \log Q_t - 0.35 \log V_t - 0.18\ T_t$$

where P_t = average selling price, year t
Q_t = output, year t
V_t = cumulated output up to year t
T_t = time since production began, year t

This is plotted in Figure B9.1, where for illustrative purposes, Q_t is fixed at 10×10^{12} bits per year.

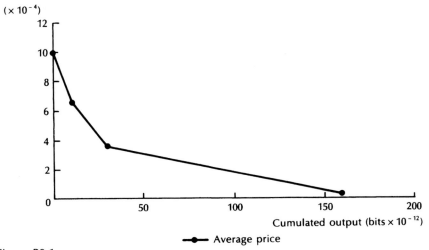

Figure B9.1

Source summarised from Gruber 1992.

9.3 Measurement of cost curves

9.3.1 Short run

Before discussing possible techniques for estimating short run (SR) cost curves we briefly recap on their nature. An SR cost curve shows the relationship between cost per period and the output per period which gave rise to it. The product is homogeneous, and input prices, the state of technology and the size of plant are fixed. A change in any of these last three variables would cause an SR cost curve to shift.

Two methods have been used to estimate SR cost curves: statistical cost analysis and the engineering approach, most studies having used the former. For ease of explanation we present the engineering approach under long-run analysis.

Statistical cost analysis

In this method, accounting data on STC or $STVC$ are regressed on the corresponding output, both having been adjusted so as to fulfil the assumptions of the theoretical curve as closely as possible. The observations may be cross-sectional or in time series. The former consist of one observation relating to one period for each of a large number of firms, all having the same plant capacity but operating at different outputs. Time series data consist of a series of observations each relating to the same firm with the same plant operated at different outputs over different periods.

Use of this technique presents a number of problems which must be overcome, and the technique itself has been criticised as not isolating the theoretical function.

Firstly, theoretical cost curves relate to opportunity costs whereas accounting data do not. What the firm forgoes when choosing the output of a product is important to know when comparing outputs of alternative products. Secondly, when using cross-section data, the accounting conventions must be the same across firms, otherwise a given output could be recorded as having incurred different costs even though all of the assumptions of the theory were fulfilled. In practice different accountants do not always classify the same items in costs.

Thirdly, theory requires the output in each period to be related to the costs it gave rise to. This involves estimating the portion of accounting costs in a period which were not due to current output and to establish the period to which they belonged. Usually this is not possible by examining what the cost entry in the accounts was attributable to, and estimates must be based on the views of engineers as to when events, which gave rise to certain costs, are likely to have occurred. For example, machinery may need repairing because of decay due to use and decay due simply to time. There may be much leeway as to when repairs may be made, hence they

---

Box 9.4

Practical use of engineering costs

R. Magee (1993) cites the case of the Best Baking Company which adopted an engineering approach to costs. The company produced 20 products per day. To estimate production costs (short run) the production workers completed forms to show the amounts of ingredients used and time taken for each batch of a line. The cost accountant converted these into total costs for each batch and so to average costs per batch. The accountant was able to correlate output with material and labour inputs and so by applying current material prices and current wage rates the cost of output could be calculated. (The company updated raw material prices and wage rates weekly).

Magee noted that the company gained the following immediate benefits when it moved to this system from standard costing procedures: the cost accountant needed to collect less data, part of the company's computer was released for other uses, production personnel no longer had to complete forms showing how long they spent on each job or raw materials they had used.

Source summarised from Magee 1993.

may be made long after the relevant output. Here there is a problem of finding which output the repairs are to be associated with (output may have varied greatly between the last and most recent repairs) and in finding how much of the accounting costs are due to usage (which is the relevant figure) and how much to obsolescence. Similarly, theoretical costs include depreciation of fixed capital due to usage but not due to obsolescence and time. But in practice, accountants usually adopt a method or methods of depreciation, which are intended to recapture the historical expenditure on the machine. The value which was estimated for usage cannot be extracted by examining the calculation of such figures because such a value was never separately estimated.

Fourthly, theoretical costs relate to a homogeneous output but most firms produce several products. In many cases separate cost and output figures for each product have not been collected and/or the products jointly use some of the same processes, so the collection of such data would be difficult. Two commonly used methods of solution are to add independent variables into the cost function which represent the differing characteristics of each product which might affect costs, and secondly to create an index of multiproduct output. The latter usually consists of a weighted average of the outputs of each product in which the weights consist of an index of each product's average direct costs. Staehle has criticised this multiproduct index by arguing that a spurious correlation of output with costs is created, because costs are entering both the independent and dependent variables. A virtual identity is being 'tested'.

Fifthly, when time series data are being used, the analyst must decide on the unit of time to which each observation relates. The shorter the period, the more difficult it is accurately to match output with cost. The longer the period the greater the chance of omitting fluctuations in output during such a period because a total would be taken instead of a separate figure for each subperiod. Staehle (1953) has argued that use of an average output rate during an accounting period rather than a smaller unit of time (so short that the ratio of output to inputs is constant in each) biases the cost curve towards linearity. Johnston (1960) has shown that the occurrence of this is likely to be rare.

Sixthly, the *STVC* curve is constructed under the assumption that technology is fixed. Therefore to identify this curve, each firm in a cross-section study must be using plant with the same technology and so must the firm at every period in the sample when time series are used. In neither case is this condition likely to hold. In a time series regression the assumption of constant technology may be false, despite the fact that the firm has the same capacity because more productive parts and improvements may have been introduced. If such changes are not allowed for in the function, one would obtain a curve which really crossed successive SR curves as they shifted downwards due to change. Also in practice this problem may render the selection of the total observation period very difficult. The greater the period's length the greater the probability that plant size will change.

Johnston (1960, p. 27) argues that in cross-section studies, the residual term of the regression equation[5] would incorporate differences between firms in the degree of efficiency with which each uses its stock of knowledge. Those which use it well would be averaged with those which do not. Therefore when using regression analysis a weaker requirement is adequate: that each firm has the same stock of knowledge.

Seventhly, the *SRTC* curve is constructed on the assumption that factor prices and quality and managerial efficiency, are given. In practice, when using time series data these assumptions are also unlikely to hold. Changes in factor prices are likely over months, or even within a day in some cases such as fuel. Greater labour skill and changing raw material quality are likely, as is a change in the degree to which management pursues efficient use of a plant to produce a given output and changes in factor prices, both over the business cycle. A rise in factor prices would, everything else being equal, cause the same output to be produced at different levels of cost over the observation periods. The usual procedure in this case is to deflate expenditure on each factor in each period so that all SR expenditure is calculated at the prices of a specific period, i.e. in pounds of constant purchasing power. Alternatively, the input quantities are calculated and multiplied by their prices in a given period. Johnston (1960, pp. 170–6) has shown that these procedures may cause bias by raising costs above their true value.

Johnston also argues that the net effect of other changes which persist over time can be taken into account by including, *t*, a time trend as an independent variable. For example, as time passes the educational standard of the labour force may increase. This is usually not done for factor price changes because their effects are important and may more accurately be included by the above procedures.

In cross-section data, factor prices may differ between firms in different locations (as may the quality of inputs obtainable for the same price). Such differences would distort the results because, again, everything else equal, output at different locations would be produced at different costs. In these cases Koutsoyiannis (1979) argues that accuracy may be partially restored by including an independent variable relating to location.

Having decided what to do about the above difficulties, the analyst proceeds to specify the cost function which he or she wishes to estimate. The theoretical cost function is cubic in form with output as the independent variable:

$$STVC_t = \beta_1 Q_t + \beta_2 Q_t^2 + \beta_3 Q_t^3 + \varepsilon_t$$

Inclusion of a constant, α, and changing the dependent variable to STC would enable an estimate for costs which do not vary with output, i.e. TFC, to be made.

If the econometrician believes that other functions are more appropriate to his or her firm then the econometrician should estimate these. Most studies have estimated cubic, quadratic and linear functions with respect to output.

9.3.3 Long-run cost curves

A long-run cost function represents the relationship between cost and output when all inputs are variable in quantity. It is constructed under the assumption that only current technology is used and factor prices and quality are both fixed. Output units are assumed to be homogeneous, produced at the lowest possible cost and using any quantities of inputs which are necessary. Three measurement techniques have been used: statistical cost analysis, the engineering approach and the survivor technique.

Statistical cost analysis

As in the estimation of short-run curves TC or LAC may be regressed against the relevant output, both adjusted to fulfil the above assumptions as closely as possible. Again time series or cross-sectional observations may be used. Each observation of the former type would relate to the costs and outputs of a single firm, but the total observations would be taken over a sufficiently long period that output levels and all inputs have varied considerably. Each cross-sectional observation would relate to a different firm during a short period and the sample would be chosen so that the range of capacity outputs would be considerable. Hence, firms with different quantities of inputs which are fixed in the short run would be included.

Many problems which are likely to occur in the estimation of short-run curves also occur when long-run curves are estimated. The first five problems cited in the case of SR cost curve estimation also apply to long-run cost curves. Similarly factor prices must be constant for all firms in a cross-section sample and for each time series observation. In addition, as in the short-run case, the theoretical long-run cost curve requires only the current technology to be used. Since time series observations in long-run estimation need to be very long, this assumption is especially unlikely to hold. In cross-sectional data the assumption is also unlikely to be valid because many firms will be using technologies of different ages. Plants are almost certainly not continually updated. However, greater division of labour which large size may allow, may enable large firms to use current technology more efficiently. It may allow them to use larger and more productive machines. This effect should not be removed since it does not represent a difference between firms in the modernity of the technology available to them.

Further, the theoretical curve is constructed on the assumption that each output is produced using the plant which produces it at lowest cost. In cross-section data, even if every firm used current technology, many firms at a point in time will not have adjusted their plant size(s) to fulfil this assumption: output may fluctuate much faster than plant size and/or some or all managers may be inattentive to possible cost reductions. Therefore in some cases the output may be produced on an SAC curve at a point away from the LAC i.e. Q_0 with SAC_1 in Figure 9.20. Since costs which are below the LAC (or LTC) for a given output are by definition unattainable, the observation can only lie on or above the long-run cost curve. Hence the estimated curve is likely to lie above the true one. This is shown in Figure 9.20 where points A, B, C and D are observed, cost–output combinations to which the incorrect LAC curve, LAC^*, has been fitted.

When cross-section data is used an incorporation problem may arise. If the LAC is estimated to have an L shape, as most studies have found, it is not clear which of two hypotheses is correct. That is whether (a) economies of scale exist, or (b) economies of scale do not exist and those firms which have operated on the LAC have grown to their currently large size leaving those who operated above the LAC to remain so at their original size. Johnston (1960, p. 188) has argued that in general, for past studies, the former hypothesis is more likely than the latter for three reasons. Firstly, many past studies have related to public utilities which because of their legal monopoly have not grown by competing with other firms. Secondly, it is not necessarily the case that a small low cost firm remains low cost when it expands. Low cost after expansion often necessitates complete reconstruction of a plant. Thirdly, a conclusion must be based on all of the relevant evidence. Both the empirical results *and* theory indicate economies of scale.

Finally Friedman (1955) has argued that relating cost to output rather than to say, capacity, renders the 'regression fallacy' likely. It is argued that on average small firms are likely to produce at relatively low percentages of capacity, whilst large firms are likely to produce at relatively high percentages of capacity. Even if the SAC curves of all firms lie along a horizontal LAC curve, the lower capacity utilisation of

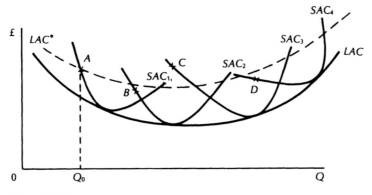

Figure 9.20

Table 9.1

Company number	Average cost (£ per ton)	Output (tons per week)	Wage rate (£ per week)	Cost of capital (£ per sq foot)
1	140	100	200	10
2	60	600	180	8
3	90	2400	160	7
4	35	1750	150	6
5	45	1050	170	6
6	60	2300	150	5
7	120	150	150	6
8	60	200	110	4
9	35	2100	120	7
10	40	900	100	3
11	50	400	120	5
12	100	100	170	6
13	130	2600	210	12
14	75	300	150	10
15	120	2500	170	11
16	85	150	160	8
17	100	2500	170	10
18	50	700	190	12
19	80	2500	150	6
20	50	2100	180	9
21	30	1900	150	7
22	30	1500	130	8
23	45	1500	190	8
24	40	1200	150	6
25	60	900	210	14

small firms would be likely to cause them to have higher average costs than large firms. The resulting *LAC* indicates economies of scale despite a horizontal *LAC* curve.

Because of the particular problems of changes in technology and in the characteristics of the product over time, time series data is used less often in the estimation of *LTC* curves than cross sectional data. As an illustration of the use of regression analysis to estimate long-run cost curves consider the (hypothetical) data shown in Table 9.1 relating to a specialist steel manufacturing industry. Each observation relates to a different company. We have estimated two alternative specifications of the *LAC* function:

Model 1

$$LAC_i = \alpha + \beta_1 X_i + \beta_2 P_L + \beta_3 P_K$$

and

Model 2

$$LAC_i = \gamma + \delta_1 X_i + \delta_2 X_i^2 + \delta_3 P_L + \delta_4 P_K$$

where LAC_i = average costs, company i;
X_i = output, company i;
P_{Li} = wage rate, company i;
P_{Ki} = cost of capital, company i.

The results are shown in Tables 9.2 and 9.3.

Notice that Model 1 explains a much lower proportion of the variation in *LAC* than does Model 2 as indicated by the relative values of the R^2. Furthermore by considering the values of the *t*-statistics it can be seen that none of the coefficients on the variables in Model 1 are statistically significant from zero. We cannot reject the hypothesis that each of output, wage rate and cost of capital have no effect on average costs. However in the case Model 2 all of the variables except the cost of capital are statistically significant, that is they do have an effect on average costs. Figure 9.21 shows the predicted values of *LAC* plotted against output (with the wage rate and the cost of capital equal to their mean values in the data). The predicted curve is a U shape. Notice that if we differentiate the estimated equation (using the rules from Chapter 2) it can be seen that the value of output at which *LAC* is a minimum is 1,349 tons per week. This would indicate the optimum size of firm in this industry.

Engineering cost curves

In its purest form the technique involves the derivation of a relationship between output and inputs for each stage of production on the basis of physical, chemical and

Table 9.2. Model 1

Ordinary Least Squares Estimation

****

Dependent variable is   LAC
25 observations used for estimation from   1 to   25

****

Regressor	Coefficient	Standard Error	T-Ratio [Prob]
C	−7.7381	39.3406	−.19670 [.846]
X	−.0029953	.0071402	−.41950 [.679]
PL	.48628	.35675	1.3631 [.187]
PK	.41358	3.8869	.10640 [.916]
R-Squared	.20688	*F*-statistic F(3,21)	1.8259 [.173]
R-Bar-Squared	.093572	S.E. of Regression	31.5369
Residual Sum of Squares	20886.1	Mean of Dependent Variable	69.2000
S.D. of Dependent Variable	33.1248	Maximum of Log-likelihood	−119.5730
DW-statistic	1.4870		

****

Table 9.3. Model 2

Ordinary Least Squares Estimation

****

Dependent variable is   LAC
25 observations used for estimation from   1 to   25

****

Regressor	Coefficient	Standard Error	T-Ratio [Prob]
C	54.6233	18.2123	2.9993 [.007]
X	−.12767	.013343	−9.5685 [.000]
X2	.4732E−4	.4926E−5	9.6049 [.000]
PL	.38694	.15465	2.5020 [.021]
PK	.14003	1.6814	.083281 [.934]
R-Squared	.85869	*F*-statistic F(4, 20)	30.3834 [.000]
R-Bar-Squared	.83043	S.E. of Regression	13.6404
Residual Sum of Squares	3721.2	Mean of Dependent Variable	69.2000
S.D. of Dependent Variable	33.1248	Maximum of Log-likelihood	−98.0102
DW-statistic	2.5076		

****

$x2$ is x_i^2

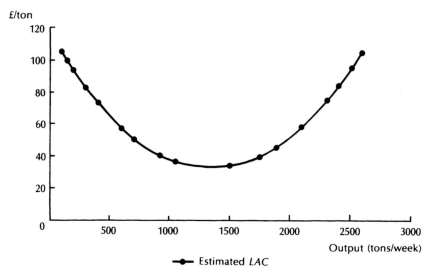

Figure 9.21

engineering 'laws'. This 'production function' may, if there are only two inputs, be presented as a series of isoquants. Stage two is to find the minimum level of total costs which, given factor prices, is necessary to produce each output. If there are only two inputs, an isocost line may be applied to the 'isoquants' as in Section 9.2. The minimum total cost necessary to produce each output may be plotted against that output to derive the total cost curve.

To derive short-run cost curves the plant etc., is assumed given and the production function for the variable inputs is calculated. The minimum costs of producing each output are correspondingly deduced. In practice, it is usually impossible to derive production functions from scientific laws. Instead engineers, managers and cost accountants are asked to calculate the lowest costs of producing selected hypothetical levels of output on the basis of their experience of working with the techniques of their industry. They are told to assume that any currently available production technique may be incorporated. Some items within the estimate may be based on scientific laws, others not.

This method has several weaknesses. The first two relate to the measurement of *LAC*s, the third to *LAC*s and *SAC*s. Firstly, engineers have less knowledge of the costs at scales which differ greatly from those in which they work, even if these techniques are known by others. Therefore inaccuracies are likely to occur when estimated LC curves are extrapolated to scales at which no respondents operate. Secondly, common procedure is to extrapolate from the verified technical relationship which holds for a small pilot plant to one for a large scale plant. Such extrapolation may involve error and many past studies which have adopted this approach have subsequently been shown to have underestimated the levels of *LAC* at extrapolated outputs.

Thirdly, since the technique essentially involves consideration of technical relationships associated with production processes, it does not yield estimates for managerial, administrative or research costs. Similarly, it is unlikely to give accurate estimates for service industries which are relatively labour intensive rather than relying on, for example, relationships between surface areas and volumes of receptacles.

However, the engineering approach has the advantages of deriving cost curves on the basis of a given state of technology and given factor prices.

The survivor technique

Use of this technique (as proposed by Stigler, 1958) assumes that the firm (or plant) operates in a highly competitive market. It also assumes that only those firms which produce at the minimum average cost possible will, in the long run, survive. Others will make less than normal profits and leave the size class either by exit from the industry or growth or contraction. Hence firms in those firm-size classes which are losing their share of industry capacity have higher average costs than firms in those size classes which are increasing their share. Therefore, by determining the firm sizes in the latter category, one determines the range of sizes over which costs are lower than those at any other sizes. Firm size is measured by *share* of industry capacity or of output, rather than by absolute capacity or output because this will nullify the effects of changes in factors which affect all size classes.

An advantage of this technique is that it can relate only to a *plant* rather than to a firm. Therefore the difficulties of dividing joint costs of different products produced by a firm and of constructing a multiproduct output index, do not exist (provided the plant produces a single product).

Shepherd (1967) points out several limitations of the technique. Firstly, survival depends on profits and not just costs. Profits may be influenced by non-minimal costs due to market imperfections, for example restrictive agreements or barriers to entry preventing potential competition from potential entrants. Firms of non-optimal size could exist and may even grow. Similarly, if a range of sizes is found to have an increasing market share, one cannot assume the *LAC* is flat in this region. Cost may vary with size, but, due to some impediment to competition, so may revenue.

In addition, multiplant and single-plant firms are not distinguished. Plant-level survival may be due to parent companies financing losses of plants which are too small or too large to have minimum average costs.

Thirdly, the technique does not indicate the level or shape of the *LAC* but only the range of firm (or plant) sizes at which average costs are lowest.

Fourthly, the technique yields implausible results if the firm (or plant) size distribution remains unchanged: all sizes of firm would be predicted to have minimum average costs.

Fifthly, factor prices and technology are likely to change over the observation period. Depending on the nature of the technical changes, the output at which firms (or plants) achieve lowest average costs may be changing. The same applies to factor prices. In addition, on a practical note, if a firm uses the Census of Production in the United Kingdom, the most relevant size measure available is employment. Technical change may alter the employment–output ratio. Therefore, even if the predicted optimum firm size in terms of *employment* remained constant, the lowest cost *output* may have been changing.

Sixthly, the technique assumes that all firms (or plants) experience the same environmental conditions. Lower input prices in one region may enable suboptimally sized firms to exist there. However an advocate of the technique would reply that in the long run such inefficiency would be competed away.

The technique also assumes that all firms have the same objectives. If they do not, inefficient firms may exist. But notice that if one firm is a profit maximiser and inefficiency is well known, only other firms whose behaviour is close to profit maximisation will survive.

Finally, because survival depends on factors which are excluded from the traditional theory of *LAC*, the concept of efficiency to which the technique relates differs from that of the *LAC* curve. Examples of such factors which are implicitly considered by the technique but which are explicitly excluded from the traditional analysis are *size-related* flexibility to uncertainty, economies in R&D and labour relations.

Appendix 9

Mathematical derivation of cost minimising combination of inputs

We may write the production function as:

$$Q = f(I_1, I_2 \ldots I_n)$$

where Q is total output and I_i is the quantity used of commodity or factor $i (i = 1 \ldots n)$. The total cost equation (equation 9.2) may be generalised to:

$$TC = P_1 I_1 + P_2 I_2 + \ldots P_n I_n$$

Suppose the firm wishes to minimise the total cost of production subject to the constraint that $Q = Q^*$. Therefore we may use the Lagrangian multiplier technique of Chapter 2:

$$TC_\lambda = P_1 I_1 + P_2 I_2 + \ldots P_n I_n + \lambda [Q^* - f(I_1, I_2 \ldots I_n)]$$

$$\frac{\partial TC_\lambda}{\partial I_1} = P_1 - \lambda \frac{\partial f}{\partial I_1} = 0 \tag{A9.1}$$

$$\frac{\partial TC_\lambda}{\partial I_2} = P_2 - \lambda \frac{\partial f}{\partial I_2} = 0 \tag{A9.2}$$

$$\vdots \qquad \vdots \quad \vdots \quad \vdots$$

$$\frac{\partial TC_\lambda}{\partial I_n} = P_n - \lambda \frac{\partial f}{\partial I_n} = 0 \tag{A9.3}$$

$$\frac{\partial TC}{\partial \lambda} = Q^* - f(I_1, I_2 \ldots I_n) = 0 \tag{A9.4}$$

This system of $n + 1$ simultaneous equations can be solved and values of I_1 to I_n obtained (provided second order conditions are satisfied). To solve the system, the price term is made the subject of equations (A9.1) and (A9.2) for example, and the first equation is divided by the latter:

$$\frac{P_1}{P_2} = \frac{\partial f / \partial I_1}{\partial f / \partial I_2}$$

Since $\partial f / \partial I_1$ is the marginal product of input 1, MP_1, and similarly $\partial f / \partial I_2$ equals MP_2 we have:

$$\frac{P_1}{P_2} = \frac{MP_1}{MP_2} \Rightarrow \frac{MP_1}{P_1} = \frac{MP_2}{P_2}$$

Note that in the case of the Cobb–Douglas function for K and L (see equation (9.1)) it can be shown that[6]

$$\frac{K}{L} = \frac{\text{Exponent on } K \times P_L}{\text{Exponent on } L \times P_K}$$

This allows us a short cut for finding the inputs to maximise output given TC, or to minimise TC given output. Thus, for the function $Q = 1.2 L^{0.6} K^{0.4}$, the ratio of K/L which does this is:

$$\frac{K}{L} = \frac{0.4 P_L}{0.6 P_K} \tag{A9.5}$$

If the TC equation is:

$$1000 = 2L + K \tag{A9.6}$$

that is, $P_L = 2$ and $P_K = 1$, we have from (A9.5) that:

$$K/L = 0.4 \times (2/0.6) \times 1 \Rightarrow K = 4/3L \tag{A9.7}$$

Substituting (A9.7) into (A9.6) we have:

$$1000 = 2L + \tfrac{4}{3}L \Rightarrow L = 300$$

$K = 400$ (by substitution in (A9.6) and $Q = 403.9$.

The maximum output which can be produced with a given budget of £1,000 is approximately 404 units per period.

Notes

1. Note a homogeneous function always has a given value of v (returns to scale). A non-homogeneous function may exhibit varying returns to scale. For example, if L and K are multiplied by λ, we cannot factorise λ^v out from: $Q = 80L + 50K + 40LK - L^3 - K^3$. Notice that by substituting various values of K and L into this equation, at relatively low inputs a doubling of each input more than doubles output (*IRS*) whereas at higher levels of inputs doubling both results in less than double output (*DRS*) as follows:

L	K	% Δ in both inputs	Q	% Δ in Q
1	1		154	
2	2	100	404	262
.	.		.	
.	.		.	
7	7		2184	
14	14	100	4172	91

2. To reduce process *B*'s output below 20, either some of the inputs will have to stand idle for some period or output is destroyed.
3. Also at very high output rates due to higher machinery breakdowns, etc.
4. This can be understood more clearly by noting that, from the shape of the *ADC* curve in Figure 9.15, the shape of the *TDC* curve is:

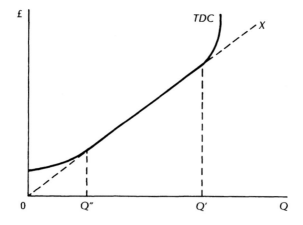

At outputs below Q'', *ADC* exceeds that above Q'' hence the *TDC* curve lies above line *OX* for these outputs. But, since *ADC* is constant over the outputs Q'' to Q', $TDC/Q = k$

where k is a constant, so $TDC = k$. Q thus $ADC = MC(= k)$. Hence in this region TDC has a constant slope. Above Q' ADC exceeds the level between Q'' and Q' so TDC is greater than that given by line OX. By examining the slope of the TDC line itself and of rays from the origin to the TDC line, the shape of the MC curve in Figure 9.15 can be deduced.

5. See Chapter 8 for an explanation of the residual term.

6.
$$\frac{MP_L}{P_L} = \frac{MP_K}{P_K} \Rightarrow \frac{MP_L}{MP_K} = \frac{P_L}{P_K} \Rightarrow \frac{baL^{b-1}K^c}{caL^b K^{c-1}} = \frac{P_L}{P_K}$$

$$\Rightarrow \frac{bK}{cL} = \frac{P_L}{P_K} \Rightarrow \frac{K}{L} = \frac{cP_L}{bP_K}$$

Bibliography

Abell, D. F. and Hammond, J. J. (1979) *Strategic Market Planning*, Prentice Hall.

Alchian, A. (1963) 'Reliability of progress curves in airframe production', *Econometrica*, vol. 31, 4.

Andrews, P. W. S. (1949) *Manufacturing Business*, Macmillan.

Bain, J. S. (1965) *Barriers to New Competition*, Harvard University Press.

Baloff, N. (1966) 'The learning curve – some controversial issues', *Journal of Industrial Economics*, vol. 14.

Boston Consulting Group (1972) *Perspectives on Experience*, BCG.

Dean, J. (1976) *Statistical Cost Estimation*, Indiana University Press.

Done, K. (1993) 'Hard slog to make the marriage work', *Financial Times*, 2 September.

Friedman, M. (1955 'Comment' in Universities National Bureau Committee for Economic Research, *Business Concentration and Price Policy*, Princeton University Press.

Fuss, M. A. and Gupta, V. K. (1981) 'A cost function approach to the estimation of minimum efficient scale, returns to scale and suboptimal capacity', *European Economic Review*, vol. 15.

Glass, J. L. and McKillop, D. G. (1992) 'An empirical analysis of scale and scope economies and technical change in an Irish multiproduct banking firm', *Journal of Banking and Finance*, vol. 16.

Gravelle, H. and Rees, R. (1992) *Microeconomics*, 2nd edn, Longman.

Gropper, D. (1991) 'An empirical investigation of changes in scale economies for the commercial banking firm 1979–86', *Journal of Money, Credit and Banking*, vol. 23.

Gruber, H. (1992) 'The learning curve in the production of semiconductor memory chips', *Applied Economics*, vol. 24.

Haldi, J. and Whitcomb, P. (1967) 'Economies of scale in industrial plants', *Journal of Political Economy*, vol. 75, 4.

Hibdon, J. E. and Mueller, M. J. (1990) 'Economies of scale in petroleum refining 1947–1984: A survivor principle time series analysis', *Review of Industrial Organisation*, Autumn.

Johnston, J. (1960) *Statistical Cost Analysis*, McGraw-Hill.

Keeler, T. C. (1989) 'Deregulation and scale economies in the US trucking industry: An econometric extension of the survivor principle', *Journal of Law and Economics*, vol. 32(2), part 1.

Koutsoyiannis, A. K. (1979) *Modern Microeconomics*, Macmillan.

Magee, R. (1993) 'Valuing production using engineering costs', *Management Accounting* (US), March, pp. 50–3.

McPhee, C. R. and Peterson, R. D. (1990) 'The economies of scale revisited: Comparing census costs, engineering estimates, and the survivor technique', *Quarterly Journal of Economics and Business*, vol. 29(2), Spring.

Pratten, C. F. (1971) *Economies of Scale in Manufacturing Industry*, Cambridge University Press.

Rees, R. (1973) 'Optimum plant size in United Kingdom industries: some survivor estimates', *Economica*, vol. 40.

Robidoux, B. and Lester, J. (1992) 'Econometric estimates of scale economies in Canadian manufacturing', *Applied Economics*, vol. 24.

Rogers, R. P. 'The minimum optimal steel plant and the survivor technique of cost estimation', Federal Trade Commission Bureau of Economics Working Paper 197.

Saving, T. (1961) 'Estimation of optimum size of plant by the survivor technique', *Quarterly Journal of Economics*, vol. 75.

Scherer, F. M., Breckenstein, A., Kaufer, E. and Murphy, R. D. (1975) *The Economics of Multiplant Operations*, Harvard University Press.

Shepherd, W. G. (1967) 'What does the survivor technique show about economies of scale?', *Southern Economic Journal*, vol. 34.

Shoesmith, G. L. (1988) 'Economies of scale and scope in petroleum refining', *Applied Economics*, vol. 20.

Siberston, Z. A. (1972) 'Economies of scale in theory and practice', *Economic Journal*, Supplement, vol. 82.

Silk, A. J. and Berndt, E. R. (1993) 'Scale and scope effects on advertising agency costs', *Marketing Science*, vol. 12.

Smith, C. A. (1955) 'Survey of the empirical evidence on economies of scale', in Universities National Bureau Committee for Economic Research, *Business Concentration and Price Policy*, Princeton University Press.

Staehle, H. (1953) 'The measurement of statistical cost functions: an appraisal of some recent contributions', in Stigler, G. J., *Readings in Price Theory*, Allen & Unwin.

Stigler, G. J. (1958) 'The economies of scale', *The Journal of Law and Economics*, vol. 1.

Tomkins, R. (1993) 'Dinosaurs on the runway', *Financial Times*, 8 December.

Varian, H. (1993) *Intermediate Microeconomics*, 3rd edn, Norton.

Williamson, O. (1967) 'Hierarchical control and optimum firm size', *Journal of Political Economy*, vol. 75.

Williamson, O. (1970) *Corporate Control and Business Behaviour*, Prentice Hall.

Williamson O. (1975) *Markets and Hierarchies*, Collier Macmillan.

Williamson, O. (1986) *Economic Organisation*, Harvester Wheatsheaf.

Chapter 10

Linear programming

Linear programming is a technique used to solve maximisation or minimisation problems in the presence of constraints. This is precisely the intention of the Lagrangian multiplier techniques described in Chapter 2. Why then did we not discuss linear programming in Chapter 2, and what distinguishes it from the calculus techniques described there? Firstly, Lagrangian techniques can only handle *exactly equal* constraints. Thus, a Lagrangian problem might be formulated so as to minimise cost, subject to the constraint that exactly 100 units of total output were produced. A corresponding linear programming (LP) problem would be formulated so as to minimise cost provided that *no less* than 100 units of total output were produced. Secondly, the Lagrangian technique can be applied when both the objective function and the constraints are non-linear, whereas the LP method requires that both sets of equations be linear.

Thirdly, the LP technique has much in common with production theory, and comprehension will be increased if it is examined now, after we have studied the economic theory of production, rather than before. Initially, however, we will examine the dissimilarities.

10.1 Least-cost input combinations

What differences are there between LP analysis and the classical production function? Firstly, the classical production function assumes that there is an infinite number of processes available to choose from. In turn, this implies that the firm can smoothly and continuously substitute one input factor for another. More realistically, LP analysis restricts the number of alternative processes to whatever finite number is relevant, and the possibility of continuous substitution is thus disregarded. Secondly, LP analysis restricts itself to one particular variant of the production function, namely the linear homogeneous production function. The expansion path of such a production function is always a straight line through the origin. That is, at given input prices, the optimal proportions of the firm's input factors will not change with the size of the input budget. Economies and diseconomies of scale are not present in such a situation since costs rise linearly with output.

Assume the firm is producing a single product using two input factors Y and Z. Also assume there are three alternative production processes A, B and C, available to the firm each of which uses a different but fixed combination of Y and Z. In Figure 10.1 the three 'process rays' OA, OB and OC join up points representing units of output. Thus A_2, B_2, and C_2 all represent two units of output, but are produced by processes A, B and C respectively, using the quantities of inputs which are indicated by their respective positions on the YZ plane. Because there are constant returns to scale $OA_1 = A_1A_2 = A_2A_3$, and so on. Similarly, $OB_1 = B_1B_2 = B_2B_3$ and $OC_1 = C_1C_2 = C_2C_3$. (There is, however, no reason why OA_1 should equal either OB_1 or OC_1 in geometric distance.)

If we now join the points of equal output, A_1 with B_1 with C_1, and so on, then we have constructed a family of production isoquants, identical to the isoquants of our discussion in the last chapter. This statement requires both qualification and expansion. Each point on B_6C_6 (for example) corresponds to a *combination* of processes B and C which produces the same output as OB_6 units by process B or OC_6 units by process C.

This is proved by taking any point P on line B_6C_6 and drawing a line through P parallel to OB (the result would be the same if the line were drawn parallel to OC). This intersects OC at C_4 indicating that four units should be produced using process C and the remaining two using process B, since $C_4P = B_4B_6$ as opposite sides of a parallelogram, and $B_4B_6 = OB_2$. (This implies the important economic assumption that simultaneous use of two processes will neither enhance nor detract from input–output relationships of the two individual processes.) A similar exercise could be performed on any of the isoquant segments connecting points such as A_6 and C_6 on rays OA and OC which would represent combinations of processes A, B and/or C which produced the same output as OA_6 or OC_6. This, however, is

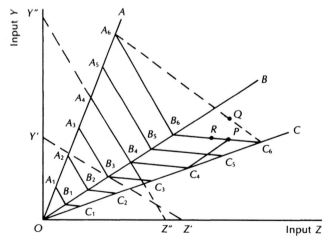

Figure 10.1

wasteful and will never occur in an optimal situation. For consider any point Q on A_6C_6. Corresponding to any such point there will be points such as R on $A_6B_6C_6$ which lie below and to the left of Q. Thus R uses less of *both* Y and Z than does Q, but both R and Q yield the same outputs. Therefore Q can be ignored as far as the $A_6B_6C_6$ isoquant is concerned.

This conclusion points to another similarity between LP analysis and production theory. Although the LP production isoquants have kinks or corners (which calculus techniques cannot handle) their slopes are generally negative and they are convex to the origin. In other words, while LP analysis rules out diminishing returns to scale, the type of diminishing returns associated with the diminishing marginal rate of substitution of one input for another is embraced by it.

To Figure 10.1 we can add isocost lines. $Y'Z'$ and $Y''Z''$ represent two possible such lines. For the relative price levels indicated by $Y'Z'$, process B is optimal at output level B_3. $Y''Z''$ is drawn parallel to the isoquant segment A_4B_4. Here either process A or B, or any combination is optimal, with a total output of 4 units.

So far we have assumed that there are no constraints imposed on the ability of the firm to obtain inputs at constant prices. Clearly this is unrealistic. Firms have access only to limited amounts of machinery, floor space, labour or whatever at any one time, irrespective of their cash resources. The effects of such limitations are illustrated graphically in Figure 10.2. The maximum obtainable amounts of Y and Z are indicated by the Y and Z constraints respectively. The production possibilities open to the firm are represented by the shaded area bounded by the constraints and the process rays OA and OC. (Y and Z cannot be combined in proportions other than those on the rays, or between the rays, when processes are combined.) The area $ORST$ is known as the *feasible space*. If the firm is trying to maximise output subject to the Y and Z constraints, it should operate where the feasible space touches the highest possible isoquant. This will be at point S. By constructing the relevant parallelogram the appropriate combination of processes B and C can be found which will enable this isoquant to be reached.

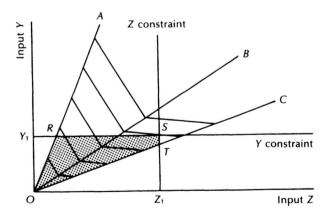

Figure 10.2

10.2 Optimising the output mix

Here we will broaden our discussion and move away from the single product situation to the more common multiproduct firm. We will consider a firm with three inputs X, Y and Z, and two outputs, products A and B. The firm wishes to maximise profits and, subject to input availability constraints, needs to determine the optimal quantities of A and B which will achieve this goal.

We will first examine the position geometrically, then algebraically and finally using the Simplex method. Clearly, the list of variables could be extended well beyond five, were it not for geometric complexity.

10.2.1 The geometric approach

The typical LP problem is set out under the following headings:

> The objective function
> The constraints
> The non-negativity requirements

Let us set these out for our hypothetical example.

The objective function

The objective is to maximise profits. In LP problems 'profits' refer to 'contribution profits' (i.e. total revenue less variable costs). Fixed costs are ignored. However, since fixed costs are constant irrespective of output, the output level which maximises contribution profits also maximises profits net of fixed costs. (See Chapter 19 for a fuller discussion on contribution analysis.) Unit contribution equals price less average variable cost; if this is £2 for A and £3 for B then the objective function can be written thus:

$$\text{maximise } \pi_c = £2Q_A + £3Q_B \tag{10.1}$$

where π_c is total contribution profit and Q_A and Q_B are the quantities produced of A and B respectively.

The constraints

To obtain the constraint equations we need to know how many units of the inputs X, Y and Z are available in each period. Say these are 20, 25 and 30 respectively. Coupled with this we need to know how many units of each of X, Y and Z are required to produce, respectively, one unit of the outputs A and B. Say these are

2, 3 and 0 for A and 5, $2\frac{1}{2}$ and 12 for B. The constraint equations can now be written thus:

$$2Q_A + 5Q_B \leqslant 20 \text{ (available units of } X) \tag{10.2}$$

$$3Q_A + 2\tfrac{1}{2}Q_B \leqslant 25 \text{ (available units of } Y) \tag{10.3}$$

$$12Q_B \leqslant 30 \text{ (available units of } Z) \tag{10.4}$$

The non-negativity requirements

Clearly no one making a graphic analysis would ever recommend negative outputs. However, in a complex algebraic problem solved by means of a computer, it may appear 'logical' to recommend certain negative outputs to maximise the objective function. Mathematically this might be possible; in practice it is nonsense. (Graphically it implies merely going to the left of the vertical and below the horizontal axis.) To ensure that this nonsense result does not occur, the following equations are included in the system:

$$Q_A \geqslant 0 \tag{10.5}$$

$$Q_B \geqslant 0 \tag{10.6}$$

Geometrically, the first step is to determine the feasible space. Figure 10.3 illustrates how this is done by drawing the corresponding lines of equations (10.2), (10.3) and (10.4) on the AB plane. The shaded area $OPRST$ represents the feasible space. Only points within this area meet all the constraints and also the non-negativity requirements.

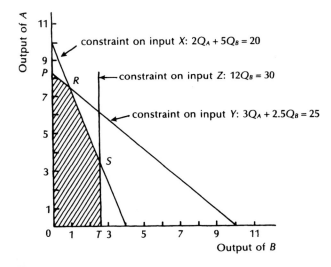

Figure 10.3

Next we must graph in the objective function, equation (10.1). This is illustrated in Figure 10.4 by the family of isocontribution lines. Each such line satisfies equation (10.1) and plots all possible contributions of A and B which produce a constant total contribution profit.

The solution to our problem becomes obvious when the feasible space $OPRST$ is superimposed in Figure 10.4. Maximum contribution profits are £18 which are achieved by the output mix of products A and B indicated by point R.

If $\pi_c = £18$ had the shape indicated by the dashed line parallel to segment RS, the optimal solution would then have been any point between and including R and S. For the algebra involved in LP analysis this last conclusion is important. Given the linearities involved in the analysis, optimal solutions occur at 'corners' of the feasible space, or along the whole of one boundary face (R to S in Figure 10.4, A_4 to B_4 in Figure 10.1). Since the firm will be indifferent as to where on the highest attainable isocontribution line it lies, it can restrict its algebraic computations to only the corner points of the feasible region and, accordingly, ignore the near infinite number of solutions within that region.

10.2.2 The arithmetic approach

To the LP format with which the previous subsection was introduced, one other concept must be added: *slack variables*. These account for that amount of any input which is unused. In our example the firm had three inputs X, Y and Z. Consequently we introduce three slack variables S_X, S_Y and S_Z, one for each input. This enables us to rewrite each constraint relationship as an equation, not an inequality.

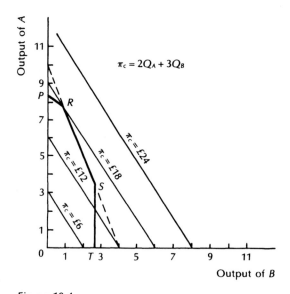

Figure 10.4

Box 10.1

Optimising wood inputs in cabinet manufacturing

Wellborn Cabinet Inc. owns a facility which manufactures wooden cabinets. This consists of a sawmill, four dry kilns and a cabinet assembly plant which includes a sawmill for producing blanks. To make blanks Wellborn has been buying no. 1 and no. 2 grades of hardwood logs to produce lumber from its sawmill. (A lower grade number indicates a higher quality.) It also buys common-grade timber. After the conversion of logs into lumber both this wood and lumber bought from outside the firm must be dried before it is made into blanks. Wooden raw materials make up 45% of total material costs of manufacturing cabinets.

The company wished to know how much of each grade and type of lumber to buy from outside sources and what volume of logs of each diameter, length and grade to buy to minimise total costs for producing blanks. Here we will simplify the problem by supposing that all logs are of the same diameter and length. So the objective function is:

$$\text{Minimise } \sum_i C1_i Q_i + \sum_j C2_j L_j$$

where $C1_i$ = cost of purchase, sawing, converting into lumber and converting into blanks per unit volume of grade i logs;

$C2_j$ = cost per unit volume of delivery plus converting outside lumber grade j into blanks;

Q_i = volume of logs required per week, grade i;

L_j = volume of outside lumber of grade j required.

The constraints faced by the firm were as follows. Firstly, the sawmill had a capacity of 1,500 logs per week. Expressing this in terms of their volume gives:

$$\sum_{i=1}^{2} Q_i \leqslant M$$

Secondly, the drying capacity of the kilns was fixed at a certain number of hours per week, S. Thus the firm must fulfil:

$$\sum_i R_1 Q_i + \sum_j R_2 L_j \leqslant S$$

where R_1 = the drying rate of lumber per unit volume of logs grade i
R_2 = the drying rate of outside lumber grade j.

Thirdly, the total supply of lumber must be at least equal to the volume of blanks required per week, Q. Therefore:

$$\sum_i b_i Q_i + \sum_j d_j L_j > Q$$

where b_i = volume of blanks per unit volume of logs grade i
d_j = volume of blanks per unit volume of lumber grade j bought from outside.

In addition two further constraints were imposed to ensure that the volumes of logs and lumber purchased did not exceed previous average values.

This model was developed by researchers working with Wellborn. It was expected that when the company implemented the linear programming solutions they will give savings of 32% in wood raw material costs.

Source summarised and simplified from Carino and Le Noir 1988.

Clearly, any slack variable which has a zero value at the optimal solution point is a possible bottleneck or limitation on production and profitability increases. Conversely, a positive value for a slack variable at the optimal point is indicative of possible excess capacity. Slack variables can never have negative values so this must be built into the non-negativity requirements.

Our illustrative problem can now be specified as follows:

$$\text{maximise } \pi_c = £2Q_A + £3Q_B \tag{10.1}$$

subject to the constraints

$$2Q_A + 5Q_B + S_X = 20 \tag{10.7}$$

$$3Q_A + 2\tfrac{1}{2}Q_B + S_Y = 25 \tag{10.8}$$

and

$$12Q_B + S_Z = 30 \tag{10.9}$$

where

$$Q_A \geqslant 0 \tag{10.5}$$

$$Q_B \geqslant 0 \tag{10.6}$$

$$S_X \geqslant 0 \tag{10.10}$$

$$S_Y \geqslant 0 \tag{10.11}$$

$$S_Z \geqslant 0 \tag{10.12}$$

The problem at this point is underdetermined. There are more unknowns (Q_A, Q_B, S_X, S_Y, S_Z) than there are equations to be solved (10.7, 10.8, 10.9).

This dilemma is overcome by two basic propositions underlying linear programming. First, in almost all LP problems, an optimal solution can be found by considering only the corner locations of the feasible space. This point has already been explained. Second, at each corner the number of variables with a non-zero value exactly equals the number of constraint equations. Consider again Figure 10.3. At O, Q_A and Q_B are zero but S_X, S_Y and S_Z must have positive values. At P, Q_B and S_Y are zero but Q_A, S_X and S_Z must have positive values. Similarly at R, only S_Y and S_X are zero. At S, only S_Z and S_X are zero and at T, only S_Z and Q_A have zero values. Such solutions are called 'basic'. Given the first proposition it can be seen that we require the optimal 'basic feasible solution' (BFS).

We can say that, in almost all cases, the optimal BFS will have as many non-zero valued variables as the number of constraints. But how to find it? One method might be to calculate the profit at every corner and choose the largest. Hence consider corner O, the origin. Substituting Q_A and Q_B equal to zero in equations (10.7), (10.8), and (10.9) we obtain:

$$S_X = 20$$

$$S_Y = 25$$

$$S_Z = 30$$

π_c in equation (10.1) equals zero

At P, Q_B and S_Y equal zero, so we have:

$$2Q_A + S_X = 20$$
$$3Q_A = 25$$
$$S_Z = 30$$

Thus

$$Q_A = 8\tfrac{1}{3}$$

and by substitution

$$S_X = 20 - 16\tfrac{2}{3} = 3\tfrac{1}{3}$$

π_c in equation (10.1) equals £$16\tfrac{2}{3}$

At R, S_Y and S_X equal zero, so we have:

$$2Q_A + 5Q_B = 20$$
$$3Q_A + 2\tfrac{1}{2}Q_B = 25$$
$$12Q_B + S_Z = 30$$

Thus

$$Q_A = 10 - 2\tfrac{1}{2}Q_B$$

and by substitution

$$3Q_A + 10 - Q_A = 25$$

Thus

$$Q_A = 7\tfrac{1}{2},\ Q_B = 1,\ S_Z = 18$$

π_c in equation (10.1) equals £18

At S, S_Z and S_X equal zero, so we have:

$$2Q_A + 5Q_B = 20$$
$$3Q_A + 2\tfrac{1}{2}Q_B + S_Y = 25$$
$$12Q_B = 30$$

Therefore

$$Q_B = 2\tfrac{1}{2}$$

and by substitution

$$2Q_A = 20 - 12\tfrac{1}{2}$$

Therefore

$$Q_A = 3\tfrac{3}{4}$$

and by substitution

$$11\tfrac{1}{4} + 6\tfrac{1}{4} + S_Y = 25$$

Therefore $S_Y = 7\tfrac{1}{2}$

π_c in equation (10.1) equals £15

At T, S_Z and Q_A have zero values, so we have:

$$5Q_B + S_X = 20$$
$$2\tfrac{1}{2}Q_B + S_Y = 25$$
$$12Q_B = 30$$

Therefore

$$Q_B = 2\tfrac{1}{2}$$

and by substitution

$$S_X = 20 - 12\tfrac{1}{2} = 7\tfrac{1}{2}$$
$$S_Y = 25 - 6\tfrac{1}{4} = 18\tfrac{3}{4}$$
$$\pi_c \text{ in equation (10.1) equals £7}\tfrac{1}{2}$$

This confirms our geometric result that the optimum level of π_c is £18 at point R. S_Y and S_X equal zero there and so indicate potential bottlenecks in the use of resource inputs Y and X. S_Z, on the other hand, has a value of 18, signifying possible idle resources which could be more fruitfully employed. The optimal output mix is 1 unit of B and $7\tfrac{1}{2}$ units of A.

10.2.3 Simplex method

A limitation of the arithmetic method in practice is that the number of corners may be *very* large indeed. Fortunately, a method of selecting corners which yield progressively higher profits is available: the Simplex method. We firstly explain the algebraic version of the technique and, secondly, a quicker matrix version.

Algebraic version

Stage 1 To choose an initial *BFS* from which to progress to other corners one might choose that of producing neither *A* nor *B*. The slack variables then equal the total available quantities of each input: $S_X = 20$, $S_Y = 25$, $S_Z = 30$. This *BFS* may be represented as:

$$Q_A = 0$$

$$Q_B = 0$$

$$S_X = 20 - 2Q_A - 5Q_B = 20 \tag{10.13}$$

$$S_Y = 25 - 3Q_A - 2\tfrac{1}{2}Q_B = 25 \tag{10.14}$$

$$S_Z = 30 - 0Q_A - 12Q_B = 30 \tag{10.15}$$

$$\pi_c = 2Q_A + 3Q_B = 0 \tag{10.16}$$

and this represents the origin in Figure 10.4.

Stage 2 But profits can be increased. From equation (10.16) it can be seen that every additional unit of *B* produced would give an additional £3 of profit, and every additional unit of *A*, £2 of profit. From equations (10.13) to (10.15) one can see that sufficient inputs are available to produce several units of *B* and/or of *A*. To select which of *A* or *B* to produce we compare their marginal profits: £2 and £3 respectively. *B*'s marginal contribution exceeds *A*'s. Therefore we increase Q_B. But by how much?

If we increase Q_B from zero we add Q_B to our basis (the non-zero variables). To keep the solution 'basic', i.e. a corner, we must reduce the value of an existing non-zero solution variable to zero. But which? The question of which existing basis variable to reduce and by how much Q_B is to be increased, are solved together.

In equation (10.13), if we keep Q_A equal to zero, each additional unit of *B* will reduce S_X by 5 units. Only 20 S_X units are available. Therefore if we use all of S_X to produce only *B*, we could produce only $20/5 = 4$ *B* units. From equation (10.14) each additional unit of *B* will reduce S_Y by $2\tfrac{1}{2}$ units. Since only 25 S_Y units are available, if we use all of them to produce only *B*, we could produce only $25/2\tfrac{1}{2} = 10$ units. Similarly if we used all of S_Z to produce *B* the maximum we could produce is only $30/12 = 2\tfrac{1}{2}$ units. Because output of *B* requires inputs *X*, *Y* and *Z*, each of which has a limited supply, the maximum *B* which can be produced is the smallest of 4, 10 and $2\tfrac{1}{2}$, i.e. $2\tfrac{1}{2}$. Greater output than this would violate constraint (10.12). Therefore Q_B is increased by $2\tfrac{1}{2}$ units and S_Z reduced to zero.

To examine the effects of changes in the values of variables which now equal zero on those variables which are currently included in the basis, we wish to have equations (10.13) to (10.15) with only Q_A and S_Z on the right-hand side. To do this, the variable which has just been introduced into the basis is made the subject of the equation whose dependent variable has been reduced to zero. This is substituted into the other constraint equations. Hence since Q_B is being introduced and S_Z reduced to zero equation (10.15) becomes:

$$Q_B = \frac{30}{12} - S_Z/12 = 2\frac{1}{2} - S_Z/12 \qquad (10.17)$$

which is substituted into equations (10.13) and (10.14). So we have, for inputs X, Y and Z respectively:

$$S_X = 20 - 2Q_A - 5(2\frac{1}{2} - S_Z/12) = 7\frac{1}{2} - 2Q_A + \tfrac{5}{12}S_Z \qquad (10.18)$$

$$S_Y = 25 - 3Q_A - 2\frac{1}{2}(2\frac{1}{2} - S_Z/12) = 18\frac{3}{4} - 3Q_A + \tfrac{5}{24}S_Z \qquad (10.19)$$

$$Q_B = 2\frac{1}{2} - S_Z/12 + 0Q_A \qquad (10.17)$$

The expression for Q_B is also substituted into the profits function:

$$\pi_c = 2Q_A + 3(2\frac{1}{2} - S_Z/12) = 7\frac{1}{2} + 2Q_A - \tfrac{1}{4}S_Z \qquad (10.20)$$

Since Q_A and S_Z are zero, by substitution into equations (10.17) to (10.19) the values of S_X and S_Y can be derived (we already know $Q_B = 2\frac{1}{2}$). Hence our second BFS is:

$$Q_A = 0, \ Q_B = 2\frac{1}{2}, \ S_X = 7\frac{1}{2}, \ S_Y = 18\frac{3}{4}, \ S_Z = 0$$

Notice that this solution relates to point T in Figure 10.4.

Stage 3 Profits can again be increased. From equation (10.20) it can be seen that every additional unit of Q_A will contribute £2 to profits. To decide the value of Q_A and the variable in the BFS to be replaced, we proceed as before. From equations (10.18) and (10.19) the maximum amounts of A which can be produced by reducing S_X or S_Y to zero are $\dfrac{7\frac{1}{2}}{2} = \dfrac{15}{4}$ and $\dfrac{18\frac{3}{4}}{3} = 6\frac{1}{4}$ units respectively. Equation (10.17) is unusual. Additional A does not affect Q_B, so an 'infinite' amount of Q_A could be produced and still fulfil the constraint. The maximum Q_A value which can be produced within all constraints is $3\frac{3}{4}$ units. Producing $3\frac{3}{4}$ units of A uses all of the slack in input X, i.e. $S_X = 0$.

To examine the effects of changes in basis variables on non-basis variables, we wish to have equations with S_X and S_Z on the right-hand side. Since Q_A is being introduced and S_X removed from the basis, equation (10.18) is rearranged to become:

$$Q_A = \tfrac{15}{4} - \tfrac{1}{2}S_X + \tfrac{5}{24}S_Z = 3\tfrac{3}{4} - \tfrac{1}{2}S_X + \tfrac{5}{24}S_Z \qquad (10.21)$$

This is substituted into equations (10.19) and (10.17). These, together with equation (10.21) become, for inputs X, Y and Z respectively:

$$Q_A = 3\tfrac{3}{4} - \tfrac{1}{2}S_X + \tfrac{5}{24}S_Z \qquad (10.21)$$

$$S_Y = 18\tfrac{3}{4} - 3(3\tfrac{3}{4} - \tfrac{1}{2}S_X + \tfrac{5}{24}S_Z) + \tfrac{5}{24}S_Z = 7\tfrac{1}{2} + 1\tfrac{1}{2}S_X - \tfrac{10}{24}S_Z \qquad (10.22)$$

$$Q_B = 2\tfrac{1}{2} - \frac{S_Z}{12} \qquad (10.23)$$

The expression for Q_A is also substituted into equation (10.20):

$$\pi_c = 7\tfrac{1}{2} + 2(3\tfrac{3}{4} - \tfrac{1}{2}S_X + \tfrac{5}{24}S_Z) - \tfrac{1}{4}S_Z = 15 - S_X + \tfrac{4}{24}S_Z \tag{10.24}$$

Since S_X and S_Z are zero, by substitution we find $S_Y = 7\tfrac{1}{2}$ and $Q_B = 2\tfrac{1}{2}$. Q_A is known to be $3\tfrac{3}{4}$. So our third BFS is:

$$Q_A = 3\tfrac{3}{4}, \; Q_B = 2\tfrac{1}{2}, \; S_X = 0, \; S_Y = 7\tfrac{1}{2}, \; S_Z = 0$$

Notice that this represents point S in Figure 10.4.

Stage 4 Again profits can be increased. The coefficient on S_Z indicates that by using one unit less of input Z, i.e. increasing S_Z by one unit, π will increase by $\tfrac{4}{24}$ units. By how much should S_Z be increased? From equation (10.23) we can see that the maximum by which S_Z could be increased is $2\tfrac{1}{2}/\tfrac{1}{12} = 30$ since then B is no longer produced. From equation (10.22) the maximum value which S_Z could take is $7\tfrac{1}{2}/\tfrac{10}{24} = 18$, then all slack in Y would be used and S_Y would become zero. From equation (10.21) additional S_Z allows additional B to be produced, not less. Therefore equation (10.21) does not indicate a constraint on the increase in S_Z. The lowest of 18 and 30 is 18. Therefore S_Y is reduced to zero.

To investigate the effects of changes in the two zero-valued variables S_X and S_Y on the positive variables, S_Z is made the subject of equation (10.22):

$$S_Z = 18 + \tfrac{18}{5}S_X - \tfrac{12}{5}S_Y \tag{10.25}$$

This is substituted into the other two constraints and the profits function. Equations (10.21) to (10.24) become respectively:

$$Q_A = 3\tfrac{3}{4} - \tfrac{1}{2}S_X + \tfrac{5}{24}(18 + \tfrac{18}{5}S_X - \tfrac{12}{5}S_Y) = 7\tfrac{1}{2} + \tfrac{1}{4}S_X - \tfrac{1}{2}S_Y \tag{10.26}$$

$$S_Z = 18 + \tfrac{18}{5}S_X - \tfrac{12}{5}S_Y \tag{10.25}$$

$$Q_B = 2\tfrac{1}{2} - \tfrac{1}{12}(18 + \tfrac{18}{5}S_X - \tfrac{12}{5}S_Y) = 1 - \tfrac{3}{10}S_X + \tfrac{1}{5}S_Y \tag{10.27}$$

$$\pi_c = 15 - S_X + \tfrac{1}{6}(18 + \tfrac{18}{5}S_X - \tfrac{12}{5}S_Y) = 18 - \tfrac{2}{5}S_X - \tfrac{2}{5}S_Y \tag{10.28}$$

Substituting $S_X = S_Y = 0$ into these equations the fourth BFS is derived:

$$Q_A = 7\tfrac{1}{2}, \; Q_B = 1, \; S_X = 0, \; S_Y = 0, \; S_Z = 18$$

Notice that this represents point R in Figure 10.4

In equation (10.28) the coefficients of both variables are negative. If S_X or S_Y is increased π_c would fall. Therefore the BFS is the optimal one.

The matrix version

The algebraic method of substituting one equation into others may be very time-consuming when the number of constraints, and hence equations, is large. When using the matrix version all of the above steps are performed, but by setting out the constraints and objective function in a matrix-like tableau and by using certain rules, time is saved.

Stage 1 A Simplex tableau is constructed representing the constraints and objective function. Table 10.1 shows the first tableau in our production problem. Essentially it represents equations (10.13) to (10.16) of our first BFS above. The row beginning 'Basis' names the variables to which each column relates. The column marked 'Basis' contains the names of variables with non-zero values in the solution, i.e. the current 'basis'. Q relates to the constants of each constraint equation. Hence the constant in the equation of which S_X is the subject is 20. The columns marked Q_A, Q_B, S_X, S_Y and S_Z (excluding the Z_j and $C_j - Z_j$ rows) all contain the corresponding (negative of the) coefficients of the constraint equations (10.13) to (10.15). Hence the number '2' in column Q_A, row S_X indicates that in the equation whose subject is S_X, (10.13), the coefficient of Q_A is -2, etc. This implies that if Q_A increases by one unit, S_X *decreases* by 2 units. If the tableau figure had been -2 corresponding to a value in the equation form of $+2$, a one unit increase in Q_A would have necessitated an *increase* in S_X by 2 units. Whenever the sign in these tableau rows is positive (negative), then a one unit increase in the column variable indicates a decrease (increase) in the row variable.

The row and column marked C_j contains the coefficients of each variable in the objective function. Each of these coefficients shows the increase in profit due to a unit increase in the corresponding variable, provided that no profit is sacrificed when the variable is increased. Such a sacrifice may occur when, to fulfil a constraint, an increase in one variable is only possible when the value of another is reduced. The row marked Z_j shows these sacrifices. The value of Z for a column is calculated by multiplying each element in the column by the corresponding C_j value of the basis variable in its row, and summing the results. Hence Z for the Q_A column equals $(2 \times 0) + (3 \times 0) + (0 \times 0) = 0$. The reason for this is as follows. If Q_A increases by one unit, S_X is reduced by 2 units, as explained above. But variations in S_X do not affect profits: it has a coefficient of zero in the original profit function. Therefore a 1-unit rise in Q_A, though reducing S_X by 2 units, would not alter profits because of its effects on S_X. Similarly, a 1-unit rise in Q_A would reduce S_Y by 3 units. But again S_Y does not affect profits, so this reduction would not affect profits. Finally, a 1-unit rise in Q_A does not affect S_Z. Summing these reductions in profits totals zero. This is repeated for every column including the Q column. The Z value in the Q column equals total profits for the current BFS. It is the sum of the

Table 10.1 First tableau

C_j			2	3	0	0	0
	Basis	Q	Q_A	Q_B	S_X	S_Y	S_Z
0	S_X	20	2	5	1	0	0
0	S_Y	25	3	$2\frac{1}{2}$	0	1	0
0	S_Z	30	0	12	0	0	1
	Z_j	0	0	0	0	0	0
	$C_j - Z_j$		2	3	0	0	0

products of the value (the Q) of each variable in the basis and their coefficients in the profits equation.

Since a change in net (contribution) profits equals the increase in gross (contribution) profits (C_j), minus the sacrifice necessary to achieve it (Z_j), $C_j - Z_j$ represents the change in net profits due to a unit increase in the column variable. Thus in the Q_A column, a unit increase in Q_A does not necessitate a reduction in a profit-adding variable (as explained above, $Z = 0$) but does directly increase gross profit, as shown by its $+2$ coefficient in the profit function (the C_j row). Therefore a unit increase in Q_A results in a net profit increase of $£(2 \times 1) - (2 \times 0)$ which is $C_j - Z_j$. Similarly, a unit increase in Q_B results in a net profit increase of $£(3 \times 1) - [(5 \times 0) + (2\frac{1}{2} \times 0) + (12 \times 0)] = £3$.

Stage 2 The $C_j - Z_j$ row indicates that because the signs of the figures for Q_A and Q_B are positive, an increase in either will increase net profits. Since the figure for Q_B exceeds that of Q_A, the marginal contribution of the former exceeds that of the latter and therefore should be increased. To decide which slack to reduce to zero we compare the maximum amounts of B which can be produced if all of each slack is used, as was done in the algebraic method. Each element in the Q column (the constant in the constraint equations) is divided by the corresponding element in the column of the replacing variable. Hence the maximum amounts of B which can be produced by reducing S_X, S_Y or S_Z to zero are 4, 10 and $2\frac{1}{2}$ respectively. (Notice that we wish to rank only the non-negative values of these maxima because a negative value of any choice variable or slack is contrary to the non-negativity constraints.) Therefore to avoid violating constraint (10.9) S_Z is to be reduced to zero.

In the algebraic version, the next step was to make Q_B the subject of the S_Z equation and to substitute this into the other constraint and profit equations. Exactly the same process is completed in the matrix version by 'pivoting'. Firstly, one finds the element which is in the column of the variable to be introduced (Q_B) and the row of the variable to be replaced (S_Z), i.e. 12. This is the 'pivot'. In each tableau the pivot has been marked by a box.

The second tableau (Table 10.2) (which represents the equations in Stage 2 of the algebraic method) is derived thus:

1. *To find the new elements in the new pivotal row*: divide each element in the old pivotal row by the pivot.
2. *To find the new elements in every other row including the ($C_j - Z_j$) row*:

$$\begin{pmatrix} \text{new element} \\ \text{in row } i, \\ \text{column } j \end{pmatrix} = \begin{pmatrix} \text{old element} \\ \text{in row } i, \\ \text{column } j \end{pmatrix} - \frac{\begin{pmatrix} \text{old element} \\ \text{in row } i, \\ \text{pivotal} \\ \text{column} \end{pmatrix} \times \begin{pmatrix} \text{old element} \\ \text{in pivotal} \\ \text{row,} \\ \text{column } j \end{pmatrix}}{\text{pivot}}$$

Table 10.2 Second tableau

C_j			2	3	0	0	0
	Basis	Q	Q_A	Q_B	S_X	S_Y	S_Z
0	S_X	$7\frac{1}{2}$	[2]	0	1	0	$-5/12$
0	S_Y	$18\frac{3}{4}$	3	0	0	1	$-5/24$
3	Q_B	$2\frac{1}{2}$	0	1	0	0	$1/12$
	Z_j	$7\frac{1}{2}$	0	3	0	0	$1/4$
	$C_j - Z_j$		2	0	0	0	$-1/4$

Hence the row corresponding to input X in the first tableau becomes, in the second tableau:

Q	Q_A	Q_B	S_X	S_Y	S_Z
$7\frac{1}{2}$	2	0	1	0	$-\frac{5}{12}$
$S_X = 20 - 5(\frac{30}{12})$	$= 2 - 5(\frac{0}{12})$	$= 5 - 5(\frac{12}{12})$	$= 1 - 5(\frac{0}{12})$	$= 0 - 5(\frac{0}{12})$	$= 0 - 5(\frac{1}{12})$

3. *To find the new elements in the Z_j row*: multiply each element in one column by the corresponding new value in the C_j column and sum. Repeat for each column.

The Z_j row would be calculated as in Tableau 1. In each column each new element would be multiplied by the coefficient in the original profits equation of the variable in the same row, but in the column marked 'Basis'. These products would then be summed. Hence the Z value for the Q_A column would become $(2 \times 0) + (3 \times 0) + (0 \times 3) = 0$. Again each element except in the Z_j and $C_j - Z_j$ rows, if it has a positive sign would correspond to a negative in the constraint equation. Thus the $+2$ in the Q_A column S_X row, indicates that a one unit increase in Q_A *decreases* S_X by (2×1) units. But from the profits equation we can see that S_X does not affect profits. So the 3-unit decrease in S_X has a £$(2 \times 0) \times 3$ effect on profits.

The $(C_j - Z_j)$ row could also be calculated as for Tableau 1. However, including $(C_j - Z_j)$ in the pivoting procedure saves time. Notice that in Tableau 2 the net marginal profit of Q_B of £0 differs from the marginal gross profit in the profit function of £3. The reason for this is that the former equals $C_j - Zj$, the latter C_j. A unit increase in Q_B does not necessitate a reduction in S_X or S_Y: the elements in the Q_B column, S_X and S_Y rows, are zeros. But the rise in Q_B would violate the third constraint unless one unit of Q_B was simultaneously removed: the element in the Q_B column, Q_B row is 1. This reduction would cause a £3 loss in gross profits since the coefficient of Q_B in the profits function is £3. However, the 1-unit rise in Q_B would raise profits by £3 for the same reason. The result is a net rise of £0 in profits. It is this net rise which is indicated by the $C_j - Z_j$ row.

Since only those variables in the 'basis' are non-zero, the column shows the values of the non-zero solution variables. Thus our second BFS is:

$$Q_A = 0, \ Q_B = 2\frac{1}{2}, \ S_X = 7\frac{1}{2}, \ S_Y = 18\frac{3}{4}, \ S_Z = 0$$

Notice that the second tableau is analogous to equations (10.17) to (10.20) of the algebraic method.

Stage 3 The $C_j - Z_j$ marginal net profit row shows that profits can again be increased by increasing Q_A. To decide which of the basis variables to reduce to zero, we again divide the Q column elements by the elements in the Q_A row. The smallest of these quotients is $3\frac{3}{4}$ corresponding to S_X. Therefore S_X is reduced to zero and Q_A increased to $3\frac{3}{4}$.

Again to examine the effects on the new basis variables of further changes in the new non-basis variables, we pivot and form the third tableau, Table 10.3. Since Q_A is being increased and S_X reduced, the pivot is the element in the Q_A column, S_X row: 2. Hence the elements in the pivotal (top) row are all divided by 2. Those in other rows follow procedures (2) and (3) above. Thus the new elements in the second row become:

Variables	Q	Q_A	Q_B	S_X
	$7\frac{1}{2}$	0	0	$-1\frac{1}{2}$
	$18\frac{3}{4} - \dfrac{3 \times 7\frac{1}{2}}{2}$	$3 - \dfrac{3 \times 2}{2}$	$0 - \dfrac{3 \times 0}{2}$	$0 - \dfrac{3 \times 1}{2}$

	S_Y	S_Z
	1	10/24
	$1 - \dfrac{3 \times 0}{2}$	$-5/24 - 3\,\dfrac{(-\frac{5}{12})}{2}$

The $C_j - Z_j$ row is similarly found.

Again since all non-basis variables are zero, the coefficients in the third tableau give the third BFS: $Q_A = 3\frac{3}{4}$, $Q_B = 2\frac{1}{2}$, $S_X = 0$, $S_Y = 7\frac{1}{2}$, $S_Z = 0$. Notice that the third tableau is analogous to equations (10.21) to (10.24) of the algebraic method.

Stage 4 The marginal net profits row indicates that profits can still be increased if S_Z is increased. Dividing each element in the Q column by the corresponding element in the S_Z column suggests that S_Y is to be reduced to zero and S_Z increased to 18.

Table 10.3 Third tableau

C_j			2	3	0	0	0
	Basis	Q	Q_A	Q_B	S_X	S_Y	S_Z
2	Q_A	$3\frac{3}{4}$	1	0	$\frac{1}{2}$	0	$-5/24$
0	S_Y	$7\frac{1}{2}$	0	0	$-1\frac{1}{2}$	1	10/24
3	Q_B	$2\frac{1}{2}$	0	1	0	0	1/12
	Z_j	15	2	3	1	0	$-4/24$
	$C_j - Z_j$		0	0	-1	0	4/24

Again to examine the effects on the new basis variables of further changes in the new non-basis variables, we pivot. Since S_Y is being reduced and S_Z increased, the pivot is the element in the S_Z column, S_Y row: $\frac{10}{24}$. Table 10.4 shows the fourth tableau. Thus the fourth BFS is:

$$Q_A = 7\tfrac{1}{2},\ Q_B = 1,\ S_X = 0,\ S_Y = 0,\ S_Z = 18$$

In the fourth tableau there are no variables with positive coefficients in the net marginal profits $(C_j - Z_j)$ row. Therefore profits cannot be increased by increasing any variable. The negative elements relating to S_X and S_Y indicate that a reduction in their values would increase profits. But S_X and S_Y cannot be reduced: they are already zero and negative values would violate the non-negativity constraints on them. Therefore the fourth BFS is the optimal solution. Notice that the fourth BFS as calculated by the matrix version is identical to that of the algebraic version and the graphical and arithmetic methods.

Finally notice that to decide whether the replacement of one variable in the basis by another would increase π_c we looked for variables whose marginal net profit, i.e. whose coefficient in the $(C_j - Z_j)$ row was positive. Since the elements in this row can be derived by pivoting without separate calculation of the Z_j row, there is no need repeatedly to recalculate the latter. (Calculation of the Z_j row was included to facilitate our interpretation of the $(C_j - Z_j)$ row.)

Table 10.4 Fourth tableau

C_j	Basis	Q	2 Q_A	3 Q_B	0 S_X	0 S_Y	0 S_Z
2	Q_A	$7\tfrac{1}{2}$	1	0	$-1/4$	$1/12$	0
0	S_Z	18	0	0	$-18/5$	$24/10$	1
3	Q_B	1	0	1	$3/10$	$-1/5$	0
	Z_j	18	2	3	$4/10$	$2/5$	0
	$C_j - Z_j$		0	0	$-4/10$	$-2/5$	0

Box 10.2

LP resolves office overload

IFS, a unit within Canada Systems Incorporated, provided a processing service for fund management companies. Its main activity was the processing of transactions and accounting activities associated with shareholders for brokerage houses, dealers and fund managers. Its business was very seasonal because most of the transactions associated with registered retirement savings plans (RRSP) contributions occurred between late January and early March. In 1984, the volume of transactions grew unexpectedly by 100% and the company was short of staff. To overcome the problem *ad hoc* solutions with additional costs of $500,000 were implemented.

→

New staff were hired to plan business in spring 1985. The problem as to how many additional clerical staff to hire, for each shift, from each source, for each task was modelled as a linear program. Here we describe a simplified version.

Clerks could be hired from two sources: a bureau called Manpower Temporary Services and directly from the labour market. Each clerk could be hired for a day, an afternoon or a night shift. The objective was to minimise the total cost of the number of hired clerks. This total cost equalled the cost per clerk from each source for each shift multiplied by the corresponding numbers of clerks and added up across all sources and shifts. That is:

$$\text{Minimise} \sum_{ij} H_{ij}C_{ij}$$

where H_{ij} = number of clerks hired for shift i, from source j
C_{ij} = cost per clerk hired for shift i from source j.

The number of clerks hired for each task and shift was constrained by the number of computer terminals available in each shift for them to work at. This can be expressed as:

$$\sum_{j} H_{ij} \leqslant N_i$$

where N_i = number of terminals available in shift i.

There was a maximum limit to the number of clerks which each source could supply for a particular shift, U_{ij}. Thus:

$$H_{ij} \leqslant U_{ij}$$

There was also a limit on the available office space for the hired clerks during each shift:

$$H_i \leqslant M_i$$

The number of transactions which the clerks could process in each shift had to be at least as large as the number of RRSP transactions expected in the 1985 peak period plus any backlog:

$$D + B \geqslant \sum_{ij} H_{ij}P_{ij}$$

where D = number of RRSP expected
B = backlog of transactions
P_{ij} = productivity of each clerk during shift i from source j.

In fact the model allowed for two separate tasks: data preparation which preceded data entry; the need to accumulate a backlog on Friday and Sundays since no deliveries of transactions were received until Monday afternoon, yet clerks worked Sundays and Mondays. In total the model consisted of 202 constraints and 226 variables.

In spring 1985 IFS hired the number of clerks which the linear program recommended. The result was a reduction in incremental costs of processing RRSP transaction from $500,000 in 1984 to $170,000. This improved the company's reputation for reliability which resulted in the renewal of most of its contracts and the successful bidding for new ones.

Source summarised and simplified from Haehling Van Lanzenauer et al. 1987.

10.3 The dual

For every LP problem (the primal) there is a corresponding dual problem. The dual consists of the primal problem which has been changed in five respects.

1. If the objective function in the primal is to be maximised (minimised), that of the dual is to be minimised (maximised).
2. The primal variables are replaced by new variables.
3. The maximum (or minimum) value of each input in the constraint equations in the primal become the coefficients of the new variables in the objective function in the dual.
4. Whereas the coefficients in each column in the primal constraint equations are related to the same (old) variable, each is placed along a row and relates to a different new variable.
5. The $\leqslant$ ($\geqslant$) signs are reversed (but of course, the non-negativity conditions remain).

Hence the primal and dual of our production problem are:

Primal

Maximise: $\pi_c = 2Q_A + 3Q_B$

subject to: $2Q_A + 5Q_B \leqslant 20$ (availability of input X)

$3Q_A + 2\frac{1}{2}Q_B \leqslant 25$ (availability of input Y)

$12Q_B \leqslant 30$ (availability of input Z)

$Q_A \geqslant 0$
$Q_B \geqslant 0$

Dual

Minimise: $C = 20P_X + 25P_Y + 30P_Z$

subject to: $2P_X + 3P_Y \geqslant 2$ (available π_c from A)

$5P_X + 2\frac{1}{2}P_Y + 12P_Z \geqslant 3$ (available π_c from B)

$P_X \geqslant 0$
$P_Y \geqslant 0$
$P_Z \geqslant 0$

In matrix form the primal can be read horizontally and the dual vertically from the following matrix:

Primal

	Variables	A	B	Relation	Constants
	X	2	5	$\leqslant$	20
Dual	Y	3	$2\frac{1}{2}$	$\leqslant$	25
	Z	0	12	$\leqslant$	30
	Relation	$\geqslant$	$\geqslant$		Minimise C
	Constants	2	3	Maximise π_c	

To interpret the dual problem economically, we begin with the constraints of the production example. In the primal the coefficient of the Q_B term in each constraint equals the number of units of the corresponding input which are needed to produce a unit of B. Hence 5 units of X are needed to produce one unit of B (from constraint 1) as are $2\frac{1}{2}$ units of Y and 12 units of Z. Let P_X represent the shadow price for input X. (The 'shadow price' is the imputed profit each unit of X yields. Corresponding interpretations relate to shadow prices P_Y and P_Z). Then the total value of inputs which are needed to produce a unit of B is $5P_X$ for X plus $2\frac{1}{2}P_Y$ for Y plus $12P_Z$ for Z.

Turning to the right-hand side of each inequality in the dual, notice that this was originally the coefficient of the corresponding variable in the objective function in the primal. Hence from the π function of the primal, £3 of profit were made for every unit of B produced overall. Therefore, the second inequality in the dual states that the total value of inputs needed to produce a unit of B must be greater than or equal to the profit which the B unit yields. A similar interpretation applies to the first constraint in terms of the output of A.

Finally, the coefficients in the objective function of the dual were originally the maximum available quantities of each input in the primal. Therefore when multiplied by the corresponding shadow prices and summed, one obtains the total value of all inputs which are available to the firm. This is the objective function of the dual. Hence the dual problem is to choose values of the shadow prices for each input which minimise the total cost of inputs, subject to the requirement that the value of inputs to produce a unit of each product is no less than the profits which that unit yields.

To solve a minimisation problem, such as the dual of a maximisation primal, one can again use the Simplex method. When the constraint inequalities show the right-hand side to be 'greater than' the constant, we must add surplus variables to change the inequality to an equation. These are negative slack variables analogous to the positive slack variables of the primal. We will call these surplus variables $L_1 \ldots L_n$.

Secondly, in the (maximising) primal, a readily available first basis existed: the slack variables (i.e. the graphical origin). When the problem is one of minimisation, if we try to take $Q_A = Q_B = 0$ as our first BFS we would obtain only the surplus variables as having non-zero values. But these would be negative and so unfeasible. Thus to obtain our first basis we add artificial variables $A_1 \ldots A_n$ to each constraint. To these is attributed a coefficient of unity. The same variables $A_1 \ldots A_n$, are introduced into the objective function with a very large coefficient (M) relative to those of the other variables. Because these *artificial* variables are positive, they can be used as (part if not all of) our first basis.

The dual of our production problem is now:

$$\text{Minimise:} \quad C = 20P_X + 25P_Y + 30P_Z + 0L_1 + 0L_2 + MA_1 + MA_2$$
$$\text{Subject to:} \quad 2P_X + 3P_Y - L_1 - 0L_2 + A_1 + 0A_2 = 2$$
$$5P_X + 2\tfrac{1}{2}P_Y + 12P_Z - 0L_1 - L_2 + 0A_1 + A_2 = 3$$

The top section of Table 10.5 shows this problem in tableau form with the two artificial variables taken as our first basis.

The Simplex procedure is followed in exactly the same way as in the maximisation case with one exception. Since we wish to minimise a function, we introduce into the basis the variable corresponding to the most negative $C_j - Z_j$ value. Such a

Table 10.5 Tableaux for minimisation problem

C_j			20	25	30	0	0	M	M
	Basis	Q	P_X	P_Y	P_Z	L_1	L_2	A_1	A_2
M	A_1	2	2	3	0	-1	0	1	0
1 M	A_2	3	5	$2\frac{1}{2}$	$\boxed{12}$	0	-1	0	1
	Z_j		$7M$	$5\frac{1}{2}M$	$12M$	$-M$	$-M$	M	M
	$C_j - Z_j$		$20 - 7M$	$25 - 5\frac{1}{2}M$	$30 - 12M$	$+M$	$+M$	0	0
M	A_1	2	2	$\boxed{3}$	0	-1	0	1	0
2 30	P_Z	$\frac{1}{4}$	$5/12$	$5/24$	1	0	$-\frac{1}{2}$	0	$\frac{1}{2}$
	Z_j		$2M + 12\frac{1}{2}$	$3M + 6\frac{1}{4}$	30	$-M$	$-2\frac{1}{2}$	M	15
	$C_j - Z_j$		$7\frac{1}{2} - 2M$	$18\frac{3}{4} - 3M$	0	M	$2\frac{1}{2}$	0	$M - 15$
25	P_Y	$2/3$	$2/3$	1	0	$-\frac{1}{3}$	0	$\frac{1}{3}$	0
3 30	P_Z	$1/9$	$\boxed{5/18}$	0	1	$5/72$	$-1/12$	$-5/72$	$1/12$
	Z_j		25	25	30	$-75/12$	$-30/12$	$6\frac{1}{4}$	15
	$C_j - Z_j$		-5	0	0	$75/12$	$30/12$	$M - 6\frac{1}{4}$	$M - 15$
25	P_Y	$2/5$	0	1	$-12/5$	$-\frac{1}{2}$	$1/5$	$\frac{1}{2}$	$-1/5$
4 20	P_X	$2/5$	1	0	$33/5$	$-\frac{1}{4}$	$-3/10$	$-\frac{1}{4}$	$3/10$
	Z_j		20	25	12	$-7\frac{1}{2}$	-1	$7\frac{1}{2}$	11
	$C_j - Z_j$		0	0	18	$7\frac{1}{2}$	1	$M - 7\frac{1}{2}$	$M - 11$

variable would reduce cost more per unit than would any other variable. The artificial variables would not appear in the final solution because their C_j values of M would make their $C_j - Z_j$ values less negative than those of other variables.

Selection of the basis variable to be replaced is again based on a comparison of the constant (i.e. the value in the Q column) divided by the corresponding element in the pivotal column. These ratios equal the maximum amount of profit which can be ascribed to each unit of the input in the column, provided that no variables become negative. Thus since P_Z is the new variable to be introduced into the basis (on the $C_j - Z_j$ criterion) the ratios of elements in the Q column to their corresponding elements in the P_Z column are 2/0 and 3/12. Thus the maximum amount of profit ascribable to Z is £∞ and £3/12 in the case of the outputs of A and B respectively. Since we wish both constraint equations to hold with non-negative variable values, the maximum value we can give to P_Z is £3/12 indicating that A_2 is to be reduced to zero. Increasing P_Z by more than this would, as shown by the equation representing the first constraint, reduce A_Z to a negative value, so violating the non-negativity constraint.

Table 10.5 also shows the second, third and fourth tableaux. The final BFS is $P_X = 2/5$, $P_Y = 2/5$, $P_Z = 0$, $L_1 = 0$, $L_2 = 0$, which gives a value of $C = £18$. Notice that the solution value of the objective function in the primal is identical with that of the dual. This is always the case. The shadow price of Z is zero. Input Z is not fully employed, and so has a positive slack variable in the primal. Other things equal, what are additional units of Z worth to the firm? In terms of impact on profit, they would have a zero value because they could not increase total output. But X and

Y, which are fully employed (zero slack in the primal), do have a positive value, since if the firm could obtain more of them, they could be combined with Z to increase output of A and B and so π_c. What are the values of X and Y at the margin? The imputed values, or shadow prices, are equal to £$\frac{2}{5}$. That is, if an additional unit of either X or Y could be obtained, the firm could increase its π_c by £$\frac{2}{5}$ and so could afford to pay up to that price for a marginal unit input of either X or Y.

We can rewrite the surplus variable of the first constraint as:

$$L_1 = 3P_X + 2P_Y - 2$$

Since $3P_X + 2P_Y$ denotes imputed price and the 2 is the resulting profit, the surplus represents the net 'loss' of using X and Y in A production. The L value for the most profitable product is zero. Therefore all other L values represent opportunity costs of using X and Y in the production of the corresponding output. In the example, since $L_1 = L_2 = 0$, the cost of production of A and B is zero. Resources used to produce A and B could not be more profitably employed. A positive L_1 (L_2) value would indicate that X and Y would more profitably be utilised in the production of B (A).

Bibliography

Baker, A. J. (1981) *Business Decision Making*, Croom Helm.

Baumol, W. J. (1977) *Economic Theory and Operations Analysis*, 4th edn, Prentice Hall.

Carino, H. and Le Noir, C. H. (1988) 'Optimizing wood procurement in cabinet making', *Interfaces*, vol. 18.

Chiang, A. C. (1974) *Fundamental Methods of Mathematical Economics*, McGraw-Hill.

Dorfman, R., Samuelson, P. and Solow, R. (1958) *Linear Programming and Economic Analysis*, McGraw-Hill.

Hadley, G. and Kemp, M. C. (1972) *Finite Mathematics in Business and Economics*, North Holland.

Haehling Van Lanzenauer, C., Harbauer, E., Johnston, B. and Shuttleworth, D. (1987) 'RRSP flood: LP to the rescue', *Interfaces*, vol. 17.

Levin, R. I. and Kirkpatrick, C. A. (1982) *Quantitative Approaches to Management*, McGraw-Hill.

Meisels, K. (1962) *A Primer of Linear Programming*, New York University Press.

Naylor, T. H. and Vernon, J. M. (1969) *Microeconomics and Decision Models of the Firm*, Harcourt, Brace and World.

Chapter 11

Price policy

Price has always stood at the centre of economic discussion. This chapter begins in the traditional way by examining how profit-maximising business men and women set prices under conditions of varying market structures. The meaning of price discrimination is explained and ways in which firms can take advantage of discriminatory opportunities under, for example, conditions of innovation and product differentiation are detailed. The problems of oligopolistic interdependence and price leadership are looked at. Finally the question is raised as to what role, if any costs do and should play in price decisions.

11.1 Market structure and price behaviour

11.1.1 Perfect competition

The characteristics of perfect competition are well known: large numbers of buyers and sellers, none of whom is powerful enough to make a transaction (or withhold from one) which affects the going market price. Products are homogeneous, information about terms of sale is freely available on both sides of the market, and firms have perfect freedom to enter or leave the industry. Under these circumstances firms will accept the going market price, they will be price takers, not price makers, and as such their only decision is to settle on the quantity of output which will maximise their individual profit levels.

This is illustrated in Figure 11.1. Market price will be determined by the interaction of the industry supply and demand curves, SS and DD. The individual firm, which faces the horizontal demand curve of perfect competition, will accept price level P_1, and set its output level at Q_1 where price (which in this case is the same as marginal revenue) equals marginal cost.

Had the minimum point of the firm's AC curve lain below its demand curve, abnormal profits would have been earned, entrants would have been tempted into the industry, and the supply curve, SS, would have fallen downwards to the right until a new and lower equilibrium market price had been arrived at, such that

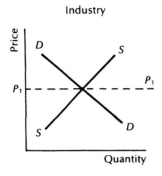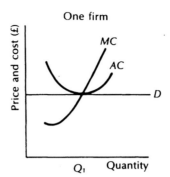

Figure 11.1

abnormal profits could no longer be earned. The reverse procedure would occur if the market price had been below the minimum level of the firm's *AC* curve. Marginal firms would leave the industry and the market price would rise.

Perfect competition, however, rarely occurs in reality. It is sometimes argued to be present in agricultural and financial instrument markets, but its prime value to the business man or woman is the insight it gives into the impact of demand conditions, competition, entry and changing supply conditions on the limits of pricing discretion.

11.1.2 Monopoly

Pure monopoly, like perfect competition, is rare. It implies the sale of a product with no close substitutes by a single firm. The firm here, unlike a perfect competitor, is a price maker, not a price taker. Given the assumption of profit maximisation, a monopolist will price at the point on the demand curve beneath which his or her marginal revenue and cost curves intersect. In Figure 11.2a this is at price level P_1, given an output level of Q_1. Figures 11.2b and 11.2c show respectively a monopolist's profit-maximising price and output positions when minimum average costs are achieved and when monopoly profits are zero.

In practice it is rare for a firm to be in a situation where it can have such freedom of action as the words 'price maker' suggest. Few products have no close substitutes. For example, coal and oil, and copper and aluminium are pairs of products between which there is a high cross-elasticity of demand, and so where, if firms set a monopolistically high price, considerable switching of consumer choice might occur. Similarly, even in the absence of close substitutes, firms may hesitate to charge the monopolistic, profit-maximising price from fear of attracting entrants into the industry and so inducing price-cutting competition.

(a)

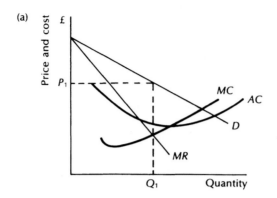

(b)

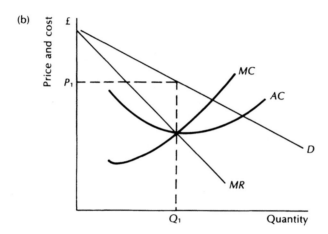

(c)

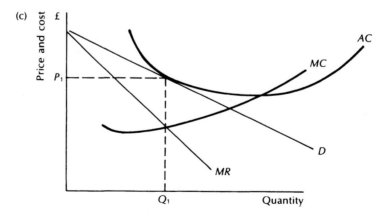

Figure 11.2

11.1.3 Monopolistic competition

The writings of Chamberlin in the 1930s on monopolistic competition were a major theoretical advance. Most firms do have competitors, but even so, most firms do produce products which are to some degree different from those of their competitors. This fact of economic life produced a degree of dissatisfaction with the polar models of perfect competition and pure monopoly, and it was hoped that the theory of monopolistic competition would improve the realism and utility of economic theory.

The main assumptions of monopolistic competition are first, the presence of large numbers of firms each of which produces a slightly different product from its rivals, thus consumer preferences and so downward-sloping demand curves emerge; second, there is keen rivalry between the firms.

Figure 11.3 illustrates the typical outcome for one such monopolistic competitor. The firm faces two types of demand curve, d_1d_1 and DD. At price P_1 and output Q_1 the firm can assume, given that it initiates a price change, one of two things. Either its rivals will match such a price change, or they will ignore the change. d_1d_1, the more elastic demand curve, rests on the latter assumption, DD on the former.

Given appropriate marginal revenue and marginal cost curves the firm may, to reach the point of marginal equivalancy, cut its price from P_1 to P_2 and hope in so doing to increase output to Q_2. It will feel safe in doing this since, given a large number of firms, it assumes that it can act independently of its rivals. As a small firm in the presence of many, it will hope to pass its price cut on unnoticed by competitors. It will hope to move down d_1d_1.

However, because of keen rivalry between firms, the price cut will inevitably be matched. The relevant demand curve is, in fact, DD; d_1d_1 is obsolete and it will 'slide' down DD to position d_2d_2, at output level Q_3. Supernormal profits attract entry. DD will move left. If losses result, exit and rightwards movement of DD will take place. This process will continue until dd is tangential to the firm's AC curve,

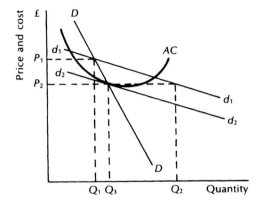

Figure 11.3

no abnormal profits are being made, and there is no incentive, either to cut prices or for new firms to enter the industry. (Note that this outcome is not unlike, indeed it is highly similar to that of Figure 11.2c.)

11.2 Discriminatory pricing

11.2.1 The theory: third degree

Any monopolist selling one product to two or more different markets or market segments with different price elasticities of demand can always earn at least as much profit as a similar monopolist selling to one market of similar aggregate size, and probably can earn more. He or she can earn as much profit by setting $MR = MC$ and subdividing the total output between the two markets at the same (profit-maximising) price. However, the monopolist also has the possibility of charging different prices in the different markets, and if this is more profitable he or she will do so. Figure 11.4 shows how this can be done. AR_1, MR_1, AR_2 and MR_2 are, respectively, the demand and marginal revenue curves for markets 1 and 2. ΣMR is the aggregate marginal revenue curve obtained by summing MR_1 and MR_2 horizontally. MC is the firm's marginal cost curve, drawn on the assumption that the firm is producing only one product in one plant location. The profit-maximising rules for the firm are as follows:

1. Set $\Sigma MR = MC$ to obtain the point of most profitable output i.e. Q_3.
2. Subdivide Q_3, between the two segments, not by equating the prices with the price which could be obtained by travelling vertically up from Q_3 to the aggregate demand curve, but by equating the marginal revenues in each segment with the marginal revenue indicated by the intersection of MC with ΣMR. (If this

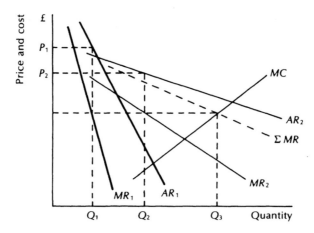

Figure 11.4

is not done then it would pay the firm to transfer output from the segment where MR is lower to that segment where it is higher, until equality was obtained, at a given fixed total output.)

3. This results in different, discriminatory prices, P_1 and P_2 being charged in the two segments provided the price elasticity of demand differs between the two markets at a common price. (We can predict which segment will pay the higher price algebraically. Given that $MR = P(1 + 1/\eta)$ then if MR_1 is to equal MR_2 the higher the value of η the lower will be the price.) Thus leakage must be minimal or customers in market 2 will buy at price P_2 and resell to customers in market 1 at a price between P_1 and P_2. Hence the seller must have some degree of monopoly power for price discrimination to be profitable. In a perfectly competitive market arbitrage would equalise price differentials.

4. The product must be homogeneous to obtain a single MC curve.

Or

5. Any cost involved in sealing off the segments to prevent leakage must be less than the extra revenue which can be obtained by practising discrimination.

Notice that the demand in each market is represented by a separate demand curve. This is not the case with two other types of price discrimination which are distinguished in theory.

11.2.2 First degree

In this case the firm is assumed to know the demand curve which each customer has for its product and charges each the highest price which the consumer is willing to pay for each unit. Hence consumer A would be willing to pay more for the first unit of a good than for the second, and so on. In terms of the aggregate demand curve for the product, since each additional unit sold increases TR by the price of that unit (the price for earlier units remaining higher), the demand curve is also the MR curve. As with third-degree discrimination, a necessary condition for profitable first-degree discrimination is that arbitrage is prevented. In addition, each customer must have a different reservation price for each unit otherwise she or he would not be willing to pay a different price for each unit. The same amount of TR and aggregate output would result if the producer offered a certain quantity to a consumer for one and only one price equal to the area under the consumer's demand curve up to that output: a 'take it or leave it price'.

11.2.3 Second degree

In second degree price discrimination there is no price distinction between consumers, but there is between 'blocks' of output. An additional block of units will be produced only if the TR from its sale exceeds the TC from its production.

11.2.4 The practice

Stigler (1966) has defined price discrimination as 'the sale of technically similar products at prices which are not proportional to their marginal costs'. This definition enables us to get away from the strictly homogeneous product examined in the figure and to understand how price discrimination can be practised more actively by actually incurring costs to seal off market segments. There are at least six different situations in which different prices can be charged for basically the same product, viz. when differences occur in: quantity, product type, location, time, product use, and stage of market development. The management task is to spot such opportunities as exist if and when there are different segments with different degrees of demand elasticity and with minimal leakage. The following list of examples is by no means exhaustive.

Quantity

Discounts are often awarded by firms to customers who buy in bulk. The granting of discounts may be made to large customers as a *quid pro quo* for the cost saving per unit the firm can make as a result of the bulk sale.

Alternatively, a discount may be awarded in return for a function which the customer implicitly carries out on behalf of the firm. Thus, a wholesaler typically receives a larger discount from a manufacturer than does a retailer since the wholesaler performs several marketing functions, such as salesmanship, storage and distribution to rail outlets, on behalf of the manufacturer. It should be noted, however, that the charging of different prices as a result of the granting of discounts is only price discrimination as strictly defined, if, and only if, the net prices are disproportional to the marginal costs of the trades made.

Product type

Market segments have different demand elasticities because buyers differ, for example, in preferences, in incomes, in tastes, in the information about products which they receive, and in the way that they process that information. These differences can be capitalised on by varying slightly the basic product, either tangibly, or intangibly through advertising, but doing so at an incremental cost less than the incremental revenue which can be gained by so doing. Thus, any price insensitivities which may be present in a market segment may be reinforced, while simultaneously the product differences make it less likely that leakage will occur.

Examples can be seen in any car manufacturer's product list where the same basic car is sold for a range of prices which are ostensibly justified to the segments concerned by the difference in engine size, numbers of carburettors, vinyl roof covering and other 'extras', which albeit adding to the manufacturing cost, generally do so by a smaller amount than can be added to the price.

Location

At least three types of price discrimination by location may be distinguished.

Uniform delivered pricing The same delivered price is charged at all destinations regardless of the buyer' location. Since the marginal costs of supplying a customer closer to a plant will be less than the marginal cost for a distant customer, price discrimination occurs. An example of this is a supermarket chain charging identical prices in each outlet for identical products.

Zone pricing In this case the seller divides a country into geographic zones and charges the same delivered price in each zone, but between zones the price differs. Two groups of buyers are discriminated against. Firstly, the marginal transport costs to those buyers nearest the seller within any one zone would be less than those to a seller on the far boundary of the zone. Secondly, two buyers, one on either side of a boundary, would have almost identical marginal transport costs but would be charged different prices.

Freight equalisation pricing The seller charges the buyer a transport cost which the buyer would pay if he bought from the nearest supplier. One way in which this may operate is where the seller quotes a delivered price which covers the transport cost from the seller's competitor's plant but absorbs the transport cost from his own plant. This issue is discussed in detail in Chapter 16.

Time

For price discrimination to be practised by time, the product must be non-storable, otherwise leakage will occur. For example most people prefer to take their holidays in July or August, not in April or October. Thus a higher price can be charged at the peak periods when demand is less elastic. The lower prices in the off-peak periods simultaneously encourage a smoothing of demand, help utilise overheads, such as aircraft and hotels, in slack times, and take the strain off overloaded facilities.

The pricing practices of the electricity industry with its on-peak and off-peak tariffs is a similar case, although in this instance we again see the danger of equating price differences with price discrimination. At off-peak periods low marginal cost nuclear powered stations are providing the bulk of the base load. As demand rises through the day gas-fired stations, and finally the coal-fired stations are brought on stream. In other words, the on-peak user is not only paying a higher price, but is consuming coal-generated electricity which has the highest marginal cost of all. The extent of price discrimination, if any, can only be identified by knowledge of the precise and relevant cost and price schedules.

Product use

The same product can be used by different people, with different price sensitivities, in different ways. Thus the same seat on a public transport vehicle is 'used' differently by a child than by an adult. If the full fare was charged for the child, however, the parent might not take the child on the journey. The demand elasticity of the two users differs. Similarly, telephones used for business purposes by business firms are 'used' differently from those of domestic households. The business firm presumably regards the telephone as a 'must', the household may regard it as more of a luxury and so a higher tariff can be charged to the business user.

New product pricing

Price discrimination can also be practised by stage of market development. This introduces the problem of new product pricing and how to price the product as it progresses through the various stages of the product life cycle (see Figure A6.1).

Joel Dean has argued that the choice lies somewhere between the two conceptual extremes of a skimming policy and a penetration policy.

Skimming policy This is a policy of relatively high prices, plus heavy promotional expenditures in the early stages, and progressively lower prices at later stages in the life cycle. Dean suggests that it will be of primary value when the following conditions hold good:

1. The product is a major departure from alternatives previously available, since then demand will be relatively price-inelastic due partly to a desire to be 'one up on the Jones's' and partly to product unfamiliarity, and so a resulting inability to link price with cost so that judgement can be made as to what sort of price is 'fair'.
2. When little is known about the elasticity of demand of the various market segments, price can be gradually lowered from a high level until the optimum level is attained; the opposite procedure, starting with a low price and discovering after the event that the market would willingly have paid a higher price is difficult to reverse without considerable loss of consumer goodwill.
3. Starting with a high price is a good way of breaking the market up into segments with different demand elasticities; the profitable 'cream' can be 'skimmed' from the least price-sensitive segment before making successive price reductions and skimming, in turn, the progressively more price-sensitive segments.
4. High initial prices may not necessarily be the most profitable long-run policy, but they may be necessary to generate the highest possible cash flow early in the product life cycle, in order to contribute to tooling-up, research and development, and promotional costs.

Penetrating pricing This is a policy of relatively low prices on market launch. Given that the product life cycle is S-shaped it should be adopted with a view to long-run not short-run profits. The bottom part of the S with low unit sales has still to be passed through, irrespective of price level. This policy, Dean suggests, is of primary value when:

1. There is a high price elasticity of demand, enabling the mass market to be penetrated quickly and so, correspondingly, abbreviating the length of time before the life cycle curve begins to accelerate upwards.
2. There are substantial unit cost savings as a result of a large throughput.
3. The firm wishes to discourage new and rival entrants.

When the life cycle reaches the stage of market maturity and saturation, however, some entrants will most probably have appeared, design and production technology will be stabilising, competing products will not be dissimilar and the situation may well be approaching the condition known as oligopoly.

11.2.5 A numerical example

The calculus can be used to accomplish price discrimination provided that the firm knows its TC functions and the demand functions for the markets it is selling to. Thus, with two markets X and Y, TR_x and $TR_y = P_x Q_x$ and $P_y Q_y$ respectively. Differentiation provides MR_x, MR_y and MC. For optimal price discrimination the three must be set equal to each other. Each of these equations are sterling values expressed in terms of Q. Thus Q_x and Q_y are found and P_x and P_y from the demand functions. As an illustration, let:

$$P_x = 2 - Q_x, \ P_y = 3 - 2Q_y$$

and $\quad MC = Q + 0.1$

where $\quad Q = Q_x + Q_y$

then $\quad MR_x = 2 - 2Q_x$ \hfill (11.1)

and $\quad MR_y = 3 - 4Q_y$ \hfill (11.2)

and $\quad MC = Q_y + Q_x + 0.1$ \hfill (11.3)

(Note: MR can be obtained from TR by differentiating.)

Solving (11.1), (11.2) and (11.3) simultaneously, we obtain:

$Q_x = 0.47$ and $Q_y = 0.49$

and from the demand equations:

$P_x = 1.53$ and $P_y = 2.02$

From this we can obtain the firm's TR, namely:

$$1.53 \times 0.47 + 2.02 \times 0.49 = £1.71$$

and if the TC equation had been $0.1 + 0.5Q^2 + 0.1Q$ then TC would be

$$0.1 + 0.5(0.47 + 0.49)^2 + 0.1(0.47 + 0.49) = £0.66$$

Hence total profit is £1.05.

What if the firm had refused to price-discriminate? This means it would have let $P_y = P_x$ at $MR = MC$. Our analysis tells us that profits would have been lower. Let us prove this. Maximise:

$$\pi = TR - TC$$

subject to $P_y = P_x$ or $P_y - P_x = 0$.

If we use the Lagrangian multiplier we have

$$\pi_\lambda = 2Q_x - Q_x^2 + 3Q_y - 2Q_y^2 - 0.1 - 0.5Q_x^2 - 0.5Q_y^2 - Q_xQ_y$$
$$- 0.1Q_x - 0.1Q_y + \lambda(2 - Q_x - 3 + 2Q_y)$$
$$= 1.9Q_x - 1.5Q_x^2 + 2.9Q_y - 2.5Q_y^2 - 0.1 - Q_xQ_y + \lambda(-1 - Q_x + 2Q_y)$$

let $\dfrac{\partial \pi_\lambda}{\partial Q_x} = 0 = 1.9 - 3Q_x - Q_y - \lambda$ (11.4)

$$\dfrac{\partial \pi_\lambda}{\partial Q_y} = 0 = 2.9 - 5Q_y - Q_x + 2\lambda$$ (11.5)

and $\dfrac{\partial \pi_\lambda}{\partial \lambda} = 0 = -1 - Q_x + 2Q_y$ (11.6)

Solving simultaneously gives $Q_y = 0.65$, $Q_x = 0.3$, $\lambda = -0.3$ and hence $P_x = 1.7$, $P_y = 1.7$ and $\pi = £0.965$.

11.3 Oligopolistic interdependence

Oligopoly exists when a few large firms compete against each other. How does this affect behaviour? In a word, interdependence – an interdependence of policies and decisions which is recognised by each oligopolist. Any decision one firm makes, be it on price, on product or on promotion, will affect the trade of competitors and so result in counter-moves. As a result, one's competitors' behaviour will depend on one's own behaviour, and this must be taken account of when decisions are made.

This interdependence makes prediction difficult and so advice as to optimal decision taking is in turn very hard to give. Kinked demand curve theory is often used to explain the behaviour patterns of oligopolists. Price leadership and non-price competition are methods used to remove or to lessen the uncertainties of interdependence which surround their decisions. Since the 1960s game theory has been increasingly applied to analyse the strategic interdependence of oligopolists.

11.3.1 The kinked demand curve

The assumption behind the theory of kinked demand is that each oligopolist will act and react in a way that keeps conditions tolerable for all members of the industry. This is most likely to occur where products are very similar. As a consequence, prices must be similar, otherwise if one firm is selling at a lower price than competitors, these competitors will be forced to lower their prices to match its price. Alternatively, the lower priced firm will raise its price to match the levels of the remaining oligopolists. The firm will probably realise that it is better to accommodate its rivals rather than start a price war. Sticky prices tend to result with firms unwilling to raise prices; and unwilling to cut prices for fear of initiating a price war.

Figure 11.5 uses the pair of demand curves dd' and DD', which are the relevant curves for one oligopolist drawn on the assumptions, with which we are now familiar, of rivals price matching in the case of DD', and ignoring price changes in the case of dd'. Given a price of P_1, the oligopolist, on the arguments laid out above, will assume that the relevant demand curve for his or her situation is the combination of the two segments dX and XD', namely dXD' with a kink indicating price stability at X.

In an inflationary situation or in a time of high demand, this analysis can possibly help explain why oligopolistic prices tend not to be stable, but to be altered frequently and that in an upward direction. In such circumstances the individual oligopolist may believe that the kink is reversed. The relevant demand curve becomes DXd'. Oligopolists will follow one another's price increase. The public

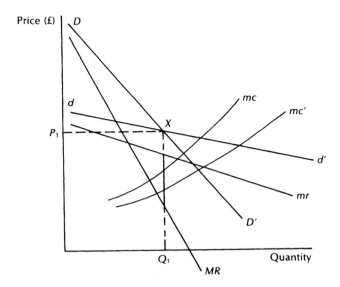

Figure 11.5

relations of this during inflation is, of course, easy. The firms merely need to express regret at the unavoidable passing on of increases, real or imagined, in the prices they pay for inputs.

Conversely, if one oligopolist has surplus capacity in conditions of high demand, he or she can cut the price to generate extra output in the relative confidence that fellow oligopolists will continue to work at full capacity at the original price.

In Figure 11.5 moreover, it is clear that cost conditions can change (e.g. from MC to MC') with no alteration of marginal equivalency. This is due to the vertical 'gap' in the relevant marginal revenue curve. Marginal revenue is denoted by mr to the left of the vertical XQ_1 (and is derived from dd') and is denoted by MR to the right of this position (being derived from DD'). Similarly, demand conditions can change (as indicated by a rightward or leftwards movement in the demand curve dXD') with no change in the pricing implications given by the equivalency of marginal revenues and costs (as in Figure 11.6.)

11.3.2 Reducing interdependence

Oligopoly tends to reduce the freedom of action a firm has in taking price decisions. One way to regain some measure of initiative is to reduce the cross-elasticity of demand between one's own products and one's rivals by means of product differentiation. The differences can be real or illusory, and will generally be backed by advertising in order to reinforce any consumer preferences, and so relative price independence, which might emerge.

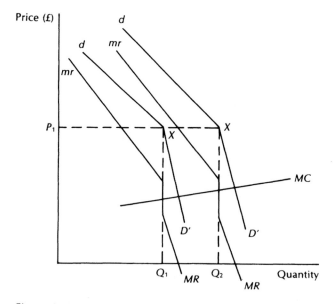

Figure 11.6

Non-price competition of this sort has considerable attractions to the oligopolist. It makes it less likely that the oligopolist will lose sales if his or her rival cuts prices, or if he or she raises them. Moreover, if a firm takes the initiative in non-price competition, the time lag which must elapse before competitors can produce an effective countermove is relatively long.

A price cut can be matched instantaneously and so the competitive advantage it brings is eliminated. A new product variation or a changed advertising campaign, however, cannot be countered so rapidly.

11.3.3 Reducing uncertainty through price leadership

Another alternative open to the firm is to opt out of the uncertainty surrounding pricing decisions in oligopoly by deliberately choosing a pattern of price parallelism. This is a situation where one firm takes the initiating role in all price changes in the relative confidence that others will follow, matching his or her lead. Three types of price leadership are commonly distinguished in the literature: dominant firm price leadership, collusive price leadership and barometric price leadership. The first of these has no apparent initial connection with oligopolistic market structure, but is still of relevance here. Firstly, it is the model for which a theory has been most elegantly developed, but secondly, and more importantly, it is a situation which has a strong tendency to devolve into an oligopoly.

Dominant firm price leadership

This model rests on the assumption that the industry is composed of one large firm and a competitive fringe of small firms. The dominant firm sets the price, the others follow and sell all they can at that price. The dominant firm, the price leader, supplies the remainder of the market which is not satisfied by the fringe companies. Thus, although the firm is a price leader, it is a quantity follower. (Implicitly the firm's price is just marginally higher than that of the fringe.)

Figure 11.7 illustrates how the leader determines its profit-maximising price given these assumptions. D_m is the market demand curve. ΣS_{cf} is the supply curve of the competitive fringe.

It is the amount estimated by the leader which will be supplied by fringe firms at various prices. It is equal to the sum of the individual MC curves of the fringe firms, in as much as they lie above their respective average variable cost curves. Thus, at price P_1 the dominant firm would sell nothing; the fringe would be willing and able to supply all the market's needs at that price.

At price P_2 total demand is equal to P_2C, the fringe would produce P_2B, leaving BC to be supplied by the dominant firm. If on the line P_2C the point A is placed such that $P_2A = BC$, then point A is on the dominant firm's demand curve where the price is P_2. This can be repeated for a series of prices and series of points like A to produce the dominant firm's demand curve, AR_d. Any price below P_3 is below the foot of the supply curve of the competitive fringe. Below this price they

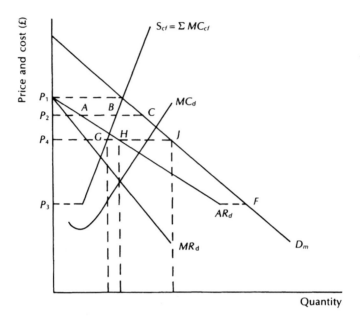

Figure 11.7

would not cover their average variable costs and so would refuse to supply. Consequently, the dominant firm's demand curve becomes the market demand curve below P_3, namely the line $P_1 AR_d FD_m$.

The dominant firm will set its price at P_4, where $MR_d = MC_d$. The fringe will accept this price, and produce the quantity $P_4 G = HJ$, leaving $P_4 H$ to be produced by the dominant firm.

This situation, however, could be one of unstable equilibrium. It may move either towards monopoly or oligopoly. If the price set allows positive profits to the fringe companies, entry will be encouraged at the expense of the dominant firm's market share; also fringe firms will be motivated to expand, either by merger or internally, to obtain the benefits of scale economies, again at the expense of the dominant firm's position.

Alternatively, the dominant firm may deviate from this pattern of leadership in price and followership in quantity, and change its objectives from short-run profit maximisation to one of aggressive long-run profit maximisation. In other words, aggressive price cutting may enable it to put many of the fringe firms out of business, enabling it to capture a monopoly or near monopoly share of the market. There are other alternatives to these strategies which are discussed below under the topic of 'entry barriers' (Section 11.4).

To apply calculus to the dominant firm model is not difficult. Consider a case where there is a fringe, c, of 20 firms. Suppose each such firm has:

$$MC = 10 + 8q \qquad (11.7)$$

where q = output for each fringe membe.

$$\Rightarrow \Sigma MC = 10 + 0.4Q_c$$

(horizontal aggregation implies an unchanged intercept and a slope 20 times as gentle as that of an individual firm.)[1] For each fringe member

$$P = MC$$

Hence

$$P = 10 + 0.4Q_c$$

$$\Rightarrow Q_c = S_{cf} = 2.5P - 25 \tag{11.8}$$

Let the market demand be:

$$P = 50 - Q \tag{11.9}$$

$$\Rightarrow Q = 50 - P \tag{11.10}$$

AR_d is equation (11.10) – (11.8) or

$$Q_d = 75 - 3.5P \tag{11.11}$$

$$\Rightarrow P = 21.43 - 0.29Q_d \tag{11.12}$$

and (with slope doubled)

$$MR_d = 21.43 - 0.58Q_d \tag{11.13}$$

Let: $MC_d = 12$
Then for profit maximisation by the dominant firm: $MR_d = 12$ and we obtain $Q_d = 16.26$ units.
By substitution in (11.12) P for the dominant firm is £16.78.
By substitution in (11.8) Q_c for the fringe is 16.71 units.
Hence total Q is 33.04 units. By substituting this value in the market demand function (11.9) we obtain a market price of £16.75 (except for rounding errors) so verifying our results.

Collusive price leadership

When oligopoly is established, collusive price leadership may emerge. The co-ordination of prices which is apparent to the outside observer may well, of course, not require explicit but merely tacit collusion. An implicit recognition by all firms that one of them is taking the initiative with group interests in mind is all that is required. The leader may well be the largest firm in the group, and historically may also have been a 'dominant firm'. Where one seller has a larger share than others, the others may feel it sensible to match any increase he or she makes. If they do not he may rescind his increase, the smaller firms will have gained little or nothing by way of increased sales, and will have forgone the increased revenue available had they raised their prices in line with the original increase. Similarly, smaller sellers are also likely to follow the leader's price reductions.

It is also probable that the leader is or has been the lowest cost seller. Low costs enable a firm to take the initiative in lowering price, and other sellers have little alternative but to follow. On the other hand, however, such cost advantages have to be tempered by statesmanship. Otherwise, setting a price which is too low for some higher cost rivals might trigger off a price war which could leave all firms, including the leader, worse off than they need have been. The beneficiary would be the firm with the greatest financial reserves, not necessarily the price leader.

Barometric price leadership

The leader with a large market share and low cost levels is not only plagued with the difficulties of exercising 'statesmanship' within the group, but it may also be regarded as highly suspect by the outside 'watchdogs' of industry such as the Director General of Fair Trading and the Monopolies and Mergers Commission. This may make it reluctant to accept the role of leader and the mantle may fall to another, smaller firm, the 'barometric' leader.

The barometric price leader is a firm which is followed even if it does not have a substantial market share. While it need not be the lowest cost firm in the industry, it certainly must be an efficient firm. The barometric firm, to maintain a leadership position, must be acknowledged by the rest of the group as a company which has a 'nose' for detecting changes in demand or cost conditions. Its price alterations in reaction to such changes must be in accord with the common interests of the other sellers in the group. The barometric leader has little or no power to impose his decisions on the group and as a result his leadership may not be prolonged. The leadership may move from firm to firm, or price leadership and parallelism may even break down.

11.3.2 Game theory

The theory of games, first published by Von Neumann and Morgenstern raised hope that a definitive solution to the oligopoly problem might be available. Game theory moves away from predictions of rivals' countermoves based on experience or on probabilistic estimates towards a deductive approach based on the determination of the most profitable countermoves which will be made towards one's own 'best' strategy and to derive the relevant defensive measures. Generally game theory is restricted to duopoly. In itself this is a major limitation to its practicality.

Game theory has been amalgamated with earlier (nineteenth-century) discussions of oligopoly originating in the work of Cournot (1838). This stream of thought has become known as the 'new industrial organisation' or 'new IO'. It has had a major impact on economic literature although as yet has had relatively little operational application. Partly this is due to the normal time lag which exists between theoretical advance and its immediate usefulness, and partly it may be that the

concepts are of value only in ordering thought for rational decisions and not ones
to which data can readily be applied.

The new IO is undoubtedly of value in strategic thinking and hence we draw on
it both here and in our discussion of entry barriers (see Section 11.4). Cournot's
analysis of duopolists is explained diagrammatically with reaction curves. Each firm
can produce outputs from zero upwards and will choose that output (and hence
corresponding price) which will maximise its profits, given its beliefs about how
much the other firm will produce (and hence at what level it will price at). Clearly
it is each firm's beliefs about the other's output behaviour which will influence its
decisions.

Appendix 11 describes the Cournot model. Here we adopt the analysis of one of
Cournot's critics, Bertrand (1883) who argued that since firms typically select price
(not output) the Cournot framework should be modified accordingly.

The first step in the Bertrand analysis is to construct each firm's isoprofit lines
(the curves in Figure 11.8). These connect points of equal profits and are valley-
shaped and convex to the relevant axes. Three assumptions underlie the slopes and
positions of these isoprofit lines. First, the two firms share the market equally when
prices are identical; when firm 1's price is high relative to firm 2 its market share falls
and vice versa. Second, total market demand is an inverse function of the two prices
weighted by respective market shares. Third, their short run cost functions are identical. Diagrammatically the firms are symmetric in price and quantity space. The
isoprofit lines of each are simply reflections of the other's against the 45° line.

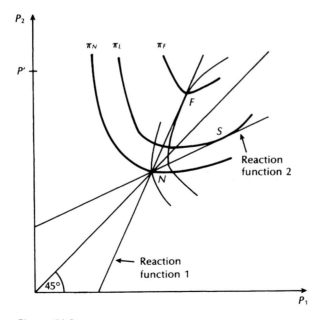

Figure 11.8

The Cournot–Bertrand problem for firm 1 is to select a profit maximising price on the assumption that firm 2 keeps price unchanged (say at P'). The answer is to raise price from zero until the highest isoprofit line is reached. After that point profits will start to fall as firm 1 forfeits sales to firm 2 to such an extent that its maximum profit point is passed. Thus in Figure 11.8 $\pi_N < \pi_L < \pi_F$. The maximum profit point will lie on reaction function 1 (RF_1) which is the locus of profit maximising prices for firm 1 for all given values of P_2. Correspondingly the reaction function for firm 2 (RF_2) is the locus of profit-maximising points for firm 2 for a series of given prices set by firm 1.

The reaction functions are also drawn on the assumptions that neither firm will charge a price below that indicated by the intersections on the respective price axes (which would be where the marginal costs of meeting the demand exceeded prices received), that the gap between the prices of the two firms never becomes unrealistically wide; and that the firms do not become involved in an apparently irrational price war, which would be the case if each followed the other in a price cutting spiral with no apparent – i.e. profit motivated – justification, as predicted by the positions of the isoprofit lines).

How then will the firms behave? There are several alternative suppositions each of which depends on beliefs about rival's behaviour. The first is the traditional Bertrand model where each firm believes its rival holds price constant. Thus in Figure 11.9 if firm 1 sets price at A firm 2 will profit maximise at the price level given by point B. But if firm 1 now assumes B is given it will react by reducing price to its revised profit maximising level of C. The process will continue to D and ultimately to equilibrium at N. The step-like process would have been reversed if

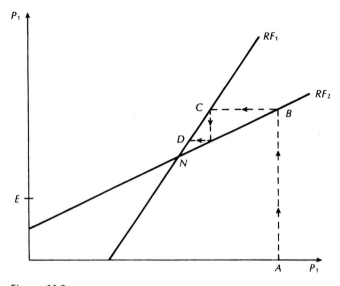

Figure 11.9

firm 2 had initially set price at point *E*. Point *N* is known as a Nash (Bertrand) equilibrium. When quantity is the decision variable (see Appendix 11) it is a Nash–Cournot equilibrium.

Two main criticisms must be directed at this model and its basic assumption that each firm regards the other's price as fixed. First, the assumption is internally inconsistent. It is only operative if, as here, each firm takes turns at setting (and resetting) different prices. Second, the assumption is then maintained and the firms are presumed never to learn that the assumption is invalid even when repeatedly proved wrong.

A second oligopoly equilibrium can be inferred from Figure 11.8. This is the Stackelberg equilibrium shown by point *S*. A Stackelberg equilibrium shows what is known as a 'first-mover advantage'. Assume that firm 1 can be identified as the market leader. By moving first it can simply choose that price which maximises its profits given that P_2 depends on firm 2's reaction function. This is given by the point of tangency between π_L and Reaction Function 2. Had firm 2 been the leader, firm 1 would have ended up at price *F* on π_F. Thus in the Bertrand framework, leader's profits exceed Nash (simultaneous move) profits. Although whichever firm is leader, the second mover is still better off ($\pi_F > \pi_L$). One difficulty with this solution is that there is no obvious reason why one or other firm should actively seek a leader's role at least if there is symmetry in competitive strengths and given that a follower's role is more profitable.

A further complexity is that if we make output the decision variable as in the Cournot model in Appendix 11, a first-mover advantage still exists relative to the Nash equilibrium but it also holds relative to the *follower*. Then the reservation is the issue of why the follower should passively accept such an unfavourable role. We have dismissed quantity as a decision variable to Appendix 11 but in reality, quantity can be a strategic variable, particularly when theory is broadened to permit innovative products and other competitive dimensions not included in the simple framework of Figures 11.8 and 11.9. We relax that assumption later in Sections 11.4 and 11.5, and also and in particular in Chapter 15.

The third set of equilibria in Figure 11.8 is given (for clarity redrawn in Figure 11.10) by the line CC$_1^1$ joining tangency points of the isoprofit lines. These represent collusive outcomes, where one firm's profits can only be increased at the expense of the other's. One of these points will be the joint profit maximising point which would exist if the firms were to merge and form a single monopoly firm or if they formed a cartel with joint profit maximisation as an objective. The end points *C* and *C*$_1$ are determined by the isoprofit lines passing through *N* since it is presumed neither firm would collude in a situation which would make it worse off than it would be in a Nash equilibrium.

If we ignore Stackelberg and concentrate on the choice between collusion along CC^1 and Nash equilibrium it is clear that while collusion is more profitable there are considerable incentives to cheat on any collusive agreement. For example, consider an agreement at *A*. Firm 1 could improve its profits by moving horizontally to its reaction function (presuming firm 2 sticks to the agreement). Firm 2's profit would then drop substantially. Firm 2, of course, would reason similarly. This reasoning

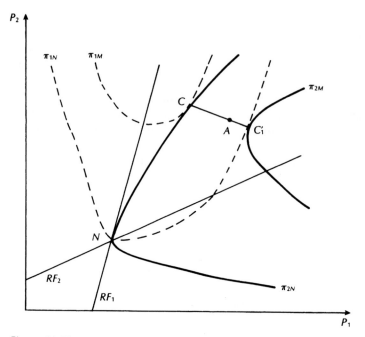

Figure 11.10

can be even better illustrated by formal game theory or by calculus. First consider a calculus example.

Assume 2 firms where:

$$\pi_1 = 4P_1 - P_1^2 + P_2 + 20$$
$$\pi_2 = 10P_2 - 2P_2^2 + P_1 + 10$$

The profit maximising Nash prices are found thus:

$$\frac{\delta\pi_1}{\delta P_2} = 4 - 2P_1 = 0$$

$$\Rightarrow P_1 = 2.0$$

$$\frac{\delta\pi_2}{\delta P_2} = 10 - 4P_2 = 0$$

$$\Rightarrow P_2 = 2.5$$

Thus:

$$\pi_1 = 25.5$$
$$\pi_2 = 23.5$$
$$\Sigma\pi = 49$$

Alternatively the joint profit-maximising price is found by adding $\pi_1 + \pi_2$ to find $\Sigma\pi$:

$$\Sigma\pi = 5P_1 - P_1^2 - 2P_2^2 + 11P_2 + 30$$

Let:

$$\frac{\delta\Sigma\pi}{\delta P_1} = 0 \quad = 5 - 2P_1 \quad \Rightarrow P_1 = 2.5$$

$$\frac{\delta\Sigma\pi}{\delta P_2} = 0 \quad = -4P_2 + 11 \Rightarrow P_2 = 2.75$$

Thus:

$$\pi_1 = 26.5$$
$$\pi_2 = 48.8$$
$$\Sigma\pi = 75.3$$

Clearly $\Sigma\pi$ is greater under collusion but firm 2 is very much better off than firm 1 (more than doubling profits while firm 1 raises them only slightly). The incentive for firm 1 to cheat to gain some of firm 2's sales and so hopefully its profits would be great.

Now consider game theory, using first a two-person zero-sum game. Such games produce Nash equilibria. That is, neither player will have an incentive to change strategy, given the opponent's strategy.

11.3.3 Two-person, zero-sum game

In the zero (or constant) sum game, what one player or firm loses the other wins; the size of the cake is fixed. Consider two profit-maximising oligopolists; A and B, with profits directly related to market share. The problem is to arrive at a price aimed at yielding the largest market share for A while bearing in mind that B has an identical aim. Assume, simplistically, that all of A's possible prices are known, and that their outcomes can be evaluated making due allowances for each of the (known) price options of B. This information is summarised in a pay-off matrix for A and analysed in terms of maximin for A and minimax for B. Table 11.1 illustrates this. A's alternative prices (or other strategies) are denoted by S_{A1}, S_{A2} and S_{A3}; B's by S_{B1} to S_{B4}. The pay-offs are the market shares A will obtain for each combination of such pure strategies. A similar pay-off matrix could be constructed for B, the basis for constructing it, given a zero-sum game, being merely that B's market share, for any given pair of prices will equal 100% less A's market share. These two pay-off matrices (Table 11.1 and its twin for firm B which is not shown here) could be used as the data source for the construction of the isoprofit lines of Figure 11.8.

A maximin approach for A will be chosen since A assumes B will be doing his or her best to ensure that, for A, the worst possible competitive situation will occur.

Table 11.1 A's market share (%)

		B's Strategies			
		S_{B1}	S_{B2}	S_{B3}	S_{B4}
A's strategies	S_{A1}	50	55	65	70
	S_{A2}	40	45	60	65
	S_{A3}	30	40	55	60

Conversely, Table 11.1 can be analysed for B on minimax principles. B will look for the best outcome for A (and so the worst for himself) in each column. The worst of these (minimax), and so the best of the worst from B's viewpoint, will be chosen. A will consequently select strategy S_{A1} and B strategy S_{B1}.

When S_{A1} and S_{B1} respectively are chosen, both A and B have their worst fears realised, but neither will wish to change their decision. Such an equilibrium is known as a saddle point. (Clearly, of course, a maximin strategy, although safe, is not the most profitable alternative when one's rival is not well informed on the available strategies and/or is not a prudent decision taker!)

Pure strategy saddle points (which occur where a value is a row minimum and a column maximum) need not exist. Consider Table 11.2. Here A has a maximin strategy of S_{A1} and B a minimax strategy of S_{B2}. This is not a saddle point since the maximin strategy combination of S_{A1}, S_{B1} does not coincide with the minimax strategy combination of S_{B2}, S_{A1}. This is not an equilibrium situation since, given the opportunity to choose anew, if B thought A would stick to S_{A1}, B would select instead S_{B1}. Acting on this, A will select S_{A2} rather than S_{A1}. But B could, in turn, anticipate this reasoning process by A and so would actually choose S_{B3}. Once again A would carry his or her reasoning a step further, and so on. In this situation unlike a saddle point, the maximin and minimax strategy combinations of the duopolists do not coincide.

One can, however, devise a *mixed strategy* for such situations. Mixed strategies are combinations of pure strategies whereby each pure strategy is selected with a given probability. The objective is to compute the relevant expected maximin (and minimax) strategy combination pay-off. This expected pay-off is the weighted average of the pay-offs which would have been obtained had the respective pure strategies been chosen. The weights are the probabilities with which the pure strategies have been chosen.

To prevent B predicting with certainty which strategy A will adopt, A will select his or her pure strategies randomly with a probability of p_i. The problem is to select

Table 11.2 A's market share (%)

		B's Strategies		
		S_{B1}	S_{B2}	S_{B3}
A's strategies	S_{A1}	50	55	65
	S_{A2}	60	45	40

p_i so as to maximise the minimum expected gain. If B should select S_{B1}, A's *expected* gain would be 50% multiplied by the relevant value of p_1, plus 60% times the relevant value of p_2, or $\Sigma_{i=1}^2 p_i \times M_{iB1}$, where M_{iB1} is A's market share under i conditions of S_{B1}. Given that *some* mixed strategy exists that will assure an expected gain of at least X, then A will want to set p_i so that $\Sigma_{i=1}^2 p_i \times M_{iB1} \geqslant X$. X is unknown but it must be greater than 50% since, given Table 11.2, 50% is the worst possible result for A under S_{B1}. In a similar manner, the choice of p_i must be made so that if B selects S_{B2} or S_{B3} then $\Sigma_{i=1}^2 p_i \times M_{iB2} \geqslant X$ and $\Sigma_{i=1}^2 p_i \times M_{iB3} \geqslant X$. As probabilities it must also be true that $p_i \geqslant 0$ and $\Sigma_{i=1}^2 p_i = 1.0$.

What we have now are the elements of the following linear programming problem:

maximise X subject to the constraints

$$0.5\ p_1 + 0.6\ p_2 - X \geqslant 0$$
$$0.55 p_1 + 0.45 p_2 - X \geqslant 0$$
$$0.65 p_1 + 0.4\ p_2 - X \geqslant 0$$
$$p_1 + p_2 = 1.0$$

and the general non-negativity requirements[2]

$$p_1,\ p_2 \geqslant 0$$

The solution of this problem is $p_1 = 0.57$ and $p_2 = 0.43$ which gives a value for X of 55%, A's expected maximin market share. Simultaneously, of course, B will be equally anxious to minimise A's expected pay-off. B's problem can be stated thus:

minimise X' subject to the constraints

$$0.5 p_1' + 0.55 p_2' + 0.65 p_3' - X' \geqslant 0$$
$$0.6 p_1' + 0.45 p_2' + 0.4 p_3' - X' \geqslant 0$$
$$p_1' + p_2' + p_3' = 1.0$$

and the non-negativity requirements

$$p_1',\ p_2',\ p_3' \geqslant 0$$

The solution to this problem is $p_1' = 0.75$, $p_2' = 0$, $p_3' = 0.25$ which gives a value for X' of 55%. It is obvious that for both A and B to reach their objectives X must equal X'. This, in fact, has been shown to hold. A and B will each choose their pure strategies at random, subject only to the values of the respective probabilities. Strategy S_{B2} will never be employed. Over a sufficiently long time period or number of observations, A will achieve an average market share of 55% and B one of 45%. The random element is essential since if A, for example, merely followed S_{A1} non-randomly for 57% of the time and S_{A2} non-randomly for 43% of the time, then a regular pattern of choice might emerge. B might detect this regularity and take advantage of it.

This result means that there will always exist a pair of mixed strategies which constitute an equilibrium pair in the sense that no one party can do any better while the other also pursues such an optimal mixed strategy.

11.3.4 Two-person non-constant-sum games

The constant-sum games considered to this point, however, are simpler than the decision of whether or not to cheat by moving off the contract curve CC_1^i in Figure 11.10. There total joint profits varied both along CC_1^i and off it. There was not the simplifying assumption we made above that they were directly related to market shares (which by definition sum to 100%). If that assumption is dropped we move to the non-constant-sum situation.

Games of this sort, in which some outcomes are more favourable to the participants jointly than others, are called non-constant-sum games or the 'prisoners' dilemma' case. Consider the combined game-theory pay-off matrix of Table 11.3. Firm A's strategies and their pay-offs are in the bottom left hand corner of the relevant square, and firm B's in the top right. Both are profit maximisers. The incentives to engage in some form of collusion are high. If both firms raise prices each will make a profit of £10. Conversely, the incentive to cheat on the collusive agreement is also present. If either A or B reduces prices alone, profits will rise from £10 to £20. The firm which does not reduce price, however, will soon follow or it would be forced into a £15 loss.

Game theory thus provides insights into oligopoly behaviour. Nash–Bertrand equilibria may, for example, help explain both where and why oligopolists demand curves are kinked. Kinked demand theory on its own, simply explains why oligopoly prices may be sticky, it gives no clue as to where the kink might be. Similarly a Stackelberg equilibrium fits well beside price leadership theory.

11.3.5 Credibility and pre-commitment

We noted while discussing first-mover advantages that one flaw in the argument was that there was no reason why firm 2 should passively accept a follower's role (in the Cournot case) or actively seek a leader's role (in the Bertrand case). There

Table 11.3

			B	
		price up		price down
	price up		10		20
A		10		−15	
	price down		−15		6
		20		6	

is a further weakness with the Stackelberg equilibrium (point S in Figure 11.8). That is that once achieved by firm 1 it can be improved upon by moving leftwards on to firm 1's reaction function. The consequence of this, together with a reluctant leader (Bertrand) or the lack of a passive follower (Cournot) of course, is that the situation again deteriorates to a Nash equilibrium.

One way out of this dilemma for a determined leader intent on gaining and retaining first-mover advantage is 'pre-commitment'.

Here we continue to look only at the Bertrand case deferring Cournot (quantity as a decision variable) to Appendix 11. Recall in the Bertrand case that

$$\pi_F > \pi_L > \pi_N$$

The dilemma faced by an intending leader intent on gaining first mover advantages (over the Nash situation) is that he would be better off as a follower (see Figure 11.8). The answer is to pre-commit by substantially raising short-run marginal costs. Conventionally firms take decisions in the long run (when they determine their capital stock) and in the short run (when they determine price and outputs). A long-run decision to reduce capital stake or investment will raise short run marginal costs. Alternatively a long-run decision to change the capital:labour ratio while maintaining capital fixed in absolute terms will also raise short-run marginal costs. This precommitment is a signal to competitors that the firm is going to behave differently in future from that behaviour pattern which would otherwise have held. In other words raising short-run marginal costs will move the firm's reaction function. One way to pre-commit by raising short-run marginal costs is to emphasise that product quality will be significantly higher due to an increase in after-sales service which is personnel dependent, or to quality of product 'finish' due to a higher degree of labour intensity in the manufacturing process.

Raising the short-run marginal cost function for firm 1 in this way would, in diagrammatic terms move Figure 11.8's reaction function to the right so that it passes through point S (as in Figure 11.11). Of course, two can play at that game and it may be that effectively over time the firms end up simply at a new Nash equilibrium, selling at higher prices and both with higher short-run marginal costs. Nevertheless, the possibility of raising short-run marginal costs by product variation does tempt an otherwise inert leader into activity when the elementary Bertrand model would suggest that no such initiatives would be taken. (In Appendix 11, where Cournot models are examined, precommitment takes the form of lowering short-run marginal cost by increasing capital investment.)

11.3.6 Collusive pricing and cartels

To avoid the uncertainties of pricing decisions and the downward pressure on prices which competition exerts (given quality) and the upward pressure on short-run marginal costs, quality and prices which precommitment exerts, firms frequently come to express or implied agreements to maintain prices at a similar level. Although express agreements are frequently declared illegal under the provisions of

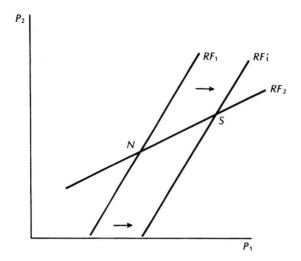

Figure 11.11

the Fair Trading Act, the same end result is often aimed at by means of tacit collusion.

Individual firms, however, frequently find it worthwhile to break out of any such agreement, whether tacit or overt. There are three reasons for this: the 'free rider' problem, varying cost conditions, and shifting demand patterns.

Figure 11.12 illustrates the first of these problems. In Figure 11.12b D_I represents the industry demand curve. S is the market supply curve, obtained by aggregating horizontally the MC curves of the numerous independent sellers in the industry. Without collusion the market price would be P and the quantity produced and sold would be Q_1 where $P = MC$. Any single seller would produce and sell Q_4 units, where $Q_4 = Q_1/n$ where n = the number of (equal sized) firms in the market. If any

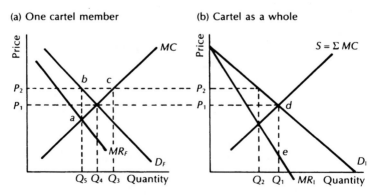

Figure 11.12

single seller were to sell an additional unit, his or her marginal revenue would be insignificantly different from P_1. For the group as a whole, however, MR would be significantly below market price. (Geometrically this is obscured in the figure since the quantity axis in Figure 11.12a is a 'stretched out' version of the same axis in the second.)

If the sellers collude as a single monopoly, the profit-maximising price–output combination is P_2Q_2 where $\Sigma MC = MR_I$. As long as all firms have identical MC curves, P_2 is also the optimum price for the individual cartel member. Since we are assuming that all sellers act in concert, when one reduces quantity there will be a perceptible effect on price. If a single seller acted alone, his or her demand curve would be almost horizontal at P_1, but since what any one does they all do, D_F, the 'share-of-the-market' curve is the relevant demand curve.

Had the two panels in the figure been drawn on the same (quantity) scale, the distance $(Q_1 - Q_2)$ would be n times as great as $(Q_4 - Q_5)$. Given concerted action the profit-maximising output for the single firm is Q_5 at the cartel price P_2 where $MC = MR_F$. Now joint profit maximisation has been made possible, 'free riding' can occur.

Each colluder is expected only to supply Q_5. This is a quota which somehow the cartel must enforce. But each firm realises that if he alone supplies more than Q_5, the effect on price will be negligible. P_2 is the price each firm must take. If a firm acts alone, P_2 is his marginal revenue curve. The quantity that then maximises profit (under these changed assumptions and given that others continue to price at P_2) is Q_3. The individual seller makes a profit gain of abc. Since this opportunity is open to all, the probability is very high that one or a few firms will seize it. A cartel may be a 'gentleman's agreement' but, as Stigler (1966) pithily pointed out, 'the participants seldom are, or long do'. Each firm will be tempted to gain a 'free ride' on the anti-competitive behaviour of his fellows. Since profits attract entrepreneurs like honey attracts bees then, unless a sufficiently powerful overseeing body can enforce the output quotas and/or inhibit new entry, the cartel will inevitably crumble. Generally only a state or government agency has such far-reaching inquisitorial powers of inspection and enforcement.

In Figure 11.12 we assumed that each firm's MC curve was in the same position so that equal quotas resulted in equal marginal costs. Suppose, however, that marginal costs vary. Assume as in Figure 11.13 that there are only two sellers and that the collusive agreement is that each will supply half the quantity demanded at each price. D_F is consequently the 'share-of-the-market' demand curve for each firm and the MR curve for the group as a whole. MR_F is each firm's perceived marginal revenue curve and MC_A and MC_B are the MC curves for firms A and B.

The optimum prices for A and B are thus different, namely P_A and P_B. They will disagree over which price should be set for the group. Moreover, the cartel's optimum price, P_C, is not the optimum for either of the two firms. Cartel profits are maximised, not when the quantity to be produced is necessarily divided equally, but rather where $MR_1 = \Sigma MC$, giving optimum output Q_1 divided so that $MC_A = MC_B$ in order that each firm might have the same marginal cost. (If $MC_A \neq MC_B$ at any output level, then output reallocation should take place between the two firms until

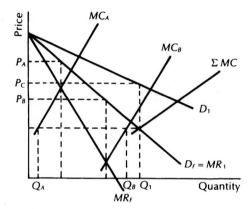

Figure 11.13

the marginal equivalency condition again holds. Without such reallocation the cartel would not be minimising costs and so would not, even if operating at the profit-maximising output level, be maximising the difference between revenue and costs.) Thus, if an output of Q_1 and a price P_c could be agreed upon, the cartel would face formidable difficulties in allocating output in the profit-maximising manner. Firm A would wish to produce more than Q_A and B less than Q_B. Again only an agency with strong powers of coercion could ensure that the cartel would not disintegrate. Again this is likely only if some governmental body exercises industrial oversight.

The problem of maintaining cartel prices is further enhanced if to the temptations of cheating and the problems of varying costs is added the hazard of shifting demand. Figure 11.14, a variant of which was first suggested by Scherer (Scherer and Ross, 1990), illustrates this and shows how the problem is at its most intense in the case of firms with high fixed or overhead costs. Figure 11.14 shows two firms with identical demand curves D_1 (representing boom conditions) and D_2

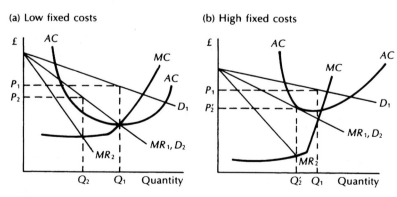

Figure 11.14

(representing slump). For simplicity D_2 and MR_1 are deemed to be graphically identical. In Figure 11.14a a firm with low fixed costs is represented and in Figure 11.14b a firm with high fixed costs.

In both cases profit-maximising behaviour in boom conditions requires identical prices of P_1 and outputs of Q_1.

Although MC is constant for both firms up to the same level of output (or designed capacity of the firms' plants) because of their different cost structures it is much higher in the low fixed cost case than in the other case. As a consequence, when demand falls to D_2, the low fixed cost firm will contract output substantially and price at P_2. The high fixed-cost firm will reduce price to P_2', and output, at Q_2', will be larger than at Q_2. However, although both firms are still pursuing profit-maximising behaviour the high fixed-cost firm is now barely breaking even, but the low fixed-cost firm is still making a significant absolute profit (albeit lower than before). If the high fixed-cost firm is a member of a cartel the temptation to free ride at P_2' will be greater than for the low fixed-cost firm. The more demand falls, the greater this temptation becomes for either firm.

11.4 Barriers to entry

It might appear that successfully colluding oligopolists can charge a price considerably in excess of their average costs. In other words, price may equal, or approach the level which would hold if the industry was a monopoly. In conditions of perfect and monopolistic competition, price cannot for long exceed average cost since the appearance of new entrants to the industry will exert downward pressure on prices. Writers such as Bain (1956) and Sylos-Labini, have extended this and argue that this relationship, between price and cost, exists throughout the entire economy; that it exists in the short run as well as the long; and that it requires merely the threat of entry, not actual entry, to enable it to hold.

If so, then relatively sticky but follow-my-leader pricing policies, ending up at a fairly high and near monopolistic level, need not necessarily occur in oligopoly, provided only that the threat of entry is strong or, what is the same thing, barriers to entry are low.

The theory of entry barriers rests on one principal assumption known as the Sylos postulate. This alleges that potential entrants expect established firms to maintain their output levels (i.e. reduce their price to accommodate the entrant) in the face of entry, and that this expectation is, in the event of entry, actually fulfilled. Figure 11.15 illustrates how a potential entrant can calculate where his or her demand will lie if the entrant is considering entering a given industry. DD is the demand curve for the industry. Existing firms are producing Q_1 units of output at price P_1. Given the Sylos postulate an entrant must increase the industry's total output and therefore the industry's price must fall by a sufficient amount to clear both Q_1, and the additional output of the entrant. Effectively, therefore, the entrant's demand curve is that segment of the total industry demand curve to the right of the ruling price. This will be P_1D_1 if the ruling price is P_1, or P_2D_2 had the ruling price–output

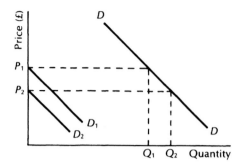

Figure 11.15

combination been P_2Q_2. To ascertain whether or not to enter an industry a potential entrant will compare this demand curve with his or her particular cost function.

Entry barriers are of three main types. Product differentiation or consumer preference barriers, absolute cost advantages, and scale economies. Analytically, the former two can be grouped together. Preference barriers and absolute cost barriers are present if established firms have lower average unit costs than potential entrants at any given output level. Thus, to overcome preference barriers, entrants might have to spend more highly on advertising or research and development than existing firms.

To overcome absolute cost barriers they may have to pay higher input prices than established firms, as, for example, when an established firm controls a scarce input such as a patent right or a raw material source from which royalties or discriminatory prices can be extracted. Scale economy barriers exist when there is a declining $LRAC$ for the product in question which makes it difficult for a smaller firm to enter the market, given its substantially higher costs; or alternatively precludes entry by a large firm if the market is of a given size, and any unsatisfied demand can only be met by a small firm. Where such entry barriers exist, 'under the Sylos postulate, there is a well defined maximum premium that oligopolists can command over the competitive price' (Modigliani). The lower are the entry barriers, the closer is the price to the (perfectly) competitive level.

This is illustrated in Figures 11.16 and 11.17. In Figure 11.16 absolute cost barriers exist. The entrant's average total cost curve, ATC_E, is higher than that of established firms, ATC_F. Established firms can produce at a price–output combination of P_1Q_1 and the demand curve confronting the entrant is consequently P_1D_1. At no point on that curve can an entrant possibly make a positive profit. Had established firms been selling at price P_1, output Q_2, then the entrant's demand curve would have been P_2D_2 and entry would have occurred, pushing price down once more to the entry-deterring level. The height of the entry barrier is measured by the difference between the entry-deterring price and the ATC_F curve. This difference is in turn dependent on the difference between the two ATC curves.

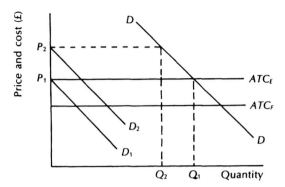

Figure 11.16

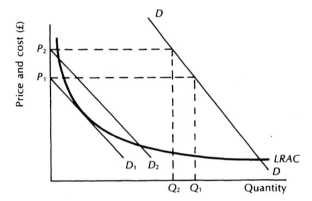

Figure 11.17

In Figure 11.17 the *LRAC* curve available to all firms in the industry is displaying scale economies. The entry-deterring price–output combination is P_1Q_1.

The demand curve P_1D_1 facing a potential entrant at no time allows him or her to make a positive profit. Again, had established firms been producing at price P_2, output Q_2, then the entrant's demand curve would have been P_2D_2 and a substantial range of output over which profits could be made would have induced entry, pushing price down again to the entry-deterring or limit price. The height of the entry barrier is measured by the vertical difference between P_1 and the *LRAC* curve at output Q_1.

The practical effectiveness of this barrier is clearly dependent upon a combination of factors including the price elasticity of demand, the scale at which the *LRAC* levels off or begins to rise, and the size of the market itself. (In other words in quantitative terms, and given the axes scales, the effectiveness of the barriers will vary with the slope of the firm's demand curve, the slope and position of the *ATC* curve, and the position of the industry demand curve.)

What of the impact of time on the price decisions? In reality a time lag will occur while a new entrant establishes his or her production capacity prior to actually moving into the market place. Prices can then be set above the limit level while still maintaining the Sylos assumption. Figure 11.18 illustrates the nature of the calculation which will be made. Assume the existence of absolute cost barriers to entry and assume also a zero discount rate. It will pay the existing firms to charge the short-run profit-maximising $(MR = MC)$ price of P_2, rather than the entry deterring price of P_1 if in so doing the profits for the period before entry, plus the profits for the period after entry, are greater than the profits which could be earned at P_1 for the total period to which the industry demand curve applies. Thus P_2 will be charged initially (and P_1, of necessity, after entry) if, in algebraic terms:

P_2ACJ (for the period before entry) + P_1BCJ (for the period after entry) is greater than P_1GHJ (for the total period)

Moreover, as Worcester has pointed out, the Sylos postulate can again hold but profit-maximising pricing and not limit pricing may be optimal even if entry barriers are low or non-existent. Thus in Figure 11.19 a monopolist (A) sets an initial profit-maximising price P_A. But because entry is easy, firms B, C and D subsequently enter the industry in successive periods. Firm A, by charging P_A initially, maximises profits over time, maintains output at Q_A and so the dominant share. To have charged the entry deterring price of P_L would not have maximised discounted profits and would simply have perpetuated a worthless (to the firm) monopoly. Over time the original firm's price falls to P_B (when B enters) to P_C (when firm C enters) and so on.

Whether or not the Sylos postulate is valid is, of course, of major relevance to entry and pricing decisions. Established firms might, for example, contract rather than maintain output levels in the fact of entry. This means, of course, that entry will be much more attractive and so more likely to occur than under the Sylos postulate assumption. The price received by an entrant would be the same as that ruling at entry, or at worst, if lower, not as low as it would be under the Sylos

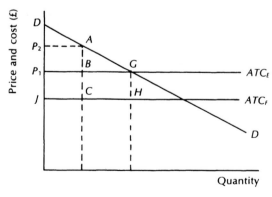

Figure 11.18

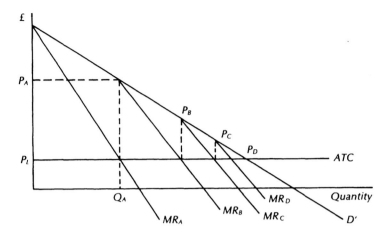

Figure 11.19

assumption. On the other hand, it could be argued that to contract output in the face of entry is a relatively unrealistic assumption. It implies that established firms will generously allow an entrant to take whatever share of the market he or she pleases while they themselves lose sales, and possibly incur higher unit costs as a result of their reduced throughput. The Sylos postulate and the discussion above seems more realistic.

The third assumption which could be made is, from the point of view of entrants, the most pessimistic of all. Established firms might be expected to and also be able to take aggressive defensive reaction in the face of entry. Heavy, but temporary price cutting, heavy advertising or other predatory tactics by established firms could well drive a relatively weak entrant out of the market. This assumption, of course, removes the possibility of obtaining definitive solutions as was sometimes done under the Sylos postulate. What the ruling price will be, whether entry will occur or not, what the post-entry price might settle at, will all depend on the relative competitive strengths of the entrant and established firms. These matters can be determined only instance by instance by observation, not a priori.

Alternatively, instead of attacking the limit price as 'too low' in wealth-maximising terms (as in Figures 11.18 and 11.19) one could argue as does McGee, that it is 'too high', in which case the Sylos postulate is again removed from centre stage. For example consider Figure 11.20. This is a typical 'limit price', 'scale economy barrier' model.

LP is the limit price. The industry is currently in the hands of a monopolist with a plant size indicated by ATC_M. To achieve a plant size of minimum efficient scale an entrant would require plant ATC_E. If the entrant constructed such a plant and the Sylos postulate held, he or she would make a loss of P_ECBA in perpetuity. But, if so, and he or she is really determined to enter, the existing firm would make the even larger loss of P_EEFC which is an irrational long-term situation.

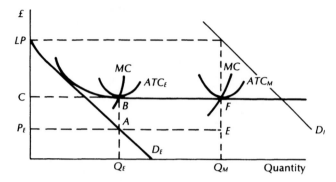

Figure 11.20

Again no definitive price policy for either entrant or existing firm is apparent. But serious doubts are cast on the logic of the limit price models.

11.5 Entry and strategic behaviour

Is a council of despair, then, the only theoretical response to the weaknesses of the Sylos postulate? Indeed it is often impossible or (as we have shown) undesirable for existing firms to maintain output. Entrants who know this will not then be deterred. Alternatively credible threats of price reductions greater than that necessary to deter entry (Sylos style) may prove to be rational. While under other conditions similar aggressive behaviour by a potential entrant may be rational.

The discussion around Figure 11.20 above suggested that the power to threaten or deter is the prerogative of the firm with financial or other resources. But strategic power is more than simply strength or even skill. Strategic power is the power to post a credible bond, the power to bind oneself, the power to make another believe that something is true.

When one threatens to fight if attacked, or to cut price if one's competitor does, more than the communication of the threat is required. To be effective the threat must be credible to the threatened. And to be effective the threatener must have and display his own incentives so as to demonstrate that he would, *ex post*, carry out the threatened action. The issue is one of credible pre-commitment. Reputation, as noted earlier, is one method of posting such a bond. But whatever means is used, for maximum credibility the threatener must be seen to have left as little room as possible for judgement or discretion in carrying out the threat.

Thomas Schelling (1984, p. 196) cites Xenephon as having explained the principle 2,000 years ago. He placed his fighting men with a deep gully at their backs, with no way of retreat. His objective was not simply to ensure his men fought well, but to let the enemy know that they would fight and fight well since there was no safe alternative for his soldiers except victory. In the terminology of modern economics

Xenophon was committed and he was signalling to the enemy that he was committed.

The prior commitment involved in standing in front of the gully was not a statement that fighting well would necessarily be optimal *ex ante*. Xenophon would have preferred to win the battle without fighting at all. What the prior commitment signalled was that fighting well would be his optimal and hence chosen strategy *ex post*, that is if the enemy did indeed choose to fight.

Avinash Dixit (1982) has used this type of reasoning to advance oligopoly theory beyond the Sylos postulate using the game theory and decision tree analysis we are now familiar with. He moves from the one-stage games discussed in this chapter to date, to a two-stage game (which in principle can be extended forward for as many stages as is usefully required).

Consider Figure 11.21, a two stage game between an incumbent monopolist and a potential entrant. The first stage is to decide whether to enter or not. If no entry occurs the monopolist continues to earn π_M. If entry occurs the monopolist has to decide whether to fight a price war where each firm ends up earning π_W or π_C where firms collude and share the resulting profits. (Thus it is assumed $\pi_M > \pi_C > 0 > \pi_W$.)

The key question posed of Figure 11.21 is: which of the three outcomes will result? Since the game is two stage and sequential, that is, each player can take a decision based on the history of the game to that point, then collusion is not a likely outcome. At stage I the incumbent will make no plans to collude or to fight until the entrant decides on his or her strategy. The incumbent will simply wait. In other words the incumbent will adopt an approach leading to a Nash equilibrium, he or she will decide on an optimising strategy (π_W or π_M) *given* the action pursued by the entrant. A similar Nash equilibrium analysis of the entrant can now be performed. Given that the entrant now knows that 'fight if entry' will occur on entry and that $0 > \pi_W$ then he or she will not enter leaving the incumbent to plan a costly price (or other competitive) war which will never occur.

This Nash equilibrium (where each optimises given the strategy pursued by rivals) is clearly unrealistic. Entry deterrence is easy since costless statements of intent (not a costly war itself) are all that have to be provided. The threat is not only cheap to make, it is empty. Since if the entrant were to ignore it and actually enter there would remain no incentive to carry it out ($\pi_C > \pi_W$: the incumbent would now be reacting to a new and revised belief about his rival's strategy).

To avoid this problem a requirement any realistic equilibrium strategy should have is that each sub-strategy should also be optimal irrespective of from which

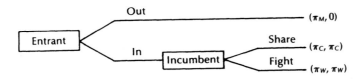

Figure 11.21

point of the game tree it arises and whether or not that contingency actually arises in the play of the game. Or to rephrase, it is more realistic to argue that at each point in time, whatever situation has arisen, firms will react rationally from that point on. This rules out empty threats and is known technically as a perfect or sequential equilibrium. In Figure 11.21 the entrant knows that the incumbent's optimal response to entry is sharing since $\pi_C > \pi_W$, and since entry would provide the entrant with $\pi_C > 0$ entry will occur. Thus this is sequential equilibrium.

Entry will therefore occur and will not and cannot be deterred unless we make the very weak Nash assumptions. However, if we allow the incumbent to act strategically like Xenophon who placed his soldiers with their back to a gulley, there are means whereby the incumbent can prevent entry. For example, if the incumbent can make a prior and irrevocable commitment, such as incurring cost K in readiness to fight a price war this will not affect his expected profits if a war does break out but will lower his expected profits by K if it does not, Figure 11.22 shows the new three-stage game. The incumbent by altering his or her own expected profits alters the entrant's expectation of the incumbent's reaction to entry. Commitment could include investment in productive capacity in excess of monopoly require- ments but which would be used in the event of a price war (breaking the Sylos assumption of constant output); or heavy advertising expenditures which would generate goodwill and customer loyalty which would persist even if entry occurred; or research and development and brand proliferation with similar consequences.

An incumbent who has made such a commitment will find it optimal to fight in the event of entry if $\pi_W > \pi_C - K$. An entrant knowing this will stay out if the incumbent is committed and enter if he or she is passive. The incumbent, aware of this in turn will indeed commit if the ultimate pay-off of doing so, $\pi_M - K$, is greater than that from being passive, π_C. Provided there exists a commitment strategy with a cost K such that $\pi_M - \pi_C > K > \pi_C - \pi_W$ then the incumbent can and will employ a credible threat and deter entry. Or rearranging, it is only if $\pi_M - K > \pi_C$ that the incumbent will find it worthwhile to deter entry by precommitment and since $\pi_W > \pi_C - K$, the incumbent will indeed choose to fight should entry occur.

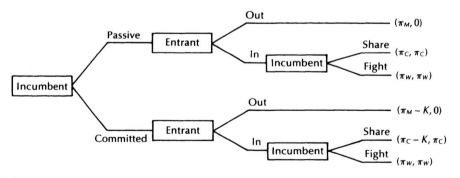

Figure 11.22

Realising this the entrant will stay out since if he or she did not he or she would end up with $\pi_W < 0$.

One point in this discussion must be emphasised. The commitment must be irreversible. K must not be easily reversible should the strategy fail. For example, expenditures on capital equipment or additional capacity would not serve as a useful entry deterrent if the entrant knows the equipment can be costlessly or cheaply resold or liquidated and the cost recovered at near the original price. In short the costs of K must be sunk.

11.5.1 The post-entry game

Of course sunk costs exist for other than strategic reasons. An entrant firm may have to incur sunk (non-retrievable) costs simply for operational purposes (and with no strategic intent to impact on the incumbent's competitive expectations). Where sunk (operational) costs are very low for an entrant and the sunk (strategic) costs of the incumbent are also low, then the incumbent must live in constant fear of what Baumol (1982) terms 'hit and run' entry. The market is then close to being what he termed 'perfectly contestable'. The incumbent does not price at a level much higher than average cost otherwise an entrant would undercut the incumbent and rapidly acquire his or her market (provided only that he can set up production facilities and switch consumer loyalty to him promptly – not a trivial consideration). A Nash–Bertrand price equilibrium would emerge with prices close to marginal costs. Only a very small sunk (operational) overhead cost is then necessary to deter entry, since with price at marginal costs there would be no surplus to cover overheads.

Most markets, however, are not perfectly contestable (where strategic behaviour cannot be indulged in by the incumbent because the costs involved would not be sunk), nor are they perfectly competitive (where the entrant must take account of his or her sunk operational costs while the incumbent need not). Since strategic behaviour and sunk costs are important a proper understanding of post-entry behaviour is essential. This the Sylos postulate failed to do.

A major weakness of the Sylos postulate was not that it necessarily made an invalid assumption about the incumbent's post-entry behaviour. Rather the flaw was that there was nothing to suggest that limit pricing behaviour and output maintenance (which clearly implied price cutting by the incumbent in the face of entry) was or was not an empty threat.

Dixit's main contribution where he modelled the post-entry game was to argue 'that the role of an irrevocable commitment of investment in entry-deterrence is to alter the initial conditions of the post entry game to the advantage of the established firm' (Dixit, 1982). The game trees of Figures 11.21 and 11.22 have already shown this. Another way of illustrating the importance of credible precommitment is to use Cournot reaction curves which we do in Appendix 11. The argument is analogous to that which we have already used above with the Bertrand assumptions where we showed how lowering the capital:labour ratio could encourage first mover behaviour. In Appendix 11 we show how the reverse behaviour, increasing capital investment and reducing short-run marginal costs can not only lead to first-mover (incumbent) advantages but also to an entry-deterring result such that it is not worth while for there to be a follower, second mover or new entrant.

11.5.2 A pricing miscellany

The role of cost

Many surveys have suggested that business men and women practice cost-plus pricing. That is, some mark-up is added to average cost to obtain unit selling price. This seems a straight contradiction of the $MR = MC$ rule. It appears totally to ignore demand and makes no concession to competition, actual or threatened. Moreover it involves circular reasoning. If volume sold depends on price (as it does in demand analysis) but price depends on cost (as in cost-plus pricing) then how can price be determined, since cost depends on volume sold (as it does in cost analysis)? However, closer inspection of mark-up pricing reveals that business men and women choose a mark-up which they deem 'necessary' or 'appropriate' and so the paradox is resolved. There need be no conflict between the accountants' rules of pricing and the economic point of view.

Recall that in profit maximisation $MR = MC$. Then:

$$MR = \frac{dTR}{dQ} = \frac{dPQ}{dQ} = \frac{Q\,dP}{dQ} + P \quad \text{and} \quad MC = \frac{dACQ}{dQ} = \frac{Q\,dAC}{dQ} + AC$$

$$\therefore \quad Q\frac{dP}{dQ} + P = Q\frac{dAC}{dQ} + AC$$

$$\therefore \quad P = Q\frac{dAC}{dQ} + AC - Q\frac{dP}{dQ}$$

$$= AC + Q\left(\frac{dAC}{dQ} - \frac{dP}{dQ}\right)$$

Now assume constant costs such that $MC = LRAC$. Then:

$$P = AC - Q\frac{dP}{dQ}$$

$$\therefore \quad \frac{P - AC}{P} = -\frac{Q}{P}\left(\frac{dP}{dQ}\right)$$

$$= \frac{1}{\eta}$$

Thus the left-hand side of this expression (the mark-up under cost-plus pricing) is higher the less elastic is demand and vice versa. The more price elastic a product is, the lower is its mark-up. Thus cost-plus pricing can simply be a synonym for $MR = MC$.

Table 11.4 Sealed-bid pricing

Bid (1) £	Profit (2) £	Probability of our bid winning the contract (3)	Expected pay-off (2) × (3) £
10	2	0.9	1.8
11	3	0.7	2.1
12	4	0.5	2.0
13	5	0.3	1.5

Sealed-bid pricing

When firms tender for contracts under a sealed-bid system the main problem is estimating the probable bids of competitors. 'Guesstimates' of these can be obtained from a variety of sources. What sort of level of bids have they submitted in the past? What are their current cost levels? Does trade gossip suggest they are working above or below full capacity? Is their plant and equipment modern and low-cost or obsolete and costly to operate? Alternatively, even if their plant is modern and their variable costs low, was the capital cost so great that they must keep the plant in continuous operation to recoup their fixed costs? In short, how keen are they to obtain business? With this sort of information a pay-off matrix of the kind shown in Table 11.4 can be constructed. Here we have hypothetical data with four price choices and an assumed unit cost of £8.

Profits, over time, will be maximised with the £11 bid. Over a run of contracts we assume that we will win 70% of them with bids of £11 and lose 30%. This provides an average or expected profit for every contract we bid for (whether we win it or not) of £2.10 per unit. Obviously this type of analysis is only useful if market conditions are fairly repetitive: this need not be the case. In addition, if our firm requires certain or near-certain profits in the short run then a bid of £10 or less should be made. This will not maximise long-run profits but it will generate near-certain business.

| Appendix 11 |

The Cournot framework of pricing analysis

The discussion in Chapter 11 concentrated on price as the decision variable not quantity. In our section on reaction curves as a means of oligopoly analysis we consequently used Bertrand reaction curves rather than the (historically older) Cournot framework. There are at least two reasons why the Cournot framework should not be ignored, however. First, the Cournot analysis is not wholly analogous to Bertrand's. For example 'first mover' advantages produce leader's profit (π_L) not only in excess of a Nash equilibrium profit level (π_N) as in the Bertrand case, but also in excess of follower's profits (π_F). This results in differing behavioural incentives for leaders and followers. Second, although we relegated Cournot's framework to the Appendix because quantity was the decision variable this was to some extent inconsistent. The Sylos postulate, after all, is based on post-entry *output* of the incumbent firm being presumed to be the same as pre-entry *output*. The pricing consequences are simply inferred. The Sylos implications and recent additions to entry theory such as the importance of precommitment may then be better, or at least more consistently understood, if developed in the Cournot (quantity adjusting) framework than in the Bertrand framework of the core chapter.

As before the first step is to construct the isoprofit lines of the two firms. Again, for simplicity we assume linear demand and cost functions for each, and identical short run cost functions. Again we assume symmetry in price and quantity space. The isoprofit lines on this occasion are higher the closer they are to the respective axes. Thus where reaction function 1 intersects axis Q_1 firm 1 would be earning its maximum possible (monopoly) profit.

How will the firms behave? The traditional Cournot view is that each firm believes its rival holds quantity constant. Thus in Figure A11.1 if firm 1 sets quantity at the monopoly profit maximising level A firm 2 will profit maximise at the output level given by B. But if firm 1 now assumes B is given it will react by reducing quantity to its revised profit maximising level of C. The process will continue to D and ultimately to the Nash–Cournot equilibrium at N.

As was with the Bertrand model a main criticism is the naivety of this sequential process where each firm's underlying assumptions are continuously falsified. However, the model's usefulness is rather in its (several) equilibrium conditions rather than in this process of attaining point N. An alternative to N is the Stackelberg equilibrium of S.

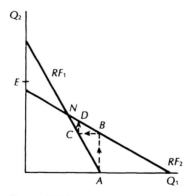

Figure A11.1

As with the Bertrand model a Stackelberg equilibrium shows what is known as a 'first-mover' advantage. Assume firm 1 is the market leader, by moving first it can simply choose that quantity which maximises its profits given that Q_2 depends on firm 2's reaction function. This is given by the point of tangency between π_L and RF_2. Had firm 2 been the leader the Stackelberg equilibrium for firm 1 (the follower) would have been at point F on π_F. Thus a first mover with π_L is better off than a simultaneous mover at π_N, who would in turn be better off than a follower at π_F. (In the Bertrand framework recall $\pi_F > \pi_L > \pi_N$.) A difficulty with this solution is that if there is comparability in competitive strengths there is no obvious reason why either firm should passively accept a follower's role.

The third set of equilibria is given in Figure A11.2 by line CC'. As before these are the collusive outcomes where one firm's profits can only increase at the expense of the other's. One of these points would be the joint profit maximising point if the firms were to form a cartel and act as if they were a monopoly. As before C and C' are predetermined by the isoprofit lines passing through N, and again, ignoring the Stackelberg solution, we can show that while collusion is more profitable than a Nash solution, the incentives to cheat are high. For example, consider a collusive agreement at A. Firm 1 could improve profits (assuming firm 2 sticks to the agreement) by increasing output by moving horizontally rightwards to RF_1. Firm 2 would, of course, reason similarly. Again game theory or calculus can be used to demonstrate this argument.

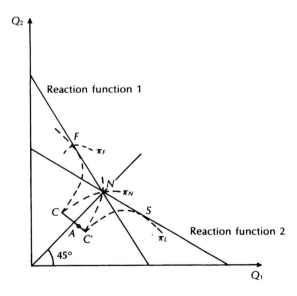

Figure A11.2

Assume two firms where

$$\pi_1 = 24Q_1 - Q_1^2 - 2Q_2^2 - 8$$

$$\pi_2 = 30Q_2 - 3Q_2^2 - 2Q_1 - 9$$

The profit maximising Nash outputs are found thus:

$$\frac{\partial \pi_1}{\partial Q_1} = 0 = 24 - 2Q_1$$

$$\Rightarrow Q = 12$$

$$\frac{\partial \pi_2}{\partial Q_2} = 0 = 30 - 6Q_2$$

$$\Rightarrow Q_2 = 5$$

Thus $\pi_1 = 86$, $\pi_2 = 42$, $\Sigma\pi = 128$.

Alternatively the joint profit maximising level is found by adding $\pi_1 + \pi_2$ to find $\Sigma\pi$.

$$\Sigma\pi = 22Q_1 - Q_1^2 - 5Q_2^2 + 30Q_2 - 17$$

let

$$\frac{\partial \Sigma\pi}{\partial Q_1} = 0 = 22 - 2Q_1 \Rightarrow Q_1 = 11$$

and

$$\frac{\partial \Sigma\pi}{\partial Q_2} = 0 = -10Q_2 + 30 \Rightarrow Q_2 = 3$$

$$\Sigma Q = 14 \text{ and } \pi_1 = 117, \ \pi_2 = 32$$

$$\text{and } \Sigma\pi = 149$$

Clearly $\Sigma\pi$ is greater under collusion but firm 2 would have a substantial incentive to cheat unless compensated in some way.

Credibility and precommitment

The Stackelberg point S (where $\pi_L > \pi_N > \pi_F$) in Figure A11.1 is not credible. Not only is there no obvious reason why firm 2 should passively act as a follower, firm 1 itself could improve profits by moving horizontally leftwards to its own reaction curve. The only credible, but less attractive, equilibrium is point N. A firm intent on gaining and retaining first mover advantages must somehow precommit its output at point S. Such a precommitment must signal to competitors that the firm is going to behave differently in future from the behaviour pattern which would otherwise have held. (In the Bertrand case this involved raising short-run marginal costs, here the opposite holds.)

If the first mover invests in additional productive capacity the first mover can shift his or her reaction function out and to the right to RF_1' such that it passes through point S. Such strategic investment reduces marginal cost and unless firm 2 is also prepared to engage in capital investment rivalry (shifting RF_2' outwards) then the Stackelberg equilibrium does become credible examined both from the leader's and the follower's perspectives. The reason for the outward movement of RF_1 to RF_1' consequential on increased capacity and lower marginal costs is readily explained. For any given output level there is a corresponding (market determined) price and marginal revenue. Given marginal revenue and a lower marginal cost the firm's profit maximising reaction is to increase output, at each and every level.

Precommitment, strategic behaviour and entry

Figure A11.3 not only helps explain oligopoly behaviour between the existing firms it throws light also on entry and entry-deterring behaviour. The Sylos situation (where incumbents choose an entry deterring output level, maintain that level, and potential entrant's accede to that belief) is essentially a Stackelberg equilibrium where firm 1 is the incumbent and firm 2 the potential entrant. The incumbent chooses point S rather than the monopoly profit-maximising point where RF_1 intersects the Q_1 axis. Entry is not then barred however, but it is limited to the level indicated by S on RF_2. Not only is S not an entry-deterring position but we saw it is also an irrational position for the leader to adopt since after entry the leader would be better off moving left to RF_1 (unless, of course, he or she credibly precommits).

Or to put it another way, Cournot reaction-function analysis also suggests as did Figure 11.22, that an uncomitted incumbent will attract entry, that the Sylos postulate will prove invalid and that a Nash equilibrium will occur. However, if the incumbent can precommit he or she can *select* a reaction function such that the entrant will remain out (diagrammatically implying that points below and to the right of S on RF_2 are non-feasible output options for firm 2, and points to the right

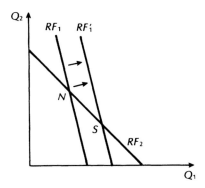

Figure A11.3

of S on RF_1^1 where output would be competitively increased as in a price war are not seriously envisaged).

Collusion and iterative games

Both in the core chapter and in this appendix we have either treated collusion as only a passing possibility, or, where we discussed it at greater length, we viewed it as an unlikely outcome. Recent game-theoretic discussions have made this general conclusion no less invalid, but they have shown how under certain circumstances the players in a prisoners' dilemma game *could* arrive at a mutually beneficial collusive outcome.

For example, players might *ex ante* sign a contract agreeing to play by certain rules and hire lawyers to ensure such collusive rules are enforced. This, of course, introduces transactions costs to the discussion. Implicitly, when regarding cartels as unlikely to survive, we have assumed that such transactions costs are too high for it to be worthwhile for participating firms to incur them.

If we move from a once-and-for-all game to a repeated or iterated game such transactions cost loom less large. For example, if a game is repeated indefinitely it usually pays the players to keep to the terms of any agreement because the gains from successive iterations will exceed the benefits to be derived from a single, one-off incident for cheating. For this argument to hold, the end of the game must be infinity otherwise the discount rate of the different players will enter into their decision processes as to whether or not to continue co-operating the closer is the perceived end of the game. The smaller is the probability of the game continuing into another round the greater must be the pay-off to sustain an agreed equilibrium. Similarly the greater the possibility of gains from short-run cheating, the greater must be the pay-off to maintain co-operation.

A continuous game reduces but does not remove transactions costs. Players must still obtain information about each other. But while several iterations may often be closer to reality than a one-off game would be a continuously repeated game with all players observing each other's actions and compliance is also far removed from real life. Self-enforcing co-operative solutions dependent on perfect information in games played into the indefinite future require assumptions just as unrealistic as the zero transactions-cost co-operation of a single play prisoner's dilemma collusive agreement.

Notes

1. When horizontally aggregating we set $MC_1 = MC_2 = \ldots = MC_n$ and add the corresponding qs. Hence from equation (11.7) $q = (MC - 10)/8 \Rightarrow Q_c = q_1 + q_2 + \ldots + q_{20} = [20/8] [MC - 10]$ $\Rightarrow MC = 10 + 0.4Q_c$.

2. In this example p_1 and p_2 must both be >0 to avoid either strategy being selected alone. It has already been noted that such a choice is unstable. Hence when introducing slack

variables into the three expressions to render them equations, we have four equations and six unknowns. The basic LP assumption for algebraic solution is that any two of the unknowns equal zero at a corner. Hence only 4 unknowns and 4 equations will exist. Solutions are then obtained for X, letting any two such variables equal zero and selecting the solution which provides the greatest value for X. Since p_1 and p_2 must be greater than zero, only equation systems with two of the slack variables equal to zero need be considered. These values can be checked by the interested reader. Manual calculation requires subtraction of the three slack variables, S_1, S_2 and S_3 from the constraints to provide four constraint equations.

Bibliography

Bain, J. S. (1956) *Barriers to New Competition*, Harvard University Press.

Baumol, W. J. (1982) 'Contestable markets: an uprising in the theory of industrial structure', *American Economic Review*, vol. 72.

Clarke, R. and McGuiness, T. (1987) *The Economics of the Firm*, Basil Blackwell.

Davies, S., Lyons, B., Dixon, H. and Geroski, P. (1991) *The Economics of Industrial Organisation*, Longman.

Dixit, A. (1982) Recent developments in oligopoly theory', *American Economic Review*, vol. 72.

Modigliani, F. (1958) 'New developments on the oligopoly front', *Journal of Political Economy*, vol. 66.

Schelling, T. (1984) *Choice and Consequences*, Harvard University Press.

Scherer, F. M. and Ross, D. (1990) *Industrial Market Structure and Economic Performance*, Houghton Mifflin.

Stigler, G. J. (1966) *The Theory of Price*, 3rd edn, Macmillan.

Waterson, M. (1988) *Economics of the Industry*, Cambridge University Press.

Chapter 12

Pricing in regulated industries

A large swathe of the economy is subject to continuous official regulation of its pricing activities.

Most obviously this is so in industries which were formerly state owned and which were subject to privatisation in the 1980s. The four most prominent regulatory bodies and the companies they monitor are:

Office of Telecommunications (OFTEL)	Mercury British Telecom
Office of Gas Supply (OFGAS)	British Gas
Office of Electricity Regulation (OFFER)	National Grid Powergen other generating and distribution companies
Office of Water Service (OFWAT)	Various water companies

These firms, their predecessors in the state sector, and indeed their opposite numbers in Europe, America and elsewhere have long been subject to regulation. Often called 'public utilities' they have frequently been assumed – not always correctly – to be either natural monopolies (that is industries where a single firm could not exhaust scale economies given the size of the market); or to be so strategically important that government ownership or control was a *sine qua non*. Given these assumptions it is not surprising that some industries often become national (not natural) monopolies with little if any competition between firms (especially from other countries) being permitted in any one economy.

Price regulation in these industries has gone through three conceptual phases:

1. marginal cost pricing   1960s and 70s
2. rate of return regulation   1970s and 80s
3. RPI-X price control   1980s and 90s

We shall look at these in turn. One major difference between the protagonists of the earlier and later types of control is that modern-day regulators (for example Little-child, the Director General of OFFER) often view controls as necessary only 'To "hold the fort" until competition arrives.' Where new competition is less likely, older forms of regulation (marginal cost pricing and rate of return regulation) may be deemed appropriate. Alternatively and additionally any of the continuously regulated industries can also be referred on an *ad hoc* basis to the Office of Fair Trading or to the Monopolies and Mergers Commission for one-off examination.

12.1 Marginal cost pricing

Traditional neo-classical welfare economics suggests that pricing where $MR = MC$ is not optimal. Instead prices should be set at marginal cost.

The rationale for this is illustrated in Figure 12.1. A private monopolist would operate at output level Q_1 and price P_1. Consumer surplus is equal to the area ABP_1 and producer surplus or monopoly profit to the area GP_1BF. If the monopolist is now compelled to operate where $P = MC$, output rises to Q_2, price falls to P_2 and consumer surplus becomes the triangle ACP_2. Producer surplus is now the area GP_2C. At P_2 the sum of producer's and consumer's surplus, ACG, is maximised. The result of the change in price policy is a net welfare gain equal to BCF. In other words, the objective of public utility pricing is assumed to be the maximisation of total social benefits over total social costs, where social benefits are measured by the willingness of the market to pay as indicated by the demand curve, and where all social costs are presumed to be embraced by the firm's cost schedules (i.e. there are no externalities).

If the marginal cost pricing rule is followed, one immediate question begged is whether the rule refers to short- or long-run MC. The answer is, that there is no conflict provided an appropriate investment rule is then adhered to.

First, it is a truism that when short-run average cost (SAC) equals long-run average cost (LAC) then at that output level both short-run (SMC) and long-run

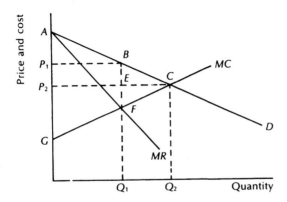

Figure 12.1

(*LMC*) marginal costs are equal. Figure 12.2 shows *SMC* and *LMC* at Q_1, Q_2, and Q_3, positions of declining, constant and rising LACs respectively. At Q_1, Q_2 and Q_3, $SAC = LAC$ and so short-run total cost (*STC*) is equal to long-run total cost (*LTC*).

Since their gradients equal their marginal values, tangencies at Q_1, Q_2 and Q_3 imply that $SMC = LMC$ at these outputs. To avoid conflict between *SMC* and *LMC* the optimum plant size occurs where the two are equal, given $P = MC$. The rule which brings this about states that either:

(a) if at the output level for existing capacity for which $P = SMC$, $SMC > LMC$, then new capacity should be constructed; or, conversely
(b) if at the output level for existing capacity for which $P = SMC$, $SMC < LMC$, then disinvestment should take place.

If this rule is obeyed, economic welfare is maximised: the marginal benefits of expansion (or contraction) are equated with the marginal costs of that expansion (or contraction). To understand this, assume that at any point $P = SMC$. The benefits of marginal output in terms of willingness to pay) are simply equal to $(P_1 + P_2)(Q_2 - Q_1)/2$, where P_1, P_2, Q_1, Q_2 are the original and revised prices and quantities respectively.

The marginal benefits of expansion would then equal the short-run marginal costs of expansion. But the cost of marginal output is $K + r(Q_2 - Q_1)$ where K is the incremental capital costs of fixed asset acquisition. Expansion is worthwhile if the marginal benefits (*SMC*) exceed the costs (*LMC*). Contraction and disinvestment is to be preferred in economic welfare terms if the costs (*LMC*) exceed the benefits (*SMC*). Thus the investment rule is justified and conflict between *SMC* and *LMC* resolved.

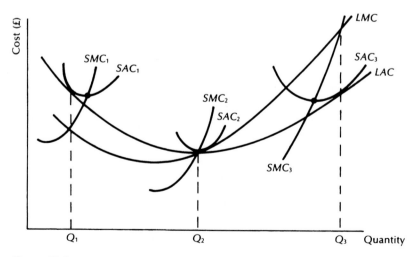

Figure 12.2

Another practical problem is natural monopoly. In decreasing-cost industries, a firm following the investment and pricing rules laid down would be unable to cover its average cost. In short, a private monopolist forced to abide by such rules would go out of business.

In Figure 12.3 with plant SAC_1 pricing at SMC results in a profit earning P_1Q_1 price–output combination. But $SMC > LMC$ at P_1Q_1 and welfare will only be maximised when investment takes place and a plant size with a cost structure equal to SAC_2 is attained. Then $P = SMC = LMC$ at P_2Q_2. However, the firm is now making a loss and given our guidelines there is no way in which it can avoid this.

One solution is to price at marginal cost and subsidise the firm. Consumers can then choose an economically optimal amount of the service or product, based on $P = MC$, and the industry will be kept solvent. This is only optimal if the money to pay the subsidy can be obtained without distorting resource allocation elsewhere. This is easier to say than to accomplish. Moreover, a subsidy redistributes income away from those who are taxed in order to raise the subsidy towards the users of the subsidised industry. This can only be equitable if those so taxed are also those who are subsidised. If a redistribution does occur, the quantity demanded may well be in excess of the quantity which would have been consumed had no subsidy been provided.

The ideal solution is for each person to pay the same price ($P = MC$) for the units he or she consumes at the margin, the deficit to be made up by each consumer

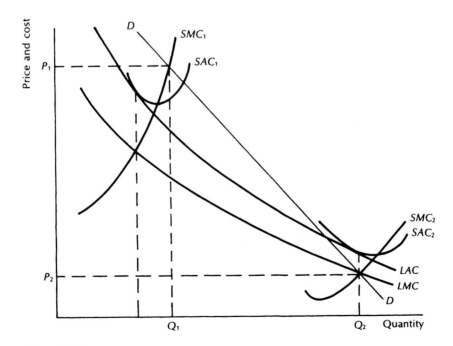

Figure 12.3

accepting a share of it according to the valuation he or she places on the goods or services consumed. This could be done either by each individual consumer paying the appropriate lump sum relevant to his or her consumer surplus, or by paying different intra-marginal prices pitched to contribute an identical net amount. These alternatives would not affect the individual consumer's marginal decision about consuming another unit. However, the information on each consumer's demand function is simply not available to enable such a system to operate at low cost.

A more practical way to leave consumers free to decide how much of a good they want to buy at MC and still pay sufficient to cover the deficit, is to operate some form of the two-part tariff. One part will be a unit price equated with marginal cost, the other a flat rate unaffected by use. This places on consumers the burden of meeting all the costs of the service they use but does not distort marginal choice, as pricing at average cost would do. However, such a system may prevent potential consumers from using the service if, at the margin, they are willing to pay MC per unit but not the flat fee for using the service at all.

Finally the whole discussion rests on the assumption that managerial and technical efficiency will be continuously maximised. The incentive effect on managerial efficiency of the provision of subsidies to eliminate deficits is ignored.

12.1.1 Peak load pricing

Marginal cost pricing theory made a major contribution to pricing practices in those public utilities where demand varies over time and the product cannot be stored. Electricity is the classic example.

Conceptually, there are two cases which can be distinguished in the peak load pricing problem. These are the firm peak case and the shifting peak case. In the firm peak case there is one peak period and differential prices (on- and off-peak) do not eliminate it. In the shifting peak case differential prices, if incorrectly applied, can result in the off-peak period becoming the period of greater consumption.

12.1.2 The firm peak case

Consider two independent demand curves for equal duration subperiods (say night and day) for electricity. Assume an inherited plant with a fixed maximum output of Q_d and constant unit running costs of r. What pricing policy will result in optimum use of the available capacity? Figure 12.4 shows that the prices should be P_N and P_D.

This pricing policy maximises the net total social benefits as measured by willingness to pay in a way no other pricing arrangement would. Geometrically these are equal to the area ($AEr + BCDr$). At night, price is equal to $SMC = r$. During the day, price acts as a rationing device to allocate the service to those consumers who place most value on it in terms of willingness to pay. Here price is equal to the vertical portion of the SMC curve.[1]

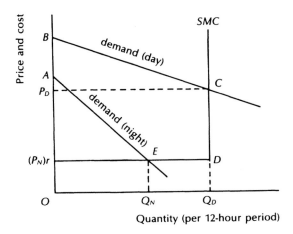

Figure 12.4

The next question is what is the optimum capacity in the firm peak case? For simplicity, assume given and constant plant lives so that capital costs can be represented in an annual equivalent form. Running costs are equal to $r = SMC$. Capital costs are equal to k, and so $LMC = r + k$ (subject to $SMC = r$, a condition which will only hold up to a given plant's output limit).

In Figure 12.5 two possible plant sizes with maximum outputs of Q_D and Q_b are shown. If capacity size Q_D was constructed, prices would be $r(P_N)$ and P_D for night and day respectively. However, this does not comply with the investment rule that SMC and LMC should be equated. In this instance, where $P = SMC$, $SMC > LMC$ and so new capacity should be constructed. The optimal size will be at Q_b where again the night price will be P_N but the daytime price will be $P_b = r + k = LMC = SMC'$. In the firm peak case, all capacity charges (k) are borne by the on-peak consumer. The off-peak consumer merely pays for his appropriate share of the running costs.

Up to this juncture we have made the implicit assumption that there are no indivisibilities in plant size. Thus if plant size Q_D is too small, in terms of the investment rule, then it is possible to build precisely the size of plant necessary so enable the conditions $P = SMC = LMC$ to be adhered to, as with plant size Q_b. Let us drop this assumption and consider the situation which arises if Q_D and Q_b are the only two plant sizes which it is commercially or technologically possible to construct over the relevant output range. All the conditions in Figure 12.5 remain unchanged, except daytime demand, which we will now assume to be represented by the line passing through the points A, B and C.

Neither plant size, under these circumstances, will permit the equating of $P = SMC = LMC$. Which plant is to be preferred? If Q_D is chosen, a daytime price of A would be selected, compared with the 'ideal' (given no indivisibilities) price of B. Net social benefits equal to the area ABE will have been forfeited. Conversely, if a plant to produce Q_b is selected, a daytime price of C would be charged compared

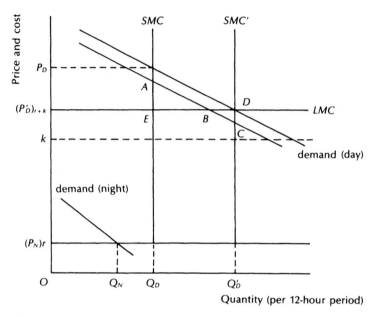

Figure 12.5

with the 'ideal' price of *B*, and a corresponding ideal plant size. Net social benefits equal to the area *BDC* will have to be forfeited. Given these circumstances, a plant will be chosen which minimises these notional losses of social benefits. Thus if *ABE* > *BDC* then the plant size with capacity Q'_D will be constructed.

12.1.3 The shifting peak case

In the shifting peak case, the nature of demand in the subperiods is such that both are responsible for capacity changes. Consequently, merely charging off-peak users for running costs can result in the quantity they demand being higher than that of the on-peak segment. In Figure 12.6, if night time users are charged *r*, the required capacity is Q_N. If daytime users are charged *r* + *k*, the required capacity is only Q_D.

The correct procedure is to use the entire 24-hour demand cycle. Vertical summation of the demand curves is required. Similarly, the cost curves must be aggregated vertically. The running costs, *r*, are consequently doubled. Capacity costs, of course, are unaffected. If an additional unit of capacity is provided for one cycle it is also available for the other. Thus the *LMC* for the 24-hour cycle is equal to 2*r* + *k*.

Optimal capacity is consequently Q_A where the aggregate demand curve intersects the 24-hour cycle *LMC* schedule and simultaneously the *SMC* curve appropriate to a plant capacity of Q_A. Optimal pricing policy can then be found by referring to the component parts of the aggregate demand curve, namely P_D and P_N for day and night respectively. In the shifting peak case, the off-peak consumers do

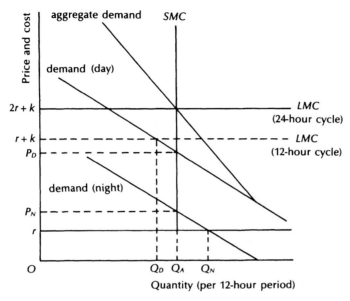

Figure 12.6

contribute to capacity costs, and do so in proportion to the strength of their demand relative to the on-peak users. Again our investment rule has been complied with: $P_N + P_D = 2r + k = LMC$ (24-hours) $= SMC$.

12.2 Controlling return on capital

An alternative approach to the natural monopoly problem is to release the public utility from the requirement to price at MC and instead require it to maximise profitability subject to a constraint on its rate of return. One possible regulatory objective is to bring profits down to the competitive level as indicated by a zero margin above long-run average costs.

How would a public utility react if such a constraint were imposed by government? Four possible alternatives suggest themselves. First, as a parallel to the natural monopoly situation with a subsidy at $P = MC$, the firm might simply raise costs above the minimum efficient level (X-inefficiency and or some other form of managerial or organisational slack would arise). Second, if the firm operated in markets other than that in which it holds a monopoly, it might reduce its rate of return to near zero in the latter and, if it possessed some market power in the former, price its products in such a way that cross-subsidisation would enable monopoly rents to be reaped in the firm as a whole, albeit not (apparently) from the public utility. Third, the firm might keep its return on capital down to the desired level, not by reducing prices and profits, but rather by raising its capital base by inefficiently and unnecessarily using excess or obsolete (and hence high-cost) capital equipment. Finally, and as a variant on this third point, the firm might even operate on its production possibility frontier (that is, at full technological efficiency on the product transformation curve) but be too capital-intensive to permit allocative (i.e. $P = MC$) efficiency.

This is illustrated in Figure 12.7. Consider a firm operating with a capital stock of K_0 at $Q_{monopoly}$ where $MR = SMC(K_0) = LMC$ and a cost of capital embodied in the short-run average cost curve $SAC_1(i)$ equalling i *together with* the relevant gap between D and SAC_1. There is no incentive for the firm to expand output at price P_1 and profits are duly maximised. The social optimum of $P = MC$ has not been obtained, however. Expansion should take place for this to occur. Now impose a return on capital constraint of $s\%$ where s, although greater than i, must not be exceeded. This has the diagrammatic effect of raising SAC_1 to $SAC_1(s)$.

P_1 must be reduced since it permits abnormal profits. Abnormal profits only disappear when plant size is raised from SAC_1 to SAC_2, a capital stock of K' against the original smaller stock of K_0. With plant size SAC_2, profit-maximising behaviour results in $SMC(K')$ being equated with MR. Price is P_2, output is Q', and the profitability constraint of $s\%$ is satisfied. Economically, the *perceived* cost of capital to the firm has been reduced. Originally it was i plus the relevant abnormal profit. After regulation the best available alternative yielded only s. The price of capital is apparently lower, consequently more capital is employed. But at Q', $SMC < LMC$ suggesting that the firm is over-invested in capital equipment. The labour:capital ratio is socially non-optimal. This is so since, if at Q' $LMC > SMC$, then what is foregone by producing with one extra unit of capital (LMC) is greater than what is

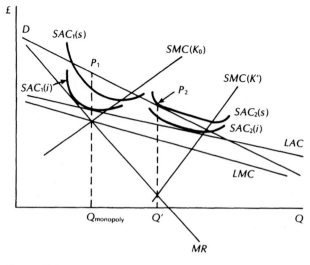

Figure 12.7

foregone by producing with one extra unit of labour (in the short run capital is a fixed input). Alternatively:

the actual cost of capital divided > the price or cost of labour divided
by its marginal product   by its marginal product

or symbolically,

$$i/MP_K > W/MP_L$$

where W is the wage rate. Rearranging,

$$MP_K/i < MP_L/W$$

which implies that output could be raised by shifting one pound of resources from capital to labour. Control of the rate of return has resulted in a production technique which is too capital-intensive.

12.3 Privatisation, regulation and RPI-X

The theoretical approach of Section 12.1 was the officially approved method of tackling nationalised industry prices in the United Kingdom from 1967 to 1978 (when one government White Paper replaced another). Rate of return control was more common in the United States, but in the 1980s the privatisation phenomenon resulted in a sea change in public utility regulation.

Discontent with marginal cost pricing rules had become widespread. The static equilibrium theory on which marginal cost pricing is based assumes that products, demands, resources, resource prices and techniques are all given before the event. In reality they are not. Managers cannot follow such rules since it is their job first to find out the alleged 'givens'. In such circumstances costs are subjective not objective since only the manager in the course of his or her job, not the regulator before the event, knows what alternatives are being foregone. One cannot therefore check that a manager is following the marginal cost rules if the marginal costs themselves only exist in the manager's mind. Another problem is the motivation of the regulators themselves. The 'public choice' as opposed to the 'public interest' school of thought argues that regulators, like everyone else, are motivated by self-interest. However, the consequent actions of such motivation do not necessarily work out for the common good (as Smith's invisible hand suggests self-interested actions do in market relationships). Rather regulators will 'rent-seek' and be liable to 'capture' by the industries they are allegedly controlling. Cost-padding will occur by the regulated industry and favours will be exchanged resulting in wealth transfer from consumers to the producer/regulator nexus rather than wealth creation consequent on informed voluntary exchange between producer and consumer.

Regulation by price-capping is the currently favoured alternative. In its detailed implementation form it was first introduced into the United Kingdom by Stephen Littlechild in 1983 and subsequently adopted for several privatised industries.

In 1987 the US Federal Communications Commission took up the idea for both AT&T and the regional telephone companies.

To recap: rate of return (ROR) regulation provides an incentive to overcapitalise (so permitting larger absolute profit); neither marginal cost pricing nor ROR regulation provide incentives to reduce costs, since if firms do prices will be reduced in step; neither ROR regulation nor marginal cost pricing encourages change, growth, cost saving innovations or new products which could be sold at lower prices. Further, prior to privatisation the stimulus or threat of competitive entry domestically, or from abroad, was generally absent since the firms often had either *de facto* or *de jure* statutory monopoly powers. Then there is an asymmetry of information inherent in the relation between the regulators and the regulated monopolies. Regulated monopolies have informational superiority in all aspects of their operations over the regulators which they can exploit to their advantage. Consequently the regulators are seldom effective in enforcing efficiency. The informational handicap of the regulators becomes particularly severe in industries in which there are rapid technological changes. Firstly, regulators may face incentives which coincide more with those of the regulated than they do with those of consumers. By contrast a price-cap regulatory regime is more market and incentive driven and less dependent on information. The principle of price-cap regulation is to regulate the monopoly so that it will have no excess profit. All factors of production including capital will have been paid for. That means capital investment will have received its normal return. When there is no excess profit, total revenue must equal total factor payments. This relation can be shown to be the same as

$$\text{rate of price increase} = \text{rate of input price increase} - \text{total factor productivity}$$

The rate of input price increase can be approximated by the retail price index (RPI). Such a proxy is necessary because it is difficult to have consensus between the regulators and the regulated monopoly on input price inflation due to problems of information, whereas RPI data are generally reliable and available. This suggests that as long as the monopoly concerned increases its prices at the rate given by the expression it will earn a normal return on its capital investment and there will be no excess profit. This serves as the basis for price-cap regulation. If the monopoly is simply regulated according to the expression, it will have no excess profit, but it will also have no incentive to increase productivity. If total factor productivity is low, the price-cap will be high and the regulated monopoly entitled to raise price until it obtains a normal return on its investment.

An aim of the regulators should be to provide incentives for the monopoly to increase productivity and to have the benefits derived from it shared among the firm and consumers. A commonly adopted proposal is to replace total factor productivity by an adjustment factor X to be determined by negotiations between the regulators and the regulated monopoly. Thus:

$$\text{Price cap} = \text{RPI} - X$$

The key features of RPI-X regulation are as follows:

1. The regulators directly set a ceiling for prices to be charged by the regulated firm according to a formula: the average price of a specified basket of services must not exceed RPI-X.
2. For a pre-specified period the regulated firm may set prices freely below the ceiling.
3. Price ceilings are defined for baskets of service provided by the regulated firm. Different ceilings may apply to different baskets.
4. The adjustment factor X will be reviewed and possibly changed at the end of some specified period.
5. The quality of service will be monitored by a regulatory agency.

The major problem of price-cap regulation is to set an appropriate adjustment factor X so as to provide incentives for the regulated firm to improve productivity and so that consumers can share the benefits of productivity increase. If the monopoly is so regulated and X is set exogenously it will have an incentive to improve its productivity so that it grows above X. This can be illustrated by a numerical example. Suppose RPI = 10%, X = 3% and total factor productivity growth = 4%. Then the rate of increase that will yield no excess profit is 6% but the price-cap is 7%. Under price-cap regulation the monopoly is entitled to increase price by 7% which is one percentage point above what is necessary for it to obtain a normal return on its capital investment. This differential will translate into excess profit for the monopoly. Therefore, the monopoly will have an incentive to improve productivity once X is fixed. The problem with this simple approach, however, is that the monopoly will reap all benefits of this higher productivity and not share them with the consumers (at least absent competition).

A more sophisticated way of determining X is needed to induce sharing of benefits arising from higher productivity while maintaining the incentive for the monopoly to achieve such an increase. X has to be related to the expected rate of productivity of growth reported *ex ante* and the actual rate of productivity growth achieved *ex post*. Due to an asymmetry of information the regulated monopoly has superior information on its cost structure and the technology of production *vis-à-vis* the regulator. It is in a better position to estimate and report on its expected rate of productivity growth. However, if the monopoly is left to do this, it will have a strong incentive to under-report in order to get the smallest X possible.

To solve this type of incentive compatibility problems, economists devise self-revelation mechanisms to induce truth-telling. The idea is to devise a mechanism so that the party that has the superior information will report truthfully because it is in its interest to do so. In other words, the monopoly in maximising its profit, will also maximise society's objective so that the incentives of both parties become compatible.

The interest of the monopoly is to have X as low as possible while the interest of the rate-payers is the reverse. The idea is to devise a formula so that X is the smallest if the monopoly reports an expected rate of productivity increase which turns out to be realised exactly afterwards. This will induce the monopoly to report as best it can its expected rate of productivity growth for the coming year. Parameters for the formula can also be carefully chosen so that once the monopoly reports truthfully its expected rate of productivity growth, it will have continuing incentives to achieve as high a rate of productivity growth as possible and that both the monopoly and the rate-payers will share the benefit.

The advantages of price-cap regulation are numerous. First, under price-cap regulation, the regulated firm will take the maximum price as given and seek to minimise costs and invest at levels that are efficient given the levels of demand resulting from the ceiling prices. The regulated firm is motivated to do this because it gets to keep whatever profits it can earn (and must also absorb any loss that may emerge). The incentive for productive efficiency under unconstrained maximisation is preserved. Second, since it gets to keep all profits, the regulated firm has the incentive to innovate and to introduce new products and services which will increase profits. Third, rate-payers also gain as part of the expected increased efficiency will be passed on to them via sharing. Fourth, prices are likely to be lower than they would be under ROR regulation. As long as X is positive, the rise in price will always be slower than the general inflation rate, thus helping to slow down inflation. In fact under price-cap regulation, the regulated firm is more willing to lower its price, since a subsequent increase in price cannot be denied as long as it stays below the ceiling. Fifth, the administrative costs of price-cap regulation are lower than that of ROR regulation as price-cap regulation is simpler to operate by the regulators and the firm.

Box 12.1

Price competition and regulation in electricity

There are several generators of electricity all of whom supply on a wholesale basis to the National Grid Company (these include National Power, Power Gen, the still state-owned Nuclear Electric, North of Scotland Hydro and one or two other suppliers in Scotland and on the Continent who are also connected to the grid). Each of these companies is also free to compete on a contractual basis for any consumer whose usage of power exceeds a given wattage per year (approximately the size of a medium-sized supermarket). The various distribution companies purchase from the Grid and are subject to RPI-X regulation.

At the core of the industry, however, is the wholesale market. Each day the generators submit bids to the National Grid Company giving the minimum prices at which they are willing to supply from each generating unit (or 'Genset'). The bids are then reviewed in ascending order and a despatch schedule is determined to match supply and predicted demand for each 30 minute period of the following day. System marginal price (SMP) is determined by the bid price of the marginal despatched set and a capacity element is then normally added to SMP. Clearly any consistently unsuccessful bidder will have to either make his or her bid more attractive or move into the retail (contract) market. While conversely, if spot prices are sufficiently attractive relative to the contract market, bidders will move out of retailing as soon as contracts end and undercut existing successful spot bidders.

Price-cap regulation is particularly suited for industries which experience rapid technological changes and which are, but need not be, monopolised. Box 12.1 outlines the form the practice assumes in the British electrical supply industry.

Note

1. This portion of the *SMC* curve is not equal to the cost of producing one extra unit, which is *r*. However, at Q_D it is not possible to produce a further unit owing to the rigidity of the plant. The relevant cost concept after Q_D is that of the opportunity cost of the marginal user, not that of the next best productive use of the resources. At Q_D the marginally excluded consumer puts the value of the resources in their current use at P_D.

Bibliography

Brittan, S., Kay, J. A. and Tompson, D. J. (1986) 'Privatisation', *Economic Journal*, vol. 96.

Cmnd 3437 (1967) *Nationalised Industries, A review of Economic and Financial Objectives*, HMSO.

Cmnd 7131 (1978) *The Nationalised Industries*, HMSO.

Kay, J., Mayer, C. and Thompson, D. (1986) *Privatisation and Regulation: The UK experience*, Oxford University Press.

Stein, J. L. and Borts, G. H. (1972) 'Behaviour of the firm under regulatory constraint', *American Economic Review*, vol. 62.

Veljanovski, C. (1991) *Regulators and the Market*, Institute of Economic Affairs, London.

Williamson, O. E. (1966) 'Peak load pricing and optimal capacity under indivisibility constraints', *American Economic Review*, vol. 56.

Chapter 13

Advertising decisions

Here we examine one of the most publicly visible business activities: advertising. It is also controversial. First, we discuss how advertising budgets are set. Second, once the budget is determined, the issue as to how that budget is allocated between different media is addressed. Strong emphasis is placed on how the marginal equivalency principles of managerial economics are actually applied in practice. Because of the wealth and sophistication of market and advertising research data in the real-life market-place, the practical usefulness of managerial economics is seldom exceeded in any other decision making area.

Finally, we look at the strategic role which advertising can play given its apparent close relationship with price and market structure.

13.1 Budget setting: the theory

Figure 13.1 shows how sales and profits may vary with advertising expenditure. Even with zero advertising, some sales will be achieved. Little impact on sales is made when advertising is indulged in at fairly low levels, since the expenditure is so low as to pass unnoticed by the majority of potential customers. After a point, however, successive increments in advertising will produce more than proportionate increments in sales. The sales response curve begins to rise steeply. The firm has crossed the threshold level below which advertising will pass unnoticed, and is reaching the stage where it can take advantage of economies of scale. Specialists in copywriting and design can be employed. Advertising research can be engaged in. More efficient media can be used. For example, a firm with £5,000 to spend may be able to purchase for that sum one page in a paper with 10,000 readers, giving it a cost per contact of 50p. Such a firm would be precluded from taking a page in a 5 million readership paper at a cost per page of £50,000, but an average cost per contact of only 1p. Eventually, the sales response curve moves out of this exponential phase, diminishing returns to advertising expenditure set in, and while the curve will continue to rise, it will do so less than proportionately and, as a whole, will take on an S-shaped appearance. The diminishing returns are due to fixity

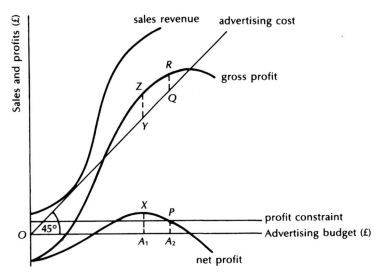

Figure 13.1 The S-shaped sales response function

in size of the target market. Sales saturation will be approached; those customers most amenable to persuasion have already bought, and only less willing prospects remain.

If the two axes of Figure 13.1 are drawn on the same scale, a $45°$ line can be drawn through the origin, and the vertical distance from any point on it to the x-axis can then be represented as advertising cost. This equals the distance on the x-axis from where the intersection occurs to the origin. With knowledge of costs other than advertising for each sales level, the profit curve gross of advertising expenditure can be drawn. The net profit curve can also be inserted. The boat-shaped area between the gross profit curve and the $45°$ line equals net profits.

The profit-maximising firm will consequently produce at that sales level where net profits are maximised, XA_1, which is where advertising costs will equal YA_1 which is a budget of OA_1. The model can readily be adapted to aid budget determination in firms with motives other than profit maximisation. For example, consider a Baumol-type profit constraint. A single-period sales maximiser would then set a budget equal to OA_2, a level which would achieve a higher sales response than OA_1, but a lower resulting profit.

This model, however, has several practical and theoretical disadvantages.

1. It assumes that advertising can be varied smoothly and continuously. In fact, this is not so. An advertising campaign may be increased or decreased in extent. But this can normally be done only by discrete 'lumps'. One insertion more or less in a magazine campaign, for example can represent an increase or decrease of thousands of pounds in expenditure.
2. It takes no account of the fact that sales vary with elements in the marketing mix other than advertising: price and product quality, choice of distribution channel

and product variety can all produce a different pattern of outcome under varying circumstances.

3. No account is taken of variations in other costs, such as manufacturing or distribution expenditures.
4. It assumes that revenue and cost functions can be constructed, that the relationship between advertising and sales is known. This is not often the case.
5. No account is taken of the possible strategic reactions of rivals.
6. The fact that advertising today can result in sales tomorrow, and that today's sales in their turn may depend on past advertising is ignored. It is a single-period model.
7. Advertising varies in quality, effectiveness and appeal, often in a manner unrelated to the level of monetary expenditure.

We discuss these critiques in more detail in the next few pages. First, however, we examine points (5) and (6).

The pay-off to advertising depends not only on how the market responds to the firm's advertising, but also upon how competitors react. One way to embrace this difficulty is to use a matrix as in Table 13.1. Here we have three alternative budget levels, one other competitor and three alternative advertising responses by that competitor.

The pay-offs in the table can be resulting profits (as here), sales, market share, attitude change by consumers, or whatever criterion the firm decides to set as the objective of its advertising effort. The advertising budget for firm A can now be selected by whatever decision rule is most appropriate given the managerial circumstances. (For example any of the maximax, maximin, minimax regret, maximum likelihood, or the expected value rules can be employed.) The profit figures in each cell which lie above the diagonal are firms A's pay-offs.

The analysis can also be developed to take account of the problem of outguessing the intelligent competitor. In other words, a game-theoretic approach could be

Table 13.1 Profits from advertising in a two competitor, zero-sum game with alternative advertising budgets

		Firms B's budgets (£'000)					
		100		200		300	
	100	5000		3000		1500	
			1200		3200		4700
Firms A's budgets (£ 000)	200	4600		3300		2900	
			1600		2900		3300
	300	3800		3500		3100	
			2400		2700		3100

adopted. For example, assume a two-person constant-sum game, with a total available profit of £6.2 million. This implies, somewhat unrealistically, that the total profits available in the market are unrelated to advertising expenditures, but that each firm's share of these total profits is directly proportional to its relative advertising budget.

The figure below the diagonals in each cell indicates firm B's pay-offs, under these circumstances, and given that both firms adopt the maximin criterion, firm A would set its budget equal to £300,000. Competing firm B would do so also. This would be the equilibrium position. Neither firm could improve its pay-off by altering its budget.

Another defect that the model of Figure 13.1 does not take into account is the time factor. Advertising can be likened to capital expenditure in that it not only generates sales and profits today, but will continue to do so into the future as a result of the creation of the asset of goodwill. Like all capital assets, the carry-over effects of advertising will wear out. Consumers will forget the original advert, future competitive advertising will obtrude, and so on. Consequently, advertising budgeting can be likened in a way to the capital investment decision.

A simple example of this approach has been suggested by Simon (1969) who suggests that the asset advertising creates will depreciate at a constant rate into the indefinite future. In addition, there will be sales in the current period even if present advertising is zero, due to the carry-over effects of past advertising. His model runs as follows:

let k = the rate of depreciation
r = the firm's cost of capital
A_0 = the advertising budget in the current period
ΔS_0 = the increment in sales (net of all costs except advertising) generated in the current period by A_0
PV_s = the present value of all present and future incremental sales generated by A_0

Then

$$PV_s = \Delta S_0 + \frac{\Delta S_0(1-k)}{1+r} + \frac{\Delta S_0(1-k)^2}{(1+r)^2} + \ldots$$

$$+ \frac{\Delta S_0(1-K)^\infty}{(1+r)^\infty}$$

$$= \sum_{t=0}^{\infty} \frac{\Delta S_0(1-k)^t}{(1+r)^t} = \frac{\Delta S_0(1+r)}{r+k}$$

which is a variant of Simon's basic formula.[1]

The principle of marginal equivalency then tells us to continue advertising in the current period until the increase in PV_s due to ΔA_0 is just equal to ΔA_0. The present value of the additional profits earned by current-period advertising is:

$$PV_\pi = PV_s - A_0$$

This model is attractive and conceptually simple. However, to the normal difficulties of specifying the sales response from a given volume of advertising is added the need to award a depreciation rate, k, and a cost of capital, r. Not all advertising will have the same decay or depreciation pattern. Some, such as institutional advertising or corporate image advertising (e.g. sponsorship of Grand Prix racing cars by cigarette companies) will have little immediate impact on sales and so a low ΔS_0, but such promotion will presumably also have a low value for k. Conversely petrol advertising tends to have a high k value and, if successful, a high ΔS_0.

13.2 Budget setting: the practice

The approaches to advertising budget determination examined so far are imperfect. Many firms turn to less rigorous but more practical methods for setting their advertising budget. Four of the more common ones have been described by Joel Dean (1951). These are:

1. The percentage-of-sales approach.
2. All-you-can-afford approach.
3. Competitive-parity approach.
4. Objective-and-task approach.

13.2.1 Percentage-of-sales

Ease of decision taking is a major advantage in this approach. The budget is set at a level equal to some predetermined percentage of past or anticipated sales. The added attraction of apparent safety is present in that sales receipts and advertising outlays tend to coincide. However, no guide is given as to what percentage should be chosen. The 'dead hand of the past' will be a likely powerful influencer of choice. Firms will tend to choose that percentage which they traditionally use. Ideally, of course, the budget should be set in such a way that the outlay maximises the return from resulting sales. There is no reason why some arbitrary and consistent percentage of sales will achieve this aim.

The approach rests on some other illogicalities, particularly with regard to the sales base from which the budget is calculated. The use of future sales as the base from which to calculate the percentage has at least some rationale (although achieved sales will depend on many other factors as well as advertising expenditure). The same cannot be said for the use of past sales. Advertising is meant to cause sales in the future, not be the result of sales in the past. Yet this is the circular implication made when budgets are set at some percentage of past sales.

13.2.2 All-you-can-afford

Here the firm spends on advertising up to the limits of its cash resources. The reasoning behind this approach bears a strong resemblance to newer models of the firm.

Oliver Williamson (1963), for example, suggests that firms must meet some 'minimum profit' level in order to maintain expected shareholder earnings and equity prices in the stockmarket, and to carry out essential investment expenditure. Above this minimum level, however, management will spend corporate resources on factors which increase its own utility. In so much as each manager obtains utility from the number of staff personnel reporting to him or her, then managers will attempt to increase the size of the firm in order to increase, in turn, the size of their staff establishment. As we saw in Chapter 5, one means of increasing firm size is to spend beyond the profit-maximising level on advertising.

In practical terms this could mean that the advertising budget is set as the result of some sort of dialogue between the firm's financial and marketing directors. Certainly, one apparent advantage is that the approach sets a definite ceiling on what will be spent. The ceiling, of course, may be well above the profit-maximising level. Conversely, the ceiling may be below the optimal level. Profitable market openings might be present in forthcoming periods for which past profit levels are insufficiently high to support an optimal advertising budget. In such cases the firm might be better advised to borrow resources for advertising, rather than be limited to 'what-it-could-afford'.

13.2.3 Competitive-parity

This method also has the attraction of apparent security. The firm spends on advertising at the same percentage of sales, assets, market share or some other variable, as do its competitors in the same industry. On the assumption that the relevant data can be obtained, the method has the advantage of simplicity. However, with the differing degrees and directions of corporate diversification, it seems unlikely that any one firm can identify itself completely with a group of firms all of whom are allegedly in the same market.

For example, a paint manufacturer mainly selling to the painting trade will require different levels and styles of advertising from another firm selling to the do-it-yourself market. Further, the first firm could be diversified into wallpaper production, the second might be operating in a wholly unrelated industry. Even if appropriate comparisons can be made, there is no reason why the budget selected should be optimal.

The method can also breed complacency. This could be rudely shattered if one aggressive firm decided to break ranks, and gained a substantial competitive advantage before sleepier rivals reacted. Similarly, a smaller firm which unthinkingly followed the industry pattern might find itself below a threshold level of advertising where its voice just could not be heard. Such a threshold is an absolute not a relative barrier.

13.2.4 Objective-and-task

The previous three methods implied that allocation of the total budget by product, region and advertising medium followed the determination of the total budget. This approach tackles budget determination in the reverse order. The firm first defines the objectives it wants the advertising to attain. For example, the objective may be to achieve sales of product A in territory Z of some specified amount. Secondly, the advertising tasks which must be done to reach the objective are defined. The programme could, for example, take the form of a media campaign, say, six inserts in the local paper serving territory Z in a specified period. Finally, the tasks are costed, the costs aggregated and so the budget obtained.

Up to a point, of course, this is only a slight advance over the percentage-of-sales approach. Once again, the tasks to attain a given objective will usually be defined in terms of what it apparently took to attain some similar objective in the past. Thus, in the example given, six inserts in the paper serving territory Z will probably be chosen to attain the specified sales of product A only because six inserts had achieved that result in the preceding period. The question of whether five or seven inserts would be more profitable than six will probably not be asked, and if it were, the choice to change from six might well be made more in hope than in certainty. But, given the current state of knowledge (or lack of it), this is rather an unfair criticism. Ideally, the tasks to be determined should be related to the objective to be attained, and not to any recorded relationship between the two in past periods. However, past relationships are very often the only starting point from which to work, given the difficulties involved in predicting future sales response to future advertising.

One slight modification to this approach would, apart from the practical constraints already mentioned, bring it closer to the theoretical ideal of marginal equivalency of revenues and costs. The relevant question is whether an objective is worth pursuing in terms of the cost. With this considered in the approach, then only the more profitable objectives would be chosen, and the firm would be moving towards attainment of a profit-maximising advertising budget. The company would, of course, still be none the wiser as to whether marginal increases or decreases in expenditure on prescribed tasks would result in any particular objective becoming more or less profitable.

13.2.5 An experimental alternative

This method is very similar to using a test market (see Chapter 6). A different level of advertising expenditure is set in different representative markets or market segments. The price, product quality, and so on are held fixed. The difference in

Table 13.2. Percentage of firms which use which method regularly

	Sample	Consumer goods	Industrial goods	Services
What we can afford	48.8	50.5	54.1	41.8
Objective and task	39.6	43.0	39.8	35.8
Percentage of expected sales	38.3	56.6	33.0	28.7
Experimentation	13.7	16.6	7.3	17.0
Desired share of voice	11.5	17.5	5.4	11.3
Match competition	8.5	12.8	4.3	8.2
Accept agency proposal	4.3	4.0	4.6	4.1
Number of replies: 1.690				

Source: Derived from Hooley and Lynch 1985.

sales between the markets is assumed to be the effect of the difference in advertising spend. Alternatively the advertising expenditure can be varied over time in one market, the differences in sales being ascribed to the advertising. The optimum budget is then chosen. The limitations of this technique are similar to those of test marketing in general: high cost, extraneous factors may nullify the results and a long time period may be required, so rendering the results possibly out of date. (The petrol case of Box 13.2 illustrates this approach.)

13.2.6 Usage

Surveys suggest that the popularity of these methods has changed over the last 10–15 years in both the United States and the United Kingdom. Table 13.2 shows some of the results from a recent UK study. This shows, firstly, that many firms actually use a combination of methods. Secondly, the most popular methods overall are the 'all-we-can-afford', 'objective-and-task' and 'percentage-of-expected-sales' methods. Thirdly, service firms use the 'what-we-can-afford' approach less than consumer or industrial goods firms, whilst a greater proportion of consumer goods firms uses 'percentage-of-expected-sales' than the percentage of firms in the other two industries. 'Experimentation' and 'desired share of voice' are more popular among consumer goods and service firms than among industrial firms. The 'objective-and-task' method is equally popular for all groups.

13.3 The theory and practice of the optimum promotional mix

13.3.1 Sales response isoquants and marginal equivalency

For any given advertising budget, the principle of marginal equivalency states that it will be optimally allocated between the media when

$$MSR_1/P_1 = MSR_2/P_2 \ldots = MSR_n/P_n$$

where MSR represents the marginal sales response resulting from the last unit of advertising, in one particular medium, denoted by the appropriate subscript from the series $1, 2, 3, \ldots n$, where n represents the total number of available media. P represents the price of purchasing one unit of the medium in question.

This is so, since if the ratios are not equal as in

$$MSR_1/P_1 > MSR_2/P_2$$

then it would pay to remove some advertising effort from medium 2 and transfer it to medium 1. This may be more clearly understood if numbers are assigned. Consider that medium 1 is TV and 2 is newspapers. Assume that, in each, an extra showing or insert costs £100. Assume that spending an extra £100 on TV will bring in an extra £2,000 sales, but in newspapers an extra £100 will only produce an extra £1000 sales. Thus:

$$£2000/£100 > £1000/£100$$

With a fixed budget it would pay to switch £100 from newspaper to TV advertising. £1,000 of sales would be forfeited through less advertising in the press, but £,2000 would be gained from the higher level of TV advertising. A net gain of £1,000 would result. Ultimately, continuing to switch advertising from the press to TV will produce diminishing returns to TV advertising. The ratio MSR_1/P_1 will fall. Conversely, spending less on the press will tend to raise the ratio MSR_2/P_2. When the two ratios are equal the budget is optimally allocated.

The same conclusion can be illustrated graphically. Here we use isoquants to join up points of equal sales response to advertising.

Figure 13.2 shows an example of an isoquant map constructed for this purpose. The budget line MM joins up those combinations of full-page press adverts and 15-second TV slots which can be purchased with the given budget. On the assumption that the costs of the media to the firm do not vary with the amount spent, MM will be a straight line.

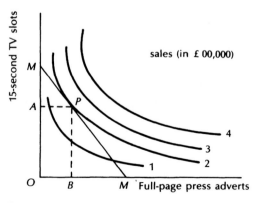

Figure 13.2

The profit-maximising advertiser will allocate his or her budget in such a way that he or she purchases A units of TV time, and B pages of press space. At this point, P, the budget line is tangential to the highest attainable (£200,000) sales response isoquant.

At P, the slope of the isoquant and the slope of the budget line are equal. That is, the marginal rate of substitution of press for TV equals:

$$\frac{MSR_{Press}}{MSR_{TV}} = \frac{\Delta TV}{\Delta Press} = \frac{P_{Press}}{P_{TV}} \text{ or } \frac{MSR_{Press}}{P_{Press}} = \frac{MSR_{TV}}{P_{TV}}$$

which is again the position of marginal equivalency (ignoring the negative signs implied by the slopes).

Up to this juncture we have merely adapted the production function for advertising purposes. Now we must move beyond the normal stopping point of these expositions. The production function assumes a given technology, but any technology embraces a variety of possible and known techniques. In real-life manufacturing there are always a variety of techniques open to the manager, not merely a variety of capital–labour input combinations. For example, the sources of supply for capital equipment are themselves diffuse. Thus items of machinery which are fundamentally similar often vary slightly one from the other in manner of use, quite apart from the range of labour inputs the manager can select to work each machine. Similarly, in real-life advertising there is always a variety of known message designs available for use, not merely a variety of, say, press–TV combinations using only one design type.

The typical graphical production function isoquant is oversimplified. In order to take account of differing techniques of manufacturing or, in this case, differing message designs, some modifications are essential. In the area of general production theory, Feller (1972) has suggested the use of an arrangement of isoquants similar to that of Figure 13.3. We will adapt this figure specifically for advertising purposes. The isoquants represent the same level of sales response obtainable not only with

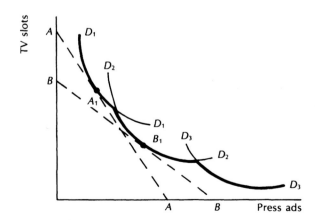

Figure 13.3

differing media combinations, but also with differing message designs. D_1, D_2 and D_3 represent three different design types. The thick 'envelope' isoquant, D_1D_3, is the only isoquant relevant for the manager, since any part of an isoquant lying above the envelope curve would require at least more of one medium, and not less of the other medium, to produce a given sales level, than would be required by some other known, existing message design. (The isoquants in Figure 13.2 are all implicitly envelope isoquants for the relevant sales responses, as in Figure 9.3 they are 'envelopes' for a range of techniques.)

With a budget line, AA, the profit-maximising advertiser would select message design D_1, and would combine his or her media in the proportions indicated at the point of tangency A_1. If the costs of TV and press advertising altered, say press became cheaper and TV more expensive, then the same budget could possibly buy the input combinations indicated by BB. Not only will media substitution take place as the advertiser moves to B_1, from A_1, but message design will also alter from D_1 to D_2.

This analysis is not in the least inconsistent with reality. It is rather an attempt to bring theory closer to real life.

Theory neglects advertising creativity. Yet the sales effect of advertising depend very heavily on it (see Box 13.1). The term 'creativity' refers to what the advertiser says (message content) and to how he decides to say it (message form).

Some flesh may now be put on the bones of Figure 13.3 by means of the following highly simplified illustration. Consider an advertiser with problems of media selection and message design (content and form). The content decision could involve a choice, say, between a highly descriptive advertisement with a lengthy exposition at one extreme, and a cryptic, abbreviated presentation of product-associated attributes at the other. The form decision could imply a choice, say, between a 'hard sell' approach and a witty, playing down of the advertised product.

Thus, isoquant D_1D_1 could represent varying combinations of press and TV advertisements which result in an equal sales response, given a message design D_1, which is a combination of minimum information and maximum wry wit. D_2 could represent a message design which is a combination of lengthy exposition and the 'hard sell'. D_3 could be maximum humour plus maximum information, and so on.

So with media cost line AA, message design D_1 would be chosen – minimum information, maximum wit – at media combination point A_1. This is not an implausible position. When TV is cheap relative to the press, as it is with cost line AA, then other things equal, TV will tend to be used relatively more by the advertiser than will the press. If this is so, then the message design which will be the most effective will be that which is relatively most suited to TV, and least to the press. Conversely, when the press is cheap relative to TV, as with cost line BB, then media substitution will take place as indicated in the shift from A_1 to B_1. When such a movement is made towards buying relatively more press advertisements and fewer TV ones, then it should not be unexpected that a change in message design will occur from one suitable to TV to one more suited to the press.

D_2 is a more suitable message design than D_1 if the press is the more attractive medium economically, and vice versa. Closely reasoned arguments require relatively large amounts of supporting information, and time for that information to be digested by the potential consumer. Newspapers provide the advertiser with the ability to put over large amounts of information and give the reader as long as is necessary to assimilate it. TV ads, on the other hand, are of necessity brief, and cannot be perused in depth at the discretion of the individual viewer.

D_1, however, is probably a more suitable message design when TV is the more economically attractive. Here TV will tend to be used relatively more than the press, and the strengths of TV can be exploited by the appropriate message design. Voluminous information is precluded, but a lesser quantity of information may be all that is required, given the added impact of visual motion and aural stimulation. Moreover, if, as some have suggested, people tend to be less willing to accept the credibility of advertising messages on TV than they do in the press, then it could be that the 'hard sell' will generate ill will towards the advertiser, while a humorous approach might knit in better with the credulity attitudes people bring to their advertisement viewing habits.

13.3.2 Media planning in practice

The difficulties involved in predicting the sales response from any advert or run of adverts often forces managers to turn to highly pragmatic, imprecise tools of media planning.

Media characteristics (such as colour, motion, sound and print) and suitability for promoting the product in question will be assessed. Costs will be obtained, and a decision taken on the basis of whether or not the appropriate potential consumers are being reached at an acceptable level of expenditure. Within a fixed budget this (reach) must in turn be balanced against frequency of advert appearance, and both against continuity, or length of campaign. Media scheduling, in other words, is often solely a matter of managerial intuition, albeit based on close and intimate knowledge of the product, the market and the available media. In short, there are four variables in media planning and (given a budget) an expenditure change in one implies a corresponding expenditure reduction or increase in one or more of the others, namely:

1. reach
2. frequency
3. continuity
4. impact

Sinclair (Barrenblatt and Sinclair, 1989) defines 'impact' as the physical media characteristics required for the product given either its nature or the nature of the target market.

Given the application of production function theory to the problem of the media mix, it is not surprising that one of the most commonly used tools is linear programming. Figure 13.4 illustrates the application of linear programming to the media-mix decision. The process rays D_1, D_2, D_3 and D_4 can now more properly be

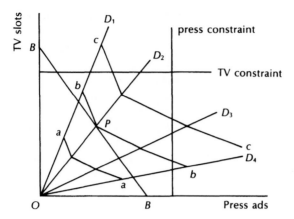

Figure 13.4

regarded as representing the differing message-design types of Figure 13.3. The press and TV constraints indicate the physical limits of insertions in each of these media. If the press was a weekly paper, for example, the constraint would be 52. The TV constraint might be 312 slots given a six-evening week (for some products manufacturers consider it worthwhile advertising on TV only on the nights before a possible shopping day, namely Sunday to Friday evenings inclusive). *BB* is the budget line and, within the constraints, the highest attainable sales response isoquant is *bb*, on process ray D_2, at the media mix indicated by point *P*.

More generally this can be written as follows:

$$\text{maximise sales} = \sum_{i=1}^{n} R_i Q_i \tag{13.1}$$

subject to the constraints

$$\sum_{i=1}^{n} C_i Q_i \leqslant B$$

$$Q_i \leqslant L_i$$

$$Q_i \geqslant 0 \text{ for } i = 1, 2, 3, \ldots n$$

where Q_i = the number of unit adverts or insertions in medium i; R_i = the sales response of a single insertion in medium i; C_i = the cost per insertion in medium i; B = given total advertising budget; L_i = a predetermined (or physical) limit of insertions in medium i.

Unfortunately, the situation is not quite so straightforward as the above discussion implies. Some of the obstacles to the immediate application of production function theory in this way are intrinsic in the linear programming technique, others are implicit in the uncertain nature of the relationship between advertising and sales. For example, the following (false) assumptions have been made:

> the sales response to a medium insertion is constant
> the time factor is non-relevant
> sales response per insertion is known
> costs of media insertions are constant
> there is no media interaction
> the number of insertions is a continuous variable.

We will now examine each of these assumptions in more detail.

13.3.3 The S-shaped sales response function

We have already seen, in Figure 13.1, that there comes a point when there are diminishing returns to scale of advertising. The linear programming model ignores this possibility. The unrealism of this assumption can be readily and intuitively shown. Consider equation (13.1). The model can be solved by finding the value R_i/C_i, the sales response per pound, for each medium.

The optimal solution is then to select the medium with the highest value of R_i/C_i and spend on it up to the limit of either B or L. If B is not exhausted then the remainder should be spent on the medium with the second highest R_i/C_i ratio.

However, it is highly unlikely that spending the budget on only one, or a few, media represents the 'true' optimum. One way out of this difficulty is to adopt the procedure of 'piecewise' linear programming. The non-linear response function is split up into a piecewise linear equivalent. Figure 13.5 illustrates this discussion and equation (13.2) shows how the linear programming model of equation (13.1) would be adapted accordingly, thus:

$$\text{maximise sales} = \sum_{i=1}^{n} [R_{i1}Q_{i1} + R_{i2}(Q_{i2} - Q_{i1}) + R_{i3}(Q_{i3} - Q_{i2})] \tag{13.2}$$

subject to the constraints

$$\sum_{i=1}^{n} C_i Q_i \leqslant B$$

$$Q_i \leqslant L_i$$

$$Q_{i3} > Q_{i2} > Q_{i1} \geqslant 0$$

13.3.4 The time factor

The problem of media scheduling (whether to advertise more heavily, for example, on a Monday or a Friday, in January or October) can be overcome by adding a time subscript to each Q_i, so specifying the total exposure, $R_{it}Q_{it}$, over each medium and

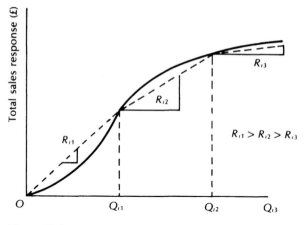

Figure 13.5

over time. This does not, however, cope with the second aspect of time, namely the positive impact of replication and the negative one of forgetfulness. We will offer one possible counter to this criticism in the next few paragraphs.

13.3.5 Exposure and awareness as a proxy for sales response

The exact relationship between advertising and sales is rarely if ever known. Econometric demand equations and test marketing exercises are two common means of attempting to ascertain what the sales response to any given level of advertising might be. Both, however, are essentially *post hoc* in nature. For *ante hoc* decision making, exposure to an ad, or awareness of its appearance, are commonly used proxy measures of advertising effectiveness, the plausible rationale behind this being that exposure of a potential customer to an ad is more likely to result in a sale than non-exposure.

Unfortunately, readership survey data (or viewership for TV) is of limited assistance to most advertisers wishing to measure the extent of exposure to their campaign. Most campaigns have more than one insertion in the media. As a result, while readership may give some idea of the reach of a one-shot campaign, it will prove to be inadequate for measurement of reach and of frequency of exposure in a campaign with two or more shots.

The term 'opportunity to see' (OTS) means just that. For example, consider a campaign with four inserts in a women's weekly magazine, which has an average readership of 7.5 million. The total target population is all women, say 20 million. Assume the same 7.5 million read the magazine week by week, and the other 12.5 million never see it. Then the situation in Table 13.3 case 1 exists. This is a very unlikely distribution. In reality, some women will subscribe to the publication faithfully week by week, others will see it frequently but not consistently, while still

Table 13.3

Total population of women 20 million = 100%	Members of total population with:				
	zero OTS	one OTS	two OTSs	three OTSs	four OTSs
Journals with identical average readership of 7.5m					
Case 1: Totally loyal readership	12.5m (62.5%)	–	–	–	7.5m (37.5%)
Case 2: High readership loyalty	50%	5%	10%	15%	20%
Case 3: Low readership loyalty	40%	20%	20%	10%	10%

others will be only spasmodic readers. Furthermore, some journals will have a more loyal readership than others. The results that this might have on the frequency distribution of OTSs throughout the target population are illustrated in cases 2 and 3 of the table.

In all three cases illustrated, the total readership potential is 4×7.5 m = 30 million readers. But, in fact, in case 1, only 7.5 million read the magazine, albeit on four consecutive occasions. In case 2, 10 million people saw the magazine at least once, but only 4 million saw it four times, while in case 3, 12 million saw it at least once, but only 2 million four times. Clearly, the advertiser with a run of adverts in a medium is interested in these sorts of data, the total and distribution of OTSs throughout the population, and not merely readership.

The data in Table 13.3 can be obtained from the National Readership Survey (NRS). Thus in column 1 of the table we have the *reach* figures. (Similar data are available for TV viewers and radio listeners from the Broadcasters' Audience Research Board (BARB). Further, the real-life data collected are broken down regionally and by socio-demographic groups. In other words, Table 13.3 is unrealistically simple. Collection techniques range from questionnaires to electronic meters attached to TV sets.

To return to our example, given that the target market is all 20 million women, reach is $7.5/20 = 37.5\%$ in each of cases 1, 2 and 3. However, reach alone is not enough, and the NRS questionnaire results provide the type of data required to construct the remaining columns of Table 13.3. Namely the OTS (or in the case of radio and TV, OTH (hear) or OTV (view)) figures, thus we obtain the *frequency* data.

At this juncture many media planners would stop and set themselves tasks (as in the objective and task budget setting exercise) embodying also the impact and continuity variables. Typical objectives could be schedules such as (a) to reach a minimum of 37.5% of the target market over the campaign period or (more complex), (b) to reach a minimum of 20% of the target market with a frequency of 4 occasions per month between August and December and a monthly frequency of 3 times between January and July. These tasks would then be costed against the rate cards of the selected media and the budget chosen. To evaluate schedules against each other comparing permutations of reach, frequency, and continuity, a *Gross Rating Point* (GRP) can be used. GRP is simply reach times frequency summed over the campaign duration. Thus, in cases 2 and 3 of Table 13.3 respectively, the GRPs are:

$$5\% + 2 \times 10\% + 3 \times 15\% + 4 \times 20\% = 150$$

$$20\% + 2 \times 20\% + 3 \times 10\% + 4 \times 10\% = 130$$

So the case 2 journal has a higher GRP value than case 3, despite having identical average readership figures. (Note: the neat whole number OTS figures of Table 13.3 will not occur in practice – rather, on average, fractional figures will be obtained.)

We can now go one stage further, however. The information in Table 13.3 can be converted into a projected advertising effectiveness (not sales) response function. From the UK Gallup Organisation (in the United States, Daniel Starch Inc.), regularly published survey data provide average noting (or awareness) scores in the particular publication in some past period by ads similar in style, size, colour, position, and so on, to the one the firm is considering inserting. This average is then taken as the probability that such an ad's OTS potential will or will not be transformed into 'opportunities taken'.

Consider an ad with a predicted noting score of, say, 50%. A prediction of the response function for a four-insertion campaign in the women's magazine described in case 2 is required. The first step is demonstrated in Table 13.3 which indicates how the OTS distribution is converted into the more relevant distribution of opportunities taken, or exposures actually received by readers. By the normal theory of probability, half of those having one OTS will see the ad, and half will not. Similarly, of those having two OTSs, one half will see it once, one quarter twice and one quarter not at all, and so on for the higher values of OTSs.[2]

The next stage is to 'specify the response function' from the 'ad exposures received' figures.

This is done by assigning values to the different numbers of exposures. Manifestly, the 15.63% of the total population in Table 13.4 who receive two exposures will be more affected by the advertising than the 18.13% who receive only one exposure. To transform each exposure datum to an appropriate effectiveness equivalent or response value requires modifying it by an appropriate weight. The weights should reflect the S-shaped sales response function, thus taking into account increasing, then ultimately decreasing, returns in advertising effectiveness. Table 13.5 shows how a response function can be specified using arbitrary weights to transform the advert exposure data of Table 13.4.

Column 4 of Table 13.5, marginal response values, refers only to that incremental proportion of the population effectively reached by one more or one less exposure. The cumulative response values are then easily calculated from the marginal data.

Table 13.4

Estimate of opportunities taken (ad exposures received)	All housewives	Members of population with:				
		zero OTS	one OTS	two OTSs	three OTSs	four OTSs
	100%	50%	5	10%	15%	20%
0	58.12%	50%	2.5%	2.5%	1.87%	1.25%
1	18.13	–	2.5	5	5.63	5
2	15.63	–	–	2.5	5.63	7.5
3	6.87	–	–	–	1.87	5
4	1.25	–	–	–	–	1.25

Table 13.5

(1) Ad exposures	(2) Relative effectiveness of exposures (arbitrary weights)	(3) % Target group reached	(4) Marginal response value 2 × 3	(5) Cumulative response values
0	0	58.12	0	0
1	0.1	18.13	1.813	1.813
2	0.4	15.63	6.252	8.065
3	0.8	6.87	5.496	13.561
4	1.0	1.25	1.25	14.781

The cumulative data can be compared with the S-shaped sales response function of Figure 13.1. Intermedia comparisons and decisions can then be effectively made on lines very similar to those suggested by the marginal-equivalency formula. The disadvantages of using arbitrary weights will be partially neutralised for comparison exercises of this sort if an identical system of weighting is used for calculating each medium's response function. Furthermore, it is highly probable that assigning weights in this manner provides more realistic information for decision takers than not doing so at all. Failure to do so implies constant returns to advertising exposure, a most unlikely situation.

Column 4 provides values for R_{i1}, R_{i2}, and so on, for equation (13.2) which can be used as proxies for (the otherwise unknown) sales response data, and which also embrace the impact of replication of advertisement exposure. It does not, however, take into account the fact that exposure effectiveness *per capita* diminishes over time due to forgetfulness.

13.3.6 Media discounts

The linearity assumptions of linear programming models ignore the not uncommon practice of media owners to award volume cumulative discounts to customers after a given size of purchase in a medium. This gives rise to sharp discontinuities in the total cost function. This inability is a significant problem at all times but particularly when a multiproduct firm is deriving its media plan. (In the theory of production the budget line is no longer straight but becomes convex to the origin.)

13.3.7 Media interaction

Linear programming also makes the unrealistic assumption that there is no media interaction. Media interaction can be of two varieties. First, there is straightforward audience duplication. Thus a potential customer can be exposed to an ad for the same product in both the *Daily Express* and on television. Conceptually, this is relatively easy to embody in the media planning model. For example, if the probability of a *Daily Express* reader noting a given ad is 0.8, and the probability of that same reader noting the relevant TV ad is 0.6, then the probability of that individual (or group of individuals) noting them both is the product of the two probabilities, namely 0.48.

More problematically, there is the problem of media synergy, or its obverse. For example, if £1,000 of press advertising in isolation results in 10 units of effectiveness and, similarly, £1,000 of TV advertising in isolation results in 10 units of effectiveness, but £2,000 of advertising evenly split between the two media and carried out simultaneously results in more or less than 20 units of effectiveness then synergy or its obverse has occurred.

For example, a person who normally ignores press advertising may be encouraged to study a press ad in some detail if he has seen the same product advertised on TV the previous evening. He might, perhaps, want to digest at leisure product information in the press which is something the transience of a TV ad precludes. When this occurs in production theory, the convexity of the output isoquants to the origin becomes more pronounced. Thus a given budget line would be tangential to a higher isoquant. The converse would occur if the advertising response functions reacted in a negative manner. Box 13.1 briefly summarises how the use of linear programming helps Mundra Communications Ltd to prescribe media plans for clients.

13.3.8 The integer nature of insertions

Linear programming is unable to cope with non-continuous input variables. The only (imperfect) practical way to overcome this is the somewhat unsatisfactory method of 'rounding off' to the nearest whole input unit. This weakness also highlights the inappropriateness of our linear programming analogy of Figure 13.4,

---

Box 13.1

MCL uses a decision support system for media planning

Mundra Communications Ltd (MCL) is one of the three largest advertising agencies in India with billings of over $20m. It has adopted a decision support system, Mundraplan, to help it to prescribe and evaluate media plans for clients.

The problem which faces many clients is to choose the number of insertions in each media to minimise the total cost of an advertising campaign, given certain constraints. To devise a multimedia plan would require data on the listening and viewing behaviour of the population as well as their reading habits. Such data did not exist in India and would be too expensive to collect. However, readership data was available and 55% of all advertising expenditure was spent on printed media. Therefore the model was built to find the number of insertions, Q, in each publication, j, Q_j, which minimised the cost of printed media advertising subject to a number of constraints:

$$\text{Minimise} \sum_{j=1}^{m} c_j Q_j$$

where C_j denotes the cost per insertion in publication j.

The constraints were the following. An advert would be placed in different publications. The number of people within each target group, i, exposed to the advert, the reach of the advert, R_i, had to be at least equal to a desired number, $\bar{R}_i$. Thus:

$$R_i \geqslant \bar{R}_i \text{ for each of } s \text{ target groups} \tag{1}$$

Secondly, the actual number of people in target group i who received exactly k OTS, N_{ik}, must be at least as large as the desired level, $\bar{N}_{ik}$. So:

$$N_{ik} \geqslant \bar{N}_{ik} \text{ for each of } s \text{ target groups} \tag{2}$$

Thirdly, the frequency of each publication, the minimum number needed to have any useful effect and the availability of discounts for multiple insertions meant that the number of insertions in publication j had to be within a certain specific range.

Unfortunately the media planners could not gain data on the number of people who read three or more publications which was needed to relate N_{ik} values to the number of insertions in each publication. Instead they estimated the attained OTS values for each target group in terms of the number of insertions in each publication. Constraints (1) and (2) were then replaced by the following:

$$\Sigma A_{ij} Q_{ij} > \bar{O}_i$$

where A_{ij} = readership in target group i of publication j
$\bar{O}_i$ = desired OTS in target group i.

The model was placed on PCs. To use the package the planner chooses the number and identities of publications, the target audience and their number, the minimum and maximum number of insertions in each publication, the minimum

$\rightarrow$

reach and maximum OTS for each target group. The package would read data from the National Readership Survey which is stored on the PC to estimate cost and overlapping audience data.

Use of Mundraplan reduced costs of campaigns by substantial amounts compared with traditional methods. For example, when designing a plan when the target group consisted of 6.5m women, the reduction of cost ranged from 25% to 50% depending on the reach of the campaign.

Source summarised from Rathnam et al. 1992.

Box 13.2

Advertising decay: the petrol case

The experimental approach to budget setting requires laboratory conditions. In economics such circumstances are rare. One example where most things were held constant was in the South African retail petrol market in the 1970s and 1980s.

The main brands included Shell, BP, Esso, Mobil, Caltex, Total and SASOL. The latter is the product derived from South Africa's giant oil-from-coal refineries which were established in the 1950s through the 1970s to provide the country with strategic and political independence. SASOL petrol accounts for around 40% of all petrol produced, but around only 8% of petrol discharged from pumps. The paradox is resolved when it is recalled that the country only has three main refining groups: SASOL, Shell-BP and Mobil. Marketing and distribution of the output of these three groups takes place through an intricate network of cross licenses and physical pooling of the product by the various marketing companies.

In essence, the basic product sold through the pump is identical, product differentiation is minimal. Price is also unimportant as a commercial tactic since price is controlled by law. Place or locational differences can impact on brand share of one firm relative to another if that firm has more conveniently sited filling stations. However, place is not a competitive factor for SASOL since each company's filling station, again by law, must have one SASOL pump. There are no SASOL filling stations as such. Thus SASOL both gains and loses from other firms' high-quality and low-quality locations. SASOL management cannot raise market share by decisions relating to any of the product, price or place variables. They can only do so by varying the promotion or advertising spend.

SASOL's share of total industry advertising was correlated with SASOL's market share on a monthly basis from 1980 to 1988. To ascertain if advertising did or did not impact on market share (all other things equal – which *ex hypotheus*; they were) and to estimate its decay the following model was built:

$$S_t = a + bA_t + cA_{t-1} + dA_{t-2} + eA_{t-3}\ldots \tag{1}$$

which suggests sales share is dependent on advertising share in that period and in all preceding periods. If we assume that ever earlier advertising has an ever smaller effect on current sales, and does so on a geometrically declining basis then we can say that:

$$c = \lambda b, d = \lambda^2 b, e = \lambda^3 b, \text{ etc.}$$

→

where $0 < \lambda < 1$, $1 - \lambda$ is the decay rate of current advertising and b the immediate effect of advertising on sales. Thus:

$$S_t = a + bA_t + \lambda bA_{t-1} + \lambda^2 bA_{t-2} + \lambda^3 bA_{t-3} \ldots \tag{2}$$

now lag (2) by one period;

$$S_{t-1} = a + bA_{t-1} + \lambda bA_{t-2} + \lambda^2 bA_{t-3} + \lambda^3 bA_{t-4} \ldots$$

and multiply by λ

$$\lambda S_{t-1} = a\lambda + \lambda bA_{t-1} + \lambda^2 bA_{t-2} + \lambda^3 bA_{t-3} + \lambda^4 A_{t-4} \ldots \tag{3}$$

Now subtract (3) from (2)

$$S_t - \lambda S_{t-1} = a - a\lambda + bA_t$$

or

$$S_t \quad = a(1 - \lambda) + bA_t + \lambda S_{t-1} \ldots \tag{4}$$

where S_t is known from the monthly data series, as is S_{t-1}, as is A_t leaving the coefficients b, λ and $a(1 - \lambda)$ to be estimated from the regressions. $a(1 - \lambda)$ is the constant figure and once λ has also been estimated a can be disaggregated leaving $(1 - \lambda)$ as the decay rate of advertising per month.

Equation (4) is known in literature as the Koyck distributed lag model. In this exercise one variable proved to be omitted. SASOL's advertising campaign theme varied over the 99 months of the study. That is advertising 'quality' or copywriting impact varied. To account for this equation (4) was re-estimated using a zero:one dummy variable for the differing campaigns thus:

$$S_t = a(1 - \lambda) + bA_t + \lambda S_{t-1} + cD \ldots \tag{5}$$

where D was the campaign dummy and c the coefficient estimated from the data. Including the dummy improved the r^2 and the t-statistics and showed which campaign themes were successful and which not.

The rate of decay of advertising effort $(1 - \lambda)$ proved to be 33% per monthly period while the value of b, the coefficient which showed the immediate impact of SASOL's advertising on its market share was 0.002. That is, a 10% increase in advertising share produced an immediate 0.02% increase in market share which in turn declines at 33% per period. Conversely, although the immediate effect of advertising on market share is a 0.02 increase per 10% increase in spend, the long run (and larger) cumulative share increase would be $0.02/(1 - \lambda)$ or 0.06.

The r^2 for the study was 0.869 and the value of c (with a t-statistic of 3.9) was 0.28 for a particular 16-month campaign with the slogan 'Rustblock'. In other words the 'Rustblock' campaign produced a 28% greater increase in market share than did the average campaign. To put it another way, the use of the 'Rustblock' theme had more than double the long-run impact of advertising which a 20% rise in advertising share expenditure would have had (at 0.33). 'Quality' creativity of advertising appears to be of substantially more consequence than does quantity of expenditure.

Source Leach and Reekie. Thanks are due to the McAnn advertising group and to SASOL for the data on which this case is based.

where we compared the process rays with the message design envelope isoquants of production theory in Figure 13.3. Message designs, however, cannot be uniquely identified; they merge imperceptibly. Moreover, in practice, the message design which, by all rational reasoning, is most appropriate for a given media mix, might prove to be highly successful if used in a wholly unconventional media pattern. Such is the unpredictability of the creative factor.

Nevertheless, despite these many difficulties because of the vast availability of survey and other market research data, advertising is an area where the reasoning of managerial economics can readily, and fruitfully, be applied. Box 13.2 illustrates the use of the advertising decay concept discussed earlier, and its use, together with known advertising quality variation, in setting budgets.

13.4 Advertising and price

So far, in the discussions on price and advertising, we have generally held price constant while varying advertising, and vice versa. The Dorfman–Steiner theorem permits variation in both. (Indeed, other variables, such as research and development expenditures, which also affect output, can be embodied in the general model – see Needham 1975).

Algebraically, the theorem states that profit maximisation occurs when

$$\eta = \mu$$

where η = price elasticity of demand
μ = marginal sales effect of advertising (i.e. the marginal change in sales revenue due to a marginal change in advertising expenditure)

Let p = price
q = quantity demanded
a = advertising expenditure
c = average production costs (assumed constant)
π = profits

During the proof process several interesting implications emerge. The firm desires to maximise profits

$$\pi = pq - cq - a \tag{13.3}$$

where $q = f(p, a)$
and $\partial q/\partial p < 0$ (the demand curve slopes down)
and $\partial q/\partial a > 0$ (advertising shifts the demand curve outwards)

Price and advertising are independent variables, so $\partial p/\partial a = 0$, while total cost (cq) is a function of output, so:

$$cq = C = g(q) = g[f(p, a)].$$

But production cost is also independent of advertising, so $\partial(C)/\partial a = 0$. With these assumptions we can rewrite equation 13.3 as:

$$\pi = p[q(p, a)] - C(q) - a \qquad (13.4)$$

To choose the values of p and a that will maximise profits, equation (13.4) must be differentiated with respect to each and the resultant equations set equal to zero:

$$\frac{\partial \pi}{\partial a} = \left(p\frac{\partial q}{\partial a} + q\frac{\partial p}{\partial a}\right) - \left(\frac{\partial C}{\partial q} \times \frac{\partial q}{\partial a}\right) - 1 = 0$$

using rules (5) and (6) from Chapter 2. Hence:

$$\frac{\partial \pi}{\partial a} = p\frac{\partial q}{\partial a} - \frac{\partial C}{\partial q} \times \frac{\partial q}{\partial a} - 1 = 0 \qquad (13.5)$$

(Recall p and a are independent variables.) And

$$\frac{\partial \pi}{\partial p} = \left(p\frac{\partial q}{\partial p} + q\frac{\partial p}{\partial p}\right) - \left(\frac{\partial C}{\partial q} \times \frac{\partial q}{\partial p}\right) = 0 \qquad (13.6)$$

Equation (13.5) can be rearranged by factorising $\partial q/\partial a$ out of the expression and recalling that $\partial c/\partial q$ equals MC. Since AC is assumed constant, i.e. not varying with output, $MC = AC$. Hence:

$$\frac{\partial q}{\partial a}(p - c) = 1$$

Now multiply through by a/pq to obtain:

$$\left(\frac{a}{q} \times \frac{\partial q}{\partial a}\right)\frac{(p - c)}{p} = \frac{a}{pq} \qquad (13.7)$$

The first term in brackets is the advertising elasticity of demand, η_a. The second term is the mark-up obtained over average costs, and the right-hand side is the firm's advertising: sales (or A/S) ratio. If c is regarded as marginal costs, then the second term is known as the Lerner index of monopoly power, which records the firm's 'power' to raise its price above marginal cost.

Thus we can see from equation (13.7) that profit-maximising advertising expenditure depends on:

1. The advertising elasticity of demand. The greater this is, the greater advertising should be (to maintain the equation's equality).
2. The firm's sales revenue (pq). The greater this is, the greater advertising will be.
3. The firm's monopoly power as measured by the Lerner index. The greater this is, the greater advertising will be. If we now return to equation (13.6) and multiply through by p/q we obtain:

$$\left[p \times \left(\frac{p\partial q}{q\partial p}\right) + \frac{pq}{q}\right] - \left[\frac{\partial C}{\partial q}\left(\frac{\partial q}{\partial p}\frac{p}{q}\right)\right] = 0 \qquad (13.8)$$

Given that the expressions in curved brackets are by definition equal to price elasticity of demand $(-\eta)$ we can rewrite equation (13.8) as:

$$p(-\eta) + p - c(-\eta) = 0$$

or

$$(p-c)(-\eta) = -p$$

which, if divided throughout by $(-p)$ and by η, results in:

$$\frac{p-c}{p} = \frac{1}{\eta} \tag{13.9}$$

So, by substituting (13.9) into (13.7), we have:

$$\frac{\eta_a}{\eta} = \frac{a}{pq} = \frac{a}{S} \tag{13.10}$$

The firm's a/S ratio will be higher, the lower is price elasticity of demand. To obtain the formal Dorfman–Steiner result of:

$$\eta = \frac{p\partial q}{q\partial p} = \mu = p\frac{\partial q}{\partial a}$$

we simply expand and manipulate equation (13.10). Thus:

$$\frac{a}{q}\frac{\partial q}{\partial a} \times \frac{1}{\eta} = \frac{a}{p \times q}$$

$$= \frac{p\partial q}{\partial a} = \mu = \eta$$

QED

An alternative geometric approach to the joint advertising/price decision was provided by Buchanan (1942). Two factors become apparent from his model which are not overt in a study of the Dorfman–Steiner theorem. First: advertising shifts demand out and to the right. Second: this may or may not result in a price fall. Third: total costs (production plus advertising) also may or may not fall as a result.

The outcomes depend on the intersection of MR and MC and on the elasticity of demand and degree of scale economies – if any – which are present.

Figure 13.6 is the starting point of Buchanan's model. He assumes that D is the consequence of a given level of advertising (thus the $P{:}Q$ relationship of D is drawn on the normal *ceteris paribus* assumption). Since advertising is given, it is equivalent to a fixed cost, and average advertising costs (AAC) will trace out the rectangular hyperbola shown falling as Q rises. With an assumption of zero production costs the optimum quantity to produce is Q^* at price P, with a corresponding AAC of A.

If advertising expenditures are now raised, D shifts out to D' and MR' intersects the quantity axis at Q', while the new higher level of advertising has an average function or AAC' and a corresponding average value of A'.

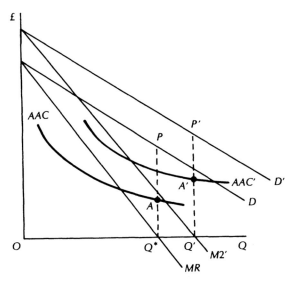

Figure 13.6

This reasoning can be continued and a series of optimal price (average revenue) points such as *P* and *P'* can be traced out for a series of given average advertising cost points such as *A* and *A'*. These series can be traced out graphically as in Figure 13.7.

Harold Demsetz (1964) calls the locus of the price points a *mutatis mutandis* demand curve, where both price and advertising change accordingly (*MMD*) while the locus of average advertising costs at given optimal prices we shall call *LAAC*. Figure 13.7 shows these loci.

The assumptions underlying the S-shaped sales response function are built into Figure 13.7 and explain why *MMD* and *LAAC* bend towards each other. Furthermore, as Demsetz emphasises, after a point even increasing advertising cannot increase output without accompanying price reductions. The relevant *ceteris paribus* demand curve will have become ever more elastic due to advertising, rendering price not advertising the more efficient means of generating extra volume. Since each of *LAAC* and *MMD* are loci or average values, each will have correspondingly marginal curves, such as *MAAC* and *MMMR* respectively. Where these coincide we have the profit-maximising price, advertising and output levels shown as P^{11}, A^{11} and Q^{11} respectively. A conventional *ceteris paribus* demand curve, of course, passes through point *X* albeit we have not shown it here.

Now if we drop he assumption or zero production costs we must add a conventional *MC* schedule to *MAAC*. Irrespective of whether *MC* is rising or falling, clearly, since *MC* must be positive, the new intersection point will be to the left of Q^{11} and the related profit maximising price will be below the hypothetical P^{11}. Whether or not total costs will be higher or lower than they would have been without advertising depends on whether achieved average production cost savings (if any) due to a

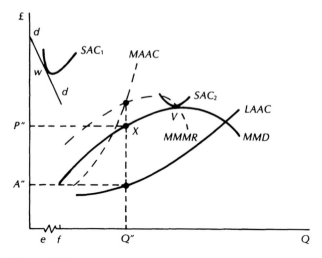

Figure 13.7

higher Q exceed the average advertising costs incurred to achieve that Q. Similarly the relevant profit maximising price in the presence of advertising depends where on *MMD* it is selected. Again this could be higher or lower than it would have been on a *ceteris paribus* demand curve without advertising. For example, in Figure 13.7, *dd* may be (part of) that curve intersecting the Q axis somewhere to the left of *ef*. If the profit maximising Q is to the left of *e* then there is no price on *MMD* (with advertising) which could be as high as that price (without advertising). Clearly the question is empirical and depends on the case not on the theory.

Another inference from Figure 13.7 which Demsetz drew is that advertising can remove the apparently inevitable tangency solution of monopolistic competition with output levels at above minimum average cost (see Chapter 11). The conventional tangency solution is shown by point W on SAC_1. Advertising, however, by shifting the *ceteris paribus* demand curve outward, by permitting the gaining of scale economies (e.g. on SAC_2) could well permit a tangency solution at minimum short-run average costs, at, for example, point V.

13.5 Advertising and strategy

Casual observation suggests that advertising can be a means to entry. It can reduce prices through increased competition and by encouraging large-scale, low-cost production. By increasing consumer information it can facilitate price comparison, increase demand elasticity and so result in competitively induced lower prices. Box 13.3 contrasts advertising as a strategy for entry and maintenance of market position with vertical integration.

The alternative argument is that advertising can and does encourage brand loyalty and so lowers consumer price sensitivity. Branding provides consumers with

---

Box 13.3

Advertising and Guinness

Brewers have long been among the top two hundred British companies. They invested heavily in retail outlets because of the need to ensure throughput, partly necessitated by the heavy capital investment involved in brewing technology, and partly because pubs were limited in number by law. The large investment in forward integration resulted in high asset values in real estate which contributes to the brewers' prominence in the top companies' lists.

By contrast Guinness owns no pubs. It exploited scale economies and invested heavily in advertising, marketing and distribution. By the 1890s it was the largest brewer in the British Isles, a position it would retain for the next century, aided by continued aggressive advertising coupled with heavy investment in temperature-controlled distribution and transportation facilities.

Source abstracted from Chandler 1990, p. 266.

---

a guarantee of product quality and consistency – poor brands can be avoided. Such 'quality information' may not be so cheaply accessible by any other route.[4]

The next few paragraphs show how advertising can raise prices. But it must be remembered that the discussion assumes, with no justification, that demand for the product could exist without advertising (and if demand did not exist there would be no price to raise!). Figure 13.8 (based on an argument by Williamson (1963) provides a summary of the considerations leading businessmen to advertise in order to permit an entry-deterring price strategy. L is the entry-deterring or limit price in the absence of advertising, where entry barriers are limited to scale economies or absolute cost advantages. In the absence of advertising, entry will occur if price is raised above L. If only a small amount of advertising is engaged in, the limit price will be little affected since the advertising will not be particularly effective, or if it is, entrants will find it easy to equal. This is illustrated in Figure 13.8a by the relative flat shape to the curve LB (plotting entry-deterring price) when only a small movement has been made along the x, or advertising, axis. As existing firms increase their advertising, however, new entrants would also have to incur substantial advertising investment in order to break down existing firms' goodwill, while simultaneously creating their own.

This makes it possible for existing firms to charge a higher price than L without attracting entry, and the entry-deterring price curve LB rises quite sharply. After a point, diminishing returns to advertising may set in, and the curve begins to level off. Curve LA has a similar, but gentler shape. This curve would apply in industries where advertising is not so effective as an entry barrier (e.g. compare cigarettes, where brand loyalty induced by advertising is high, with flour sales to the bakery trade, where customer choice is made largely on the basis of price or service).

Figure 13.8b shows a group of equal output curves. Each is a locus of price-selling expense combinations which are capable of inducing sales of the same output level. They slope upwards from left to right initially, because more advertising is required

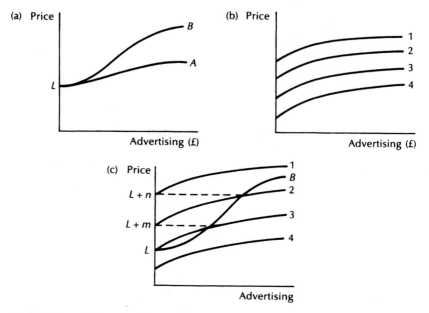

Figure 13.8 (a) How the limit price may vary with advertising. (b) Sales isoquants at different price – advertising combinations. (c) Maintenance of output and raising of price through advertising

to sell the same output at higher prices. After a point, increasing advertising is less effective as a compensating mechanism for price increases, and the slope becomes less steep. Higher curves represent lower outputs since, given advertising, as price rises, output falls. Figure 13.8c superimposes the two diagrams. This shows how a firm originally producing quantity 3 at price L can raise its price to level $L+m$ without inducing entry, while maintaining constant output. (Price could be raised still further to $L+n$, but in this instance sales would have to be forefeited by moving from isoquant 3 to isoquant 2.)

Notes

1. This is proved as follows:

$$PV_s = \Delta S_0 + \frac{\Delta S_0(1-k)}{1+r} + \frac{\Delta S_0(1-k)^2}{(1+r)^2} + \ldots + \frac{\Delta S_0(1-k)^{\infty}}{(1+r)^{\infty}} \qquad \text{(i)}$$

Now multiply throughout by $(1-k)/(1+r)$:

$$\frac{PV_s(1-k)}{1+r} = \frac{\Delta S_0(1-k)}{(1+r)} + \frac{\Delta S_0(1-k)^2}{(1+r)^2} + \frac{\Delta S_0(1-k)^3}{(1+r)^3} + \ldots +$$

$$+ \ldots + \frac{\Delta S_0(1-k)^{\infty}}{(1+r)^{\infty}} \qquad \text{(ii)}$$

Now if equation (ii) is subtracted from equation (i) we obtain:

$$PV_s - \frac{PV_s(1-k)}{1+r} = \Delta S_0$$

Therefore

$$PV_s = \Delta S_0 \left[\frac{1}{1-(1-k)/(1+r)} \right]$$

$$= \Delta S_0 \left[\frac{1+r}{(1+r)-(1-k)} \right]$$

$$= \frac{\Delta S_0(1+r)}{r+k}$$

which is the desired result.

2. These proportions relate to the products of (a) the corresponding binomial probabilities of a certain number of successes from a given number of opportunities (where the probability of success in each case is 0.5); and (b) the percentage of the population with 0, 1, 2, 3 . . . OTS values. Hence they can be determined from the binomial probabilities table in a statistics text.

3. For illustrative purposes it has been assumed that for a four-insert campaign, increasing returns to advertising inserts have been succeeded by diminishing effectiveness. Clearly, the use of the entire length of the S-shaped function to base weights on in this way may not be valid until many more inserts have been made. This can only be judged on the merits of the case. It is possible, for example, that a pattern such as 0.1, 0.6, 0.8, 1.0 would have been more appropriate here (increasing followed by constant returns).

4. If a cheaper route were readily and universally available, entrepreneurs would provide product information *and* the product at a lower price than is paid by consumers when they buy the product and the advertisement as a joint and inseparable package. This, of course, does happen, although not frequently. For example, for years Marks & Spencer never advertised the St Michael brand. Restaurant and hotel information is provided by organisations separate from the firms themselves; for example the motoring organisations' handbooks. Similarly, the Consumers' Association publishes *Which?* However, these are exceptions.

Bibliography

Barrenblatt, M. and Sinclair, R. (1989) *Make the Other Half Work Too*, 2nd edn, Macmillan.

Broadbent, S. (1980) *Spending Advertising Money*, 3rd edn, Business Books.

Buchanan, N. S. (1942) 'Advertising expenditures: a selected treatment' *Journal of Political Economy*, vol. 50.

Chandler, A. D. (1990) *Scale and Scope*, Belknap Press.

Dean, J. (1951) *Management Economics*, Prentice Hall.

Demsetz, H. (1964) 'The welfare and empirical implication of monopolistic competition', *Economic Journal*, vol. 74.

Dorfman, R. and Steiner, P. (1954) 'Optimal advertising and optimal quality', *American Economic Review*, vol. 44.

Economist Intelligence Unit (1986) *Is your Advertising Budget Wasted?*, Economist Intelligence Unit.

Feller, I. (1972) 'Production isoquants and the analysis of technological and technical change', *Quarterly Journal of Economics*, vol. XXCVII.

Hooley, G. J. and Lynch, J. E. (1985) 'How UK advertisers set budgets', *International Journal of Advertising*, vol. 4.

Leach, D. F. and Reekie, W. D. (1994) 'The effect of advertising in a controlled environment', University of the Witswatersrand, Research Monograph.

Needham, D. (1976) 'Entry barriers and non-price aspects of firms' behaviour', *Journal of Industrial Economics*, vol. 25, 1.

Rathnam, S., Arum, M. R., Chandhury, A. and Shukla, P. R. (1992) 'MUDRAPLAN – a decision support system for media planning: from design to utilisation', *Interfaces*, vol. 22.

Simon, J. (1969) *The Management of Advertising*, Prentice Hall.

Williamson, O. E. (1963) 'Selling expense as a barrier to entry', *Quarterly Journal of Economics*, vol. 77, 1.

Medium-/long-term decisions

Chapter 14

Capital budgeting

There are three main problems involved in financial economics: investment selection, method of funding investments once selected, and dividend policy towards corporate shareholders when investments begin to bear fruit.

14.1 Traditional methods of investment appraisal

Investment appraisal handles three main types of capital outlay problem. First, is expansion advisable? Would it be profitable to add to our existing stock of plant or equipment? Second, is replacement of obsolete, but mechanically adequate, capital stock worthwhile? Finally, if the answers are positive, should we rent or buy the new machinery or factory space? There are two traditional methods of solving these problems, the return on capital employed and the payback period. The more theoretically correct method is to use one of the discounted cash flow techniques which we explain in the next section.

14.1.1 Return on capital employed

This is the estimated average profits of a project after taxes and depreciation have been deducted, divided by the average value of the investment. For example, consider two machines with the accounting values shown in Table 14.1. The initial capital outlay is £400 and the machine is worth nothing in year 4 which is the end of the economic life of the machine. Depreciation has been calculated by the straight-line method; that is the reduction in value of the outlay has been divided by the length of life of the investment. If the company had to make an accept or reject decision then if it considered 40 per cent to be adequate, the project would be accepted. If the company had to select between alternative projects from which only a limited number could be chosen (because of shortage of funds or because projects were mutually exclusive) then the return on capital employed (ROCE) would be ranked and those with the highest values accepted.

Table 14.1

Year	0	1	2	3	4	Sum	Average
Capital flow	−400	0	0	0	0		
Revenue		540	270	200	150		
Costs		260	80	70	30		
Depreciation (400/4)		100	100	100	100		
Profits		180	90	30	20	320	80

$$ROCE = \frac{\text{Average annual profit}}{\text{Average value of investment}} = \frac{80}{200} = 0.40$$

Note: For simplicity we assume taxes are zero.

As detailed here this technique has a number of drawbacks. First, there are many different ways of defining 'profit' and 'capital outlay'. For example, there is no prescription as to which system of depreciation the firm should use. In our example we used the straight-line method. But there is no reason why the reducing balance method would not have been equally appropriate; nor why 24% or 26% as depreciation rate would be more or less appropriate than the 25% used. Some experts (Brealey and Myers 1991) specify that tax should be deducted from profit (as we have done); others (Lumby 1988) state that it should not be. The technique does not indicate whether receipt of government investment grants or tax allowances should be deducted or included.

A second problem with the ROCE is that it ignores differing lengths of life of different projects. A firm may wish to choose between a project giving an ROCE of 40% for four years after which the profit opportunity ended and another project giving 39% over 10 years. It might be that the second project is more desirable for shareholders, but the technique would not show this. Thirdly, the technique ignores the fact that £1 received early in the life of a project is worth more than £1 received later. Thus consider the profit streams of two projects as shown in Table 14.2. Both have the same capital outlay and zero scrap value, both have the same length of life. But the earlier profits of A are bigger than those of B. Therefore if the profits of A and B were separately reinvested, at the end of the project the value of A's profits

Table 14.2

Project	Year	0	1	2	3	4	ROCE
A	Capital flow	−400	0	0	0	0	
	Profits		180	90	30	20	0.40
B	Capital flow	−400	0	0	0	0	
	Profits		20	30	90	190	0.41

Table 14.3

Year	0	1	2	3	4	5
Capital flow	−100					
Cash inflows		50	30	20	20	20
(gross of depreciation)						

plus interest would exceed those of B. Nevertheless the ROCE would indicate project B as being more desirable than project A because its ROCE is 41% compared with 40% for A.

14.1.2 Payback period

A project's payback period is the number of years required for the accumulated profits, gross of depreciation, to equal the capital cost of the asset. For example in Table 14.3 the payback period is 3 years. If the company has to decide whether to accept or reject this project without a need to rank it with others it would compare the project's payback period with a cut-off period and if the project paid back in less time than the cut-off period it would be accepted. If a choice had to be made between projects, then the projects with the shortest payback periods would be accepted.

There are two major difficulties. First, no account is taken of earnings received after the payback period expires. Thus, a project with no further net cash inflows after its payback period of five years would be regarded as more attractive than a project which pays back in six years but which continues to give positive net cash inflows for a further ten years. Second, all net cash inflows are given the same weight; the possibility of reinvestment of earlier net cash inflows is ignored. Thus no distinction would be made in the relative attractiveness of two projects, each with a three-year payback period and a capital outlay of £1,000, where the net cash inflows were in years 1, 2 and 3. £900, £50 and £50 for project A; and £50, £50 and £900 for project B.

14.2 Discounted cash-flow methods of investment appraisal

Discounted cash flow (DCF) techniques overcome the difficulties associated with the two traditional methods. Each deficiency is taken into account and net cash inflows reduced consistently to one figure which is truly comparable, project by project.

Both DCF methods make use of the present value formula of Chapter 2, viz:

$$PV = \frac{\pi_1}{1+r} + \frac{\pi_2}{(1+r)^2} + \frac{\pi_3}{(1+r)^3} + \cdots + \frac{\pi_n}{(1+r)^n} = \sum_{i=1}^{n} \frac{\pi_i}{(1+r)^i}$$

To work through the full formula is tedious and a common short-cut is to use a table of discount factors (see Appendix 14 at the end of this chapter). This enables us to give a value to each term provided that π and r are known.

There are three basic steps. First, profits are calculated for each year of the project's estimated life. These are obtained from sales and cost forecasts, calculated after tax. Thus, variability of profit year by year is explicitly taken into account. Second, the depreciation is not deducted. All capital expenditure will be included in the final cash flow calculation, so no provision to build up a fund to cover the original outlay will be required. Thus the problems of how to handle depreciation in the traditional methods are taken account of. Third, investment grants and allowances are included in the appropriate year's cash flow. The relevant future receipt or cash flow for each year can then be calculated as in the example in Table 14.4.

Table 14.5 shows what the present value of the project would be at three given and different interest rates (r). The discount factors are taken from the Appendix – they are, quite simply, the values of $1/(1 + r)^i$.

The two alternative DCF techniques, net present value (NPV) and internal rate of return (IRR), both generally provide the same outcome or result. The rules for the use of the two are as follows:

1. A project is worthwhile if the NPV is greater than zero (where NPV is defined as the project's present value less its capital outlay),[1] or

Table 14.4

Year	Profits (sales-cost less tax)	Investment allowances	Proceeds from sale of plant as scrap	Cash flow
1	10	20	–	30
2	30	10	–	40
3	30	–	–	30
4	25	–	–	25
5	10	–	–	10
6	10	–	10	20

Table 14.5

Year	(1) Cash flow	(2) Discount factor for 5%	Relevant PV (1 × 2)	(3) Discount factor for 6%	Relevant PV (1 × 3)	(4) Discount factor for 7%	Relevant PV (1 × 4)
1	30	0.952	28.56	0.943	28.29	0.935	28.05
2	40	0.907	36.28	0.890	35.6	0.873	34.92
3	30	0.864	25.92	0.840	25.2	0.816	24.48
4	25	0.823	20.57	0.792	19.8	0.763	19.1
5	10	0.784	7.84	0.747	7.47	0.713	7.13
6	20	0.746	14.92	0.705	14.1	0.666	13.32
	£155		£134.09		£130.46		£127.0

2. A project is worthwhile if its *IRR* is greater than the cost of capital to the company (where *IRR* is defined as that discount rate which will render the project's *NPV* equal to zero).

Box 14.1 illustrates the importance of discounting net cash inflows in the context of Lockheed's Tristar aircraft project. Box 14.2 shows the details of a net present value calculation.

Box 14.1

The Lockheed Tristar

During the 1971 Congressional hearings Lockheed sought a federal guarantee for an additional $250m. of bank debt to finance the remaining development and production costs of its three-engined wide-bodied passenger jet: the Tristar. Lockheed argued that the break-even point would be reached when 195–205 aircraft had been sold. Reinhardt (1973) has argued that this break-even number was equal to the number of aircraft where simulated sales revenues equalled cumulated development and production costs, without taking into account the opportunity cost of money. Using publicly available information Reinhardt has estimated the *NPV* of the Tristar under alternative assumptions and so suggests that the failure to discount led to an underestimate of the true break-even number, that is the number of aircraft at which *NPV* equals zero.

The costs of research, development, testing and evaluation plus initial investment were estimated and it was assumed that they were divided equally between the number of months that Lockheed probably assumed these stages would take. The production costs were assumed to follow a 77% learning curve with the first aircraft costing $100m. and the output rate was approximately 3 aircraft per month. The revenue in each month of production was assumed equal to the price for each aircraft ($15.5m.) multiplied by the number sold.

The discount rate was estimated by calculating a weighted average cost of capital (WACC). The long-term proportion of debt to equity (30:70) for the company was taken as its desired future ratio and the cost of debt was set at 4.5%. The cost of equity was estimated using the Gordon growth formula (see equation 14.1) with Lockheed's historic dividend yield of 5% and forecast growth rate of earnings per share of 7% taken to give a cost of equity of 12%. This gave a WACC of 9% to 10%.

Since the level of WACC is uncertain, the effects of different values were considered. It was found that if the net cash inflows were not discounted then, if 287 Tristars were built, cumulative revenue would equal cumulative costs. If the discount rate was 5% the number of aircraft to give a zero *NPV* was 360. By October 1972 Lockheed had only 184 orders.

Reinhardt believed that at the time of the hearings the company had hoped to gain a 35% to 40% share of the free world market in wide-bodied passenger aircraft, with orders for 271–310 of them. However this number is based on an assumed growth rate of air passengers of 10% when 5% may have been more realistic.

Source see Reinhardt 1973.

Box 14.2

The expansion decision

ABC Electronics is trying to decide whether or not to buy an additional machine which makes microchips and which costs £100,000. The machine will have an economic life of 5 years at which point it will have no scrap value. The machine will enable the company to increase significantly its output of chips and the predicted additional revenues and operating costs which the machine will generate are shown in Table B14.1. The company pays tax at 34% of taxable profit. The company is financed entirely by equity and will be eligible to receive an investment allowance of £10,000 in year 1 only. The company's cost of capital is 12%.

Table B14.1 Incremental cash inflow calculation

Year	0	1	2	3	4	5
1. Capital investment and disposal	−100,000	0	0	0	0	0
2. Sales revenue		50,000	60,000	65,000	50,000	30,000
3. Operating costs		10,000	15,000	16,000	10,000	7,000
4. Pre-tax profit (2 − 3)		40,000	45,000	49,000	40,000	23,000
5. Depreciation		20,000	20,000	20,000	20,000	20,000
6. Interest		0	0	0	0	0
7. Investment allowances		10,000	0	0	0	0
8. Taxable profit (4 − 5 − 6 − 7)		10,000	25,000	29,000	20,000	3,000
9. Tax payable (0.35 × 8)		3,500	8,750	10,150	7,000	1,050
10. Change in working capital		−1,000	0	0	0	0
11. Net cash inflow (1 + 4 − 9 + 10)	−100,000	35,500	36,250	38,850	33,000	22,950

$$NPV = = -100,000 + \frac{35,500}{(1+0.12)} + \frac{36,250}{(1+0.12)^2} + \frac{38,850}{(1+0.12)^3} + \frac{33,000}{(1+0.12)^4} + \frac{22,950}{(1+0.12)^5}$$

$$= 3,367$$

Table B14.1 shows the full calculation of the incremental net cash inflow from this additional machine. Notice the following:

1. Taxable profit is sales revenue less operating costs less depreciation less interest on debt used to finance the project less investment allowances.
2. Depreciation and interest are shown only because they enable the value of tax to be calculated. They are not added or subtracted from pre-tax profit to calculate the net cash inflow but only to calculate the value of taxable profit on which tax is calculated.
3. Depreciation has been calculated by the 'straight line' method. This method consists of calculating the difference between the initial outlay and final scrap value and divide it by T, the length of the economic life of the machine.

→

4. The operating costs do not include money which has been used to fund inventories and accounts receivable less accounts payable, that is working capital. The table shows that in year 1 inventories and accounts receivable increased by £1,000 more than accounts payable. Inventories were accumulating and customers did not pay their bills immediately. In years 2, 3 and 4 the level of working capital remained constant (changes were zero). In year 5 when the economic life of the machine ended the accounts receivable increased by £1,000 more than inventories and accounts payable as customers paid their bills.

5. If the funding of the project had included debt with interest, the value in row 6 would have been the interest rate on the debt multiplied by the book value of the debt.

The *NPV* of the additional machine is positive (£3,367) therefore shareholders would benefit from its purchase.

Reconsider Table 14.5, given that the capital outlay required is exactly £130.46. The *NPV* is positive (£134.09 − £130.46) at a 5% interest rate. The project is worthwhile. At 7%, *NPV* is negative (£127.00 − £130.46) and so the project is not attractive. Alternatively, the project's *IRR* is exactly 6%. Thus the project is worthwhile at any cost of capital to the company below 6%. At a cost of capital over 6%, the company would be paying more for the capital than it would receive as a return from the project.

Figure 14.1 shows the *NPV* function for the project of Table 14.5 varying with the discount interest rate, *r*. Both methods indicate that the project is worthwhile at any cost of capital less than 6%. The *NPV* is positive at all points to the left of the 6% discount rate. The *IRR* is 6% exactly, the point where the *NPV* function cuts the discount rate axis.

In Figure 14.2 the firm is faced with three alternative projects, *A, B* and *C*. In this situation of project choice, either technique provides the same answer. At a discount

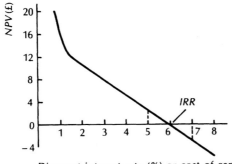

Discount interest rate (%) or cost of capital

Figure 14.1

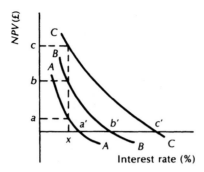

Figure 14.2

Table 14.6 Discounted cash flow formulae and their uses

(a) Expansion decisions

Go ahead if *NPV* > 0

$$\text{i.e. if } NPV = \sum_{i=1}^{n} \frac{FR_i}{(1+r)^i} - \text{capital outlay} > 0$$

or Go ahead if *IRR* > cost of capital

(b) Rent or buy decisions

Rent if the *PV* in this case is greater than the *NPV* in case (a) and is also > 0.

$$\text{i.e. if } PV = \sum_{i=1}^{n} \frac{(FR\text{-rental charge})_i}{(1+r)^i} > 0$$

Clearly, no capital outlay is deducted from the *PV* in this case. *or* Rent if *IRR* is greater than the *IRR* in case (a).

(c) Decisions on replacement or continuity with existing plant

Here the book value of existing plant should be ignored. It is irreversible and cannot be altered by today's decisions. Marginal equivalency principles will be adhered to and sunk costs ignored if actions are taken only when the benefits exceed the costs. Thus it pays to replace existing plant if the following condition holds (and vice versa):

$$\sum_{i=1}^{n} \frac{(\text{Cost savings due to new equipment})_i}{(1+r)^i}$$

+ scrap value of old plant today

$$+ \frac{\text{scrap value of new equipment in year } n}{(1+r)^n}$$

> capital outlay on new equipment

$$+ \frac{\text{scrap value of old plant in year } n}{(1+r)^n}$$

Note: All of the above formulae can be adjusted for risk and uncertainty using the techniques described in Section 3.8. Alternatively, if the capital asset pricing model is used to calculate 'r', then risk is explicitly embodied in the formulae (see pp. 398–419).

interest rate of *x*, each project has a positive *NPV*, yet the *NPV* of *C*(*c*) is more attractive than *b* or *a*, the *NPVs* of *B* and *A* respectively. Similarly, *C's IRR*, *c'*, is greater than either *a'* or *b'*.

One disadvantage of the *IRR* technique is that it requires trial-and-error calculation until a zero *NPV* is reached and so the *IRR* discovered. This is laborious, but it does mean that it can be calculated before a decision is taken on what the cost of capital is, against which the *IRR* is to be compared. The *NPV* calculation is a one-off job, but only if the cost of capital, the discount rate *r*, is known.

Table 14.6 summarises much of this discussion.

14.3 Conflict between the DCF techniques

14.3.1 Capital rationing

Although the *NPV* and *IRR* techniques appear to be simply the opposite sides of the same coin they can and do give conflicting results. Consider Figure 14.3. A group of projects is arranged in descending order of attractiveness by their respective *IRRs*. *MCC* is the marginal cost of capital. The heavy line on the histogram shows the *IRR* of the marginal project. Clearly the firm should invest £7,000 up to and including project *E*.

However, in any given period the firm is unlikely to have an unconstrained budget available for capital investment, in which case it may prove better to accept

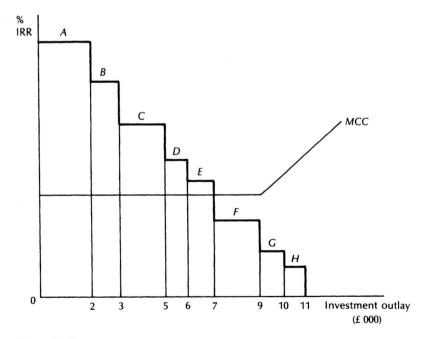

Figure 14.3

several smaller projects which fully utilise the budget, rather than accept one large project which leaves part of the budget unused. Thus in Figure 14.3 the firm might have only £4,000 to invest. Should it undertake A, B and D, A and C, or A and B with an unused £1,000? Each of these three courses of action is acceptable by the *IRR* method. The appropriate choice is the one which provides the highest *NPV* to the firm. Suppose the *NPVs* and other relevant information are as summarised in Table 14.7. The profitability index (i.e. the ratio of the gross present value of future cash flows to the original outlay) is clearly a useful shorthand device when appraising projects using the *NPV* method: it merely needs to exceed unity for us to know that the *NPV* will be positive, thus the higher the index, the more attractive in relative (but not absolute) terms is the project. The index emphasises not only the *NPV* of a project, but also the efficiency with which the project generates that *NPV* from each pound invested. In this example, the optimal choice is A and C, providing an *NPV* of £1,700, rather than A, B and D providing an *NPV* of only £1,650.

14.3.2 Mutually exclusive projects

On other occasions also, the *IRR* and the *NPV* methods can give contradictory results. This is not of importance if there is no capital rationing, and if we are merely trying to find out whether a project is worthwhile. If both methods say the project is attractive, then it can be gone ahead with. But it does matter if two or more mutually exclusive projects are being compared and a rank order is desired to permit choice of one and rejection of the others. Graphically, this situation is illustrated in Figure 14.4. With a cost of capital of V, project A has a higher and more attractive *NPV*. Yet project B, with an *IRR* of Z is more attractive than project A with an *IRR* of only Y.

The conflict arises because of differences in the time patterns of the cash flows of each project. In *NPV* terms project A is preferred at lower interest rates because its receipts are achieved relatively later. (Tomorrow's cash is worth less than today's because of discounting, and the higher the discount rate and/or the further away 'tomorrow' is, the more true this becomes.) Project B, with cash flows received

Table 14.7

Project	Initial outlay (£)	NPV	Profitability index	Ranking Profitability index	NPV	IRR
A	2000	1000	1.5	1	1	1
B	1000	400	1.4	2	3	2
C	2000	700	1.35	3	2	3
D	1000	250	1.25	4	4	4
E	1000	200	1.2	5	5	5
idle balance*	1000	0	1.0	6	6	6

* Invested at cost of capital, i.e. *MCC* in Figure 14.3.

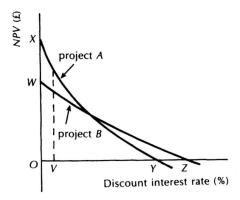

Figure 14.4

relatively earlier, consequently becomes more attractive at higher discount rates. In IRR terms, project B is consistently more attractive at Z% > Y%.

Consider the two projects C and D outlined in Table 14.8, given a cost of capital of 3%.

If correct assumptions are made about the implicit compounding of interest, the NPV and IRR techniques can be reconciled. Several methods of comparing like with like are available. First, and most simply the NPV method compares today's pounds with today's pounds, thus favouring project D. Secondly, the two projects can be compounded forward to a *common terminal date*. (Project C's income of £120 in year 1 is available for reinvestment at that point at the cost of capital.) In year 3 project D yields £140 less £120.2 (the initial £110 outlay compounded forward to year 3) which equals £19.8. Project C's £120 compounded forward is worth £123.6 by year 2 and £127.3 by year 3 from which we subtract £109.3 (the initial £100 outlay's value in year 3) to obtain £18. Again project D is preferred. Third, project D's IRR is 8.5%. Project C, however, returns 20%, but only for one year. Subsequently it returns 3%, the cost of capital or the return on the best available alternative investment opportunity. In addition, D has a greater initial outlay than C. The return from this additional £10 must be included with those of the £100 to facilitate comparison. We assume this £10 is invested at (the best available rates) the cost of capital to give an inflow of £10.9 in year 3 only. By adding this to the £127.3 to give £138.2 and finding the rate which discounts this to equal the £110 initial outlay, the *corrected IRR* of C is found to be 7.9%. This is less favourable than D's 8.5%. Finally, the NPV and IRR

Table 14.8

	Year	Outlay (year 0)	1	2	3	NPV	IRR(%)
(i)	Project C	100	120	0	0	16.4	20
(ii)	Project D	110	0	0	140	18.1	8.5
(iii)	D – C	10	– 120	0	140	1.7	4

techniques can be reconciled using the method known as the *incremental hypothetical project*.

If project C is chosen at the opportunity cost of D, then the implication is that the £10 'saved' by not investing in D is invested at 3%, the best alternative use. If D is chosen, however, that 'incremental' £10 has an *IRR* greater than 3%, namely 4% (calculated as in row (iii) of Table 14.8). In other words, D provides all that C can provide in terms of *NPV* (18.1 = 16.4 + 1.7) but provides 1% more (4% – 3%) on the additional £10 which is required to finance it. Again project D is the optimal choice.

14.3.3 Dual rates of return

Simultaneous calculation of two *IRRs* for one project is not common but it can happen and ambiguity arises. Figure 14.5 illustrates the phenomenon. With a cost of capital of Z, the project has a positive *NPV* of C. Yet two *IRRs* are present, A and B. Since OZ > OA, this project should be rejected. Yet, if OB is taken as the *IRR*, the project should be gone ahead with. The reason for the duality of answers is the two reversals of sign in the net cash flow during the project's life. When this occurs, the *IRR* method will often (not always) produce ambiguous results. The reason this happens lies in the mathematical construction of the discounting formula itself. Consider a three-period project with outlay K and income π. The *IRR* is that value for r which renders:

$$K - \frac{\pi_1}{1+r} - \frac{\pi_2}{(1+r)^2} = 0$$

or $K(1+r)^2 - \pi_1(1+r) - \pi_2 = 0$

Let $(1+r) = x$, and K, π_1, and π_2 be a, b and c respectively, then

$ax^2 - bx - c = 0$

In short, this is merely a quadratic equation where two possible values for x, i.e. $1 + r$, may occur. In short, the *IRR* formula has the same number of roots as the power value of the discounting denominator. Most of these multiple roots will be either negative or hypothetical (e.g. $\sqrt{-2}$). The Change of Sign Rule described by

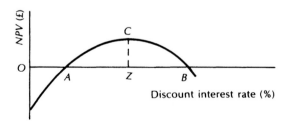

Figure 14.5

the mathematician Descartes can be adapted to the *IRR* formula to state that there will be as many positive roots for $(1 + r)$ as there are changes in the sign of the cash flow. Thus, if after the initial outlay there are only positive cash flows, there will be only one positive root for $(1 + r)$ and hence only one value for r itself. On occasions, however, negative cash flows can be expected in a project's life.

For example, some North Sea oil rig construction yards on the West Coast of Scotland were built in deep water sea lochs. Permission to build these yards during the height of the rig construction boom in the 1970s was given on the understanding that the firms would return the countryside to its original condition when the yards were closed. Open cast coal mining has similar environmental reclamation constraints. Consider a project with the following cash flow and a cost of capital of 10% as in row 1:

	Outlay	Year 1	Year 2	Year 3	Year 4
Row 1	−1000	+1000	+2000	+1500	−1100
Row 2	−1000	+1000	+2000	+ 500	0

The problem of multiple roots can be avoided by limiting the number of sign changes to one as in row 2. In *NPV* terms rows 1 and 2 are identical. £1,100 spent in year 4 is the same as £1,000 spent in year 3. The former is simply discounted to year 3 values using the 10% discount rate. An example of the context in which the *NPV* criterion has been used is given in Box 14.3.

14.4 Capital structure

So far we have not considered how the cost of capital is selected for use in the discounting approach. Here we will discover that the value for r is intimately connected with the decision as to how to raise the capital with which the firm is funded.

14.4.1 The cost of capital

The cost of capital is the discount rate which should be used in the formula for calculating a project's *NPV*. It is the yardstick with which the *IRR* of a project is compared. It enables the manager to apply marginal equivalency principles to the investment decision. Projects can be ranked in diminishing order of attractiveness by *IRR* and each undertaken until the *IRR* of the marginal project equals its cost of capital.

Thus, it is a marginal cost. It is the cost of capital of the marginal project. This project will only be gone ahead with if the benefits it will produce are equal to the benefits foregone by failing to invest in (and so forfeiting the return from) the best available alternative investment opportunity. It is, therefore, an opportunity cost. It is the return available on the best alternative project. This is a figure which is easier to describe than to determine, however. It is not, for example, the ruling market interest rate. That would only be the cost of capital if there was a perfect capital

---

Box 14.3

Skye Bridge project

In 1991 the UK parliament passed the New Roads and Street Works Act. This allowed private companies to initiate, fund and construct roads, motorways and bridges and to charge drivers tolls for their use. One of the earliest projects approved by the government was the private funding, construction and operation of a bridge between mainland Scotland and the Isle of Skye, one of the nearest Hebredean islands. Prior to construction of the bridge there were three crossings to Skye: two which were not connected to a trunk road on the mainland and the main crossing which was by ferry between the Kyle of Lochalsh on the mainland and Kyleakin.

On 26 October 1989 the Highland Regional Council decided to support the provision of a privately funded bridge crossing. Tenders were invited and three consortia offered them. Proposals had to fulfil a number of conditions including that (a) the bridge toll in any one year must not exceed the toll which would be charged on the ferry; and (b) the operator may operate the bridge until the present value of the tolls equalled the value of the bid made to gain the concession, subject to a maximum of 27 years from that in which it first opens. Thereafter ownership of the bridge would revert to the Regional Council. The successful tender was proposed by Miller Group which offered a concrete box design which would cost £23.63m. Construction began in mid-1992 and the bridge is expected to be open in mid-1995.

The calculations performed by Miller group are commercially confidential. However, by using publicly available data, Moles and Williams (1993) have estimated the NPV of the gains which shareholders would be expected to receive over the value of the bid under alternative assumptions: a sensitivity analysis. The variables about which the greatest uncertainty existed and for which alternative values were examined were the predicted growth rate of traffic over the bridge and the rate of price inflation.

Source see Moles and Williams 1993.

market. Then a firm could borrow or lend without limit and without risk. Given unlimited capital, any project yielding a rate higher than the market rate would already have been undertaken. Only then would the highest obtainable rate anywhere, the opportunity cost, be the market rate.

Even if the capital market was perfect, a further difficulty would arise. Lending rates and borrowing rates tend to differ. Borrowers usually have to pay more than they would receive as lenders. At its simplest, this is accounted for by the presence of a middleman. Which rates should be chosen? If the only alternatives are borrowing and lending, then the lending rate is the cost of capital, if the money to be invested would otherwise have been lent out to the market given an absence of outstanding debt. The borrowing rate is the best available alternative return (or avoidable cost) if the money to be used in the project would otherwise have been allocated to repay a debt.

In addition, the cost of obtaining money is not always static as the quantity borrowed rises. Sometimes the cost rises as more is borrowed. In such circumstances it is the marginal cost of borrowing which is the cost of capital.

Finally, the cost of capital cannot equal the market rate for the simple reason that the market rate is not unique, but can have a range of values depending on the source from which funds are raised. Each source (for example, debentures, ordinary shares, loans, retained earnings, and so on) has a different interest requirement. There is no reason why any of them should be equal to the rate offered by the best available alternative investment opportunity. Moreover, which source of new capital a firm will use will depend upon its attitude to capital gearing, to fixed interest charges and to any tax advantages which may accrue by using one method rather than another. (Current tax law permits the charging of loan interest against profits before the levying of Corporation Tax. Dividends, however, are deducted from profits after the calculation of Corporation Tax. Other things being equal, for this reason alone loan stock is a more attractive form of financing than equity. It reduces the base figure on which Corporation Tax must be paid and so reduces the firm's tax bill and, correspondingly, increases the after-tax income available for distribution or for reinvestment.)

14.4.2 The debt:equity ratio and gearing

The practical advantages and disadvantages of one method of financing *vis à vis* another are, of course, taken into account in the theoretical concept of the cost of capital. Since this theoretical cost is difficult to determine for reasons discussed above, practical alternatives have been devised which are useful approximations to the firm's true cost of capital.

The so-called 'traditional' approximation is to take the weighted average of the firm's earnings yield calculated before tax[2] and the rate of interest payable on any fixed interest capital.

This is illustrated in Figure 14.6 for a continuous range of gearing (loan:equity) ratio alternatives. The cost of capital of a company financed solely by equity would be the earnings yield itself. The 'average' and the 'equity' cost curves intersect at this point. In the impossible event of a company being solely financed by debentures, the 'average' and 'loan stock' cost curves would intersect at a loan:equity ratio of 100%. Why do the curves have the positions and shapes indicated? The fixed interest on loan stock cost curve starts off at a relatively low level. Since loan stock holders legally have first call on the profits of a company in the pecking order of distribution, they are traditionally assumed to have chosen a less risky form of investment alternative than equities and consequently they expect and are entitled to a lower rate of return than the equity holder. As the gearing ratio increases, however, the degree of risk assumed by loan stock holders also increases. By definition, the surplus of total profits accruing to equity holders will have become absolutely smaller. Since this is the bond holder's 'cushion' in the event of a downturn in the fortunes of the firm, they will demand a slightly higher return to

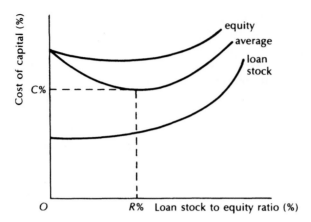

Figure 14.6

compensate for this. After a point this increase in reward will not compensate for increasing risk and the gentle rise in the early stages of the loan stock curve will become dramatic and sharp. Table 14.9 expresses this argument in figures.

Two firms are shown each with £1,000 of capital assets, each experiencing a profits fall from £200 to £100 in a given 2-year period. Each distributes its total surplus to its shareholders. The only difference between the two is in their gearing ratios. Hi-Gear Ltd, the firm with the higher debt:equity ratio, is less favourably placed to maintain payments of loan interest in the face of a profit downturn. (The initial cushion is £110, compared to Lo-Gear's £100; for a similar profit downturn, this falls to only £10, a proportionately larger fall than Lo-Gear's which drops only to £90.)

The equity cost curve in Figure 14.6 will be higher to begin with because of the intrinsic difference in risk. As the debt:equity ratio rises, the return demanded by shareholders will also rise. Higher gearing increases the risk to the equity holder as

Table 14.9

Hi-Gear Ltd Capital structure			Low-Gear Ltd Capital structure		
100 £1 Ordinary shares		100	900 £1 Ordinary shares		900
900 10% Debentures		900	100 10% Debentures		100
		£1000			£1000
	Year 1	Year 2		Year 1	Year 2
Profits	200	100	Profits	200	100
Less loan interest	90	90	Less loan interest	10	10
Dividend	110	10	Dividend	190	90
Dividend yield	110%	10%	Dividend yield	21%	10%

well as to the debenture holder. In this case, the increased risk is due to the increased variability of the residual left to pay shareholders with. (Hi-Gear Ltd, for example, experiences a 100% fall in dividend yield between years 1 and 2. Lo-Gear suffers a drop, under identical circumstances, of only 11%.)

The traditionalist view, therefore, is that moderate levels of gearing reduce the cost of capital, higher levels increase it. Just as management tries to minimise production and marketing costs at any given output level, so too it should try to minimise financing costs. This means, first, selection of the appropriate gearing structure. Cost of capital is minimised at C%, a gearing ratio of R%. Second, the average cost of capital curve is dependent on the positions of both the loan stock and the equity cost curves. If either of these can be shifted downwards, then the average itself will fall.

14.4.3 The Modigliani–Miller view

The main challenge to the above arguments has come from Modigliani and Miller (MM (1958)). They argue that the cost of capital is independent of capital structure. The main MM proposition is that the average cost of capital is constant (not U-shaped) and is equal to the cost of equity in a company with a zero loan:equity ratio.

They argue that this must be so since, if otherwise equally risky companies differ in market value and gearing ratio, then investors will sell investments (shares or debentures) in the higher valued firms and buy investments in the lower valued. This arbitrage process is profitable so long as differences in market value (and so total yield from any one firm) persist. Given that ungeared firms are in the list of options open to investors, then the uniform level at which the cost of capital will settle will be the cost of equity in such firms. Figure 14.7 illustrates the MM view of the cost of capital. Figure 14.8 compares the MM and traditional views of how the value of the firm varies.

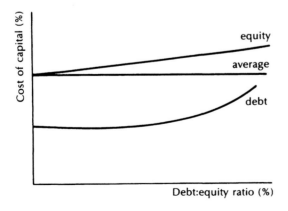

Figure 14.7

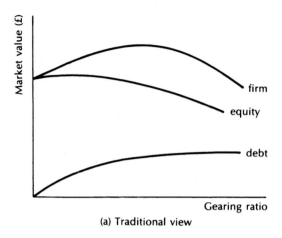

(a) Traditional view

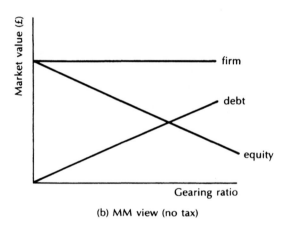

(b) MM view (no tax)

Figure 14.8

The MM model rests on a number of highly restrictive assumptions. Corporate taxation is disregarded. Earnings retention and so corporate growth is zero. Total assets are given, only their method of funding may change. For any firm, each investor has the same expectations as to earnings before interest (π_{BI}). π_{BI}, in turn has a zero growth rate. Company operating risk is deemed constant over time and independent of gearing. The firm's life span is infinite. Investors operate rationally in a perfect capital market, and each individual is able to borrow or lend at the same rates as would quoted companies. To show the model in operation let:

S = total market value of equity
B = total market value of debt
V = $B + S$
I = interest payments

g = growth rate
N = number of shares outstanding
P_0 = current share price
D_0 = current dividend
$I/B = K_d$ = cost of debt (see pp. 391 and 397)

$$\frac{D_0}{P_0} = K_e = \text{cost of equity given that } g = \text{zero (see pp. 391–2 and 397)}$$

$$= \frac{D_0(N)}{P_0(N)} = \frac{\pi_{BI} - I}{S} = \frac{\pi}{S}$$

where π = earnings after interest, and all of the above expressions are in their perpetuity form. The weighted average cost of capital, K_w, under either the traditionalist or MM views is:

$$K_w = (W_d \times K_d) + (W_e \times K_e)$$

where $W_d + W_e = 1.0$

$$\therefore \quad K_w = (B/V \times K_d) + (S/V \times K_e)$$

$$= (B/V \times I/B) + (S/V \times \pi/S)$$

$$= I/V + \pi/V = \pi_{B1}/V$$

Now suppose that 2 firms exist identical in every respect except market values and gearing. The share price of the more highly valued company will be bid down by shareholders selling their shares, and the share price of the lower valued company will be bid up by shareholders buying its shares. This will continue until the market values of both companies are equal. This is because, without increasing his or her risk, each shareholder can increase his income by such arbitrage. When the market values become equal, shareholders can no longer increase their income in this way and equilibrium is reached. K_w is now the same for each firm irrespective of gearing.

To see this, recall that

$$K_{w1} = \frac{\pi_{BI1}}{V_1} \text{ and } K_{w2} = \frac{\pi_{BI2}}{V_2}$$

for firms 1 and 2. If they are identical for V_1, V_2 and their gearing ratios, then because V_1 comes to equal V_2 through arbitrage, and since $\pi_{BI1} = \pi_{BI2}$ because the firms are identical, then the weighted average costs of capital, K_{w1} and K_{w2} must also be equal.

Numerically, consider firms A and B prior to an MM arbitrage process. Each has a par and market value as shown. This assumes an identical equity capitalisation rate of 10% despite gearing differences. Thus:

	A		B	
	Par value	Market value	Par value	Market value
Equity	5,000	7,500	10,000	10,000
Debt (5%)	5,000	5,000	–	–
	£10,000	£12,500	£10,000	£10,000

B has a dividend of £0.1 per share, a pay out of £1,000 for an earnings yield of 10%. A has a dividend of £0.15 per share, a pay out of £750 for an earnings yield of 10%. In addition A must pay out £250 in interest. As a consequence of A's higher gearing, its total market value is higher at £12,500, reflected in this example exclusively in equity prices. As the traditional approach would predict A's weighted average, cost of capital at 8% is lower than B's at 10%. These have been calculated as follows:

$$\text{for } A, \ K_w = \frac{\pi_{Bl}}{V} = \frac{1,000}{12,500} = 8\%; \text{ for } B, \ K_w = 10\%.$$

But any individual investor who held, say, 50 A shares in his personal portfolio, could improve his position by selling them and acquiring B shares in their place. Thus as in columns (i) and (iii):

	Before sale		After sale	
	(i)	(ii)	(iii)	(iv)
		(equilibrium)		(equilibrium)
A shares (50)	£75	£50	nil	nil
B shares	nil	nil	125	100
dividend received	£7.5	£7.5	£12.5	£10
debt (personal)	nil	nil	50	50
gearing ratio of portfolio	75:50	50:50	75:50	50:50
interest due (personally)	nil	nil	£2.5	£2.5
income (net)	£7.5	£7.5	£10	£7.5

The investor in this case has maintained the gearing ratio of his portfolio at 75:50 by borrowing £50 to enable him to purchase a total of 125 B shares. As a consequence his net income rises from £7.5 to £10. He will continue to do this until no further gain can be made. Thus, at its simplest, if B's market price and par values remained the same, but A's share price fell to par because of continuous selling, then when A's total market value reached £10,000, no further arbitrage would take place, and both firms would have a weighted average cost of capital of 10%. Columns (ii) and (iv) show how arbitrage would no longer be worthwhile in such circumstances. Note that in both comparisons the gearing ratios are held constant in order to hold portfolio risk constant.

14.4.4 The cost of debt

The cost of debt, $I/B = K_d$, in the weighted average cost of capital equation is obtained by adjusting it for tax. Thus the after tax cost of debt is $K_d = I(1 - t)/B$ where t is the rate of corporation tax. Thus, for tax reasons, debt is cheaper than equity and MM and traditionalists agree that the overall cost of capital is U-shaped when gearing takes place. MM, however, attribute this solely to the tax effect, and not at all to the pure leverage effect. More precisely, I should equal the present value of all interest payments and any principal repayment and K_d should be the IRR which equates the value of I with the proceeds to the firm of the issue of debentures.

14.4.5 The cost of equity

The cost of ordinary shares in the cost of capital calculations is 'the minimum rate of return' the firm 'must earn on the equity-financed portion of its investments in order to leave unchanged the market price of its stock' (Van Horne, 1980). This is the firm's expected earnings yield or rate of return shareholders expect to earn over the years from holding shares of the firm.

Thus it can be found by calculating the value of r in the following equation:

$$P_0 = \frac{D_0}{1+r} + \frac{D_0(1+g)}{(1+r)^2} + \frac{D_0(1+g)^2}{(1+r)^3} + \cdots + \frac{D_0(1+g)^n}{(1+r)^{n+1}}$$

which simplifies to $P_0 = D_0/(r - g)$, or

$$r = \frac{D_0}{P_0} + g = K_e \qquad (14.1)$$

where D_0 is the current level of dividend, P_0 the current market price and g the expected constant growth rate of dividends per share.

This model (often known as the Gordon dividend growth model) assumes, of course, that dividends will grow at a rate of g compounded to infinity. It also assumes an efficient capital market: that is, that P_0 reflects all available information about the economy, the financial markets and the particular company concerned. In turn this implies that P_0 adjusts quickly and smoothly to new information. P_0 thus only moves randomly (the random walk) around its 'intrinsic value', the intrinsic value itself adjusting solely to informational changes. Neither of these assumptions is necessarily correct, and although modifications to g can be embodied in the original equation before solving for r, these too must involve inexact estimation. Several surveys of the popularity of different investment criteria have been conducted. Box 14.4 gives details of one of the latest surveys.

Box 14.4

Which appraisal criterion is most popular?

In 1981 and 1986 Pike conducted a questionnaire survey to investigate the proportion of firms which used various capital budgeting criteria. The popularity of different criteria is shown below:

	1981	1986
Number of firms	150	100
Appraisal Criteria		
Average accounting rate of return	49	56
Payback	81	92
Net present value	39	68
Internal rate of return	57	75
Risk Analysis Techniques		
Sensitivity analysis	42	71
Analysis under different assumptions	n/a	93
Reduced payback periods	30	61
Increased discount rates	41	61
Probability analysis	10	40
Beta analysis	0	16

Pike comments that managers appear to use a combination of appraisal techniques. Using data relating to 1975 as well as the above he performed various statistical tests to see if the apparent increase in the proportion of managers using DCF-type techniques had increased between 1975 and 1986. He concluded that for all of the financial appraisal criteria except the average rate of return, there had been an increase in the proportion of the largest firms which used them. By regressing the perceived changes in the effectiveness of evaluating and controlling projects on the use of each appraisal technique and other explanatory variables, Pike concluded that the use of *NPV* and *IRR* had indeed increased appraisal effectiveness.

Source Pike 1988.

14.5 The cost of equity and portfolio theory

An alternative approach to measuring the cost of equity, r, is the capital asset pricing model (CAPM) approach. Given certain assumptions, the required rate of return is the same as the discount rate calculated using the Gordon dividend growth model. Moreover, it also embraces any risk involved in the potential shareholding (or investment project). Hence no further adjustment for risk to the *NPV* formula is required.

When an investor decides to adopt a certain mix of securities (or range of investment projects), he or she does so under conditions of less than full information. If we ignore uncertainty and assume that conditions of actuarial risk apply, then it is conceptually possible that a decision taker could use the expected utility maximis-ation model of Chapter 3. To do so would require knowledge of each individual project's or security's risk and return profile. The entire probability distribution of the possible returns of each security or project would have to be known and so would the utility function of the decision maker.

Furthermore, since the returns of different securities may or may not be correlated over time, any particular portfolio's returns will vary according to its mix of securities. Thus the expected utility maximisation model would have to be extended to the choice of the optimal portfolio or set of securities. Each set in turn would have an expected (mean) return and risk (standard deviation). The firm or decision maker would then choose the portfolio which maximises his or her expected utility.

In principle this requires that every possible portfolio mix be examined, and that the expected utilities be calculated from the total probability distribution of possible returns given the utility of wealth of the investors. The investor can then choose the portfolio providing the highest expected utility. To obviate this enormous data requirement, Markowitz suggested that the possible values of a security's risky *NPV* will have a *normal* probability distribution. Such a distribution is, of course, identi-fiable by only two elements: the mean and the variance. (The variance, σ^2, is the square of the standard deviation, σ.) This, as we shall see, reduces the data requirement problems to a more manageable level.

Since the mean and variance provide in summary all the information about a normal frequency distribution for one asset or project, we can move on to consider a two-or-more security portfolio.

14.5.1 Expected returns

Let proportion x of the investor's resources be invested in firm A and $(1 - x)$ in firm B. The portfolio's expected return $\bar{r}_P$ can then be expressed as:

$$\bar{r}_p = x\bar{r}_A + (1 - x)\bar{r}_B \tag{14.2}$$

The *portfolio's* mean return is simply the weighted average of returns on *individual shares* (or investments) where the weights are the percentages of resources attributed to each. Thus, if the returns for A and B are as shown in Table 14.10 then $\bar{r}_A = 9.5\%$ and $\bar{r}_B = 12\%$ respectively.

Table 14.10

Probability (p)	A(%)	B(%)
0.25	12	22
0.25	20	10
0.25	10	4
0.25	− 4	12

14.5.2 Variances

The variances for A and B are calculated from the general formula:

$$\sigma^2 = \sum_i (r_i - \bar{r})_p^2 \qquad\qquad (14.3)$$

Hence $\sigma_A^2 = 0.25(0.025)^2 + 0.25(0.105)^2 + 0.25(0.005)^2 + 0.25(-0.135)^2$

$\qquad\qquad = 0.007475 \qquad (\sigma_A = 8.6\%)$

Likewise $\sigma_B^2 = 0.0042$

The relevant risk measure of the portfolio (in terms of its standard deviation around $\bar{r}_P$) will clearly depend not only on $\bar{r}_A$, $\bar{r}_B$, on σ_A and σ_B, but *also on whether all possible returns for A and B are or are not expected to be positively or negatively correlated with each other*, and on the strength of that correlation. Thus, unlike the calculation of $\bar{r}_P$, portfolio risk is *more than* just the weighted average of the relevant securities' standard deviations or variances. Rather, we are interested in how the distributions of returns do or do not move in unison.

This is the basis of what is now called portfolio theory. It distinguishes between two types of risk: systematic and unsystematic. The former (systematic risk) cannot be avoided by security investors, since it affects financial markets in totality (e.g. general economic conditions, government policy changes at a macro level, and so on). Unsystematic risk, however, is peculiar to the security or firm concerned. This type of risk will include strikes, innovations, management quality, the state of industry rivalry and the like. Unsystematic risk can be 'diversified away' in any individual's portfolio. Shares which are not perfectly positively correlated can be combined. Figures 14.9, 14.10 and 14.11 illustrate the effect of such diversification.

In Figure 14.9 the returns for firms A and B fluctuate over time. Their returns are perfectly inversely correlated and equally risky. Notice that the investor does not know whether returns on A or B will be high or low next period, but only that *if* they are high for A, they will probably be low for B and vice versa. By appropriately

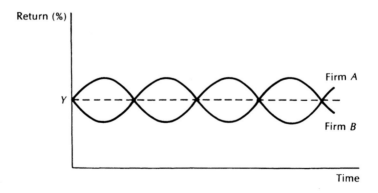

Figure 14.9

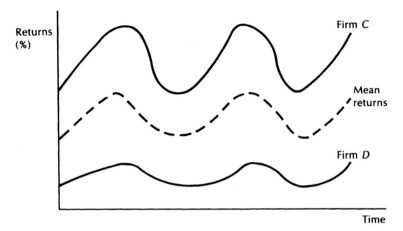

Figure 14.10

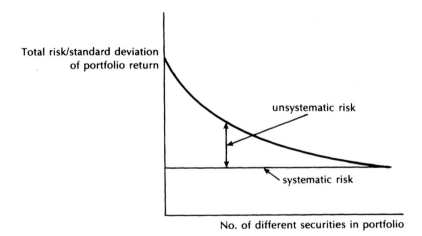

Figure 14.11

diversifying ownership between *A* and *B* an investor can guarantee for himself (assuming a perfectly negative correlation) an unvarying (i.e. riskless) return of *Y*%. This is known as risk removal or *risk reduction*. Risk was reduced because the correlation between the returns did not equal 1.

It should be noted that this is not the same as risk averaging. For example, in Figure 14.10, firms *C* and *D* have perfectly positively correlated returns over time (albeit *C* has both bigger returns on average and a higher level of risk as indicated by their variability). By appropriately diversifying his or her portfolio between *C* and *D* an investor can decrease risk by just risk averaging. The fluctuation amplitude of the dashed line is less than that of the returns pattern for *C* but greater than that for *D*.

The risk which can be reduced (or averaged) is, of course, limited to unsystematic risk. Thus even an investor with a portfolio such as that in Figure 14.9 will not actually find that his or her returns are static and consistent over time as the figure indicates. Rather, the dashed line at Y will continue to rise and fall in line with the stock market as a whole. That is, the systematic risk component cannot be eliminated.

Figure 14.11 shows how appropriate portfolio diversification can reduce unsystematic risk close to zero, but never risk as a whole. That is, if the capital market is efficient (i.e. investors are rational and well informed, transaction costs and obstacles to investment or disinvestment are zero, no participant is large enough to affect a security's price, and all investors have similar expectations) then it follows that at the margin investors will have constructed portfolios whose overall risk is effectively limited to the systematic component (Figure 14.11).

This explains why, in Table 14.10, the σ for a diversified portfolio of A and B is less than σ for a specialised holding of either A or B. This is what we would expect successful diversification to accomplish. But we would also expect riskier assets to have higher returns as in Figure 14.10. However, A with a σ of 8.6% has a lower return at 9.5% than B with σ of 6.5% and return of 12.0%. This paradox is resolved when we discover that σ is not an appropriate measure of risk when individual securities can be combined (as in most cases in real life they can) with others into portfolios. As Brealey and Meyers put it: 'Since investors can diversify away unique risk, they will not demand a higher return from stocks that have above-average unique [i.e. unsystematic] risk. But they *will* demand higher return from stocks with above-average *market* [i.e. systematic] risk.' (1988, p. 149).

In statistical terms the reason is that covariance, rather than variance or standard deviation, is the appropriate measure to gauge the riskiness of an individual security relative to a diversified portfolio. This can be proved or illustrated numerically, intuitively, or with more sophisticated statistical theory. Here we will use numerical and intuitive illustrations.

The covariance is simply a measure of the way the two random variables, for example r_A and r_B, move in relation to each other. When the covariance σ_{AB} is positive the variables move in the same direction, and when negative in opposite directions. The covariance is important since it measures the contribution of a single security's returns to total portfolio risk.

There are two factors which, statistically, affect the value of σ_P, given the returns on each stock. These are (a) the proportion of resources devoted to each stock; and (b) the correlation between these returns. We shall consider these in turn.

Proportion of resources in each stock (x)

As the number of securities in a portfolio rises and the share of each (x) decreases, the portfolio variance decreases and approaches the average feasible covariance. The 'average feasible' covariance is, of course, at the limit, the covariance of the stock market as a whole.

Consider first a numerical example based on the securities A and B of Table 14.10. A 50:50 mix of products A and B provides a return midway between the returns to be expected from specialisation, but in addition a lower level of risk (as measured by σ_P) than specialisation in *either* A or B (measured by σ_A and σ_B) would provide. A and B have standard deviations of 8.6% and 6.5% respectively, whereas σ_P is only 5.3% (see Table 14.11). Risk reduction, not risk averaging, has taken place.

Naturally, the manager need not choose to have a product mix composed only of A or B on a 50:50 basis. Any mix is possible. Some possibilities are listed in Table 14.11, and Figure 14.12 plots the resulting mean and standard deviation. It can be shown that

$$\sigma_P^2 = x^2\sigma_A^2 + (1-x)^2\sigma_B^2 + 2x(1-x)\rho_{AB}\sigma_A\sigma_B \tag{14.4}$$

σ_A and σ_B are known from Table 14.10, and that ρ_{AB}, the correlation coefficient, is calculated from the returns data relating to r_A and r_B in Table 14.10, and it equals -0.04, while $\sigma_A\sigma_B = 8.6\% \times 6.5\% = 0.0056$.

Column 3 ($\bar{r}_P$) of Table 14.8 is simply the weighted average of $\bar{r}_A$ and $\bar{r}_B$ taken from the results of Table 14.11 ($\bar{r}_A = 9.5\%$ and $\bar{r}_B = 12\%$). Column 4 (σ_P), however, is not the simple weighted average of the individual σ_A and σ_B values derived from Table 14.10 ($\sigma_A = 8.6\%$ and $\sigma_B = 6.5\%$). That would only be so if the returns were perfectly correlated (pure risk *averaging* would have taken place). But we have already seen (Figures 14.9 and 14.10) that risk *reduction* is achieved by diversification, not simply risk averaging.

Why does this result in the use of equation (14.4) for σ_P^2 in Table 14.11 rather than the intuitively apparent use of a weighted average? To understand equation (14.4) consider a two stock portfolio. The variance, σ_P^2 is calculated from the following four cell matrix which shows the covariation between any two stocks.

	A	B
A	$\sigma_{A,A}$	$\sigma_{A,B}$
B	$\sigma_{B,A}$	$\sigma_{B,B}$

This can be re-expressed as:

	A	B
A	σ_A^2	$\rho_{AB}\sigma_A\sigma_B$
B	$\rho_{AB}\sigma_B\sigma_A$	σ_B^2

since it is a statistical definition that the correlation coefficient, $\rho_{AB} = \sigma_{AB}/\sigma_A\sigma_B$. Each of these cells is respectively the covariance between A's returns and A's returns, between A's and B's returns, between B's and A's returns and between B's and B's returns. The portfolio variance is obtained by summing the four cells having first weighted each cell by the relevant proportions of total funds invested in A, (x), and B, (1 − x). Thus in the top-left cell the weight is x^2 and in the bottom-right it is $(1-x)^2$. (Since we are dealing with σ_P^2 not σ_P.) In the top-right and bottom-left cells the appropriate weighting factor is $x(1-x)$ in each cell. Hence equation (14.4) is derived. Notice from Table 14.11 that given ρ_{AB}, increasing the proportion of the portfolio which is devoted to B (from 0%) increases the value of $\bar{r}_P$ but leads at first to a reduction in σ_P before an increase (see Figure 14.12).

Table 14.11

Percentage in *A*	Percentage in *B*	$\bar{r}_P(\%)$	$\sigma_P(\%)$
100	0	9.5	8.6
75	25	10.0	6.4
50	50	10.75	5.3
25	75	11.5	5.6
0	100	12.0	6.5

Note: The product portfolio risk and return figures were
calculated thus (for the 50:50 case):

$$\bar{r}_P = (0.5 \times 0.095) + (0.5 \times 0.12)$$
$$= 10.75\%$$
$$\sigma_P^2 = (0.25 \times 0.007475) + (0.25 \times 0.0042)$$
$$+ 2.0 \times 5.0 \times 5(-0.04)\ 0.0056$$
$$= 0.001869 + 0.001 - 0.000112$$
$$= 0.00276$$
$$\Rightarrow \sigma_P = 5.3\%$$

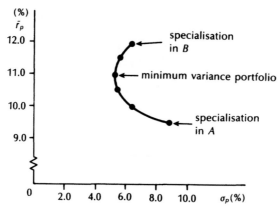

Figure 14.12 Trade-off between mean and standard deviation

In the multi-security case, the number of possible covariances, of course,
increases. This can be illustrated in a matrix thus:

$$
\begin{matrix}
\sigma_{A,A} & \sigma_{A,B} & \sigma_{A,C} & \ldots\ldots & \sigma_{A,n} \\
\sigma_{B,A} & \sigma_{B,B} & \sigma_{B,C} & \ldots\ldots & \sigma_{B,n} \\
\sigma_{C,A} & \sigma_{C,B} & \sigma_{C,C} & \ldots\ldots & \sigma_{C,n} \\
\vdots & \vdots & \vdots & & \vdots \\
\sigma_{n,A} & \sigma_{n,B} & \sigma_{n,C} & & \sigma_{n,n}
\end{matrix}
$$

In a two-product portfolio, we have two variances (σ_B^2 and σ_A^2) and two covariances ($\sigma_{A,B}$ twice). In a three-product portfolio, the top left-hand corner, there are nine possible covariances, three are variances (σ_A^2, σ_B^2 and σ_C^2) and six are 'pure' covariances ($\sigma_{A,B}$, and $\sigma_{A,C}$ and $\sigma_{B,C}$, all twice). Similarly, a four-asset portfolio has four variance terms and twelve covariance terms. As the number of variance terms equals the number of securities (n) while the number of covariance terms equals ($n^2 - n$) then, as we form ever larger portfolios, the covariance terms become relatively more and more important.

So, as n increases, the value σ_P^2 approaches the average covariance: first, because equation (14.4) becomes ever more dependent on the covariance rather than on individual variances; second, the individual variances not only become less numerous relative to the number of covariances but also less important, given that they are weighted by the squares of the fraction of the portfolio they comprise and this fraction is an ever diminishing one. So, if the average covariance were zero, then all risk, not only unsystematic risk, could be eliminated by sufficiently broad diversification. Since security returns do not move wholly independently, however, market or systematic risk will never fall to zero.

Thus not only numerically, but also intuitively, it is clear that a covariance measure, rather than standard deviation alone, is the appropriate risk measure for a security relative to a diversified portfolio.

The correlation between returns

Now that a method has been developed for calculating the risk and return for a portfolio, we must ask: (a) what happens if A and B are independent of each other, i.e. if σ_{AB} is zero? (b) What if they are perfectly correlated? (c) How do we find the product mix which minimises risk? And (d) are we limited to the series of points traced out by the curve in Figure 14.12?

The statistical definition of the correlation coefficient, ρ, helps answer some of these questions. The correlation coefficient ρ_{AB} between two independent variables is:

$$\rho_{AB} = \frac{\sigma_{AB}}{\sigma_A \sigma_B} \qquad (14.5)$$

Clearly, if the returns from the two products or securities are independent, namely if σ_{AB} is zero, then so too will be ρ_{AB}. Conversely, if the returns are perfectly correlated, ρ_{AB} will equal unity.

In the example of Tables 14.10 and 14.11 the covariance was negative. This indicated that r_A and r_B tended to move in opposite directions. (Had σ_{AB} been positive it would have indicated the returns moved simultaneously in broadly the same direction.) Hence if both securities are purchased, there is less risk than if only one is. The gains appearing at any one time on A tend to offset the losses (or relative downward profit movements) occurring at the same time for B, and vice versa. A and B had returns which were negatively correlated.

What would have been the situation had they been *perfectly* correlated (positively or negatively)? Consider the data given in Table 14.12 for securities Y and X respectively. If we were now to plot a mean–variance return trade-off graph as in Figure 14.13, given differing levels of investment in the products in question, we would obtain the dashed line joining points X and Y. If $\rho_{xy} = +1$ this can be shown to be a straight line. The expected return on the portfolio mix as x changes from 100% to 0% moves from 2.25% to 0.625%. The standard deviation also changes from that of X to that of Y. The slope of this line can be found thus:

$$\text{slope of } XY = (r_y - r_x)/(\sigma_y - \sigma_x)$$

$$= \frac{2.25 - 0.625}{1.92 - 0.96} = 1.69$$

Table 14.12

Probability	$r_Y(\%)$	$r_X(\%)$
0.25	−0.5	0.0
0.25	0.0	1.0
0.25	1.0	3.0
0.25	2.0	5.0
$\sigma_x = 1.92$	$\sigma_Y = 0.96$	$\rho_{xy} = 1.0$

$$\sigma_{xy} = \rho_{xy}\sigma_x\sigma_y$$

$\bar{r}_x = 2.25$ $\bar{r}_y = 0.625$

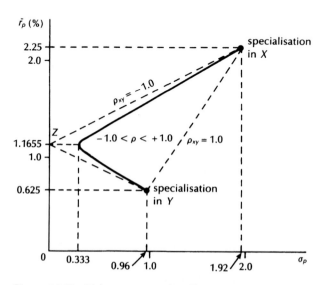

Figure 14.13 Risk–return trade-off: two products

Conversely, if the returns between X and Y are perfectly *inversely* correlated ($\rho_{xy} = -1$), the trade-off between mean and standard deviation would be the dashed line XZY. At the appropriate security mix one security's fluctuation of returns would be exactly offset by the others. This can also be proven mathematically. Usually, however, since securities never vary wholly independently of each other because of systematic risk, neither extreme holds and correlation is less than perfect. The general slope of the mean–variance opportunity set will be the solid curve XY.

14.5.3 The opportunity set

This *opportunity set*, or *minimum variance boundary*, is the locus of risk and return combinations offered by a portfolio of risky products which yield the minimum variance for a given rate of return. The line is normally convex, i.e. bounded by triangle ZXY. Indeed, any set of portfolio combinations formed by two risky products, less than perfectly correlated, must lie inside this triangle, and hence must be convex.

Figure 14.14 (originally devised by Eleanor Morgan) provides a simple way of understanding how the two-security opportunity set is derived (with given values

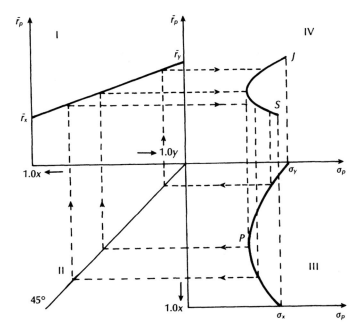

Note: This figure was based on an idea originally devised by Eleanor Morgan of the University of Bath.

Figure 14.14

of $\bar{r}_x$, $\bar{r}_y$ and ρ_{xy}). In quadrant I the horizontal axis shows how portfolio returns (given securities x and y) can range from $\bar{r}_x$ when the investor has 100% of his or her funds invested in x, to $\bar{r}_y$ when the investor specialises in y. Alternative portfolio mixes provide a portfolio return, $\bar{r}_p$, which is a weighted average of $\bar{r}_x$ and $\bar{r}_y$.

Quadrant II contains a 45° reference line with both axes displaying the proportion of x and/or y the investor holds. Quadrant III plots the portfolio risk σ_P, which can range from σ_x to σ_y. But here the relationship is not linear as in quadrant I. Since by assumption the returns on x and y are at least partly negatively correlated, *portfolio risk is not averaged* between σ_x and σ_y, *it is reduced.* (Had the correlation been negative unity, point P, the point of minimum risk would have lain on the vertical axis). The risk–return opportunity set can now be constructed graphically in quadrant IV by selecting any points in quadrant III, tracing them to their corresponding values in quadrant I and linking the relevant horizontal lines in quadrant I with the appropriate verticals from quadrant III. If this is done for sufficient points the minimum variance boundary, JS, is obtained.

14.5.4 The capital market line and efficient portfolios

Figure 14.15 illustrates the opportunity set of an investor showing all possible portfolios of securities as perceived by him or her, not simply two. The efficiency boundary, XZ, is convex to the upper left of the figure (note that the phrases efficiency boundary, opportunity set, and minimum variance boundary tend to be used interchangeably). Any portfolio below and to the right of this line is a possibility to the investor, given the investor's available funds. They are not, however, 'efficient' in that other portfolios on XZ are possible with lower levels of risk (given an expected return) or higher returns (given a level of risk).

The opportunity set is made up of a series of convex curves, each representing different portfolio blends of a given list of securities. Thus the addition to or deletion

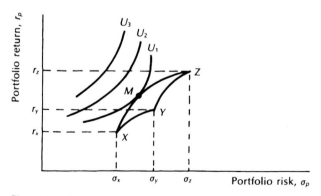

Figure 14.15

of a particular security from a portfolio might result in a curve such as *XY* as opposed to *YZ* or *XZ*.

The line *XY* could represent all combinations of securities *X* and *Y*, *YZ* all combinations of securities *Y* and *Z*, *XZ* all combinations of securities *X* and *Z*. The *area* enclosed by *XYZ* represents all possible combinations of all three securities. Portfolios composed of only one security are indicated by the points *X*, *Y* and *Z* respectively, and have the return and risk values indicated in the figure. (In this simplified example a two-security portfolio of some mix of *X* and *Z* is everywhere superior to any three-security portfolio composed of *X*, *Y* and *Z*. This, of course, need not be the case. It will depend on each security's risk and return characteristics and their covariances with each other. It is more probable that *XZ* would be a multi-security portfolio.) The optimum portfolio, given any investor's utility function and degree of risk aversion or preference, is obtained by superimposing the risk–return indifference curves (see Figure 3.9) on Figure 14.15. In this instance the highest attainable utility is given by point *M* on U_1, where U_1, U_2, U_3, are the investor's indifference curves.

We saw that, as the number of products in a portfolio increases, the risk which any one contributes to the portfolio reduces exclusively to the covariance risk. That is, the portion of a security's risk not correlated with the portfolio as a whole can be avoided at no cost. No rational investor will pay a premium for a security with diversifiable risk. But since *covariance* risk cannot be diversified away, the investor will pay such a premium: or what is the same thing, expect a higher return.

14.5.5 CAPM and the cost of equity

The *capital asset pricing model* (CAPM) uses this principle to price risky securities. If it is assumed that all investors hold an effectively diversified or 'market' portfolio, then part of a security's risk – the 'unsystematic' component – will have been diversified away. Only the undiversifiable 'systematic' risk will remain, as measured by the covariance between the returns on the security and those on the market portfolio, which by definition cannot be diversified away. Thus securities will be priced in equilibrium, according to their non-diversifiable systematic risk (normally termed their beta (β) coefficient). A risk-free security earns a return equal to the risk-free rate, and a risky product earns an additional premium in proportion to its beta coefficient. For any individual security, *j*, then, the total expected rate of return is the completely risk-free rate *i* plus some premium, r^*. Thus:

$$i + r^* = \bar{r}_j \tag{14.6}$$

What is the value r^* (the price of systematic risk), and how can it be calculated? It is to this question we now turn.

Unfortunately, most investors are unlikely to be aware of the efficiency boundary, far less the optimum point on it. The concepts can be given greater practical usefulness, however, if we add to our analysis the possibility of risk-free securities such as government bonds, where the cash return is certain. When this alternative is available, in order to determine the optimal portfolio we draw a straight line from the risk-free rate, i, tangential to the efficiency boundary as in Figure 14.16. The line itself shows the proportions of the risk-free security and portfolio N which can be held. Now only one portfolio mix of risky securities, N, not an infinite number as before, is considered. If the investor is also able to borrow or lend at the risk-free rate, then this line has a higher utility than the efficiency boundary. To the left of N the investor would invest part of his or her funds in the portfolio mix designated by N and the remainder in the risk-free security. To the right of N, the investor would hold only portfolio N and borrow additional funds at rate i to invest still further in it.

Thus, for example, investor A cannot improve his or her utility by either borrowing or lending. A will invest all his or her resources in portfolio N. Investor C, however, has a different utility function. U_{C1} indicates the highest level of utility he can achieve while remaining on the efficiency frontier. But if C moves from the portfolio mix indicated by that tangency point and instead invests all his or her resources in portfolio N and borrows funds at the risk-free rate i, and invests this sum in N, C can increase his or her return (and probably his or her risk) and his or her utility to the tangency point of U_{C2} and the straight line. (A numerical example for C might be an individual with wealth of £100, initial interest of £20 = 20%, who borrows £50 at i = 5% and invests the £150 in N at 18%, giving a return of £27 less the servicing charge on his or her borrowing of £2.50, so providing £24.50 as a return on his or her personal wealth of £100, i.e. 24.5%.)

Conversely, B, who is probably more risk-averse, would initially choose a portfolio indicated by the tangency point of U_{B1}. B could be earning, say, 8% or £8 on an investment of £100. B could increase his utility by moving to U_{B2} as follows. B takes, for example, £50 out of his or her original portfolio and lends it at the risk-free rate of 5%. B puts the remaining £50 into portfolio N at 18%, so obtaining a total income of £2.50 plus £9.50 = £12 or 12% on £100 invested at the original 8%.

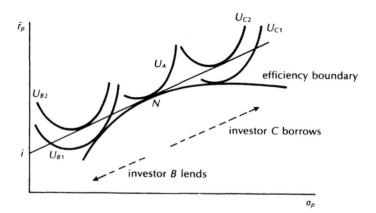

Figure 14.16

Given this reasoning, *all* investors are deemed to hold portfolio N in order to maximise their individual utilities. N is the 'typical', 'average' or 'market portfolio' and so only N need be considered in our analysis from now onwards, not the infinite number of portfolio mixes possible on and within the efficiency frontier.

What are the proportions in which investor A will allocate his or her funds between portfolio N and the riskless security? Obviously, at point i in Figure 14.17, 100% would be invested in the risk-free bond. At point N, 100% would be invested in the security mix of that portfolio. If A invested 25% of his or her available funds in N he or she would expect a mean return of: $\bar{r}_P = 0.75i + 0.25\bar{r}_N$. To obtain this A would accept a risk of $0.25\sigma_N$. Similarly, on a 50:50 split A's risk would be $0.5\sigma_N$. If A were to borrow to invest an additional 25% of cash in N his or her risk would be $1.25\sigma_N$. The straight line through i and N is known as the capital market line (*CML*). It illustrates the extra return which is expected for each extra unit of risk, i.e. the measure $(\bar{r}_N - i)\sigma_N$ is also the market price of risk, the slope of the *CML* (which we shall call α).

The *CML* dominates the efficiency boundary. That is, it is everywhere superior (except at N) to the efficiency boundary in indicating optimal portfolios of a mix of risky and risk-free securities. Thus, not only has the *CML* concept enabled us to limit the analysis to only one risky portfolio (N), it has also provided a way of isolating that portfolio from the individual's indifference curves. This is known as the separation theorem. The security mix indicated by N is now chosen irrespective of any individual's risk preferences. Only the amount lent or borrowed at rate i is affected. The optimal portfolio of risky securities (in this case N) depends only on $\bar{r}_N$ and σ_N. It is *not* the minimum variance portfolio.

The individual can thus be seen as taking a two-step decision: first, deciding on the optimal portfolio of risky assets; and second, determining the proportion of his or her portfolio which will consist of risk-free securities and the market portfolio. Only the latter depends on his or her utility function. Risk averters will choose points to the left of N (i.e. will lend), risk preferrers to the right (i.e. will borrow).

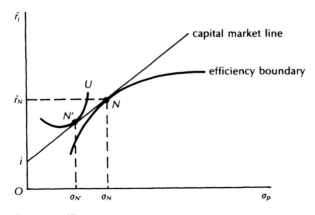

Figure 14.17

All investors consequently hold the same mix of risky stocks. This is the market portfolio. This may appear unrealistically presumptive, but since all the risky securities available must be held by someone, and since the market is assumed perfect, then their individual prices will adjust so that the expected return and risk characteristics of each ensure it will be bought by someone. If, given its risk, a security's price is too high, it will be sold until its price is lower, and vice versa if the price is too low. (Thus the assumption of complete divisibility of risky securities is made, and at the limit the proportion which the market portfolio may amount to of a risk-averse investor's total portfolio can be zero.)

From this we can say that when investors contemplate their portfolios:

1. They are usually better off if they borrow or lend to change the mix of the given portfolio N to N *plus or minus* a risk-free security. This does not always hold (e.g. if it is tangential at N) but provided their decisions are correct they will not be worse off by borrowing or lending.
2. *Two-fund separation* exists: that is, every investor regardless of his or her risk preferences will hold some combination of two funds (the so-called 'market portfolio' N, and the risk-free security).
3. In equilibrium, the marginal rate of substitution (MRS) between return and risk is the same for all managers, regardless of their individual risk preferences. (The MRS is, of course, simply the slope of the indifference curve U.)

Now if the MRS between risk and return is the same for *every* manager or investor in equilibrium, then the slope of the *capital market line* is the equilibrium or the market price of risk:

i.e. $\alpha = MRS$ (14.7)

(bearing in mind that the MRS of risk for return is defined as the extra return required per additional unit of risk borne by the investor and that each investor will have the same MRS in equilibrium).

We have already shown that in equilibrium all portfolios (as now defined) must lie on the CML, and that the slope of the CML is the market price of risk. We have also shown that the return required for any mix of the market portfolio, N, and riskless securities in equilibrium is dependent on the weighted average return of N and the risk-free investment. Thus if $(1 - x)$ is invested at risk-free interest rates, x is invested in N and α is the slope of the CML, then:

$$\alpha = \frac{\bar{r}_N - i}{\sigma_N}$$ (14.8)

and $\bar{r}_P = (1 - x)i + x\bar{r}_N$ at a risk of $x\sigma_N$

and $\sigma_P^2 = x^2\sigma_N^2 + (1 - x)^2\sigma_i^2 + 2x(1 - x)\rho_{Ni}\sigma_i\sigma_N$

$= x^2\sigma_N^2$ (since $\sigma_i = 0$)

The extra return per unit of risk required by an individual for investing in N is calculated by dividing the change in overall return by the change in total risk. So, if we assume our investor moves from a totally riskless portfolio to the one described, then the resultant calculation is:

$$\frac{(1-x)i + x\bar{r}_N - i}{x\sigma_N} = \frac{-xi + x\bar{r}_N}{x\sigma_N} = \frac{\bar{r}_N - i}{\sigma_N} = \alpha$$

Each unit of risk accepted by an individual will thus be rewarded by a premium over i of α, or generally:

$$\bar{r}_P = i + \alpha\sigma_P \tag{14.9}$$

which is simply the equation of the CML (P is any portfolio of N plus or minus an unknown number of risk-free securities). The premium thus reflects the portfolio's unique risk (σ_P) and the market's own risk–return trade-off (α).

14.6 The capital asset pricing model

The capital asset pricing model is derived directly from portfolio theory and the notions of systematic and unsystematic risk. It provides (if one accepts all the underlying assumptions) a superior measure of the cost of equity because, unlike the equation $K_e = D_0/P_0 + g$, it explicitly embraces the risk attached to a security as well as future returns.

The CML equation (14.9) as a whole can now be used to derive a valuation model for each individual security in the market portfolio. The CML applies only to efficient *portfolios*. It does not describe the relationship between individual *securities* and their riskiness.

The CAPM states that the expected return on any *security* (or portfolio) is related to the riskless rate of return and the expected market return. The general expression summarising this is:

$$\bar{r}_j = i + \beta_j(\bar{r}_N - i) = i + r_j^* \tag{14.10}$$

where r_j is the expected return on security j, and β_j, the beta coefficient, is a measure of the sensitivity of that security's return to movements in the overall market's return. Figure 14.18 plots this equation which is known as the security market line (SML). Obviously, if a value for β can be obtained for a security, then its rate of return can be calculated. Under the CAPM all portfolios (*efficient or otherwise*), including the market portfolio as well as all individual securities, lie on the SML. Thus in the case of the market portfolio where ($\bar{r}_N - i$) is known already from overall market data:

$$\bar{r}_N = i + \beta_N(\bar{r}_N - i)$$

$$\therefore \quad \beta_N = 1 \tag{14.11}$$

The risk premium of security j is (from 14.10):

$$\bar{r}_j - i = \beta_j(\bar{r}_N - i) \tag{14.12}$$

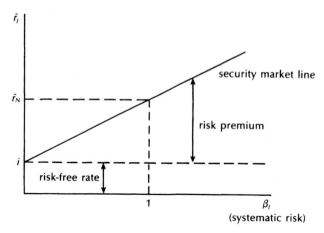

Figure 14.18

or β_j times the risk premium on the market portfolio. Given that all efficient portfolios, including the market portfolio, lie on the *CML* and the *SML*, then for any efficient portfolio, *P*, we obtain:

$$CML \equiv \bar{r}_P = i + \frac{(\bar{r}_N - i)}{\sigma_N}\,\sigma_P \qquad (14.13)$$

and

$$SML \equiv \bar{r}_P = i + \beta_P(\bar{r}_N - i) \qquad (14.14)$$

and so, for efficient portfolios like *P* where the *CML* = the *SML*:

$$\beta_P = \frac{\sigma_P}{\sigma_N} \qquad (14.15)$$

where either β_P or σ_P can be used as a risk measure. But since individual securities and most portfolios will rarely lie on the *CML*, their spread of returns will not be perfectly correlated with the market's. In terms of Figure 14.18 neither their returns nor their β will lie exactly on the *SML*.

Equation (14.15) is thus an inadequate measure of β for individual securities. Any variation of return on such assets not explained by market movements is unsystematic risk. β explains only systematic risk since as we saw in Figure 14.11, most unsystematic risk will be diversified away by careful portfolio construction. As a corollary, only systematic risk should be considered in determining the risk premium of a security.

To calculate β as a measure of a security's systematic risk in practice involves plotting expectations about the future responsiveness of that share's return against changes in the market's return. Since the future is unknown, historical data must be used as a substitute (say monthly returns as measured by dividend yield plus capital appreciation for the share for a period of years). The market portfolio is also unknown, but some widely accepted share index could be used as a proxy. From such data a *characteristics line* can be plotted and its equation estimated by normal OLS analysis. Thus in Figure 14.19 the characteristics line for a particular share is shown. Point X, for example, is an observation in a given month when the security provided a return of 5% less than risk-free treasury bills and the market a return of 10% more than such a risk-free security surrogate.

Both intuitively and empirically one finds that the characteristics line typically slopes up from left to right. That is, the greater the expected return for the market, so too one would expect a greater expected excess return over the risk-free rate for the stock. Theoretically the line passes through the origin since the excess return on the market portfolio not due to market movements is diversified to zero. Similarly, since the market portfolio's average of zero is simply the weighted average of shifts in the non-market inspired individual share returns, these too will sum to zero. Arbitrage will ensure that no individual share has a negative average excess return over time. Thus each share's average must in turn equal zero.

Where $\beta_j = \sigma_{jj}/\sigma_N = 1$, it means that the stock has the same systematic risk as the market (see equation (14.11)). Where $\beta_j > 1$, the stock's excess return varies more than proportionately with the excess return of the market portfolio, and vice versa. Historically calculated Betas have proved useful proxies for calculating future Betas. Thus if a stock's β in a given month was 2.5, and the market excess return was 2%, this would imply an expected excess return for the stock of 5%. This 5% cannot be diversified away.

Beta's significance as far as stock market buying and selling is clear. High-value shares should be bought if the market is expected to rise since they will rise faster than the market. They have a high 'upside potential'. Conversely, if the market is expected to fall, high β value shares are unattractive prospects. They have a high 'downside risk'. The opposite holds in both cases for low β value securities.

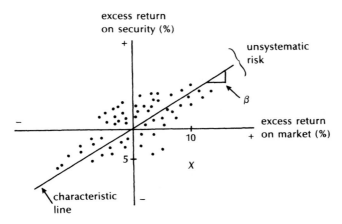

Figure 14.19

14.6.1 The cost of equity again

We noted (equation (14.6)) that the expected rate of return for security j was $i + r_j^* = \bar{r}_j$ where r^* was the price of systematic risk. We also now know (equation (14.10)) that $K_e = \bar{r}_j = i + \beta_j(\bar{r}_N - i)$. Geometrically β_j can be measured by the slope of the characteristics line. The slope of any line $(y = \hat{m}x + c)$ where y is regressed on x is:

$$\hat{m} = \rho_{yx}\frac{\sigma_y}{\sigma_x}$$

which in this specific instance implies that $\hat{\beta} = \rho_{jN}(\sigma_j/\sigma_N)$

$$\therefore \frac{\sigma_N}{\sigma_N}\hat{\beta} = \rho_{jN}\frac{\sigma_j\sigma_N}{\sigma_N^2} = \hat{\beta} \tag{14.16}$$

and so (recall equation (14.5)):

$$\beta = \frac{\sigma_{jN}}{\sigma_N^2} \tag{14.17}$$

Algebraically, what equations (14.16) and (14.17) tell us is that both in theory and in the way the estimate of β, $\hat{\beta}$, is derived, β, the measure of responsiveness of j's excess returns to the market's excess returns, is the ratio of the covariance between the possible returns for j and for the market divided by the variance of the market's probable returns (where $\rho_{jN}\sigma_j\sigma_N$ is the covariance of returns for j with the market's returns, and ρ_{jN} is the correlation coefficient between the relevant expected returns). By substitution of this result in equation (14.15) we obtain:

$$K_e = i + \frac{\bar{r}_N - i}{\sigma_N^2}(\rho_{jN}\sigma_j\sigma_N)$$

The significance of this equation as far as *capital* investment appraisal is concerned is that each project should be evaluated in terms of its expected return and its own unique systematic risk in relation to the market portfolio. The traditional weighted average cost of capital equation provides only one discount rate applicable to all projects. The cost of capital calculated using the CAPM, however, will vary from project to project. Thus projects acceptable by one yardstick may prove unacceptable by the other and vice versa.

The difference between the two criteria is highlighted in Figure 14.20. Assume that the weighted average cost of capital (WACC) is given a constant value for all projects being considered. That is, we are assuming either that the firm is optimally geared, as in the traditional approach, or that gearing is irrelevant, as in the Modigliani–Miller approach. Under WACC the cost of capital calculation provides only one discount rate for all projects being considered. Under CAPM, the higher the project's systematic risk (β_j), the higher is the required rate of return. The equation for SML (from equations (14.14) and (14.6)) being:

$$SML = \bar{r}_j = i + \beta_j(\bar{r}_N - i) = K_{ej} = i + r_j^*$$

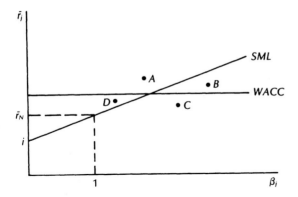

Figure 14.20

Clearly, a constant WACC and varying CAPM criteria will result in conflicting results. Thus in Figure 14.20 the WACC yardstick would accept projects A and B, reject C and D, while the CAPM approach would differ, by accepting D but rejecting B as being respectively above and below the relevant risk-adjusted cost of capital.

Several objections to the CAPM can be raised. First, it rests on the very dubious assumptions of a perfect capital market. Second, as so far developed, it is essentially only a single-period problem. Third, it assumes that firms should diversify their portfolio of investment projects in the same way as investors diversify their portfolios of securities. But if investors can diversify to minimise their risk, there seems little point in firms doing so too. Under portfolio theory, corporate diversification and individual investor diversification are effectual substitutes. Of course, if one relaxes some of the assumptions then clearly diversification by firms can result in higher profits or lower risks for the firm given its own peculiar resource and opportunity situation. Similarly, individuals cannot always hold a portfolio large enough to diversify away all unsystematic risk. Thus, although portfolio theory and the CAPM are still in their infancy in assisting managers to assess the cost of capital, their practical and conceptual weaknesses at the level of the individual investor may mean that their strengths should not be ignored by corporate managers in investment appraisal. Finally, and a major weakness for capital budgeting purposes, relative to stock exchange portfolio analysis, the β values for each investment proposal must of necessity be far more subjective in their construction and in their comparisons with the portfolio of ongoing projects than will the β values calculated from historic stock market data.

14.7 Dividend distribution

The level of dividends paid to equity holders is the most obvious link between a firm and its owners. Moreover, given that the objective of the firm is to maximise shareholder wealth we know from equation (14.18) just how important dividends are to that objective:

$$P_0 = \frac{D_0}{r - g}$$

(14.18)

Consider Figure 14.21. The curve AB is the *physical investment line* (*PIL*) open to the firm in a two-period model and connects all possible physical investment: dividend distribution combinations in time t_0. Thus at point D, OC is distributed, CA is retained, and OE is the amount available for distribution in t_1 as a consequence of retaining and reinvesting AC. Projects available to the firm are assumed to be ranked in descending order of attractiveness.

Thus projects which could be funded with AC are more attractive than those which can be funded with OC. Hence the curve is simply a variant of a product transformation curve, the two axes representing shareholder consumable income in t_0 and t_1. The appropriate dividend can be obtained by superimposing on the figure shareholder indifference curves which would reflect owners' time preferences. (These would be convex to the origin.)

The highest indifference curve (U_3) would then indicate the optimal level of distribution. However, if we introduce the *financial market line*, FG, it is possible because of the presence of capital markets, where shareholders can borrow and lend to increase shareholder utility, and/or take account of different shareholders having different time preferences. This development is a corollary of the separation theorem employed in Figure 14.17.

It enables us in this instance to ignore all possible distribution:retention combinations except the existing one at point D. It assumes a perfect capital market and the angle GFO is consequently equal to $1 + r$ where r is the rate of interest in that

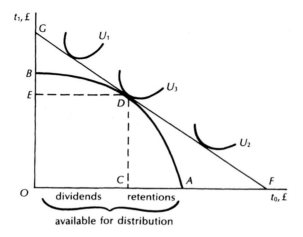

Figure 14.21

market. Thus to the left of C, U_1 is a utility indifference curve of a shareholder still receiving his or her proportion of OC in dividends, but whose time preference indicates that he or she will lend to the capital market to reduce his or her income today in order to increase it tomorrow. U_2 is a utility indifference curve of a shareholder dissatisfied with the current level of dividends (and so his or her proportion of OC) but who borrows today to increase his or her current income.

Thus if shareholders can use the capital market in this way, firms should simply invest all available distributable funds in all projects with a positive NPV, i.e. they should always move from A to D. This notion underlies the Modigliani and Miller 'dividend irrelevancy' notion.

Again MM depends on the assumptions of a perfect market and again their propositions have provoked controversy. If we introduce market imperfections into the discussion, the argument that dividend policy is irrelevant as a financing decision becomes less tenable. First, there are information effects. Managers are generally reluctant to cut dividends. Thus, any rise in the dividend rate carries with it the presumption that it will be maintained. The increase itself consequently carries information to investors that management has higher expectations for the future, due to the manager's possession of more intimate knowledge of the firm's prospects. Conversely this information perceived to be carried by the dividend can be faulty or misinterpreted. Static dividends may conceal more than they reveal.

Second, we have tax effects. Depending upon the individual investor's marginal tax rate, he or she will or will not prefer frequent income distributions to capital accretion. Clearly, this will depend upon the mix of both current and potential shareholders in the firm. Finally, transaction costs exist. It is much cheaper administratively for a firm to retain profits than to raise sums through the new issue market. Conversely, the individual investor may prefer generous dividends since, to the investor, to realise capital for current consumption purposes involves the brokerage costs of selling shares. The picture is very muddy.

This concludes our discussion of capital budgeting. Of all the topics covered in this book, this is the area where the theoretical advance has been most rapid in the last two decades. Whether practitioners have kept up with these advances, indeed whether it is practical so to do, is regarded by many as an open question.

| *Appendix 14* |

Table of discount factors

Table A14.1 shows the present value of £1 discounted for different numbers of years and at different rates of discount.

Table A14.1

Year	5%	6%	7%	8%	9%	10%	12%	14%	16%	18%	20%
						Rate of discount					
0	1.000	1.000	1.000	1.000	1.000	1.000	1.000	1.000	1.000	1.000	1.000
1	0.952	0.943	0.935	0.926	0.917	0.909	0.893	0.877	0.862	0.847	0.033
2	0.907	0.890	0.873	0.857	0.842	0.826	0.797	0.769	0.743	0.718	0.694
3	0.864	0.840	0.816	0.794	0.772	0.751	0.712	0.675	0.641	0.609	0.579
4	0.823	0.792	0.763	0.735	0.708	0.683	0.636	0.592	0.552	0.516	0.482
5	0.784	0.747	0.713	0.681	0.650	0.621	0.567	0.519	0.476	0.437	0.402
6	0.746	0.705	0.666	0.630	0.596	0.564	0.507	0.456	0.410	0.370	0.335
7	0.711	0.665	0.623	0.583	0.547	0.513	0.452	0.400	0.354	0.314	0.279
8	0.677	0.627	0.582	0.540	0.502	0.467	0.404	0.351	0.305	0.266	0.233
9	0.645	0.592	0.544	0.500	0.460	0.424	0.361	0.308	0.263	0.225	0.194
10	0.614	0.558	0.508	0.463	0.422	0.386	0.322	0.270	0.227	0.191	0.162
15	0.481	0.417	0.362	0.315	0.275	0.239	0.183	0.140	0.108	0.084	0.065
20	0.377	0.312	0.258	0.215	0.178	0.149	0.104	0.073	0.051	0.037	0.026
25	0.295	0.233	0.184	0.146	0.116	0.092	0.059	0.038	0.024	0.016	0.010

Notes

1. The underlying reason for the NPV rule is that NPV is the value today of the surplus which the project earns over the amount the firm could earn by putting its money into the next-best project (which would give a rate of return equal to r). To understand this, consider a project costing £10 with a single cash inflow of £22 in year one. Let the return on the best alternative project be 10%. The cash inflow of the £22 is worth only £20 (= 22/1.10) today, that is, after we have removed the amount we could have earned with the best alternative project during our one year's wait. But our project cost £10. So the value today, of the project net of its outlay *and also after the opportunity cost has been removed*, is £20 – £10 = £10. But notice how this was obtained:

   $$-10 + [22/(1 + r)]$$

   in other words: NPV.

2. The earnings yield is the net profit earned per share expressed as a percentage of the market price of a share. Generally, it is calculated after Corporation Tax, hence the use of the word net. For cost of capital purposes, it is usually grossed up to include Corporation Tax liability. This is done to ensure that the cost difference between the two sources of funds due to differences in tax treatment is not overlooked.

Bibliography

Brealey, R. and Myers, S. (1988) *Principles of Corporate Finance*, 3rd edn, McGraw-Hill.
Bromwich, M. (1976) *The Economics of Capital Budgeting*, Penguin.
Copeland, T. E. and Weston, J. F. (1988) *Financial Theory and Corporate Policy*, 3rd edn, Addison Wesley.

Hawkins, C. J. and Pearce, D. W. (1971) *Capital Investment Appraisal*, Macmillan.

Hirst, I. R. C. (1988) *Business Investment Decisions*, Philip Allan.

Levy, H. and Sarnat, M. (1978) *Capital Investment and Financial Decisions*, Prentice Hall.

Lumby, S. (1988) *Investment Appraisal*, Nelson.

Modigliani, F. and Miller, M. H. (1958) 'The cost of capital, corporation finance and the theory of investment', *American Economic Review*, vol. 48.

Moles, P. and Williams, G. (1993) *Privately Funded Infrastructure in the UK: An analysis of the Skye Bridge Project*, Centre for Financial Markets Research, Working Paper 93.3.

Pike, R. H. (1988) 'An empirical study of the adoption of sophisticated capital budgeting practises and decision-making effectiveness', *Accounting and Business Research*, vol. 18.

Reinhardt, U. E. (1973) 'Breakeven analysis for Lochheed's Tristar: an application of financial theory', *Journal of Finance*, vol. 28.

Samuels, J. M., Wilkes, F. M. and Brayshaw, R. E. (1990) *Management of Company Finance*, 5th edn, Chapman & Hall.

Van Horne, J. (1980) *Financial Management and Policy*, Prentice Hall.

Chapter 15

Product, market and corporate strategies

Traditionally neo-classical economics has addressed itself to problems of value allocation. Whether buyers and sellers have been many or few, relationships between them have been examined as though they were impersonal and as though the participants were indifferent to the characteristics of their opposite numbers in the market-place. All of the factors which go to make up transactions costs were ignored. So too were the characteristics and relationships which existed within the firm. Yet it is these characteristics (and the fact that buyers and sellers are not indifferent to their fellow traders) which result in value creation by the business enterprise as opposed to value allocation by some abstract market mechanism.

Certainly real life exchange (in the market-place) creates value, but only because successful firms have produced high quality (desirable) products at low (affordable) costs and have done so either more successfully (with higher quality attributes) than competing firms and/or done so at lower costs. To create value, firms must continuously be involved in the strategic process of examining how best to satisfy their unique and varying customers' requirements, given their own technological base and with the understanding that their ever-changing rivals are also intent on doing so. Neither customers' rivals, nor their technology can be regarded as impersonal 'givens'. In earlier chapters we have examined how contracts can be designed to facilitate exchanges, minimise transaction costs and maximise resultant joint value or wealth (the Coase Theorem in practice) between traders. In this chapter we tend to look rather at how heterogeneous traders strive continuously to differentiate themselves not only from their rivals but also from what they themselves were in the immediate past.

There are three broad strategic decisions firms can take. These are horizontal, vertical and lateral integration. Horizontal integration can refer to the action by which a firm introduces new products which, while not contributing to the present product line, cater for market needs which lie within the industry of which the firm is a member; requiring similar manufacturing and production know-how. For example, if a car firm extended its interests to the light commercial-van market different vehicles would be required. None the less cross-elasticity of supply is high. The same engines could be used for both vehicles. The wheels and tyres could be common and production workers on the assembly line could be readily and cheaply switched from one vehicle to the other with few learning costs. Vertical integration can be either backward or forward in nature. Backward integration is where the firm begins to manufacture products previously purchased from others in order to utilise them in making its original product line. (A vehicle firm moving into glass windshield production would be an example.) The firm begins to carry out different but successive stages in the production of its original output. Where the firm moves nearer the final market for its product and carries out a function previously undertaken by a customer, the activity is called forward integration. Vertical integration means that the firm has chosen to conduct certain activities within its organisation rather than through the market place. (An example would be the decision by a car manufacturer to own its own dealership outlets.) When and why a firm will prefer administered transactions to arm's length trading will depend on the costs and consequences (both technological costs and transactions costs). Lateral integration or 'pure' diversification occurs when the firm moves into areas totally unrelated to its existing activities, either on the side of supply or demand. (For example, on the supply side – a car firm moving into book publishing, or on the demand side, a firm which previously only sold in Europe deciding to begin car sales and/or production in the Americas.)

15.1 The decision to integrate vertically

Recall that the Coase Theorem asserts that absent transactions costs joint value-maximising decisions will be taken and trading will occur. Recall also that transactions costs are crucial in real life markets and that 'production' costs (Matthews), while perhaps predominant, are not the only decision parameter when deciding whether to trade, not to trade, or to arrange one's business affairs in some other manner such as vertical integration.

When production costs take centre stage the decision of whether to vertically integrate depends on three main groups of reasons: security, efficiency and strategic or predatory causes.

15.1.1 Security

Austin Robinson has argued that traditionally the main reason for vertical integration is 'a search for security'. When demand conditions are high and competing manufacturers are outbidding each other for supplies it may make good sense to integrate backwards and have an assured source of materials of a quality and quantity one can dictate. Conversely, if demand is slack and manufacturers are competing for business it can be sensible to integrate forwards and so be assured of 'customer' loyalty.

15.1.2 Efficiency

Where vertical integration results in 'production' cost reduction it is a form of scale economy since, *ceteris paribus*, a vertically integrated firm is larger than a non-integrated one. Four main sources of such increased efficiency are available:

1. *Engineering economies*: the classic example is the combining of iron production with rolling-mill operations into a single integrated steel manufacturing process. The need to reheat the iron is removed if the processes are carried out in quick succession.
2. *Marketing economies*: clearly delivery charges are reduced if plants are located in close proximity. Savings are also possible without physical nearness. Advertising and sales promotion expenditure can be pruned when the loyalty of 'customers' is guaranteed. Economies also arise when transactions are carried out continually between the same people. Search and negotiation efforts are reduced when transactions become habitual. Repetition fosters the development of routine, reliable, and so low-cost, information flows.
3. *Financial economies*: capital costs are lower in an integrated firm because stocks can generally be held at lower levels. An integrated firm can co-ordinate rates of production and consumption in the various stages of the firm so as to lessen the need to hold contingency and buffer stocks. A firm can also find it easier and cheaper to raise capital if it can gain investors' confidence by indicating that one particular element of risk has been reduced (namely by a guaranteed source of supply or a captive market).
4. *Administrative economies*: strategic reasons for vertical integration can be seen as the desire for security writ large. Forward integration can secure a market but it can also foreclose it to competitors. One cannot buy McEwans beers in a pub owned by Watneys. Backward integration can guarantee a reliable source of supply but it can also prevent rivals gaining access to that source; or it can ensure that their costs are raised disadvantageously if the price charged to them is higher than the price charged in an intra-firm transfer. By this analysis, vertical integration is a deliberate investment in entry barriers.

Box 15.1 gives a typical example of vertical integration (forwards and backwards carried out for security and efficiency reasons.

Transactions costs writers, however, would argue that the decision to vertically integrate is dependent more on transactions costs than on production costs. Indeed they would redefine many of the above production-cost savings as having transactions costs roots. (Even the heat-saving iron and steel example has been analysed in this way.) In transactions costs analysis the objective of economic actors is not assumed to be that of optimising the allocation of scarce resources to obtain a particular output, rather the objective is to ascertain the costs of trade and to set up transactions in such a way that the gains of trade are maximised.

The two underlying assumptions of transactions costs analyses are first that buyers and sellers contract with each other subject to bounded rationality. Information is incomplete, is costly to acquire, and while all participants think full

---

| Box 15.1 |

Vertical integration in milling, bread baking and food retailing

Although bakers existed in London in the 11th century, in non-metropolitan areas as late as 1804 even towns such as Manchester (population 100,000) had no commercial bakers. By 1850, however, the number of commercial bakers had risen to 50 000, bread being baked and sold on the premises.

By the 20th century economies of scale in manufacture and distribution resulted in dramatic changes in this structure. Technological advances such as 'travelling ovens' (hot tunnels with a conveyor running through them) permitted large scale plants while the constraint of perishability was overcome by road transport.

Plant bakeries supplying a number of branches grew from 11 firms serving 265 outlets in 1906 to 69 firms serving 2659 outlets in 1950. In addition the plant bakers sold through dairies, grocers and general stores (22% of their output in 1938, rising to 60% by 1965).

Simultaneously retailers such as Lyons integrated backwards into bread production in 1939, becoming a major producer by 1950.

Meanwhile scale economies in flour milling (due to the development of the roller mill) encouraged the emergence of larger and fewer mills. By 1935, only 2,600 millers remained, 39% of the output being controlled by Ranks, Spillers and the CWS (Co-operative Wholesale Society). By 1944 this had risen to 66%.

On the retailing and baking side Garfield Weston, a Canadian entrepreneur, formed Allied Bakeries which by 1954 owned 72 plants and 642 shops. Weston was refused discounts on his purchases of flour, and so once postwar bans on flour imports were lifted, promptly imported cheaper flour, so eventually wresting price concessions from local mills. The domestic millers reacted too late in giving price concessions, and Allied began to integrate backwards, by 1962 owning 29 mills.

In the next 20 years Ranks merged with Hovis McDougall to form RHM Ltd and its subsidiary British Bakeries acquired an additional 700 production or distribution firms by 1976. In 1970 the CWS merged its interests with Lyons, and in 1971 with Spillers. The resulting merged firm was insufficiently competitive, successfully to rival RHM and ABF (Allied's revised title Associated British Foods), in a market with declining demand. (Bread is an inferior good). In 1978 Spillers ceased operations closing 10 bakeries and selling off the remaining 13 to RHM and ABF.

Source abstracted from Reekie 1978.

information would be 'nice to have' they perceive that it is more economical (less costly) to initiate and monitor trading relationships with each other under some governance structure such as vertical integration which departs from the classical, market contracting mode.

Second, transactions costs economics assumes opportunism. This is a stronger assumption than the normal classical belief that individuals are self-seeking. Here 'self-seeking with guile' is admitted. That is individuals trade with each other not only with incomplete information but each is motivated to a greater or lesser degree to conceal information which he does have to make the terms of trade finally agreed upon less favourable to the other. *Ex ante* opportunism, or adverse selection and *ex post* opportunism, moral hazard, both exist.

As Williamson points out (p. 67) where opportunism and bounded rationality are both absent a 'state of bliss' can exist. There are no transactions costs. Admit opportunism and long-term 'comprehensive contracts' between traders are required if the problems arising from opportunistic behaviour are to be eliminated. The drawing-up and monitoring of such contracts or alternative governance structures involves incurring transactions costs. Admit bounded rationality without opportunism and the comprehensiveness of the contracting procedure can be replaced with 'general clause contracts' where the traders agree freely to divulge all pertinent information to each other and to behave co-operatively during contract execution and at contract renewal. Allow both opportunism and bounded rationality to be present and the transactional problems or costs become very high.

The transactions costs problem then becomes one of devising a governance structure other than a perfectly classical trading market which economises on bounded rationality whilst simultaneously safeguarding transactions against opportunistic hazards.

Even in transactions costs economics, a key issue is still choice among alternatives. Given non-zero transactions costs, *which* governance structure (including standard, perfect market classical contracting) will maximise the net gains from trade (given that trading involves planning and adapting contracts, executing and monitoring them through to completion, and contract renewal)? The passage of time is seen as important (as with experience and learning curves, but unlike conventional cost theory).

Time is crucial in transactions costs analysis due to what Williamson calls the 'fundamental transformation' (p. 61). When contracts or trades are initiated there are typically large numbers of bidders. The terms of the trade will depend on the degree to which collusion exists or could exist between the varying suppliers (or demanders). This much is mainstream and reaches its ultimate in monopoly or monopsony. Transactions costs analysis, however, goes beyond the day on which the contract is drawn up to the periods beyond, namely, contract execution, and indeed renewal. The fundamental transformation (not taken account of in conventional analysis) is that the relatively large numbers of bidders at the date of contract agreement could well become a relatively small number during the execution and renewal stages. The reason (not always present) is that once a trade has been entered into suppliers will be supported by transaction-specific human or physical assets. (Human assets include know-how but also know-who. Thus familiarity and trust are opportunism-attenuating assets.) Once such assets are in place (the asset-specificity condition), existing market participants are more likely to continue meeting with each other than with outsiders. (On the supply side the asset will have a much higher value in use in contract renewal than in alternative uses; on the demand side the buyer presumably will be unable to find a supplier with such a transaction specific asset, or if the buyer can find one who is willing to create it, it is presumably unlikely that it would be available on terms as favourable as those provided by existing suppliers.) There are hold-up problems.

Thus the presence of bounded rationality and opportunism both encourage the emergence of the fundamental transformation especially when asset specificity is present. Indeed asset specificity is a necessary (but not sufficient) condition for vertical integration (or at least for some substitute governance structure). Economics, and most especially industrial economics then may well reduce to what Buchanan called a 'science of contracts' rather than a 'science of choice' (cited in Williamson, 1985, p. 29). The contracting process can be one of centralised planning, mutual co-operation, conventional competition or governance structure selection. Planning requires full information. Co-operation (promise) requires the absence of opportunism while competition is infeasible over time given asset specificity. Table 15.1 summarises this discussion. Economising on bounded rationality while safeguarding against opportunism requires a non-competitive contracting process, such as vertical integration in the presence of asset specificity.

Thus this line of argument shows why even vertical integration of a smelter and a rolling mill can be explained in transactions costs and not merely production cost terms.

15.1.3 Alternatives to vertical integration

What openings are available to firms which enable them to capture some of the benefits without incurring the costs of formal integration? We will examine three: partial vertical disintegration, exclusive franchising and the exercise of contervailing power.

Partial vertical disintegration

Here the firm would vertically integrate large portions of its business, but it would stop short of total integration. One example of this is provided by the Walls ice cream division of Unilever. Walls is also in the transport business with a large fleet of refrigerated trucks. In order to avoid having large numbers of expensive lorries lying idle in winter (when demand is low) Walls own a basic fleet, but in times of high demand, rents refrigerated vehicles.

Table 15.1 Attributes of the contracting process

Behavioural assumptions			
Bounded rationality	Opportunism	Asset specificity	Implied contracting process
No	Yes	Yes	Planning
Yes	No	Yes	Promise
Yes	Yes	No	Competition
Yes	Yes	Yes	Governance

Source: Williamson, 1985, p. 31.

Exclusive franchising

The granting of sole rights of resale to a particular customer in a specific trade or locality provides many of the economies in transportation and promotion which are obtained by ownership of outlets without the associated costs of capital outlay and day-by-day management. Moreover a poor dealer can probably be dispensed with and replaced more readily than a poorly located but wholly owned retail site. Motor car distributorships and dealerships are common examples of this type of franchising operation. Car firms tend only to award franchises to garages who adhere to certain standards of stock holding and who provide specified service facilities.

'Exclusive franchising is a good example of how transactions costs analysis explains an activity better than conventional theory. Transactions costs are the economic equivalent of friction in physical systems' (Williamson, 1985, p. 19), therefore what might be regarded *prima facie* as a market or monopolistic imperfection in a no-transactions costs framework, might simply be observation of a governance structure created to gain the benefits of trade at least cost. For example, franchising, which is essentially a refusal to supply non-approved potential buyers, could well be regarded as anti-competitive in traditional analysis (or predatory or strategic). Under transactions costs analysis the probability is that the contract exists to safeguard transactions. For example non-franchisees cannot free ride on franchiser promotion, nor can they shift costs of lower quality on to the whole franchise network since strict quality controls are implemented, for example, by purchase inputs agreement as well as by inspection.

Thus, in fast-food franchising such as MacDonalds or Kentucky Fried Chicken, franchisees get the benefits of national advertising, while the franchiser, in structuring the contract will ensure that clauses are inserted providing for quality inspection so that no one franchise holder can readily damage the brand image of the network (the specific asset). Contracts will be drawn up so that benefits and costs are concentrated on those who make the relevant investments (failure to concentrate benefits means others can 'free ride', failure to concentrate costs invites incomplete compliance).

The exercise of countervailing power

A firm may be able to exercise buying strength if it is large relative to suppliers. It can force prices down to a near competitive level. Simultaneously it can ensure that supplies are tailored to its own specification and requirements. This is a relationship not unlike that which Marks & Spencer had for many years with the then highly fragmented garment manufacturing industry. The benefits for the manufacturer were continuity of custom and access to technological and administrative know-how. Alternatively countervailing power may be used to offset the monopoly or monopsony selling or buying power of the other party to a trade.

5.1.4 Loyalty rebates

Price discriminatory practices such as 'loyalty rebates' (where the buyer gets a lower price not because of order size but because of cumulative purchase volume to date) may be seen (traditionally) as anti-competitive on a pre-contractual basis, or less conventionally, they may be a means of lowering transactions costs over both pre- and post-contractual periods The seller has to expend less resources in marketing and the buyer gains by having his search costs lowered and has the incentive of a lower price to participate.

All of these (and other) institutional alternatives to vertical integration may well be required for transactions costs reasons but be more efficient as governance struc- tures than integration as such. Forward integration may be less efficient if the distributors are highly diversified into slots alien to the manufacturer's expertise. Similar products might not be readily available to customers from other manu- facturers if they in turn felt uneasy about possible opportunistic behaviour by a fully integrated retail firm. Finally, management of self-owned outlets may (or may not) have less incentive to provide the same standard of service that franchisees would have.

15.2 Managerial implications of vertical integration

Two main areas of managerial discretion are of interest once the integration decision has been taken. How should the firm price in its final market? Under what conditions should the divisions of the newly integrated firm trade with each other? Or, to phrase it differently, what interdivisional transfer price policies should be pursued?

15.2.1 Final market behaviour

Whether price (and conversely output) should rise, fall or remain unchanged after integration depends on the firm's original decision and the reasoning behind it.

15.2.2 Security motivation

If an integration exercise is carried out for security reasons alone (i.e. if recorded cost schedules are unchanged) then price will remain unchanged. We need consider only three cases under differing initial conditions or market structure to illustrate this.[1]

1. *Vertical integration between two perfect competitors*: consider the perfect competitor operating at the earlier stage of production (Stage I) and the similar firm operating at the later stage (Stage II). After integration the combined firm faces an unchanged final demand situation and since costs are unchanged has an identical

aggregate cost function. The price and output of Stage II will consequently remain unaltered. If the price at which the intermediate product is transferred from Stage I to Stage II changes as a result of integration, this will affect the profits earned by the individual stages but not the aggregate profit of the firm.

2. *Vertical integration between a monopoly and one perfect competitor*: the outcome in this situation would be the same as in case (1) above and for analogous reasons.

3. *Vertical integration between a monopoly and all firms in a perfectly competitive industry*: consider, firstly, the situation where the monopolist is operating at Stage II and the competitive industry is responsible for the earlier stage. Given his or her costs of production, including the cost of purchasing the output of Stage I, the monopolist will already be operating at the profit-maximising $MR = MC$ output level. That part of the monopolist's average cost (AC) curve which represents the inputs bought from the competitive industry will be equal to the competitive industry's supply curve (i.e. the prices at which the competitive industry would supply certain outputs). After integration this is still the case, except that these inputs will no longer be bought in but will be manufactured within the one firm. The AC curve and so the MC curve will remain unaltered.

Consider secondly, the situation where the monopolist is operating at Stage I, and integrates forward. It might seem in this situation that output would be reduced as Stage II is monopolised. However, the impact of monopoly at Stage I will already have affected the price:output decisions of the competitive industry at Stage II. Integration will merely result in a change of ownership of Stage II (again assuming no cost change as a result of monopolisation).

Figure 15.1 explains case (3). For simplicity we assume that one unit of output of Stage I is required to produce one unit of output of Stage II. This enables us to make direct comparisons between the revenue and cost functions of each stage. Also we assume a horizontal AC_{II} curve. Before integration the monopolist's demand curve (D_I) is derived from the given market determined final demand (D_{II}) by deducting the cost (AC_{II}) of transforming the monopolist's output into the final product. AC_{II} is defined so as *not* to include the purchase costs of inputs from Stage I, it is

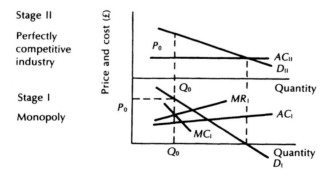

Figure 15.1

the AC of *processing* raw materials bought from Stage I. Since Stage II is perfectly competitive, each firm's price level will be equal to its marginal and its average costs in equilibrium. Thus at any price, say P_0, that price will equal average processing costs (AC_{II}) plus the monopolist's raw material selling price – the average costs of buying raw materials. Given this derived demand curve the monopolist will produce at output level Q_0 where $MR_1 = MC_1$ at price P_0. After integration the monopolist's demand curve becomes D_{II} (i.e. $D_1 + AC_{II}$) and his or her unit cost curve becomes $AC_1 + AC_{II}$. For both D_{II} and ($AC_1 + AC_{II}$) there will be corresponding marginal functions (MR_{II} and MC_{II}). Where these functions are equated the monopolist will maximise profits. This must be at output level Q_0. At that output level the corresponding marginal values for D_1, and AC_1, were equated. But if at Q_0 $MR_1 = MC_1$ (which it did) then the slope of $TR_1 =$ the slope of TC_1 at Q_0, but both D_1 and AC_1 have been increased by the identical value AC_{II} in order to obtain D_{II} and ($AC_1 + AC_{II}$). If at any Q both TR_1 and TC_1 have been raised by the identical amount $Q \times AC_{II}$ to give the corresponding total values TR_{II} and TC_{II} for the integrated firm, then between any two output levels, say a and b, the increase in TR_b minus the increase in TR_a equals the change in the slope of TR between a and b (ΔMR) as a consequence of integration.[2] By analogy between a and b the change in TC, pre-, and post-integration, is merely the change in MC. Therefore since the changes in TR and TC at any output level result in identical changes in MR and MC, the output level where $MR = MC$ is also unchanged.

15.2.3 Cost reduction

If the motivation behind the vertical integration is that of increasing efficiency the AC function of the integrated firm will be lower than the sum of the AC functions of the individual stages. If the cost saved is an overhead or fixed cost, then output will remain unchanged. For example, if two firms at succeeding stages integrate and the combined firm does away with a fixed cost such as a now redundant head office for one of the stages. The TC curve is reduced by an identical amount at each and every output level. The slope of the TC curve is consequently unchanged, marginal cost remains the same. With unchanged demand conditions, the output level where $MR = MC$ will also be unchanged. If the cost saving is one which varies with output (e.g. the elimination of the need to reheat each unit of output between Stages I and II) then MC will be altered. Generally when the cost saving rises with output, MC will shift to the right, price will be lowered and output will be increased. Alternatively on the rarer occasions when the costs saved fall with output, MC will move to the left and output will be reduced.

15.2.4 Strategic and predatory reasons

Two sets of circumstances exist where a vertical integration exercise can result in a changed pattern of industrial behaviour without any accompanying change in

demand or cost conditions. One is where an opportunity to practise price discrimination emerges as a result of the integration exercise. The other is where the
integration is between the two sides of a bilateral monopoly.

The emergence of an opportunity to practise price discrimination

Forward integration may make price discrimination possible for the first time. If a
monopolist in Stage I acquires some customers operating in Stage II, he or she can
ensure that there will be no leakage or resale between subsidiaries and extra-group
customers operating independently in other segments of the market which is Stage
II. Before integration the segments might have been insufficiently sealed off, one
from the other, to enable the monopolist to charge discriminatory prices.

In some conditions (for example those of Figure 11.4 in Chapter 11) output will
remain unchanged, only the allocation of that output between market segments will
differ as a result of the price discrimination. In others, however, the given cost and
demand conditions facing Stage I may be such that the practice of price discrimination will result in output being increased. This is illustrated in Figure 15.2.

Consider first the situation before integration. There are two (or more) market
segments with differing demand elasticities, but price discrimination is not possible.
For practical purposes the firm is consequently faced not with two differing demand
curves, but with one, ΣAR which is obtained by summing the individual demand
curves in each segment horizontally. The relevant marginal revenue curve for ΣAR
is the discontinuous version of ΣMR (represented by a dashed line). The finite
discontinuity in ΣMR is caused by the kink in ΣAR which in turn has resulted from
the horizontal summation of the demand curves in the individual segments.

The unintegrated firm with a marginal cost curve of MC_a will produce at output
level ΣQ_1 and price P_1. Similarly the unintegrated firm whose marginal cost curve
is MC_b will produce at output level ΣQ_2 and price P_2. In both cases these are the

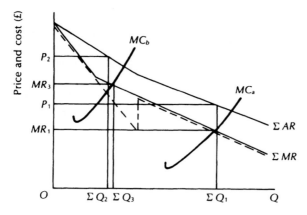

Figure 15.2

relevant price:output combinations indicated by the intersection of the relevant MC curve and the discontinuous version of ΣMR.

After integration and the appearance of the opportunity to price discriminate between segments, ΣAR ceases to have practical relevance. The firm is now interested in and can take advantage of the demand curves in the individual segments. For decision making purposes the relevant ΣMR curve is now obtained by summing the MR curve in each segment horizontally to obtain the continuous line version of ΣMR.

The integrated firm with MC_a as its MC curve will continue to produce ΣQ_1. The prices charged in the market segments will be found by setting output in each segment at the level where the respective MRs equal ΣMR and the prices then obtained from the segment demand curves accordingly. The integrated firm whose cost conditions are represented by MC_b, however, will increase its output from ΣQ_2 to ΣQ_3 where MC_b intersects the continuous version of ΣMR. Price and output levels in each segment will be found in the usual way by equating each segment's marginal revenue at MR_3.

Vertical integration between a monopolist and a monopsonist (bilateral monopoly)

Consider a monopolist at Stage I before integration, with marginal cost curve MC_1 in Figure 15.3. At fixed or agreed prices the monopolist would be prepared to supply the quantities indicated by this curve, since then his or her marginal cost would equal his or her (constant) marginal revenue. A monopsonist at Stage II must then regard MC_1 as the unit (net of processing) purchase cost curve facing him or her for the product (AC_{II}). The curve marginal to this, MC_{II}, is consequently the marginal purchasing cost of the product to the monopsonist. Given that the monopsonist's net marginal revenue curve (net of processing costs) is indicated by NMR_{II}, the unintegrated monopsonist would profit maximise at output level Q_2 where NMR_{II} and MC_{II} intersect. This would require an agreed transfer price of P_2.

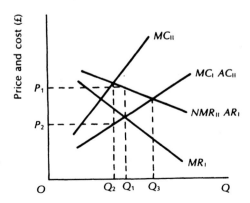

Figure 15.3

On the other hand NMR_{II} indicates the quantities the monopsonist would be willing to purchase at any given fixed or agreed price, since then his or her net marginal revenue would equal his or her (constant) marginal purchasing cost for the product. A monopolist at Stage I must then regard NMR_{II} as the demand curve facing him or her for the product (AR_I). The curve marginal to this MR_I is consequently the seller's marginal revenue curve. As a result, the monopolist's profit-maximising output level is Q_1 where MR_I and MC_I intersect. This would require an agreed transfer price of P_1.

The objectives of the two firms are inconsistent. Without integration we can only indicate that the agreed price will lie somewhere between the two extremes of P_1 and P_2. Where the agreement will be will depend on factors such as bargaining skill and negotiating expertise. After integration, however, output will be higher than either Q_1 or Q_2. The two stages will then maximise joint profits by exploiting their suppliers and customers and not as in the above discussion also attempting to exploit each other. This case is discussed more fully under transfer pricing below.

15.2.5 Transfer pricing

When firms integrate vertically they may suffer from managerial diseconomies of scale. One way out of this problem is to employ an M-form (multidivisional) organisation rather than a U-form (unitary) structure. Managers become responsible for their own profit and loss account.

Each division is a profit centre in its own right. The inefficient manager is then no longer 'concealed' in the overall accounts of the company, and the efficient manager is more highly motivated because his or her merits are highlighted. However, divisional autonomy creates its own problems, one of which is transfer pricing. What price should be charged by one division for the products it sells to another? Should the sister division be compelled to buy at the price asked? The way these questions are answered will influence overall profits. They will also affect divisional profitability and so management morale and the long-run efficiency of the integrated firm.

Transfer pricing policy should have as its prime objective the maximisation of group profits. A second objective is to permit divisional managers to profit maximise as autonomous units. The transfer price rules which group management lay down must be such that both of these objectives can be pursued simultaneously. The general rule to accomplish these goals is that the transfer price should be equal to marginal cost, except when the transferred product can be bought and sold in a competitive market when it should equal the market price.

Transfer pricing of a product with a competitive market

Consider two independent firms: T, the earlier firm in the production process and F, the final or transferee firm, which processes the transferred product before selling it in the final market. In Figure 15.4 let D_T be the demand curve in the perfectly

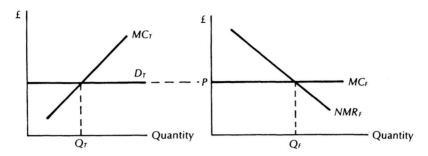

Figure 15.4

competitive market for the transferred product. MC_T is the marginal cost curve of firm T and NMR_F is the net marginal revenue curve of firm F.

It is obtained by deducting from the marginal revenue curve of F the marginal costs of processing and distribution which F incurs (i.e. all F's marginal costs but exclusive of the costs involved in purchasing the transferred product). MC_F is consequently equal to P, and is the cost of purchasing the good to be processed. The quantity axes are drawn on the same scales and unit for unit production is assumed. Both firms operate at their respective $MR = MC$ points, i.e. at Q_T and Q_F.

Now assume the firms integrate vertically. This is illustrated in Figure 15.5 where the panels of Figure 15.4 are superimposed on each other. The transfer price rule tells us that the divisions should continue to behave as if they were independent firms. The market price P should be selected as a transfer price and Q_T and Q_F produced by the respective divisions. This results in a shortfall of the transferred product of $Q_F - Q_T$. This should be made up by purchasing on the open market. No other position results in the group as a whole profit maximising. If, for example, T was compelled to make up the difference $Q_F - Q_T$, then the additional costs to T can be represented by the polygon $Q_T X Z Q_F$. Purchase in the open market, conversely,

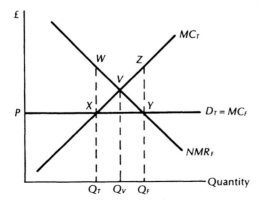

Figure 15.5

merely costs F the area $Q_T XYQ_F$. Group profits would be diminished by the triangle XYZ if T was compelled to produce Q_F. Similarly, if F restricted its output to Q_T units, then the group would suffer a loss in net profits equal to the triangle WXY. Q_V might appear to be the optimal output at first glance since there $MC_T = NMR_F$, or, adding the marginal costs of processing to both sides of this equation, it is where the group's $MC = MR$. But this is only the case if the external market is ignored, and to produce at Q_V would lose the firm XVY in profits. If, as in Figure 15.6, the optimal solution results in overproduction of the transferred product for F's requirement of $Q_T - Q_F$, then the surplus is merely sold in the open market.

If T restricted its output to Q_F it, and so the group, would forfeit net profits equal to area WXY. If F were compelled to absorb, process and sell Q_T units then the overall loss of profits would equal XYZ. (The additional net marginal revenue F would gain would equal the polygon $Q_T XZQ_F$. The addition to total costs of buying in the transferred product would, however, equal $Q_T XYQ_F$.) Similarly, where group MR = group MC, at Q_V, XYV would be forfeited if the external market were ignored.

When there is a perfect external market, transfer pricing is accomplished in practice by following the above rules and using the relevant calculus. Thus Stage I equates its own MR and MC. For this its own TC function is required and differentiation applied to obtain MC. Stage II's demand function is transformed in the usual manner into MR by differentiating TR (or with a linear demand curve doubling the slope). Since MR is a sterling value expressed in terms of Q – for example

$$MR_F = 100 - 0.5Q_F$$

then, to obtain NMR by deducting processing costs, the entire MR curve must be lowered on the monetary axis by that amount. Thus if the marginal processing costs are:

$$MC_F = 10 + 0.1Q_F$$
$$\Rightarrow NMR_F = MR_F - MC_F = 90 - 0.6Q_F$$

the MR_F curve has been lowered by 10 along its length and the gradient increased by $0.1Q$. If the market price of the transferred product is $P = 10$, then this is set equal to NMR_F of Stage II and the optimal output of Stage II is found. Thus:

$$10 = 90 - 0.6Q_F$$
$$\Rightarrow Q_F = 133.33$$

If the MC_T of Stage I is

$$MC_T = 5 + 0.01Q_T$$

then Stage I's output is where

$$P_T = 10 = 5 + 0.01Q_T$$
$$\Rightarrow Q_T = 500$$

(a surplus of approximately 366 units to be sold on the open market.)

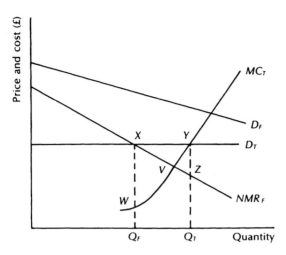

Figure 15.6

Transfer pricing with no external market

Here interdivisional transfers should be priced at the level of the marginal cost of production. Operating independence for the divisions implies a situation of bilateral monopoly. Figure 15.7 illustrates that group profit maximisation is at output Q_V where $MC_T = NMR_F$. This is true because if we add the marginal costs of processing and distribution to both sides of the equation we deduce that group marginal costs equal MR_F which in this case is also group marginal revenue since the only demand

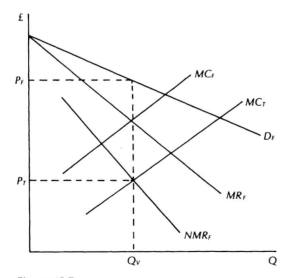

Figure 15.7

curve the group faces is D_F. The objectives of the group in this instance include the desire to prevent the divisions exploiting each other at group expense as the firms did in Figure 15.3. To achieve this, two additional constraints are required. Either F or T must have its pricing freedom removed, and conversely and simultaneously T or F must not be permitted monopolistically to restrict output or monopsonistically to restrict purchasing by constructing marginal curves to NMR_F and MC_T respectively (as happened in Figure 15.3). This is explained below.

Figure 15.8 shows the alternative group and divisional profits if either of T or F depart from the transfer pricing rules. In Figure 15.8b T can increase π_T by exploiting the purchasing division, drawing a marginal curve to NMR_F and setting price and output where that marginal intersects MC_T. Group π, however, falls by

(a) following transfer price rule $\pi_f + \pi_T = $ group π

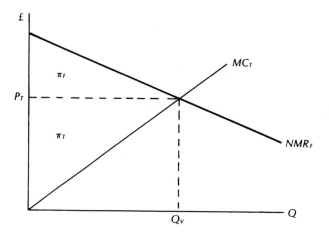

(b) breach of rule profit maximising by T   (c) breach of rule profit maximising by F

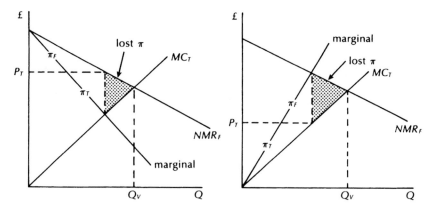

Figure 15.8

the amount of the shaded area. Alternatively in Figure 15.8c the purchasing division could exercise buying power by drawing a marginal to MC_T and restricting output to where that curve intersects NMR_F, forcing price down to P_T. π_F is then increased partly at the expense of π_T but partly as a consequence of lost group π.

To avoid these problems and accomplish simultaneously the objectives of group profit maximisation with divisional independence the transfer price rule can be implemented in either of two ways.

Either T can be given the NMR_F schedule and told to use it as a demand curve in the certain knowledge that F has already been instructed to be a price taker. That is T can be assured that F will accept whatever price T sets (but will of course, only purchase the quantity indicated on NMR_F). F's freedom is thus partially restricted. T's independence is likewise limited. It must be instructed not to draw a marginal to NMR_F. Given these limitations, in order to maximise its profits T will travel up its own (known) MC_T schedule until it intersects NMR_F. A transfer price of P_T (Figure 15.8a) will then be set since this maximises π_T given the constraints. Clearly T still has incentives to improve efficiency since if it can lower costs (and MC) it can expand output, increase π_T and lower P_T, thus simultaneously increasing $\pi_F + \pi_T$, namely group π.

Alternatively the same outcome can be arrived at by providing F's managers with the MC_T schedule and instructing them to regard it as their supply schedule to determine the transfer price they are willing to pay. Analogously they will know T is a price taker and that they must not exploit buying power by drawing a marginal to MC_T. Since NMR_F is effectively a gross marginal profit curve (gross only of the costs of the transferred product) inspection of Figure 15.8a shows they will willingly travel down NMR_F until it intersects MC_T, there π_F is maximised and P_T selected. Again incentives remain for F to increase its own processing efficiency. Since if it can reduce its own marginal costs of processing, NMR_F will shift up (recall $NMR_F = MR_F - MC$ processing), Q_V will be raised, P_T will rise, and π_F will also increase.

Transfer pricing with an imperfect external market

This case is simply an extension of the arguments put forward in the last example. The rule again is to price at the marginal cost of production of the transferred product. Figure 15.9 illustrates how this results in an optimal position for the group, while permitting profit-maximising autonomy for the divisions within the transfer pricing rules and constraints. Figure 15.9a shows the demand curve for the final division. D_F, and also NMR_F. In deciding on its profit-maximising level of output, division T will, as in the previous example, know that NMR_F is T's given demand curve. Again T will be instructed not to exploit F monopolistically by constructing another curve marginal to NMR_F in order to restrict output to maximise T's profits at the expense of F and the group. Figure 15.9b shows the demand curve for division T in its external market D_T, and the accompanying marginal revenue curve MR_T. Figure 15.9c has been constructed in a manner analogous to Figure 11.4 which illustrated how to obtain the profit-maximising output level when charging

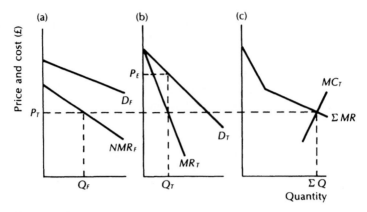

Figure 15.9

discriminatory prices between different market segments. NMR_F and MR_T have been horizontally aggregated to give ΣMR with which T can compare its marginal cost curve, MC_T.

The profit-maximising output level for T is ΣQ. Given that T must price at marginal cost when selling to F, T's profit-maximising distribution of ΣQ is where $\Sigma MR = NMR_F = MR_T$, that is, at output levels Q_F and Q_T. Price P_E will be charged in the external market, and P_T will be the relevant transfer price. A price of P_T will ensure that division F voluntarily purchases Q_F from T and so the group as a whole maximises profits.

15.3 **The decision to diversify**

15.3.1 Avoidance of risk

One major reason to diversify is to spread risk. The probability of loss in two markets simultaneously is always less than the probability of loss in either individually. Moreover, we know from equation (14.4) that the less closely markets (or securities in that instance) are correlated in terms of profit variability, the more stable will be the profit performance of a firm operating in each.

More specifically, firms can be affected by seasonal, cyclical and irregular factors. and by the direction of the overall market trend itself. If the trend is falling, a specialised firm will clearly wish to diversify so that total sales will not decline along with those of its primary market. Diversification to minimise the impact of seasonal, cyclical and irregular factors can also be undertaken.

Firms in seasonal-goods industries will diversify in order to keep plant fully utilised for the 12 months of the year; or to avoid having to build up stocks in seasons of lean demand; or to avoid the need to shed and re-engage labour, none of which is a costless alternative. The ideal is obviously to produce goods with a seasonal fluctuation inversely related to that of the original product (e.g. Christmas card firms may diversify into summer postcards). Pure risk *reduction* is preferable to pure risk averaging.

Firms in industries with a cyclical pattern of demand may diversify into areas with a sales pattern the reverse of the original. This may not prove as easy as with seasonal fluctuations but another way to obtain a sales cushion is to diversify into a cyclically stable industry. Irregular factors, of course, are wholly unpredictable. Diversification to avoid such uncertainty rests on the desire of the firm to avoid having all its commercial eggs in the one basket.

15.3.2 Growth and diversification economies

Firms also diversify because it appears to be a suitable route for corporate growth. Figure 15.10 illustrates the concept of why on occasion straightforward expansion of the existing product line is more profitable, and why at other times diversification is to be preferred. In Figure 15.10a, the firm's product transformation curve is FF'. Profit (or sales) maximisation occurs at point F, with production of OF units of Y and zero output of X. If the firm now expands its production capacity, its product transformation curve will shift out and up, say to GG'. If there are constant returns to scale then the curve must move outwards exactly in the same proportion along any straight line through the origin. This must be so to enable output to increase in exact proportion with the extra input resources. The curvature of GG' will be the same as that of FF'. The marginal rate of product transformation ($MRPT$) will consequently be the same at G as it was at F. Given unchanged prices, the point of tangency between GG' and an isorevenue line, such as TR', must then again be at the intersection with the y-axis. In this case it pays to remain a single product firm.

Now consider Figure 15.10b. Here the curvature of GG' is greater than FF'. Constant returns to scale are not present. If output of Y (or X) alone was increased by movement along the y- (or x-) axis, this could only be done by a smaller

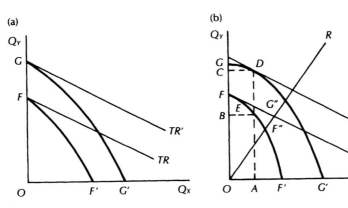

Figure 15.10

proportionate amount than could an increase in output of any combination of the two products by moving along a straight line such as OR (i.e. $FG/OF < F''G''/OF''$)

When diminishing returns are present the $MRPT$ will not be the same at G as at F. Expansion of the scale of operations will result in diversification. The optimal tangency point is now at D and production of both X and Y has become worthwhile.

What realities underlie those concepts? Why does GG' have a different curvature from FF'? Two interlinked factors are operating simultaneously. Diminishing returns have arisen in the production of Y, and economies not previously available have become present in the production of X. Even if there are economies of large-scale manufacture, the marketing costs associated with any particular output will probably rise with scale of production. Markets will become increasingly saturated. Advertising and promotion will become progressively less successful and the firm will move well up its S-shaped sales response function. (Alternatively, price will have to be reduced to clear the extra output. This changes the shape of the isorevenue line not the product transformation curve, but the result is the same.) Consequently, as the costs of producing Y increase, it is becoming cheaper, in opportunity cost terms, to produce X. In Figure 15.10b OA = one unit of X. Before growth, on curve FF', to move from F in order to produce one unit of X, FB units of Y had to be foregone. After growth, at G, in order to produce one unit of X only GC units of Y have to be forfeited.

In addition there is what Penrose (1980) called 'the continuing availability of unused productive services'. This can be subclassified as follows. First, there is the balance of processes. This is a principle generally explained by reference to the size of manufacturing plant required to utilise fully a range of machine types with differing and indivisible throughput capacities. Throughput must be large enough to equal the least common multiple (LCM) of the various maximum outputs from each machine type.

However, if we consider the whole range of resources in a firm, (managers, accountants, market researchers, sales force workers, engineers, research and development staff, and so on) it becomes apparent that to utilise fully all of these resources, human and/or physical, the LCM will be very large indeed in terms of output. Given market saturation for any one product, it is not surprising that diversification may often prove to be the most profitable way to achieve this large LCM.

Second, there is the similar economy of fully utilising specialised services. For example, if two products have common costs, a specialised firm in one product may diversify into the other so that it can achieve economies at the stage of common cost. This need not mean taking up slack as in the LCM case; it can do, but it can also include the attainment of any scale economies available at that point of common cost. Thus, a tinned soup manufacturer with his or her own tin-can factory may diversify into tinned fruits in order to lower the unit costs of the can factory.

15.3.3 The product life cycle and the experience curve

The above two reasons for diversification tend to depend on a static view of markets. A blend of two products with regular but non-correlated sales patterns is less risky

| Box 15.2 |

The early story of General Motors and the demand/technology product life cycle

In 1900, fifty-seven surviving American automobile firms, out of hundreds of contenders, produced some 4,000 cars, three-quarters of which ran on steam or electricity. Companies famous for other products were entering the fray. Among them were the makers of the Pope Bicycle, the Pierce Birdcage, the Peerless Wringer, the Buick Bathtub, the White Sewing Machine, and the Briscoe Garbage Can. All vied for the market with stationary-engine makers, machine-tool manufacturers, and spinoffs of leading carriage firms, Durant and Stude-baker. Among the less promising entrants seemed a lanky young engineer from Edison Illuminating Company named Henry Ford, whose Detroit Automobile Company produced twenty-five cars and failed in 1900. ...

Americans seemed willing to try anything – by 1900, there were some 200 different types of vehicles, from motorized Quadricycles to plush horseless broughams, using perhaps one hundred different modes of propulsion. Many of the early companies even propelled themselves without capital. Like the personal computer buffs to come – and the deluded DeLorean of the early 1980s – these early venturers would get the necessary cash from their own mail-order customers and dealers, and build the product only after the payment arrived.

As in virtually every new industry, it was impossible to tell, in the early years, who would prevail. Even after the gasoline motor was established, enterprises rose and fell frantically. In 1901, Ford began another company. But he soon left it after a conflict with the other shareholders. The companies that made five of the ten best-selling automobiles in 1903, including the leader, Colonel Pope's bicycle firm, went out of business within the decade. Ford, back again with $28,000 in capital and a new company named after himself, sold 658 cars of a two-cylinder design. He returned dolorously to the drawing board, an entre-preneurial failure for the third time. Of the ten top producers of 1924, only three had entered the industry by 1908. ...

The technological turning point, perhaps, was a fire in 1901 in the plant of Ransom Olds that destroyed all his elaborate equipment for producing electric Oldsmobiles, but allowed recovery of one rejected gasoline prototype. It became the first mass-produced car, selling 7,000 during the next three years. ... Ransom Olds was himself only a partial success. But ... played a seminal role in Michigan's auto industry. Not only did he assemble the strong men of varied disciplines needed for success, but he committed the industry to the internal combustion motor ... the gasoline motor freed autos from a chaos of competing fuels and engines. Finally the auto companies could offer a settled product. They could lure in the talent for mass production and marketing that was needed to bring cars from machine shops to mass consciousness ... and incidentally, drive most of the pioneers out of the business.

Willie Durant, who knew all about production and selling from his carriage business, decided it was time to move into cars after several months of driving a prototype containing David Buick's valve-in-head engine – the most powerful in the world for its size – through rural Michigan in 1904. Within four years, Durant was to parlay his sturdy Buick vehicle into domination of the automobile industry, with a 25 percent share of the market in 1908, the year he founded General Motors.

than specialisation. Secondly, costs may be lower even by comparative static analysis if a smaller less diversified firm is changed to a larger less specialised one.

This section concentrates on two complementary reasons for diversification which explicitly embrace the passage of time and do not simply examine two alternative time periods.

The first is the product life cycle: or as some writers (e.g. Ansoff 1984) define it: the demand/technology/product life cycle. Box 15.2 describes a good example of how an emerging industry, motor vehicles, was subject to all three aspects of the cycle. In the emergent phase of the industry there were a plethora of companies using a variety of technologies. Eventually a single technology was settled on (the internal combustion engine) and firms which did not adapt disappeared. Accelerating growth occurred as surviving competitors reaped the fruits of demand growth, and in particular General Motors came to dominate the industry.

However, not only does demand change during the product life cycle so too do costs. Although long understood by successful managers, one of the first to formulate the notion formally was Alchian (1963).

Figure 15.11 shows the product life-cycle S-shaped curve, with sales rising slowly at first, then accelerating as markets become familiar with the products, prices are reduced, then levelling off as the product matures and markets become saturated. Variant I shows product sales going into decline as tastes change or a new product supersedes the old. Variant II in Figure 15.11 shows static sales on maturity as the product matures but does not decline, while Variant III shows that the producers of the product have discovered and exploited previously untapped market segments for the product (for example, two-car or two TV-set households after each household has purchased one and the market had 'settled' to simply a replacement level) or had discovered new uses for the product (for example, nylon, after having been heavily used in the clothing industry, was taken by its innovator, du Pont, and successfully introduced to tyre manufacturers as a product which could be successfully combined with rubber in the manufacture of tyres).

The life-cycle curve has its characteristic shape, as can be inferred from the above discussion, both because of consumer and producer changes in tastes, costs,

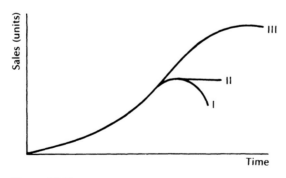

Figure 15.11

technologies and prices (and other myriad factors) over time. When producers introduce a new product not only are they aware of the S-shaped life-cycle curve they are also aware that one of the main factors underlying its position and shape (actual and potential) are the costs of production. But costs of production themselves are not simply a matter of mechanistically forecasting average cost curves and making allowances for varying volumes over time and hence distinguishing between short- and long-run curves, diminishing returns to scale and diseconomies of scale as in conventional analysis. Such forecasts are predictions of a static point in time only. When the dynamics are taken account of what is known as the 'learning' or 'experience' curve comes into play. Examples of the shapes such a curve can take are given in Figure 15.12.

We have already discussed the learning curve on pp. 244–5. The experience curve is a direct derivative. With the learning curve where direct labour costs per unit are plotted against total accumulated units produced, every time production occurs, unit labour costs fall. The experience curve extends this concept to all manufacturing costs. The reasons include learning, but also embrace increased specialisation and improved methods, redesigned products, standardisation, scale and factor substitution. Clearly, like the learning curve, the experience curve is different from the conventional *LAC* curve where experience accumulation is precluded by definition; technology is constant and the product is homogeneous and constant.

The crucial difference to note between the conventional *AC* curve and the unit costs indicated in Figure 15.12 is that the quantity axis in the former relates to a given period of time (albeit that period is typically unspecified except for the 'short'-run and 'long'-run distinctions where some costs are 'fixed' in the short run, and all costs are 'variable' in the long run). Even then however, the quantity axis still relates to the same time period, it is only the inputs *within* the diagram which are or are not allowed to vary. The learning or experience curve, however, is not concerned with these disparities, nor even with time as such, but rather with the impact on costs as experience is gained as production accumulates at some optimal rate.

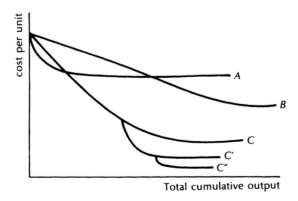

Figure 15.12

When a new product or process is initiated by a firm a learning process commences and, by trial and error and the accumulation of expertise, as more and more units are produced the firm and its labour force learn the least-cost ways of carrying out the manufacturing or production process. People gain dexterity, machinery is adapted to be more appropriate for its tasks, faulty or stupid (in the light of events) habits or machine processes are removed. 'De-bugging' takes place. Other things equal, the first movers in an industry will have a cost advantage over later entrants for as long as the curve is declining.

Figure 15.12 shows examples of three different kinds of experience curve. The nature of the curve is one factor which will determine how successful later entrants can expect to be. For example, curve A is very steep and innovators will quickly reach minimum unit costs, but because it levels off rapidly that advantage will be short-lived relative to a firm in an industry with a learning curve shaped like C, where the 'first mover' can (other things equal) keep one step ahead of followers for a longer period (this assumes equal rates of progress down the curve). Even with curve B, which is much less steep, a firm which reaches the steady-state, horizontal section of the curve before a competitor enters the market will have a large and significant cost advantage over an entrant.

What the experience curve shows is that whatever the market or product a firm is involved with it will usually have to sell more than its rivals over the long run in order to have lower costs and potentially higher profits. Moreover, in a growing market it will have to grow too, by retaining or increasing market share, otherwise rivals with larger shares will experience lower costs and thus be able to lower prices in a spiral of ever-growing commercial success.

The examples of firms which have used the curve (or its underlying concept) are legion. Moreover, it is difficult if not impossible to measure the nature of the curve in advance of the event. This immeasurability is where entrepreneurial judgement is at a premium. Box 15.3 expands on the motor industry case using the Ford example. Gilder (1986, p. 159) gives several examples. He quotes Henry Ford's autobiography:

> Our policy is to reduce the price, extend the operations, and improve the article. You will note that the reduction in price comes first. . . . Then we go ahead and try to make the prices. We do not bother about costs. The new price forces the costs down . . . so one knows what a cost ought to be. One of the ways of discovering [it] . . . is to make a price so low as to force everybody in the place to the highest point of efficiency.

Texas Instruments followed the same strategy of 'aggressive pricing' and 'extending capacity ahead of demand' in the semi-conductor industry (Gilder 1986, p. 154). It rapidly descended the experience curve. The examples are endless. And just as firms (as in Figure 15.11) must either innovate into a totally new area or find new uses or users for their product (curves II and III) to avoid the decline in the product life cycle, so they, must be alert to the fact that the 'steady state' on the learning curve is probably more apparent than real. New processes will suddenly appear, or the product will have to be modified to meet changing consumer tastes and a whole new family of experience curves can emerge (Figure 15.12) as, for example, curves C' and C" enabling later entrants to overtake the first mover and/or providing the innovator with continuous challenges.

Box 15.3

Ford's exploitation of the experience curve

The 1908 selling season found Buick the only company with a full line of cars, from a $2,500 Model 5 touring car to a $900 'white streak'. The streak doubled its sale to 8,485, gave Buick experience in 'mass' production, and set the stage for one of the decisive confrontations in the history of capitalism.

Henry Ford made a portentous announcement: 'I will build a motor car for the great multitude...' Nonetheless, during the first year, at a selling price of $850 the Model T had lost money and market share to the dashing $900 Buick. To increase his profits the next year, Ford raised his price by a full $100 to $950 and saw his sales more than double to 12,292 in a mushrooming market. But his share of this market declined again as Buick, Oldsmobile, and other companies proceeded to underprice him.

This was the key entrepreneurial moment for Henry Ford: the moment when the central but often secret laws of enterprise came into play most decisively in the car business. Focusing on the rising profits that followed his price hike, his advisers urged him to raise prices again in 1910 to take advantage of a market exploding beyond the ability of the firms to fulfil it. This was the course chosen by General Motors, which raised the price of Buick to $1,150, leaving Ford plenty of room to follow.

Indeed, in the usual accounting analysis, Ford had no plausible alternative to continuing the strategy that had worked for him in the past. Most analysts denied the existence of a large market for low-priced vehicles and dismissed the possibility of manufacturing them; costs were simply too high. Personal incomes, moreover, were too low for such a luxury product, which could be used only in the warmer months; the working class was not ready. ...

Automotive history might have taken a different course, at least for a while, if Ford had followed the GM example and raised his prices. But rather than raising his price as Buick did, Ford dropped it by nearly one-fifth, to $780. At this price Ford could break even only if he vastly expanded sales or lowered production costs.

This strategy of the self-fulfilling price is a classic gambit in the repertory of entrepreneurs. Contrary to the cliché, a company losing money on every unit sold can indeed make it up by volume. It is a prime law and governing experience of capitalism. In effect, Ford set his price not on the basis of his existing costs or sales but on the basis of the much lower costs and much expanded sales that might become possible at the lower price. The effect in the case of Henry Ford in 1910 was a 60 percent surge in sales that swept the Model T far ahead of Buick. ...

Ford had learned his lesson. In the recession year of 1914, he cut prices twice, and sales surged up while other companies failed. By 1916, he had reduced the price of a Model T to $360 and increased his market share from 10 percent to 40 percent, while the share commanded by General Motors slipped from 23 percent to 8 percent. By 1921, after cutting prices 30 percent during the 1920 economic crisis, Ford commanded a 60 percent share of a market that had grown by a factor of twelve in a decade. By 1927, he had sold 15 million cars, with a sales volume of $7 billion, and the company's net worth, with no new infusions of capital since the original $2,000, had risen to $715 million, including some $600 million in cash.

(Reproduced, with permission, from *The Spirit of Enterprise*, George Gilder, published by Penguin, 1986. © George Gilder, 1984.)

The experience curve and the need for entrepreneurial judgement in advance, of course, poses a problem for managerial economists, and for public policy makers such as anti-trust authorities. Predatory pricing or dumping are two business activities which are often condemned as anti-competitive. The definitional problems of when pricing at a low level is non-competitive are difficult at the best of times (is it when prices are below marginal costs, below average total costs, below average variable costs, or below the costs of competitors?). But when, as with the entrepreneurial use of the experience curve, pricing is in anticipation of some immeasurable cost reduction in the future to enable the firm to move rapidly down what Gilder called 'the curve of growth' then business advisors on the one hand and government policy makers on the other can only wait till after the event (by which time the price-reducing firm will either have successfully captured a large market share or unsuccessfully made an error of judgement resulting in rivals increasing *their* market shares). Ford reduced its prices in anticipation of (a) increased demand; and (b) of rapidly falling unit costs due to the simultaneous impact of the experience and learning curve effects. The product life cycle of Ford's offering eventually matured and went into decline as General Motors offered alternatives, and in the consumer's eyes more valuable products. While ultimately the market became saturated and both Ford and General Motors had either to diversify into alternative products or internationalise out of America to maintain their pattern of growth.

15.4 Managerial implications of diversification

15.4.1 Optimising the product mix

Eli Clemens (1951) argued that firms should expand output on each product to the point where the least profitable unit will be produced at marginal cost. His model, reproduced in Figure 15.13 assumes a low cross-elasticity of demand between a firm's products.[3] Each product is produced until its MR is equal to the MR of every other product, and prices are selected accordingly. At the limit, EMR (equal marginal revenue) = the firm's MC curve. (The products whose demand is most elastic have the lowest margin over MC. Only on products which have some sort of differential advantage can more monopolistic prices be charged.)

The two-product model of Figure 15.14 is more restrictive, but shows implicitly how linear programming can be applied to the problem, and hence how the multi-product Clemens model can be applied in practice. FF is a product transformation curve. It is the locus of output or product mix combinations of products Y and X which can be obtained from a given amount of input. The input could be regarded as the firm's total resources at a given point in time. If the firm produces, say, at point P then it is underutilising its resources. The firm, however, is unable, through lack of resources, to produce any combination of Y and X above and to the right of FF.

FF slopes downwards since any increase in output of X must be accompanied by a decrease in output of Y. FF is also concave to the origin. This is indicated by the

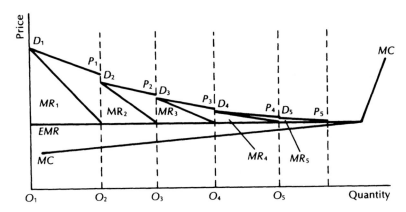

Figure 15.13

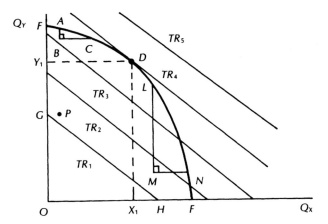

Figure 15.14

rising *MRPT* of *X* for *Y*, which is the direct outcome of the presence of heterogeneity in the fixed input. Thus, for example, as output of *X* increases, resources which previously were used to produce *Y* will have to be transferred to the production of *X*. More and more of *Y* will have to be foregone to provide the resources which are required to produce (in an increasingly technologically inefficient manner) one unit of *X*. The reverse will hold as the output of *Y* is increased at the expense of *X*. This argument is illustrated geometrically. $BC = MN =$ one unit of *X*. At *A*, to increase the output of *X* by one unit, *AB* units of *Y* must be foregone. At *L*, however, *LM* units of *Y* must be foregone to increase the output of *X* by one.

We can now determine the optimal output mix of the firm by superimposing on Figure 15.14 isorevenue lines. These represent the locus of all possible combinations of the two outputs which result in the same total revenue. They will be higher in value the further they are from the origin. They are straight on the assumptions that the products are unrelated on the demand side of the market and that they are sold in perfectly competitive conditions with prices which are invariant with respect to quantity. The point of tangency, D, between TR_4 and FF determines the optimal output mix of Y_1X_1, which gives the firm the highest total revenue for its given level of expenditure on input resources.

The highest total revenue, given costs, automatically implies that profits are also maximised. Thus both a profit maximiser and a sales maximiser will, given the level of costs, choose an output mix where the marginal rate of product transformation between every pair of outputs is numerically equal to the inverse ratio of their prices.

Algebraically the slope of TR_4 (the same as the slope of TR_1) $= OG/OH = P_X/P_Y$. But the slope of $FF = \partial Q_Y/\partial Q_X$. Thus at D:

$$\frac{\partial Q_Y}{\partial Q_X} = \frac{P_X}{P_Y} \text{ or } P_X\partial Q_X \ (= MR_X) = P_Y\partial Q_Y \ (= MR_Y) \tag{15.1}$$

for both types of firm. Any differences between the output mix or resource allocation of the two types of firm must consequently be due not to reallocation of a given level of costs or revenues, but to the larger outputs (and so larger TC and TR) which can be expected to accompany sales maximisation. This is a trite conclusion as it stands. However, when one bears in mind that a sales maximiser 'forfeits' profits in order to operate up to a profit constraint, that fact that equation (15.1) is valid indicates that profit optimising behaviour will still be pursued. In the case of the sales maximiser, however, absolute profits will not be maximised, but relatively unprofitable input and output mixes continue to be avoided.

If we now compare Figure 15.14 with Figure 10.4 it will be apparent that once again there is a close relationship between marginal analysis and linear programming. In the two-product examples of the figures, the boundary of the feasible space is analogous to the product transformation curve. Similarly the iso contribution lines are analogous to the isorevenue lines. (Revenue $= P \times Q$, Contribution $= (P - VC \times Q)$. Both concentrate on incremental revenues and costs, and recognise the irrelevance of fixed costs. LP concentrates on contribution maximisation, conventional economic analysis concentrates on $MR = MC$, where MC is the benefit foregone at the margin by cutting back output on one product to increase output of the other. Both thus implicitly or explicitly take opportunity cost into account. With LP, the iterative corner-by-corner comparison of the additional revenue gained by bringing a new product into the solution (or increasing output of an existing one) is contrasted with the sacrifice of earnings from the products that must be given up (or outputs that must be reduced).

The major differences in the two approaches are that the boundary of the LP feasible region is curvilinear only because it is composed of segments each of which is perfectly linear in its own right. Each input type is assumed to be homogeneous. Product transformation curves permit input heterogeneity *within* groups of inputs. Second, linear isorevenue lines require a fixed output selling price and zero demand cross-elasticity between outputs. But linear isorevenue lines are *not* essential to economic analysis. Linear isocontribution lines *are* necessary to LP, and in addition constant variable costs are assumed which in turn implies constant input prices and constant input marginal productivity. Third, product transformation curves assume that output mixes can be smoothly and continuously varied. LP restricts itself to a finite number of alternative mixes which may be more realistic and certainly facilitates calculation. Finally, scale economies are not possible with LP, constant returns are essential.

15.4.2 Joint product pricing

When a multiproduct firm sets a price for any one product it must also consider the impact on revenues of any other member of its product range which is related to the original: either as a substitute or as a complement. In short, *cross-elasticities of demand* must be taken into account.

Consider a simple two-product case, where a firm produces x and y. The firm's total revenue function is:

$$TR = P_X Q_X + P_Y Q_Y$$

The values of MR_X and MR_Y are obtained using the addition and multiplication rules of differentiation, thus:

$$MR_X = \frac{\partial TR}{\partial Q_X} = P_X + Q_X \frac{\partial P_X}{\partial Q_X} + P_Y \frac{\partial Q_Y}{\partial Q_X} + Q_Y \frac{\partial P_Y}{\partial Q_X}$$

$$MR_Y = \frac{\partial TR}{\partial Q_Y} = P_Y + Q_Y \frac{\partial P_Y}{\partial Q_Y} + P_X \frac{\partial Q_X}{\partial Q_Y} + Q_X \frac{\partial P_X}{\partial Q_Y}$$

The first two terms of each equation are the marginal revenues directly arising from each product. The final two terms arise from the presence of demand cross-elasticities. If the products are substitutes, the sum of these two terms will be negative; if complements, the net sum will be positive. Thus, for example, the third and fourth terms of the MR_X equation show the change in revenue from product y when an additional unit of x is sold.

In addition to demand cross-elasticities, firms must consider supply cross-elasticities. Joint products can be produced in fixed proportions, as in the case of sides of beef and cow hides, or pineapple rings and pineapple juice; or in variable proportions, where a decision can be taken as to how many units of product A should be produced and the decision does *not* have a corresponding effect on the output of product B.

15.4.3 Pricing joint products produced in fixed proportions

For marketing and pricing purposes, joint products produced in fixed proportions are separable entities. From a production viewpoint, however, it makes sense to regard them as one package. Appropriation of costs to one product or the other is both an impracticable and an unnecessary exercise. Determination of separate and individual prices, on the other hand, is necessary to enable the firm to maximise total profits in the two distinct markets in which the products are sold.

Figure 15.15 shows how the theory of marginal equivalency can be applied to this problem. D_1 and D_2 are the demand curves for products 1 and 2 in their respective markets. MR_1 and MR_2 are the corresponding marginal revenue curves. MR_1 is not continued below the quantity axis, because under no circumstances does it make sense to sell more than Q_2 units of product 1. Beyond Q_2 marginal revenue for product 1 becomes negative, that is, total revenue decreases. ΣMR is obtained by aggregating MR_1 and MR_2 vertically. At Q_2 and beyond, MR_2 and ΣMR are, of course, one and the same.

The summation of marginal revenue curves is vertical, not horizontal as when the practice of price discrimination was examined in Figure 11.4. Vertical summation gives the added revenues for both products. In the case of joint product pricing, we wish to ascertain the total marginal revenue obtainable at any given output level, and how that ΣMR is distributed. In the case of price discrimination, we wished to ascertain the total quantity at a given MR level, and how that quantity was divided.

Note also that since the two products are assumed to be produced in fixed proportions, the units of measurement on the quantity axis refer to both goods 1 and 2. The profit maximising output level is Q_1 where $MC = \Sigma MR$. Q_1 units of each product are sold and are priced at the levels indicated by the relevant demand curves, P_1 and P_2 on D_1 and D_2 respectively.

It is possible that with a given cost schedule, the marginal cost curve could intersect ΣMR to the right of Q_2, as does MC_a. In this case profit-maximisation procedures require a total production of Q_3 units, with product 2 selling at price P_3. Total revenue from product 1, however, is maximised at output Q_2, not Q_3. Given

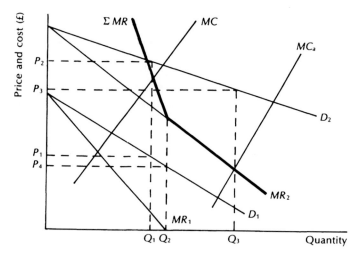

Figure 15.15

this, product 1 should be sold at price P_4 which would leave a quantity equal to $Q_3 - Q_2$ as surplus to requirements. This surplus must be withheld from the market in some way (e.g. dumping or destruction) to permit product 1's total revenue to be maximised. Alternatively, it may be more profitable to advertise and increase demand for product 1 so that redundant output is avoided.

The calculus can be used to accomplish optimal joint product pricing. Suppose A and B are produced on a 1:3 basis with the following demand functions:

$$Q_A = 1 - P_A$$
$$\Rightarrow P_A = 1 - Q_A$$

and
$$Q_B = 2 - P_B$$
$$\Rightarrow P_B = 2 - Q_B$$

The latter must be re-expressed as:

$$P_B = 2 - 3.0Q_B'$$

where the prime sign is an indicator of 3 units of B, the amount produced in relation to A in the joint product. The demand function for B is rearranged as shown since the monetary intercept is unchanged. (Zero units of B will be sold at a price of 2 whether B is sold singly or in the larger packages of $Q_B' = 0.333 Q_B$.) The new demand function, however, relates to packages which number Q_B' where Q_B and Q_A are going to be compared on a diagram with the same horizontal scale. Namely each of Q packages contains one unit of A and three units of B, i.e. $Q = Q_A = Q_B' = 0.333Q_B$. The slope of the demand function with respect to Q_B' must, therefore, be three times as steep as that for Q_B, if Q_A and Q_B are to be compared on the same diagram where the quantity axis relates to the fixed proportion joint product.

$$\Rightarrow TR_A = P_A Q_A = Q_A - Q_A^2$$
$$\Rightarrow TR_B = P_B Q_B' = 2Q_B' - 3Q_B'^2$$
$$\Rightarrow \Sigma TR = Q_A - Q_A^2 + 2Q_B' - 3Q_B'^2$$

But since $Q_A = Q_B'$

$$\Sigma TR = 3Q - 4Q^2$$

The firm's TC function is, of course, constructed for Q_A and Q_B' jointly and $\pi = TR - TC$. Assume:

$$TC = 100 + 2.75Q + 0.1Q^2$$

then
$$\pi = 3Q - 4Q^2 - 100 - 2.75Q - 0.1Q^2$$
$$= 0.25Q - 4.1Q^2 - 100$$

$$\Rightarrow \frac{d\pi}{dQ} = 0 = 0.25 - 8.2Q$$

$$\therefore Q = 0.03$$

The optimal solution, therefore, is to produce

        0.03 units of A

and   0.09 units of B (recall $Q'_B = 0.333Q_B$)

provided that the values of MR_A and MR_B are positive at these outputs. This can be ascertained by evaluating MR_A and MR_B from the relevant demand curve as follows:

$$MR_A = 1 - 2Q_A = 1 - 0.06 = +0.94$$

$$MR_B = 2 - 6Q'_B = 2 - 0.18 = +1.72$$

Both values are positive and hence $Q = 0.03$ is the appropriate solution. The respective selling prices are found by substitution in the demand equations. Thus

$$P_A = 1 - 0.03 = 0.97$$

and $P_B = 2 - (3 \times 0.03) = 1.91$

Had either A or B had a negative MR at 0.03 and 0.09 units of output respectively then an excess production problem would have existed. In which case the relevant MR equation for determining optimal output is that for the other product. That is, MC for the joint product would be set equal to MR for the single product with no excess production problem. This would give optimal output. The output rate for the product with the excess production problem would be determined by setting MR equal to zero.

15.4.4 Pricing joint products produced in variable proportions

We know that optimally $MR_X = MR_Y$ in a two good situation.

In Figure 15.16 a given product transformation curve appears (flipped 180° over on the X-axis) together with demand and MR curves for product X and for product Y, (in the latter case flipped 180° to the left). Quadrant (iii) contains a 45° line for guidance purposes. The problem is to find the prices P_X and P_Y which will equate MR_X and MR_Y while remaining on the firm's product transformation curve. No other rectangle other than the one traced in on the figure satisfies these conditions. In practice, in a multiproduct world, the problem can be solved either by the calculus or by linear programming.

In both diagrammatic expositions (Figures 15.13 and 15.16) we arrived at the same equimarginal result. That is, firms should produce and price two goods, X and Y, where $MR_X = MR_Y$. This is somewhat simplistic, however. In Figure 15.13 the Clemens model defined the quantity axis in terms of inputs not outputs, hence permitting an identical and diagrammatically uniform MC schedule for each product, whence $MR_X = MR_Y$ was inferred. In Figure 15.10 the problem was one of selecting scale, not price. This can result in a least-cost product mix, but not necessarily in profit maximisation. In Figure 15.16 again $MR_Y = MR_X$ and from quadrant iv one could analogously deduce that when this is so, $MR_Y = MC_Y$ and

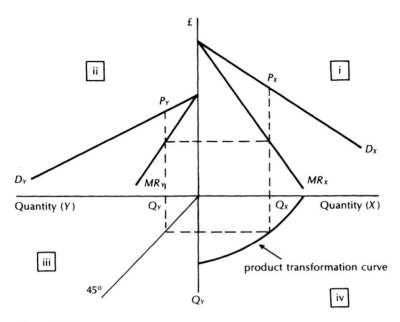

Figure 15.16

$MR_X = MC_X$. Similarly, in quadrants i and ii, if the functions MC_X and MC_Y were to be inserted, they would intersect MR_X and MR_Y above Q_X and Q_Y respectively. But Figure 15.16 is contrived with optimal scale given. Scale may not be optimal.

In brief, the equimarginal revenue per product rule assumes too much. Rather, price quantity decisions should be taken so that, first, the ratios MR_X/MC_X and MR_Y/MC_Y should be equal (verbally the firm should receive the same incremental revenue per pound spent on each product) and second, MR should equal MC for each product, otherwise a profit maximising (as opposed to a least-cost) product mix and scale will not have been achieved. This can be more elegantly phrased using calculus. Assume zero cross-elasticity of demand. Then:

$$\pi = P_Y Q_Y + P_X Q_X - TC(Q_Y, Q_X)$$

To maximise profits take the partials and set equal to zero:

$$\frac{\partial \pi}{\partial Q_Y} = P_Y + Q_Y \frac{\partial P_Y}{\partial Q_Y} - \frac{\partial TC}{\partial Q_Y} = 0$$

$$\frac{\partial \pi}{\partial Q_X} = P_X + Q_X \frac{\partial P_X}{\partial Q_X} - \frac{\partial TC}{\partial Q_X} = 0$$

or

$$P_Y + Q_Y \frac{\partial P_Y}{\partial Q_Y} = \frac{\partial TC}{\partial Q_Y}$$

and

$$P_X + Q_X \frac{\partial P_X}{\partial Q_X} = \frac{\partial TC}{\partial Q_X}$$

or

$$MR_Y = MC_Y \text{ and } MR_X = MC_X \text{ (see Note 4)}$$

As an example, assume $TC = 500 + 5Q_Y^2 + 2Q_X^2 - Q_X Q_Y$

$$P_Y = 100 - Q_Y$$

$$P_X = 200 - 2Q_X$$

Hence

$$\pi = 100Q_Y - Q_Y^2 + 200Q_X - 2Q_X^2(500 + 5Q_Y^2 + 2Q_X^2 - Q_X Q_Y)$$

$$= 100Q_Y - 6Q_Y^2 + 200Q_X - 4Q_X^2 - 500 + Q_X Q_Y$$

$$\frac{\partial \pi}{\partial Q_X} = 200 - 8Q_X + Q_Y = 0$$

$$\frac{\partial \pi}{\partial Q_Y} = 100 - 12Q_Y + Q_X = 0$$

Solving these equations and substituting to obtain prices:[5]

$$Q_Y = 10.5, \quad Q_X = 26.0, \quad P_Y = 89.5 \text{ and } P_X = 148.0$$

15.4.5 Innovation and product differentiation

Figure 15.17 depicts the firm in Figure 15.13 in a subsequent period when it has successfully introduced a new product significantly better in consumers' eyes than existing products. Demand curve D_6 represents this innovation. While the firm was developing this product, competitors could readily see the profit potential of the product associated with say D_1. They had an incentive to enter with products of their own, and such entry would cause the elasticity of D_1 to become greater. The introduction of the new product, D_6, alerts competitors to the profit potential of the innovation also. At the same time as the firm in the figure is introducing its significant new product it could also be entering product areas of competitive firms (D_7) with demand curves like D_5 in Figure 15.13 or any other product area in which price is greater than marginal cost. This in turn increases the elasticity of the demand curves faced by these competitors. This approach to innovation or brand addition to a product range is a straightforward development of conventional theory.

Box 15.4 illustrates this type of comparative static approach in practice using the example of the British and American drug industries.

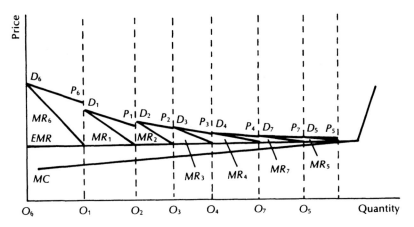

Figure 15.17

Box 15.4

Pricing new drugs in Britain and America

Figures 15.13 and 15.17 conceptualise neatly how new drugs are priced. In the UK the National Economic Development Office categorised pharmaceutical innovations as follows:

1. fundamental new medicines, of major clinical significance
2. important innovations for a majority of patients
3. useful new products for minorities
4. new medicines of marginal incremental usefulness
5. new medicines with little or no advantage over existing products.

The US Food and Drug Administration also categorises drug innovations using a similar (but three point) scale from major innovations to 'me-toos'.

Surveys of all new products introduced in both the UK and the USA from 1950 onwards, using these official categories, showed that major new products in both countries tend to be priced mostly at very high (skimming) prices or (in the case of 'me-toos') at penetration prices. High priced products tend to fall over time as subsequent competitive innovations are introduced and price remains the major competitive weapon to retain sales obtained initially on the basis of incremental quality. Furthermore, demand elasticities tend on launch to be low but rise over time. Patients and prescribers are not very price sensitive when good health is at stake, but when better alternatives are available they do become price conscious and will tend not to use costly medicines if cheaper alternatives are adequate for the purpose.

Source condensed from Reekie 1972 and Reekie 1978b.

15.5 The product portfolio

A diversified firm by definition has a range of products. One purpose of generating a range is to optimise the risk–return mix of the overall product portfolio. Diversification can thus be analysed analogously with security diversification as in our discussion surrounding Figure 14.9.

Box 15.5

The entrepreneurial business

'Big businesses don't innovate,' says the conventional wisdom. This sounds plausible enough. True, the new, major innovations of this century did not come out of the old, large businesses of their time. The railroads did not spawn the automobile or the truck; they did not even try. And though the automobile companies did try (Ford and General Motors both pioneered in aviation and aerospace), all of today's large aircraft and aviation companies have evolved out of separate new ventures. Similarly, today's giants of the pharmaceutical industry are, in the main, companies that were small or non-existent fifty years ago when the first modern drugs were developed. Every one of the giants of the electrical industry – General Electric, Westinghouse, and RCA in the United States; Siemens and Philips on the Continent; Toshiba in Japan – rushed into computers in the 1950s. Not one was successful. The field is dominated by IBM, a company that was barely middle-sized and most definitely not high-tech forty years ago.

And yet the all but universal belief that large businesses do not and cannot innovate is not even a half-truth; rather, it is a misunderstanding.

In the first place, there are plenty of exceptions, plenty of large companies that have done well as entrepreneurs and innovators. In the United States, there is Johnson & Johnson in hygiene and health care, and 3M in highly engineered products for both industrial and consumer markets. Citibank, America's and the world's largest non-governmental financial institution, well over a century old, has been a major innovator in many areas of banking and finance. In Germany, Hoechst – one of the world's largest chemical companies, and more than 125 years old by now – has become a successful innovator in the pharmaceutical industry. In Sweden, ASEA, founded in 1884 and for the last sixty or seventy years a very big company, is a true innovator in both long-distance transmission of electrical power and robotics for factory automation.

To confuse things even more there are quite a few big, older businesses that have succeeded as entrepreneurs and innovators in some fields while failing dismally in others. The (American) General Electric Company failed in computers, but has been a successful innovator in three totally different fields: aircraft engines, engineered inorganic plastics, and medical electronics. RCA also failed in computers but succeeded in colour television. Surely things are not quite as simple as the conventional wisdom has it. (Drucker 1986, pp. 168–9.)

Note: Early 1993 some of the above successful examples had shown signs of decline in the nominated markets (IBM and RCA).

Risk–return analysis is not enough on its own, however. It generally assumes investors are buying securities in a secondary financial market – i.e. the shares are already being traded and a market in each of them is well developed with concomitant fullness of information. Diversification is also carried out with innovations (i.e. the product life cycle has still to develop) where consumer unfamiliarity and procedure unfamiliarity exist (i.e. the slope of the experience curve is still an unknown). In short, while risk–return analysis provides a static, snapshot effect of optimal diversification given a known actual or potential product range, entrepreneurial flare becomes crucial in deciding on what a balanced portfolio should be, given unknown and probably unknowable future rises and declines in sales and/or costs.

The literature on corporate strategy attempts to envelop and codify these problems. Some of the prescriptions in this literature are set out below. But readers should examine Box 15.5 before proceeding further. This book has relied heavily on techniques using the principles of marginal equivalency and transactions cost analysis. These are inadequate guides to entrepreneurial analysis. The strategic planning literature is less modest. After reading our survey and the success and failure studies of Box 15.5 we would caution that the literature be viewed as 'descriptive' not prescriptive.

One of the first codifications of the strategic diversification problem was the growth:share matrix developed by a firm of American managerial consultants (the Boston Consulting Group) displayed in simple form in Figure 15.18. Products are identified as 'stars', 'cash cows'. 'problem children' or 'dogs' and placed in the relevant quadrant.

Market growth is measured, in real (inflation-adjusted) terms, as the growth rate per year of the overall market for the product. The rate can be calculated either as an *absolute* figure or *relative* to that of real GNP.

Market share of the product in its own industry can also be measured in two ways: either as a straight percentage or as that percentage deflated by that of the leading firm. (Thus a product that has 10% of a market might be reckoned to have a 'high' share relative to one with only 5%. On the other hand, the former product might be competing against a brand leader with a 50% share, $10/50 = 0.2$; the latter might have no competitor stronger than a rival with a 2% share, $5/2 = 2.5$. This would reverse the quadrant allocation.)

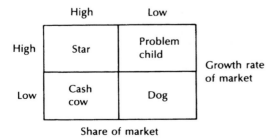

Figure 15.18

There are no hard and fast rules on how to place products in the growth:share matrix – the law of the situation must hold. That is, the yardstick chosen should be the most helpful to the decision maker and not simply selected because it was successful in a previous, but possibly dissimilar, marketing environment.

Underlying the growth:share matrix is the product life cycle and the experience curve. In early (rapid growth) stages, purchasing behaviour and brand loyalty are deemed to be fluid and a large market share can be obtained at a relatively low cost in marketing expenditures. In maturity, an increase in market share is more difficult to obtain: consumers are more inert and firm growth involves obvious encroach-ment on competitors who will therefore be provoked to resist. In this situation (cash cow) funds should be redirected to research and development (R&D) for totally new products, to finding new uses or new markets for the existing product to prevent decline (a move to a dog), or towards other existing products in the right-hand column.

Figure 15.19 illustrates how this process can appear from the perspective of a given product over time, from product launch to the position where (it may be hoped) a product rapidly becomes a star, albeit initially a relatively small part of a firm's total sales. As maturity approaches the product becomes a cash cow. A moderate or high share has been obtained but growth has ceased or slowed. The company hopes it will remain in or reach that quadrant and not be a problem child on launch, nor degenerate into one. The marketing tools to adopt for problem

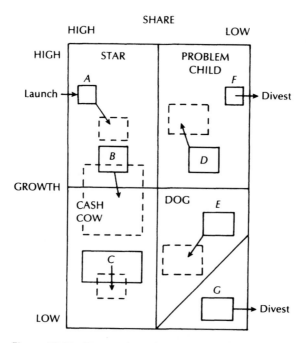

Figure 15.19 (Source based on Day 1977)

children or dogs range from identifying new target segments and exploiting them (which is costly although it may ultimately prove worthwhile) to cutting losses by divesting oneself of the product by sale to another firm which itself wishes to diversify.

In Figure 15.19 the solid squares indicate a current position. The dotted squares indicate forecast positions. The areas are approximately and hypothetically suggestive of contributions to corporate sales.

Day (1977) suggests that when a firm is using the growth:share matrix to help assist in corporate strategy it should use cash to support A (in order to achieve the higher forecast sales indicated by the dashed lines); adopt policies to maintain B and C which are about to achieve, or have already achieved, significant sales volumes; and aid D by further product acquisition or range widening (hence increasing its growth rate and its sales contribution). Conversely, with E, which has a lower initial growth potential than D had, Day suggests a narrowing of range in order not to dissipate managerial effects but rather harvest what can be obtained from those specialised market segments where E is doing well, and hence, as the dotted lines indicate, increase total sales contribution of E. In the cases of F and G, Day's diagram suggests divestment since market share and sales are either so small or growth so low that potential returns would appear to be less than are further development costs.

Again we must emphasise that these are only conceptualised guidelines, which may well need to be varied situation by situation. Furthermore, even if the suggested strategies are correct, they are not clear-cut for products in the centre of the matrix. For this reason the McKinsey management consulting group developed a 3×3 or 9-cell matrix, plotting 'industry attractiveness' (as measured by a check list) against the business' 'competitive position' (gauged by a similar check list) and not merely a 2×2 growth:share analysis. Once a product or division is categorised there are additional problems. For example, there is the human or behavioural problem that managers may not like being associated with dogs, and leave: or conversely growth may be excessively costly but be embarked upon by managers wishing to 'save' their products from divestment or abandonment and so their jobs.

15.6 The decision to invest abroad

The McKinsey matrix can be adapted to aid planners in deciding whether to invest abroad. At an international level this implies focusing on markets (or countries) and their attractiveness and on the firms *total* strength in such markets rather than on individual products. To attack the international problem, Harrel and Kiefer (1981) suggest using the matrix of Figure 15.20. The axes are linear combinations of factors determined from check lists relating to the country's commercial attractiveness and the firm's competitive strength in that country. Country attractiveness can be gauged, for example, by awarding points to market size, market growth rate, and degree of government regulation in areas such as price control, local content rules, dividend repatriation possibilities, and economic and political stability in terms of

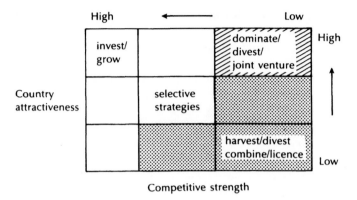

Figure 15.20 Product plotting matrix (Source Harrel and Kiefer 1981)

inflation, balance of trade and political unrest. For competitive strength, firms could examine factors such as market share, market ranking (thus, to be firm number one with a 20% share is qualitatively different from being firm number two in size with a 40% share), product fit (i.e. how well does the domestically designed product fit the needs of the foreign market?), contribution profit per unit, and the degree of market visibility and dealer or after-sales or promotional support. Using a numerical check list for the firm's product portfolio and for countries, national markets can be plotted on the matrix. Those countries falling in the right upward-sloping cells require selective funding strategies, while those in the upper left should receive resources for growth and those in the bottom right are candidates for harvest or divestment.

'Investment and growth' countries require commitment to a strong market position. A high share of a fast-growing market requires considerable financial backing, and commitment to personnel. Local production will often be required for the sake of prompt delivery and good service. Adaptation of products to fit local requirements may be necessary. Marketing support must be strong.

'Harvest/divest/licence/combine' nations should not see profits forfeited to maintain market share. Short-run profits should be concentrated in such low-growth, low-potential situations until the operation can be sold or terminated. Cash flows can be increased by cutting support costs and possibly even raising or maintaining prices.

'Dominate/divest/joint venture' nations provide alternative strategic choices. The firm is weak, yet the market is attractive. Moving the firm to a position of strength could be costly, yet if this cost is avoided by divestment the opportunity cost of selling out at a low price and the forfeiting of future profits may be incurred.

'Selectivity strategy' nations also pose difficult choices: should the firm regard the national market as a cash cow or as a potential star with further investment expense required?

Can this somewhat pragmatic framework for deciding on the nature and direction of foreign operations be given greater rigour? It can if we appeal first to the simple theory of international trade, and supplement that with the product life cycle and experience curve, we have come to rely on so heavily in recent pages.

International trade, of course, has never been overlooked even in early work by industrial economists. Adam Smith argued for it on the basis of the advantages of division of labour and absolute cost differences. David Ricardo took the argument one stage further and showed that, even if a country was absolutely disadvantaged in the output of two commodities, specialisation and trade were still worthwhile because of the principle of *comparative* advantage. The Ricardian comparative advantage was due to differential labour productivities between two countries (due in turn to varying national technologies and production functions). The latter was not explained by Ricardo, but his basic model still helps explain the pattern of trade flows. Hood and Young (1979, p. 137) explain that it was because of this deficiency that the Heckscher–Ohlin theory (H–O) was developed.

Heckscher and Ohlin were Swedes who attempted to explain the pattern of international trade as being consequential on a country's endowments of inputs, in particular the labour and capital factors of production. A nation will have a comparative advantage in those products in which its most abundant factor is used relatively intensively (and hence will export that product). Conversely, it will import those products which tend to require factor inputs with which the country is relatively poorly endowed.

Thus a country which is capital-rich but short of labour (relative to its trading partners) will have a comparative advantage in products which require a high capital:labour input ratio. Such goods will be exported, and products which require a high labour:capital input ratio will be imported. The rationale, of course, is that capital abundance will be reflected in a low (relative to other countries) price of capital and a high (relative) price of labour. Capital intensive goods will thus have a relatively low price. H–O theory obviously assumes international factor immobility, but, unlike Ricardian theory, uniform production functions across nations and hence free flows of information.

Despite the factor immobility constraint in H–O theory, factor prices still tend towards equality because of international trade. Thus, for example, a labour-rich country will export labour-intensive goods. This will increase demand for labour in the exporting country thus raising wages in that country (and depressing them in the importing country). In 1954 the H–O theory was subject to a major shock when in an empirical study Leontief (1954) produced evidence contradicting its predictions. His results are now known as the 'Leontief Paradox' and it will be seen below that the Paradox is (at least partly) due to the factor immobility constraint imposed in H–O theory. Relaxation of that constraint is, of course, necessary if we are to examine the phenomenon of the multinational enterprise (MNE) and foreign direct investment (FDI) For the moment let us examine the paradox in more detail and list explanations put forward for its existence.

Leontief applied input–output analysis to the US economy for 1947. He attempted to ascertain how much capital and how much labour was required to produce a given value of US exports on the one hand, and of US home-produced goods which competed with US imports on the other. Intuitively the United States is a capital-rich/labour-poor country, and so, by H–O theory, it should specialise in and hence export capital-intensive products and import labour-intensive goods.

Leontief's results, however, showed that US exports required a greater ratio of labour:capital than did production of import-competing goods. The United States was apparently a capital-short country specialising in labour-intensive production.

Hood and Young (1979, p. 138) summarise several explanations put forward to resolve the paradox. First, H–O theory assumes similar consumption patterns at different income levels. But the United States is a high-income country with a strong demand for capital-intensive goods resulting in a higher price in the United States for such goods despite relative capital abundance. Second, input–output analysis itself has deficiencies. There are fixed technological coefficients. That is, for a given type of product, irrespective of output level, the ratio of capital:labour is invariant. This flaw is magnified if (as Leontief did) US exports are compared not with US imports from other countries but with US produced import substitutes. The capital:labour ratios of actual imports in their countries of origin might have produced a different picture. Third, labour is not homogeneous, although it is assumed to be in both H–O and input–output analysis. Leontief himself argued that US labour may in fact be plentiful and hence cheap (in productivity wage terms) because of differences in skills, training, scale economies or superior technology.

In short, international trade theory as developed through to the H–O level has proved deficient as a satisfactory description of reality. The Leontief Paradox has highlighted some of the deficiencies. H–O was too abstract from reality, particularly in allowing for factor mobility, while input–output analysis, albeit spotlighting deficiencies, has weaknesses in handling the richness, diversity and heterogeneity of real-life business inputs and outputs, and this may be especially so when we turn away from international flows of trade towards international flows of (equity or risk) capital through the MNE.

Three main types of MNE predominate. First, the European-based firms (e.g. Shell, Dunlop, Unilever) which undertook backwards integration into agriculture and minerals in colonial territories in the early decades of the century. Second, the US-based MNEs which were a phenomena of the 1950s and 1960s and which undertook import-substituting investments (most obviously in Europe) and third, Japanese firms which emerged in the 1970s and 1980s using low wage, 'Pacific Rim' countries as export sources. These categories are, of course, drastically simplified and caricature reality but they are conceptually helpful.

We have seen that international trade theory is not comprehensively helpful in explaining trade patterns. Nor did it allow for the movement of equity capital between nations which is so commonplace. What then are the economic reasons for the existence of FDI? Several have been put forward which we shall examine in turn. These are the need for supply security (backward integration), the product life-cycle approach, the proprietary knowledge model, and the integrative or 'eclectic' theory.

Backward integration to secure supply sources is a common feature of industrial structure not just international industrial structure. Why does it occur in some industries and not in others? Clearly there are additional costs involved in international as opposed to domestic backward integration (e.g. the costs of learning about operating in an alien commercial and political environment, the costs of communication which to some extent even with modern communications increase with distance, and so on). These transactions costs must, in certain instances, be perceived as lower than the benefits to be obtained by internationalisation. Casson (1987, pp. 3, 30) points out that only in some industries is backward FDI deemed worthwhile. Thus it is common in aluminium, copper, oil and bananas. It is rarer with metals such as tin, minerals such as coal, or agricultural industries such as grain or cotton. The benefits which outweigh the transactions costs of FDI in the minerals case are due not to the presence or absence of scale economies in smelting. (These are present in all three examples.) But rather to the greater degree of uncertainty present in securing supplies at the desired price in the case of aluminium and copper. Sources of these metals are concentrated while those of tin are diffuse. Bilateral monopoly uncertainty is best overcome by backward FDI in the case of aluminium and copper. Tin industry smelters do not perceive such a requirement. Similarly there are economies in the continuous and guaranteed flow of oil through pipelines (or ship) to the oil refineries which operate on a 24-hour-day basis (which do not exist with coal). With coal, storage is perceived to be a lower-cost method of industrial organisation to minimise uncertainty than internalising transactions in order to obtain the benefits of centralised monitoring (as with multinational oil companies). Again security of supply is paramount. In the agriculture areas the security or assurance of quality is the spur. Casson (1987, p. 30) points out that unlike grain or cotton, bananas pose serious problems of quality control which can best be resolved through skilled plantation management and the integration of growing, ripening and shipping. The much more homogeneous grains, which are readily storable, relatively non-perishable and have many alternative supply sources do not pose such a quality control security problem to millers who consequently perceive market transactions to be less costly than in-firm integrated operations.

Vernon's (1966) life-cycle explanation for the existence of the MNE moved attention away from the European-originating, backward-integrating MNE to the post-war US-originating phenomenon. Simultaneously, he put forward reasons why his views might help resolve the 'Leontief Paradox'.

Vernon's argument commences with the axioms that the United States is a high-income country characterised by high wages and plentiful capital. These facts impact on the demand for both consumer and industrial products. There will be a demand for innovations which are labour-saving in the workplace (as producers try to economise on high-cost labour) and also for income-elastic consumer goods (due to high-consumer incomes). There are, therefore, incentives to invest in product developments in such areas in the United States. The initial manufacturing of the resulting innovations will also take place in the United States even if a superficial examination of the comparative cost suggests otherwise. This will be so, argues Vernon because innovations are generally non-standardised, either in their process of manufacture or as products *per se*. (For example, early motor cars were petrol-driven, steam-driven, electrically-driven, had camshafts or chain drives, and so on.) Unit production costs will consequently be high until the optimum product and process in terms of market demand is arrived at. In turn this requires close co-ordination with the market itself. The benefits of this will outweigh any costs involved in initial non-optimal production technologies. Second, demand for innovations is generally price-inelastic in the early stages of marketing. Consequently, any such cost differentials will be relatively unimportant to the innovators. However, as the product matures, standardisation of design, production technology, and the like set in. Prices fall as the market widens and scale economies appear. Exports may begin. Demand will appear next in high income-elastic countries such as Western Europe. Simultaneously the high labour costs involved in US production will come to play an increasingly important role in corporate decisions (as they form an ever-increasing proportion of declining selling prices). Overseas manufacture will come to be seen as an attractive possibility. (Partly due to the shift in location of the market, partly due to the decrease in importance of immediate market liaison, and partly due to the rising importance of labour costs.) FDI will thus come about with eventual exports from the overseas subsidiaries back into the United States provided only that labour-cost savings exceed the transportation-cost differential.

Vernon sees this scenario as at least partially resolving the Leontief Paradox. In the early stages of the above process high value-added items with an unusually high labour cost component were being produced in the United States. This was not because US labour was necessarily more skilled as suggested above but rather, simply because at that stage in the product life-cycle production is labour-intensive and it is economically more efficient to produce in the innovating and high income US market. As the cycle progresses, the demand for the product becomes more price-elastic, and capital-intensive mass production methods set in, the cheaper location becomes non-US and imports from subsidiaries arise. Again (and naturally) this is also at odds with H–O trade theory which suggests that the exports of labour-rich countries would be of labour-intensive products. The Vernon view is that at advanced stages of standardisation less developed countries may offer a comparative advantage as production locations. Certainly the Vernon view also fits in with Japan's use of Pacific Rim nations as 'export platforms'.

Vernon's view is certainly plausible but it leaves unanswered the question of why this international relocation of production is done through the means of FDI (or close variants such as joint ventures or licensing) rather than by straight imitation by entrepreneurs in the other nations. Caves (1971) was one of the first to provide a convincing answer to this question. He answered the question by first eliminating a series of alternative but unsatisfactory answers. FDI might be explained by equity (or risk) capital flowing from low-return countries to high-return countries. (Rather like labour migrating from Turkey to West Germany from Mozambique to South Africa, or Mexico to the United States as workers seek higher wages in foreign markets.) However, equity capital does not appear to flow systematically in such directions. Indeed, even a casual glance at MNEs shows a network of equity capital flowing to and from virtually the same nations. The capital-exporting nations are not obviously low-profit ones and indeed are often capital-importing and exporting simultaneously. Likewise, the desire to get under tariff barriers is a plausible but far from universal or even prime empirical reason for FDI. Moreover FDI is not selected by firms because it is a low-cost alternative to exporting. It may be on occasion, but there are high costs involved in establishing and operating a foreign subsidiary.

Indeed, other things being equal, it would be cheaper and easier for a firm to expand domestically since it would not have to incur the costs of learning about a new and alien socio-economic culture. This suggests that MNEs will tend already to be large in their own domestic markets and so have reached the stage where diminishing returns have set in to expansion in their home country. Otherwise the cheaper, local expansion option would be selected. Nor is it likely, argues Caves, that MNEs come into being because they have low-cost access to a particular input such as organisational skills or finance. If that were so then in the former case MNEs would tend to be consultants and not exist, as they do, in a multiplicity of industries; while in the latter instance if low-cost finance were the key, then conglomerate expansion domestically (in a known milieu) would be preferable to horizontal foreign expansion (in a strange and costly environment).

Rather, Caves suggests equity capital is transferred between countries as part of a package of capital plus proprietary knowledge. Both words are required. 'Knowledge' is costless to transfer (whether that knowledge is due to R&D expenditures, patenting, marketing skills, advertising expertise, or whatever) and so can be shifted with equity to another market at no cost to the owner of the equity. The word 'proprietary' is also required, however, if FDI is to be explained under Caves's scheme. The asset of knowledge can provide a return to the firm, but that return can only be maximised if the firm goes multinational. For that to be so implies that either the knowledge is difficult for foreigners to use (because they lack the technological or marketing expertise), or if they can use it then the original owner would find it difficult to capture maximum returns unless an equity stake was also held. These conditions are more likely to hold in industries typified domestically by product differentiation, whether that differentiation is due to high levels of R&D expenditures, brand-image advertising, marketing expenditures adjusting the product to consumers' needs, or whatever. In such industries local skills and expertise will either be inadequate or, the other side of the coin, be all too adequate from the viewpoint of the firm wishing to profit-maximise by selling a readily copiable product.

Sometimes, of course, proprietary knowledge can be capitalised on without FDI but by exporting or licensing. A classic example is syrup for soft drinks. Provided the originating company is satisfied with the quality control arrangements of its importer or licensee who adds carbonated water to the syrup, it can capture the rents from the transfer of its proprietary knowledge in a 'syrup plus brand name' package rather than a 'capital plus brand' package.

Caves's model goes a long way to explaining the existence of FDI and thus why MNEs will tend to be large firms with an oligopolistic home market operating with large R&D and/or advertising and other product differentiation expenditures.

For direct investment to be worthwhile, not only must the foreign firm have some more than compensating advantage over an indigenous company, it must also find foreign production preferable to either exporting or licensing. In its decision the firm must not only weigh this balance of advantage, but also take into account tariff barriers, tax structures transport costs and not least the stage of the foreign market's development. The model depicted in Figure 15.21 draws all of these threads together and is based on arguments put forward by Buckley and Casson (1981).

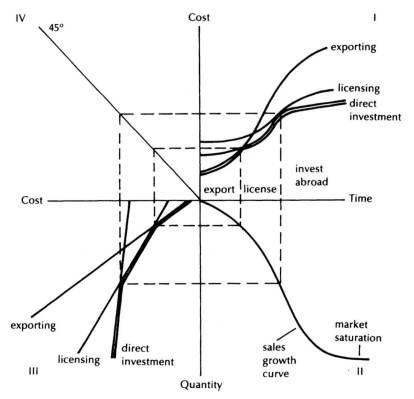

Figure 15.21

Consider quadrant III which is a normal cost–quantity diagram whose axes have been twisted (to the right) through 180°. When the firm is exporting, fixed costs are low and limited possibly to the establishment of a distribution network. Variable costs will be high and will embrace production costs 'at home', agent's commission (if appropriate), international transport costs and tariffs. Because licensing excludes the last two costs, it will have lower variable costs than exporting, hence the slope of the licensing-cost function is less than that of exporting. The fixed costs of licensing are likely to be lower than direct investment because of the start-up and sociological learning costs already mentioned. On the other hand, the variable costs of foreign direct investment are likely to be lower than under a licensing agreement; at the very least the cost of a per unit royalty to the licensee will be avoided. Thus in quadrant III the cost functions take the positions and shapes indicated. (Average variable costs are assumed constant, hence the functions are straight; this simplification is not essential even diagrammatically.)

In quadrant II the normal S-shaped market or product life-cycle curve is plotted, flipped over on the time axis by 180°. The combination of quadrants II and III enables the construction of quadrant I to be carried out. This illustrates dynamic cost functions for the overseas trading decisions, and shows how the costs of trading overseas vary with the stage of market development.

At any one output level, as shown in quadrant I, there is one optimal method of trading overseas. (The thick line connecting the lowest segments of each cost function shows which.) However, the quantity sold depends also on the maturity of the market, and the various market strategies being followed through the sales growth curve. These strategies, and time itself, influence the position and shape of the S-shaped curve. Given this, the least-cost method of servicing overseas markets varies not only with quantity sold, but quantity sold varies with time. Thus the decision as to invest directly, license or export depends on when the 'least-cost envelope' of quadrant I's dynamic cost functions indicates that each is optimal.

Figure 15.21 is, of course, stylised. Each method of overseas trading would be engaged in in turn. This need not be the case, and either cost or demand conditions could indicate, for example, an immediate market entry via the licensing route and ignoring the exporting mode altogether. The decision is further complicated by currency market fluctuations, varying international tax treatments, non-identical input costs at international level, the growth or decline of rivalry, and so on. Again we have restricted ourselves to the partial equilibrium approach. Full corporate optimisation is, as remarked earlier, either improbable or is an achievement of indefinite complexity as a modelling objective. Nevertheless the combination of the 'check list' approach of Figure 15.20 with an understanding of why factors of production flow or do not flow abroad can together order thought on how, when and where a decision to go multinational should be taken. Without a structured thought pattern (even if only implicitly adopted by management) success and failure in overseas activities would simply be randomised events.

Notes

1. Under any other type of market structure combination than those considered here (e.g. the combination of two oligopolists, or a monopolist integrating with an imperfect competitor) there would exist, to a greater or lesser extent, predatory or strategic benefits from integration. If costs are reduced (production or transaction) then a *de novo* situation arises where a case by case examination of the marginal equalities of MR and MC would be required.

2. This is proved as follows: consider the figure at the top of page 470 $\Delta TR_a - \Delta TR_b = WZ - XY = WV + VZ - WV - WU = VZ - WU$. And new slope less old slope equals change in slope or ΔMR. That is $(VZ/a - b - WU/a - b) = \Delta MR = (VZ - WU/a - b)$. At $a - b$ equal to unity $\Delta TR_a - \Delta TR_b = MR_{II-1}$. QED.

3. Note the quantity axis is somewhat unusual in the Clemens model. It is obviously not measuring homogeneous output units. Rather, the demand curves relate price received to the number of units of homogeneous production inputs used in order to provide for the successive markets.

4. The MC functions for each of the joint products can thus be identified although the average costs can still not be disentangled.

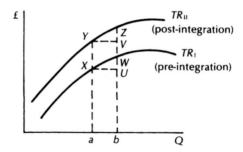

5. We can now demonstrate our verbal conclusion that, given scale, the profit-maximising prices are where the marginal revenues are proportionate to the marginal costs of production. Maximise:

$$\pi = P_x Q_x + P_y Q_y + \lambda(TC_k - TC(Q_x Q_y))$$

where TC_k is fixed total expenditure as given by the product transformation curve.

$$\frac{\partial \pi}{\partial Q_x} = P_x + Q_x \frac{\partial P_x}{\partial Q_x} - \lambda \frac{\partial TC}{\partial Q_x} = 0$$

$$\frac{\partial \pi}{\partial Q_y} = P_y + Q_y \frac{\partial P_y}{\partial Q_y} - \lambda \frac{\partial TC}{\partial Q_y} = 0$$

or

$$MR_x = \lambda MC_x \text{ and } MR_y = \lambda MC_y$$

Hence

$$MR_x/MR_y = MC_x/MC_y \text{ or } MR_x/MC_x = MR_y/MC_y$$

QED

Scale should be altered, and the constraint should be increased or decreased in the long run should either $MR_x \neq MC_x$ or $MR_y \neq MC_y$. When this long-run optimal scale situation is accomplished, then the equimarginal revenue position of $MR_y = MR_x$ of Figure 15.16 must be attained.

Bibliography

Abell, D. F. and Hammond, J. S. (1979) *Strategic Market Planning*, Prentice Hall.

Alchian, A. (1963) 'Reliability of progress curves in airframe production', *Econometrica*, vol. 31.

Ansoff, I. (1984) *Implementing Strategic Management*, Prentice Hall.

Brownlie, D. (1985) 'Strategic marketing concepts and models', *Journal of Marketing Management*, vol. 1.

Buckley, P. J. and Casson, M. (1981) 'The optimal timing of a foreign direct investment', *Economic Journal*, vol. 91.

Casson, M. (1987) *The Firm and the Market*, Blackwell.

Caves, R. (1971) 'International corporations, the industrial economics of foreign investment', *Economica*, vol. 38.

Clemens, E. W. (1951) 'Price discrimination and the multiple product firm', *Review of Economic Studies*, vol. 19.

Day, G. S. (1977) 'Diagnosing the product portfolio', *Journal of Marketing*, vol. 41, 2.

Drucker, P. (1986) *Innovation and Entrepreneurship*, Pan.

Gilder, G. (1986) *The Spirit of Enterprise*, Penguin.

Harrel, G. D. and Kiefer, R. O. (1981) 'Multinational strategic market portfolios', *MSU Business Topics*.

Hood, N. and Young, S. (1979) *The Economics of Multinational Enterprise*, Longmans.

Hirshleifer, J. (1956) 'On the economics of transfer pricing', *Journal of Business*, vol. 29.

Leontief, W. (1954) 'Domestic production and foreign trade: the American capital position re-examined'. *Economica Internazionale*, vol. VII.

Needham, D. (1978) *The Economics of Industrial Structure, Conduct and Performance*, Holt Rinehard & Winston.

Penrose, E. T. (1980) *The Theory of the Growth of the Firm*. Blackwell.

Porter, M. E. (1989) *Competition Strategy*, Free Press.

Reekie, W. D. (1972) *Pricing New Pharmaceutical Products*, Croom Helm.

Reekie, W. D. (1978a) *Give Us This Day ...*, Hobart paper 79, Institute of Economic Affairs, London.

Reekie, W. D. (1978b) 'Price and quality competition in the United States Drug Industry', *Journal of Industrial Economics*, vol. 27.

Robinson, E. A. G. (1959) *The Structure of Competitive Industry*, Cambridge.

Vernon, R (1966) 'International investment and international trade in the product cycle, *Quarterly Journal of Economics*, vol. 81.

Williamson, O. E. (1985) *The Economic Institutions of Capitalism*, Free Press.

Chapter 16

Location decisions

Industrial firms are not spread evenly over the globe, nor even throughout heavily industrialised nations such as Britain, Germany or the United States. They are concentrated in dominant centres such as towns, cities and regions. Why is this so? Why do firms decide to locate in one area rather than another? Why do different firms from different industries locate in different areas? Why do still others locate together?

16.1 Factors influencing location

The manager faced with a location decision must take four variables into account: input costs; the location of the market, transportation costs, and miscellaneous factors.

16.1.1 Input costs

Inputs include land, labour, capital, power, materials and enterprise. Only rarely are the attributes of a particular piece of land critical in determining the location of a firm. Bedrock may be essential if heavy equipment is used. A plentiful supply of water may be required in some industries for cooling or waste disposal purposes. But more generally, other features of land costs such as access roads, sewers and power supply lines can be minimised easily by careful choice *within* an area or region and can be regarded as roughly and ubiquitously uniform, at least in an advanced economy such as Britain.

Capital is a highly mobile resource with an insignificant cost of transfer. It is risk differences rather than location differences which result in varying costs of capital. Power, too, is a relatively mobile resource. Gas and oil pipelines, and the electric grid system have reduced the importance of pithead location for the power-hungry, formerly high coal-consumption, company.

For socio-cultural reasons labour is a relatively less mobile input than capital or power. Skill availability will depend in part on the nature and history of employment of any given area; in part on the schools and technical colleges of that area; in part on current levels of employment and unemployment; and given the joint supply of male and female labour, on the mix of male and female employment opportunities already present in the area. Labour costs will obviously depend on the ruling wage rates in the area but caution must be exercised in wage-rate comparisons. Productivity differences may more than offset any apparent gain in lower wage levels. It is not uncommon to find that the regions with the lowest wage *rates* are the regions with the least favourable efficiency wages.

Clearly, all raw materials are not uniformly available everywhere. Yet they vary enormously both in their bulk and in their perishability. The more costly they are to transport, the more firms will be attracted to locate near to them. Nevertheless, over the last few decades, the importance of raw materials as a location factor has been falling. Firstly, cartage costs have been steadily declining with improving transportation technology. Secondly, those industries with a low material content, but high 'brain' content in the finished product (e.g. electronics), have been taking a steadily larger share of total industrial output and are, by their nature, less dependent in cost terms on transportation inwards of bulky raw materials. Thirdly, large numbers of modern industries draw on a multiplicity of raw material sources and then engage in complex assembly or process operations. This diminishes the need to be irrevocably linked to *one* main material source. Finally, finished goods often tend to be bulky and relatively valuable and so require greater care in transportation than do the raw materials. For this reason, a one-ton motor car is costlier to transport than the one ton of sheet steel and other materials which go into its manufacture. These reasons all combine to minimise the 'pull' of the raw material source *vis à vis* that of the market.

Finally, enterprise. There is little one can say with confidence about this particular input. By definition, the supply of enterprising people should be highly mobile. If we restrict the definition to highly qualified personnel, however, then it is often said that these are relatively immobile. For example, graduate scientists and engineers, and other higher calibre executive staff are allegedly more readily attracted to the southeast of England than to other parts of the country.

16.1.2 The market

In the last few decades 'being close to the market' has become of increasing importance as a location factor. Materials, power, and high transportation costs are no longer major factors keeping firms *away* from large urban centres. Conversely, the affluence of the town as a market, the relatively high costs of transporting bulky, but valuable and complex finished goods to that market, and the advantages of being close to customers for service purposes, especially in high technology industries, have all combined to pull firms towards their major sales locations.

16.1.3 Transportation costs and miscellaneous factors

Transportation costs

It has been seen above how transportation costs, although an important variable in location decisions, are not as critical as they have been in the past.

Historical accident

In many instances no rationale can be given for a location decision. For example, what causes other than historical accident, or possibly personal preference, can be cited for the location of Player's tobacco works and Morris's motor factory at Nottingham and Oxford, respectively?

Agglomeration economies

Agglomeration is one of the most obvious features of economic activity. Firms tend to cluster together in cities and towns. There are three main types of cost saving open to a firm as a result of such clustering or agglomeration. First, *internal economies*, as the firm takes advantage of scale economies open to it due to the size of the immediate market. The firm moves down its long-run average cost curve. Second, *localisation economies*; these are economies which are external to the firm but internal to the industry. Thus, if several closely related firms are located together they benefit, since common facilities which all can draw on would not have been available had the agglomeration not existed. Examples of such economies include common research facilities; technical colleges with specialist courses tailored for the industry in question; the presence of a component supplying industry and other specialised service and consultancy industries made possible by the aggregate demand of the firms. Third, *external economies* to the industry itself; these are gains to all firms in all industries which result from locating together. They include the presence of a highly developed infrastructure of roads, railways, ports and airline facilities; a well-developed banking and capital market; financial, management, and market-research consultancy industries; a pool of management expertise which can be 'poached' from other firms if necessary; and pleasant and developed social and cultural amenities. There are, of course, diseconomies of congestion. But the balance of advantage is probably still heavily in favour of net cost savings.

16.2 Theories of location

The conventional theory of price, as depicted, for example, in Chapters 7 and 11, is spaceless. We now outline theories which predict the location of a firm.

16.2.1 Weber's theory

The father of industrial location theory is generally acknowledged to be Alfred Weber. He assumed perfect competition in all respects except that labour, materials and markets had fixed and immobile locations. Implicitly there are no physical constraints on the supply of inputs or demand for outputs at the ruling market prices. In this situation only transport and labour costs, and any agglomerative economies or diseconomies, influence location.

The least-transport-cost ($LTrC$) location can be obtained by resort to the locational triangle. For example, in Figure 16.1a, take one point of consumption C, select the most advantageous deposits of the two necessary raw materials, M_1 and M_2, and the $LTrC$ location (P) is found by minimising the total ton-miles involved in getting materials to the factory and the end product to the market. If the pull of any one

(a) A locational triangle

C = point of consumption
M_1 = source of material 1
M_2 = source of material 2
L = a cheap labour location

a, b and c are mileages
x, y and z are tons

the least transport cost location
is where $xa + yb + zc$ is
minimised.

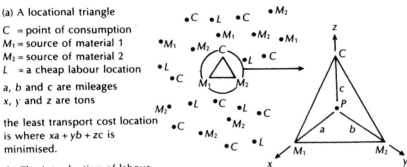

(b) The introduction of labour
cost difference requires the use of
isodapanes (i.e. curves of equal
marginal transport costs)

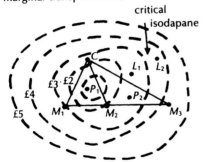

L_1 is a source of cheap labour which
would save £3 on labour costs per unit.

The critical isodapane is that which has
the same value as the savings in labour
costs

Figure 16.1

(c) Economies of agglomeration

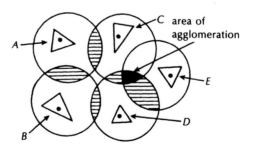

A minimum of three firms could attain
economies of £20 per unit through
agglomeration. Only the critical (£20)
isodapanes are shown in the diagram

corner is greater than the sum of the pulls of the other two, then P will be at that corner.

P, however, will not be optimal if a suitable supply of labour is unavailable. This would be so if any labour cost savings gained by relocating more than offset any incremental transport costs incurred. To analyse this situation Weber introduced isodapanes. These are lines joining points of equal marginal transport costs if the factory was located anywhere other than P_1, the $LTrC$ location, in Figure 16.1b. Assume that isodapanes are known per unit of production from £1 to £5. Then, since L_1, a location where cheap labour is available, is nearer P_1 than the £3 isodapane, it would be worth relocating at L_1 if labour cost savings there were £3 per unit. If L_1 lay outside this critical isodapane, like L_2, movement would not take place. Movement, of course, introduces further complications. Assume M_1 is a source of material 1. Then M_3 becomes a possible source of material 1 which previously had been too distant. A new locational triangle must be set up, CM_2M_3 and P_2 becomes the $LTrC$ location with a unique set of isodapanes. The process must then recommence until a final and optimal solution is obtained.

Finally, agglomeration economies are treated in a similar manner, namely as reason for movement from the $LTrC$ point. In Figure 16.1c, A, B, C, D and E are five firms located at the $LTrC$ points of their respective triangles. The firms find they can cut unit costs by £20 if at least three of them have the same location. But in order to gain from this, their average marginal transport costs must not exceed £20. The critical £20 isodapanes show that only C, D and E will find it worth their while to relocate.

16.2.2 Hoover's theory

Hoover's theory can be explained with the aid of Figure 16.2. In practice transport costs are rarely linear. That is, although they increase with distance they tend to do so less than proportionately. Not only will the cost per ton-mile decrease the greater the distance, but probably also more efficient forms of transport will be used (rail rather than road, sea rather than rail and so on).

In Figure 16.2 the firm uses one raw material, located at M, and serves the one point of consumption, C. The line $a'a$ is the transfer cost gradient of transporting the finished goods to the market. Thus, if the plant were situated at C, the transfer costs would be limited to Ca', the so-called 'terminal costs' of distribution, off-loading from factory pallets and so on, into the hands of consumers. The distance Ma indicates the total transport costs of moving the finished goods to the market if the factory were located at M. The line $a'a$ has the curvature indicated because of a diminishing transport cost rate per ton-mile. The line $b'b$ is the transfer cost gradient of transporting the raw materials to the factory. Clearly, such assembly costs would be minimised if the plant were located at the material source and maximised if the plant was located at the market. The distance Mb is the terminal loading and off-loading charge incurred in transferring the raw material from the source to the plant.

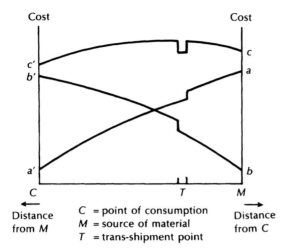

Figure 16.2

The total transport cost of assembly and distribution of raw materials and finished goods is given by $c'c$, the aggregate of $a'a$ and $b'b$. Given the curvatures of the latter two lines, the least-cost location must be at an end point, such as C or M.

The introduction of a trans-shipment town T, because, say, the goods must be transferred from sea to rail, results in both $a'a$ and $b'b$ 'jumping' by the amounts involved in the appropriate terminal charges of off- and on-loading. A location at T, however, avoids such additional terminal or trans-shipment charges. (A location *away* from T means that Ca' and Mb must be incurred again, namely at T.) Thus the most favourable location can now be either an end point, or a trans-shipment point. Thus, on Hoover's analysis, a location within the Weberian triangle is unlikely except where trans-shipment junctions occur.

16.2.3 Spatial demand curves

A normal demand curve is spaceless. It depicts a relationship between price and quantity at a point and imposes no further constraints, making the implicit assumption of perfect resource and factor mobility. In fact, a consumer positioned nearer a seller will purchase more than one further away because the price for the latter includes the cost of movement to the seller. The sloping demand curve has not one, but two determinants – price and location.

August Lösch was the first writer to attempt to develop a theory of spatial demand. In his initial model Lösch assumed an agrarian economy on a uniform plain with uniform transportation costs in all directions, and an even distribution of population and raw materials. Trade is introduced for the first time when some of Lösch's self-sufficient farmers attempt to sell a surplus of their home-made beer to others.

His arguments are illustrated in Figure 16.3. Assume a Löschian plain with a retailer wishing to sell good X at price p. It costs consumers mt to visit the store, where m is the distance in miles and t represents the transport cost rate. So the price paid by each consumer is $p + mt$. Each (identical) consumer has an identical demand curve for X (Figure 16.3a). Thus, at price $\bar{p}$, a consumer living next to the store will buy q_1 units, a consumer m miles away will buy q_2, and a consumer r miles away will buy nothing. Since consumers are distributed evenly around the store r is the radius of a perfect circle depicting the market boundary. Thus, as in Figure 16.3b, it is possible to draw a demand *cone* around the seller, according to which quantity bought drops off with distance. The volume of this cone multiplied by an indicator of population density gives the quantity demanded in the market area at price $\bar{p}$. If the exercise is repeated at different prices, differently sized demand cones which are associated with a specific location of a firm will be obtained. Hence a price:quantity schedule can be calculated which takes into account transport costs and distance. DD in Figure 16.4 represents such a schedule, or *spatial demand curve*.

16.2.4 Profit-maximising theory

Since Lösch assumed uniform transport costs in all directions, an even distribution of population and that all consumers have identical demand curves, total revenue is the same in all locations. The revenue maximisation location is indeterminate. Since it is additionally assumed that factors are perfectly mobile and uniformly distributed, total costs are the same everywhere. The profit-maximising location is also indeterminate.

In contrast, the profit-maximising theory argues that both TR and TC vary with location. This has been most eloquently explained by Smith and Richardson who we follow here. Figure 16.5 shows curves of these variables.

The TR (or Space Revenue) curve shows TR, as given by an (adjusted) Löschian demand cone, when the plant, and hence the origin of the cone, is located at different places. Some of Lösch's assumptions concerning the demand cone are

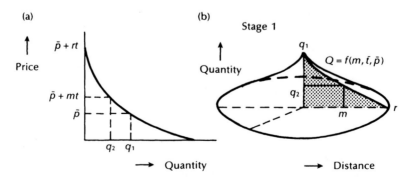

Figure 16.3

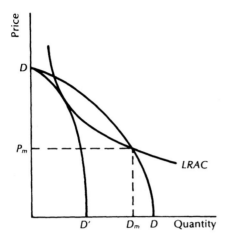

Figure 16.4

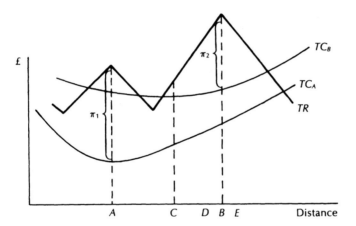

Figure 16.5

relaxed. Firstly, we allow population to be more concentrated in some areas than in others. *Ceteris paribus*, the greater the population density within a market area, the greater the total revenue it yields. In addition, the volume of the cone would not be multiplied by a simple population density indicator. Population density is likely to be higher closer to the plant rather than further from it and each of those living close to the plant would be expected to buy a greater quantity than each of those living further from it (due to differences in transport costs). Therefore the population density factor would have to be weighted to reflect the locational distribution of population within the area. Market areas with different distributions of population, even if both had the same total population within their boundaries, may have different population density factors.

Secondly, we relax Lösch's assumption of identical individual demand curves by allowing average income to vary with location. Assuming that the income elasticity of demand is positive, quantity demanded is positively related to mean income. Thirdly, if the transport cost rate decreases with distance from the plant, *ceteris paribus*, the gradient of the cone's upper surface will become flatter as m increases.

Combining these factors and assuming that price is fixed, a slice through a modified demand cone may appear as in Figure 16.6. The flattening of the edges is due to assumed decreasing transport rates. The kinks in the edges are due to differing population densities and average incomes.

If, instead of plotting Löschian demand cones at points along the distance axis, we plot the Richardson style total revenue associated with each cone, as in Figure 16.6, we derive for a given price, the space revenue curve, *TR*, of Figure 16.5. (This figure may be regarded as a slice through a three-dimensional diagram with distance coming out of the page.) The peaks correspond to locations of relatively high density population, high mean incomes, etc.

Each space cost curve, TC_A and TC_B in Figure 16.5, is constructed under the assumption of a given output. It may be derived from the corresponding average (per unit of output) space cost curve. Average costs in space equal the sum of average basic and average location costs. The former are the average production costs if the firm pays the lowest possible price for each input. Location costs are the premium over these prices which must be paid to gain the factors in a particular spot, rather than where they have the lowest price and the necessary transport costs of these inputs. (Note the output transport costs to market are included in the *TR* curve.)

If we assume that all inputs are available at all locations at the same price except one which is available only at *K* in Figure 16.7, and suppose the only additional costs of using this resource at other locations are those of transport, then the line *AC* of Figure 16.7 represents average space costs. If we now relax the assumption of uniform availability of resources and assume that they may occur in isolated locations, then as one moved, average location costs would at first rise, then fall, then rise, etc.

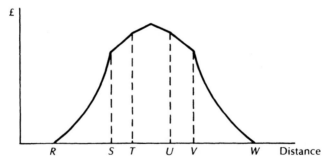

Figure 16.6

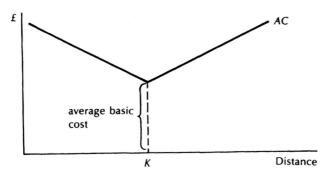

Figure 16.7

Multiple minima may then occur. (This assumes factor ratios are unchanged.) In addition, if at different places the ratio of average costs of two (or more) inputs changes, the isocost line in an isoquant figure will change gradient and the constant output could be produced at different cost levels. Again multiple minima may exist. If we assume that there is only one AC minimum and that transport costs are not linear with distance the average total cost curve can be U-shaped. Since the AC curve is drawn for a given output, if we multiply AC by this output we gain a curve of the same shape but representing TC.

Now return to the TR curve of Figure 16.5. Given price, this shows how output, i.e. the volume of a demand cone multiplied by a population density factor, differs between locations. But the TC curve relates to a single output. Therefore corresponding to each single point on the TR curve, and hence each single output, there is a complete TC curve. Hence in Figure 16.5, to simplify the figure we show only two curves. TC_A relates to the TR level at location A, and TC_B relates to the TR level of location B. The minimum of different TC curves *may* occur at different outputs because of possibly differing optimum factor ratios. The profit-maximising location occurs at location A where the difference between the TR level and the corresponding TC curve is greatest. Notice that one cannot compare the TR at C with either of the two TC curves drawn. Neither TC curves relates to the output corresponding to the TR level at that place.

If an input is subsidised in certain locations, but not in others, the total costs of producing the same output in that location will decrease. The TC curve over those locations will be lower than it would otherwise be. For example in Figure 16.5, if an input was subsidised in locations between D and E, both TC curves would fall in that range *only*. π_2 would then increase and may exceed π_1. (We have ignored any effect on the TR curve of a movement of employment into the area DE which may increase the population density there.)

16.2.5 Locational interdependence

A criticism of all of the previous theories is their lack of consideration of rivalry.

Using a simplified analysis (see Figure 16.8) we explain Hotelling's discussion of locational rivalry. To facilitate analysis a homogeneous product, perfect market information and linear transportation rates are assumed. A linear market (rather than a point of consumption) and *given* plant locations are also assumed. The two sellers are identified as, and located at, A and B respectively. The arms beginning at A' and B' represent the (linear) transportation costs from the two locations. The boundary between the two market areas is at X where the delivered product price from A and B is equal, where the gradients of delivered price intersect. Thus, on the linear scale, A's market is OX, B's market extends from X to some boundary undefined in this figure.

The assumption of a linear market can be readily relaxed if one visualises Figure 16.8a as being merely a cross-section through a three-dimensional diagram. Figure 16.8b represents a bird's eye view of such a situation. The lines surrounding A and B join points of equal delivered price and are known as isotims. The market boundary, where consumers are indifferent as to the source of supply, is formed by the intersection of isotims of equal value.

Let us now relax the assumption of given locations and ascertain how competitive interdependence affects the location decision. Hotelling used a model consisting of two ice-cream vendors, with uniform production costs, selling their products to a uniform linear market (a beach) with inelastic demand where each consumer would

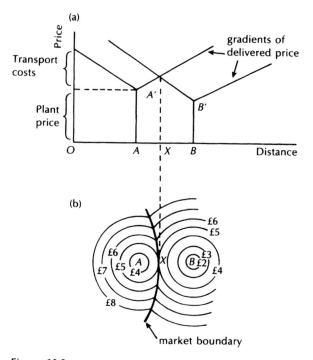

Figure 16.8

buy exactly one ice-cream. He postulated that the two vendors would end up in the middle of the beach in a back-to-back situation (Figure 16.9a). One firm could capture the entire market by locating anywhere, but two could only share the market equally by locating together. Thus in Figure 16.9b, firm *B* is located non-optimally.

This model can be criticised on a number of grounds, however, as being too restrictive. Firstly, the market can be shared evenly if the firms locate at the quartiles, as in Figure 16.9c. If a third firm entered the market, this type of symmetrical dispersion is even more likely, since the back-to-back situation would be inherently unstable with more than two competitors.

If we relax the assumption of infinitely inelastic demand, price reductions will increase quantity sold. A two-plant monopolist or two firms in collusion would then reject the back-to-back situation and locate at the quartiles in order to minimise transfer costs. In Figure 16.9c, continuing our ice-cream analogy, the average distance walked to purchase a cone is halved compared with Figure 16.9a's back-to-back situation. Superimposing Figures 16.9a and 16.9c in 16.9d illustrates graphically this net saving in transfer costs. The cross-hatched areas (transfer cost

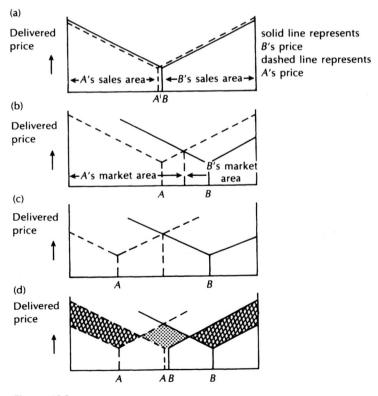

Figure 16.9

savings) exceed twice the dotted area (transfer cost increases as a result of quartile location).

We can now relax two further assumptions in our model, those of uniform production costs and identical price policies. In Figure 16.10 firm A sets up in the centre, and consumers buy at the prices indicated by the gradients of delivered price. If B enters, locates at B and has production costs of BB' B will be unable to compete with A and has chosen an unprofitable location. At C, a firm's costs are again higher than A's, but low enough to enable C to undercut A from O to X. C can now attempt to extend his or her market by geographic price discrimination. In area OC, price can be raised to OC'', provided OC'' is below A's gradient of delivered price. The extra revenue so obtained can be used to lower prices to the right of C, giving a gradient extending from, say C''', thus moving the market boundary to Y. A would inevitably react by price cutting also and the process would continue until an equilibrium situation was reached.

One assumption that we cannot relax is that of homogeneous products. If product differentiation is introduced to our model then, instead of rigid market boundaries, only blurred and uncertain areas are predicted.

Lösch, in later models, also introduced concepts of competitive interdependence, profit maximisation and customer reaction. Consider again the spatial demand curve of Figure 16.4. If the retailer's $LRAC$ curve is now added, the conclusion is that the optimum size of store is one providing for an aggregated demand of D_m at price p_m (otherwise, there would be either excess supply or demand, and given a situation of free industry entry this would be a situation which could not persist).

Lösch believed that with the entry of competitors, circular market areas would become hexagonal and so all unclaimed space would be occupied and no market overlaps would occur. As a result DD must fall to DD' (Figure 16.4) tangential to $LRAC$ for perfect hexagonal matching. Figures 16.3b, 16.11a and 16.11b illustrate the derivation of this pattern.

The market radius differs for different goods. Partly this is due to the need, on the supply side, for different scales of production. Partly it is due, on the demand side, to consumer preference to search for and to compare different sources of

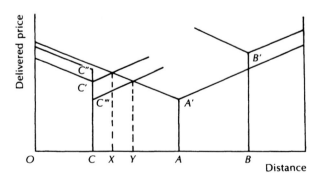

Figure 16.10

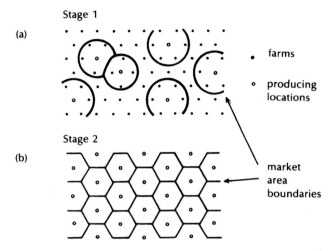

Stage 1

(a)

farms

o producing
locations

Stage 2

(b)

market
area
boundaries

Figure 16.11

expensive and/or infrequently purchased goods or services. Thus, some centres in Lösch's 'economic landscape' (the metropolii) will have each and every industry's hexagonal pattern centred on them. Others, villages, towns and cities, will each have relatively fewer such coinciding producing locations.

Greater appreciation of the importance of time, distance and market boundaries can be obtained from Figure 16.12. Assume a homogeneous product, two producing areas, perfect information, consumer immobility, and linear transportation costs. Region A's supply and demand curves are shown in the traditional manner. Region B's are reversed and juxtaposed with region A's. The transfer costs between the two regions are shown by the distance MN. Since B is the lower priced region, any product movement would be from B to A, and B's portion of the figure is elevated against A's by MN, the unit cost of transfer.

The 'excess supply' curves ES_a and ES_b can be obtained for the relevant regions by subtracting the quantity demanded at any price from the quantity supplied at that price. These show the amount by which regional supply exceeds demand at any given price. Clearly, there is zero excess supply in each market at their respective equilibrium prices. The intersection of the excess supply curves indicates the unique price at which B will willingly supply a surplus to its own regional requirements ($GF = LM$) and at which A will willingly purchase that surplus to match its supply deficit ($DE = LM$). Thus, provided the difference in market prices in the two regions is greater than the transport costs, trade will occur. Conversely, *prices can differ between two regions* and trade will not occur *provided the differential is less than the transfer cost.*

This is the rationale behind the basing point[1] or uniform delivered price system operated for many years by the Portland Cement Makers Federation in the United Kingdom. The system provides for the same delivered price at the same point of delivery for all brands of cement, irrespective of the works from which the cement

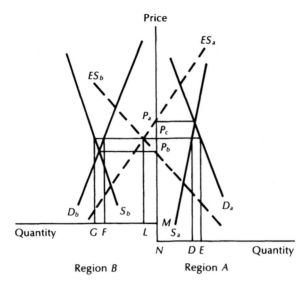

Figure 16.12

may come. The number of cement works in Britain and the number of prices have not always been identical. Factories near each other, for example could have the same base price. Radiating from each basing point is a series of concentric circles at four or five mile intervals. The circles from each point continue until they meet the circles radiating from another point. The delivered price per ton increases within each of the circles by an agreed increment. The map of Britain is covered with a network of isotims after the fashion of Figure 16.8b. Thus every buyer at a particular point will pay exactly the same price for cement. Every manufacturer is encouraged to minimise transportation costs by selling as close to his works as possible. The further away he delivers, the more likely it is that he will run into isotims controlled by another basing point and the amount he receives will begin to decrease.

For the system to be effective, the isotims and the base prices must be known to everyone in the trade; the product must be homogeneous and so be perfectly substitutable; and spatial differentiation of the product, namely high levels of transfer costs relative to delivered price, is essential.

16.2.6 Central place theory and gravity models

Central place theory developed directly out of the arguments underlying the spatial demand curve. Each larger central place performs all or most of the central place functions of smaller centres and other functions as well. Functions that can be performed only in a city or metropolis are said to be 'nested in' or 'layered upon' lower order functions that can be performed in towns which in turn are layered upon those performed in villages.

Central places are supported or maintained by the incoming flows of people to purchase the goods or services available there. Both buyers and sellers can be argued to work according to the principles of marginal equivalency in the amount of effort they spend to purchase and distribute their wares. The pattern of spatial availability of goods and the shopping efforts to get them depend upon their value relative to the cost of negotiating an exchange transaction.

Consumption, the lowest order function, takes place wherever people live. Retailing appears in towns, villages and hamlets. Wholesaling, manufacturing and government services only become characteristic at the town level. Trans-shipment of goods appear in towns and cities. Agglomeration economies are present in cities with a concomitant reduction in transaction and distribution costs. Consumers can cluster purchases and sellers maximise their volume of trade from a single point.

The principle of marginal equivalency ensures that as the variety of goods that can be profitably stocked at any one central place rises, the higher is its order. Assortments are broadest in cities and narrowest in villages. On the supply side, a retailer will expand his or her assortment to the point where the marginal profit added by the last item added tends towards zero. On the demand side some goods are so unique or so expensive that the consumer will only willingly hazard risk of money loss after diligent comparison shopping. High order central places provide the opportunity, at a low cost, for such comparison in closely located stores. Other products are purchased frequently, or are low in value. In these cases consumer knowledge is already high, and the risk of monetary loss low, so that the marginal utility of time to the consumer is of more value than the small money savings which might be obtained by time-consuming search activity. Such goods will be purchased in the closest, low order, central place.

Thus the movement of people towards goods in a given central place of whatever order is a function of at least three variables. First, there are the characteristics of the goods themselves: whether they be luxuries or necessities, price or income elastic or inelastic, and whether, as a result, they merit comparison and search before purchase. Second, the necessity for movement depends on the order of alternative central places which are available for the consumer to choose from, given the combined cluster of purchases the consumer wishes to make on any one occasion. Third, the relative desirability of movement depends on the personal cost of visiting the central place. This cost will be some combination of each of time, money and effort outlays.

So central places attract people in from the hinterland, and also from other central places of the same or different orders. Gravity models have been developed to give operational meaning to this and to the term 'market area'; and to ascertain what catchment area or hinterland a given central place draws upon. The task of a gravity model is to relate in a quantifiable fashion the costs incurred and benefits gained by consumers as they move towards a central place.

Specifically, gravity models answer such questions as:

- From how large an area will a particular type of distributor draw custom?

- Where should a distributor locate to minimise personal consumer costs from his or her potential market area?
- How many plants and distribution outlets are required to serve consumers in a given region or regions?
- From how large an area can a single customer draw supplies?

The 'market area' or trading area of a central place can be circumscribed by the use of isolines. An isoline is a line dividing the combined population of two centres along which the 'gravitational pull' of the two is equal. The size of the circumscribed area will be a function of population, income per capita, and personal cost outlays involved in reaching the central place. Some, empirically verified, models plot isolines which are equiprobability contours that consumers will shop in a specific centre. Probabilities decline as the distance from the centre increases and the distance to other centres becomes correspondingly less.

For example, Huff calculated that the probability that consumers in each homogeneous statistical area will go to a particular shopping centre for a particular type of purchase was:

$$P_{ij} = \frac{S_j}{T_{ij}^x} \bigg/ \sum_{i=1}^{n} \frac{S_j}{T_{ij}^x}$$

where P_{ij} is the probability that a consumer from the ith area will go to centre j, S_j is the size of shopping centre j, T_{ij} is travel time from customer's base in i to centre j, and x is a parameter to be estimated empirically and which would vary product by product.

The discussion in this chapter has provided a logical framework to show how the location decision is made. Whether or not the individual firm will consciously go through the steps outlined here is a moot point. However, the prudent manager will certainly take into account the range of variables we have highlighted and will investigate in depth those most relevant to the conditions in his or her particular industry. Should the manager have a specialist staff department aiding him or her in his decision, or call on outside consultants, then the formal logic which we have detailed will certainly be employed, albeit with adaptations and modifications to meet the needs and data availability of the situation.

Note

1. Basing point pricing has been held to be illegal in the United States. The British attitude depended on the circumstance of the case. The Cement Makers Federation agreement was upheld in 1961 and 1973 by the Restrictive Practices Court, but formally terminated in 1987.

Bibliography

Armstrong, H. and Taylor, T. (1985) *Regional Economics and Policy*, Philip Allen.
Berry, B. D. L. (1967) *Geography of Market Centres and Retail Distribution*, Prentice Hall.

Huff, D. L. (1962) 'A probabilistic analysis of consumer spatial behaviour', in W. S. Decker (ed.), *Emerging Concepts in Marketing*, American Marketing Association.

Needleman, L. (1968) *Regional Analysis*, Penguin.

Richardson, H. W. (1969) *Elements of Regional Economics*, Penguin.

Smith, D. M. (1971) *Industrial Location: An Economic Geographical Analysis*, John Wiley.

Public policy and regulation of business

Chapter 17

Competition policy legislation

Managerial knowledge of competition policy legislation is important for several reasons. Firstly, the manager who has such knowledge has an idea as to which actions are illegal or are likely to be prohibited. Secondly, an examination of past investigations by the Monopolies and Mergers Commission (MMC), Restrictive Practices Court and European Commission (EC) helps the manager decide whether, if the activity of his or her company was referred, it would or would not be likely to be sanctioned. Hence the questions arise: why does monopoly policy exist? What is the current legislation? What criteria have the MMC, Restrictive Trade Practices Court (RTPC) and EC used to decide whether or not to allow an activity to proceed?

17.1 Rationale

Government policy is usually aimed at improving economic performance. This presupposes that such performance is poor. Why might this be so, and what defects is policy aimed at? The concept of consumers' surplus can help provide an answer. Consumers' surplus is the value (or utility) consumers obtain from buying goods, which is over and above the total price they pay the supplier. It arises because of the fact that the price paid for each unit is the same, but is, in turn, equal to the utility of only the last unit bought, while earlier units have all provided greater utility. (This is explained by the two economic laws, the law of diminishing marginal utility and the marginal equivalency principle of consumer equilibrium which states that the marginal cost (price paid) must equal the marginal benefits obtained (or utility).) Geometrically, in the special case where utility can be measured by money, consumer surplus is the triangular area DP_1A under the demand curve and above the revenue rectangle OP_1AQ_1 in Figure 17.1.

Now assume that the perfectly competitive industry of Figure 17.1 is monopolised and that a higher price is charged by virtue of the monopolist's increased market power. Output is reduced from Q_1 to Q_2. The original consumer surplus triangle is considerably reduced in size to DP_2B. Part of the original triangle, the rectangle P_2P_1CB, is transferred to the monopolist as additional profits at output

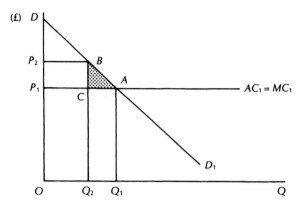

Figure 17.1

level Q_2; the remainder is lost to society as a whole, to both consumer and producer. This area, the shaded triangle ABC, is the deadweight loss from monopoly.

However, the monopolised industry may get the benefits of scale economies, and so lower costs, say AC_2 in Figure 17.2. In this case the net welfare loss (or gain) to the economy is the difference between the two shaded areas, ABC and P_1CDE. The shaded area P_1CDE is a further addition to monopolistic profits. (We have ignored the fact that the profit-maximising output with scale economies would be greater than Q_2 because the original MR curve would cut the lower AC curve at a greater Q.) Because of the scale economies arising from monopolisation, Q_2 can be produced with fewer real resources than otherwise. Resources are released to increase output of other products elsewhere in the economy.

On the other hand, monopolisation may have the reverse effect. Market power often enables high-cost producers to remain in business. Competition, by mounting pressure on firms' profits, tends to discipline both management and employees to

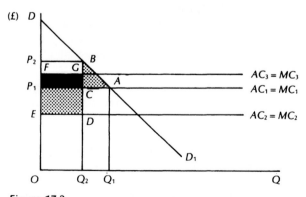

Figure 17.2

utilise their inputs and to put in more effort more effectively and more energetically than is the case when this pressure is absent. Thus monopolisation may raise costs, say to AC_3 (see Note 1). The solid rectangular area P_1FGC is here a deduction from maximum monopoly profits at Q_2 (see Note 2). The net welfare loss is now represented by this area plus the deadweight loss triangle. More real resources are being used to produce Q_2 than would have been in perfect competition.

The case for anti-monopoly thus rests in the first instance on the presence of deadweight loss resulting from monopolistic price and output practices. When scale economies are present as a result of the monopoly, however, the situation is less clear cut. A welfare trade-off is required between the dead-weight loss to the consumer and the cost savings accruing to the producer. Simplistically, a merger should be allowed if the cost savings which will result are greater than the consequent loss of consumer surplus, and vice versa. Where scale economies do not exist, the presence of X-inefficiency reinforces the arguments in favour of anti-monopoly policy. By extension, when X-inefficiency and scale economies are both present, then any welfare trade-off must be less favourable to the monopolist than it would be in the absence of X-inefficiency.

This is a very abstract explanation of the rationale behind government competition policy. More practically, we can summarise the case for and against increased industrial concentration and monopoly power as follows:

Factors in favour of increased concentration:
1. increased monopoly profits provide both the incentive and the wherewithal to conduct research and development and to innovate;
2. attainment of scale economies;
3. avoidance of capacity duplication.

Factors in favour of diminished concentrations:
1. avoidance of X-inefficiency;
2. avoidance of red tape;
3. avoidance of price:output levels leading to resource misallocation.

It should be noted, of course, that these sets of arguments are *not* restricted to the polar extremes of pure monopoly and perfect competition, and consequently are not necessarily mutually exclusive.

17.2 UK competition policy

17.2.1 Restrictive practices

British legislation against restrictive practices dates back to 1948, to the Monopoly and Restrictive Practices Act; but current legislation, the Restrictive Trade Practices Act 1976, consolidated earlier legislation beginning with the Restrictive Trade Practices Act of 1956. This 1956 Act set up the Restrictive Practices Court, composed of High Court Judges and experts to replace the Monopolies and Restrictive

Practices Commission (MRPC) for the consideration of restrictive practices. The Act required any agreement between two or more persons who manufactured or supplied goods in the United Kingdom where the agreement related to the prices charged or paid, the terms or conditions on which goods were to be produced or supplied, the quantities or descriptions of the goods, the manufacturing process or the persons to be supplied, to be registered with the Registrar of Restrictive Trade Agreements. The Registrar would take proceedings against the persons involved, in the Restrictive Practices Court (RPC).

All agreements which were taken to court were *presumed* to be against the public interest unless the Court was persuaded that two conditions held. Firstly, the agreement had to fulfil at least one of seven 'gateways':

1. that the restriction is necessary to protect the public where the use of the goods requires special knowledge or skill;
2. that the removal of the restriction would deprive buyers and users of substantial benefits;
3. that the restriction is a necessary defensive measure against other restraints imposed on the trade by persons outside it;
4. that the restriction is a necessary defensive measure against an outside monopoly;
5. that the removal of the restriction is likely to have an adverse effect on the general level of employment in some area;
6. that the removal of the restriction is likely to cause a substantial reduction in the export trade of the United Kingdom;
7. that the restriction is necessary to maintain another restriction which the Court finds to be not contrary to the public interest.

Secondly, the Court must also be satisfied 'that the restriction is not unreasonable, having regard to the balance between those circumstances and any detriment to the public or to persons not party to the agreement . . . resulting from or likely to result from, the operation of the restriction'.

Experience since the 1956 Act, especially the possibility of operating unwritten price agreements, resulted in the Restrictive Trade Practices Act of 1968, which amended the 1956 legislation in three ways. First, price *exchange information* not registrable under the 1956 Act, can have much the same effect as a *price fixing agreement*, although only the latter was registrable (and usually declared illegal). The 1968 Act empowered the Board of Trade to call up any such information agreements for registration (i.e. this would still not be compulsory). Second, an additional 'gateway' was added. A restriction can now be defended on the grounds that:

8. it does not directly or indirectly restrict or discourage competition.

Thirdly, the government was permitted to make orders providing exemptions for certain agreements from registration provided that either:

1. (a) the agreement is aimed at promoting a scheme of substantial importance to the economy;

(b) its main object is to promote industrial efficiency or to improve production capacity;

(c) an agreement is necessary to achieve this object within a reasonable time;

(d) only those restrictions which are reasonably necessary to achieve this aim will be allowed; and

(e) on balance the agreement is in the national interest; or

2. the agreement was designed to restrict price increases or to gain price reductions.

The 1973 Fair Trading Act repealed the 1948 Monopolies and Restrictive Practices Act and amended the 1956 and 1968 Acts. The Registrar of Restrictive Practices was replaced by the Director General of Fair Trading. The Director's duties were 'to keep under review commercial activities with a view to becoming aware of, and ascertaining the circumstances relating to, monopoly situations or uncompetitive practices'. In addition, restrictive agreements and information provisions within service industries were brought under the 1956 Act.

Finally and currently in force is the Restrictive Trade Practices Act 1976 which consolidated and only slightly amended earlier legislation. All agreements and information provisions relating to prices charged or recommended, terms and conditions of supply, quantities to be supplied, process of manufacture (form of provision), persons or areas to be supplied or purchased from for both manufacturing and service industries are, with certain exceptions, to be registered with the Director General of Fair Trading (DGFT). Information provision on costs is also included. The exceptions include those first exempted under the 1968 Act and certain others. The unexempted registrable agreements or provisions are *presumed* to be contrary to the public interest unless the RTP Court is persuaded that at least one of the previously existing 'gateways' applies and that the 'tailpiece' of the 1956 Act is also fulfilled. If the DGFT believes that an agreement is not sufficiently significant to merit court proceedings, he can apply under Section 21(2) of the Act to the Secretary of State to issue directions to this effect.

17.2.2 Resale prices

The 1956 Restrictive Trade Practices Act prohibited *collective* enforcement of resale price maintenance. However, it effectively increased the powers of manufacturers enforcing *individual* resale price maintenance (RPM) (namely the practice whereby the manufacturer stipulates the resale prices of his goods and where he can enforce these prices by withholding supplies from retailers who do not adhere to his terms). The 1964 Resale Prices Act prohibited RPM on all but 'exempted' goods.

The Restrictive Practices Court was allowed to exempt goods where it believed that without RPM:

1. the quality or variety of available goods would be reduced 'to the detriment of the public'; or

2. the number of outlets for the goods would be 'substantially' reduced 'to the detriment of the public'; or

3. the price would in the long run rise 'to the detriment of the public'; or
4. 'the goods would be sold by retail under conditions likely to cause danger to health'; or
5. necessary after-sales service would be reduced to the detriment of the public.

The Resale Prices Act 1976 consolidated earlier legislation. The same conditions for exemption apply.

17.2.3 Monopolies

The 1948 Monopolies and Restrictive Practices Act was the first UK legislation against monopolies. Its provisions have been described above.

The 1956 Restrictive Trade Practices Act, dissolved the MRPC and for 'monopolistic' situations created the Monopolies Commission to which the Board of Trade (BOT) could again refer the same situations as it could under the 1948 Act. The onus was still on the Monopolies Commission to show that the situation was against the 'public interest', the definition of which remained unchanged from the 1948 Act. The 1965 Monopolies and Mergers Act made service industries subject to the 1948 Act.

The most significant change in monopoly legislation since 1948 was contained in the 1973 Fair Trading Act which is currently in force. The Director General of Fair Trading may, subject to veto by the Secretary of State, refer monopoly situations which are believed to exist to the Monopolies and Mergers Commission (the MC, renamed under this Act). The Act altered the definition of a monopoly situation to a situation where:

1. one person supplies or buys at least 25% of a market in the UK; or
2. a group of interrelated companies supplies or buys at least 25% of a market; or
3. agreements exist which prevent parts of the UK from being supplied with the good at all; or
4. at least 25% of the UK market is supplied by several persons who restrict or distort competition.

The same criteria apply to services. Monopoly situations in exports may be referred, where these occur when at least 25% of UK production of the expected good is produced by one person or a group of related firms. The MMC may be asked to investigate whether a monopoly exists and if it does whether it is in manufacturing services or exports, who benefits, whether any uncompetitive activities are maintaining the monopoly and whether the monopoly allows the firm(s) to operate in a particular way. The MMC may additionally be asked whether any of the monopoly's activities 'may be expected to operate against the public interest'.

The Act made the 'definition' of the 'public interest' which was hitherto contained in the 1948 Act, more specific:

the Commission shall take into account all matters which appear to them in the particular circumstances to be relevant and, among other things, shall have regard to the desirability

(a) of maintaining and promoting effective competition ...
(b) of promoting the interests of consumers, purchasers and other users of goods and services in the United Kingdom in respect of the prices charged for them and in respect of their quality and the variety of goods and services supplied;
(c) of promoting, through competition, the reduction of costs and the development and use of new techniques and new products, and of facilitating the entry of new competitors into existing markets;
(d) of maintaining and promoting a balanced distribution of industry and employment in the United Kingdom; and
(e) of maintaining and promoting competitive activity in markets outside the United Kingdom on the part of producers of goods and of suppliers of goods and services, in the United Kingdom.

If the MMC finds that a monopoly's activities are against the 'public interest', the Secretary of State may ask the DGFT to gain voluntary Undertakings from the party(s) concerned or he may issue Orders preventing or modifying the practices concerned.

Notice that it was only after the passing of the 1973 Act that antimonopoly policy explicitly stated that the process of competition should be regarded as a normative goal.

17.2.4 Anticompetitive practices

In 1980 the Competition Act broadened the scope of anticompetitive legislation. The Director General, with the Secretary of State's approval, was given power to carry out an investigation into any conduct which appears to be 'anticompetitive', regardless of whether or not a monopoly situation might exist. A person is acting 'anticompetitively' according to the Act if either his or her conduct alone or when considered with that of others has, or is intended or likely to have, the 'effect of restricting, distorting or preventing competition in connection with the production, supply or acquisition of goods in the UK'. If the Director decides that anticompetitive behaviour exists, those concerned may give undertakings of restraint. If these are rejected by the Director he may again, subject to approval, make a 'competition reference' to the MMC. The MMC will investigate whether the person referred had in the preceding 12 months acted as the Director claims, whether such action was 'anticompetitive' and whether the action was 'expected to operate against the public interest'. The MMC may add suggested remedies and, if the referred person does not act upon these suggestions from the Secretary of State, the latter may legally prohibit the activity.

The 1980 Act also empowered the Secretary of State to refer any question of the efficiency, service provided or possible misuse of monopoly situation by a bus service, water authority, agricultural marketing board or any body whose members are government appointed and any organisation with a statutory duty to supply any of these goods or services. By December 1985 the Director General had initiated 18 investigations, in which three companies were found not to have acted anti-competitively. In nine cases the firm concerned gave acceptable undertakings or the practice was too insignificant to merit a full reference.

17.2.5 Mergers

Anti-merger legislation began with the 1965 Monopolies and Mergers Act. The BOT was empowered to refer mergers to the MC who would be asked to investigate whether acquisition 'operates or may be expected to operate against the public interest', the definition of the 'public interest' being that of the 1948 Act. Notice that the onus is again on the MC to show that the merger is against the public interest.

Currently in force is the 1973 Fair Trading Act which, in repealing the 1948 and 1965 Acts, redefined the circumstances in which an acquisition may be referred. Nowadays the Secretary of State may refer a merger involving manufacturing or service industries – again, which is only proposed, or which occurred within the preceding six months, but where either the value of acquired assets exceeds £5m. or the resulting combine supplies or is supplied by 25% of the market. Unlike the case of monopoly, the Director General may only advise the Secretary of State as to which firms to refer. The MMC would be asked to decide whether the situation qualified for investigation and, if so, whether the creation of the combine would be likely to operate against the 'public interest' as redefined in the Act. In 1980 the £5m. size limit was raised to £15m. and in 1984 to £30m. Again, if the MMC finds the merger against the public interest the Secretary of State may require undertakings from the firms concerned or prohibit the merger or require the firms to separate.

Following a government review of mergers policy and publication of a Blue Paper (1988), the 1989 Companies Act contained two procedural changes. Firstly, firms can be told whether a referral is likely by voluntarily submitting a completed question-naire, a Merger Notice, to the DGFT, thus speeding up this decision. In the light of this 'prenotified' information the DGFT advises the Secretary of State on whether or not an acquisition should be referred to the MMC. The Secretary of State has 20 working days after receipt of the prenotification in which to make public his decision as to whether a referral will take place. Secondly, in place of a MMC reference the DGFT is able to accept *legally binding* undertakings by parties to a merger to act in ways thought by the DGFT to be in the public interest, an example might be divestiture of specific assets so reducing a particular market share.

The Commission is usually allowed six months in which to make its prediction of the likely state of the post-merger market and to come to a judgement on the basis of that prediction. Once a reference has been made there is an automatic prohibition on each firm buying further shares in the other. Enforced delays of this sort have resulted in the firms calling off the merger. The possibility of a negative verdict or changed market conditions can explain such breakdowns.

17.3 European Union competition policy

17.3.1 Restrictive agreements

Restrictive practices legislation is contained in Article 85 of the Treaty of Rome. This states that

> all agreements between undertakings, decisions by associations of undertakings and concerted parties which may affect trade between Member States and which have as their object the prevention, restriction or distortion of competition within the Common Market are incompatible with the Common Market.

The article gives, as examples of outlawed behaviour, price fixing, restrictions on output, restrictions on technical development, market sharing, price discrimination and contracts contingent on supplementary obligations. Restrictions are exempt if they are found to improve 'the production or distribution of goods or to promote technical or economic progress while allowing customers a fair share of the benefit' provided they are necessary for the attainment of the objective and do not remove competition for a substantial part of the goods concerned.

17.3.2 Dominant positions

Article 86 of the Treaty of Rome states that: 'any abuse ... of a dominant position within the Common Market or in a substantial part of it shall be prohibited as incompatible with the Common Market in so far as it may affect trade between Member States'. The article gives examples of abuses. These include imposition of 'unfair' purchase or selling prices, restrictions on output, technical development, etc., price discrimination, contracts contingent on supplementary obligations.

17.3.3 Mergers

Until 21 September 1990 mergers were dealt with under Article 86 of the Treaty of Rome. However from September 1990 Regulation 4064/89 became effective. This regulation applies to all 'concentrations' which have a 'Community dimension', that is when (a) the combined world turnover of the firms involved is over 5 billion ECU, and (b) the aggregate turnover within the European Community of each of at least two of the companies is over 250m. ECUs, unless each of the companies has over 66% of its aggregate Community turnover within one state. (Following a review in October 1993 it was decided that these thresholds still stand.) A 'concentration' occurs when either two or more firms merge or one firm gains control of another.

Certain joint ventures come under this regulation. Concentrations which restrict competition in the Common Market or in a substantial part of it will be declared incompatible with the Common Market 'unless authorised on the ground that their contribution to improving production and distribution, to promoting technical or economic progress or to improving the competitive structure within the Common Market outweighs the damage to competition'. In deciding whether a concentration does restrict competition the Commission must consider the market power of the firms, their economic and financial power, the position of suppliers and users, the structure of affected markets, entry barriers and the supply and demand trends for the goods concerned, and the development of technical and economic progress provided it is to the advantage of consumers.

Individual states are not allowed to take a merger to their own national investigative committee if the merger has a community dimension (subject to certain exceptions). If a merger does not reach the EU thresholds it may be referred to the antitrust organisation within its own state by the relevant nation state authority, for example, in the United Kingdom, by the Secretary of State. Thus the regulation is said to provide a 'one-stop shop' whereby companies know that they will be investigated by the Commission or by their national organisation but not by both.

All mergers which have sizes above the thresholds must be notified to the European Commission within one week of the announcement or agreement of the bid. Thereafter for three weeks the merger may not be put into effect and within one month the Commission must tell the parties whether or not the merger will be referred to the Commission for a Phase II investigation. At this stage the Commission conducts hearings, consults member states, etc. and must within four months decide whether the merger is or is not compatible with the European Community.

After investigation, the Commission may require that the firms divest, or any other action to restore competition. The regulation also allows the firms to make commitments voluntarily to the Commission to modify the original plan to make the merger acceptable.

17.4 Evaluation of UK policy

17.4.1 Restrictive practices

Various criticisms have been made of existing legislation and procedures. We shall consider firstly, the prevalence of restrictive practices; secondly arguments relating to the appropriateness of the gateways; thirdly, arguments concerning registration; fourthly arguments concerning justiciability; fifthly arguments concerning the rulings of the RTPC, sixthly empirical evidence concerning the effects of the legislation, and finally recent proposals for replacing the Restrictive Trade Practices Act.

Prevalence

Elliot and Gribbin (1977) have argued that in the early 1950s some 50 to 60 per cent of manufacturing output was cartelised. Between 1956 and December 1992, 10,600 agreements were registered (Office of Fair Trading 1992).

Appropriateness of the gateways

The eight gateways of the 1976 Act (the first seven from the 1956 Act and the last from that of 1968), through one of which a restrictive practice must pass before the Court will declare it legal, have varying degrees of support in economic logic.

Gateways (1) and (2) are unexceptional in terms of economic theory. But as the first Green Paper on restrictive practices (1979) reported, Stevens and Yamey (1965) have argued that the first gateway is redundant because legislation exists against situations which may put the public at risk, and where it does not the gateway is insufficient anyway.

Gateways (3) and (4) both pertain to countervailing power and a restrictive practice allowed through either can be justified on the grounds that the monopoly power so permitted is necessary to offset monopoly power existing elsewhere. Despite the view suggested to the first Green Paper group by the National Federation of Retail Newsagents that gateway (4) should be widened, the group concluded that it would appear that this gateway already deals sufficiently with equality of bargaining power.

Gateway (5) relates to employment. It can be argued that the general level of employment in an area is a responsibility of either macro- or regional economic government policy and not that of a group of firms operating in a restrictive practice. The reverse argument could also be made that the provision of employment may often benefit many and therefore, in a decision on the desirability of an agreement, such an effect should be allowed to offset any detrimental effects which restriction might have.

The first Green Paper argued that the two tests of gateway (6) are 'discriminatory'. The first test, that removal of the agreement would reduce export earnings or volume by a substantial amount relative to aggregate UK exports, it argued, favours firms in industries with a relatively large share of UK exports over those in industries with a relatively small share. The second test that removal would reduce export earnings or volume by a substantial amount relative to the total business of the industry was argued to 'discriminate against large industries especially where they have a small export trade'. The Green Paper adds further that the gateway was not presented in a way which would achieve its intended objective of improving the balance of payments. This is because there is no gateway which would enable a restriction to pass due to its causing a reduction in imports, due to greater efficiency, although greater inefficiency *per se* is included in gateway (2).

In its evidence to the first Green Paper group The National Consumer Council argued that the final gateway (8) was unnecessary because it undermined the legal presumption against restrictive practices. The Green Paper replied that the clause should be retained because it allowed insignificant agreements which reached the Court to be continued.

The first Green Paper also noted that the current legislation deterred some significant agreements, which were in the public interest, from being made. Such agreements would have either to pass through a gateway which some firms may believe to involve great expense and time, or to be sanctioned on the grounds of efficiency in the national interest which applies only to agreements 'of substantial importance to the national economy'.

Registration

The Green Paper noted a further problem with the Act; that many registrable agreements are not registered. A failure to register is not a criminal offence but it does mean the agreement cannot be legally enforced and does render the colluding parties open to civil proceedings by anyone who has consequently suffered a loss.

In addition if an unregistered agreement is discovered and brought before the RTPC then normally the Court will make an order preventing the parties continuing with the agreement. If the parties do continue they may be charged with contempt of court. But the second Green Paper (1988) argued that these procedures have only a 'slight' deterrent effect. This has been because such contempts have been difficult to prove; when proven the fines have been too low; in the case of civil proceedings all known cases have been settled out of court; and any registrable agreements which have not been registered are difficult to detect.

The second Green Paper argued that the fact that the criterion for registration relates to the legal form of an agreement and not to its actual or possible effect on competition has certain undesirable effects. Firstly, many agreements which have no effect on competition or may even increase it have to be registered so imposing an administration cost on firms and on the Office of Fair Trading (OFT). Secondly, certain agreements with anticompetitive effects have been so phrased as to obviate the need for registration. For example a necessary condition for registration is that both parties accept the restriction; if the 'agreement' is drafted so that only one party accepts it, it is not registrable. Williams (1993) gives as an example, the case of Lyons which he states agreed to supply Schweppes with 43 per cent of its citrus concentrates but which was not registrable because only Lyons accepted the restriction.

The 1988 Green Paper also noted that negotiations between the DGFT and parties to an agreement on how the agreement should be changed to gain exemption under 21(2) now 'dominate(s) the whole process'. But the legislation does not state precisely the criteria which the OFT must use to decide whether the remaining characteristics qualify for a referral. Furthermore the Green Paper estimated that in 1985 the average time taken for 85 cases to gain exemption was 2 years and 9 months, with 9 cases taking over 8 years.

Justiciability

Stevens and Yamey (1965) have given several reasons why they believe that a judicial court is an inappropriate forum for determining whether a restrictive practice does or does not pass through one of the gateways and the tailpiece. Firstly, some agreements may have socially beneficial or detrimental aspects and the RTPC is required to make a value judgement as to the net effect where this comparison is not based on legal logic. Secondly, since none of the members of the Court is an economist, it has been doubted whether they could correctly appreciate some of the economic arguments made to determine acceptable values for economic variables such as 'the reasonable price'. Thirdly, it has been argued that the RTPC is an inappropriate institution to set down economic policy which it does when making decisions as to the acceptability of certain economic behaviour. It is also inappropriate to lay down political policy which it would do if deciding in favour of one group rather than another on grounds of, for example, the effects of an agreement on unemployment. In its place, Hunter (1966) has suggested an Administrative Tribunal, presumably including economists and politicians. However, since one effect of the Acts has been to lead to the termination of agreements *before* they are presented to the RTPC, this issue of 'justiciability' has been less important than it might be.

Rulings by the RTPC

Much discussion has questioned some RTPC decisions. For example, in the case of the supply of magnets, some have questioned whether the price agreement allowed by the Court was necessary to maintain the existing technical co-operation and hence the rate of technical progress. In the case of the Black Bolt and Nut Association, the Association had its price-fixing agreement upheld on the ground that all sellers offered a buyer the same price. Thus the buyer was saved the cost of shopping around. No consideration was given to the benefits the buyer might get by such shopping around. And no reasons were given in the Court's verdict as to why the Association should be treated any differently from any other industry.

Effects of legislation

Finally, several empirical studies of the effects of the 1956 RTPA have been conducted. Swann *et al.* (1974) carried out case studies of 40 industries, 18 in depth, 22 less so. Of the former group, in 4, the agreement was upheld by the Court; in 6, the agreement was struck down by the Court; and in 8 the agreement was abandoned voluntarily before it was tried in Court. Swann *et al.* consider the impact of the Act at different times relative to its implementation. The study found that, of 60 agreements existing before the Act, 8 were not registered after it and were suspected of having been abandoned. Various cases of agreement modification were observed around the time of the passing of the Act. For example, in the case of batteries, agreement to engage in exclusive dealing was removed, but price fixing continued. In some industries agreements were substantially unchanged but reworded to appear more acceptable and in some, home agreements were discontinued but those on exports remained. Immediately after the passing of the Act instances of agreements breaking down were observed, probably due to anticipated additional future competition, for example in surgical dressing manufacturing.

Further, events in industries where the agreement was struck down were considered. Of 34 such industries, between 61 per cent and 53 per cent experienced competition, mainly in prices and discounts, as for example wire ropes manu-facturing. This was partly due to the entry of new substitute products and to greater import penetration. In 50 per cent of the industries, information agreements were introduced, often to prenotify other parties of a price change or of a tender price, e.g. Tile Mileage. In other cases, price leadership followed termination, e.g. electric cables (leader BICC), and in some cases, supply agreements with a large buyer.

In the longer term, after termination in some industries, behaviour paralleled the shorter-term effects. In some, information agreements were ended (frequently before the 1968 call for registration). The greater competition was found to lead to reduced capacity and greater cost consciousness. In many cases, in the long term greater competition was due to innovation. Swann et al. list 13 industries from their sample where this occurred. However, 'on a not inconsiderable scale', collusion rather than competition resulted. Price leadership became more evident in the longer term than in the short term, for instance in steel-drum manufacturing. Swann et al. also found that the Act led indirectly to greater merger activity to reduce excess capacity which followed the termination of agreements, and possibly also to reduce competition.

However, two major weaknesses of the Swann et al. study have been proposed by Clarke (1985). Firstly, case studies are not based on comparable quantitative data; comparisons are therefore made based on impressionistic interpretations. Secondly, no rigorous method of indicating that some of the observed behaviour was actually due to the Act was adopted: in many cases, such as mergers, it could have had some other cause.

Finally, O'Brien et al. (1979) selected a sample of firms in industries which were known to be affected differently by the 1956 Restrictive Trade Practices Act. These firms fell into four groups: (a) those in an industry where a restrictive practice(s) was upheld; (b) those in an industry where a restrictive practice was struck down by the Court; (c) those in an industry where agreements were voluntarily abandoned and (d) those in an industry where no restrictive practice had operated – the control group. Three subperiods were considered: a pre-Act period, 1951–8, and two post-Act periods: 1959–67 and 1968–72. By comparing the groups within any one period and the performance of groups between different periods, and by standardising variables for groups (a) to (c) by the values for the control group – to account for changes in the macroeconomy rather than the change in the law – the effects of the 1956 Act were estimated. The authors concluded that:

1. Although the rate of return on assets or on sales decreased between the earliest and later periods for groups (a) to (c), most of this could be attributed to changes in the macroeconomy and only some of it to the change in legislation.
2. The group whose restrictive practice had been struck down had slower asset growth in the earlier period than in the post-Act period, whereas the group

whose restrictive practices were upheld by the Court grew more slowly in the later period compared with the earlier period. In terms of sales, firms which retained their restrictive practices grew slowly relative to the control group in both periods, whereas firms in the groups whose restrictive practices changed grew more rapidly.

3. In case the removal of restrictive practices due to the Act made industries more competitive and hence led to firms merging to increase their profitability by economies of scale or monopoly power, comparisons of merger activities were made. For no group were significant differences in merger activity between the earliest and later periods found, and very few differences between the groups were found either. In fact, the control group had the greatest proportion of acquiring and acquired firms in all three periods.

Recent proposals

Given its criticisms of a *form*-based approach the second Green Paper proposed that an *effects*-based policy should be pursued instead. It stated that the government proposed to prohibit anticompetitive agreements which have the potential to affect the consumer or supplier. 'But this does not necessarily include agreements which only affect the ability of an individual competitor to compete. The agreements must affect competition in the relevant market taken as a whole' (para. 3.2). Compared with the current system, this effects-based approach was seen to remove the need for firms to register all agreements and to bring under control agreements which in the past had been drafted in a way which removed the requirement for registration.

Following a period of consultation the government published a White Paper (1989) which set out details of its intended legislation. The RTPA 1976 and the Resale Prices Act 1976 would be repealed. The intended legislation is as follows. Agreements or concerted practices which have the aim or effect of restricting or distorting competition in a UK market will be prohibited. This prohibition will apply to agreements which: fix prices and charges which determine net prices; may be expected to lead to the fixing of prices, for example, agreements to exchange price information; involve collusive tendering; involve sharing markets, customers, inputs, production or capacity; involve collective refusals to supply, price discrimination, tie-ins, etc. The relevant 'market' will include a consideration of entry barriers and, in effect, the cross-price elasticity of demand between different goods and services. It will not be defined in terms of a geographic area. Excluding agreements which fix prices, those agreements between firms whose combined turnover is less than £5m. will not be prohibited. (In the case of vertical agreements the *de minimus* threshold is a UK turnover of £30m. by each party.) This *de minimus* provision will be set so that firms with too small a market share to influence competition will not risk a penalty from forming an agreement. Agreements which the DGFT agrees 'make a sufficient contribution to the production or distribution of goods or the provision of services or to economic or technical progress' to negate their restrictive effects and where 'consumers share adequately' in the benefits will be exempt from prohibition for a specified period. Both the definition of the types of activities prohibited and the criteria for exemption follow those of the Treaty of Rome's Article 85.

The DGFT will investigate possible anticompetitive agreements, decide on exemptions and issue guidance on whether certain types of agreements are prohibited. But he or she will not hear appeals against his or her own recommendations. Such appeals will be heard by a restrictive trade practices tribunal drawn from membership of the MMC. Unexempted parties which breach a prohibition will be liable to fines up to the larger of £250,000 or 10 per cent of their UK turnover. Fines of up to £100,000 may also be imposed on individual directors.

The proposals would also give the DGFT powers to enter and search premises for documents to detect breaches of prohibitions, thus partially overcoming the criticism that collusion is difficult to detect. The penalties indicated above also counter the criticism that in the past the penalties for enforcing unregistered agreements were too small. The use of a Restrictive Trade Practices tribunal rather than a Court answers the criticism concerning the inappropriateness of the legal profession to make decisions requiring economic concepts.

However Williams (1993) has argued that the gains from the implementation of the White Paper's proposals may not be as great as some expect. Firstly, the proposal to change from a *form*-based criterion to an *effects*-based criterion is not as significant a change as some have suggested because when deciding whether to exempt an agreement under section 21(2), the DGFT already uses the effects on competition criterion. Secondly, the anticipated gains from preventing some anticompetitive agreements continuing as it is alleged they do under the current legislation, may also be less than anticipated because in fact restrictive agreements practised by large firms currently come under the anticompetitive criteria of Article 85 (see below). Thirdly, the proposals would be likely to lead to a large number of enquiries from firms wishing to establish whether their activity may be registered as anticompetitive thus negating some of the administrative savings expected to result from the absence of registrable agreements.

17.4.2 Monopolies

The public interest

Hay and Vickers (1988) and others have argued that the broad definition of the 'public interest' in the Fair Trading Act 1973 makes policy 'less focussed and less predictable than it might be' (p. 60) since it allows many considerations apart from competition to be taken into account. Secondly, they argue that the 25 per cent market share reference criterion will include many cases where competition is present. Whilst the OFT would be expected to discover this and so decide against a reference, this implies that the significance of competition is being given a dominant position, which is not consistent with the broad definition of the public interest given in the Act.

By considering a large number of cases Devine *et al.* (1985) have suggested the general position of the MMC to be as follows. 'Deliberately anticompetitive' conduct, for example, exclusive dealing and entry-preventing behaviour, has been consistently criticised, as have restrictions on the sale of competitors' goods, forms of discount payments to disadvantage potential competitors, tie-in sales and full-line forcing. (Full-line forcing is the requirement by a seller that if one of his or her products is to be sold, the full range must also be sold.) In addition Devine *et al.* reported that price discrimination has usually been condemned as have 'very high profits'.

The Green Paper (1978) notes that MMC investigations impose a considerable burden on the firm(s) concerned, both in time and cost. Monopoly references specify time limits: usually 18 months or 2 years. A firm's situation could change significantly during this period and additional salary and legal costs have to be expended over this period to prepare the case.

Consistency of the MMC

The consistency of MMC reports has aroused discussion. For example Clarke (1985) has argued that the Commission has been 'extremely liberal in its treatment of monopoly profits'. Thus in the Cat and Dogfoods Report (MMC 1977) the Commission accepted that Pedigree Food's average rate of return on capital (on historic costs) of 47% in 1972–5, compared with an average for all manufacturers of 16% was reasonable, despite the fact that they had 50% of the market. Pedigree had argued that their high rate of return was due to high efficiency, and the MMC found no anticompetitive practices. Other instances of MMC approval for rates of return much higher than the average for UK manufacturing industry are Rank Xerox (36% on historic cost) and tampons (55%–80%).

Effectiveness of policy

Little work has been carried out to discover the effectiveness of UK monopoly policy. However Shaw and Simpson (1989) carried out detailed case studies of 9 markets on which MMC reports were published between 1959 and 1970 and less detailed investigations of 28 markets which the MMC had investigated over the same period. They found that the recommendation of the MMC and the ensuing undertakings by the firms concerned had 'only a minor impact on the competitive process'. Whilst the average market share of the market leaders experienced a decline in share at the time of the Report their share typically remained high for ten years afterwards. Where market leaders suffered significant decline in market share this was due mainly to competitive processes not the actions of the MMC. However Shaw and Simpson cautioned that their findings did not remove the need for monopoly investigations: MMC-recommended actions can hasten the otherwise slow rate at which competitive processes reduce monopoly power and dominance; and, secondly, the threat of an MMC investigation did encourage entry-barrier reduction and price restraint in some industries.

Comparisons with alternative procedures

In 1992 the government published a Green Paper which debated the strengths and weaknesses of the current legislation aimed at restrictive abuses of monopoly power: the 1973 Fair Trading Act and the 1980 Competition Act. The paper then evaluated three alternative options for improving such legislation.

The advantages of the current approach were seen as flexibility and with a wide range of remedial provisions when abuses are found. The current legislation is flexible in the sense that it allows the MMC to consider the conduct of firms and structural factors associated with a market such as entry barriers in both dominant-firm and oligopolistic situations. The remedial action available includes behavioural (agreement termination), structural (divestiture) and regulatory (e.g. price control requirements).

Four weaknesses of current provisions were observed. Current legislation was stated to have little deterrent effect because there are no penalties which can be applied to guilty parties and no act in itself is unlawful. Secondly, there is no right for companies which have suffered due to the market power abuse by others to obtain damages. This contrasts with the position in the United States where third parties can sue for triple damages. It is not possible for third parties to obtain a temporary order to restrain abuses whilst an MMC investigation occurs which, since the latter can take twelve months or more, causes some third parties to go out of business. Thirdly, the powers of the OFT to conduct a *prima facie* investigation are weak. Fourthly, the Fair Trading Act and the Competition Act do not cover abuses of competition in the supply of certain tangible property, e.g. land.

The three alternative options which were considered were: firstly, strengthening the existing legislation, secondly a system in which abuses of market power would be prohibited – as is consistent with Article 86 of the Treaty of Rome – and the proposals for new Restrictive Trade Practices legislation. The third option was a dual system whereby the Competition Act would be substituted by a prohibition on specific abuses but the Fair Trading Act would be retained to enable an MMC investigation in the case of a monopoly.

The advantages of a prohibition scheme were seen as providing a more effective deterrent: the DGFT would have greater investigative powers than currently and guilty parties would be liable to large fines and third-party actions; and making UK procedures consistent with European Union law specifically Articles 85 and 86 of the Rome treaty. The disadvantages related to the proposed adoption of a description of prohibited actions which was the same as that of Article 86. Firstly, if the prohibitions were described in terms of Article 86, which, when it relates to several firms does so only to companies which are structurally or economically linked, then certain conduct would not be caught by the prohibition, but they would be under the Fair Trading Act. Examples of these practices include price leadership without explicit collusion and strategic anticompetitive behaviour. Secondly, the Green Paper argued that Article 86 also relates to exploitation of market power which is more difficult to prove using the rate of return criterion – as under the Article – than is determining whether pricing is operated against the public interest – as under current UK legislation. Thirdly, Article 86, unlike the Fair Trading Act, does not include structural or regulatory remedies if an abuse is found. But fines imposed on offenders may be passed on to customers and not act as a deterrent.

In April 1993, after public consultation, the government decided to strengthen existing legislation and rejected the prohibition option. Thus it proposed to give the DGFT greater investigative powers to gain the information required to establish a *prima facie* case and power to accept legally enforceable undertakings to be given by firms to avoid an MMC reference. Powers would be established to prevent an abuse continuing whilst it was being investigated by the MMC, and the use of certain property rights, for example, relating to land would be included under both the Competition Act and the Fair Trading Act. The government rejected a prohibition system because it believed that the uncertainty which firms would face over whether or not their activity was anticompetitive and the possibility of fines and private actions would restrict rather than foster competition.

Williams (1993) has also argued that, if the Restrictive Trade Practices proposals are implemented, firms may be subject to a large fine if they collude, but only measures to deter continuance in the case of an abuse of market power. This may encourage firms to become dominant by growth rather than to collude. Consistency of treatment is therefore desirable.

17.4.3 Mergers

Implementation

During the period 1988–92 the OFT found 1,021 mergers which qualified for a reference under the Fair Trading Act criteria, excluding those cases where confidential guidance was given. Of these, 67 were referred; an average of 6.9 per cent of qualified mergers per year. During this period the Secretary of State chose not to refer only one case which the DGFT had recommended should be referred (11 cases during 1965–92), but he did refer 4 cases which were not recommended by the DGFT.

In the case of mergers an obvious difficulty is that the MMC must usually pass judgement on whether their effects are *likely to be* against the public interest in the future, whereas in the case of monopolies the Commission must decide whether the past or current effects *have been (are)* against the public interest. Therefore accurate merger vetting is often more difficult than the examination of monopolies or abuses of monopoly power.

Referral criteria

Following an unpublished review of merger policy by the Department of Trade and Industry (DTI), in July 1984 Norman Tebbitt, Secretary of State, stated that 'my policy has been and will continue to be to make references primarily on competition grounds'. Thus the government's stated policy for referral differed from the criteria which the MMC are to apply when deciding if referred mergers are against the public interest. However George (1990) has argued that the Tebbitt referral doctrine is so vague that it creates uncertainty as to whether a merger will be referred and could also result in inconsistency in the cases referred. He argues that a more precise set of guidelines would be desirable.

Fairburn (1993) has criticised the Secretary of State for refusing recommendations of referral by the DGFT arguing that the Secretary of State has less time and probably less expertise to make the relevant comparisons of gains and losses than the MMC and that it is the MMC which the legislation charges with this duty not the Secretary of State. Therefore Fairburn argues that the responsibility for making references should lie solely with the DGFT.

Hay and Vickers (1988) have further criticised the referral procedures arguing that since many acquisitions which are referred are abandoned whilst the MMC investigates, in effect the decisions by the OFT and Secretary of State to refer pre-empt any subsequent decision which the MMC makes. Box 17.1 describes the arguments and issues which were considered by the MMC in a recent merger report.

Public interest criteria

A number of authors have tried to summarise the criteria which the MMC uses when deciding whether a merger is against the public interest. Fairburn (1993) found that when the MMC supported defending management it was on the grounds of reduced morale and efficiency which the merger would cause. A concern for career prospects in the regions, especially Scotland was detected, as were arguments to restrict foreign takeovers such as the offer by the Hong-Kong Shanghai Banking Corporation for the Royal Bank of Scotland. The latter was opposed because it would undermine the Bank of England's control over monetary policy. The view was also expressed that it was advantageous to have a British trans-atlantic shipping company. Fairburn also observed that in the Elders IXL/Allied Lyons case the MMC stated that the volume of debt used to finance a merger might also be a public interest issue if it overexposed the firm to an excessive financial risk.

Fairburn also considered competition issues. When, on the few occasions, cross-subsidisation has been relevant, the MMC generally accepted firms' arguments that such activity was irrational. Vertical mergers, by a firm with great market power, have caused the MMC concern. In considering horizontal mergers during 1980–6 Fairburn observed that the MMC grouped products within a market according to how close substitutes they were and delimited the geographic boundaries of a market in terms of customers' transport costs. The MMC was willing to include imported products as presenting competition within a market. However the closest correlation which Fairburn could detect between market share and merger prevention was that acquisitions involving market shares of less than 30 per cent would probably be allowed whilst those involving a share of over 60 per cent would probably not be passed. Where mergers involving market shares in excess of 40 per

---

Box 17.1

Report by the MMC on Hillsdown Holdings PLC and enterprises belonging to Associated British Foods PLC

Hillsdown was an investment holding company which owned HL Foods Ltd which canned fruit and vegetables and produced ambient stored meals. Associated British Foods (ABF) owned British Sugar and Anglia Canning. The latter also canned fruit and vegetables and produced ambient stored meals.

On 13 September 1992, Hillsdown bought the canning undertakings and assets of ABF plus some associated buildings (but not the companies themselves). The amount paid was £21.1m., largely by an issue of scrip.

On 27 February 1992, the Secretary of State for Trade and Industry referred the acquisition to the MMC. The MMC was asked to decide whether (a) a merger situation qualifying for investigation under the 1973 Fair Trading Act had been created; and (b) if it had, whether the merger operates or may be expected to operate against the public interest. The Commission had 3 months in which to deliver its Report.

Qualification

ABF told the MMC that the value of the acquired assets was £35.2m. The MMC decided that the value of the assets purchased was over £30m. and Hillsdown accepted this.

Views of the main parties

The MMC received views from the two main parties and various third parties. Here we summarise those of the main parties only.

ABF told the MMC that it had sold its fruit and canning activities because it had for several years been operating at a loss with no expected improvement. ABF entered discussions with Hillsdown and it became clear that rationalisation under one company was the best policy. Negotiations with Albert Fisher Group PLC as a potential purchaser of Anglia failed. ABF argued that the alternative to purchase by Hillsdown was closure of its canning factories. ABF argued that the removal of Anglia's competition from Hillsdown would allow Hillsdown to raise prices only in small and specialised areas, for most products competition from imports was high. Excess capacity in the EC food market still existed following rationalisation of the merger and so retailers had strong negotiating power. ABF said the exit by Anglia was unlikely to incur entry barriers. ABF argued that the merger should allow Hillsdown to increase its efficiency by reducing overhead costs of selling, buying, invoicing, administration and stockholding, and it would gain economies of scale by using machinery continuously rather than intermittently.

Hillsdown told the MMC it had decided to acquire Anglia because Anglia's activities were complementary to its own and it could rationalise the combined business to make a more efficient larger firm. Hillsdown disagreed with the MMC's argument that the merger considerably reduced the number of alternative UK suppliers of canned fruit and vegetables which multiple retailers and

→

wholesalers could buy from. Hillsdown argued that such buyers sourced from wherever prices were least including from outside the United Kingdom. Hillsdown said it regarded two other firms Co-operative Wholesale Society Ltd (CWS) and Stratford-upon-Avon Foods Ltd as active competitors as were imports. Concerning the extent to which Hillsdown could exploit its larger market share, Hillsdown said it had, in the past, been sensitive to the requirements of multiple retailers and that such retailers had great purchasing power. The ability of retailers to buy from alternative suppliers rather than competition from frozen vegetables restrained Hillsdown's pricing power. With regard to entry barriers Hillsdown argued that used canning equipment was available in the United Kingdom, that in recent years entry had not occurred and that likely decreases in profit rates in the industry would deter entry. Hillsdown stated that it had gained the synergies expected from the merger – mainly from closing Anglia's factories – but the cost of rationalisation had been higher than expected. Concerning the effects on employment, Hillsdown had made 370 staff redundant at one of Anglia's plants of which 51 had been offered new or temporary jobs.

Public interest

In assessing the likely effects of the merger on the public interest the MMC considered a number of factors.

Competition

The MMC argued that there were only four other UK canners of seasonal fruit and vegetables: Albert Fisher Group PLC, CWS, Gerber, and Mid Norfolk. Only two produced in retail pack sizes (as opposed to catering and wholesale size cans) and had spare capacity which could be taken up by extra demand from retailers who wished to buy from two independent companies after the merger. But the MMC decided they held sufficiently significant market positions to be able to restrain any attempts Hillsdown might make to raise prices. This was especially so given the expectation that the market for canned vegetables would decline. The probability that entry would occur into the seasonal fruit and vegetable canning industry was very low because of the likely low profitability.

The MMC decided that although European canners provided slightly different products, for example, baby carrots not sliced carrots, the concentrated structure of the multiple retailer market resulted in sufficient interest from foreign producers to restrain UK suppliers' prices. The MMC noted that no multiple had objected to the merger. However Hillsdown was found to have some scope to raise prices for canned raspberries where it was virtually the only UK supplier.

Interests of growers

The MMC argued that vegetable growers were large and that those who formerly supplied Anglia had been offered contracts by Hillsdown on terms and for quantities which overall did not suggest the merger had had adverse effects. After the merger Hillsdown became the only UK canner of raspberries. But the MMC argued that even if Anglia had offered its Brechin canning factory to the growers, they would still have been heavily dependent on Hillsdown for the disposal of their crop.

→

Employment
The MMC argued that the merger resulted in a loss of 370 jobs at one of Anglia's plants and 91 at the other. But if the merger had not occurred the plants would have been closed anyway with the loss of as many jobs. The trade union, Manufacturing Science Finance complained about the pension arrangements for former Anglia employees. The MMC believed that Hillsdown had not acted unreasonably.

Efficiency gains
The MMC found that Hillsdown was gaining economies in merging headquarters, reorganising warehousing, etc., but little in the canning process.

Conclusion

The MMC concluded that whilst Hillsdown initially gained market shares usually indicative of market power in some markets, the buying power of retail multiples and the threat from imports would prevent Hillsdown from gaining significant price increases. The merger had only a marginal effect on raspberry growers, not an adverse effect on employment, nor on competition for ambient stored meals. Therefore the MMC decided that the merger was *not* against the public interest.

Source summarised from Monopolies and Mergers Commission (1992).

cent have been cleared the MMC almost always argued that easy entry conditions would act as an important factor in restraining prices. Fairburn also noted that the MMC did not generally try to subtract estimates of cost savings from estimates of losses due to greater monopoly power despite the rationale of the Williamson trade-off.

In a separate study, Weir (1993) used a sample of 73 merger reports published during 1974–90 to regress a variable indicating whether a merger was allowed or not against the MMC's prediction as to the merger's effect on competition. He found that the MMC was more likely to pass a merger if it was expected to increase rather than to decrease competition and if it did not affect competition rather than decrease it. However, few specific sources of competition could be used both to predict the MMC's decision that a merger would increase rather than decrease competition and to predict whether a merger would decrease competition rather than leave it unchanged. The MMC appeared to be persuaded by particular behaviour in each case.

Evaluation of the MMC's criteria

We now turn to criticisms which have been made of the appropriateness of the criteria which the MMC has used. Williams (1993) has argued firstly, that although sometimes the MMC assesses the potential and actual managers of a target when investigating the likely effects of a merger on efficiency, it is more appropriate to allow the stock market to do this. The expectations of shareholders would affect the share price and so affect which set of managers will run the firm in the future.

Secondly, he argues that although the definition of the public interest in the Fair Trading Act includes a reference to the 'balanced distribution of employment', the MMC should ignore this. First, if a regional imbalance should be corrected, the most appropriate way to do this is through regional policy. Second, preventing a merger on these grounds may in the long run reduce employment because enhancements in efficiency which the merger would bring would not be gained. George (1990) agrees with these arguments and states that the first argument applies also to the balance of payments. He points out that the MMC have articulated such a view. For example, in the report on Car Parts (MMC 1982) the Commission argued that, even if the industry needed protection against foreign competition, this should be considered by a separate government policy and not by approving a continuation of an anticompetitive practice.

Williams (1993) also argues that the prevention of mergers by foreign companies which are state owned (and so bid-proof), for example the proposed acquisition of a division of ICI by Kemira, is also inappropriate. A better way of reducing this threat to competition is through the EC which is adopting policies to reduce the provision of state aid to distort competition. Fourthly, he argues that the volume of debt used to fund an acquisition is irrelevant to the public interest provided the Bank of England is content that the financing does not involve a risk to the viability of any financial institution, and provided that, even if the acquiring firm is bankrupt, it continues to trade and to earn operating profits.

Much debate has surrounded the burden of proof. The Green Paper (1978) argued that current legislation is biased in favour of mergers taking place because it is based on the assumption that few will be referred to the MMC. Since much empirical evidence suggests that, on average, mergers result in lower profitability (Singh 1971, Utton 1974, Meeks 1977, and more recently Kumar 1984 and Cosh et al. 1989), the possibility that mergers should not be allowed unless net benefits could be expected was considered. This possibility was rejected because (a) it would have led to around 90 per cent of mergers being referred to the MMC; (b) the MMC would find most mergers to be in the public interest; and (c) because the whole procedure may act as a deterrent to socially desirable mergers. Instead it proposed a neutral approach which would recognise both the disbenefit of reduced competition and benefits of larger size. A greater emphasis would be placed on the effects of a merger on competition. Two new clauses relating to the desirability of maintaining competition and international competitiveness of British industry were to be added to the 1973 Act's definition of the public interest. In the event, this proposal was not adopted – perhaps due to a change in government. Instead Tebbitt's referral doctrine was announced.

The 1988 Blue Paper reaffirmed the position of the Fair Trading Act arguing that to reverse the burden of proof would make it more difficult to carry out acquisitions and so would distort competition in the market for corporate control which encourages managers to run their companies efficiently.

Hay and Vickers (1988) support the conclusion of the Green Paper (1978), especially in cases of agreed mergers where both the acquirer and acquiree have more information than the MMC and have incentives to demonstrate that the merger will be socially desirable. They propose a three-stage system which they believe would give greatest weight to the competition criterion but also allows for other factors to be considered. They propose that firstly, acquisitions which 'obviously' do not reduce competition are passed; secondly, an investigation of the remaining mergers is carried out to identify those which would reduce competition; and thirdly for these cases the onus of proof is reversed: the merger is approved only if the parties concerned can show that there are sufficient compensating benefits.

George (1990) gives several reasons why he believes that the burden of proof should be reversed. First, economic theory suggests horizontal mergers may increase market power. Second, empirical evidence does not suggest that we should presume mergers are socially desirable. Third, merger partners would have more knowledge of the circumstances surrounding a merger than the MMC and may use such knowledge to demonstrate the benefits of the acquisition. He continues that the reasons given in the 1978 Green Paper and the 1988 Blue Paper for not reversing the burden are not convincing. Firstly, even with firms having to demonstrate benefits for merger approval, most would be speedily passed at the referral stage. Secondly, he argues that it is appropriate that mergers that present a threat to competition (decided by application of a threshold) would have to demonstrate the desirability of the merger on the grounds that if 'we are not prepared to accept that the greatest danger comes from the most highly concentrated industries, there is not much of a basis left for policy' (p. 104). Reversal would deter mergers which rested on 'flimsy arguments' and it would not deter those where management believed the case was convincing.

Williams (1993) also believes that none of the arguments in favour of reversing the burden of proof is acceptable. He argues that the strongest case for reversal is that it would change the type of information which would be revealed to the MMC. Certain information as to the likely effects will be possessed only by the acquirer and other information will be possessed only by the acquiree. The acquirer will reveal only positive information (information suggesting that the merger will result in a social gain) from his private knowledge. The victim will reveal only negative information (information suggesting that the merger will result in a welfare loss). If both amounts of information are approximately equal then the MMC has sufficient information to make the right decision. If the acquiring firm has planned the acquisition then the amount of privately held positive information held by the acquirer is larger than the privately held negative information held by the victim. So the MMC would need to gain more positive information from the raider than from the victim if it is to believe the welfare effect is neutral. Given the Williamson (1968) trade-off comparison of Figure 17.2, the welfare losses from an acquisition come from an increase in market power. In the case of horizontal acquisitions both the acquirer and the acquiree can calculate the market-share gain of the former and so such information is available to both firms and so to the MMC. But the MMC will not receive all of the good news about the effects of the merger. The raider will not wish to reveal his or her plans to increase the efficiency of the victim in case this raises the cost of the acquisition and the victim will not wish to tell the raider how the raider can improve the victim's efficiency. Therefore Williams argues, if the MMC receives all of the information about the welfare losses of the acquisition, but only some of the information about the benefits, the case for the reversal of the burden of proof is not proven.

In the case of agreed mergers both companies will reveal only positive news. Williams then argues that from their past experience the MMC will know that negative information will exist but is not being revealed to them and so take this into account.

A second argument considered by Williams in favour of burden reversal is that it is desirable for the MMC to allow only bids which can be shown to be in the public interest because if it accepts a bid where this cannot be demonstrated, the Secretary of State cannot prevent the merger taking place. If mergers are allowed only when positive gains are demonstrated it does not matter that the Secretary of State cannot prevent it happening. However, Williams states this is an argument in favour of removing the discretion of the Secretary of State to overrule the MMC and allowing an independent OFT to receive undertakings from the firms concerned.

17.5 Evaluation of EU policy

17.5.1 Restrictive practices

First, note that whilst Article 85 relates to competition within the Common Market, the European Commission believes it can impose (and has imposed) penalties, for example, fines, on companies registered in countries outside the Common Market if they are found to act with member firms in ways which infringe the Article. Second, the Article relates to actions which distort competition and to those which may do so at some time in the future. Third, Article 85 is phrased in the same terms as the proposed UK legislation. That is, it prohibits agreements with the aim or effect of restricting etc. competition and is not a regulation which could be criticised as only applying to agreements of a specific form.

Cases considered by the Commission show which competition-distorting behaviour has been criticised. These include the following.

1. *Price fixing agreements*: the Commission imposed fines on Fabbuca Pisana SpA, an Italian flat glass company, for, amongst other things, fixing prices and conditions of sale for flat glass for use other than in the motor vehicle industry and fixing prices and quotas for flat glass for the motor vehicle industry. The Commission also imposed fines on Groupement des Cartes Bancaire and Eurocheque International for making an agreement under which French banks charged French retailers the same commission for cashing foreign Eurocheques as they charged for payment by bank card.
2. *Application of output or sales quotas*: following investigations in 1983 and 1987, producers of PVC (polyvinyl chloride) and LDPE (low-density polyethylene)

were found to be agreeing at regular meetings to sharing the Western European market on the basis of annual volume targets, in addition to other behaviour.

3. *Exclusionary practices*: the Commission ordered the clause in an agreement made between Nutrasweet and Coca-Cola and Pepsico Inc., whereby the last two companies agreed to buy all their aspartance (a food sweetener) from the former, to be removed.

4. *Sole or exclusive distribution agreements*: the Commission prohibited an agreement whereby Grundig appointed Consten as the sole dealer of its products at the importer/wholesale stage in France. The agreement was upheld on appeal.

5. *Information exchange*: certain manufacturers in the Dutch and Belgian Paper Industry Federations exchanged information which included notification of relevant prices giving individual company's names, general terms of supply, and sales and payments received including details of discounts to particular customers. The information exchanged was so detailed that it enabled members to plan their export sales policy knowing exactly the prices charged by local manufacturers. The European Commission decided that the practice infringed Article 85.

6. *Prevention of parallel imports within the European distribution system*: Pioneer, a hi-fi equipment supplier, was fined for operating, effectively, export bans.

Also relevant to a firm are the criteria which the Commission applies to agreements which come under Article 85 but which are exempted. Examples of behaviour which has been exempted are as follows.

1. *Amadeus/Sabre*: these two firms had an agreement to provide to travel agents and others a joint product giving access to their computer reservation systems (CRSs). The Commission argued that the agreement was within Article 85(1) because price competition between the firms was reduced and the services would not be marketed independently in the Community. The agreement was given an exemption, for several reasons. Firstly, the Commission believed the agreement would improve distribution in Europe and worldwide; and secondly, the companies gave undertakings to the Commission which included a commitment that when distributing their products carriers with an ownership interest in Amadeus or Sabre would not discriminate against other CRSs. Amadeus and Sabre must not impede non-associated carriers from distributing through other CRSs and must treat equally all carriers whose products they displace.

2. *Bord Telecom Eireann/Motorola Ireland Ltd*: these two companies had formed a joint venture to set up a paging service. The Commission found that the agreement between the companies was within Article 85(1) because it included a non-competition clause, the two companies were potential independent suppliers and because the agreement prevents either firm becoming, independently of the other, a member of a competing worldwide paging service. The Commission gave an Article 85(3) exemption for 30 years because the form of the joint venture had enabled the rapid introduction of a paging service with facilities which were not previously available in Ireland. The exemption was conditional on certain changes

in the arrangements being implemented such as the eventual removal of the non-competition clause.

17.5.2 Dominant positions

Article 86 raises two substantive issues: what exactly defines a 'dominant position ... in a substantial part' of the Common Market and what counts as an 'abuse' of such a position. The Article gives no statement as to what market share constitutes a 'substantial' one. Case law suggests that this could be a proportion of the market within a single Member State and also that the size distribution of other firms in the industry is relevant. Market shares as low as 40 per cent (IBM case) and 40 to 45 per cent (United Brands) have been taken as dominant, but in both cases their competitors were very much smaller than the largest firm.

Notice that it is not dominance but its *abuse* which the Article declares as incompatible with the Common Market. The Article gives examples of such abuse and the following cases give examples of practices which have been considered abuses.

1. *Action to restrict the development of a new entrant*: British Sugar was fined 3m. ECUs for abuse of its dominant position (market share 58 per cent of the British market for granulated sugar) because it had tried to force Napier Brown – a new entrant into the market – to withdraw. British Sugar, for example, discriminated against Napier Brown by refusing to sell it pure beet sugar, whilst supplying beet sugar to other customers.
2. *Inducements to deal exclusively with suppliers*: the Commission found that British Plasterboard Industries PLC abused its dominant position in two ways, one of which was through its subsidiary British Gypsum, to put pressure on importers to stop imports of Spanish plasterboards.
3. *Charging different prices in different parts of the European Community for the same product*: the Commission found against United Brands for selling bananas at higher prices in Denmark and Germany and lower prices in the Benelux countries. In another case the Commission found that Tetra Pak (which supplies machines and cartons for packaging liquid foods) applied discriminatory pricing between member states where the differences in the price of cartons ranged between 50 per cent and 60 per cent and differences in the price of machines between 300 per cent and 400 per cent.

17.5.3 Mergers

Table 17.1 shows the number of cases considered under the Regulation during 1990–1 and 1991–2.

In 1992 it was decided that a dominant position would be created in three proposed mergers but after modifications the Commission declared them to be compatible. The only merger in the two years to be prohibited was that between Aerospatiale and DeHavilland.

Table 17.1

	No. of adopted decisions	No. which were deemed 'concentrations'	No. authorised in Stage I	No. of Stage II proceedings	No. of prohibition decisions
1991	60	55	50	1	1
1992	60	51	47	4	0

Source: Commission of the European Communities 1992, 1993.

The Commission (1993) has argued that it has allocated products to the same market if they are highly substitutable in terms of demand (not of supply), and if they are marketed along the same channel of distribution. For example in Torras/Sarrio the limited substitutability of demand between coated and non-coated papers led the Commission to allocate them into different product markets even though the producer could easily switch from the production of one type to the other. Concerning channels of distribution, in Accor/Wagon-Lits part of the reason why motorway restaurants were classified into a different market compared with other types of restaurant was that distinct operating conditions of supply apply.

The Commission argues that the market share of a merged firm is a 'significant but not a determinative factor' (2.1.c., para. 247) in its decision as to whether the enlarged firm will dominate an industry. To support this argument the Commission notes that in 1992 the largest market shares for cleared mergers were 48 per cent of the EEC and 79 per cent in one member state; whilst the lowest shares for cases where it was decided that dominance would be created were 43 per cent in the EEC and 53 per cent in one member state.

In a survey of mergers considered by the Commission in 1992, Pathak (1993) has argued that the Commission found the following characteristics indicative of dominance when high market shares were also expected:

1. market share of the leading firm is considerably greater than those of its competitors;
2. significantly greater financial power and capacity of the leading firm relative to its competitors;
3. barriers to entry;
4. little countervailing power from customers;
5. other additional structural factors such as a 'hub and spoke' route network for scheduled airlines.

Alternatively Pathak argued that even if a high market share was expected the Commission would generally not decide that the merged firm would dominate an industry if the following were observed: rapid changes such as growth, changing customer tastes; great import penetration; no entry barriers; potential entry; competitors with comparable financial power and/or significant market shares; regulations; countervailing power of buyers.

Morgan (1993) has argued that the Commission's decisions concerning mergers which led to oligopolies may be divided into three phases. In Phase I the existence of competitors with similar market shares to the merged firms was taken as indicative of their ability to pose competitive threats whilst the possibility that oligopolies so created could result in collusion was ignored. As an example she cites the truck operations of the merger between Renault and Volvo. She argues that in national markets three firm concentration ratios over 50 per cent existed. But because the combined market shares of the two companies in the *Community* market was only just over 25 per cent and because there was existing and potential competition from other financially strong firms in the national markets it was decided that the merger would not create a dominant position which would restrict competition.

In Phase II the possible application of the merger regulation to oligopolies was mentioned but a decision on this was not made, for example, in the Alcatel/AEG Kable (1991) case. In Phase III, the current phase, the possibility that oligopoly created by merger might lead to anticompetitive price parallelism is recognised. For example in the Nestlé/Perrier case (1992) the analysis by the Commission led it to believe that the elimination of Perrier would increase the chance of tacit co-ordination between Nestlé and BSN. Box 17.2 summarises the procedures and criteria adopted by the European Commission in a recent merger investigation.

Box 17.2

The Nestlé/Perrier Phase II investigation by the European Commission

On 25 February 1992, Nestlé notified the Commission of a proposal to buy all of the shares in Perrier, the largest supplier of bottled water in France. Before the bid BSN, a French food manufacturer, was the second and Nestlé the third largest suppliers respectively on the French market. Before the bid Nestlé granted BSN an option to buy Perrier's main water source (Volvic) if Nestlé's bid was successful. Therefore after the bid Perrier's activities would have been shared between Nestlé and BSN.

The Commission first considered the definition of the relevant product and geographic markets. In the former case Nestlé argued that the then relevant market was that of non-alcoholic beverages because all drinks have the function of quenching thirst. The Commission rejected this, arguing that the proposed criticism would put tea, milk, beer, etc., in the same market. The Commission argued that a separate market for bottled water existed compared with that for soft drinks. This was because firstly, bottled water is bought because of its association with purity, cleanliness, etc.; secondly, source waters are drunk in volume, soft drinks more occasionally; thirdly, the cross-price elasticity of demand between the two sectors was low; fourthly, the production and marketing of the two products are subject to different constraints; and finally, manufacturers adopt different pricing policies for the two product groups.

Nestlé argued that the relevant product market was France plus Belgium and parts of Germany because if higher prices were set in France than elsewhere,

→

parallel imports into France would occur. The Commission disagreed. It argued that the relevant product market was France. First, the demand for water varies considerably between countries, supply is usually from a large number of small suppliers and intercountry trade is low because water is relatively expensive to transport. Second, the Commission did not believe that parallel importation would be profitable because of the high transport costs, because delivered prices in Belgium and Germany were *higher* than the ex-works prices in France and because exports of French mineral waters were generally carried out by the main suppliers.

The Commission then assessed the compatibility of the merger with the Common Market under two scenarios: (1) Volvic not being sold to BSN; and (2) Volvic being sold to BSN. In case (1) the Commission decided that Nestlé's acquisition of Perrier would give Nestlé the power to act 'to an appreciable extent independently of its competitors and customers' on the French market. The reasons for this decision were that the acquisition would have involved (a) the firm with the largest water reserves, sales volumes and portfolio of brands; (b) a combined market share of over 50 per cent of the French market (twice that of the next competitor); (c) an inability of the only other supplier (BSN) to increase output if demand increased; (d) other sources being too small to constrain Nestlé; (e) retailers would become more dependent on the new firm's brands and so they could not effectively constrain the merged firm; and (f) there was no evidence that potential entry might constrain price.

Under scenario (2) the Commission concluded that Nestlé and BSN would have gained sufficient power to act jointly and independently of their competitors and customers in the French market. In coming to this conclusion the Commission first investigated the likely degree of competition between Nestlé and BSN. It took many factors into account which included the following: (a) after the acquisition Nestlé and BSN would have a combined market share of 94 per cent of the French market; (b) after the merger the two companies would have had similar capacities and market shares, a situation in which there would be 'a strong common interest and incentive to maximise profits by engaging in anticompetitive parallel behaviour' (Official Journal 1992); (c) low cross-price elasticity between national mineral waters gave an incentive for Nestlé and BSN to maintain high prices; (d) neither of the two firms had a cost advantage which would give them an incentive to compete on price; (e) innovation could not be expected to result in lower prices; and (f) the Commission saw signs of co-operative behaviour between the two firms. The Commission also decided that the threat of entry had very little effect on prices.

To avoid prohibition Nestlé made a number of commitments to the Commission. These included Nestlé making available for sale a number of springs with a capacity of 3,000m. litres (20 per cent of those held by the three companies) and their brand names. The buyer must have no relationships with the three companies which might lead it to compete ineffectively. Provided Nestlé carries out its commitments the Commission believed that the sale of 3,000 litres of capacity would be sufficient to create an effective competitor and the acquisition would be declared compatible with the Common Market.

Source summarised from the *Official Journal* (1992).

Jacquemin (1990) has criticised the regulation by arguing that turnover is an inappropriate criterion for deciding whether the regulation applies: turnover relative to market size would give a more accurate indication of market power. In fact he argues that the threshold levels were set so high as to allow some 3-digit industries to be completely monopolised without reference to the Commission.

George (1990) has argued that the burden of proof should rest with the merger partners since only those which are likely to restrict competition will be referred to the Commission. He also argues that when mergers are prevented property rights are allocated and this should be a political decision. However in the regulation the decision is not made by the Council of Ministers but by the Commission.

Overbury (1993), the Director of the Merger Task Force in the Directorate General for Competition, European Commission, counters the criticism that the Commission has been too lenient towards mergers. The excessive-leniency criticism is based on the fact that until the end of 1992 only one merger had been prohibited. But Overbury argues that firstly, the ratio of the number of prohibited to number of mergers considered in the EC has been similar to that in Germany and the United States. Secondly, the objective of the regulation is not prohibition, but to ensure that firms which propose any mergers which might reduce competition implement remedial action so that competition is not, in the event, weakened.

Overbury also defends the Commission's record against the criticism that it has made inconsistent decisions. He argues firstly that a small difference between cases can lead to a different decision (and presumably that those who make the criticism do not notice the difference between what they regard as comparable cases). Secondly, he argues that since the regulation is new, the Commission must modify its attitudes with experience if necessary.

Notes

1. This is the concept of X-inefficiency. It is nothing more than the normal 'inefficiency' which business men and women, and non-experts have always talked about. Economists, however, have reserved the word 'efficiency' for discussions relating to allocative efficiency. They have, moreover, made the assumption that firms always employ all factor inputs in the technically most efficient manner. Our discussions in Chapter 9, for example, rested on this assumption and suggest that in imperfectly competitive circumstances firms may well work within their production possibility frontiers.
2. We again ignore the fact that the profit-maximising output would now be less than Q_2.

Bibliography

A Review of Restrictive Trade Practices Policy, (1979) Green Paper, Cmnd 7512, HMSO.
Bergson, A. (1973) 'On monopoly welfare losses' *American Economic Review*, vol. 63.
Clarke, R. (1985) *Industrial Economics*, Blackwell.

'Commission decision on 22 July 1992 relating to a proceeding under Council Regulation (EEC) no 4064/89 (case no IV/M, 190–Nestlé/Perrier', *Official Journal of the European Communities*, vol. L356.

Commission of the European Communities (1992) *XXIst Report on Competition Policy 1991*, Official Publications of the European Communities.

Commission of the European Communities (1993) *XXIInd Report of Competition Policy*, Official Publications of the European Communities.

Cosh, A., Hughes, A., Lee, K. and Singh, A. (1989) 'Institutional investment mergers and the market for corporate control', *International Journal of Industrial Organisation*, vol. 7.

Cowling, K. and Mueller, D. (1978) 'The social costs of monopoly power', *Economic Journal*, vol. 88.

Curwen, P. (1993) 'Merger control in the European Community: an analysis of scope, subsidiarity and duopoly', *European Business Journal*.

Devine, P. J., Lee, N., Jones, R. M. and Tyson, W. J. (1985) *An Introduction to Industrial Economics*, Allen & Unwin.

Department of Trade and Industry (1988a) *Mergers Policy*, Blue Paper, HMSO.

Department of Trade and Industry (1988b) *Review of Restrictive Trade Practices Policy: A Consultative Document*, HMSO Cmnd 331.

Department of Trade and Industry (1989) *Opening Markets: New policy on restrictive trade practices*, HMSO, Cmnd 727.

Department of Trade and Industry (1991) *Merger Control in Europe: The main provisions of EC regulation 4064/89*, HMSO.

Department of Trade and Industry (1992) *Abuse of Market Power – A Consultative Document on Possible Legislative Options*, Green Paper, Cmnd 2100.

Elliot, D. C. and Gribbin, J. D. (1977) 'The abolition of cartels and structural change in the United Kingdom', in A. P. Jacquemin and H. DeJong (eds), *Welfare Aspects of Industrial Markets*, vol. 2, Martinus Nijhoff.

European Commission (1989) 'Council regulation (EEC) 4064/89 of 21 December 1989 on the control of concentrations between undertakings', *Official Journal of the European Communities*, vol. 32, L395.

European Commission (1994) *Community Competition Policy in 1993*, Office for the Official Publications of the European Community.

Fairburn, J. (1993) 'The evolution of merger policy in Britain', in M. Bishop and J. Kay (eds), *European Mergers and Merger Policy*, Oxford University Press.

George, K. D. (1990) 'Lessons from UK merger policy', in P. H. Admiraal (ed.), *Mergers and Competition Policy in the European Community*, Blackwell.

George, K. D. and Joll, C. (eds) (1975) *Competition Policy in the UK and EEC*, Cambridge University Press.

Harberger, A. C. (1954) 'Monopoly and resource allocation', *American Economic Review*, Papers and Proceedings, vol. 44.

Hay, D. and Vickers, J. (1988) 'The reform of UK competition policy', *National Institute Economic Review*, August.

Hunter, A. (1966) *Competition and the Law*, Allen and Unwin.

Jacquemin, A. P. (1990) 'Mergers and European Policy', in Admiraal, P. H. (ed.) (1990) *Merger and Competition Policy in the European Community*, Blackwell.

Jenny, F. and Weber, A. P. (1983) 'Aggregate welfare loss due to monopoly power in the French economy: some tentative estimates', *Journal of Industrial Economics*, vol. 32.

Kumar, M. S. (1984) *Growth, Acquisition and Investment*, Occasional Paper no. 51, Cambridge University Press.

Littlechild, S. C. (1981) 'Misleading calculations of the social costs of monopoly power', *Economic Journal*, vol. 91.

Masson, R. T. and Shaanon, J. (1984) 'Social costs of oligopoly and the value of competition', *Economic Journal*, vol. 94.

Meeks, G. (1977) *Disappointing Marriage*, Cambridge University Press.

Monopolies and Mergers Commission (1977) *Cat and Dog Foods, A Report on the Supply in the United Kingdom of Cat and Dog Foods*, HMSO.

Monopolies and Mergers Commission (1982) *Car Parts: A report on the matter of the existence or the possible existence of a complex monopoly situation in relation to the wholesale supply of motor car parts in the United Kingdom*, HMSO.

Monopolies and Mergers Commission (1992) *Hillsdown Holdings PLC and enterprises belonging to Associated British Foods PLC*, HMSO, Cmnd 2004.

Morgan, E. (1993) 'Controlling "concentrations": the treatment of oligopoly under the EC Merger Control Regulation, EARIE Conference Paper.

O'Brien, D. P., Howe, W. S. and Wright, D. M. with O'Brien R. J. (1979) *Competition Policy, Profitability and Growth*, MacMillan.

Official Journal (1992) vol. L356, Section 123.

OFT (1990) *Restrictive Trade Practices: Provisions of the Restrictive Trade Practices Act 1976*, HMSO.

OFT (1992) *Annual Report of the Director General of Fair Trading*, HMSO, HC719.

Overbury, H. C. (1993) 'Politics or policy? The demystification of EC merger control', in B. Hawk (ed.), *Institutional Antitrust Law and Policy*, Fordham Corporate Law Institute, Kluwer.

Pathak, A. S. (1993) 'Merger regulation enforcement during 1992', *European Law Review*, vol. 18.

Robertson, A. (1992) 'Enforcement of the UK Restrictive Trade Practices: judicial limitations and legislative proposals', *European Competition Law Review*, vol. 2.

Sawyer, M. (1980) 'Monopoly welfare loss in the United Kingdom', *Manchester School of Economics and Social Studies*, vol. 48.

Shaw, R. and Simpson, P. (1989) *The Monopolies Commission and the Market Process*, Institute of Fiscal Studies, Report Series No. 33.

Singh, A. (1971) *Takeovers: Their relevance to the stockmarket and the theory of the firm*, Cambridge University Press.

Stevens, R. B. and Yamey, B. S. (1965) *Restrictive Trade Practices Court: A study of the judicial process and economic policy*, Weidenfeld and Nicolson.

Swann, D. P., O'Brien, D. P., Maunder, W. P. J. and Howe, W. S. (1974) *Competition in British Industry*, Allen & Unwin.

Utton, M. A. (1974) 'On measuring the effects of industrial mergers', *Scottish Journal of Political Economy*, vol. XXI.

Weir, C. M. (1992) 'The Monopolies and Mergers Commission merger reports and the public interest: a probit analysis', *Applied Economics*, vol. 24.

Weir, C. (1993) 'Merger policy and competition: an analysis of the Monopolies and Mergers Commission's decisions', *Applied Economics*, vol. 25.

Williams, M. E. (1993) 'The effectiveness of competition policy in the United Kingdom', *Oxford Review of Economic Policy*, vol. 2, 9.

Williamson, O. E. (1968) 'Economies as an antitrust defense: the welfare trade-offs', *American Economic Review*, vol. 58.

Chapter 18

Pollution and the environment

What managers should know

In the late 1980s 'greenery' became an important topic in the media, boardrooms and in parliaments. 'Recycling', 'acid rain' and 'the hole in the ozone layer' were topics of some controversy. Frances Cairncross of *The Economist* magazine in her book *Costing the Earth* (1992) provides a checklist of Do's and Don't's for corporations (Box 18.1). There seems little doubt that the issues will not go away. Business men and women must be aware of them, respond sensibly and constructively and, given the level and intensity of public policy debate they must be able to understand it and contribute to it. This chapter provides an economic framework within which the issues can be better understood and uses the Coase Theorem discussed in earlier chapters to do so (see Chapter 4).

18.1 Public goods and externalities[1]

To this point we have restricted our discussions solely to private goods (i.e. goods which are scarce, or (which is the same thing) economic goods). When a good does not suffer from reduced availability due to consumption it is called a *public good*. As consumers increase in number the same given amount is available. National defence is a classic example; so too is the Thames flood barrage, a television broadcast or a football game. In addition, people often cannot be excluded from the benefits provided by the good. Thus if the authors' houses are saved (or not saved) from nuclear extinction by the effectiveness (or ineffectiveness) of Britain's defence forces the same result will also occur for our next door neighbours. Similarly the Thames flood barrage provides flood protection equally to all inhabitants in the area it protects. However, it becomes ever more possible to exclude outsiders as human ingenuity grows. In the simple case of the football game, the match is a public good until the point when someone decides to erect enclosures and stadia with only a few gates at which would-be spectators must pay. Similarly, cable-transmitted television (as opposed to wireless transmission) not only permits a wider choice of programmes but provides access to those programmes only if the viewer pays for

---

Box 18.1

A checklist for companies

1. **Put the most senior person possible in charger of environmental policy.**
   A member of the board should have clear responsibility and there should be a well-defined management structure. All the golden intentions in the world are pointless unless the chairman cares and is known to care.

2. **Draft a policy and make it public.**
   Do not make it woolly. If possible, include clear targets with dates. That will not be possible unless you also:

3. **Measure.**
   Nothing concentrates the mind like numbers. In particular discover what wastes you are creating and what energy you are using.

4. **Institute a regular audit to check on what is happening.**
   While an outside consultant may be a help with Numbers 1–3 above, this one can be home-grown. Pay particular attention to the follow-up: there is no point in knowing what is wrong if nothing happens to fix it.

5. **Communicate.**
   Tell everybody – your workers, your shareholders, local people, green groups, the press – about your environmental problems and how you are solving them. When possible, involve them in helping you to choose solutions.

6. **Consider ways to reduce the range of materials you use that could do environmental harm.**
   Do you really need so many toxic chemicals?

7. **Think about the materials in your product.**
   If you had responsibility for disposing of it when your customer threw it out (and one day, legislators may well dump that burden on your firm), could you do so? In an environmentally benign way? If not, consider changing the design and materials you use.

8. **Remember that you may be able to make a business opportunity out of disposing of your product when the customer has finished with it.**
   If your customer brings back used paint drums or old refrigerators, it offers a chance to build a new link and to make your customer dependent on you in a new way.

9. **If you invest in a country where environmental standards are low, do not expect them to stay that way.**
   If one country finds a way of forcing companies to clean up, others will follow. Better assume that standards everywhere will rise rather than risk an expensive and disagreeable surprise.

10. **Accept that green regulations will tend to converge upwards.**
    What is compulsory in the most energetically environmental markets (California, Germany, Scandinavia) will probably reach your home market, too. If you accept the highest standards before they are compulsory, you steal a market advantage.

→

11. **Be flexible.**
    When making investments or designing products, remember the speed with which environmental understanding can change.

12. **Remember that greenery is often a proxy for quality in the eyes of your customers, your workers and your managers.**
    A truly green company is unlikely to be badly managed. Conversely a well-managed company finds it relatively easy to be green.

the rental of the cable, or alternatively has a meter built into the set which registers the amount owing by the viewer to the broadcast company.

Another assumption we have made so far is that whenever a trade occurs all the costs and benefits from the exchange accrue only to the transactors. This need not be the case. For example, one consumer may heat his or her house with oil and pay the fuel company for the oil consumed. But the cost of the consumer's central heating may not be fully reflected in his or her fuel bill if the oil refinery produces a large amount of air pollution.

In effect, part of the cost of heating the consumer's house is being borne by others. They are subsidising the consumer. They may not use oil-fired central heating themselves but are involuntarily consuming dirty air. This is an external cost or *negative externality* (since it is external to the transaction which resulted in it). External benefits or *positive externalities* arise if, for example, a householder goes to his or her local garden nursery, purchases flowering shrubs for the garden and makes the property pleasant and appealing to look at.

Externalities only occur if property rights do not exist. When private property rights are well defined and easily enforced there is no cause for concern about externalities. We shall examine this situation first, and then the problems of government policy when externalities persist.

Recall the Coase Theorem. The theorem states that efficiency will always be realised in the absence of transaction costs no matter how property rights are assigned.

The first main lesson from the Coase Theorem is that externalities can often be 'internalized' if property rights can be established and means of charging devised. Thus public goods may not be so common as supposed. The classic lighthouse example is not necessarily a public good. In America it is provided by government. But in Britain, Trinity House in England and the Commissioners for Northern Lights in Scotland, plus other bodies, built substantial numbers of lighthouses in the nineteenth century, collecting tolls from ships when they entered the harbour. Cable television has already been mentioned.

Another textbook example is that of beekeepers whose bees receive nectar free of charge from fruit tree owners (an external benefit) but provide cross-pollination services without charge (a negative externality to the beekeeper). In fact Steven Cheung (1978) has also dismissed this example. He discovered that in California there were three groups of fruit orchards: those which provided nectar with a high honey potential; those with a moderate honey potential; and those which provided little or no honey potential. All, however, required pollination and cross-fertilisation by bees and other insects. Cheung found a well-developed market, contrary to the textbook writers. Orchard owners with fruit trees of the first type charged the apiary owners a site rental to leave their hives in the orchard. Those of the third type paid apiary owners to leave their hives in the orchards during the relevant seasons. The middle grouping came to more or less no-charge agreements because the respective alleged externalities cancelled out.

The second lesson from the Coase Theorem is that externalities can still occur, and if property rights cannot be established or transaction costs minimized then market failure will arise. How can it be minimized? What does the demand curve look like for a public good? Unlike the market demand curve for a private good (obtaining by adding each individual's demand curve horizontally), to obtain the market demand curve for a public good the addition is vertical. For private goods if one extra unit was made available only one individual could consume it (so we moved along the Q axis of the demand diagram) and this consumer would value the good at its market price (so we remained at the same position on the P axis). With public goods, however, everyone benefits if one extra unit is provided, so the value of that unit is the sum of the values that all consumers place on it. To reflect this we must move up the P axis.

With this tool-kit we can now look at some of the problems of public good provision. What is the optimal provision of the public good? Figure 18.1 shows a three-citizen community where the demand curves D_1, D_2 and D_3 represent their relevant marginal valuation curves. Curve D is equal to $D_1 + D_2 + D_3$ added

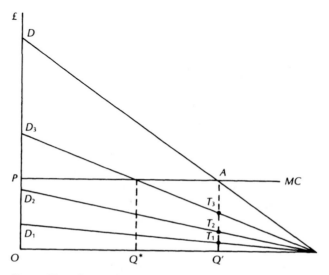

Figure 18.1 Optimal provision of a public good under conditions of different marginal valuations

vertically at any given Q. MC is the marginal cost of providing the good. At output Q' social marginal benefits received equal social marginal costs; Q' is consequently the optimal output.

But here we encounter the next difficulty. Although output Q' is socially optimal, only one individual values the good sufficiently highly to pay a price for the first few units which will cover the marginal cost. This is individual 3. He will buy to Q^* and then cease purchasing. In short, with public goods, everyone wants them but few, and sometimes none, are prepared to pay for them.

In addition. if individual 3 does pay for Q^* units then the other two members of the community are *free-riding* at his expense. They are obtaining the benefits without incurring any costs. All three members of society would prefer Q' units, which would increase their net benefits to equal the area DPA, the maximum net benefit they can collectively obtain.

With three individuals a collective agreement could possibly be hammered out to ensure that Q' units were produced. With a large nation the solution to the problem is usually obtained by handing the task over to government who will fund the provision through taxation. Again Figure 18.1 can be used to show the difficulties arising from this approach. People will still wish to free-ride, if they can. So they will attempt to conceal their preferences (in a private good situation the act of purchase reveals them). Thus although at Q' the optimal solution is to raise marginal taxes of T_1, T_2 and T_3 from each individual respectively (where $T_1 + T_2 + T_3 = P$), and although Q' is the desired goal of all, it is clear that if people believe their share of total taxes will be based on their desire for the good then they will understate that desire to minimise their tax bills and hope, again, to free-ride. This difficulty may be viewed as real but practically insurmountable unless somehow the good can be privately supplied and the Coase Theorem invoked.

Another and more difficult case is not only when people have genuinely different marginal valuations of the good, but when agreement on the optimal quality and the optimal tax is impossible because of this (quite apart from any free-riding propensity or the practical difficulty of determining individual demand curves). This can occur with defence expenditures where pacifists would under no circumstances willingly support the military.

It can also occur with less obvious goods. Consider government expenditure on a new airport (this is not strictly a public good, but it has some of the characteristics; the provision of travel facilities for other people also results in their being provided for oneself). In Figure 18.2 a two-consumer community has a demand for an airport as shown. Individual 2, a salesperson, is a frequent traveller. Individual 1, an infrequent traveller but a keen gardener, with a house in the vicinity of the proposed airport, does not value the airport highly at all, given the noise and inconvenience it will cause him or her compared with the slight benefits which might accrue to him or her. Moreover, individual 1 has a much higher income than individual 2 and knows that, in reality, his or her marginal tax rate is related to his or her income and not to his or her preferences for public goods of whatever nature. If their marginal tax rates are T_1 and T_2 respectively then, given the two marginal valuation curves, the marginal values of the new airport to individuals 1 and 2

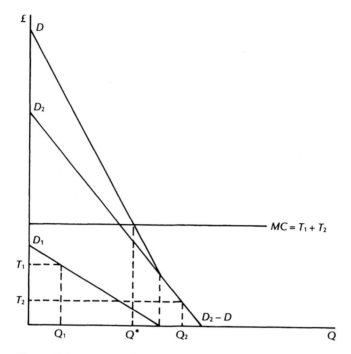

Figure 18.2 Optimal provision of a public good under conditions of lack of agreement on quality and tax

exceed their marginal costs up to Q_1 and Q_2 units of airport (or flight arrivals or other subdivision).

Unfortunately, an airport is indivisible and both individuals must benefit from and pay for the chosen size of airport. With normal tax structures disagreement is inevitable, irrespective of preference distortion for public relations purposes. Moreover, neither party would be satisfied with the social optimum, Q^*, albeit that is the only output that both individuals could desire and still collectively pay a tax covering the cost of the good. Thus individuals 1 and 2 would desire the public good – airport, national defence, industrial subsidies or whatever – up to the apparently, and probably factually, irreconcilable levels Q_1 and Q_2. This is a major advantage of private goods and attempts to internalise so-called externalities: that polarisation of opinions and social disharmonies are minimised and individual diversity is permitted and accommodated.

18.2 Environmental pollution

With these basic principles about externalities and public goods in mind, what can we learn about economic policy problems in issues such as pollution? Private motorists pollute the atmosphere with their exhaust emissions; farmers do so with insecticides and weed killers; firms in heavy industry produce sulphur dioxide and other fumes from their factory chimneys.

Every activity we engage in, from breathing to steel production, generates a by-product discharged into the atmosphere. The pollution 'problem' could thus be easily solved by banning all these activities but the opportunity cost would be too great. We would die. The real issue is how much pollution we are prepared to accept in order to obtain the benefits we want. How much of these benefits are we prepared to sacrifice to obtain a cleaner environment? What is the optimal level of pollution?

In principle the answer is given in Figure 18.3. *MB* shows the marginal benefits from polluting. *MB* has a negative slope since the first units provide enormous benefits (to individuals or firms); the last few units are near to irrelevant in the benefits they provide. The *MC* curve slopes up since the first few units of pollution impose negligible environmental costs; at higher levels an extra unit can impose extremely high additional costs. (Thus a little carbon monoxide in the atmosphere is almost harmless; a little more produces headaches; a little more still will result in death.)

The optimal level of pollution to society is P^*. This is positive, and will be so for most products. However, in some cases it either is or is presumed to be negative, as with curves *MC'* and *MB'*. When this occurs the government may ban the polluting activity altogether. Examples of such bans are the use of the drug thalidomide; the use of cyclamates, a very popular food additive in the 1960s as a sweetener; and the dumping of nuclear power station waste in unprotected heaps.

However, although the concepts of Figure 18.3 are useful, they are difficult if not impossible to use. Moreover, the *MB* and *MC* schedules are society's valuations of the costs and benefits, and very few individuals in society are likely to agree over any average outcome even if it could be shown to be 'correct' in that statistical sense. What we can infer, however, is that pollution is likely to be in excess of the social

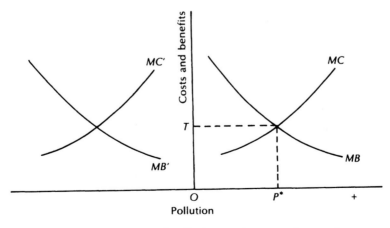

Figure 18.3 Optimal level of pollution under a taxation system

optimum P^*. Why? The reason lies in the frequent absence of property rights and resulting negative externalities.

A firm with a factory chimney emitting noxious fumes will move (in Figure 18.2) from the origin rightwards. As the factory emits more and more pollution it earns more and more profit (represented by MB) but the firm will not stop at P^*. Other things equal, it could continue until MB hits the horizontal axis. Although MC is rising the firm itself is bearing none of the costs of the polluted air. The community as a whole is (hence the rising MC) but the firm is only one small part of the community. If the firm introduced pollution abatement procedures, the benefits to the community would be large, but the firm would bear the total cost of this abatement and there is thus a positive externality for pollution abatement. From our discussion of public goods we know that pollution abatement is a form of public good and as such is unlikely to be purchased.

What then is the appropriate policy response to the pollution problem? There are three alternatives. First, and probably best, is to bear in mind the Coase Theorem, and look for ways to permit *trading between the polluter and polluted*. If the individuals or groups of individuals who suffer from the negative externalities can agree with the polluter on a price they should receive in compensation, or alternatively a price they will pay to make him cease or reduce polluting activities, then the optimal level of pollution is likely to be reached. Certainly this requires assignation of property rights in the atmosphere and a mechanism whereby the damaged can sue the damager (or pay the damager depending on how the courts assign the rights) and this permits variation in individual evaluation of the costs and benefits of pollution.

This flexibility is not so readily present in the second alternative, namely *taxation of the polluter*. Thus, in Figure 18.3 a tax of T, levied on the polluter, would ensure that he did not move down the MB curve beyond P^*. But the heights of the MB and MC curves can vary. Thus the demand for pollution (MB) is likely to be higher in cities and towns than in the country. (There are more people wishing to drive more cars, there are more firms wishing to be located close to their labour force and to their market.) Similarly the demand for a clean environment (i.e. the costs of pollution represented by the MC schedule) will be lower in country areas. This is because (a) there are fewer people anyway, and so the vertical aggregation of the curves results in a lower total schedule; and (b) the intensity of each individual's demand for anything, the height of the curve at a given quantity, is less the lower is his income. Country dwellers have a lower average per caput income than town dwellers, and so the MC curve is again lower.

In short, even if the situation of Figure 18.4 existed, where P^* is the same in both town and country, varying taxation levels (T and T') would be required to attain it. Given the extremely large numbers of alternative situations, it is unlikely that any one tax, or even any range of taxes, could possibly cover all the different situations in the way that individual contracting, under the Coase Theorem assumptions, could.

Taxation, however, is probably a better policy tool than the third alternative, which is that of *setting standards*. Taxation will motivate the polluter to reduce pollution as cheaply as possible and to do so until the MB schedule equals the

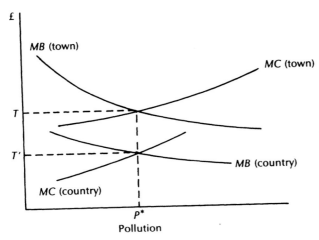

Figure 18.4 Pollution and taxation in town and country

marginal tax rate. Even if the tax rate is not optimal or variable there are still significant advantages over the standards approach. The reason is due again to varying
situations and therefore lack of complete information by the standard-setting
authority.

For example, the typical anti-pollution law requires all polluters to reduce their
emissions by a given percentage. Thus in Figure 18.5 firms 1 and 2, which before
the standard was set were polluting at P_1 and P_2 respectively (where their MB
schedules equal zero, since they themselves assumed none of the costs of pollution),
reduce their pollution levels by the same percentage to P_1' and P_2' after the law is
passed. To do this each must incur a cost. This cost is represented by the sacrificed
MB of the polluting activity and is achieved by installing pollution abatement
machinery, adopting new processes, or most simply by reducing output. In any

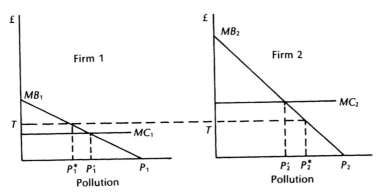

Figure 18.5 Pollution under a standards system

event the cost is still the opportunity cost of the sacrificed MB. These costs are represented by MC_1 and MC_2 respectively. For whatever reason, firm 1 is more efficient than firm 2 in reducing pollution levels ($MC_1 < MC_2$). Thus the same amount of pollution reduction could have been achieved at less social cost than it has been by the imposition of standards. For example, say $MC_1 = £5$ and $MC_2 = £8$, then if firm 1 is asked to restrict its output of pollution from P'_1 by one further unit, the cost is £5. If firm 2 is permitted to produce one further unit of pollution above P'_2 then the total pollution is unchanged, but £8 of pollution abatement expenditure has been saved, a net social gain of £3.

A uniform tax, for all its faults, is thus better than uniform standards. It encourages the lowest-cost pollution abaters more than the high-cost ones to reduce pollution. This is seen in Figure 18.5 where a uniform marginal tax rate is imposed on both firms at T. Firms 1 and 2 will now alter output to P_1^* and P_2^* respectively. The total pollution reduction remains the same but the total cost of pollution abatement has been lowered.

Not only does a tax motivate reduction of pollution more cheaply than do standards, it also encourages still further reductions by motivating a search for new technologies, and does so in a way that the setting of standards fails to do. If the long run is important, this is a major advantage of the taxation approach. Consider Figure 18.6. The MB schedules are identical in each. The pollution produced by the firm in Figure 18.6a is identical with that in Figure 18.6b. The only difference is that in the first case the level of P achieved is accomplished by virtue of a tax, whereas in the second it is the result of a legal standard.

Now assume that a new technology becomes available which lowers the marginal costs of pollution abatement (i.e. it reduces the marginal benefits sacrificed by reducing the polluting activity). Diagrammatically MB shifts to MB'. In case (a) the firm subject to the tax is further motivated to reduce pollution to P'. There the MB of pollution (MB') equals the marginal cost (T) of pollution abatement. Any other position is not one of profit maximization. In case (b) the firm will continue to pollute

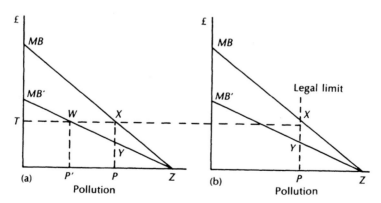

Figure 18.6 Pollution and the search for new technology under systems of (a) taxation and (b) standards

up to the legal limit of P and any costs saved by the introduction of the new technology (XYZ) will simply be additional profits to the firm. (Furthermore, experience indicates that legislative changes are relatively infrequent and often lag behind technological improvements.)

But, of course, not only does the tax result in reduced pollution; somehow research into the new technology itself must be encouraged. The incentive to do such research is greater in (a) than (b). In case (b) the incentive to introduce the new technology is the additional profit XYZ. In case (a) the savings from introducing cheaper pollution abatement also include XYZ, but since the tax bill of the polluter is also reduced (by $P'WXP$) this must be added to XYZ; moreover, of course, the benefits forgone by reducing pollution from P to P' ($WYPP'$) must be deducted. Thus the tax-paying polluter is better off by WXY as a consequence of introducing technology, *vis-à-vis* the regulated polluter. The tax-paying polluter thus has the stronger incentive to search for and introduce the new technology.

Note

1. This chapter draws heavily on a discussion in Reekie, Crook and Allen 1988, *The Economics of Modern Business*, pp. 387–98, and is used with permission of Blackwell Publishers.

Bibliography

Cairncross, F. (1992) *Costing the Earth*, Economist Books.
Coase, R. H. (1961) 'The problem of social cost', *Journal of Law and Economics*, vol. 4.
Cheung, S. (1978) *The Myth of Social Cost*, Hobart Paper 82, Institute of Economic Affairs.

Decision evaluation and control

Chapter 19

Profits and control

In Chapter 2 we outlined some differences between the economist's definitions of profits and costs. In this chapter we expand on these differences and explain how managers can use profits figures for planning and control.

19.1 Economic interpretation of accounts

Here we examine three specific problems met by economic analysts of company accounts as a result of certain accounting conventions.

19.1.1 The problem of depreciation

To the economist, depreciation is capital consumption. (Economically depreciation also includes the opportunity cost of capital equipment, namely, the most profitable alternative foregone by putting it to its present use.) The cost of capital consumption is the replacement cost of equipment that will produce comparable earnings. To the accountant, depreciation is an allocation of capital expenditures over time. Allocating the historical capital expenditure on the original plant over time will only equal replacement cost under wholly unrealistic assumptions of stable prices and certain obsolescence. Moreover, the methods of allocating original cost themselves differ and so in turn produce varying levels of profits as reported by accountants.

To illustrate this, consider a firm purchasing a new machine for £1,000, with an estimated life of 10 years. The firm has a choice of at least three alternative methods of allocating this expenditure over time. Under the straight line method the cost of the machine is spread equally over its expected life (i.e. £100 per annum). Under the reducing balance method the firm can choose among an infinite range of depreciation rates (say $x\%$). Instead of deducting the same amount of profits annually, $x\%$ of the price of the machine is allocated against year 1 profits, $x\%$ of the balance is allocated against year 2 profits and so on. Clearly, under this system the £1,000 will never be wholly written off. The sum-of-the-year's digits approach is a variant on the reducing balance method. The years of expected asset life are aggregated $(1 + 2 + 3 + \ldots + 10 = 55)$ to give an unvarying denominator. In year 1 the depreciation ratio used is 10/55. As a fraction of £1000 this is £181.80. In year 2 the depreciation ratio becomes 9/55; 9/55 of £1,000 is £163.60. This process continues until year 10 when the depreciation has fallen to 1/55. None of these methods bears any relationship to charging depreciation according to the replacement cost of the asset. Moreover calculated profit must vary widely according to which of the three accounting conventions are used.[1]

19.1.2 The treatment of capital gains or losses

The way capital gains or losses ('windfalls') are handled also affects a company's reported profits. Examples of windfalls include the bankruptcy of a major creditor not allowed for in bad debt reserves, or the unanticipated rise in share price of a firm in whom the company has a minor stake. By traditional accounting practice a capital gain is not made until the property is sold, irrespective of fluctuations in its value during the period it is held. Thus the entire gain or loss is treated as though it had occurred in the ultimate year of ownership. Clearly, were the actual loss or gain reported annually, whether or not it was realised, this would have an impact on the firm's reported profits over the years in question. The economist is not concerned with which accounting convention is selected for the recording of historical events. The important fact is that management should be aware of the magnitude of such windfalls, long before they become precise enough to be acceptable to accountants. Only then can the manager make valid decisions with regard to the future based on the value of net assets which he or she will have at his or her disposal when the decision is activated.

19.1.3 The evaluation of inventory and stocks

The Inland Revenue requires, and most British accountants practise, even in internal accounts, the evaluation of stocks and inventory by the FIFO (first in first out) method. Stocks consequently appear in a firm's balance sheet at their actual cost price – or market value, if lower. This system correctly represents the physical facts. It assumes that the raw materials which a firm consumes during the course of a year will always be the oldest in stock. Only when earlier purchases have been consumed will later purchases be turned to. However the FIFO system results in an exaggeration of reported profits over 'true' profits in a time of rising prices.

The system known as LIFO (last in first out), on the other hand, more closely approximates the economist's desire to see replacement costs used in the calculation of profits rather than historic costs. LIFO assumes that the most recently purchased stocks will be the first to enter the manufacturing process. Under LIFO the prices of the most recently purchased stocks become the costs of the raw materials in current production. Given stable inventory levels, the costs of raw materials applied at any point in the calculation of profits is always close to market or replacement value; only when stocks fall do the prices paid for earlier purchases enter into the calculation. Consequently, in times of rising prices the LIFO approach results in a higher level of costs being used in the calculation of profits and thus deflates profits closer to their 'true' level. Conversely in times of falling prices, LIFO shows a higher profit than would FIFO.

LIFO has certain disadvantages, however. If stock levels fall, the figure 'cost of materials' becomes increasingly obsolete. If stock levels rise, the figure 'cost of materials' becomes a jumble of different figures, possibly as complex as that produced by the FIFO method. It can also be argued that FIFO produces a more realistic (closer to replacement value) figure for stocks in the balance sheet. At its simplest, if stock levels are static then under LIFO the financial value of stocks in the balance sheet will remain unchanged year by year. This is not a serious objection since LIFO can still be used for the calculation of 'cost of materials' in the profit and loss account, while closing stocks at the year end can be revalued for balance sheet purposes, putting the excess to a capital reserve.

Both LIFO and FIFO, however, are historic cost accounting techniques. To attain full economic realism stocks should be valued in constant pounds.

19.2 Accounting for inflation

Discontent with conventional accounting standards is not new. But it has spread and with the rising rates of inflation common to most of the western world in the later 1960s and 1970s, it has been accentuated. Profits, as reported by accountants and as inflation has increased, have departed further and further from reality. Figure 19.1 highlights and summarises some of the major areas of concern.

Current operating profit is defined as the excess of current sales over the current costs of inputs. This plus realised capital gains (or losses including the accountant's depreciation charge) in the current period is accounting profit. The difference between accounting profit and money income is made up of those accrued capital gains (or losses) which have not yet been realised, less those capital gains (or losses) which accrued in previous accounting periods but were realised in the current period.

Neither money income nor accounting profit make allowances for the change in the general price level. Real income does. How can we move in practice, from accounting profit figures to real income figures? For planning and control purposes this is the critical question to which the manager needs an answer. Several alternative routes have been suggested – none is uniquely agreed upon. Ideally replacement cost accounting is the optimal method, the difficulty is to find an operational definition which would be universally accepted. Replacement cost (RC) accounting is not one technique. It is a term which covers a range of alternative methods of accounting for inflation.

The advocates of RC accounting argue that adjusting figures in the balance sheet by the Retail Price Index, or even some less aggregated but still high-level Index

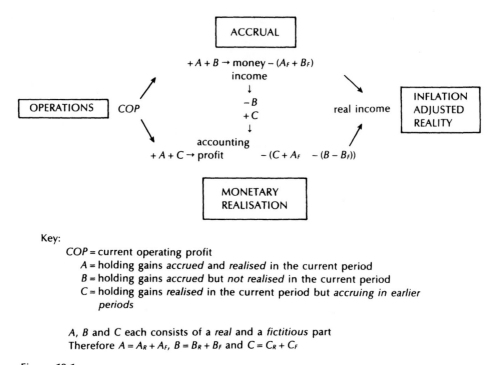

Key:

COP = current operating profit
A = holding gains *accrued* and *realised* in the current period
B = holding gains *accrued* but *not realised* in the current period
C = holding gains *realised* in the current period but *accruing in earlier periods*

A, B and C each consists of a *real* and a *fictitious* part
Therefore $A = A_R + A_f$, $B = B_R + B_f$ and $C = C_R + C_f$

Figure 19.1

Number, has little relationship with the replacement costs of stocks of finished or semi-finished goods or of raw materials.

Replacement costs, they claim, vary widely, and often whimsically, from firm to firm and year to year, depending on the mix of finished goods, work-in-progress, and raw materials in any particular company. In like manner, no one Index can be regarded as an adequate substitute for the replacement costs of capital assets. Indices are merely weighted averages of the prices of selected goods. They are prisoners of the selected items whose prices go to make them up; and whose prices in any event themselves deviate from the Index they make up. A cursory comparison of the RPI and other indices, such as the various wholesale and commodity price indices would indicate frequent and irregular differentials between their respective trends. Thus for some firms index number adjustments in given years might still leave their accounts far from realistic reflections of market values. And in some industries, indexed corrections might move firms away from greater accuracy rather than towards it.

A further problem is the treatment of monetary items, or net indebtedness. The consequences of failure to take account of losses on monetary assets (and profits on current liabilities) as a result of shifts in the general level of prices can be illustrated by the following abstract example. Consider a firm with no transactions between the two dates t_0 and t_1, and let p be the percentage rise in prices between t_0 and t_1. The firm's financial position at t_0 is:

$$N + M - L = C \tag{19.1}$$

where N is the firm's non-monetary assets, M is monetary assets, L is current liabilities and C is the value of the shareholders' interest or net worth. Now multiply equation (19.1) throughout by $(1+p)$ to recognise the effect of the rise in prices between t_0 and t_1:

$$N(1+p) + M(1+p) - L(1+p) = C(1+p) \tag{19.2}$$

By assumption, however, the firm's holding of physical assets is the same at both times, and, in particular, the 'counts' of both monetary assets and current liabilities are the same. Transpose Mp and Lp to the right-hand side of equation (19.2) and the position of the firm in t_1 becomes:

$$M - L + N(1+p) = C(1+p) - Mp + Lp \tag{19.3}$$

So, in a situation of rising prices, so long as current liabilities exceed monetary assets $(L > M)$, the measure of shareholders' interest or net worth (the right-hand side of equation (19.3)) will represent a larger command over goods and services than did C in equation (19.1). If $L < M$ the reverse is true. This complies with the well-known fact that in conditions of inflation it is better to be a borrower than a lender. So, in order to assess the real value of the shareholders' interest in the company in t_1, it is necessary not only to supplement it by Cp, but also to subtract from it $(Mp - Lp)$, the loss on the holding of monetary assets after allowing for the gain on current liabilities. In extreme situations, companies which calculate apparently attractive profits on the basis of historic costs may distribute them all as dividends to shareholders and ultimately discover that when machines have to be replaced, the cash flow is no longer available to permit asset purchase. Alternatively, its entire cash flow might be absorbed by high replacement costs, high profits would be indicated by the accounts, but no cash would be available for dividends. In this situation the shares would be worthless, high profits would be shown in the accounts and the firm could only be valued on a break-up basis. These are absurdities which can arise through the practice of historic cost accounting. The basic objective of inflation accounting then is to provide a measurable yardstick, unaffected by changes in the real value of money, which can enable objective comparisons to be made between the changes in the real net worth of a business firm.

The economist's version of profit requires an estimate of the present value of all future cash flows. This is an impossible attainment in an uncertain world, and if it were attainable, management would cease to be a decision making task and become merely one of stewardship. RC accounting shows fixed assets and stocks, with depreciation and cost of sales at current replacement values. The shareholders' equity interest is also adjusted for the general price level change, as is net monetary indebtedness. Replacement costs can be arrived at by estimating current market values for replacing each individual asset; or (less satisfactorily) by applying one of the many available specific price indices relating to capital goods and published by the government, each of which was believed to be a reasonable indicator of the replacement cost of the asset or group of assets concerned.

An alternative (or variant) of RC accounting is the net realisable value (NRV) method. Here assets are priced in the balance sheet at the value they would realise if sold on the open market, not at the price a replacement asset would cost. The attractions of *NRV* to the economist are that it embraces the concept of opportunity cost and, secondly, particularly in the case of current assets held for realisation in the short term, it must come close to *PV*, the discounted present value of the cash flow to be expected from their sale price in the near future.

19.2.1 Adjusting the discounting formula for inflation

Failure to correct the *DCF* formulae for inflation can result in biased estimates and hence incorrect project choice. The solution is to be consistent in both numerator and denominator. That is if future cash flows do not take account of inflation, then neither should the discount rate. If they do then so should the discount rate. Which approach is the easier? Since the numerator in the DCF formulae contains a multiplicity of different figures (revenues and costs) before it is reduced to a single value in each time period, it is probably more difficult to estimate all outlays and inflows in today's pounds (i.e. in real terms) for every future period. If the numerator is, therefore, expressed in current pounds in each period, then to be consistent, this requires that the value $(1 + r)$ in the DCF formula also be expressed in nominal terms. But today's interest rates on which capital costs are based already embody anticipated changes in the price level (i.e. inflation). Irving Fisher argued that:

$$r_n = r_r + I_r$$

where r_n, r_r and I_r are the nominal and real interest and inflation rates respectively. Thus, instead of employing a figure based on r_r, in the DCF formulae, the denominator should simply be expressed in terms of r_n: the nominal rate which already accounts for inflation.[2]

Now that we have examined the meaning, significance and measurement of profit we turn to two of the ways in which managers use profitability figures for purposes of planning and control: the break-even chart and the rate of return on investment.

19.3 Profit planning and control

19.3.1 Break-even analysis

Break-even analysis studies the relationship between the volume and cost of production on the one hand, and the revenue and profits obtained from the sales of the product on the other.

The break-even point, price being given, occurs where total cost equals total revenue. Figure 19.2 depicts a linear break-even chart. The similarities between this figure and the economist's single-period, profit-maximising cost and revenue diagram (Figure 5.1, Chapter 5) are readily apparent. The main differences are the assumptions of a given price and constant variable costs. Over certain ranges of output for brief periods of time these additional assumptions may not be too restrictive.

The break-even production volume can readily be determined from the chart by dropping a perpendicular from the intersection of TR and TC to the Q-axis. Altern-atively, it can be calculated algebraically by the following formula:

$$Q = F/(P - V)$$

where Q is the quantity produced and sold, F is total fixed costs, P is the price per unit sold, and V is unit variable cost. (The break-even quantity occurs where $TR = TC$ or $P \times Q = F + (V \times Q)$ which becomes $(P - V)Q = F$ which produces the desired result.)

Contribution analysis

In the short run, where many of the firm's costs are fixed, business men and women are often interested in determining the contribution additional sales make towards fixed costs and profit. Contribution analysis provides this information. Total contri-bution profit is defined as the difference between total revenues and total variable costs, which equals price less average variable cost on a per unit basis. Figure 19.3 rearranges Figure 19.2 to highlight the meaning of contribution profit. Total contri-bution profit, it can be seen, is also equal to total net profit plus total fixed costs. Figure 19.3 contains most of the information needed for contribution analysis.

Contribution profit analysis provides a useful format for examining a variety of price and output decisions. For example, consider the situation where the variable costs of a product are £5 per unit and the selling price is £12. The unit contribution

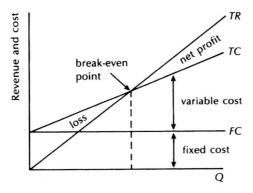

Figure 19.2

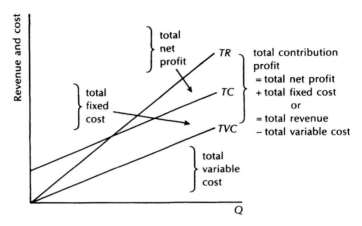

Figure 19.3

profit is consequently £7. Assume the company has a profit target of £12,000. How many units of the product must it sell to meet the target? The answer is found by using the following formula:

$$Q = \frac{(F + \pi^*)}{A\pi_c} = \frac{(F + \pi^*)}{(P - V)}$$

where F is total fixed costs, π^* is the total profit and $A\pi_c$ is the unit contribution profit. With total fixed costs of £9,000:

$$Q = \frac{(£9,000 + £12,000)}{£7} = 3,000 \text{ units}$$

(This can be easily corroborated. 3,000 units produce a total revenue of £36,000. Total cost equals F plus $V \times Q$ equals £9,000 + £15,000, i.e. £24,000, leaving a profit $(TR - TC)$ of £12,000.)

Operating leverage

Break-even analysis can also be useful in appraising the financial merits and demerits of differing production systems. In particular, it highlights how total costs and profits vary with output as the firm operates in a more or less mechanised manner and so substitutes fixed for variable costs.

Operating leverage reflects the extent to which fixed inputs are used relative to variable inputs in production operations. Consider the three alternative production techniques, X, Y and Z, which can be used in producing any given product. X is a highly automated technique, Y is labour intensive, and Z is moderately auto-mated. The break-even charts for the three techniques are given in Figure 19.4. The TR line is the same in each case, given an identical product sold at the same price. The fixed costs, however, differ according to the degree of automation, with X having the highest TVC. The variable costs also differ. The labour-intensive

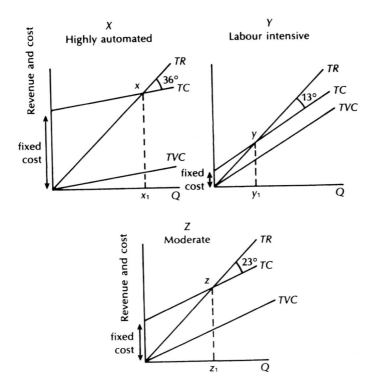

Figure 19.4

technique, Y, has the most rapidly rising level of total variable costs. X, conversely, has a TVC line which rises more slowly than either Y or Z. As a result of these differences the break-even points occur at different volumes of output. Given that the three pairs of axes are drawn on the same scale:

X breaks even at $x_1 > y_1 < z_1$

Y breaks even at $y_1 < z_1 < x_1$

Z breaks even at $z_1 < x_1 > y_1$

Other things equal, capital intensive operating procedures have higher break-even points than labour intensive procedures. Once break-even point is reached, however, the profits of the capital intensive operation, X, rise more rapidly than either of the other two, Y and Z. This is indicated visually by the rise of the angles at x, $(36°)$, y, $(13°)$, and z, $(23°)$.

Operating leverage is measured more precisely as the percentage change in profits that results from a percentage change in units sold. That is:

$$\text{degree of operating leverage} = \frac{\Delta \pi \times Q}{\Delta Q \times \pi}$$

Effectively, operating leverage is an elasticity concept relating to profits.

Since it is based (here) on linear *TR* and *TC* curves it will vary along the length of any particular pair of curves, and will be largest near the break-even point where π is close to zero.

More generally, operating leverage at any level of output Q, is measured thus:

$$\text{degree of operating leverage at point } Q = \frac{Q \times A\pi_c}{(Q \times A\pi_c) - F}$$

where $A\pi_c$ is unit contribution profit, and F is total fixed costs.[3]

If we calculated the operating leverage for our three alternative procedures X, Y and Z for any given output level Q, we would discover that X had the highest leverage and Y the lowest. The profits of procedure X are much more sensitive to changes in sales volume than those of either Y or Z.

Break-even data are consequently of considerable value to decision makers, both in their provision of information relating to contribution profit, and in the assistance they give in analysing the implications of different degrees of operating leverage. However, they often require to be modified before they can be of practical use. To embrace different prices, either a series of charts with different TR functions must be constructed, or a curvilinear analysis used. Cost changes, either once for all or varying with output, can be embraced in similar modifications.

19.3.2 Ratio analysis

Return on capital employed is one of the most common methods of appraising business performance. It is a ratio and, like all ratios used for control purposes, it will generally be compared either with the same ratio at other points in time, or the same ratio for other fiirms at the same time. Ratio analysis rests on the belief that some normality or abnormality will be found in the process of such a comparison and that managerial action will be taken accordingly.

Ratio analysis makes for readily quantifiable inter or intra-firm comparisons. The ease with which it can be carried out has encouraged its use. Like all management tools, however, ratio analysis is no stronger than the accuracy of the information on which it rests. Since most ratios spring from the ubiquitous profit expressed as a rate of return on assets, it will be obvious from our earlier discussion that ratios should be used with considerable care. Ratios can only be fully understood in practical use. However, we will list some of the more common. They fall into two groups: line management and financial ratios; both are related to return on capital employed.

Line management ratios

Line management ratios are of value to top management and the relevant line managers. Return on capital is the root of all line management ratios. It can be defined as the percentage of:

$$\frac{\text{profits (before deduction of interest and Corporation Tax)}}{\text{total assets less current liabilities}}$$

or

$$\frac{\text{profits}}{\text{shareholders' interest (including reserves) plus fixed interest capital}}$$

Return on capital employed indicates how effectively the firm's resources are being utilised. Both the numerator and the denominator are within the control of management. Figure 19.5 indicates how any deterioration in return on capital employed can (in theory) be traced through the firm. Any change in the return on capital ratio depends on a change in one or both of the ratios 'rate of asset turnover' and 'profit margin on sales'.

The profit margin on sales ratio depends in turn on one or more of the various cost/sales ratios. If any one of these have altered for the worse over time, or compare unfavourably with similar ratios in comparable firms, then specific management action to reduce, say, the administrative cost/sales ratio will, other things being equal, raise the profit margin on sales and so the return on capital.

The rate of asset turnover indicates how often the profit margin on sales has been earned on each pound of assets. The higher the figure (i.e. the lower the value of the denominator given a level of sales) the higher is the return on capital. Again, if a deterioration in the return on capital is perceived to arise from a change in the

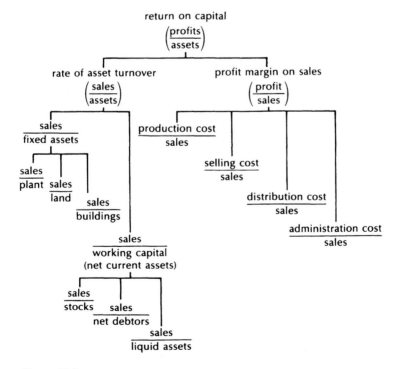

Figure 19.5

rate of asset turnover, then the specific asset class which has caused this can be pinpointed and managerial action taken to right the situation (say by reducing the value of net debtors by urging more rapid payment from debtors and delaying payments to creditors, or by pruning stock levels).

Financial ratios

Financial ratios are of value to top management, financial managers and outside investors. We have already defined return on capital employed. It will be recalled that in Chapter 14 (page 420) we defined the earnings yield as the percentage of:

$$\frac{\text{profits (after interest and after Corporation Tax) per ordinary share}}{\text{current share price}}$$

The inverse of the earnings yield is the price/earnings or P/E ratio. Financial vernacular talks of the P/E ratio as representing the 'purchase of x years' profits'. The higher the P/E ratio, other things being equal, the greater is the expected future growth of earnings and dividends.

Dividend yield indicates the current income that a shareholder can expect in the absence of any alteration in dividend policy, share price or taxation rates. It is the percentage of:

$$\frac{\text{dividend per share (after Corporation Tax)}}{\text{current share price}}$$

A useful additional ratio which increases the usefulness of dividend yield and earnings yield is dividend cover. This is the ratio:

$$\frac{\text{profits per share}}{\text{dividends per share}}$$

It indicates the extent to which the company retains earnings and does not distribute them to shareholders. It thus also indicates the extent to which the company's profits can fluctuate without it being forced either to prune its dividend payment or to dip into reserves in order to maintain it.

This chapter concludes our discussion of managerial economics. As a conclusion few topics could have been more appropriate than the above discussion concerned with the measurement of income and with the elements of profit management.

Notes

1. It should be noted that the Inland Revenue accepts neither the economist's nor the accountant's version of depreciation cost. Standardised capital allowances are permitted as charges against profits for tax purposes. Accountants consequently compile two computations of profit – one for shareholders and management and one for the Inland Revenue, where the internal depreciation charge is 'added back' to profits and the legally permitted capital or investment allowance is deducted, producing a net figure on which tax is computed.

2. If inflation is not correctly treated, profitable projects may be rejected, or vice versa. For example, for much of the 1970s, real interest rates were negative. That implies possible project profitability even if the sum of undiscounted cash flows is less than the outlay. For example, consider a negative real rate of 8%, outlay of £100 in t_0, and income of £50 and £40 in t_1 and t_2 (all in constant pounds). Present value $= 50/0.92 + 40/0.92^2 = 54.35 + 47.3 = £101.65$.

3. This is proved as follows:

the initial profit is $(Q \times A\pi_c) - F$

Thus the percentage change in profit is

$$\frac{\Delta Q \times A\pi_c}{(Q \times A\pi_c) - F}$$

but the percentage change in output is $\Delta Q/Q$ so the ratio of the change in profits to the change in output is

$$\frac{\Delta Q \times A\pi_c}{(Q \times A\pi_c) - F} \times \frac{Q}{\Delta Q} = \frac{Q \times A\pi_c}{(Q \times A\pi_c) - F}$$

Bibliography

Baxter, W. T. (1962) 'Inflation and accounts', *Investment Analyst*, vol. 43.

Dean, J. (1951) *Managerial Economics*, Prentice Hall.

Edwards, E. O. and Bell, P. W. (1972) *The Theory and Measurement of Business Income*, California University Press.

Hayes, W. W. and Henry, W. R. (1974) *Managerial Economics*, Richard D. Irwin.

Hill, S. and Gough, J. (1982) 'Discounting for inflation', *Managerial and Decision Economics*, vol. 2.

Merrett, A. J. and Sykes, A. (1974) 'How to avoid a liquidity crisis', *Economist*, 3 August.

Newbould, G. D. (1969) *Business Finance*, Harrap.

Study questions

Chapter 2: Introduction to maximisation and optimisation

1. Find the first derivatives with respect to x of the following:

    (a) $y = 15$

    (b) $y = 7x^4$

    (c) $y = 4x^2 - 3x^3$

    (d) $y = 6x(x^2 - 2)$

    (e) $y = \dfrac{x^2 - 1}{2x^3 + 3}$

    (f) $y = \sqrt{(x + 4)}$

2. A firm has the following profits (π) function:

$$\pi = 10\,000Q + 150Q^2 - 0.25Q^3$$

where Q denotes output per period (units)

    (a) Derive the average and marginal profits equations.
    (b) Find the outputs at which profit is at an extremum and identify which is a maximum and which a minimum.
    (c) Show that average profits equal marginal profits when average profits are at a maximum.

3. A firm has estimated its demand function to be:

$$Q = 1000 - 0.5P + 2A + 0.01Y$$

where Q = Quantity demanded per period (units)
          P = Price (£)
          A = Advertising expenditure per period (£)
          Y = consumers' *per capita* income per period (£)

    (a) find $\partial Q/\partial P$, $\partial Q/\partial A$, and $\partial Q/\partial Y$;

(b) defining the price, advertising and income elasticities of demand as

$$\eta_P = \frac{\partial Q}{\partial P} \frac{P}{Q}, \; \eta_A = \frac{\partial Q}{\partial A} \; \text{and} \; \eta_Y = \frac{\partial Q}{\partial Y} \frac{Y}{Q}$$

respectively, calculate η_P, η_A and η_Y when $P = 10$, $A = 400$ and $Y = 4000$

4. A firm's production function is:

$$Q = 3K + 2L - LK - 0.5L^2 - 1.5K^2$$

   where Q = output per period
         L = labour inputs per period
         K = capital inputs per period

Find the (unconstrained) maximum output which the firm could produce. (Assume the second order conditions are fulfilled.)

5. Solve the following maximisation problem using a Lagrangian multiplier: a firm has £100,000 to spend on labour and materials in the coming year; the cost of labour is £2,000 per unit per year; the cost of materials is £1,000 per unit. The firm, therefore, has the following budget constraint:

$$2L + M = 100$$

where L is the quantity of labour and M the quantity of materials purchasable.
   The firm's output (Q) is related to inputs thus:

$$Q = 5LM$$

(i.e. this is the production function). What input mix of L and M will maximise Q? What is the value of λ? (You may assume that the second order conditions for a maximum are satisfied.)

Chapter 3: Decision analysis under risk and uncertainty

1. A firm's management wishes to maximise profits. It must choose from three investment strategies I_1, I_2 and I_3 and knows that its profits will depend on which of three future states of the economy S_1, S_2 or S_3 prevail. The company's payoff matrix in £ 000 profit is:

	S_1	S_2	S_3
I_1	12	8	5
I_2	10	20	0
I_3	1	10	15

Which strategy should the management choose if it used:

(a) the maximin criterion
(b) the minimax regret criterion
(c) the Principle of Insufficient Reason
(d) the Hurwicz α-criterion (assume $\alpha = 0.4$)?

2. Repeat Question 1 but suppose that, instead of aiming to maximise profits, the management aimed to maximise utility where:

(a) $U = 2\pi$,

(b) $U = \log_{10}(1 + \pi)$

where U = managerial utility (in 'utils')

π = profits (in £ 000)

3. Using the same data as in Question 1, which alternative would have the highest EMV if S_1, S_2 and S_3 had probabilities of 0.3, 0.4 and 0.3 respectively?

Calculate the standard deviation of the returns for each strategy. Plot the standard deviation EMV point for each on a graph and arbitrarily apply indifference curves to show project 1 with the greatest utility.

4. Suppose that the probabilities of S_1, S_2 and S_3 are again 0.3, 0.4 and 0.3 respectively, that the payoffs *in £000 profits* are given in Question 1 and that the cardinal utility function of a manager has been found to be:

(a) $U = 2\pi$,

(b) $U = \log_{10}(1 + 2\pi)$

Using the Von Neumann–Morgenstern *expected utility* criterion, which strategy would the manager prefer?

5. When considering two projects a firm has estimated the following payoffs:

	S_1	S_2	S_3	S_4	S_5
P_i	0.15	0.20	0.30	0.20	0.15
I_1	25	50	100	50	25
I_2	10	20	100	70	50

Calculate the standard deviation, coefficient of variation and the semi-standard deviation of the payoffs for each project. Which do you consider to be the riskier project?

Chapter 4: Strategic decision taking and transactions costs

1. (a) Consider a port authority wishing to lease land to a chemical tank farm operator. Both have made profit forecasts in present value terms. The harbour's profits are what would have been achieved if the land had been leased for the most profitable alternative use different from the projected trade. The tank farm's profits are what it would have made from renting and handling charges levied on petrochemical importers and exporters in the least costly alternative harbour. The firms assume these profits will be as indicated (in billions) over the next ten years:

Port

		10	40
Tank farm	15		
	50		

The projections depend on whether the parties assume high or low growth for the economy.

Indicate when and when not the two parties might agree to a lease agreement, and what the terms of the lease would be. (Hint: refer to Table 4.2 in text.)

(b) Now introduce bounded rationality such that the tank farm firm, instead of *knowing* that the port authority is presuming low or high growth forecasts that there is a 33% chance and a 66% chance of each respectively. Similarly the harbour, instead of knowing that the tank farm is presuming low or high growth, forecasts that there is a 75% chance of low and a 25% chance of high growth respectively. How does this affect when and when not lease agreements would be made and their terms?

(c) Next introduce opportunism where each respectively but untruthfully claims (tank farm) he or she cannot pay more than £15 billion or (port) afford to accept less than £40 billion. When this is so the No Lease situation is inevitable.

What incentive compatibility constraints are required to ensure joint value maximisation?

2.

		Port	
		Honours agreement	Cancels agreement
Tank farm	Honours agreement	40 / 40	50 / 10
	Moves elsewhere	10 / 50	−10 / −10

Now assume that the same two firms can either honour any long-term lease agreement or break it. Thus the port authority may have agreed to provide sole rights to the tank farm company *ex ante*, but *ex post* permits a new competitor to build a similar tank farm in the dock side area. Alternatively the tank farm may have agreed to provide long-term usage of the harbour but decides to use an alternative port several hundred miles distant.

If both firms practice this type of hold-up, each loses, say £10 billion, while if both honours the agreement, each earns £40 billion. If only one party behaves opportunistically the respective profits are £10 billion and £50 billion. What outcome is therefore likely?

3. Consider a manager with a utility function $U = f(s, e)$ where s is salary and e effort. Let the specified function be $U = s^{0.33} - e^2$. Assume effort can be at two alternative levels, 1 and 2.

The owner of the firm wishes to maximise profits which depend on the manager's effort and on the state of the economy. Let expected profits be as follows:

	Boom	Slump	$E\pi$
	0.6	0.4	
$e = 1$	800	700	760
$e = 2$	1500	700	1180

Let the manager's opportunity salary be £9.

(a) What is the manager's minimum level of utility which would prevent him or her working elsewhere?

(b) If the owner could observe and costlessly monitor the manager's effort would the owner instruct the manager to provide e_1 or e_2? Why?

(c) What salary would the owner have to provide for the manager to make this instruction worthwhile to the owner, and worthwhile to the manager to obey?

(d) Is paying this salary worthwhile for the owner? What is the bonus to the manager? What is the owner's net profit?

(e) If the owner cannot observe the manager's effort the manager would select e_1 and blame the outcome on the economy (still claiming the effort bonus). What incentive contract can the owner design to encourage the manager to share some risk and so volunteer $e = 2$?

(f) What net expected profit is the owner then left with?

Chapter 5: Business objectives

1. Defining Q as output produced and sold and given the following total cost and demand functions:

$$TC = 150 + 10Q - 0.5Q^2 + 0.02Q^3$$

$$Q = 37.7 - 0.91P$$

(a) find the total profit function in terms of Q
(b) find the profit-maximising output level
(c) find profits and price at that level
(d) if fixed costs rise from 150 to 200, determine the effects of such an increase on the profits of the firm, on its price policy and on its output level.

2. Using the cost and demand functions of Question 1 determine the MR and MC functions. Show that at the output level determined in (b) $MR = MC$.

3. For the company in Question 1, what are its:

(a) unconstrained price and output levels if its objective is sales maximisation and its profit at that output?
(b) its price and output level if a profit constraint of 100 is imposed?

4. An owner/manager initially owns 100% of the equity in CLV Enterprises. The market value (V) of his or her firm if the owner/manager takes no perks is £10. The owner/manager maximises his or her utility by taking a value of perks whose present value (P) is £0.50, with the market value of his or her equity consequently being £9.50. Now suppose the owner/manager sells 10% of his equity to a Pension Fund for a mutually acceptable price and that at that price the manager's indifference curve is given by the equation $V = P^{-1} + 0.5$. What is the monetary value of the 'residual loss' due to the new agency relationship? (Hint: find the coordinates of the relevant points in Figure 5.15 in the text.)

Chapter 6: Forecasting

1. This month and last month the quantities demanded of a firm's product were 1,000 units and 990 units respectively. Estimate next month's demand using the following naive forecasting techniques:

(a) $\hat{X}_{t+1} = X_t + \Delta X_t$
(b) $\Delta \hat{X}_{t+1} = 1.09(\Delta X_t)$
(c) $\hat{X}_{t+1} = 900 + 100(t + 1)$ (currently $t = 0$)

2. XYZ Ltd has presented you with the following sales data. Plot the data on a graph.

UNITS SOLD (X_t)

	Quarter			
	1	2	3	4
1990	800	900	900	950
1991	1900	2600	3100	2900
1992	3200	3000	2650	2300
1993	2600	2550	2500	2800
1994	3350			

Using the time series model

$$X_t = T_t C_t S_t$$

predict sales in quarter 1, 1995.
Note: To find $\hat{a}$ and b in the equation $T_t = \hat{a} + bt$ use the formulae analogous to equations (8.8) and (8.9).

$$b = \frac{n \sum_{t=1}^{17} X_t t - \sum_{t=1}^{17} t \sum_{t=1}^{17} X_t}{n \sum_{t=1}^{17} t^2 - \left(\sum_{t=1}^{17} t \right)^2}$$

$$\hat{a} = \frac{\sum_{t=1}^{17} X_t}{n} - b \frac{\sum_{t=1}^{17} t}{n}$$

and where $n = 17$ (the number of observations)

3. XYZ has presented you with the following data. Plot the data on a graph and establish what, if any, cycle exists.

Sales in month (£ 000)	1992	1993	1994
January	10	11	12
February	12	13	15
March	13	14	16
April	15	15	18
May	16	17	20
June	15	17	19
July	14	16	19
August	17	18	22
September	18	19	23
October	20	23	27
November	21	25	29
December	22	26	33

Calculate the 12-month moving averages and forecast the value for January 1995.

4. In mid-1994 Grampian Aluminium Ltd was evaluating the merits of building a new factory, in order to meet the needs of the North Sea oil industry's component supplies. The alternative is to use additional overtime and/or to reduce other production. The company already supplies the aircraft, motor, agricultural equipment and domestic appliance industries and will want to add new capacity only if the total economy appears to be expanding. Forecasting UK economic activity is consequently an essential input to the firm's decision process.

The firm has collected the data and estimated the following relationships for the UK economy:

Last year's total profits (all firms)	P_{t-1}	$= £50$ million
This year's government expenditure	G	$= £100$ million
Annual consumer expenditure	C	$= £40$ million $+ 0.5Y$
Annual investment expenditure	I	$= £2$ million $+ 0.75P_{t-1}$
Tax receipts	T	$= 0.25GNP$
National income	Y	$= GNP - T$
Gross national product		$GNP = C + I + G$

Assume that random disturbances average out to zero, and forecast each of the above variables from the simultaneous relationships experienced in the equation system.

5. The Input–Output transactions matrix for the Island of Trespass for last year has been calculated to be (in £ million):

	Producers			Final demand			
	Inputs to agriculture	Inputs to manufacturing	Inputs to services	Exports	Govt	Households	Gross output
Agriculture	3	8	5	1	3	45	65
Manufacturing	7	50	20	50	40	140	307
Services	1	30	25	15	60	90	221
Government	15	29	21				
Wages	25	150	120				
Profits and Depreciation	14	40	30				
Gross input	65	307	221				

(a) Calculate the direct inputs technology matrix.
(b) Calculate the direct and indirect inputs technology matrix.
(c) Suppose that the value of output which households will take from each industry is 5% greater this year than last year. Predict this year's output for each industry.
(d) How might the manager of each firm on the island use these IO matrices?

6. Suppose that the market for washing powder is supplied by only 3 brands: X, Y and Z. Suppose that the flow of customers between these three brands between the end of the

first quarter and the end of the second quarter of this year were:

Brand	Number of customers at end of 1st quarter	Gains from			Losses to			Number of customers at end of 2nd quarter
		X	Y	Z	X	Y	Z	
X	30,000	0	5,000	20,000	0	15,000	5,000	35,000
Y	50,000	15,000	0	10,000	5,000	0	5,000	65,000
Z	65,000	5,000	5,000	0	20,000	10,000	0	45,000

(a) Calculate the market shares of each brand at the end of the first and second quarters.
(b) Calculate the number of customers which each brand retained between the two quarters. Hence calculate the probability of retention for each brand.
(c) Calculate the transition probability matrix. What does each element in this matrix represent?
(d) Using a first order Markov process, estimate the market shares at the end of the third quarter. What assumptions are you making when doing this?
(e) Calculate the equilibrium shares for each brand.

Chapter 7: Demand theory

1. A firm estimates the following demand functions for its two products as:

$$Q_1 = 200 - 2P_1 - 3P_1$$
$$Q_2 = 450 - 6P_1 - 2P_2$$

At $P_1 = £2$ and $P_2 = £4$

(a) what is the demand elasticity for Q_1 with respect to P_1
(b) and for Q_1 with respect to P_2
(c) and for Q_2 with respect to P_1
(d) are the products substitutes, non-related, or complements?

2. An analysis of income data for the Manchester area resulted in the equation $Y_m = 0.02$ $X^{0.706}$, where Y_m and X are respectively Manchester's and UK's disposable per capita income. This means:

(a) the relationship is log-linear
(b) a 1% change in the nation's disposable income may be expected to result in about 0.7% change in Manchester's disposable income
(c) the elasticity is given by the exponent in the equation
(d) the equation may also be written:

$$\log Y_m = \log 0.02 + 0.706 \log X$$

(e) all of these

3. Hazzods, the department store, found that the average daily demand for shirts was given by the equation $Q = 60 - 5P$.

(a) How many shirts per day will the store sell at £3?
(b) If the store has a target of 20 shirt sales per day what price should it charge?

(c) What would demand be if the shirts were given away?
(d) What is the maximum price at which shirts can be sold?
(e) Plot the demand curve.

4. Kuzzy's Ltd, a major TV chain store, does not rent sets to customers but only sells them outright. In addition it provides an optional insurance plan for its customers whereby a one-year or two-year service contract can be entered into. The contract provides for an unlimited number of otherwise free-of-charge service calls to repair broken or faulty sets. The company has decided to review this strategy and the following data have been collected from one of the branch stores:

	Premium for 1-year contract (£)	Premium for 2-year contract (£)	No. of 2-year contracts taken out	Average household income
1970	35	50	1000	5000
1971	35	55	950	5000
1972	40	55	1000	5500
1973	45	55	1050	5500
1974	35	50	1000	5500
1975	40	50	1050	5500
1976	40	50	1000	5000
1977	40	60	1050	5500
1978	35	60	950	5500
1979	35	65	900	5500
1980	40	65	1000	6500
1981	40	65	1050	7000

What inferences can be drawn from this table in general terms? How would you back up these inferences by computing elasticity measures? Which elasticities would you calculate and what are their values? Why would you restrict yourself to these specific elasticities?

5. (a) A firm producing racks to hold CD (compact disc) collections has collected quarterly sales data together with records of its own prices, income per capita, and the price of CDs. Estimate the demand equation. Compute the relevant elasticities. Is the demand relationship linear or curvilinear? Are the signs of the various coefficients operating in the expected directions? Are they statistically reliable?
   (b) A competitor had a fire in his warehouse in 1992 quarter 2. Use a zero:one dummy variable and recompute your results to ascertain if this affects your estimates.

The raw data are given in the table where PX is the price of CDs.

obs	Q	P	I	PX	FIRE
1990.1	19.00000	5.200000	500.0000	5.500000	0.000000
1990.2	17.00000	5.320000	550.0000	5.500000	0.000000
1990.3	14.00000	5.480000	550.0000	6.000000	0.000000
1990.4	15.00000	5.600000	550.0000	6.000000	0.000000
1991.1	18.00000	5.800000	550.0000	4.500000	0.000000
1991.2	16.00000	6.030000	660.0000	5.000000	0.000000
1991.3	16.00000	6.010000	615.0000	5.000000	0.000000
1991.4	19.00000	5.920000	650.0000	5.000000	0.000000
1992.1	23.00000	5.900000	745.0000	4.500000	0.000000
1992.2	27.00000	5.850000	920.0000	5.000000	1.000000
1992.3	23.00000	5.800000	1053.000	5.500000	0.000000
1992.4	21.00000	5.850000	950.0000	5.500000	0.000000

Chapter 8: Techniques for demand estimation

1. The marketing department of Goldmine Inc. has collected the following data on the demand for its product:

Time period t	Quantity demanded (units per period) Q_t	Price (pence) P_t
1	26	2
2	4	16
3	12	13
4	16	16
5	4	13

(a) Assuming the model:

$$Q_t = \alpha + \beta P_t + \varepsilon_t$$

relates to the population of possible Q_t values at every given value of P_t, use OLS to estimate values of α and β, $\hat{\alpha}$ and $\hat{\beta}$, on the basis of this sample.
(b) Draw the resulting estimated curve and plot the observations.
(c) Calculate the price elasticity of demand at the mean values of Q_t and P_t in the sample.

2. The ABC company has estimated its demand function using OLS to be:

$$Q_t = 1992.9 - 4.845P_t \qquad R^2 = 0.949$$
$$\quad (37.776) \quad (0.264) \qquad n = 20$$

where Q_t = quantity demanded in week t
P_t = price in week t
n = number of observations
and the number in brackets is the standard error of $\hat{\beta}$.

(a) Calculate the t-statistic for H_0: $\beta = 0$.

(b) Using this t-statistic test the null hypothesis:

$$H_0: \beta = 0$$

against $H_1: \beta < 0$

(look up the critical t-statistic in a statistics or econometrics text).
(c) Interpret the R^2.

3. The market research section of your company has collected the following data on the demand for your product:

Time period	Quantity demanded (units per period) Q_t	Price (pence) P_t
1	10	45
2	30	45
3	40	30
4	60	30
5	70	15

(a) Assuming the model:

$$Q_t = \alpha + \beta P_t + \varepsilon_t$$

relates to the population of possible Q_t values at every given value of P_t, use OLS to estimate values of α and β, $\hat{\alpha}$ and $\hat{\beta}$, on the basis of this sample.
(b) Draw the resulting estimated curve and plot the observations.
(c) Calculate the t-statistic for the null hypothesis $H_0: \beta = 0$.
(d) Can the null hypothesis

$$H_0: \beta = 0$$

against $H_1: \beta \neq 0$

be rejected? (Look up the critical values of t in a statistics or econometrics text.)
(e) Calculate the R^2 and interpret it.

4. The marketing section of a firm has collected the following statistics:

Period t	(Quantity per period) Q_t	Price charged P_t
1	2800	39
2	3700	32
3	3250	32
4	3100	39
5	2750	44
6	3750	26
7	4500	15
8	4000	20
9	4750	15
10	4250	23
11	2500	47
12	4000	30
13	3400	34

Suppose that the firm *knows* that the supply but *not* the demand curve has shifted over time. Now:

(a) estimate α and β for the hypothesised demand function

$$Q_t^D = \alpha + \beta P_t + \varepsilon_t,$$

(b) test the null hypothesis

$$H_0 : \beta = 0$$

against $H_1 : \beta \neq 0$

using a *t*-test,
(c) repeat (b) using an *F*-test,
(d) calculate the R^2 and interpret it,
(e) find the price elasticity of demand at the means of Q_t and P_t in the sample,
(f) use the Durbin–Watson test to examine the possibility of autocorrelation (look up the critical values of the *t*, *F* and DW statistics in a statistics or econometrics text).

5. The following data on sales and prices have been collected by the market research section for the past five quarters:

Quantity sold (units) Q_t	Price (£) P_t
146	9.00
153	8.50
160	8.00
167	7.50
175	7.25

The supply function is *known* to be $Q_t = 110 + 4P_t + 9t$ where Q_t, P_t and *t* are quantity demanded in quarter *t*, price in period *t* and quarter *t* respectively.

(a) Plot the family of supply functions at values of *t* of $0, 1, 2, 3$ and 4. Why might *t* be included in the supply function?
(b) Plot a line *by eye* fitting data in the table.
(c) Under what conditions associated with the completeness of the demand and supply curves (i.e. excluding consideration relating to the 'by eye' estimation technique) is this line an approximation to the demand function for the product?

6. (a) Use the data of question 3 but *instead* of assuming that the model $Q_t = \alpha + \beta P_t + \varepsilon_t$ relates to the population of possible Q_t values, assume that the model:

$$Q_t = a P_t^b U_t$$

where *a* and *b* are constants to be estimated

    U is a multiplicative error term

is applicable and estimate *a* and *b*.

To estimate a and b take logarithms of both sides of the equation:

$$\log_{10} Q_t = \log_{10} a + b \log_{10} P_t + \log_{10} U_t$$

then substitute: $Q'_t = \log_{10} Q_t$

$$\alpha = \log_{10} a$$
$$\beta = b$$
$$P'_t = \log_{10} P_t$$
$$\varepsilon_t = \log_{10} U_t$$

Hence one has:

$$Q'_t = \alpha + \beta P'_t + \varepsilon_t$$

Assume this model fulfils the assumptions of the OLS technique and so estimate α and β in the usual way. Then take the antilog of $\hat{\alpha}$ to derive a.

(b) Plot the value of Q_t which the estimated equation predicts, $\hat{Q}_t$ at values of P_t given in the data table.

(c) Calculate the values of $e_t = Q'_t - \hat{Q}'_t$ at each P'_t value.

(d) Plot these e_t values against time. Can you distinguish a pattern or not?

Chapter 9: Cost theory and measurement

1. Find the input values in terms of financial outlay which lie on the firm's expansion path given the production function $Q = Y^2 X^4$ and input prices $P_y = £4$ and $P_x = £12$. (The objective is consequently to maximise Q subject to the constraint $4Y + 12X = TC$, using a Lagrangian multiplier expression.)

2. Electricity may be produced with either a high-grade coal (low sulphur content) or a low grade coal (high sulphur content), with the low-grade fuel giving off a much higher air pollution element. If XCX PLC, a large chemical firm, generates its own power, and has the choice of technology defined by the isoquants in Figure 1, find:

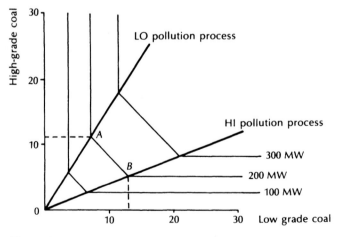

Figure 1

(a) The optimal input mix if the firm is trying to minimise the cost of producing 200 megawatts when prices are $P_L = £40$ per ton, $P_H = £80$ per ton.

(b) What price would British Coal have to sell low-grade coal at to induce XCX PLC to switch to the low pollution process?

(c) What financial penalty would XCX PLC incur if a law was passed forbidding the use of the high-pollution process at the original prices?

3. Show that the following production functions are homogeneous:

(a) $Q = aL + bK$

(b) $Q = \gamma [\delta K^{-\rho} + (1 - \delta)L^{-\rho}]^{-1/\rho}$ (a Constant Elasticity of Substitution production function)

where γ = an efficiency parameter
ρ = a substitution parameter
δ = a distribution parameter

4. Which of increasing, constant or decreasing returns to scale does each of the production functions of Question 3 have?

5. ABC Ltd has estimated its production function to be

$$Q = -71.202 + 63.250K - 0.078K^2 - 37.894L$$
$$(63.103) \quad (28.602) \quad (0.036) \quad (20.463)$$
$$+ 0.034L^2 - 0.00000008LK$$
$$(0.019) \quad (0.00000002)$$
$$R^2 = 0.988 \qquad n = 13$$

where the number in the brackets denotes standard errors.

(a) Using the formulae (8.8) and (8.9) calculate the t-statisics for each coefficient for the null hypothesis that each population coefficient equals zero.

(b) Test these null hypotheses against the alternative hypotheses that each is not equal to zero.

(c) Find expressions for the marginal products of labour and capital.

6. Using the engineering approach Goldrush Inc. believes that its long-run total cost function is:

$$TC = 3.54Q^{0.85}$$

(a) If this is the correct function does Goldrush have economies of scale or not?

(b) If Goldrush is a management consultancy company, what problems would it experience in trying empirically to derive its long-run average cost curve using the engineering approach?

7. Windfall Corporation has estimated its STC curve using accounting data and OLS to be:

$$STC = 380.32 + 2.72Q - 0.003Q^2 + 0.000001Q^3$$
$$(27.82) \quad (0.15) \quad (0.0002) \quad (0.00000007)$$
$$R^2 = 0.993 \qquad n = 25$$

(Numbers in brackets are standard errors.)

(a) Calculate the t-statistics for the null hypothesis that the population coefficient of each variable equals zero. Test these hypotheses for each coefficient separately against the alternative hypotheses that each coefficient is not equal to zero.

(b) The firm has also estimated its demand curve as:

$$Q = 2317.4 - 671.77P$$
$$\quad\ (47.89)\quad (19.65)$$
$$R^2 = 0.981 \quad\ n = 25$$

(Numbers in brackets are standard errors.)

Using the estimated coefficients in both regression equations, form the profits function and find the profit-maximising level of output.

(c) Why might the output which you have calculated in (b) not in fact be the level which maximises profits?

8. Hands Inc. manufactures quartz watches. The company accountant has tried to estimate the theoretical 'long run total cost' curve for quartz watches and has taken data from the last 20 six-monthly accounts. Using regression analysis the accountant has estimated the 'LTC curve' to be:

$$LTC_t = 50.00 + 111.00\ Q_t - 7.00\ Q_t^2 + 0.33\ Q_t^3$$

where LTC_t = accounting operating costs in period t

Q_t = number of watches produced in period t

What economic assumptions has the accountant made in carrying out this procedure? Which of these assumptions are unlikely to be valid?

9. The following data has been taken from the *Census of Production*. Using the Survivor technique deduce the plant sizes at which the technique would suggest the *LAC* is lowest. Discuss any sources of inaccuracy in this procedure.

Plant-size distribution for the UK printing and publishing industry

| Size range | Net output (£ million) | |
(No. of employees)	1980	1989
1– 99	1483.5	4078.3
100– 199	402.9	1147.2
200– 299	255.9	735.4
300– 399	214.5	433.6
400– 499	170.6	404.4
500– 749	314.1	813.4
750– 999	132.5	692.8
1000–1499	238.4	884.9
1500–1999	150.8	375.0
2000–2499	221.0	733.6
2500 and over	642.6	233.4
	4,223.2	10,532.1

Sources Business Monitor, *Census of Production*, 1980, vol. PA475 Table 4 and Business Monitor, *Census of Production*, 1989, vol. PA475, Table 4.

Chapter 10: Linear programming

1. For the following linear programming problem for π_C, Q_A and Q_B:

$$\text{Maximise } \pi_C = 3Q_A + 2Q_B$$

$$3Q_A + Q_B \leqslant 16$$

$$Q_A + 2Q_B \leqslant 20$$

$$Q_A \geqslant 0$$

$$Q_B \geqslant 0$$

π_C = contribution profits from the production of A and B

Q_A, Q_B = output of products A and B respectively

   (a) Represent the two constraints graphically, indicating the set of feasible solutions.
   (b) Solve the problem using the arithmetic method.
   (c) Solve the problem using the Simplex algebraic method.
   (d) Solve the problem using the Simplex matrix method.

2. Offequip Ltd produces two types of spring clip, the Bulldog and the Poodle are their brand names. Bulldogs sell for £10 per pack. Poodles for £9.50. The VC of Bulldogs is £5 per pack and of Poodles £5.50. Both products go through the stamping department and the assembly and packing department. The former has 9,600 minutes per day available, the latter 12,000. Each Bulldog pack takes 4 minutes to stamp out and 2 to assemble and pack. Each Poodle pack takes 2 minutes to stamp and 10 minutes to assemble and pack. What is the optimum product mix? Find the optimal outputs of both types of clip if their selling prices changed so that the contribution became £7 per Bulldog pack and £3 per Poodle.

3. Potbanks Ltd manufactures two types of vase, Tall and Spherical. The prices of Tall and Spherical are £9 and £7 per vase respectively. The VC of Tall and Spherical are £5 and £4 per vase respectively. The production of each vase requires inputs of labour time, machine time and clay. Each Tall vase requires 2 minutes of labour time, 1 minute of machine time and 2 pounds (weight) of clay. Each Spherical vase requires 1 minute of labour time, $3\frac{1}{2}$ minutes of machine time and 4 pounds (weight) of clay. Potbanks has only 1,000 minutes of labour time, 4,000 minutes of machine time and 2,100 pounds of clay available per day. What is the optimal daily output of each type of vase?

4. (a) Find the dual of the primal shown in Question 2. Interpret the new objective function, the constraints and the new variables. Represent the constraints of the dual as a graph and indicate the set of feasible solutions.
   (b) Formulate the dual of the dual which you found in part (a). Interpret its objective function, constraints and new variables. Compare this formulation with Question 2.

5. (a) Solve the dual problem of the primal given in Question 3. Interpret the dual variables.
   (b) Calculate the values of the slack variables and interpret them.

6. A revenue (R) maximiser manufactures two types of towel: a bath towel and a hand towel. The prices of each are *fixed* at £7 and £4 respectively. Each towel must pass through three production stages: weaving, printing and cutting. Each bath towel requires 4 minutes of weaving, 5 minutes of printing and 3 minutes of cutting, whereas each hand towel requires 3 minutes of weaving, 2 minutes of printing and 3 minutes of cutting. There are only 70,000, 50,000 and 60,000 minutes of capacity per week available for weaving, printing and cutting respectively.

(a) Find the optimal value of R, R^*.

(b) Formulate the dual of this primal.

(c) Find the optimal value of the objective function of this dual and compare it with R^*.

7. Solve the following linear programming problem for C by solving its dual:

$$\text{Minimise } C = 60P_X + 100P_Y + 55P_Z$$

$$\text{subject to } 5P_X + 3P_Y \geqslant 5$$

$$2P_X + 4P_Y + P_Z \geqslant 4$$

$$P_X, P_Y, P_Z \geqslant 0$$

Chapter 11: Price policy

1. A firm selling the same commodity to two or more groups of customers who cannot trade between themselves (because of cost, information imperfection, or characteristics of the commodity) is in a position to practise price discrimination if not restricted. Suppose two markets are geographically separated, with demand schedules $Q_1 = 20 - P_1$ and $Q_2 = 50 - 2P_2$, where the firm's marginal cost schedule is $MC = 2Q$ where $Q = Q_1 + Q_2$. What are the profit-maximising prices in each market? What are the demand elasticities in each market at the selected prices? Are profits with price discrimination more than profits without? If so, by how much? (Assume fixed costs are equal to £2.) Note that this problem has an interesting twist; it will be discovered that one segment is not worthwhile selling into if uniform prices are charged. (This type of situation often exists, for example, when considering whether to export or not. Exporting is often only profitable if the price overseas is much less than the price charged at home. On the other hand, consciously deciding *not* to export or to do so only if identical – and high – prices are received, both at home and abroad, may prove non-optimal.)

2. Welcome Brewers dominates the liquor industry, although there are 50 small competitors scattered throughout the country and strongly supported by the Campaign for Real Beer (CAMRB). The CAMRB brewers each have an identical total cost function: $0.03 + 2Q + 1.75Q^2$. The market demand for beer has been found by Welcome's market research arm to be $P = 3 - 0.03Q$. Welcome's total cost function is $1 + Q + 0.01Q^2$. What price should Welcome set in order to maximise profits? What price level should the CAMRB brewers set? What will be the profits made by Welcome? What quantity will Welcome produce? And the small firms?

3. Two grocery groups control virtually all food sales in a given local newspaper area. Each Thursday evening they provide the local paper with advertising material indicating which product will be on cut price offer that weekend. Experience has indicated that detergent or coffee is the most effective good with which to attract customers for the weekend sales. Suppose that past data show that sterling sales over all goods are gained or lost as shown:

		B cuts price on:	
		detergent	coffee
A cuts	detergent	0	100
price on:	coffee	150	-50

Given sales gains as an objective, what price strategy will A, settle on? What do you think B would do?

Chapter 12: Pricing in regulated industries

1. Here are some regulated average price increase formulae for 1994–5: British Telecom: RPI-7.5; British Gas: RPI-4; Water companies: RPI + K where K varies from 1.9 to 11.0 between companies. Why do these pricing formulae differ between these industries? Do some customers face greater price increases and some less than these formulae? If so which?

Chapter 13: Advertising decisions

1. Suppose there are two large supermarkets in Inverness. The nearest similar shops are 90 miles away in Aberdeen. Both begin to consider heavy advertising and/or price cutting in order to take business away from their rival. Both firms are assumed to be astute market share maximisers. The following market share pay-offs are estimated to be the outcomes from various combinations of actions:

| | Supermarket A | | | |
	Doubles advertising	Cuts prices	Both	Neither
Supermarket B				
Doubles advertising	+ 2	– 10	– 20	+ 10
Cuts prices	+ 10	+ 4	– 10	+ 15
Both	+ 15	+ 5	+ 6	+ 20
Neither	– 5	– 10	– 15	0

What decision will each firm come to?

2. Suppose a press and TV advertiser calculates that by spending an extra £1,000 on TV he or she can increase the number of viewers who see his or her ads by 600. For an extra £500 in either of two papers (or both) the advertiser can increase the number of readers by 400, each of whom has an average probability of noting of 0.5. What should the firm do, assuming no audience overlap, homogeneity of viewer and reader characteristics and equal probable purchase response? Would your view be altered if the advertiser had engaged an extremely creative copywriter?

3. Calculate the marginal advertising response function for a four-night TV campaign with adverts appearing at 9.00 p.m. (when on average 50% of all viewers recall advertisements). The product is toilet soap. There are 20 million housewives in the population, of whom 6 million watch ITV one night in four, 4 million watch two nights in four, 3 million watch three in four and 2 million nightly. Assume constant returns to scale from repetition.

4. Express your answer to the last question in the form of a linear programming problem, given a total budget of £10,000, a choice of a TV or press campaign with a maximum of five TV nights and/or six press pages. One night's TV advertising costs £1,500, one press page costs £1,000. The marginal response function for press is 20%, 20%, 20%, 15%, 2%, 0.3%.

5. A necktie manufacturer estimates his demand function to be:

$$Q = 100,000P^{-3}A^{0.5}$$

Unit costs are £6.66. What are the optimal price and advertising levels? (Hint: in the Demand theory chapter we find that elasticities are given by exponents in multiplicative expressions.)

6. A firm making electronic games forecasts that its required turnover next year will be a sales figure of £5 million. It estimates that price and advertising elasticities respectively will be 0.9 and 0.08. At what level will it set its advertising budget for the coming year?

Chapter 14: Capital budgeting

1. A firm makes the following cash flow calculations for two mutually exclusive projects, X and Y; cost of capital is 10%:

Year:	0	1	2	3	NPV	IRR
X	− 1000	475	475	475	181	20%
Y	− 350	0	0	684	164	25%

Which project should it choose?

2. A firm makes the following cash flow calculations:

Year	0	1	2	3	4	IRR
Cash flow	− 200	100	100	173.3	− 110	20%

Its cost of capital is 10%. How should the calculation have been performed? Why?

3. An investor is considering purchasing loan stock which pays interest of £10 a year for ten years and a capital repayment of £100 simultaneously with the last interest payment. The first interest payment is in one year's time.

If the investor requires a return of 12% what is the maximum amount he or she would be willing to pay for the stock?

4. A company is introducing a new product, whose production run will be 10,000 units/year for the next 10 years. The manufacturing process requires welding which may either be carried out on the company's existing equipment or by the purchase of new equipment. Two sorts of new equipment are available, depending on whether a low or high level of automation is selected. The company's cost of capital is 10%. The existing equipment has a book value (original cost less accumulated depreciation) of £50,000, though if sold on the open market it could only fetch £20,000. Equipment that would introduce low-level automation would cost £240,000, though the supplier in this case would be willing to give an allowance of £40,000 if he took the existing equipment in part-exchange. Equipment for a high degree of automation would cost £300,000. (Assume no taxation and that neither of the two new machines will be replaced.)

Costs of production with the different processes would be as follows. All costs are direct. None of the equipment would have any value at the end of 10 years.

	Existing	Low automation	High automation
Material			
cost/unit (£)	5.00	4.00	4.00
Labour			
cost/unit (£)	7.00	3.50	2.00

(a) What are the payback periods of the two investments?
(b) What *IRR* does each offer?
(c) What is the *NPV* of each investment?
(d) What is the company's optimal investment decision? (Hint: when using IRR remember to correct for the different outlays.)

5. A landowner is considering whether to plant oak or pine on land which he is committing to forestry. Oak can be sold for £8 per cubic metre and pine for £4. These prices are expected to remain constant. The land will carry equal numbers of oak or pine trees to the acre and the growth expected from the two types of tree is as follows:

Cubic metres of wood	Pine	Oak
after 5 years' growth	1.5	0.5
10	5.0	2.0
15	9.0	4.0
20	12.0	7.5
25	14.0	10.0

Costs of planting and felling the trees may be ignored. The landowner's cost of capital is 10%.
(a) What is the optimum length of time to let oak trees and pine tress grow (consider only the values given in the table)?
(b) What is the present value of the cash flow from each type of tree if it is planted now and allowed to grow for the optimum period?
(c) Which type of tree is more profitable to grow?

6. In the last 5 months excess returns over (or under) the risk-free rate were the following (i) for the market index and (ii) for XYZ Ltd.

	1	2	3	4	5
(i)	0.04	0	0.08	-0.02	0.06
(ii)	0.02	0	0.04	-0.04	0.12

Using this historic data as a proxy for the future and given that the risk-free rate was 5% what is:

(a) the value of XYZ Ltd's Beta coefficient?
(b) XYZ Ltd's cost of equity capital under the assumptions of the capital asset pricing model?

7. In the context of *CAPM* what is the expected return for ABC Ltd if it and the market have the following characteristics?

σ_{ABC}	$= 0.2$
σ_N (market portfolio)	$= 0.1$
$\bar{r}_N$ (market portfolio)	$= 0.15$
i (risk free rate)	$= 0.03$
ρ between possible returns between security ABC and the market portfolio	$= 0.9$

What happens if $\rho = 0.9$ changes to $\rho = 0.1$?

If ρ remains at 0.9, but σ_{ABC} rises what happens to the required rate of return, $\bar{r}_{ABC}$?

8. Securities A and B have the following characteristics:

	$\bar{r}$	σ
A	0.2	0.1
B	0.12	0.3

ρ_{AB} is expected to be 0.8

Calculate the risk and return of the following portfolios:

(a) 100% of A
(b) 50% A, 50% B
(c) 25% A, 75% B

Which portfolio is optimal? What results would be obtained if $\rho_{AB} = 0.2$?

Chapter 15: Product, market and corporate strategies

1. Kezzoggs Ltd has a farming division and a cereals division. The corn grown by the farming division can be sold (or bought) on the open market at £20 per 100 kilograms. The farming division's cost function is $TC = 10,000 + 0.0005Q_f^2$ where Q_f is in hundreds of kilograms. The cereal division can process corn into flakes which will cost £30 per 100 kilograms, exclusive of the cost of corn. Assume one kilogram of corn produces one kilogram of flakes. The demand schedule for the cereal division is $P = 85.5 - 0.00002Q_c$. What should be the transfer price? How much corn should the farming division produce? How much cereal should be produced? Where should it be sold? What price should it be sold at?

2. IBI Ltd is divisionalised into a fine chemicals and a pharmaceutical division. The latter sells a patented drug which requires a unique raw ingredient made by the former. No other firm has been licensed to sell the drug. The demand equation for the drug is $P = 20 - 0.003Q_p$. The tableting process costs £0.005 per unit. The cost function for the fine chemical ingredient is $TC = 400 + 0.005Q_f^2$. What quantity of the medicine should be produced? At what price? What should the transfer price be? Assume unit for unit production.

3. MacSporran Publishers Ltd has best-selling textbooks in both History and French subject areas. Each has about 65% of the market. A recent market study suggests that the elasticity of demand for each is about the same. Moreover, the MC of production of each text is equivalent and constant over the relevant range. About twice as many copies of the History book are sold as of the French, yet the prices are the same. Is the firm's pricing

policy correct? (Hint: recall the definition for MR given by equation (7.11)). Assume (a) that the firm is working at capacity (i.e. that output level at which the firm is working on its constant and flat MC curve has now reached the point where the MC curve becomes a vertical line); and (b) that the firm has slack resources for both printing and distribution.

4. Whisky Distillers Ltd produces malt whisky of two grades, special and rest. Rest is considered to be a relatively low-quality variant of special and is sold to the large household brand bottlers for blending with grain whisky. Special is bottled by Whisky Distillers Ltd for direct sale under their own label. The demand functions for the two are:

$$Q_s = 500 - 5P_s$$
$$Q_r = 2500 - 10P_r$$

Total cost is:

$$200 + Q_s = TC$$

What is the optimal output ratio? At what prices should the products be sold?

5. Chicken farmers have two products to sell: feathers and meat. If each bird produces on average 2 kilograms of meat and I kilogram of feathers, if storage is not practicable, if each chicken costs £0.50 to rear, and if the demand schedules for meat and feathers are $Q_m = 4000 - 1000P_m$ and $Q_f = 2000 - 1000P_f$ respectively, determine the optimal quantity of birds for the industry to produce and the prices of meat and feathers. (The demand schedules are specified for price per kilo.)

Chapter 17: Competition policy legislation

1. Is it socially desirable for an economy to have Dominant Firm and Merger policies?

2. Should the 'burden of proof' in MMC investigations under the Fair Trading Act 1973 be changed?

3. If you were managing director of a large UK company with a market share over 35% and you wished your company to acquire another firm in the same industry, what undertakings would you offer to the OFT to try to avert a reference to the MMC?

4. 'A complete assessment of firm conduct and market performance is so fraught with difficulties that a purely structural approach to monopoly and merger policy is more desirable than a cost–benefit approach.' Discuss.

5. Are the definitions of the 'public interest' in the case of UK Competition Policy and 'compatibility with the Common Market' in the case of European Union policy consistent?

Chapter 19: Profits and control

1. For ABC Ltd the following relations exist: for each unit, selling price is £75; for output up to 25,000 units fixed costs are £240,000, and variable costs are £35 per unit.

   (a) What is the firm's gain or loss at sales of 5,000 units and of 8,000 units?
   (b) What is the break-even point?
   (c) What is ABC's degree of operating leverage at sales of 5,000 units and of 8,000 units?
   (d) What happens to the break-even point if price rises to £85? What significance does this have?
   (e) What happens to the break-even point if variable costs rise to £45 per unit (price £85)?

Index

Student's notes

Student's notes

Student's notes